An Introduction to Computer Science Using Java

Second Edition

Samuel N. Kamin
University of Illinois at Urbana–Champaign

M. Dennis Mickunas
University of Illinois at Urbana–Champaign

Edward M. Reingold
Illinois Institute of Technology

Boston   Burr Ridge, IL   Dubuque, IA   Madison, WI   New York   San Francisco   St. Louis
Bangkok   Bogotá   Caracas   Kuala Lumpur   Lisbon   London   Madrid   Mexico City
Milan   Montreal   New Delhi   Santiago   Seoul   Singapore   Sydney   Taipei   Toronto

McGraw-Hill Higher Education

A Division of The **McGraw-Hill** *Companies*

AN INTRODUCTION TO COMPUTER SCIENCE USING JAVA
SECOND EDITION

Published by McGraw-Hill, a business unit of The McGraw-Hill Companies, Inc., 1221 Avenue of the Americas, New York, NY 10020. Copyright ©2002, 1998 by The McGraw-Hill Companies, Inc. All rights reserved. No part of this publication may be reproduced or distributed in any form or by any means, or stored in a database or retrieval system, without the prior written consent of The McGraw-Hill Companies, Inc., including, but not limited to, in any network or other electronic storage or transmission, or broadcast for distance learning.

Some ancillaries, including electronic and print components, may not be available to customers outside the United States.

This book is printed on acid-free paper.

International   1 2 3 4 5 6 7 8 9 0 QPF/QPF 0 9 8 7 6 5 4 3 2 1
Domestic   1 2 3 4 5 6 7 8 9 0 QPF/QPF 0 9 8 7 6 5 4 3 2 1

ISBN 0–07–232305–1
ISBN 0–07–112232–X (ISE)

General manager: *Thomas E. Casson*
Publisher: *Elizabeth A. Jones*
Developmental editor: *Emily J. Lupash*
Executive marketing manager: *John Wannemacher*
Senior project manager: *Susan J. Brusch*
Production supervisor: *Kara Kudronowicz*
Coordinator of freelance design: *Rick D. Noel*
Cover designer: *Emily Feyen*
Cover image: ©*Image Bank, #459416, White Mouse in Maze/Garry Gay*
Senior supplement producer: *Tammy Juran*
Media technology senior producer: *Phillip Meek*
Compositor: *Techsetters*
Typeface: *10/12 Times*
Printer: *Quebecor World Fairfield, PA*

Credit Lines: For: "As Time Goes by" p. 57 "AS TIME GOES BY, by Herman Hupfeld. ©1931 (Renewed) Warner Bros. Inc. All rights reserved. Used by Permission. WARNER BROS. PUBLICATIONS U.S. Inc., Miami, FL 33014." For: Piet Hein p. 77 "Copyright©Piet Hein Grooks:-Reprinted with kind permission from Piet Hein a/s (HPH/Middlefart)" For: Piet Hein p. 128 "Copyright©Piet Hein Grooks:-Reprinted with kind permission from Piet Hein a/s (HPH/Middlefart)" For: "Little Boxes" p. 263 From the song, "Little Boxes: Words and music by Malvina Reynolds. ©Copyright 1962 Schroder Music Co. (ASCAP) Renewed 1990. Used by permission. All rights reserved."

Library of Congress Cataloging-in-Publication Data

Kamin, Samuel N.
    An introduction to computer science using Java / Samuel N. Kamin, M. Dennis Mickunas. — 2nd ed.
        p. cm.
    Includes index.
    ISBN 0–07–232305–1 — ISBN 0–07–112232–X (ISE)
    1. Computer science. 2. Java (Computer program language). I. Mickunas, M. Dennis.
II. Title.

QA76 .K262   2002
005.13′3—dc21

2001044970
CIP

INTERNATIONAL EDITION ISBN 0–07–112232–X
Copyright ©2002. Exclusive rights by The McGraw-Hill Companies, Inc., for manufacture and export. This book cannot be re-exported from the country to which it is sold by McGraw-Hill. The International Edition is not available in North America.

www.mhhe.com

Contents

1 WHAT IS PROGRAMMING?

2 CLASSES AND METHODS I: BASICS

3 FUNDAMENTAL DATA TYPES OF JAVA

4 DECISION MAKING

5 CLASSES AND METHODS II: CLASSES WITH MULTIPLE METHODS

6 ITERATION

7 CLASSES AND METHODS III: WORKING WITH OBJECTS

8 ONE-DIMENSIONAL ARRAYS

9 NESTED LOOPS AND TWO-DIMENSIONAL ARRAYS

10 CLASSES AND METHODS IV: STATIC METHODS AND VARIABLES

11 THE JAVA AWT PART I: MOUSE EVENTS (*OPTIONAL*)

12 INHERITANCE AND EXCEPTIONS

13 JAVA AWT PART II (*OPTIONAL*)

14 RECURSION

15 TEXT PROCESSING AND FILE INPUT/OUTPUT

16 CASE STUDY: THE GAME OF REVERSI

A OTHER JAVA FEATURES

B PRECEDENCE RULES

C CLASSES IN CSLIB AND THE JAVA API

D UML CLASS DIAGRAMS

E JAVADOC AND CSLIB

List of Figures

List of Tables

List of Bug Alerts

Preface

Read not to contradict and confute, nor to believe and take for granted, nor to find talk and discourse, but to weigh and consider.

—from *Essays, 50. Of Studies*,
Francis Bacon

In the preface to the first edition of this book, we explained why we thought Java was a good choice for a language with which to teach programming. We argued that Java was a clean and simple object-oriented language; that it would be fun for students to learn because of the ability to program graphics and post programs on their websites; that it was freely available for all major platforms; that its compilers would be friendlier to beginners than the compilers for other languages such as C and C++; and that, by virtue of its similarities to C++, it would make a good jumping off point for learning that very popular, but complex, language.

These arguments have become commonly accepted truisms. The questions about introductory programming have turned to two primary issues: how, and how much, to cover object-oriented programming; and how to cover the fun parts of Java, such as applets, without drowning in details. The goal of an introductory computer science book, after all, is not to teach Java or C++ or any other specific language. It is, as we said in the first edition, "to give the reader the tools to develop correct, efficient, well-structured, and stylish programs and to build a foundation for further studies in computer science."

In considering the revision of the text, we came to two conclusions concerning those questions: that object-oriented programming is an important part of the foundation of computer science; and that there is a way to cover the fun stuff without the details—indeed, in a way that *reinforces* the principles we are teaching, rather than distracting from them. Accordingly, we have substantially rewritten and reorganized the book. The treatment of object-oriented programming has been greatly expanded, and the use of graphics is now pervasive (in the first edition it was optional). Like some other authors, we have written a class library, CSLib, that permits the use of graphical elements in programs without the raft of details associated with applets.

What's New in the Second Edition?

To be specific about the changes from the first edition:

- Object-oriented programming is used from the beginning of the book. The four "classes and methods" chapters—2, 5, 7, and 10—form the backbone of our coverage. CSLib allows us to use objects in our very first complete program, and then it allows us to provide the student with considerable practice *using* objects before delving into their design and implementation.
- We use class diagrams from the Unified Modeling Language (UML) to illustrate the relationships between classes. The UML is rapidly gaining widespread acceptance, and it has been adopted as a standard by the Object Management Group (OMG).
- Our examples and exercises involve writing *graphical applications* using CSLib. Compared to programming applets using the standard Abstract Windowing Toolkit (AWT) or Swing components, this involves much less "bureaucracy," while allowing use of essentially the same graphical elements. Once all the requisite language elements have been presented, we show how to transform graphical applications into applets (Chapter 13).

Aside from these changes, much of our approach and style follow the first edition. In particular, since our goal is to introduce computer science, not Java programming, we place a heavy emphasis on the development of algorithms. That object-oriented programming is now considered fundamental does not mean that topics previously considered fundamental have lost any of their importance. Conditional execution, iteration, and recursion are still the basic control structures in computer programming; the design and analysis of efficient algorithms are hardly possible without using arrays; the classic sorting algorithms are still the best and simplest examples of algorithm development. We have not wanted to sacrifice these and other fundamental topics. It is no surprise, then, that the present book is 50% longer than its predecessor!

What This Book Covers

Most of the Java language is covered eventually, with more advanced features naturally receiving a less expansive treatment than essential concepts. All the concepts we would normally consider essential to an introductory programming course—using any language—are covered, of course. These include the basic object-oriented programming paradigm; conditional execution, iteration, and recursion; integer, double, String, character, and Boolean data types and associated operations; one- and two-dimensional arrays; and the best-known sorting algorithms. Specifically, the chapter-by-chapter coverage is as follows:

Chapter 1 introduces the broadest principles of computing, including such notations as *algorithm, object,* and *compiler.*

In **Chapter 2**, we begin to write Java programs, using the CSLib classes for input and output. These simple programs use no language features other than those needed for object creation and message sending. This chapter serves as an introduction to those concepts, as well as to Java syntax and the mechanics of compilation and execution of Java programs. An important CSLib class introduced in this chapter is DrawingBox, which incudes graphical operations exactly like those used in applets. It is worth noting that using this class is of no greater conceptual difficulty than using text-oriented output would be—arguably less, in fact—and allows us to retain a purely object-oriented view of programming.

Chapter 3 presents the primitive data types int, double, and char, as well as String.

Chapter 4 is a fairly conventional treatment of conditionals, including if and switch statements, Boolean expressions, and the boolean data type.

Chapter 5, which is comparatively short, fills in a crucial gap in the previous coverage of classes and objects, by discussing the construction of classes with multiple methods. Up to this point, the student has *written* classes with a single method—in effect, the "main" method of the program—while *using* objects (such as DrawingBoxes) that respond to multiple methods.

Chapter 6 is devoted to the treatment of iteration, including for, while and do-while loops. At that point in the book, quite a few interesting programs can be written, using CSLib. (One might say that at this point the ability to do interesting graphics is determined mainly by the students' *mathematical* knowledge.)

Chapter 7 presents for the first time the design and implementation of classes with constructors, instance variables, and multiple methods. By this time, the two earlier "classes and objects" chapters (2 and 5) and the numerous examples will have prepared students for their first construction of "real" classes.

Chapters 8 and **9** are fairly conventional (except, that is, for the use of graphic-oriented examples) introductions to one-dimensional and two-dimensional arrays, respectively. (We have chosen not to cover higher-dimensional arrays.)

Chapter 10 completes the treatment of classes (short of inheritance) by introducing static (or "class") variables and methods as well as interfaces (required for the next chapter).

Chapter 11 describes how to write programs that respond to mouse clicks. It is labeled "optional" because it concerns only the Java Application Programming Interface (API) and not general concepts of computer science. However, considering that this part of the API is extremely useful without being terribly complicated, we expect that most instructors will want to cover this chapter.

Chapter 12 concerns inheritance and exceptions. Opinions on the importance of these features at the introductory level vary, but the features are in any case prerequisites for the study of applets and other aspects of the Java API that are covered in subsequent chapters.

Chapter 13 introduces the Java AWT package in earnest, including components, events, and layout managers. We show how to transform the applications we have been writing into applets.

Chapter 14 covers what we consider to be among the most essential topics in computer science: recursion. As shown in the dependency chart in Figure 1, this chapter does not depend upon any advanced language or API features.

Chapter 15 introduces the part of the Java API that concerns file input and output. Although many instructors will want to cover this topic earlier, it is unfortunately rather complicated and makes heavy use of advanced language features such as inheritance and exceptions.

The final chapter, **Chapter 16**, gives our "valedictory," in the form of a large applet that implements the game of Reversi. This program uses virtually every feature introduced in the book, introduces a few new ones (such as the `Vector` class), and implements a pretty good game-playing strategy.

How to Use This Book

A dependency chart of all the chapters in the book is shown in Figure 1. The optional chapters, 11 and 13, are shown as dashed ovals.

Numerous selections of chapters and orders of coverage are possible. One can use the book to teach a pure Java programming course by covering Chapters 1–8, 10–13, and 15; this omits material on, for example, two-dimensional arrays and recursion. On the other hand, a selection better suited to beginning computer science majors might be Chapters 1–10 and 14, which omits some Java arcana in favor of more traditional topics.

In this edition we have added several web chapters covering topics which most instructors will consider too advanced for an introductory class. These are

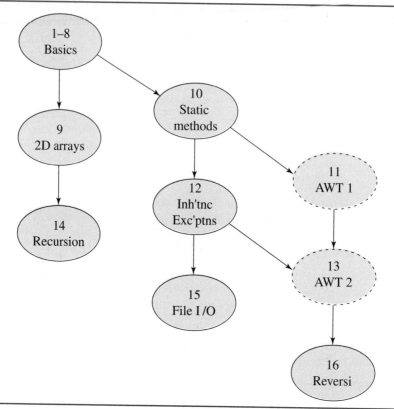

FIGURE 1   Chapter Dependency Diagram.

the Swing classes; threads and synchronization; and collection classes. These chapters are available on our website.

All of the important Java classes are covered to some extent in this book. Of course, the `java.awt` and `java.awt.event` classes are covered only in the AWT chapters (11 and 13). In particular, following are the classes that are covered in each of the indicated packages.

Classes in the `java.lang` package

```
Double          Integer          Math
Object          String           StringBuffer
System
```

Classes in the `java.util` package

```
Calendar        Enumeration      Vector
```

Classes in the `java.awt` package

BorderLayout	Button	Canvas
Checkbox	CheckboxGroup	Color
Component	Container	Dimension
FlowLayout	Font	FontMetrics
Graphics	GridLayout	Label
Panel	Point	Polygon
Scrollbar	TextArea	TextComponent
TextField		

Classes in the `java.awt.event` package

ActionListener	AdjustmentEvent	AdjustmentListener
EventObject	ItemEvent	ItemListener
MouseEvent	MouseListener	MouseMotionListener
TextListener	WindowListener	

Classes in the `java.applet` package

Applet	URL

Classes in the `java.io` package

BufferedReader	BufferedWriter	FileReader
FileWriter	PrintWriter	Reader
Writer		

Pedagogical Features

We have retained all of the pedagogical features from the first edition that were judged effective, we expanded some of them, and we introduced new features that were requested by instructors. The main features are

- In the first edition, we included in most chapters a "debugging section," in which a complete program development was illustrated, warts and all. We have continued that policy in this book, as we have found that students find it useful and encouraging to see how even experienced programmers can struggle with errors, both silly and subtle.
- We also had occasional "bug alert" boxes, pointing out common pitfalls of a language feature or programming idiom being introduced; again, we have retained this feature.
- In this revision, however, we have changed somewhat our approach to exercises. Instead of placing exercises after each section, we have placed exercises only at the ends of chapters.
- However, we have added numerous "quick exercises" throughout the text. These are easy problems intended to reinforce the concepts being introduced; in many cases, their main purpose is to encourage readers to try out on the computer what they've learned from the text. In principle, readers should do—or at least completely understand—every quick exercise.

- The outside margins contain keywords and phrases from the nearby text. The outside margins are visible on both left- and right-hand pages as one flips through the text, making it easy to locate a particular discussion.
- The inside margins are used occasionally to display a "curvy road" sign. Such a sign warns the reader that the nearby material is more subtle or difficult than other material and deserves special attention. More than one curvy sign warns that more care should be taken in reading the material. Naturally, we have tried our best to smooth and widen all the roads, but some curvy ones are unavoidable.

Obtaining a Java Compiler

All our programmers are based on version 1.3 of the Java 2 system, available from Sun Microsystems (website: java.sun.com). The naming of the different versions has been a source of confusion. For the most part, our programs will run on any version as recent as 1.1 (the change from 1.0 to 1.1 having been the most significant as far as the essential elements of the Java language go).

Use of Integrated Development Environment (IDE) greatly simplifies the edit-compile-execute cycle. There are a number of commercial IDEs for Java, one of which—Code Warrior—is supplied with this book.

Feedback to the Authors

In the introduction to his *Guide to the Perplexed*, the great 12th-century philosopher, physician, and rabbinic commentator Moses Maimonides outlines seven categories of contradiction or error to be found in books:

1. The author quotes various sources that disagree.
2. The author has changed his mind on a point but neglects to remove all the rejected material.
3. Something is not to be taken literally but has inner content.
4. An apparent (but not real) contradiction stems from the necessity to explain one thing before another.
5. A simplification is made for purposes of explanation but later the point is explained in full.
6. A contradiction escapes the author.
7. The author is intentionally concealing something.

Maimonides avers that all the errors in his *Guide to the Perplexed* are of the fifth and seventh types. Would that the present authors could make such a claim!

There undoubtedly are errors of substance, style, spelling, and grammar in this book, try mightily as we did to prevent and eliminate them. All the programs and segments of programs were compiled and thoroughly tested before incusion in the text.

If you should happen to notice an error, please bring it to our attention. We also welcome any ideas or feedback from our readers. We can be reached at the e-mail addresses

```
kamin@cs.uiuc.edu
mickunas@cs.uiuc.edu
reingold@cs.uiuc.edu
```

or by regular mail at:

Department of Computer Science
University of Illinois at Urbana–Champaign
1304 West Springfield Avenue
Urbana, IL 61801-2987

Web Page

The web page for this book is

```
www.mhhe.com/engcs/compsci/kamin
```

There you will find

- Javadoc documentation for CSLib.
- Source code for the CSLib.
- Source code for all the examples given in the text.
- Answers to quick exercises.
- Runnable versions of solutions to the end-of-chapter programming exercises. (Source code is, of course, not included!)
- The "bonus" chapters covering the Swing classes; threads and synchronization; and collection classes.
- A list of errata.
- Links to the Java documentation and download pages at Sun Microsystems.
- Instructions on using the Code Warrior IDE.

To the Instructor

A separate password-protected instructor's web page is also available. Please contact your McGraw-Hill Higher Education representative to obtain access to it. There you will find

- Solutions to all the end-of-chapter exercises.
- Chapter by chapter Powerpoint presentations.
- An alternate version of CSLib to assist with grading student assignments.

Acknowledgments

First Edition

Our Sponsoring Editor for the first edition was Betsy Jones. Betsy, together with our Developmental Editor, Brad Kosirog, diligently shepherded us through our last year of effort. They were ably assisted by Emily Gray. Beth Cigler (Senior Project Manager) efficiently handled copyediting, composition, and proofreading.

We prepared the original manuscript using LaTeX, drawing many of the figures with the powerful `pstricks` macros written by Timothy Van Zandt of Princeton University.

We were fortunate to get feedback from a number of highly qualified and perceptive outside reviewers. Although we may not always have agreed with—or even enjoyed seeing—their comments, we always found them thoughtful and thought provoking. Many thanks to Ann Ford (University of Michigan), Ephraim Glinert (Rensselaer Polytechnic Institute), Michael T. Goodrich (Johns Hopkins University), William Hankley (Kansas State University), Lily Hou (Carnegie Mellon University), Dale Johnson (Gadsen State Community College), Michael Johnson (Carnegie Mellon University), Brian Malloy (Clemson University), David Poplawski (Michigan Technological University), Brent Seales (University of Kentucky), Stephen Slade (Yale University), Don Smith (Rutgers University), Lou Steinberg (Rutgers University), David Teague (Western Carolina University), and Dawn Wilkins (University of Mississippi).

We received feedback from many readers. Those who were the first to point out errors were Maryam Abbassian, Mark Blanchard, Lawrie Brown, Miranda Callahan, Chuck Ehlschlaeger, Yuval Feinstein, Eric Han, Bharat Kharadia, William Knight, Jonathan Kozolchyk, Naomi Lindenstrauss, Jiten Patel, Neil Rhaods, Sam Rhoads, Nan Schaller, Arie Schlesinger, John A. Trono, William Voss, Ali Yazici, and Eliyahu Yona.

Second Edition

Our Sponsoring Editor for the second edition was again Betsy Jones, and Emily Lupash was our Developmental Editor. They were both very helpful with all the details involved, and also incredibly patient as deadlines approached (and sometimes passed). Susan Brusch (Senior Project Manager) provided quick, efficient turnaround on copyediting, composition, and proofreading.

As with the first edition, we received a great deal of very perceptive feedback from outside reviewers. Their suggestions were always well-reasoned, and have resulted in a vastly improved second edition. Many thanks to:

Byron Weber Becker (University of Waterloo), Kenneth D. Blaha (Pacific Lutheran University), Jonathan E. Cook (New Mexico State University), James H. Cross (Auburn University), Walter C. Daugherity (Texas A & M University), Roger Ferguson (Grand Valley State University), Philip Gilbert (California State University, Northridge), Scott Grissom (Grand Valley State University), Joanne F. Houlahan (Johns Hopkins University), Eliot Jacobson (University of California, Santa Barbara), Stan Kwasny (Washington University), Alan Saleski

(Loyola University, Chicago), Dale Shaffer (Lander University), David Surma (Valparaiso University), Phil Ventura (State University of New York, Buffalo), Jennifer L. Welch (Texas A & M University), and Lan Yang (California Polytechnic University, Pomona).

As before, our families and friends endured cancelled plans, inattention, late nights, and crisis deadlines. We are truly indebted to them.

S.N.K.
M.D.M.
E.M.R.

1 WHAT IS PROGRAMMING?

CHAPTER PREVIEW

Before writing programs in the Java language, we demonstrate the thought processes and problem-solving techniques necessary for programming. We present a problem—leading a mechanical mouse through a maze—and work through the design of an *algorithm* to solve the problem, and a *program* to implement the algorithm. We discuss the importance of *object-oriented programming*. To provide some grounding in the operation of computers, we discuss the architecture of computers, the representation of various kinds of data, and the mechanics of entering and running Java programs.

"Again, it [the Analytical Engine] might act upon other things besides numbers, were objects found whose mutual fundamental relations could be expressed by those of the abstract science of operations, and which should be also susceptible of adaptations to the action of the operating notation and mechanism of the engine …Supposing, for instance, that the fundamental relations of pitched sounds in the science of harmony and of musical composition were susceptible of such expression and adaptations, the engine might compose elaborate and scientific pieces of music of any degree of complexity or extent."

—Lady Ada Augusta, Countess of Lovelace
Commenting on Babbage's Analytical Engine
In: *Scientific Memoirs, Selections from the Transactions of Foreign Academies and Learned Societies and from Foreign Journals,* edited by Richard Taylor, F.S.A., Vol III
London: 1843, Article XXIX.

The popular perception of the computer is as an all-powerful entity that, with seemingly little human effort or input, is responsible for running business, government, science, and many more mundane aspects of our lives. But a computer is no more than an inanimate collection of wires and silicon, organized so that it can quickly perform simple operations such as adding numbers. So how does it come to have such power? What sleight of hand transforms this box of electrical components into a powerful tool?

Programming performs the magic. A *program* is a set of directions that tells the computer exactly what to do; a program thus is the medium used to communicate with the computer. Programs can be written in many *programming languages*—languages for specifying sequences of directions for the computer. In this book we use the language Java. *program*

programming language

Our first job in programming is to clarify the problem. *Exactly* what is required? How can the job be broken down into manageable pieces? What *algorithm*—sequence of steps—is appropriate to solve the problem? How can this algorithm be turned into a program? Does the program work? Is it written as clearly as it can be? Is it fast? Can it be changed easily if needed? Does it demand too great a fraction of the computer's resources? These are the questions confronting the *computer programmer*, the person who designs and writes the program. *algorithm*

computer programmer

3

1.1

Mechanical Mouse in a Maze

We start learning to program by analyzing a problem that contains, in miniature, the basic components of any programming problem. We want to give instructions to a mechanical mouse so it can get through a maze. For our purposes, a *maze* is a rectangular arrangement of square rooms; adjacent rooms may be separated by a wall, or the boundary between them may be open. We place the mouse facing the entrance to a maze in which solid lines represent walls between rooms and dotted lines represent open boundaries:

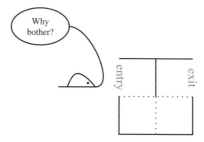

The mouse is like a computer in that it knows how to follow only certain very simple instructions: `step forward` into the next room, `turn right` in place, or `turn left` in place. We must *program* the mouse by writing the precise instructions it must follow to get through the maze. For this simple maze, the instructions are

```
step forward;
turn right;
step forward;
turn left;
step forward;
turn left;
step forward;
turn right;
step forward;
```

This sequence of instructions is comparable to a computer program.

What happens if the maze has a different configuration? For example, what if we had the following?

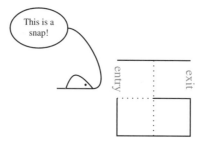

Then our preceding program would not work correctly, but the simpler program

```
step forward;
step forward;
step forward;
```

would work.

It is easy to write out instructions to the mouse for any specific maze as long as we know the maze's internal configuration. But what if the inside of the maze is hidden from view, beneath an opaque cover? All we see is a mouse-eye view of things:

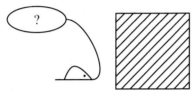

Now our problem is to give the mouse proper instructions to get it through *any* maze. In fact, we have to approach the problem from a completely different perspective. In the language of computer programming, it is our task to figure out an *algorithm* to solve this task—a general method precise enough to be turned into a mouse program — and then to write the corresponding *program*, the exact sequence of mouse instructions.

algorithm
program

The first step in computer programming always is to make the problem as precise as we can. Where is the mouse initially placed with respect to the maze? What should happen if the maze has no exit? We'll assume the mouse is placed in front of the entrance to the maze so that a single `step forward` instruction takes it into the maze. Our instructions to the mouse must get it out the exit of the maze or back out the entrance if there is no path to the exit or no exit at all. This problem, of course, is impossible to solve unless the mouse is capable of examining the inside of the maze and making decisions based on what it finds as it goes along; the three instructions `step forward`, `turn left`, and `turn right` are not sufficient. The mouse, however, also can look forward myopically to see whether there is a wall immediately in front of it, and it can detect when it is inside the maze. These, then, are five instructions that the mouse can follow:

```
step forward
turn right
turn left
facing a wall?
inside the maze?
```

We are limited to these instructions to get the mouse through the maze.

First, we must design an algorithm for getting through an unspecified maze, and then we need to express the algorithm in terms that the mouse can follow. For the mouse in the maze, the algorithm we will use is a familiar trick for going through a maze:

Have the mouse walk hugging the wall to its right.

In our first example above, the mouse would travel like this:

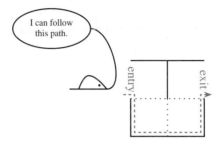

Our first job is to convince ourselves that this algorithm actually works. As is often the case, this is not obvious. A careful argument would hinge on the observation that the mouse never hugs the same wall twice. We will not prove this, but you should run the algorithm on enough examples to convince yourself.

QUICK EXERCISE 1.1	Follow this algorithm on the second example above. (Note that the path given by this algorithm is longer than the path we chose for this maze, which was just to walk straight ahead from entry to exit. We never said this algorithm would always find a *good* path.)

QUICK EXERCISE 1.2	What does this algorithm do if there is no separate exit from the maze?

QUICK EXERCISE 1.3	An alternative algorithm would be to have the mouse walk hugging the wall to its left. Give a maze for which this algorithm gives a better result—that is, a shorter path through the maze—than our "hugging the wall to the right" algorithm. Then give a maze for which this algorithm gives a worse result.

We have an algorithm—a precise method that will always get us through the maze—but that is not enough. We need to express this algorithm with the set of five instructions available to our mouse. This is always the situation in computer programming: First we need to discover an algorithm, then we need to express the algorithm using the limited repertoire of actions that the computer has available to it.

For example, the algorithm directs us to keep the wall to the mouse's right, but the only instruction the mouse understands about walls is `facing a wall?`. How can it check if there is a wall to its right? It must `turn right` first and then ask whether it is facing a wall. If it is, then it originally had a wall to its right, so it should turn back. Now the question is, Can it move forward? If it is facing a wall, then it has a wall to its right *and* a wall in front, and it should keep turning left to find an opening. Thus, the instructions to tell the mouse to find an opening with a wall to its right are

```
turn right;
if facing a wall? then
   turn left and if facing a wall? then
      turn left and if facing a wall? then
         . . .
```

continuing as long as necessary—that is, turn right and then keep turning left until no wall is in front. Since the mouse got into this room to begin with, there must be at least one opening; eventually the preceding instructions will have it facing an opening with a wall to its right.

We're not done, of course. We've figured out how to perform one part of the algorithm—finding an exit from any room in the maze, being sure that a wall is to our right—but not the entire algorithm. Before finishing it, we introduce another aspect of computer programs: their notation. If our mouse spoke Java, it would not understand the above set of instructions, because they are not in Java notation. Instead, we would—and will, from now on—write it as

```
turn right;
if (facing a wall?) {
   turn left;
   if (facing a wall?) {
      turn left;
      if (facing a wall?) {
         . . .
      }
   }
}
```

omitting the words *then* and *and*, and using { and } to indicate the grouping of instructions and (and) to denote a question or condition.

We still haven't said what the . . . means. It means to continue with the same instructions while the mouse is facing a wall, stopping only when the mouse is *not* facing a wall. So we write it instead as

```
turn right;
while (facing a wall?) {
   turn left;
}
```

which means, "after turning right, repeat the process of checking whether you're facing a wall, and if you are, turn left." The distinction between *while* and *if* is that *while* means "continue checking as long as" and *if* means "check the current state of things just one time."

After following these instructions, the mouse will be facing an opening. In other words, it can now step forward (without crashing into a wall).

```
turn right;
while (facing a wall?) {
  turn left;
}
step forward;
```

This is all there is to making a single move. However, we must consider one small detail. What happens if the mouse reaches the end of the maze, that is, manages to exit the maze? What is the meaning of the code when the mouse is *outside* the maze? The mouse must be able to detect when it is outside the maze and simply do nothing if asked to make a move in that circumstance:

```
while (inside the maze?) {
  turn right;
  while (facing a wall?) {
    turn left;
  }
  step forward;
}
```

This raises another small problem. What happens with the very first move? The mouse cannot execute the code just shown, since initially it is outside the maze. The solution is that the mouse's very first move is simply step forward, and subsequent moves are given by the preceding code. Here is the final version of the program:

```
1    step forward;
2    while (inside the maze?) {
3      turn right;
4      while (facing a wall?) {
5        turn left;
6      }
7      step forward;
8    }
```

How simple and elegant this program is! It reads almost like English, but it expresses exactly how the mouse (with its limited abilities) can be made to trace its way, step by step, through a maze by keeping its right paw on the wall.

Let's follow the mouse's trip for a bit to make sure we understand the algorithm. The first few steps are shown in Figure 1.1. The mouse begins by following the first instruction and steps forward into the entry (*a*). Since it is inside the maze, the mouse follows the next group of instructions, starting by turning right (*b*). It is not facing a wall (that is, its nose is not touching a wall), so it doesn't turn left, but instead steps forward (*c*). It is still inside of the maze, so it again follows the group of instructions between lines 3 and 7. First, it turns right (*d*). Since it is facing a wall, it turns left (*e*) and checks again; still facing a wall, it turns left again (*f*) and checks again; *still* facing a wall, it again turns left (*g*). Finally, it is no longer facing a wall, so it skips to line 7 and steps forward (*h*).

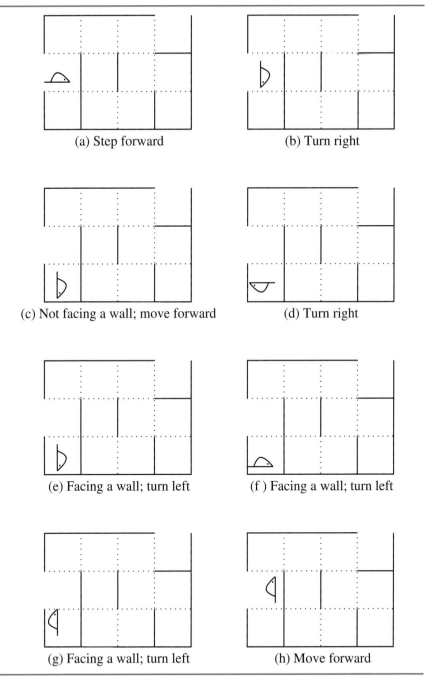

(a) Step forward

(b) Turn right

(c) Not facing a wall; move forward

(d) Turn right

(e) Facing a wall; turn left

(f) Facing a wall; turn left

(g) Facing a wall; turn left

(h) Move forward

FIGURE 1.1   The start of the mouse's trip through the maze.

In the end, the mouse follows the path shown by the dashed line in the following picture:

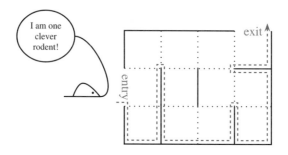

QUICK EXERCISE 1.4   Complete the next eight steps in the narrative of the mouse's trip that was begun in Figure 1.1.

The mouse takes a rather circuitous route to the exit, going through every room once and through three of the rooms twice! We could have taken a different approach to this problem, leading to a different, possibly shorter, path through the maze. With programming, the only limit is our ingenuity.

This program is the result of breaking down the problem at hand into a workable *algorithm*. The algorithm was then expressed using the five simple instructions available to our mechanical mouse. By expressing the algorithm in the very precise syntax of Java, we obtained a *program*.

QUICK EXERCISE 1.5   Rewrite the maze-walking program using the "walk hugging the wall to your left" algorithm.

This example illustrates what beginners find to be perhaps the most difficult and even disconcerting aspect of programming: It requires a degree of precision quite unknown in ordinary human activities. The *algorithm* must be correct and carefully designed; in real life, algorithms are rarely written with the same level of precision—anyone who has ever tried to follow a recipe that says "Season to taste" knows that. The *program*—the written expression of the algorithm—must be written in the language that the mouse understands, with parentheses, brackets, semicolons, and so on, in just the right places.

In this book, we teach you how to design algorithms and how to express them in the Java language. To beginners, mastering the syntax of Java seems like the hard part, but as you get more practice, the syntax will become second nature. The development of algorithms, on the other hand, is a deep intellectual challenge and always will be. Indeed, the study of algorithms is one of the major research areas in computer science. This book contains many algorithms. Most are simple, like the mouse's algorithm, but a few are famously ingenious (e.g., the "quicksort" algorithm, page 550), and some are even historic (e.g., Gaussian Elimination, page 558).

While you are learning the Java syntax and learning how to design algorithms for a variety of problems, we hope you will develop a sense of *programming style*. Style is the intangible quality that makes programs easy to read, elegant, and even admirable. Donald Knuth of Stanford University, one of the leading practitioners of the art of algorithm design, has written, "The chief goal of my work as educator and author is to help people learn to write *beautiful programs*."[1] We cannot claim that you will be writing beautiful programs when you have finished this book, but we hope that you will at least understand what Knuth means.

1.2

Object-Oriented Programming

Java is one of the modern programming languages that encourages the use of *object-oriented programming (OOP)*, which is a way of organizing programs. In object-oriented programming, a program is structured as a collection of *classes*, where each class describes a type of *object*. The objects represent the entities naturally occurring in the program, like the mouse and the maze.

object-oriented programming
classes

Every Java program is nothing but a collection of classes. When a Java program runs, it uses these classes to create a collection of *objects* that interact with one another by sending *messages*. For example, if we wrote the mouse-in-the-maze program in object-oriented form, the mouse would be an object (Figure 1.2), and so would the maze. The mouse would exchange messages with the maze to

objects
messages

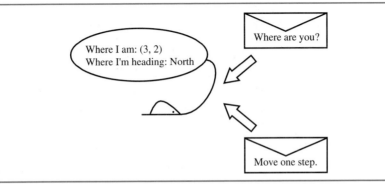

FIGURE 1.2   A mouse object receiving messages.

---

[1]Computer Programming as an Art, 1974 ACM Turing Award Lecture.

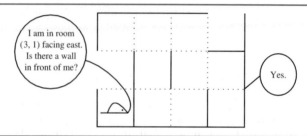

FIGURE 1.3   The mouse in the maze in object-oriented form.   The algorithm is the same as before, but now the mouse and the maze are both objects that communicate by sending messages.

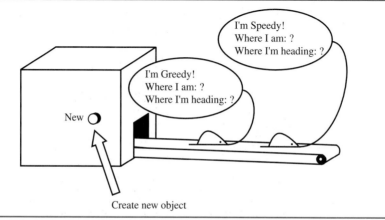

FIGURE 1.4   Relationship between a class and its objects.

determine where it can move, as illustrated in Figure 1.3. Note that the mouse still follows an algorithm—in this case, the "wall to the right" algorithm—but the way we think about and organize the program is quite different.

The main job of the Java programmer, then, is to describe the objects that need to be created when the program runs. This is done by writing a class for each type of object, which we can think of as an *assembly line* for that type of object. The relationship between classes and objects is illustrated in Figure 1.4. For the mouse in the maze, the programmer would write a `Mouse` class and a `Maze` class. (It is conventional in Java to capitalize the names of classes.)

To be more specific, the Java programmer would create two classes by entering the following:

```
public class Mouse {
    we'll see what goes inside the class later in the book
}

public class Maze {
    ditto
}
```

Then, in a different part of the program, the programmer would write something like this:

```
Mouse righty = new Mouse();     ← ── create Mouse object
Maze bigmaze = new Maze();      ← ── create Maze object
righty.enter(bigmaze);          ← ── tell mouse to enter maze
righty.getout();                ← ── tell mouse to find a way out
```

These four lines, or *statements*, are executed in sequence. The first two create the object described by the classes we defined above and give the objects the names `righty` and `bigmaze`, respectively. The third line "sends the `enter` message" to the mouse object and provides the maze as an *argument*; this tells the mouse object to enter the maze. The last line tells the mouse to find a way out of the maze.

The use of object-oriented structure is pervasive in Java. This structure has many advantages: It makes it easy to create multiple objects of the same type; for example, we could have two mice finding their way through the maze at the same time. It also makes it easy to create a variety of *similar* objects; for example, we could create one kind of mouse that follows the "wall to the right" algorithm and another that follows the "wall to the left" algorithm, without having to rewrite the first mouse class completely. Using object-oriented programming helps to make programs simpler to understand and more reliable, because it prevents one kind of object from knowing more than necessary about the structure of other kinds of objects. We will begin using objects in the very first real Java program we write in Chapter 2, and very shortly after that we will begin writing our own classes.

1.3

Computers and Data Representations

Although computers are amazingly complicated machines, the basic principles upon which they operate are fairly simple. Knowing something about these principles will help you understand how programming languages such as Java fit into the picture. It is especially useful to know something about how the computer represents different types of data: text, pictures, sound, and so on.

1.3.1 Bits, Bytes, and Binary Numbers

To a computer, everything is a number. Numbers are used to represent all kinds of data: pictures, sounds, characters, and, of course, numbers themselves. Numbers are also used to represent your program inside the computer as the computer executes it.

Throughout this book, we use the decimal representation of numbers, just as we all do in everyday life. Recall that our normal notation for numbers is called

Base 10:　　3　　　9　　　7_{10}
　　　　　　　|　　　|　　　|
　　　　　　　×　　　×　　　×
　　　　　　10^2　　10^1　　10^0
　　　　　$= 300_{10} + 90_{10} + 7_{10}$

Base 2:　　1　　1　　0　　0　　0　　1　　1　　0　　1
　　　　　　|　　|　　|　　|　　|　　|　　|　　|　　|
　　　　　　×　　×　　×　　×　　×　　×　　×　　×　　×
　　　　　　|　　|　　|　　|　　|　　|　　|　　|　　|
　　　　　2^8　2^7　2^6　2^5　2^4　2^3　2^2　2^1　2^0
　　　　　‖　　‖　　‖　　‖　　‖　　‖　　‖　　‖　　‖
　　　256_{10}　128_{10}　0　　0　　0　　8_{10}　4_{10}　0　　1_{10}
　　　$= 256_{10} + 128_{10} + 8_{10} + 4_{10} + 1_{10}$
　　　$= 397_{10}$

FIGURE 1.5　Positional notation.

positional notation. The value of each digit depends upon its position within the number. Thus, the four numerals 5427 represent the value $5 \times 1000 + 4 \times 100 + 2 \times 10 + 7$. In general, the digit that is i positions from the right is multiplied by 10^i.

　　　Numbers in positional notation are so convenient that their invention is considered one of the greatest technical innovations in human history. *Base 10*, on the other hand, is a mere accident. Any number can be used instead of 10. *binary* In building computers, *binary*, or *base 2*, representation is most efficient. In *bits* base 2, there are two digits—0 and 1—which are called *bits* (for binary digit). In general, the digit that is i positions from the right is multiplied by 2^i. For example, the number 1010100110011 in base 2 has the value: $1 \times 4096 + 0 \times 2048 + 1 \times 1024 + 0 \times 512 + 1 \times 256 + 0 \times 128 + 0 \times 64 + 1 \times 32 + 1 \times 16 + 0 \times 8 + 0 \times 4 + 1 \times 2 + 1 \times 1$, which happens to add up to the same number as 5427 in base 10. The translation from binary to decimal is further illustrated in Figure 1.5.

QUICK EXERCISE 1.6

Convert the following binary numbers to decimal:

1. 1010101

2. 1010110

3. 1111111

　　　The use of binary rather than decimal in computers is confusing at first, but is not of fundamental significance. More important is that numbers in computers are of *fixed size*. In most computers, each integer is restricted to 32 bits (commonly *word* called a *word*). If you do the conversion $(1 \times 2^{31} + \cdots + 1 \times 2^0)$, you will see

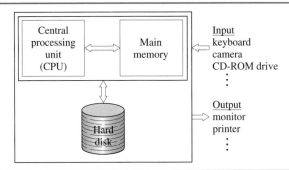

FIGURE 1.6 Block diagram of a computer. Computation is done by the CPU working with program and data in main memory; data move between these components at extremely high speed. New programs and data can be brought in from the hard disk; it is much larger and much slower than the main memory.

that this allows for numbers ranging from 0 up to a maximum of 4,294,967,295. This range is quite large enough for most purposes, so the restriction is rarely a problem in practice. However, it can result in some puzzling results on occasion. An example is given in Chapter 2.

Computer memories are commonly divided into 8-bit numbers called *bytes*. Thus, a word consists of 4 bytes. In describing the size of computer memories, one commonly uses the terms *megabyte* (2^{20}, or a little more than a million, bytes) and *gigabyte* (2^{30}, or a little more than a billion, bytes).

bytes

megabyte
gigabyte

1.3.2 Computer Organization

Internally, a computer consists of three major components: a central processing unit, or *CPU*, that does all the actual work of executing the program; a *main memory* that holds all the data and the program while it is executing; and a long-term storage device, usually a *hard disk*, that holds the programs that are not currently executing and the data that are not currently being used. See Figure 1.6. (Think of the CPU as an office worker, the main memory as the worker's desk, and the hard disk as the items on her or his shelves. All real work is done while sitting at the desk, but items are frequently pulled down off the shelves and placed back onto them.) There are numerous additional parts, called *input/output devices*, that let the computer communicate with the outside world (without which the computer is pretty useless). The three we've mentioned are the key internal components.

CPU
main memory
hard disk

input/output
devices

The main memory, unlike an average desktop, is not a disorganized collection of documents. Rather, it is a long list of binary numbers; in most modern computers, it is a list of bytes. Each byte can have a different value, and the CPU can tell the memory to change the value of any byte in memory. To do this,

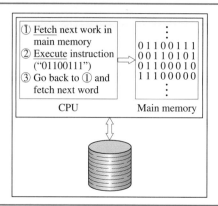

FIGURE 1.7   The fetch/execute cycle. The CPU repeats this cycle, fetching its instruction from the next memory location, until the program is finished.

address   each byte has an *address*, namely, its position in the memory. Thus, the CPU can direct the main memory to change byte 345 (the 346th byte in memory, since the first address is 0) to 45 (that is, 00101101). Location 345 will then continue to hold number 45 until the CPU tells it to change to something else. The CPU can also direct the main memory to return to it the number stored at a given location (just as you recover the value stored in the memory of a calculator). On most computers, the CPU actually reads and writes entire words (groups of 4 bytes) at once; this is more efficient than reading and writing individual bytes.

Nowadays, main memories are quite large. Their sizes are usually measured in megabytes. Thus, a 64-megabyte computer has 64×2^{20}, or about 64 million, bytes, or about 16 million words, or about 512 million bits. Disk memories are much larger. New personal computers (PCs) have disks that hold at least 10 gigabytes, about 10 billion bytes.

The action of the computer when it runs a program can be summarized roughly as follows: First, the program and all the data it uses must be loaded from the hard disk into the main memory. The program is placed in one part of the main memory and the data are placed in another; keep in mind that both the program and the data are nothing but a sequence of numbers. The CPU goes to the location of the first word of the program and reads that word. Each different number—that is, each different pattern of bits—tells the CPU to do something different. It may tell the CPU to load a number from a certain location in the data area and increment it, or to place a character at a certain location on the computer's screen, or to read a number from the disk and place it into a certain location in memory. The CPU performs that action and then goes to the next location in the program area of memory, reads that number, and executes it. This
fetch/execute cycle   is known as the *fetch/execute cycle* (Figure 1.7).

Computers can do amazing things, but only by performing many, many tiny actions, one at a time. Even relatively inexpensive home computers nowadays can run through the fetch/execute cycle about 100 million times per second.

The correspondence between the number in a word and the action that the CPU takes when it sees that number is determined by the type of CPU. It is called the *machine language* of the processor. All PC-compatible machines have the same machine language, based on the Intel x86 line of CPUs,[2] so programs can be run on any such machine regardless of the manufacturer. On the other hand, Apple Macintoshes have been built with two different processors. Programs from earlier Macs, based on the Motorola 680x0 CPUs, will not run on today's Macs, which use the Motorola PowerPC. None of the programs, from either generation, will run on a PC-compatible computer. It is possible to write programs directly in machine language, but this is much more difficult than writing them in Java, and, of course, a program written in machine language can run on only one type of computer.

machine language

The main thing to remember is that only programs in machine language can be executed by the computer, which raises the question: How does a Java program become a machine language program? We discuss that in Section 1.4.

1.3.3 Data Representations

You might ask, If all the CPU can do is to take numbers and perform arithmetic operations on them, how can it print documents, or play music, or perform computer animations? What do documents or music or animated pictures have to do with numbers?

Indeed, in the early years of computation, all that computers were ever used for was numerical calculations. But it gradually became clear that numbers could be used to represent just about any kind of information:

Text. This is easy: Just choose a correspondence between *numbers* and *characters*. We can represent an entire book in memory by placing the characters of the book in sequence. Furthermore, since normal writing in English uses fewer than 256 characters (including letters, digits, and all the usual punctuation marks), we can represent each character in a single byte. (Shakespeare's complete works have a total of about 5 million characters; at 1 byte per character, we can easily fit them into the main memory of a modern computer; in fact, we could fit 10 copies or more.)

QUICK EXERCISE 1.7

The most common code for characters used in English is ASCII, an abbreviation of American Standard Code for Information Interchange. Look up "ASCII" on the Internet. What are the codes for the characters "a", "z", "A", "Z", "0", "9", and "&"?

---

[2]Actually, the machine languages for the newer processors, such as the Pentium 4, are somewhat different from the machine languages of earlier processors, such as the 8086. Programs being written today may not run on CPUs of an earlier generation.

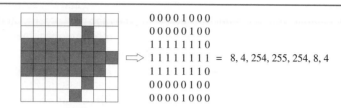

FIGURE 1.8   Representation of black-and-white pictures using numbers. Here, an arrowhead is drawn on a screen with 7 × 8 = 56 pixels. (Real screens have sizes closer to 1000 × 1000 = 1,000,000 pixels, so they need many more numbers and produce much better images.)

pixel

Pictures. Most readers probably already know the answer to this one. A picture can be reduced to a collection of dots, or *pixels*. This is how computer screens and computer printers work. In the simple case of a pure black-and-white picture, each pixel is either black or white, so it can be represented by a single bit. See Figure 1.8. A 1000 × 1000 image, which is quite a detailed image, can thus be represented in 1,000,000 bits, or 125,000 bytes. If the image is "gray scale" or color, it will need several bits per pixel; so the memory requirement will go up substantially, but the principle is the same. Modern digital cameras represent pictures using as many as 3000 × 2000, or more than 6 million, color pixels.

Animations. Since an animation is just a sequence of pictures, we can represent animations easily. Memory space will be stretched, and we might have to apply some cleverness to "compress" the images. But the point is that animations can be represented using numbers (Figure 1.9).

Sounds. You have undoubtedly seen pictures of sound waves (Figure 1.10*a*). Such curves can be *digitized*—turned into sequences of numbers—very easily: Just record the numerical values at regular intervals. If the interval is small enough, you can get as faithful a copy of the curve as you could possibly want. Hardware devices known as analog-to-digital (A/D) converters can perform this sampling (Figure 1.10*b*), and digital-to-analog (D/A) converters can convert this sequence of numbers back to the wave and thereby reproduce the sound. This is exactly how digital music formats like compact disks (CDs) work.

files

Data stored on your computer are kept on the hard disk in *files*. Each file is a collection of bytes, with a name and a type. See Figure 1.11. Thus, a file containing a picture might be called `my_new_car.jpg`. On many systems, the type of a file is indicated by the last part of its name (`jpg`, in this case). Every file takes up some space on the hard disk, and, of course, a large file takes up more space than a small one. As the discussion we've just had might suggest,

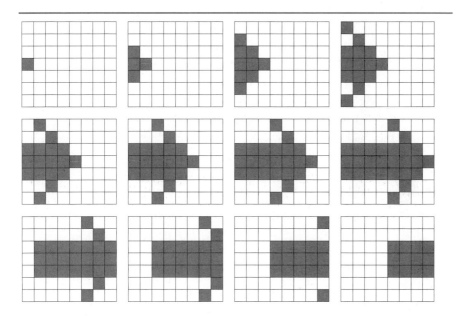

Animation is represented as a sequence of pictures. Each picture is a sequence of numbers. First picture: 0, 0, 0, 128, 0, 0, 0; Second picture: 0, 0, 128, 192, 128, 0, 0; Third picture: 0, 128, 192, 224, 192, 128, 0. Place two numbers at beginning, giving height and width of each picture: 7, 8, 0, 0, 0, 128, 0, 0, 0, 0, 0, 128, 192, 128, 0, 0, . . .

FIGURE 1.9 Representations of animations using numbers.

files containing sound and animations tend to be very large, while files containing text are usually of more modest size.

1.4

Compilers

Let's talk about the mechanics of programming. After you have designed the algorithm and written the program on paper, you begin the process of entering it into a file on the computer's hard disk. Entering and modifying your program in a file are done using a *text editor*, or just *editor*, a program provided to you that permits the storage and retrieval of what you have written on the disk. Learning how to use an editor well can make the job of entering a program much easier.

text editor

The program you have entered is written in Java. Java is not the same as the machine language of your computer. Rather, it is a *high-level language* designed

high-level language

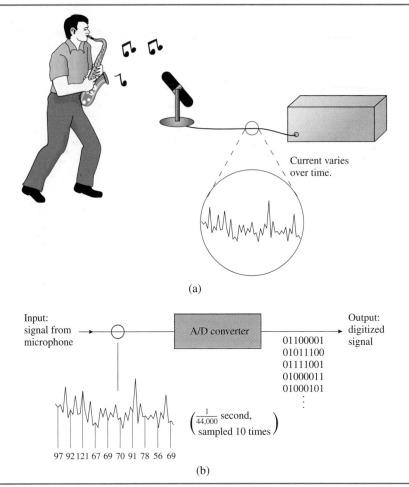

(a)

(b)

FIGURE 1.10 (a) Sound is carried through the air. Microphone turns sound into electrical impulses of varying strength. (b) Analog-to-digital (A/D) converter samples signal at regular intervals ($\frac{1}{44,000}$ second intervals in this illustration). The sampled values (in binary, of course) are sent to the device that will process the digitized signal.

to make programming easier than using machine language. Most programming is done in such high-level languages; other examples of high-level languages include C, C++, and Visual Basic. However, as we have indicated above, only machine language programs can be executed by a computer. Somehow, the Java program needs to be translated to machine language. In the very early history of computers, programmers might do such a translation by hand, but now it is done *compiler*   by another program called a *compiler* (see Figure 1.12). The Java program you

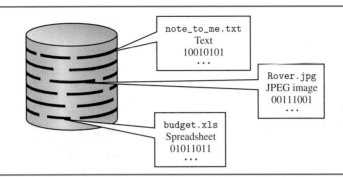

FIGURE 1.11 **Files occupy space on the hard disk. Files consist of many binary digits. A file also has a name and a type. In most systems, the type is given as the latter part of the name; for example, "xls" indicates a spreadsheet created by Excel.**

enter is called the *source code*; the compiler translates it into machine language and stores the result in another file; it is called the *object code*. The object file can be loaded into the computer's main memory and executed by the CPU. *source code* *object code*

In summary, to create and run a Java program, you need to enter the program using a text editor; execute a special program, the compiler, to translate the Java to machine language; and then load the machine language into main memory and execute it. The process is illustrated in Figure 1.12.

Actually, this process doesn't apply to Java in exactly the same way as it does to most high-level languages. Java is different because one of the goals of the Java language is to be *platform-independent*, that is, to be able to execute on a wide variety of different types of machines *after* it has been compiled. It follows that we cannot translate it to machine language, because each program in machine language only runs on one type of machine. Instead, Java is translated into an intermediate-level language called *Java Bytecode*. Java Bytecode is subsequently interpreted in the exact same way on every computer, so that a Java program does the same thing whether run on an IBM PC, an Apple Macintosh, or whatever. *platform-independent* *Java Bytecode*

So the process of creating and executing a Java program is modified a bit: Once you have the file containing the Java program, you use a compiler to translate it to a program in the Java Bytecode language, and then you use another special program, called an *interpreter*, to *execute* the Java Bytecode. A particularly attractive feature of Java is that many modern Internet browsers (such as Netscape Navigator and Microsoft's Internet Explorer) incorporate Java interpreters. *interpreter*

The precise steps you will follow—what editor you use, how to save files, how to invoke the compiler, etc.—depend on the system you are using. The simplest case occurs when you are writing an application on a *command-oriented* system (such as DOS or UNIX). In this case, you place your program in a file called `whatever.java` (`whatever` can be anything you choose, but `java`

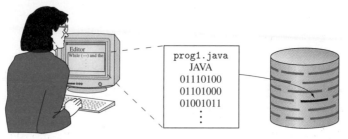

Programmer types program using a *text editor*. File is stored on disk with type "JAVA." Text is represented in binary.

Programmer invokes Java compiler. Compiler reads source file and produces object file.

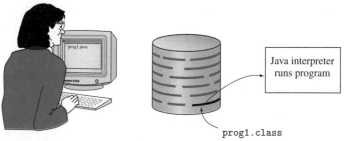

Programmer invokes Java interpreter to run object file.

FIGURE 1.12   Entering, compiling, and executing a Java program.

must be java). Then type the command

    javac whatever.java

to *compile* the program, and then

    java whatever

to execute it.

Again, you must always *compile* your program first. You can then execute it (as many times as you like).

1.5

Debugging

In reality, the "enter/compile/execute" process rarely runs as smoothly as we've described it. In fact, most of the time the program you enter will fail either to compile correctly or to execute correctly. In that case, you will have to go back to the editor and fix the problem, then again compile and execute. The creation of programs is referred to as the *edit/compile/execute cycle*, because those three steps are repeated many times.

edit/compile/execute cycle

Your program will fail to compile if it has *syntactic errors*, meaning that it fails to adhere to the grammatical rules of Java. The compiler will be unable to "understand" your program, and it will tell you so, usually in a terse, unfriendly way. Something as simple as omitting a semicolon or entering a letter in uppercase when it should be in lowercase, or vice versa, can easily cause the compiler to reject your program. You must figure out what needs to be changed, use the editor to change it, and then try compiling again. After a few iterations of this process, the program will compile properly into Java Bytecode form.

syntactic errors

Just because the program compiles without errors does *not* guarantee that it will work correctly! You may have written something that is grammatically correct but that doesn't do at all what you expected. Errors that occur during the execution of the program are called *run-time errors* or *logic errors*; they need to be fixed, too, just as the syntax errors do. Run-time errors can result from simple typing mistakes or from flaws in the algorithm. In either case, it's back to the editor to revise your program and back to the compiler until the algorithm is correct, your program compiles, and finally it executes to completion. Did it get the right answers? If so, try enough additional data to be sure it really works; if not, find the errors, correct them, and recompile and rerun the program. This whole process of removing bugs (errors) from a program is called *debugging*.

run-time errors
logic errors

debugging

The edit/compile/execute cycle is illustrated in Figure 1.13. Just below the Editor is a Java program. The Compiler translates this Java program into Java Bytecode, shown in the figure as a sequence of numbers, which, of course, it is. The Java Bytecode produced by the compiler is then loaded and interpreted by the Java Interpreter, producing the output shown.

If you're working in an *integrated development environment*, or *IDE*, instead of a command-oriented system, you're lucky! An IDE allows you to edit, compile, and run programs by clicking on command buttons, rather than by typing commands. The procedures for compiling and executing programs will differ from those just described for command-oriented systems; consult the manual or your local guru for details.

integrated development environment

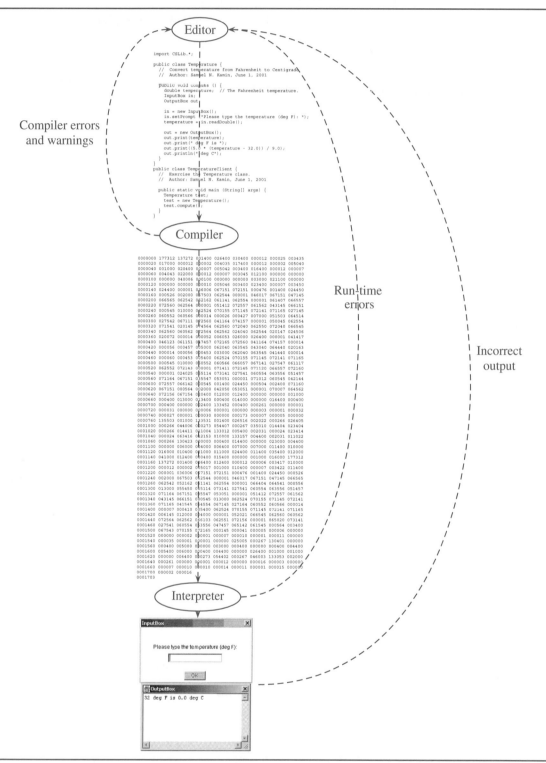

FIGURE 1.13 The cycle of editing, compiling, and debugging a program. The Java program shown is the temperature program from Section 3.3 (pages 67 and 68).

Applications and Applets

In Java, you can write two kinds of programs: applications and applets. *Applica-*   *applications*
tions are stand-alone programs that run on your own computer. They are no
different from the kinds of programs that you might write in other programming
languages, such as C++. Applications can read and manipulate data stored on your
computer's disk, as well as data that you enter through the keyboard. Applications
can also write data on your disk, display output on your screen, and print on
your printer. All the programs you normally run, including word processors,
spreadsheet programs, and games, are applications.

Unlike applications, *applets* are executed from within a *browser*, such as   *applets*
Netscape Navigator or Internet Explorer. Once you've written an applet, not   *browser*
only can you execute it from within your browser, but also you can make it
available for others to execute from within *their* browsers. Correspondingly, you
can execute applets that other programmers have written. The ability to execute
applets really brings the World Wide Web to life, and it is its ability to write
applets that has made Java the sensation that it is.

The difference between applications and applets is illustrated in Figure 1.14.

(a) Application is a stand-alone program
    that runs in its own window:

(b) Applet runs in a window within the
    browser's window:

FIGURE 1.14 Applications versus applets.

We will teach you how to write both applications and applets. Applets are more fun, because you can easily show your work to the entire world. On the other hand, since creating and running applets require slightly more work than creating an application (for example, you have to create a web page to run an applet), we will begin by focusing on applications. Applets are covered in detail in Chapter 13. In any case, the differences between them are mainly superficial; an application and an applet, if they do the same computation, will differ only slightly.

Summary

The computer can do extraordinary things in the hands of a skillful programmer. By now you should have some idea of the steps involved in programming. The *problem* must first be clarified and an appropriate *algorithm* developed; the algorithm must be stated in a specific computer language, such as Java, to become a *program*. Object-oriented programming is a modern paradigm that allows the programmer to model the problem in a real-world fashion. Objects interact with one another by sending messages.

The most important internal parts of a computer are the *central processing unit, main memory,* and *hard disk.* In addition, *input/output devices* allow the computer to receive input from, and provide results to, the outside world. A program executes only when it and all the data it needs are in the main memory; programs and data can be read from the hard disk when needed, and results can be written out to the hard disk.

Computers use *binary numbers.* Numbers can be used to represent any conceivable kind of data. Text is represented as a sequence of numbers by choosing a code for each letter. Pictures are represented by dividing them into numerous *picture elements,* or *pixels,* and representing each pixel by a number. Video images are represented by placing numerous pictures one after another. Sounds are represented by *sampling* the sound wave at regular intervals. All data are stored in *files* on the hard disk.

To run a program, enter it into a file using an *editor,* then *compile* it to transform it to machine language. *Debugging* is the process whereby errors in a program are detected and fixed. Errors can be *syntactic,* meaning that the compiler cannot understand the program; or they can be *logical,* meaning that the program compiles to machine language but an error occurs when it is executed. Errors that occur during execution of a program will sometimes cause the program to stop prematurely with an (obscure, usually) error message; other times, they will simply give incorrect results with no warning. Programs must be thoroughly tested and debugged to ensure that neither of these errors can occur.

In Java parlance, *applications* are ordinary programs that are run from a computer's desktop, and *applets* are programs that run within a window inside a web browser. Java can be used to write either kind of program.

Exercises

1. To familiarize yourself with the notion of an *algorithm*, write specific, detailed, procedures for the following activities. Use the Java "if" and "while" constructs where appropriate.
   (a) Fill your car with gas.
   (b) Place the initial set of red and black pieces on a standard 8×8 checkerboard.
   (c) Generalize the algorithm in part (b) so that it works for a checkerboard of any given size n, so long as n is even.
   (d) Add two three-digit decimal numbers.
   (e) Generalize the algorithm in part (d) to add two decimal numbers of any length n.

2. The central programming structure in any object-oriented language is the *class*. However, some languages use different terminology. Use the Internet to look up each of the following computer languages. For each, determine whether or not it is an object-oriented language and, if it is, the term used for what Java calls a class:
   (a) Fortran
   (b) Cobol
   (c) C
   (d) C++
   (e) JavaScript
   (f) Eiffel
   (g) Visual Basic

3. Using the Internet, find a computer you can buy for between $900 and $1000. Describe the computer, giving the type of its CPU, the amount of main memory and the size of its hard disk.

4. In addition to binary (base 2) and decimal (base 10), computer programmers frequently use *octal* (base 8) representation. Numbers in octal use digits 0–7, and the multiplier for the ith digit is 8^i. For example, $370_8 = 3 \times 8^2 + y \times 8^1 + 0 \times 8^0 = 248_{10}$.
   (a) Convert 370_8 to binary.
   (b) Convert 101111000_2 to octal.
   (c) Octal numbers are popular in computing because there is a simple way to convert them to and from binary. Can you find the algorithm? After doing several more conversions the hard way (translating to and from decimal), you should be able to see it.

5. Continuing with the previous exercise, there is another base commonly used in computing: base 16, or *hexadecimal*. Since this base needs 16 numerals, we use the orginary numerals 0–9 and the letters A–F for the numbers from 10 to 15. For example, $1FF_{16} = 511_{10}(1 \times 16^2 + 15 \times 16^1 + 15 \times 16^0)$. As with octal notation, the main attraction of hexadecimal is that it is easy to convert to and from binary. Redo part (c) of exercise 4 using hexadecimal in place of octal.

6. Although ASCII is a very widely used code for English text, it is quite limited because, as a one-byte code, it can represent only 256 different characters. Java uses the more modern Unicode representation, which is a two-byte (16-bit) code, allowing for 65,536 different characters. Find the Unicode code for these characters:

A: ordinary capital A
ç: c with "cedilla"
π: Lower-case Greek letter "pi"
£: British pounds sterling
¥: Japanese Yen symbol

7. A black-and-white image uses a single bit per pixel. A gray-scale image might permit 16 levels of gray (from pure white to pure black). Many computers allow three options for representing colors: 256 colors (one byte per pixel), "thousands of colors" (two bytes per pixel) and "millions of colors" (four bytes—one word—per pixel). If a 1000×1000-pixel image is stored in a computer, how much memory will it occupy if it is represented in each of these ways?

2 CLASSES AND METHODS I: BASICS

CHAPTER PREVIEW

We look at some sample Java programs and use them to illustrate the structure of a Java program. We illustrate techniques for creating and using objects—instances of a class. We introduce two particular classes that are used throughout the book for doing output: `OutputBox` for text output and `DrawingBox` for graphical output. With the `DrawingBox`, we lay the foundation for doing sophisticated graphical output.

Three blind mice,
Three blind mice,
See how they run!
See how they run!

—Mother Goose

The first step in learning to *write* programs is learning how to *read* them. If a program is simple, well written, and arranged neatly on the page, reading it can be a pleasure. In this chapter we read several simple programs and use them to illustrate the fundamental parts of a Java program.

2.1

Some Simple Programs

We begin with some complete but simple working programs. These programs are *applications* rather than applets, meaning they are run outside of a web browser. However, these applications *do* use a graphical interface for communicating with the user. Here is our first Java program:[1]

```
1    import CSLib.*;
2
3    public class HitWall {
4        //  Exterminate a rodent.
5        //  Author: Elizabeth Baranowicz, September 8, 2000
6
7      public static void main (String[] args) {
8        TrickMouse morte;
9
10        morte = new TrickMouse();
11        morte.hitWall();
12      }
13    }
```

To summarize what this program does, it creates a `TrickMouse` object (line 10) and sends it the `hitWall` message (line 11). The object responds by displaying the window shown in Figure 2.1. This application, like all the

---

[1] The small line numbers are *not* part of the program; they are shown here so that we can refer to them in our discussions.

FIGURE 2.1   The output of the `HitWall` application.

applications in this book, are executed from a command line and write output to an output window.[2]

We first type this program into a file named `HitWall.java`. (The name is chosen to match the name on line 3 of the program, including choice of lower- and uppercase.) Next we compile the program by typing the command

```
javac HitWall.java
```

Then we execute the program by typing the command

```
java HitWall
```

Now a window pops up on the computer screen and displays a mouse performing the "hit the wall" trick, as shown in Figure 2.1.

BUG ALERT 2.1

Each Class Requires a Separate File

Java imposes the restriction that the name you use following the word `class` must also be used as the base name for the file into which you type the program. The last part, or *extension*, of the file name must be `.java`. It is important that the file name and class name match *exactly*, upper/lowercase and all! (Later we'll see that there are some exceptions to this rule.)

QUICK EXERCISE 2.1

Enter, compile, and execute the `HitWall` program. Remember that the small line numbers are not part of the program, but you type everything else exactly as we've shown it. (*Warning*: Make sure you have downloaded the `CSLib` package from our website; see page xxvii or consult your instructor.)

---

[2]If you are using an IDE, as discussed in Chapter 1, your method of invoking the program will be different from what we show; consult your local guru.

```
1    import CSLib.*;
2
3    public class HitWall {
4        // Exterminate a rodent.
5        // Author:   Elizabeth Baranowicz, September 8, 2000
6
7        public static void main (String[] args) {
8            TrickMouse morte;
9
10           morte = new TrickMouse();
11           morte.hitWall();
12       }
     }
```

FIGURE 2.2 Structure of the HitWall program.

The program is pretty cryptic, to be sure. We will look over every line in detail, but first a few words about the overall layout and appearance of the program. The blank lines are there strictly for aesthetic reasons and have no effect on the operation of the program. They provide what is called *white space* to make the program more easily readable by a human. Lines 4 and 5 are *comment lines*, meaning lines whose only purpose—but a very important one!—is to help other humans to read the program; the computer ignores them. Line 4 identifies the author and date of the program; often there are additional comment lines at the beginning of a program to explain such things as its purpose and intended usage and to give other *documentation*. Comment lines are those that begin with a double slash //.

The "working part" of the program consists of all the lines that are not blank or comment lines. Line 1 (highlighted in Figure 2.2) is an *import directive* that tells the Java compiler which *packages* our program will use. Packages are predefined collections of programs providing services used by many programmers; they exist so that programmers don't have to keep reinventing the same code. An import directive always consists of the word import and the name of a package. The CSLib.* package is one that we've produced to support the examples in this book. It contains the "trick mouse" class that we've written. CSLib also contains the graphical interface that we use for output in our examples (which you will also use in doing the exercises). The complete source for the CSLib package is available for download on our website.

Line 3 (see Figure 2.2) is a *class heading* that needs to be included at the beginning of every program; this heading consists of the words public class and the name of the class (which must exactly match the root portion of the file name).

The *main method* appears in lines 7 through 12 (see Figure 2.2). You can tell it is the main method because of its *method heading* on line 7. A method

white space

comment

documentation

import directive

packages

class heading

main method

method heading

function   (also called a *function*) with the name `main` represents the main computation of an application; it is what is first executed when the application is run. The individual parts of this line will be explained in various places in this book, but you needn't worry about them: This method heading will always appear *exactly as shown here* in every application.

body   The important part, called the *body*, of the main method is between the { on line 7 and the matching } on line 12. These lines do the real work of the application, and we now discuss them in detail.

Lines 12 and 13 really do little, but they must be there or the compiler (`javac`) will issue error messages. Note that lines 3 and 7 contain *opening braces* {. Lines 13 and 12 contain corresponding *closing braces* }. Specifically, the braces on lines 3 and 13 are a matching pair, indicating that everything between them (lines 4 through 12) is part of the class called `HitWall`. The braces on lines 7 and 12 match up, indicating that everything between them comprises the body of the `main` method. Note how the braces are nested: The entire `main` method is contained within the class. We will see this sort of nesting—one part of a program containing other parts of the program—repeatedly, and it is usually represented, as here, by matching braces.

QUICK EXERCISE 2.2	You will see the Java compiler, `javac`, print numerous error messages as you work through the examples and exercises in this book. To get used to this, make the following changes in the `HitWall` program, one at a time, and see what the compiler does in each case.

1. Omit one of the semicolons.
2. Add an extra semicolon at the end of a line.
3. Change `main` to `mian`.
4. Change one occurrence of { to [.

A full understanding of Java programs, even simple ones like this, relies on the closely related concepts of *classes* and *objects*. It will take some time for you to understand these concepts completely, but we start introducing them now and continue to use them, gradually explaining them in greater depth.

The last few pages explain the structure of the `HitWall` program, but we haven't yet explained the details of *how* the program accomplishes its task, namely, the production of the output shown in Figure 2.1. The program accom-
execute   plishes its task(s) when we *execute* the program by typing the command

```
java HitWall
```

When this, or any, application begins running, the computer starts in the `main` method. The name `main` is very special, and there must be only one use of it—in the method heading identifying the main method. In the main method, line 8 says that the program will use a `TrickMouse`, and that the trick mouse will be called

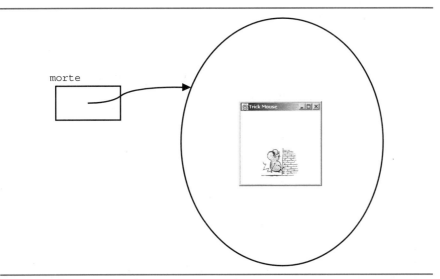

FIGURE 2.3 **The variable** `morte` **is made to refer to a** `TrickMouse` **object.**

`morte`. (Just as in elementary algebra when you say, "Let x be the number of bananas we buy and y be the cost per banana," here we are saying, "Let `morte` be the name of the trick mouse.") The word `morte` is called a *variable*, and line 8 is a *declaration* saying that the program intends to use the variable called `morte`.

variable declaration

The heart of the program is in the two *executable statements* on lines 10 and 11. The compiled program executes these statements one after the other. All Java programs consist of declarations and executable statements that are executed in this fashion. You should be able to guess what line 10 does—it creates the new `TrickMouse` object that we declared would be used. In addition to creating the `TrickMouse` object, line 10 stores a reference to the newly created object in the *variable* `morte`. In Java parlance, we say that the reference to the new `TrickMouse` is *assigned as the value of the variable* `morte`, or simply *assigned to* `morte`. Figure 2.3 depicts this assignment. Finally we get to line 11. This line "sends the `hitWall` message" to the object that the variable `morte` refers to. Note the syntax here: the name of the object (`morte`) followed by a period, followed by the name of the message. Other terminology is also used. It is sometimes said that the `hitWall` method is *called* or *invoked*. In response to this message, the `TrickMouse` will display the window shown in Figure 2.1.

executable statements

variable variable assignment

To summarize, this sequence of actions takes place when the `HitWall` application is executed:

1. The Java run-time interpreter transfers control to the `main` method.
2. The executable statement at line 10 is executed, which
   (a) Creates a new instance of a `TrickMouse`.

(b) Stores a reference to the newly created `TrickMouse` object in the variable `morte`.

3. The statement at line 11 is executed, invoking the method `hitWall` on the object referred to by `morte`. The method `hitWall` causes a window to appear picturing a mouse performing the hit-the-wall trick. (It does this, in turn, by sending messages to the computer's "desktop" object; that code is in `CSLib`.)

4. The `main` method reaches the end of its body (line 12) and returns control to the Java run-time system.

The Java run-time system will continue to remain active until you either close the output window or explicitly terminate the program.

Just where is all the code for the class `TrickMouse`? It's in the `CSLib` package that line 1 imported! How did we know that a `TrickMouse` object would respond to a `hitWall` message, and how did we know just what would be displayed as a result? Every class defines a set of methods, and these are precisely the set of messages that objects of the class can handle. *We* know which these are because we wrote the `TrickMouse` class; *you* know it because we told *documentation* you! In general, classes have *documentation* that tells you what messages their objects respond to and how they respond. Are there other messages to which a `TrickMouse` will respond? You must look at the documentation to decide. In this book, we introduce classes gradually, and we include brief documentation describing the methods that are defined for each class.

2.1.1 Identifiers

Our `HitWall` program used three names that were chosen by the programmer: `HitWall` was the name of the class, `morte` was the name of the `TrickMouse`, and `main` was the name of the main method. In addition, some *other* programmer chose the name `TrickMouse` for the class that was placed in the `CSLib` package for our use, and *still another* programmer chose `CSLib` for the package name itself.

identifier   These names, or *identifiers*, are used for various purposes. Identifiers such
variable   as `morte` are called *variables*; they give names to data that can be manipulated,
method name including objects. Identifiers such as `main` are called *method names*; they give names to the messages that can be sent to objects. Identifiers such as `HitWall`
class name   are called *class names*. Identifiers such as `CSLib` are called *package names*.
package name   Not every possible identifier is legal. For example, it is an error to write

        import 4.7;

because `4.7` is not a proper name for a package. Similarly,

        import !%--;

is not legal. Rather, an identifier must consist of a letter (upper- or lowercase) followed by any number (including zero) of letters and digits. Thus, legal identifiers are

        temperature   temp1   TEMP23   T

abstract	boolean	break	byte	byvalue	case
cast	catch	char	class	const	continue
default	do	double	else	extends	false
final	finally	float	for	future	generic
goto	if	implements	import	inner	instanceof
int	interface	long	native	new	null
operator	outer	package	private	protected	public
rest	return	short	static	super	switch
synchronized	this	throw	throws	transient	true
try	var	void	volatile	while	

TABLE 2.1   Keywords in Java.

Also, for this purpose, the characters underscore _ and dollar sign $ are considered letters, so that

      $temp_1   T$$0   low_temp

are legal identifiers.

Note that lower- and uppercase letters are considered *distinct*, so that identifiers temp and Temp are different.

Some sequences of letters appear to be legal identifiers but are not, because they are reserved by the language for special uses. These are called *keywords*.   *keyword*
The keywords of Java are listed in Table 2.1. For example, you cannot use class or int as variable names.

QUICK EXERCISE 2.3

Which of the following are valid Java identifiers? In each case, explain why or why not.

first_entry	2nd	dataType	right-hand
FATHER	break	a<b	last one
____	this	1.2.3	a.b.c

There is a *convention* in Java for distinguishing some of the kinds of iden-   *convention*
tifiers. Like all conventions, this is not a firm rule, but a rule of thumb that most Java programmers follow.

1. Variable names and method names begin with lowercase letters. Those that read as multiple words are run together, with each successive word capitalized. Examples are morte and hitWall.

2. Class identifiers begin with uppercase letters. Class names that read as multiple words have each successive word capitalized. Examples are TrickMouse and HitWall.

FIGURE 2.4 The output of the `HelloMorte` application.

Notice that in our program, the names `hitWall` and `HitWall` are *different names*—one is a method name, and the other a class name.

2.1.2 Another `TrickMouse` Program

For the `TrickMouse` class, there are two other methods that we can use:

- The `setTitle` method changes the string that appears in the window's title.
- The `speak` method displays a mouse "speaking" a phrase.

The following program, which is a slight modification of our `HitWall` program, uses both of these methods.

```
1   import CSLib.*;
2
3   public class HelloMorte {
4      //  Author: Dan Ries, December 25, 2000
5      //  Have Morte say hello.
6
7      public static void main (String[] args) {
8         TrickMouse morte;
9
10        morte = new TrickMouse();
11        morte.setTitle("I'm Morte");
12        morte.speak("Hello, world!");
13     }
14  }
```

The program's output is shown in Figure 2.4. This program is almost identical to the previous `HitWall` program. The name of the class has changed from `HitWall` to `HelloMorte`, as has the file which contains the code. The change to the code itself involves replacing the former line

```
11        morte.hitWall();
```

with the two method calls:

```
11        morte.setTitle("I'm Morte");
12        morte.speak("Hello, world!");
```

These two method calls are different from the hitWall() call. With hitWall(), there was no additional information that we needed to transmit to the TrickMouse object morte. However, for the two new methods, we must provide additional information by providing text inside the parentheses of the method call. So setTitle("I'm Morte") causes the characters *I*, *'*, *m*, , *M*, *o*, *r*, *t*, and *e* to be displayed one by one in the title bar of morte's window, thereby forming the displayed title. Likewise, the call speak("Hello world!") draws the appropriate picture and causes those characters to be displayed in the window. Such a sequence of characters is called a *string* in Java. A specific string is written   *string* as a sequence of characters enclosed in a pair of double quotes (" ").

QUICK EXERCISE 2.4

Create a GoodbyeMorte program the same as the HelloMorte program, but saying Goodbye instead of Hello. Make sure to change the name of the file to Goodbye.java and to change all uses of Hello to Goodbye in the program.

QUICK EXERCISE 2.5

Add a new line to the HelloMorte program just after line 12 that is identical to line 12 except for replacing Hello by Goodbye. What do you think will happen? Call this program HelloGoodbyeMorte.

Having seen how the methods of the TrickMouse class behave, you can now understand the brief documentation that would normally be given for the class. An example of brief class documentation is given in Table 2.2. The word void indicates that the method doesn't return any value to the calling program, but after it does its work, it merely causes its caller to resume executing. Also, the documentation tells us that the setTitle method requires that we supply a string to specify exactly what the title should be. This is called an *argument*;   *argument* the word String is Java's formal *type* that corresponds to the string literals that   *type* we've been writing. The specification for the argument, String t, says that "I, the method setTitle, expect the caller to supply an argument of type String, and I'll call it t." Likewise, speak requires a String to specify exactly what the mouse should "speak." When the method is actually called, the caller must supply some value to be used as the argument. This is analogous to mathematical functions, such as sin, where you are required to supply an argument, for example, $\sin(2 \times \pi)$.

Often the basic features of a class can be summarized in a concise drawing.   *Unified Modeling* One popular mechanism for doing this is the *Unified Modeling Language*, or   *Language* *UML*. Over the years, a number of notations were developed for describing the   *UML*

Name	Description
`void hitWall ()`	Plays dead
`void setTitle (String t)`	Sets the window title to t
`void speak (String s)`	Speaks the phrase s

TABLE 2.2   Methods of the `TrickMouse` class.

UML Class Diagram

relations in object-oriented programs. However, since 1999, UML has emerged as a popular standard. We gradually introduce many of the UML features that will help us to document our programs. Although the diagrams may seem trivial at first, we'll soon find that they are very useful when designing classes and their relationships. The first UML tool that we use is the *class diagram*. The class diagram for `TrickMouse` is

```
┌─────────────────────────┐
│       TrickMouse        │
├─────────────────────────┤
│                         │
├─────────────────────────┤
│ hitWall()               │
│ speak( :String)         │
│ setTitle( :String)      │
└─────────────────────────┘
```

In the top line of the class diagram, the name of the class is given. In the bottom line, the class's methods are listed. If a method requires an argument, then the type of that argument is shown. By examining the diagram, you can see that for each `speak` and each `setTitle`, an argument of type `String` is required. In the center line of the diagram, the class's internal data are detailed. Often we know little more about a class than the methods that we're allowed to invoke on its objects. In this case we see that the middle line is empty, indicating that we do not know (or do not wish to disclose) anything about the internal data for a `TrickMouse`.

2.2   Building Simple Classes

There is much more to discuss regarding classes, objects, and methods. However, we now have enough ammunition to *build* our first useful class! It is simple, to be sure, but it illustrates what is to come.

Imagine that you are writing a large program, say an adventure game, and when certain circumstances occur, you need to present instructions or warnings to the player. Suppose that you'd like to use the `TrickMouse` to give a warning, causing it to be displayed with a "WARNING" title, and having it "`speak`" the message "Look Out!" as shown in Figure 2.5. We know what must be done, since

FIGURE 2.5 **The output of the** `WarningMouseClient` **application.**

that's exactly how we wrote the `HelloMorte` program. But `HelloMorte` is a *stand-alone* program; it cannot be "called" from our adventure game program. What we would like is a new class, call it `WarningMouse`, with one method:

Name	Description
`void shout ()`	Gives the "Look Out!" warning.

If we were to draw a class diagram for our `WarningMouse`, it would look like this:

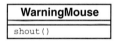

Since *we* are going to build the `WarningMouse` class, we know all the details about it. In particular, there will be one method, called `shout` with no required arguments.

All we need to do is to adapt the code from `HelloMorte`:

```
1   import CSLib.*;
2
3   public class WarningMouse {
4     //  Exterminate a rodent.
5     //  Author: Courtney Mickunas, November 21, 2000
6
7     public void shout () {
8       TrickMouse alert;
9
10      alert = new TrickMouse();
11      alert.setTitle("WARNING");
12      alert.speak("Look Out!");
13    }
14  }
```

This class is quite similar to the earlier `HelloMorte` program. The primary difference is that instead of the `main` method, we have a method called `shout` in lines 7 through 13. This time we've used a variable `alert` rather than morte, but that is merely the programmer's choice of which name to give to the TrickMouse object. The important distinction is that the method shout is defined with particular properties:

- It is public, meaning that it is one of the methods that other classes may use. Other classes that use the methods of the WarningMouse class are *clients*   called *clients* of WarningMouse.
return type   - It has a *return type* of void, meaning that it does not return any value to the caller.

How would a client use our WarningMouse class? The programmer would write a program very much like the two we've already written, except that instead of creating a TrickMouse object ("instantiating" TrickMouse) and sending it messages, he or she would create an instance of our newly crafted WarningMouse and send it messages. Here's an example:

```
1   public class WarningMouseClient {
2       // Exercise the WarningMouse class.
3       // Author: Courtney Mickunas, November 21, 2000
4
5       public static void main(String[] args) {
6           WarningMouse snitch;
7           snitch = new WarningMouse();
8           snitch.shout();
9       }
10  }
```

To run this client successfully, we must

- Compile the WarningMouse class: javac WarningMouse.java
- Compile the WarningMouseClient class: javac WarningMouseClient.jav
- Run the WarningMouseClient program: java WarningMouseClient

You should make sure that both the WarningMouseClient class and the WarningMouse class files are in the same folder, or directory.

The foregoing example is typical of the applications that we write throughout this book. The general layout of all of our classes is the same, and it should look like

```
public class Classname {
    public void methodName () {



    }
}
```

with the bulk of the work done in statements contained in the shaded region. The typical use of such a class by a client will look like this:

```
class ClassnameClient {
    public static void main (String[] args) {
        Classname variable;
        variable = new Classname();
        variable.methodName();
    }
}
```

As we increase our knowledge of classes, we'll add more and more details to them.

Text Output

The process of displaying data, either in printed form or on the computer screen, is called *output*. In Java, there are a number of ways to produce output. For now, the programs that we write will produce output on the computer screen, using objects from the CSLib package. In particular, the CSLib package defines a class OutputBox to which we can write lines of text. The brief documentation for OutputBox is given in Table 2.3.

output

We know how to read some of these method descriptions. For example, the first one says that the method setTitle expects the caller to supply a string argument that will be called t. But what about the next description? What is the meaning of int i? In the same way that String t says that the setTitle method expects an argument of type String that it will call t, the notation int i says that the method print expects an argument of

Name	Description
void setTitle (String t)	Sets the window title to the string "t"
void print (int i)	Prints the integer "i"
void print (String s)	Prints the string "s"
void print (double d)	Prints the double "d"
void print (boolean b)	Prints the boolean "b"
void print (char c)	Prints the char "c"
void println (int i)	Prints the integer "i" then a newline
void println (String s)	Prints the string "s" then a newline
void println (double d)	Prints the double "d" then a newline
void println (boolean b)	Prints the boolean "b" then a newline
void println (char c)	Prints the char "c" then a newline

TABLE 2.3 Some methods of the OutputBox **class. Those for** double, boolean, **and** char **are explained in subsequent chapters.**

int literals

type int that it will call i. There are many ways that a caller can supply something of type int, but for now, we supply only *int literals*. The int literals are the positive and negative counting integers 0, 1, −1, 2, −2, 3, −3, ... Then there is the fourth method, void print (double d). Obviously this says that the print method expects an argument of type double that it *double literals*   will call d. The *double literals* are decimal numbers, such as 3.45, −47.2, and 33.0.

So we can send the print or println message to an OutputBox object to display output on the computer screen. The two messages behave similarly, *new-line*   with println supplying an ending *new-line* character. The new-line character behaves as a carriage return and paper advance on a typewriter. The new-line *output cursor*   character does not actually appear on the computer screen, but it causes the *output cursor* (often a blinking vertical bar) to be positioned at the beginning of the next line. We use print (without the new-line) when we know that there is more printing to be done on the present line.

When an int is given as the argument to print or println, it is converted to characters for printing. Likewise a double is converted to characters, with an appropriate number of decimal places. Strings are printed directly, just as the speak method of a TrickMouse did. As an example, this is a program to print the weather forecast:

```
1    import CSLib.*;
2
3    public class Forecast {
4       // Give the weather forecast.
5       // Author: Edward M. Reingold, November 12, 2000
6
7       public void predict () {
8          OutputBox out;
9          out = new OutputBox();
10         out.print("The temperature will be ");
11         out.print(-10);
12         out.println(" degrees.");
13         out.println("That's cold, folks!");
14      }
15   }
```

The output of this program is shown in Figure 2.6. The actual output is somewhat larger, but to conserve space, we've manually adjusted the size of the OutputBox before capturing it for printing.

QUICK EXERCISE 2.6	Type in the Forecast program and run it. Manually adjust the size of the OutputBox so that it matches what is shown in Figure 2.6.

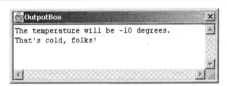

FIGURE 2.6 Output for the Forecast program.

As always, execution begins with line 9 in the main method, which creates the OutputBox object and causes the variable out to refer to it; in line 8, we declare that we will be using an OutputBox, and that we will refer to it by the name out. In line 10, we send the print message to the out object, supplying a string literal as an argument; this causes the string to be displayed in the OutputBox, without a new-line character at the end. Then in line 11, we send the print message to the out object, supplying an integer literal as an argument; this causes the integer to be converted to the three characters −, 1, and 0, which are then displayed in the OutputBox. These three characters continue on the same line as the previous printing. Then in line 12, we send the println message to the out object, supplying a string as an argument; this causes the string to be displayed continuing on the same line as the previous printing, but this time a new-line character is added to the end. Finally, in line 13, we send the println message to the out object, supplying a string as an argument; this causes the string to be displayed on a new line (why?). Then it is followed by a new-line character.

QUICK EXERCISE 2.7

1. What would happen if in the Forecast program the first print were changed to out.print("The temperature will be"), eliminating the blank character following the word be?
2. What if the first println were changed to print?
3. What if all the prints were changed to printlns?

It is not necessary for you to understand at this time how the code works within these CSLib objects. As you learn more about Java, you will understand more and more about the code for these objects; the complete Java code for them is available from our website.

2.4

Drawing in Java

> Our father, Adam sat under the Tree and scratched with a
> stick in the mould;
> And the first rude sketch that the world had seen was joy
> to his mighty heart.
> Till the Devil whispered behind the leaves, "It's pretty,
> but is it Art?"
>
> —Rudyard Kipling
> *The Conundrum of the Workshops*

In addition to simple dialog boxes for doing output, the CSLib package provides the ability to draw simple pictures on the screen. This is done using the class DrawingBox. The DrawingBox class is used in a manner similar to the OutputBox: You declare a variable to be of type DrawingBox, build a new object of type DrawingBox, and send various messages to the DrawingBox object. The methods do such things as draw lines, draw circles, and draw rectangles.

pixel   The DrawingBox window is divided into a rectangular grid of *pixels* (picture elements), as shown in Figure 2.7. The size of a pixel depends on the resolution of your computer monitor, but it can be as small as $\frac{1}{100}$ inch on each *resolution*   side. The number of pixels in the grid—its *resolution*—varies; 1000×1000 is the approximate resolution of workstation screens. By increasing the resolution, the amount of detail in displayed images can be increased; the disadvantage is the additional memory and the greater time needed to draw an image.

Another variable quantity is the number of available colors for each pixel. Some systems have only two—black and white—whereas others have 256 dif-

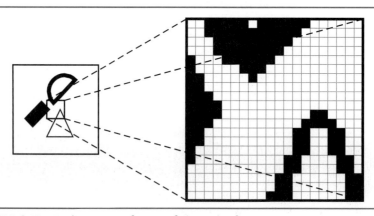

FIGURE 2.7   A picture made up of tiny pixels.

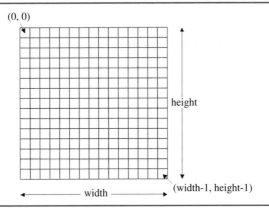

FIGURE 2.8 **The `DrawingBox` window as a grid.**

ferent colors and still others have millions. The more colors, the better; but again it requires additional memory if each pixel has a wide range of values.

To draw lines and figures on the screen, you must consider the `DrawingBox` to be a grid of small squares, with square (0, 0) at the upper left and some point with positive coordinates (x, y), depending upon the size of the `DrawingBox` window, at the lower right, as shown in Figure 2.8. (Therefore, y values increase as you go down, in contrast to Cartesian coordinates in mathematics. Note that a window of size, say, 200 × 300 has pixels numbered (0, 0), …, (199, 299).)

Some of the graphical operations provided as methods in the `DrawingBox` class are shown in Table 2.4. The integer arguments to the various `draw...` methods are in units of pixels. For example, the following code fragment draws about a 1-inch horizontal line about $\frac{1}{2}$ inch from the top of the window.

```
DrawingBox g;
g = new DrawingBox();
g.drawLine(0, 25, 50, 25)
```

As a simple first example, let's write a program to draw three concentric circles. The output is shown in Figure 2.9, and here is the program:

```
1    import CSLib.*;
2
3    public class Concentric {
4       // Draw concentric circles.
5       // Author: Adrienne Baranowicz, December 2, 2000
6
7       public void drawThem () {
8          DrawingBox g;
9          g = new DrawingBox();
10         g.setDrawableSize(300, 300);
11         g.drawOval(110, 110, 80, 80);
12         g.drawOval(95, 95, 110, 110);
13         g.drawOval(80, 80, 140, 140);
14      }
15   }
```

Example	Explanation
void drawLine (int x0, int y0, int x1, int y1)	Draws a line from point $(x0, y0)$ to $(x1, y1)$.
void drawRect (int x, int y, int w, int h)	Draws the outline of a rectangle with upper left corner at (x, y), having width w and height h.
void fillRect (int x, int y, int w, int h)	Draws a rectangle as with drawRect, but fill it in with the current color (see page 50).
void drawOval (int x, int y, int w, int h)	Draws an oval inscribed in the rectangle with upper left corner at (x, y), having width w and height h.
void fillOval (int x, int y, int w, int h)	Draws an oval as with drawOval, but fill it in with the current color.
void drawString (String s, int x, int y)	Draws the string s with its baseline (bottom left corner) at (x, y).
void setTitle (String t)	Sets the window title to t.
void setSize (int w, int h)	Sets the window size to w pixels wide by h pixels high.
void setDrawableSize (int w, int h)	Sets the window size large enough that the *drawable portion* is w pixels wide by h pixels high.
void setColor (Color c)	Sets the drawing color to c.

TABLE 2.4   Some methods of the DrawingBox class.

with the client:

```
1   import CSLib.*;
2
3   public class ConcentricClient {
4
5     public static void main (String[] args) {
6       Concentric circles;
7       circles = new Concentric();
8       circles.drawThem();
9     }
10  }
```

In line 10 we see a new message that can be sent to a DrawingBox, the setDrawableSize message. This message ensures that the size of the DrawingBox is large enough that its drawing region is 300×300 pixels. There is also a method setSize that sets the *overall* size of the DrawingBox, including the borders. The OutputBox also can be resized with the setSize message.

The program draws three concentric circles with their centers at (150, 150) and with radii of 40, 55, and 70. The three statements that do the drawing, the method calls in lines 11 through 13, simply draw three ovals. The first one has

FIGURE 2.9 Drawing concentric circles.

the upper left corner of its circumscribing rectangle at (110, 110) and its height and width are each 80. (Thus, the "oval" is a circle with a diameter of 80. You can do the math to see that the *center* of that rectangle, and hence the center of the circle, is at (150, 150).) Similarly, the second circle is centered at (150, 150), but with a diameter of 110, while the third concentric circle has a diameter of 140.

QUICK EXERCISE 2.8

Write a program that first creates a DrawingBox of size 250 × 300 and then draws an X from corner to corner in that DrawingBox.

QUICK EXERCISE 2.9

Write a program that sets the drawable size of a DrawingBox to 300 × 500, then draws as large an oval as possible in that DrawingBox.

2.4.1 Color

Take a look at the description for the setColor method of the DrawingBox class (in Table 2.4). This method expects an argument of type Color. Color is one of the classes that is predefined in Java. The Java package java.awt contains the class Color. This class defines *symbolic constants* Color.black, *symbolic constants* Color.white, Color.red, Color.blue, and several others. Recall from Section 1.3.3 that several bits are needed to represent a colored pixel. By using symbolic constants, you do not need to know what those bits are—you can simply use the symbolic constant.

As Table 2.4 shows, you use `setColor` on the `DrawingBox` object to set the current color; everything will be drawn in that color until you change it again. This code draws a rectangle in blue with a black outline:

```
1   import CSLib.*;
2   import java.awt.*;
3
4   public class Rectangle {
5      // Draw a blue rectangle with a black border.
6      // Author: Erica Little, March 19, 2000
7
8      public void drawIt () {
9         DrawingBox g;
10        g = new DrawingBox();
11        g.setSize(300, 300);
12        g.setColor(Color.blue);
13        g.fillRect(0,0,50,25);
14        g.setColor(Color.black);
15        g.drawRect(0,0,50,25);
16     }
17  }
```

and here is the client:

```
1   public class RectangleClient {
2
3      public static void main (String[] args) {
4         Rectangle r;
5         r = new Rect();
6         r.drawIt();
7      }
8   }
```

There is one important thing to notice about this program. In line 2 we must import the `java.awt` package, since the `Color` class (and consequently the definitions of the `Color` symbolic constants) is found there.

QUICK EXERCISE 2.10

Modify the `Concentric` program on page 47 so that the circles are drawn in red.

QUICK EXERCISE 2.11

Examine the online Java documentation for the class `java.awt.Color` to determine which other colors are predefined.

> ### *Erroneous Punctuation*
>
> The most common mistakes made by both new and experienced programmers are mismatching opening and closing braces and omitting a semicolon. The computer is unforgiving if you fail to follow its grammatical rules; unaware of your intent, it will try to run statements together in pursuit of a semicolon or closing brace. This results in peculiar and sometimes grotesque behavior. To help avoid this problem and to make your program more intelligible, the statements should be placed on the screen (or paper) with consistent, easily read indentations, as illustrated throughout this book.

2.4.2 Program Layout

Let's review the "physical" structure of Java applications.

A simple class definition starts with the words `public class` *Classname* and an opening brace {, then contains one method and finally a }. The body of the method is also enclosed within braces, and it contains declarations of *variables* and various *executable statements*. So far, the only executable statements that we have seen are the creation, and assigning to a variable, of a new object using the `new` statement, and statements that send messages to such objects. In each case, these statements, called *atomic statements*, were terminated by a semicolon.

executable statements

atomic statements

The form in which a program is laid out on the page (or monitor) is not important to the Java compiler; the compiler cares only about the keywords and punctuation (parentheses, commas, braces, and semicolons). The program can be compressed to have almost no blanks at all. Here is what the concentric circles program looks like when compressed into dense lines of characters with no comments.

```
1   import CSLib.*;public class Concentric{public void
2   drawThem(){DrawingBox g;g=new DrawingBox();g.
3   setDrawableSize(300,300);g.drawOval(110,110,80,
4   80);g.drawOval(95,95,110,110);g.drawOval(
5   80,80,140,140);}}
```

This form of the program works just as well as the original version on page 47; the compiler does not object. To the compiler, any division into lines is acceptable as long as strings are kept on one line and names (class names, method names, and identifiers) aren't split across lines. However, from the point of view of a person reading it, this last form of the program is a disaster!

Common sense dictates that a program should be laid out consistently in a way that clarifies, rather than obscures, its purpose and its method. Identifier names should be descriptive of their roles, statements should be properly aligned, blank spaces and lines should be included for readability, and matching pairs of braces and parentheses should be apparent at a glance. As we present each Java statement, we show reasonable layouts and arrangements of braces, as appropriate.

comments

We can make our programs more readable by including *comments*. Comments consist of any text following the symbol // to the end of the line. (Comments may also be enclosed within the symbols /* and */ and may extend over any number of lines, though we never use this form.)

At first you will want to spend your energy only on writing, debugging, and polishing a program; you will be tempted to avoid commenting or to add comments only *after* writing the entire program. Don't do it! The comments should be an integral part of the program, written, modified, and debugged, just as the program is. You'd be surprised how quickly you can forget the details of some section of code, and other people almost always need comments to understand your program. Reading a program should not be a detective game. Begin *every* program with a comment giving your name, the date, an explanation of the purpose of the program, and the method of solution used. Each section of a program should have comments covering a description of its purpose.

Summary

An identifier in Java is a string of letters and digits, starting with a letter. The dollar sign $ and underscore _ are considered to be letters.

The essential parts of a Java class definition (so far) are

```
public class  Classname {
 //  Author, date, explanation

public void  methodName () {

    declarations of variables

    executable statements with relevant comments
  }
}
```

A typical client looks like this:

```
public class  ClassnameClient {

  public static void main (String[] args) {

    Classname  variable;

    variable = new  Classname ();

    variable. methodName ();

  }
}
```

The file in which a Java program is written has the name *Classname*.java, where *Classname* is the name of the class that the file contains.

Every class MyClass defines a set of values called *objects*, or *instances*, *of type* MyClass, or just MyClass *objects*. You declare variables to give names to MyClass objects. For example, we've seen that the CSLib package has classes OutputBox and DrawingBox.

    OutputBox out;

declares that the variable out will be the name used to refer to an OutputBox. You create a new object of type MyClass by writing new MyClass(). Messages are sent to objects with *dot notation*: u.method(...). The *arguments* to the method are written inside the parentheses.

This chapter introduces three classes that are defined in CSLib: TrickMouse, OutputBox, and DrawingBox. TrickMouse is a very specialized class, and it was included in CSLib only for the examples in this chapter. OutputBox is used to produce text output, and DrawingBox is used for graphical output. Both OutputBox and DrawingBox are used throughout this book.

Comments, set off by //, are ignored by the computer but are essential to a person who is reading the program. Commenting is part of the development stage of a program; it should *never* be omitted or even delayed during program composition.

Program layout is essential to the reader, even though it is irrelevant to the Java compiler. Statements should be properly aligned, blank spaces and blank lines should be included to enhance readability, and pairs of braces should be apparent at a glance.

Exercises

1. Modify the Concentric program to draw a bull's-eye consisting of five concentric rings of alternately red and green colors.

2. Modify the Forecast program so that there is a call to setSize just before the first print. Experiment until you find a size that is close to the size shown in Figure 2.6.

3. Write a program to draw the International Olympic Committee logo:

   The colors of the circles, left to right, are blue, yellow, black, green, and red.

4. Write a program to draw a large circle centered in a 300 × 300 DrawingBox area. Then draw two equilateral triangles inscribed in that circle, forming a hexagram, sometimes known as the Star of David.

5. Draw a 4×4 checkerboard in a 400×400 DrawingBox area. The squares should be colored red and black.

6. Reproduce Figure 2.8, as closely as you can, in a 300×300 drawing box.

FUNDAMENTAL DATA TYPES OF JAVA

Objects and methods are central to Java programming, but so are some of the primitive data types, such as numbers. In this chapter, we expand our repertoire of programming tools by studying four important data types: integers, real numbers, strings, and characters. In Section 3.5 on debugging, we take you through the process of developing a program, including many of the pitfalls and errors you may encounter; such sections appear throughout this book.

You must remember this, a kiss is still a kiss,
A sigh is just a sigh;
The fundamental things apply,
As time goes by.

—Herman Huupfeld
"As Time Goes By"

In Chapter 2, you learned the basics of Java programming—objects and message sending—as well as program structure and layout. In this chapter, we discuss some other types of data—numbers and strings.

Although objects are fundamental in Java, so are *numbers.* Although objects are ... numbers. Numbers are not objects. Instead, they are *primitive values,* *primitive values* meaning they are built into Java and do not need to be defined by classes. The examples in Chapter 2 show how important numbers are; even producing graphical output requires the use of numbers. In this chapter, we introduce the most important types of numbers—integers and real numbers—as well as the types of strings and characters. In Section 3.5, we present our first substantial (nearly 40-line) program.

3.1

Integers

Integers are numbers without fractional parts. In Chapter 2, you saw how to write integers (3, 47, -12, etc.) and how to print them in an `OutputBox` [`out.print(47)`]. In this section, we learn to do three more things with numbers: store them in variables; read them as input from the user; and perform arithmetic operations, such as addition and multiplication, on them. Later in this chapter, we also see how to output them in `DrawingBox` objects.

Variables are used in Chapter 2 to store references to objects, such as `TrickMouse`, `OutputBox`, and `DrawingBox` objects. For example, on page 44, we used the variable `out` to store the `OutputBox` object, so that we could send it `print` and `println` messages. But variables can also be used to hold integers:

```
int daysInWeek;
daysInWeek = 7;
```

assignment
statement

As with `OutputBox` and other objects in Chapter 2, we first *declare* a variable and then use an *assignment statement* to give that variable a value. Thus, this follows the general form we have seen:

```
type-or-class-name variable;
variable = initial-value;
```

Integer variables can be used in many of the same ways as integer literals. For example, they can be passed as arguments to methods, as in

```
int diam;
diam = 140;
...
g.drawOval(80, 80, diam, diam);
// same as g.drawOval(80, 80, 140 140)
```

An extremely important feature of variables that we have not yet seen is that they can *vary*: We can change what is in a variable by using an assignment statement. Here is a version of the `Concentric` circle program from page 47 that produces exactly the same output:

```
1   import CSLib.*;
2
3   public class Concentric {
4       // Draw concentric circles.
5       // Author: Adrienne Baranowicz, December 2, 2000
6
7       public void drawThem () {
8           int coord;
9           int diam;
10          DrawingBox g;
11          g = new DrawingBox();
12          g.setDrawableSize(300, 300);
13          coord = 110; diam = 80;
14          g.drawOval(coord, coord, diam, diam);
15          coord = 95; diam = 110;
16          g.drawOval(coord, coord, diam, diam);
17          coord = 80; diam = 140;
18          g.drawOval(coord, coord, diam, diam);
19      }
20  }
```

Each time the `drawOval` message is sent, its arguments are obtained from the *current* contents of the variables `diam` and `coord`. Thus, the first call passes in arguments 80 and 110, the next call passes in 110 and 95, and the third call passes in 140 and 80. Note that each variable holds only one value at a time. The assignment statement changes that value, and the earlier value is forgotten. Each time a variable is referred to, its current value is used.

With the ability to change the contents of a variable, we can finally get some input data into our programs. `CSLib` provides an `InputBox` class, with two relevant methods:

```
void setPrompt ( String p )
int readInt ()
```

The set Prompt method is similar to the set Title method in OutputBox
except that the prompt is displayed within the window instead of in the border.
The readInt method is rather different. It has no arguments, but it gets an
integer from the user and *returns* it. This means it can be called on the right-hand
side of an assignment statement and the number it reads will be assigned to the
variable on the left, as in

```
InputBox in;
in = new InputBox();
in.setPrompt("Enter an integer:");
int i;
i = in.readInt();
```

For example, here is a program that reads an integer and prints it:

```
1   import CSLib.*;
2
3   public class EchoInteger {
4
5     // EchoInteger:  read and echo an integer
6     // Author:  S. Kamin, April 13, 2001
7
8     void echo () {
9       InputBox in;
10      int i;
11
12      in = new InputBox();
13      in.setPrompt("Please enter an integer: ");
14      i = in.readInt();
15      OutputBox out = new OutputBox();
16      out.print("The integer you entered was ");
17      out.print(i);
18      out.println(".");
19    }
20  }
```

and here is its client:

```
1   import CSLib.*;
2
3   public class EchoClient {
4     public static void main (String[] args) {
5       EchoInteger ec;
6       ec = new EchoInteger();
7       ec.echo();
8     }
9   }
```

Here is a program that reads two numbers and prints them in reverse order
(we omit the client this time; you can write it yourself):

```
1   import CSLib.*;
2
3   public class EchoTwoIntegers {
4
```

```
 5        // EchoTwoIntegers:   read two integers and print in reverse
 6        // Author:  S. Kamin, April 13, 2001
 7
 8        void echo () {
 9           InputBox in;
10           OutputBox out;
11           int i;
12           int j;
13
14           in = new InputBox();
15           in.setPrompt("Enter an integer:");
16           i = in.readInt();
17           in.setPrompt("Enter another integer:");
18           j = in.readInt();
19           out = new OutputBox();
20           out.print("The integers you entered were ");
21           out.print(j);
22           out.print(" and ");
23           out.print(i);
24           out.println(".");
25        }
26     }
```

(It is common to write all the declarations in a program at the beginning, but it is not required. Just be sure to declare each variable before it is first used.)

QUICK EXERCISE 3.1	Write the program `EchoThreeIntegers`, which reads three integers and then prints them in reverse order.

Now that we can store integers in variables and read them as input, we come to what is, after all, the most important thing we can do with them: to perform arithmetic operations like addition and multiplication. Table 3.1 lists some of the available operations. Note that an asterisk * is used for multiplication. Also note that the division operation always returns an integer, never a number with a fractional part. The remainder operation, written %, gives the remainder after dividing its first argument by its second argument. An *expression* is a literal, a variable, a symbolic constant, or some arithmetic operations applied to expressions resulting in a value of one particular type. An expression can be used anywhere that a literal can.

expression

This program (client omitted) reads an integer from the user and puts a circle of that diameter in the middle of a drawing box:

```
import CSLib.*;

public class DrawCircle {

    // Draw circle.
    // Author:  Sam Kamin, April 10, 2001

    public void draw () {
```

Type	Symbol	Operation	Example
int	+	Addition	45 + 5 = 50
	-	Subtraction	657 - 57 = 600
	*	Multiplication	7000 * 3 = 21000
	/	Division	10 / 3 = 3
	%	Remainder	10 % 3 = 1

TABLE 3.1 Integer arithmetic operations in Java. Division by zero results in an error; this includes both / and %.

```
DrawingBox g;
g = new DrawingBox();
g.setDrawableSize(300, 300);

InputBox in;
in = new InputBox();
in.setPrompt("Enter diameter (<= 300): ");
int diam;
diam = in.readInt();

g.drawOval(150-diam/2, 150-diam/2, diam, diam);
    }
}
```

Write a client for the `DrawCircle` class.

**QUICK EXERCISE
3.2**

Arithmetic operations can be used in the right-hand sides of assignment statements as well as in method calls. In the last example, we can avoid repeating the arithmetic in the arguments of `drawOval` by doing the arithmetic once and placing its value into a variable:

```
int diam;
diam = in.readInt();

int x_y_coord;
x_y_coord = 150-diam/2;

g.drawOval(x_y_coord, x_y_coord, diam, diam);
```

When you write an arithmetic expression, you need to take some care to make sure you've written what you intended. For example, suppose variables x, y, and z contain integers 4, 5, and 6, respectively. What is the value of the expression x+y*z? It depends upon whether the addition or multiplication is done first: If the addition is done first, then the value is 54 (= 9 × 6), but if the multiplication is done first, then it is 34 (= 4 + 30). In fact, writing large arithmetic expressions would be tedious if not for certain *precedence rules* that tell the computer in what order to do the operations. Just as in high school algebra,

precedence rules

Rules	1. Evaluate all subexpressions in parentheses.
	2. Evaluate nested parentheses from the inside out.
	3. In the absence of parentheses or within parentheses,
	a. Evaluate `*`, `/`, or `%` before `+` or `-`.
	b. Evaluate sequences of `*`, `/`, and `%` operators from left to right.
	c. Evaluate sequences of `+` and `-` operators from left to right.

Examples	`6 + 37 % 8 / 5`
	is the same as
	`6 + ((37 % 8) / 5)`
or	`6 + (5 / 5)`
or	`7`
	However,
	`6 + 37 % (8 / 5) = 6 + 37 % 1 = 6 + 0 = 6`

TABLE 3.2   **Precedence rules (with examples) for evaluating arithmetic expressions in Java. Use parentheses to avoid confusion for the person reading the program. See Appendix B for a comprehensive description.**

multiplication and division are given precedence over addition and subtraction. Thus, the expression above has value 34. Parentheses can be used to change the order of evaluation; if we had written `(x+y)*z` above, its value would be 54. The precedence rules are explained in Table 3.2. A fuller exposition of Java's precedence rules (which is needed because there are actually quite a few more operations than the ones we've mentioned) is given in Appendix B. However, when things get complicated, the best policy is to use parentheses to avoid ambiguity.

QUICK EXERCISE 3.3	With $x = 4$, $y = 5$, and $z = 6$, the following expression has value 63:

        `x+y+z*x+y*z`

Insert one pair of parentheses into this expression so that its value becomes 78. Remove those and insert another pair to produce 333. Do this again to get 213.

3.2

Declarations, Variables, and Assignment Statements

Suppose that we write a declaration

    `int temperature;`

variable   This declares `temperature` to be a *variable* of type `int`. Variables are of

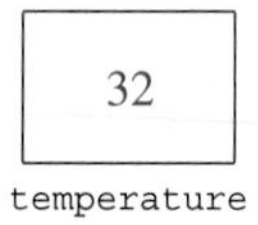

FIGURE 3.1 **Variables are like containers.**

crucial importance in computer programming, and we now take some time to explain what they are and how they are used.

Think of a variable such as `temperature` as a container for a value, as shown in Figure 3.1. The declaration creates this container; therefore, every variable must be declared (before it is used). Initially, that is, just after it is declared, it contains nothing, and it is a mistake to try to use its value.[1] Before long, however, your program will place a value into it with an *assignment statement*, which is a line containing the variable, an equals sign =, and an expression. For example, after the assignment statement

assignment statement

```
temperature = 32;
```

`temperature` contains the value 32.

Variables can have their contents changed by an assignment statement, but they always contain exactly one value. As the statements in a program are executed one by one, the contents of the variables remain the same except when altered by assignment. Thus, *the content of a variable is the value assigned by the most recent assignment statement that placed a value into it.*

3.2.1 Self-assignment, Increment, and Decrement

In general, the execution of assignment statements is simple: Find the value of (*evaluate*) the expression on the right side of the equals sign, and place that value in the variable, replacing the old value. This has a surprising result, though, in that a statement such as

```
temperature = temperature + 10;
```

appears to be legal as well. In fact, it is legal, and such statements occur very frequently. This statement retrieves the current value of `temperature`, adds 10 to that value, and then makes the result the new value of `temperature`. The net effect is that the value stored in `temperature` is *incremented* by 10.

In fact, statements that increment or decrement a variable by 1 are so common that Java allows us to write them in an abbreviated form, using operators ++ and --. The statement

```
cent++;
```

is equivalent to

```
cent = cent+1;
```

---

[1] Well, technically, it contains *something;* it's just poor programming practice to depend on the value, even if we do know what it might be!

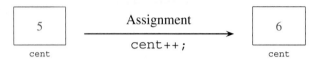

FIGURE 3.2   The effect of `cent++`.

This is illustrated in Figure 3.2. Similarly,

```
cent--;    // Decrement the Centigrade value.
```

is equivalent to

```
cent = cent-1;
```

3.2.2 Initializers

Initializers in declarations can be used to give initial values to variables. For example, rather than writing

```
int x;
int y;
x = 5;
y = 6;
```

we can write

```
int x = 5;
int y = 6;
```

Another trick for writing this more concisely is to declare more than one variable in a single declaration. You can do this as long as all the variables you are declaring have the same type, as in

```
int x = 5,
    y = 6;
```

(Keep in mind that line breaks and spaces usually don't matter to the computer, but are there only to enhance the readability of the program.)

It is not necessary that the initial value in the declaration be a literal. It can be another variable or an expression. Here are three versions of the declaration above:

```
int x, y;
x = 5;
y = x+1;

int x = 5, y;
y = x+1;

int x = 5, y = x+1;
```

QUICK EXERCISE 3.4

Forgetting to initialize a variable is one of the most common errors in programming. To see what can happen, enter the version of the concentric circles program shown on page 58, but omit line 13.

QUICK EXERCISE 3.5

Even though more than one variable can be declared in one declaration, it would be a mistake to replace lines 9 and 10 on page 59 by the single declaration:

```
InputBox in, i;
```

Why?

The form of declaration in which an initial value is provided in the declaration itself can be used for any type of value, not just integers. In particular, we can—and usually do—create objects using this form:

```
OutputBox out = new OutputBox();
InputBox in = new InputBox();
```

Since variables are such an important part of programming, a few more words about assignment statements are in order. As we have seen, the effect of an assignment statement is to *replace* the current value of the variable to which the assignment is made. Even if a variable already has a value, an assignment statement can give it a new value, as in

```
temperature = 30;
temperature = 40;
```

This is legal, although silly, and after the two statements are executed, `temperature` has the value 40.

3.2.3 Symbolic Constants

It is sometimes useful to have a variable whose value never changes. In this case, the variable doesn't serve as a true variable at all—it never *varies*—but it provides a name for the value. This way, for example, we can use the name US_POPULATION for the value 278,058,881; it makes the program easier to read and reduces the risk of mistyping the number 278,058,881 each time it is needed. To declare a variable and at the same time indicate that its value will never change, add the *modifier* `final` to the declaration, as in

final modifier

```
final int US_POPULATION = 278058881;
```

US_POPULATION cannot appear on the left-hand side of an assignment statement. It is called a *symbolic constant*. Since it cannot get a value from an assignment statement, it must get its value from an *initializer* in the declaration (= 278058881).

symbolic constant

initializer

programming
convention
It is a Java *programming convention*—an extension of the one mentioned in Chapter 2 (page 37)—to use capital letters in the names of symbolic constants, and we have generally followed that convention in this book. Multiword symbolic constants have each word separated by an underscore character.

3.3

Real Numbers

Real numbers are numbers with fractional parts, such as 3.14159. In Java, `double` is the type name used for real numbers. Thus, a Java program could contain a declaration such as

```
double pricePerPound = 3.99;
```

Like integers, doubles are primitive values, not objects.

You might ask at this point, Since an integer is just a real number whose fractional part is zero, why do we need integers at all? In other words, what is the difference between the integer 3 and the double `3.0`? This is an excellent question. Mathematically, there is no difference. However, computers use completely different representations for integers and real numbers, and operations on integers are often much more efficient than the corresponding operations on doubles. Since integers are used more often than real numbers, they are kept as a separate type.

Whatever the reason for distinguishing the types `int` and `double`, it is important that you appreciate that these *are* different types. For example, there are situations where it is legal to write 3 but not to write 3.0.

Declarations of doubles are written in the same way as integers. Just as with integers, you can declare several `double` variables at once:

```
double pricePerPound = 3.99,
       taxRate       = 0.05,
       shippingCost  = 5.55;
```

As with `int` variable declarations, the initialization part is optional, but the variable must be assigned a value before it is used. The same arithmetic operations are available on doubles as on integers, except `%`. Division on `double`s returns a result with a fractional part (i.e., a `double`). Examples are shown in Table 3.3. The precedence rules are those described in Table 3.2.

The literals of type `double` include not only numbers with fractional parts, but also numbers in scientific notation:

```
3.14159     7.12     9.0     0.5e+001     -16.3e+002
```

e notation
The `e` is the way Java signifies scientific notation (called e *notation*); the letter e separates the number from the exponent, and the integer following e is the power of 10 by which the number is multiplied. For example, the speed of light

Type	Symbol	Operation	Example
double	+	Addition	`4.50e01 + 5.30e00 = 5.03e01`
	−	Subtraction	`6.57e02 - 5.70e01 = 6.00e02`
	*	Multiplication	`7e03 * 3.0e00 = 2.1e04`
	/	Division	`9.6e01 / 2e01 = 4.8e00`

TABLE 3.3   Real arithmetic operations in Java. Division by zero results in an error.

Express these `double` values in e-notation:

   -6543210.0 $.897654321$ 3×10^{45} 0.000061 45.8×10^{-3}

QUICK EXERCISE 3.6

---

is 2.997925×10^8 meters/second, written `2.997925e8` in Java; the radius of an electron is 2.817939×10^{-15} meter, written `2.817939e-15` in Java.

Input and output for doubles are analogous to input and output for integers. Use the `print` and `println` methods on an `OutputBox` to print a `double` value, and get a `double` value from the user by sending the `readDouble` message to an `InputBox` object.

(`InputBox` has methods for reading numerous types of data, including some we haven't covered yet. The brief documentation for `InputBox` is given in Table 3.7 in the Summary section of this chapter.)

An example of a program that uses real numbers is the following program to convert temperatures from degrees Fahrenheit to degrees Centigrade. It asks the user for the temperature in degrees Fahrenheit, converts it to degrees Centigrade, and puts its output in an `OutputBox`. The user will type in the Fahrenheit temperature in an `InputBox`, as shown in Figure 3.3. If we type `32` in the `InputBox` of Figure 3.3, then the program produces the output box shown in Figure 3.4. Here is the class that produces just that dialog:

```
1   import CSLib.*;
2
3   public class Temperature {
4      //  Convert temperature from Fahrenheit to Centigrade
5      //  Author: Samuel N. Kamin, June 1, 1996
6
7      public void compute () {
8         double temperature;  // The Fahrenheit temperature.
9         InputBox in;
10        OutputBox out;
11
12        in = new InputBox();
13        in.setPrompt ("Please type the temperature (deg F): ");
14        temperature = in.readDouble();
15
```

FIGURE 3.3   The `InputBox` **of the** `Temperature` **application.**

FIGURE 3.4   The `OutputBox` **of the** `Temperature` **application.**

```
16        out = new OutputBox();
17        out.print(temperature);
18        out.print(" deg F is ");
19        out.print((5.0 * (temperature - 32.0)) / 9.0);
20        out.println(" deg C");
21      }
22    }
```

A typical client would be

```
1    public class TemperatureClient {
2
3      public static void main (String[] args) {
4        Temperature test = new Temperature();
5        test.compute();
6      }
7    }
```

The central part of this computation is in lines 16 through 20. Line 16 causes a reference to a newly created `OutputBox` to be assigned to the variable `out`. Line 17 prints the value that was assigned to `temperature`. Since line 17 is a `print` rather than a `println`, the literal that is printed by line 18 continues on the same line. So lines 17 and 18 together are responsible for printing the part of the output that says "`32.0 deg F is `".

Line 19 is executed next. It evaluates the expression, substituting whatever values are presently held in any variables that are used in the expression. So if we suppose that the user types 32 in the `InputBox`, the evaluation proceeds thus:

$$(5.0 * (temperature - 32.0)) / 9.0 = (5.0 * (32.0 - 32.0)) / 9.0$$
$$= (5.0 * 0.0) / 9.0$$
$$= 0.0 / 9.0$$
$$= 0.0$$

After we evaluate the expression, the resulting value is used as the argument to the `print` method. Since the expression (with *this particular* user input) evaluated to `0.0`, the net effect is exactly the same as if line 19 had been written `out.print(0.0)`. Finally the remaining string is printed by line 20, and the output is complete.

QUICK EXERCISE 3.7

Modify the `Temperature` program so that it computes Fahrenheit temperature from Centigrade, using the formula

$$°F = °C \times \left(\frac{9.0}{5.0}\right) + 32.0$$

QUICK EXERCISE 3.8

Rewrite the temperature program to convert from Fahrenheit temperature to *both* Centigrade and kelvins (absolute temperature). The relationship between °F and K is

$$K = (°F - 32.0)\frac{5.0}{9.0} + 273.16$$

A kelvin is identical to one degree on the Centigrade scale, (1°C), but a temperature of 0 K is equal to $-273.16°C$.

Aside from the elements we have covered, expressions can contain *method calls*. These appear as names (sometimes names with several parts connected by periods) followed by parentheses containing zero or more arguments. The arguments themselves are expressions of the proper type. If there is more than one argument, the arguments are separated by commas.   *method call*

There is a particularly useful set of methods that calculate *numerical functions*. For example, a method called `Math.sqrt` is available for computing the square root of a `double`, giving a `double` result, so we can write, for example,   *numerical functions*

Name	Description
`double Math.abs(double x)`	Absolute value of x (double version)
`int Math.abs(int x)`	Absolute value of x (integer version)
`double Math.ceil(double x)`	Ceiling (smallest integer value not less than x)
`double Math.cos(double x)`	Cosine
`double Math.exp(double x)`	Exponential (e^x)
`double Math.floor(double x)`	Floor (largest integer value not greater than x)
`double Math.log(double x)`	Natural logarithm (base e)
`double Math.pow(double a, double b)`	Power (a^b)
`double Math.sin(double x)`	Sine
`double Math.sqrt(double x)`	Square root
`double Math.tan(double x)`	Tangent

TABLE 3.4   Some of the predefined numeric methods in Java's math package. A more complete list is given in Appendix C.

`Math.sqrt(x)`. Some of Java's predefined numeric methods are shown in Table 3.4. A more complete list is given in Appendix C.

static methods   These method calls resemble those that we've made on objects, but they are different. They are the *static methods*. The difference is that the name before the dot is a class name (`Math`) rather than a variable name. We shall learn more about static methods in a later chapter, so for now we'll simply use them as needed.

As an example, suppose we want to print the value of $2.0 \times e^{\sin x + 1.0}$. A Java expression for computing this is

```
OutputBox out = new OutputBox();
out.println(2.0 * Math.exp(Math.sin(x) + 1.0));
```

Computers are very picky about data types. Java always knows what type of value any expression has and is careful about not placing into any variable a value not of that variable's type. One example is assigning a `double` to an `int` variable. If `i` is a variable of type `int` and `x` is a variable of type `double`,

```
int i;
double x;
```

the assignment

```
i = 10.3*x;
```

is illegal.

(We note that the `readDouble` method in `InputBox` allows users to enter integers, in effect adding ".0" if there is no fractional part. This is just a convenience provided by this particular method. It does not change the fact that `int`s and `double`s are fundamentally different types of values in Java. Unfortunately, such "conveniences" tend to muddy the waters and make the distinction even more confusing for beginners; Section 3.6 discusses more of these "conveniences.")

3.4

Strings

The most widely used data types in Java programs are integers (type `int`), real numbers (type `double`), and character strings (type `String`). Of these, `int` and `double` are primitive types (meaning they are not classes and their values are not objects). `String` is a class; its values are its objects, or instances. Table 3.5 gives a taxonomy of the types we have seen thus far.

`String` is, however, a somewhat special class. Unique among all the classes in Java, it has literals and operations (actually, just one operation). Like every other class, it has methods as well. We will discuss its literals, operations, and methods, in that order.

Also unlike the other classes we have used, `String` is not defined in the CSLib package. Instead, it is defined in the `java.lang` package. This package does not have to be explicitly imported, as CSLib does; the `String` class can always be used in any Java program.

The literals of the `String` type are just the character strings we have written in double quotes. Like integers and doubles, these literals can be passed to methods as arguments, as we have often done [e.g., `in.setPrompt("Please type the temperature (Deg F)")`]. They can occur on the right-hand sides of assignment statements:

```
String promptF = "Please type the temperature (Deg F):";
```

String variables can, of course, be passed as arguments to methods [e.g., `in.setPrompt(promptF)`].

The one operation on strings is *string concatenation*—joining two strings to form a new string—which is written using the plus sign +. If `t1` and `t2` are strings, `t1+t2` is the string that looks like `t1` followed by `t2`.

string concatenation

```
String t1 = "To be ",
       t2 = "or not to be.";
out.print(t1+t2);        // prints: To be or not to be.
```

Primitive types	Predefined classes in Java	Classes in `CSLib`
`int`	`String`	`TrickMouse`
`double`	⋮	`OutputBox`
⋮		`DrawingBox`
		`InputBox`

TABLE 3.5 Taxonomy of data types encountered thus far. There are a few more primitive types, a few more classes in `CSLib`, and many more predefined classes in the Java packages.

Name	Description
`int length()`	Returns the length of this string.
`int indexOf (String s)`	Returns the index within the string of the first occurrence of the string s.
`String substring (int beginx, int endx)`	Returns the substring of beginning at index beginx and ending at index endx-1.
`String toUpperCase()`	Converts all the characters of the string to uppercase.
`String toLowerCase()`	Converts all the characters of the string to lowercase.
`char charAt (int index)`	Returns the character at the specified index. Index must be between 0 and length()-1. (This method is explained on page 76.)

TABLE 3.6   Some of the predefined `string` methods.

Strings also have ordinary methods, such as `length`, which use dot notation. For example, `t1.length()` returns the integer 6, the number of characters in `t1` (spaces count!).

There are a number of other methods that you will come to use, and they are all detailed in the Java online documentation.[2] Here we summarize some of the more commonly used methods. When we speak of an *index* into the string, we mean the character positions, with the first character having position zero (0), and the last character having position $length() - 1$. (Refer to Table 3.6.) Here are some examples.

```
OutputBox out = new OutputBox();

String s1 = "Here is a test string.";

out.println(s1.indexOf("s"));    // prints '6'
out.println(s1.indexOf("x"));    // prints '-1'
                                 // (x does not occur)
out.println(s1.length());        // prints '22'
out.println(s1.substring(8,14));// prints 'a test'
```

A useful property of the concatenation operator is that it can be used to convert other types of data to strings. If n is an `int` or a `double`, and t is a string, `t+n` converts n to a string and then concatenates the two strings. This feature would have allowed us to replace lines 17 through 20 on page 68 with a single statement:

```
out.print(temperature + " deg F is " +
          (5.0 * (temperature - 32.0) / 9.0) + " deg C");
```

---

[2]The Java online documentation can be accessed from the Javasoft website http://java.sun.com/products/jdk/. It is probably available in your local installation as well; consult a guru.

What is printed by each of the following `println` statements?

```
OutputBox out = new OutputBox();
String s1 = "Here's another test.";

out.println(s1.length()/2);
out.println(s1.substring(0,s1.length()-1);
out.println(s1.indexOf("e'x"));
```

Explain why each of the following println statements is illegal.

```
OutputBox out = new OutputBox();
String s1 = "Another test";

out.println(s1.substring(1,100));
out.println(s1.substring(6,2));
```

This conversion allows numbers to be displayed in drawing boxes. Recall from Section 2.3 on page 43 that `DrawingBox` has a method `void drawString(String s, int x, int y)`. Since we now know how to convert numbers to strings, we can use this to display a number x in a drawing box: convert x to a string by writing `"" + x`, and then place it on the screen:

```
d.drawString(""+x, 100, 50);
```

To be precise, `drawString` places the string on the screen in such a way that its lower-left corner is at the indicated location. Thus, if x contains the number 1409, the call to `drawString` shown above will place the characters 1, 4, 0, 9 as:

$$\vdots 1409 \vdots$$

$$\nwarrow$$

$$(100,50)$$

The bottom left corner is called the *reference point* of the string.   *reference point*

The `InputBox` class has a method to read strings.   `String readString()` reads every character typed by the user and creates a `String` object containing those characters. For example, the `convert` method of the following class reads a string and then converts it to capital letters using the method `toUpperCase` that is available in the `String` class:

```
1    import CSLib.*;
2
```

```
3    public class UpperCase {
4       // Author: Mary Angela McDermott, December 30, 2000
5       // Convert mixed case to all upper case.
6
7       public void convert () {
8          String input;
9          InputBox in;
10         OutputBox out;
11
12         in = new InputBox();
13         in.setTitle ("Lower to Upper Case Conversion");
14         in.setPrompt ("Enter characters: ");
15         input = in.readString();
16
17         out = new OutputBox();
18         out.println(input.toUpperCase());
19      }
20   }
```

A client might look like this:

```
1    import CSLib.*;
2
3    public class UpperCaseClient {
4
5       public static void main (String[] args) {
6          UpperCase uc;
7          uc = new UpperCase();
8          uc.convert();
9       }
10   }
```

We compile both[3] using `javac UpperCase.java` and `javac UpperCaseClient.java`, and then we run it using `java UpperCaseClient`. The input dialog box is

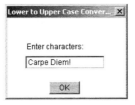

and the output box is

---

[3]If both `UpperCaseClient.java` and `UpperCase.java` are in the same directory, merely compiling `UpperCaseClient.java` will also induce a compilation of `UpperCase.java`, since `UpperCaseClient.java` *uses* `UpperCase.java`.

3.4.1 Characters

A character is any key you can strike on the keyboard or that can show up on the computer screen. This includes upper- and lowercase letters, punctuation marks, and even digits. Each time you type a key on the keyboard, the computer receives a character as input; each time a letter or digit shows up on the screen, it is because the computer printed a character.

You can store characters in your program by declaring variables of type `char`:

```
char firstLetter, middleInitial;
char MorF;
```

Character literals represent specific characters. They are written using single quotes:[4]

Character literals

```
char vitamin = 'A',
     chromosome = 'y',
     middleInitial = 'N';
```

Just as integer literals can be assigned to `int` variables, so character literals can be assigned to `char` variables.

You might think that characters are nothing but short strings. Indeed, in some programming languages, no distinction is made between characters and strings of length 1. In Java, however, characters are a distinct type. One major difference is that characters are a primitive type and strings are an object type. You cannot pass a character as an argument when a string is expected, and vice versa; similarly, you cannot assign a character to a `String` variable, and vice versa.

Input/output of characters works similarly to the other types we have seen. The `print` and `println` methods of `OutputBox` can take characters as arguments. The `readChar` method in the `InputBox` class reads and returns a character. Just as with integers and doubles, `DrawingBox` provides no direct method for printing characters; but, as with those types, characters can be converted to strings by concatenating with a string, and then `drawString` can be used to draw a character in a `DrawingBox`.

Characters seem simple enough when you think solely in terms of letters and punctuation marks, but the concept can get confusing when some other cases are considered.

One source of trouble is the *space character*, ' '. It is sometimes difficult to think of a space as a real character, but it is. A space appears between two words on the screen because the computer sent a space character to the terminal.

space character

Another source of confusion is the distinction between characters and numbers. The literals 3 and '3' are completely different (and are both different from 3.0 or "3"). We discuss this further in Section 3.6.

---

[4]Not to be confused with the *double* quotes used for strings.

nonprinting   Finally, there are the *nonprinting characters*, which don't explicitly show
characters up on the screen at all but are still useful. The most important of these is the
newline *newline* character. You send this character to the computer when you strike the
Enter or Return key. When the computer prints it, it causes the cursor to skip
to the beginning of the next line for subsequent output. The `println` method
prints a newline character at the end of a line. Newlines also can be printed by
using the character literal ` '\n' `. The literal \n is called an *escape sequence*, and
escape character \ is the *escape character*. Without the escape character, you would have just a
lowercase n; with it you have the newline character.

Because the backslash *always* is assumed to be used as an escape character, the question arises, How can you write a backslash as a character literal?
The answer is to embed it in an escape sequence by introducing it with another
backslash: ` '\\' ` represents a (single) backslash character. As another useful
example, ` '\'' ` represents a single-quote character.

Here are the character literals you need to know:

`'A',...,'Z'`	Uppercase letters
`'a',...,'z'`	Lowercase letters
`'0',...,'9'`	Digits
`'.','','!',''',` etc.	Punctuation marks
`' '`	Blank
`'\n'`	Newline
`'\t'`	Tab
`'\\'`	Backslash
`'\''`	Single right quote

We've seen that `String` literals are characters enclosed in double quotes.
You can include escape sequences in `String` literals as well. Strings and characters are distinct types, but strings are made up of characters. The method `charAt`
in the `String` class was mentioned in Table 3.6, but was not explained there,
since we had not yet introduced the character type. Its purpose is to return the
character at a particular position in a string, where positions begin at zero. For
example,

```
char firstchar = s1.charAt(0);
```

assigns to `firstchar` the first character in `s1`. If `s1` has length 10, then all
the expressions `s1.charAt(0),...,s1.charAt(9)` are legal, and any other
arguments that might be given to `charAt` are not legal.

QUICK EXERCISE
3.11

Place the following lines of code into a full program that reads input from the
user. Run it several times and explain its output.

```
String s = in.readString();
int pos = in.readInt();
out.print(s.charAt(pos));
```

3.5

Debugging

The road to wisdom?
Well, it's plain and simple to express:
Err and err and err again,
but less and less and less.

——Piet Hein
Grooks

Now let's develop a program from the beginning. We do this repeatedly throughout the book. Each time we do it, we try to reproduce faithfully the thought processes that go into the development of the algorithm and its implementation as a program. It may be misleading to start out with a badly designed algorithm or a poor Java implementation, but this is exactly the process you will be going through as you learn to write good programs, and we feel it is important to reproduce it in all its frustrating details. When we present erroneous versions of a program, you will be able to recognize them, because a warning such as WRONG will be printed.

Although the process—the spirit, so to say—of what we do in this section is just what you are likely to go through, the details will vary. You will make different mistakes, and we cannot possibly list all the syntactic or logical errors that you may have to debug. Moreover, Java compilers vary. The one you use may be more or less helpful than ours and may give you different error messages.

The program we write defines a class called Peets that has a single method, compute, that computes the price of a coffee order from Peet's, a well-known chain of coffee shops in the San Francisco Bay area that also sells coffee by mail. Peet's computes the price for an order as[5]

$$\text{Price per pound} \times \text{Weight} + \text{Shipping}$$

where

$$\text{Shipping} = \text{Rate per pound} \times \text{Weight} + \text{Fixed handling fee}$$

The price per pound and the number of pounds vary with each order, but the shipping cost per pound and the fixed handling fee do not. We want a program to calculate the total cost of a coffee order. Corresponding to this problem description, we use the variables pricePerPound and weight, whose values are to be read from the InputBox as input, and the symbolic constants FIXED_FEE and RATE_PER_POUND. We calculate and print the values of the variables shippingPrice and totalPrice.

---

[5]Not really. They use a more complicated formula in which the shipping cost depends upon several factors. Our formula is for illustrative purposes only.

Here is a typical client:

```
1  public class PeetsClient {
2    public static void main (String[] args) {
3      Peets sale = new Peets();
4      sale.compute();
5    }
6  }
```

and here is our first attempt at writing the Peets class:

```
1   import CSLib.*;
2
3   public class Peets {
4     //  Peet's Coffee
5     //  Author: Eve M. Reingold, May 10, 1996
6
7   public void compute () {
8     final int
9       RATE_PER_POUND = 1.25, // Shipping rate per pound
10      FIXED_FEE,             // Shipping rate per shipment
11    int
12      priceperPound,         // Coffee price per pound
13      weight,                // Amount ordered
14      shippingCost,
15      coffeeCost;
16    InputBox in;
17    OutputBox msg;
18
19    in = new InputBox();
20    in.setTitle("Peet's Coffee");
21    in.setPrompt("Enter price per pound: );
22    pricePerPound = in.readInt();
23
24    in.setPrompt ("Enter number of pounds: ");
25    weight = in.readInt();
26
27    shipingCost = RATE_PER_POUND + weight + FIXED_FEE;
28    totalPrice = priceperPound * weight + shippingCost;
29
30    msg = new OutputBox();
31    msg.setTitle("Peet's Coffee");
32    msg.println("Coffee total is " + coffeeCost);
33    msg.println("Shipping cost is " + shipingCost);
34    msg.println("Total cost is " totalPrice);
35   }
36  }
```

debugging   We now have to correct the program by the process of *debugging*, the identification and correction of errors until a program works and is in good form.
syntax errors   The easiest errors to identify are those of *syntax* (such as mismatched parentheses or missing or extraneous semicolons). Because the program does not compile,

the errors are pointed out by the compiler, and they are usually easy to fix. Harder to identify, and far more serious, are *logical errors*. These go unnoticed by the compiler, but they cause fatal errors in the outcome of the program. This can happen in two ways: The program might terminate as a result of performing some illegal operation, such as division by zero; or the program might simply produce erroneous results. Perhaps the most elusive errors are stylistic errors. A program may compile, run, and produce just the right results, and yet be a nightmare in form. We will repair the preceding program, fixing the syntactic and logical errors.

logical errors

Before reading further, "desk check" (examine carefully without actually running) the program by scanning it carefully to find any errors. Look for errors first in syntax, then in logic, and finally in style. Now, being optimistic, we run the preceding program. On some computers, a sufficiently serious error may stop the compilation process, and then no further errors will be discovered; in other cases one may get a long list of errors. Often, a simple error can cause the compiler to announce many errors; in effect, a single error may so confuse the compiler that it sees many errors where there is only one. Compiling the program yields

```
Peets.java:10: <identifier> expected
    FIXED_FEE,                  // Shipping rate per shipment
              ^
Peets.java:21: unclosed string literal
  in.setPrompt("Enter price per pound: );
                                        ^
Peets.java:22: ')' expected
  pricePerPound = in.readInt();
                             ^
Peets.java:34: ')' expected
  msg.println("Total cost is " totalPrice);
                                          ^
Peets.java:9: possible loss of precision
found    : double
required: int
      RATE_PER_POUND = 1.25, // Shipping rate per pound
                       ^
Peets.java:25: cannot resolve symbol
symbol   : variable weight
location: class Peets
  weight = in.readInt();
  ^
Peets.java:27: cannot resolve symbol
symbol   : variable shipingCost
location: class Peets
    shipingCost = RATE_PER_POUND + weight + FIXED_FEE;
    ^
Peets.java:27: cannot resolve symbol
symbol   : variable weight
location: class Peets
    shipingCost = RATE_PER_POUND + weight + FIXED_FEE;
                                   ^
Peets.java:28: cannot resolve symbol
```

```
symbol   : variable totalPrice
location: class Peets
    totalPrice = priceperPound * weight + shippingCost;
       ^

Peets.java:28: cannot resolve symbol
symbol   : variable priceperPound
location: class Peets
    totalPrice = priceperPound * weight + shippingCost;
                 ^

Peets.java:28: cannot resolve symbol
symbol   : variable weight
location: class Peets
    totalPrice = priceperPound * weight + shippingCost;
                                 ^

Peets.java:28: cannot resolve symbol
symbol   : variable shippingCost
location: class Peets
    totalPrice = priceperPound * weight + shippingCost;
                                          ^

Peets.java:32: cannot resolve symbol
symbol   : variable coffeeCost
location: class Peets
    msg.println("Coffee total is " + coffeeCost);
                                     ^

Peets.java:33: cannot resolve symbol
symbol   : variable shipingCost
location: class Peets
    msg.println("Shipping cost is " + shipingCost);
                                      ^

14 errors
```

Apparently we have 14 errors in our program! The Java compiler displays messages detailing the error together with a copy of the erroneous line and an indicator ^ pointing to the offending construct.

The first error in line 10 is easy enough to see—we have a comma instead of a semicolon ending the declaration. The second error is also simple: We failed to supply the closing double quote for the output string. The correct statement is

```
in.setPrompt("Enter price per pound: ");
```

The third error in line 22 is a bit puzzling. The statement looks perfectly fine; why would the Java compiler be expecting a right parenthesis? Actually, line 22 *is* fine. The compiler was confused by the error in the previous line 21; it could not tell that the literal should have been closed just before the right parenthesis, so it guessed that line 21 might have been

```
in.setPrompt("Enter price per pound: );"
```

with the closing quote at the end of the line! So the compiler was still looking for the right parenthesis that matches setPrompt(in the next line.

We also have an error in line 34. After staring at the offending statement for a while, we finally realize that it's missing a concatenation plus sign. The Java compiler didn't supply the correct error message, but it *did* point to the precise position of the error. So we correct the statement to read

```
msg.println("Total cost is " + totalPrice);
```

The fifth error in line 9 says that something is wrong with the initialization of RATE_PER_POUND—we declared it an int, but assigned it a double value. Indeed something *is* wrong, since the price of coffee per pound will be a dollar-and-cents value; that is, it must be declared as a double. The same holds true for the variable FIXED_FEE, so we change final int to final double in line 8.

The remaining errors are awfully puzzling. So let's ignore them for now—perhaps correcting the first five errors will have some effect on the remaining errors. We try the compiler again, only to find this:

```
Peets.java:22: cannot resolve symbol
symbol  : variable pricePerPound
location: class Peets
  pricePerPound = in.readInt();
  ^

Peets.java:27: cannot resolve symbol
symbol  : variable shipingCost
location: class Peets
  shipingCost = RATE_PER_POUND + weight + FIXED_FEE;
  ^

Peets.java:28: cannot resolve symbol
symbol  : variable totalPrice
location: class Peets
  totalPrice = priceperPound * weight + shippingCost;
  ^

Peets.java:33: cannot resolve symbol
symbol  : variable shipingCost
location: class Peets
  msg.println("Shipping cost is " + shipingCost);
                                    ^

Peets.java:34: cannot resolve symbol
symbol  : variable totalPrice
location: class Peets
  msg.println("Total cost is " + totalPrice);
                                 ^

5 errors
```

We still have a few "cannot resolve symbol" errors, but there are fewer than before, and they refer to different lines in our program.

BUG ALERT 3.2	*Capitalization Errors*

One of the most common mistakes is inconsistency of capitalization in identifier names. The variables named FIXEDFEE, FixedFee, and fixedfee are all different, because uppercase and lowercase letters are different characters to the computer.

The first error may take some time to understand, but after careful inspection we realize that back in line 12 we *tried* to declare the variable pricePerPound, but we failed to capitalize the *P* in *Per.* So we look for all occurrences of this typo, finding another at line 28.

The second error results from another typo—shipingCost where we wanted shippingCost. This is also the cause of the fourth error in line 33.

The third error tells us we forgot to declare totalPrice, even though we tried to use it—so we add totalPrice to our list of declared variables. This is also the cause of the fifth error in line 34.

It looks as if we've found all our errors! Here's our corrected program.

```
 1    import CSLib.*;
 2
 3    public class Peets {
 4       //  Peet's Coffee
 5       //  Author: Eve M. Reingold, May 10, 1996
 6
 7       public void compute () {
 8          final double
 9             RATE_PER_POUND = 1.25, // Shipping rate per pound
10             FIXED_FEE;             // Shipping rate per shipment
11          int
12             pricePerPound,         // Coffee price per pound
13             weight,                // Amount ordered
14             shippingCost,
15             coffeeCost,
16             totalPrice;
17          InputBox in;
18          OutputBox msg;
19
20          in = new InputBox();
21          in.setTitle("Peet's Coffee");
22          in.setPrompt("Enter price per pound: ");
23          pricePerPound = in.readInt();
24
25          in.setPrompt ("Enter number of pounds: ");
26          weight = in.readInt();
27
28          shippingCost = RATE_PER_POUND + weight + FIXED_FEE;
29          totalPrice = pricePerPound * weight + shippingCost;
30
31          msg = new OutputBox();
```

```
32          msg.setTitle("Peet's Coffee");
33          msg.println("Coffee total is " + coffeeCost);
34          msg.println("Shipping cost is " + shippingCost);
35          msg.println("Total cost is " + totalPrice);
36      }
37  }
```

Let's try to compile again.

```
Peets.java:28: possible loss of precision
found    : double
required: int
    shippingCost = RATE_PER_POUND + weight + FIXED_FEE;
                                         ^

1 error
```

Wait a minute! This is an entirely new error! Java apparently is complaining that we've confused the use of double and int. Aha—in the offending statement

```
28          shippingCost = RATE_PER_POUND + weight + FIXED_FEE;
```

we've computed a double value, because RATE_PER_POUND and FIXED_FEE are each double; but we're attempting to store the value in shippingCost, which we've declared to be int! We should change the declaration of shipping-Cost (and the other variables) to double in line 11.
Let's try compiling again.

```
Peets.java:28: variable FIXED_FEE might not have been initialized
    shippingCost = RATE_PER_POUND + weight + FIXED_FEE;
                                         ^

Peets.java:33: variable coffeeCost might not have been initialized
    msg.println("Coffee total is " + coffeeCost);
                                        ^

2 errors
```

This certainly is frustrating! One step forward and two steps back! At least the error messages are relatively clear: We forgot to give the value for the symbolic constant FIXED_FEE, which should have been $1.95. So we change line 10 to

```
FIXED_FEE = 1.95;      // Shipping rate per shipment
```

As for the second error, indeed, we never assigned a value to the variable coffee-Cost, which is just the price per pound times the number of pounds. We add a statement to compute it, using it in the calculation of totalPrice. After all these changes, our program looks like this, and we try once again to compile it.

```
1   import CSLib.*;
2
3   public class Peets {
4      //  Peet's Coffee
5      //  Author: Eve M. Reingold, May 10, 1996
6
7      public void compute () {
8         final double
9            RATE_PER_POUND = 1.25,  // Shipping rate per pound
10           FIXED_FEE = 1.95;       // Shipping rate per shipment
11        double
12           pricePerPound,          // Coffee price per pound
13           weight,                 // Amount ordered
14           shippingCost,
15           coffeeCost,
16           totalPrice;
17        InputBox in;
18        OutputBox msg;
19
20        in = new InputBox();
21        in.setTitle("Peet's Coffee");
22        in.setPrompt("Enter price per pound: ");
23        pricePerPound = in.readInt();
24
25        in.setPrompt ("Enter number of pounds: ");
26        weight = in.readInt();
27
28        shippingCost = RATE_PER_POUND + weight + FIXED_FEE;
29        coffeeCost = pricePerPound * weight;
30        totalPrice = coffeeCost + shippingCost;
31
32        msg = new OutputBox();
33        msg.setTitle("Peet's Coffee");
34        msg.println("Coffee total is " + coffeeCost);
35        msg.println("Shipping cost is " + shippingCost);
36        msg.println("Total cost is " + totalPrice);
37     }
38  }
```

Hurray! Our program compiles without errors; let's try to run it. The first thing we see is the input dialog box asking us to input the price per pound:

But when we try to enter 8.95 for the price per pound, the InputBox raises an ErrorBox, telling us that an integer is required, not a decimal fraction.

This run-time error is pretty easily explained. We tried to read the value 8.95 from the input using readInt(), whereas we should have used read-Double(). We should make that change in line 23 and in line 26 as well, since we may wish to order fractions of a pound. Remember, an integer can be transformed to a decimal. We try to run the program again, and we get two input dialog boxes into which we type the values 8.95 for the price per pound and 3 for the number of pounds desired.

It is followed by the output dialog box

Yes! It ran! We're done! Or are we? Certainly the format of the output is not pleasing, but we learn in a later chapter how to fix that. More important, is the program's output *correct*? Let's perform a quick "hand check" of our results. We find very quickly that our program has miscomputed the shipping cost, overcharging by 50 cents! What could be going wrong?

Logic Errors

The most difficult of all errors to detect are those where the program appears to run correctly but produces incorrect output. The difficulty is that the output may look deceptively correct. So it is imperative that we test our program thoroughly and *verify* that the output is correct.

Examining our computation for `shippingCost` in line 28, we see that we've typed a plus sign where we should have typed a multiplication symbol. Once we change that, our program finally runs as expected, giving the following output.

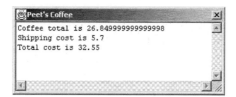

No program is ever perfect, although at this point our `Peet's Coffee` program is about as good as we can make it, given our present knowledge of Java.

```
1    import CSLib.*;
2
3    public class Peets {
4       //  Peet's Coffee
5       //  Author: Eve M. Reingold, May 10, 1996
6
7       public void compute () {
8          final double
9             RATE_PER_POUND = 1.25,  // Shipping rate per pound
10            FIXED_FEE = 1.95;       // Shipping rate per shipment
11         double
12            pricePerPound,          // Coffee price per pound
13            weight,                 // Amount ordered
14            shippingCost,
15            coffeeCost,
16            totalPrice;
17         InputBox in;
18         OutputBox msg;
19
20         in = new InputBox();
21         in.setTitle("Peet's Coffee");
22         in.setPrompt("Enter price per pound: ");
23         pricePerPound = in.readDouble();
24
25         in.setPrompt ("Enter number of pounds: ");
26         weight = in.readDouble();
27
```

```
28      shippingCost = RATE_PER_POUND * weight + FIXED_FEE;
29      coffeeCost = pricePerPound * weight;
30      totalPrice = coffeeCost + shippingCost;
31
32      msg = new OutputBox();
33      msg.setTitle("Peet's Coffee");
34      msg.println("Coffee total is " + coffeeCost);
35      msg.println("Shipping cost is " + shippingCost);
36      msg.println("Total cost is " + totalPrice);
37    }
38  }
```

A complicated program released for public use requires maintenance throughout its useful life, so debugging a large program is a task that never really ends while the program is in use. Such maintenance always involves many people over a period of many years. When is a program ready to be released for public use? Consider these headlines drawn from recent news reports:

- August 23, 1996. **Airline Crash Possibly Caused by Computer Glitch**. The crash of an American Airlines jet in Columbia may be due to a programming error in the plane's navigational system. Despite the pilot entering a correct one-letter command into the computer, a database misdirected the plane, sending it toward Bogota instead of Cali.
- January 12, 1999. **Premature Release of Data**. Key economic data for December were prematurely released by the Bureau of Labor Statistics when a "computer flaw" caused the data to appear on the Internet a day earlier than expected. The information on average prices charged by manufacturers could be worth millions of dollars to traders.
- February 24, 1999. **Computer Malfunction Downs Online Trading at Schwab**. Schwab's online system went down at 9:37 A.M. due to software problems with a new mainframe computer. Schwab's stock lost 5 percent, dropping 3.81\frac{1}{4}$ on the New York Stock Exchange. Similar problems had previously plagued ETrade, Ameritrade, and Datek.
- January 1, 2000. **Y2K Glitch Hits U.S. Spy System**. The most significant Y2K glitch caused a key U.S. Defense Department satellite to fail exactly at midnight Greenwich Mean Time. For 2 to 3 hours the Defense Department was "not able to process information from [the] system" operated by the National Reconnaissance Office, a secretive Pentagon agency run by the CIA and the Department of Defense.
- January 6, 2000. **Computer Glitch Grounds Planes**. The Washington Center that handles much of the air traffic for the northeast suffered an overload of error messages, forcing a shift to a backup system. Meanwhile, the FAA temporarily grounded planes at all airports in Boston, New York, Philadelphia, Pittsburgh, Raleigh-Durham, and Washington, D.C.. Although the main computer was restored within 4 hours, the delays continued throughout the day.

3.6

Pitfalls of Numbers, Strings, and Characters

For the most part, using integers, real numbers, strings, and characters is straightforward. Thus far in this chapter, we have tried to avoid giving too many details about them, and in the "quick exercises," we have tried to steer clear of subtleties that might cause mysterious bugs. In this section, we warn about some of the subtleties, especially when different types are used together.

3.6.1   Integers

In Chapter 1, we discussed how numbers are always represented in binary. We also said—and this is really the key point—that each number is represented in a *fixed number* of binary digits (bits). Specifically, integers use 32 bits. This allows for a wide range of numbers—$-2{,}147{,}483{,}648$ to $2{,}147{,}483{,}647$—but it is not infinite. Bug Alert 3.4 warns of the problems that can occur because of that.

BUG ALERT 3.4

Limitation of Type `int`

Integer values in the computer are limited in value by the internal structure of the computer (in the same way that there's a limit to the number of digits that your handheld calculator can display). This limitation can have unexpected consequences, and no warning is given that you have overstepped the limit. Consider

```
int x = 100000 * 100000;
out.println(x);
```

This produces the output

```
1410065408
```

instead of the correct value `10000000000`, because the correct value is too large for the computer.

3.6.2   Real Numbers

Just as integers have a limited range, so do `doubles`. However, the range of `doubles` is much larger than that of integers: They can represent numbers between $\pm 1.79769313486231570 \times 10^{308}$. Furthermore, they can represent extremely tiny numbers, with a magnitude as small as 10^{-324}.

Type double represents an approximation to what mathematicians call *double* real numbers.[6]

Like integers, doubles have a fixed size (64 bits, to be exact), and this again can cause problems. It means that doubles have a limited *precision*; some num- *precision* bers are necessarily represented inexactly. In fact, only the first 15 or so decimal digits are stored by the computer. This is called the *precision* of the number. Con- *precision* sequently, the same precision would result from using $\pi = 3.141592653589793$ as would result from using $\pi = 3.141592653589793238462 6433$. This precision is quite adequate for most purposes. Still, as with integers, funny things can happen and you should be aware of them. Bug Alert 3.5 warns of this problem.

Finite Precision of Type double   **BUG ALERT 3.5**

The computer's representation of type double with a finite number of decimal places means that computation with type double may not be exact in many cases. For example, if we write

```
double x = 1.0/5.0 + 1.0/5.0 + 1.0/5.0 - 0.6;
out.println(x);
```

then instead of the accurate result 0, we get the output

```
1.1102230246251565E-16
```

because the values 1.0/5.0 and 0.6 cannot be represented precisely with a finite number of bits. Granted, this is still a very small number, quite close to zero. But suppose we had written out.println(1e20 * x);. The output would be 11102, nowhere near the correct value of zero. Thus, very small errors can easily turn into very large ones.

3.6.3 Mixing Data Types

There are some exceptions to Java's pickiness regarding data types. Whenever a double is expected in an expression, an int can be used instead; Java will automatically convert it to a double. The philosophy is that integers can be converted to doubles *without loss of information*, so this conversion is done silently (the conversion from double to int does not share this property). Thus, if x is a variable of type double and i is a variable of type int,

```
x = i + 10;
```

---

[6]The term double is short for double-precision floating-point numbers. Java also has a type float for single-precision floating-point numbers. Double-precision numbers take twice the space, but sometimes can give better results; with computer memories as big as they are nowadays, we always use doubles.

is legal. The term i + 10 is an int, but it is converted to a double before it is assigned to x. Also legal is

```
x = i + 10.0;
```

Here, Java converts i to a double before adding it to the double literal 10.0, and this sum is assigned to x. The effect of the two assignments is the same, although the time at which the conversion occurs is different.

cast   Perhaps, you would like to convert a double value to an int. Java will never do this automatically, but it will let you do it explicitly by using the *cast* operation.

```
i = (int)(10.3 * x);
```

The cast (int) takes the expression that follows it, chops off any fractional part, and thereafter treats the value as an int. If you want to *round* the expression to the nearest integer value, you should first add 0.5 to it:

```
i = (int)(10.3 * x + 0.5);
```

When it comes to nonprimitive types (i.e., object types), Java's usual pickiness about types applies. Since InputBox and OutputBox are two different classes, their objects have different types. If you declare variables of type InputBox and OutputBox

```
OutputBox out;
InputBox in;
```

then the following assignments are illegal:

```
out = in;   // cannot assign InputBox
            // value to variable of type OutputBox
in = out;   // cannot assign OutputBox
            // value to variable of type InputBox
```

Objects (of any class) are also distinct from the primitive types, so the assignment in = 10 would also be erroneous.

3.6.4   Mixed-Mode Operations with Strings

We have emphasized the distinctions that Java draws between data types. In this regard, String can be especially confusing, because strings can look like other values. The string "13" and the integer 13 are entirely different; the fact that + can be applied to strings and between strings and integers makes matters worse. Here are some examples:

```
out.println("4"+"5");    // prints: 45
out.println("4"+5);      // prints: 45
out.println(4+5);        // prints: 9
```

The first concatenates the strings "4" and "5" and prints the result; the second converts the integer 5 to a string and then concatenates the strings "4" and "5"; the third *adds* the integers 4 and 5, and prints the result.

**QUICK EXERCISE
3.12**

Place each of these output statements into a program and execute them. Explain why each produces the output it does.

```
out.println("4"+"005");
out.println("4"+005);
out.println(1+2+"4");
out.println(1+(2+"4"));
out.println("4"*5);
```

3.6.5 Characters as Integers

We described in Chapter 1 how characters can be represented in a computer but using a fixed *code*, establishing a correspondence between characters and numbers. It is important to know how Java can sometimes confuse characters and integers.

For now, it is not important to know the precise code used for representing characters (it is discussed in Chapter 4), but a few examples will allow us to better illustrate the points we are about to make. The letter a has code 97; A has code 65; the digit character 3 has code 51, and the space character has code 32.

In understanding how characters and integers relate, it is essential, first of all, to understand that the digit characters '0', '1', . . . , '9' are *characters* and not *numbers*. These are completely different from the *integers* 0, 1, . . . , 9. It is a serious, but common, mistake to assign an integer to a character variable, as in

```
char level = 3;
```
Wrong

Here is where the tricky part comes in: Since there is an established coding of characters as integers, Java treats characters and integers as interchangeable in many cases. It is legal to assign a character to an integer variable; when this is done, the integer code of that character is assigned, as in

```
int i = 'a';  // assigns 97 to i
```

Similarly, an integer can be assigned to a character:

```
char c = 97;  // assigns 'a' to c
```

Thus, the earlier assignment level = 3, which we described as a serious mistake, is not considered a mistake by the Java compiler at all, and will not cause any error message to be printed. However, it does not assign the *character* '3' to the variable, but instead assigns the character whose code is 3 (which happens to be a nonprinting character). Thus, if you attempt to print level, the computer will not print anything; try it. The correct way to assign the *character* 3 to a variable is, of course,

```
char level = '3';
```

Name	Description
int readInt()	Returns integer entered by user.
double readDouble ()	Returns double entered by user.
String readString ()	Returns string entered by user.
char readChar()	Returns character entered by user.
void setPrompt(String text)	Makes text the input prompt

TABLE 3.7 **Some of the predefined InputBox methods.**

Note that the 3 is enclosed in single quotation marks. After this assignment, attempting to print level will result in printing 3.

Again, we will not cover the coding of characters in detail here. However, we mention that the correspondence between characters and integers can be very useful. To give a foretaste of what can be done, see if you can figure out what the second statement does:

```
char ch = 'a';
ch = ch+1;
```

The answer is that it evaluates the expression on the right by automatically converting the character 'a' in variable ch to an integer (97), adding 1 to that integer, and converting the result back to a character. Not surprisingly, 98 is the code for the character b, so after the assignment, ch contains b. Doing arithmetic on characters can be useful for doing conversions (such as uppercase to lowercase) and for interpreting user input.

Summary

Java has two major primitive numeric types: int and double. Variables of either type can be declared. Unlike objects, values of primitive types are not created by using new.

Integer arithmetic expressions are formed from integer literals (such as 37 or −409), integer variables (variables declared to have type int), and arithmetic operators +, −, *, /, and % (the remainder operator). The operators have a precedence relation (*, /, and % have precedence over + and -); it can be overridden by using parentheses. Integer expressions can also include method calls, as long as the method returns a value of type int. For example, the Math class in the java.lang package contains the method Math.abs which returns the absolute value of an integer; its argument is an integer expression.

Variable declarations give the type of a variable:

```
typename x ;
```

That variable is the name of a container, which can subsequently be filled with an assignment statement

```
x =  e ;
```

where *e* is an expression of the same type as x. Alternatively, the declaration itself can include an initializer for the variable:

```
typename x =  e ;
```

giving the same effect as the declaration and assignment. If a variable is never going to change, but is just being used as a convenient way to refer to a value, you can tell Java this by using the keyword `final` in the declaration:

```
final  typename x =  e ;
```

Such a variable is called a *symbolic constant*. Because it is prohibited to assign to a symbolic constant, it *must* be initialized in its declaration.

"Doubles" are Java's version of the real numbers in mathematics, that is, numbers with fractional part. Double literals either have a decimal point (e.g., `34.79`) or are written in scientific notation (`-17701e10`), or both (`-1.7701e14`). Double expressions consist of double literals, double variables (variables declared with type `double`), arithmetic operators, parentheses, and method calls. Again, the `Math` class contains several double-valued methods, such as `Math.cos(double)` and `Math.sqrt(double)`.

A frequently used nonprimitive type is `String`. `String` expressions are made up of string literals (sequences of characters enclosed in double quotes), `String` variables, the operator `+` (for string concatenation), and `String`-returning method calls. An example of the latter is the `String` instance method `toLowerCase`.

The primitive data type `char` is also heavily used. Character literals are single characters enclosed in single quotes, or single escape sequences—a back-slash \ followed by a character—enclosed in single quotes. An example of a char-valued method is the instance method `charAt(int)` in the `String` class.

In an assignment statement x = *e*, the type of variable x must generally be the same as the type of e. Expressions that mix types are usually not allowed either, but there are many exceptions. For example, the expression x+y is legal if:

- x and y both have the type `int` or `double` or `String` or `char`.
- x has type `double` and y has type `int`, or vice versa. The `int` will be converted to a `double` before doing the addition.
- x has type `String` and y has type `int` (or `double` or `char`), or vice versa. The `int` (or `double` or `char`) will be converted to a `String` and then concatenated to the string.
- x has type `char` and y has type `int`. And x will be treated as an integer for the addition.

Exercises

1. Your European shoe size can be determined from the length of your foot in centimeters. Take the foot length, subtract 9, multiply by 3, divide by 2, round *up*, and add 15. Write a Java class called `EuroShoe` with a single method, `convert`, to read a

person's foot length *in inches*, convert it to centimeters, and print the corresponding European shoe size. (There is 0.394 inch per 1 centimeter.) The input and output should look like this:

2. A "target" heart rate is useful in establishing a suitable exercise level. To determine this rate, subtract your age from 220. The upper limit of your target heart rate is 85 percent of this value; the lower limit is 65 percent. For example, a 40-year-old person can achieve a healthy workout by reaching a heart rate between 117 and 153 beats per minute. Write a Java class called `HeartRate` with a single method, `compute`, to read a person's age and print the range of that person's target heart rate. Your input and output should look like this:

3. The value at maturity of an initial investment P, invested over n periods at an interest rate r, and compounded at the end of each period is

$$P(1 + r)^n$$

Write a Java expression for this formula. (*Hint*: Use the method `Math.pow`.)

4. Write and debug a program to calculate the selling price of items at a discount store where

$$\text{Selling price} = \text{List price} - \text{Discount} + \text{Tax}$$

Use variables `listPrice`, `discount`, and `tax`, whose values are to be read. Print the value of a variable `sellingPrice`.

5. The area of a triangle can be calculated from its side lengths by Heron's formula:

$$\text{Area} = \sqrt{s(s - a)(s - b)(s - c)}$$

where a, b, and c are the side lengths and s is the semiperimeter; that is, $s = (a + b + c)/2$. Write a program to read the three sides of a triangle and calculate its area by Heron's formula.

6. The (Euclidean) distance between two points (x_1, y_1) and (x_2, y_2) is

$$\text{Distance} = \sqrt{(x_2 - x_1)^2 + (y_2 - y_1)^2}$$

Write a program to read the coordinates of two points and calculate the distance between them.

7. Write a program to read four numbers, representing the number of quarters, dimes, nickels, and pennies the user possesses, and print the total number of dollars and cents.

8. For this exercise, you will need to use the string operations charAt and substring, and possibly others. Write a program that reads a string of exactly eight characters from the user (use readString; you can assume that the user has entered eight characters) and writes those eight characters in an output box, in three different ways:

(a) Write the even-number characters (0, 2, 4, 6) followed by the odd-numbered characters (e.g., Polonius would come out as Plnuoois.

(b) Write all the characters in reverse (suinoloP).

(c) Write the first four characters in capital letters followed by the next four in lower-case (POLOnius).

9. It is often important to be able to *scale* a picture—shrink or expand it—to fit properly within a window. In exercise 5 in Chapter 2, you were asked to draw a 4 × 4 checkerboard in a 400 × 400 drawing box. Solve this problem again, in such a way that the size of the drawing box can be changed *easily*. The program should have the form

```
int size = 400;
d.setSize(size, size);
... statements to draw checkerboard ...
```

It should be written so that the size of the drawing box can be changed by changing *only* the initial value of `size`. Allow the user to specify this size in an input box.

10. Put the following statements into a program and execute them. Can you explain what happened in each case?

(a) out.println(3 * (1/3));

(b) out.println((2-Math.pow(Math.sqrt(2), (2))) * 10E20);

(c) out.println((char)('0' + '4' - '3'));

(d) out.println((int)('0' + '4' - '3'));

(e) out.println('0' + '4' - '3');

4

DECISION MAKING

Decisions are made in Java with the `if` statement and the `switch` statement; we introduce these statements in this chapter. *Boolean expressions* determine the outcome of decisions using `if` statements; integers determine the outcome of decisions using `switch` statements.

The prologues are over ... [i]t is time to choose."

——Wallace Stevens
Asides on the Oboe

The if Statement

All the programs that we've written so far involved "straight-line" computation. That is, they performed one thing, then the next, then the next, etc. If we were to diagram the sequence of actions, it would look like Figure 4.1. Such a *flowchart* shows the sequencing of actions that a program performs. But as we saw with the mouse in a maze in Chapter 1, a program sometimes makes decisions regarding what is to be done. For example, if only persons 18 years old or older are permitted to vote, we might write a flowchart like Figure 4.2. With this flowchart, the diamond box contains a *condition*. The logic of the program is to evaluate the condition, and then, if the evaluation is "true," to proceed to execute the code in the rectangle (the *true part*); otherwise, the true part is skipped. The two paths then converge, to continue with the program's execution. Such a computation can be expressed neatly in Java by the if statement as used in Chapter 1:

flowchart

condition

true part

```
if (age >= 18)
    out.println("You are eligible to vote.");
```

When this code is executed, the current value of the variable age is compared to 18. If the value of age is greater than or equal to 18, then the statement out.println("You are eligible to vote."); is executed. However, if the value of age is less than 18, then nothing is done. In either case, execution continues with the subsequent statement in the program. The net result is that the line of output

```
You are eligible to vote.
```

will be printed if age is 18 or larger; nothing will be printed if age is less than 18.

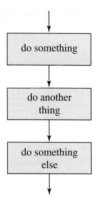

FIGURE 4.1   A flowchart for straight-line code.

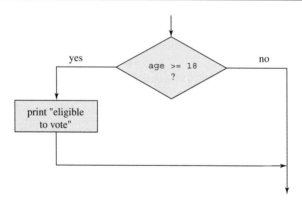

FIGURE 4.2   A flowchart for voting.

Sometimes there is one action to be taken if the condition is true and another if it is false. For example, the Social Security tax on wages used to be computed as 12.4 percent of income, up to a maximum income of $57,600. That is, it was computed using this formula:[1]

$$\text{Tax} = \begin{cases} 0.124 \times \text{wages} & \text{if wages} \leq \$57{,}600 \\ 0.124 \times \$57{,}600 & \text{otherwise} \end{cases}$$

The flowchart for this computation is shown in Figure 4.3, and the code would look like this:

---

[1]The current formula is just a little more complicated; see Exercise 4 at the end of the chapter.

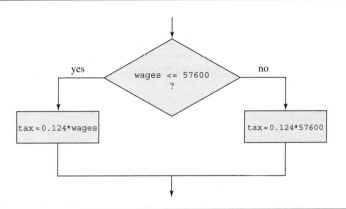

FIGURE 4.3 Flowchart for the Social Security computation.

```
if (wages <= 57600)
   tax = 0.124 * wages;
else
   tax = 0.124 * 57600;
```

When this code is executed, the current value of the variable wages (thought of as dollars) is compared to 57,000. If the value of wages is less than or equal to 57,000, the statement tax = 0.124 * wages is executed. If the value of wages is greater than 57600, the statement tax = 0.124 * 57600 is executed. Note that *just one* of the assignments is executed, *not* both.

This computation is embedded in the following complete Java application, with the values 0.124 and 57,600 replaced by suitably named symbolic constants.

```
1    import CSLib.*;
2
3    public class SocialSecurity {
4       //  Calculate and print the  Social Security
5       //  Self-Employment Tax on wages (to be read in).
6       //  Author: Deborah R. Klapper, November 6, 1994
7
8       public void compute () {
9          final double
10            MAXIMUM_WAGE = 57600, // maximum wage subject to tax
11            TAX_RATE = 0.124;     // tax rate on wages less than
12                                  // the maximum
13         double wages,            // amount of wages subject to tax
14                tax;              // amount of tax
15
16         InputBox in = new InputBox();
17         in.setTitle("Social Security Tax");
18         in.setPrompt("Your wages subject to Social Security Tax are: $");
```

```
19        wages = in.readInt();
20
21        if (wages <= MAXIMUM_WAGE)
22          tax = TAX_RATE * wages;
23        else
24          tax = TAX_RATE * MAXIMUM_WAGE;   // maximum allowable tax
25
26        OutputBox out = new OutputBox();
27        out.setTitle("Social Security Tax");
28        out.println("Your Social Security Tax is: $" + tax);
29      }
30    }
```

with the client code:

```
1    public class SocialSecurityClient {
2
3      public static void main (String[] args) {
4        SocialSecurity ss = new SocialSecurity();
5        ss.compute();
6      }
7    }
```

When run, this application gives the following sample output for the case of wages less than MAXIMUM_WAGE:

and

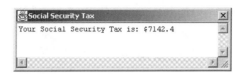

for `wages` greater than `MAXIMUM_WAGE`.[2]

An `if` statement chooses one of two alternatives based on some true/false condition. The `if` statement is made up of several parts: the keyword `if` followed by a parenthesized condition, followed by the "then" alternative (which is executed if the condition is true); this is followed by the keyword `else` followed by the "else" alternative (which is executed if the condition is false):

```
if ( condition )
    statement    ←── The ``true'' part
else
    statement    ←── The ``false'' part
```

Each alternative can be a single statement or a compound statement enclosed by braces {…}. Only the alternative chosen is executed; the other alternative is skipped entirely. If there is nothing to be done in the "else" alternative, it may be omitted:

```
if ( condition )
    statement    ←── The ``true'' part
```

QUICK EXERCISE 4.1

Write an `if` statement that checks the age of a child, contained in a variable `age`, and prints a message indicating that a child under age 8 must be secured in a car seat when traveling.

Extend the above `if` statement to print the message "Your child may use a regular seat belt" for a child age 8 or older.

Each alternative in the `if` statement for the Social Security tax calculation was a single assignment statement. Here, by contrast, is an example of an `if` statement with a compound statement for each alternative. A *compound statement* is a group of statements placed inside of braces. Given two positive integers `firstNumber` and `secondNumber`, we want to calculate the `quotient` and the `remainder` of the larger integer divided by the smaller integer:

compound statement

```
if (firstNumber <= secondNumber) {
    quotient  = secondNumber / firstNumber;
    remainder = firstNumber % secondNumber;
```

---

[2]We normally want dollars-and-cents amounts to be written with two digits following the decimal point, even if those digits are zeros. To do this in Java, you must explicitly code the output of the proper number of digits. You'll learn how to do that in Section 10.2.

```
    }
    else {
        quotient  = firstNumber / secondNumber;
        remainder = secondNumber % firstNumber;
    }
```

Suppose that a sales associate earns a monthly commission of 7 percent if monthly sales exceed $500, but only 5 percent if sales are less than $500 for the month. Write an `if` statement to assign appropriate values to the variables `rate` and `pay`, given the value of `monthly_sales`.

The *statement* in the true or false part of an `if` can be *any* statement, including another `if`. A common example is seen when the `else` statement is an `if` statement:

```
if ( condition-1 )
    statement-1
else
    if ( condition-2 )
        statement-2
    else
        statement-3
```

The flowchart that corresponds to this example is shown in Figure 4.4. Here, if *condition-1* is true, *statement-1* is executed. If not, *condition-2* is tested and if it is true, *statement-2* is executed; if it is false, *statement-3* is executed. Again, exactly one of the three statements is executed: *statement-1* is executed if *condition-1* is true (traversing the flowchart along the "true" path); *statement-2* is executed if *condition-1* is false and *condition-2* is true (traversing the flowchart along the "false" "true" path); and *statement-3* is executed if both *condition-1* and *condition-2* are false (traversing the flowchart along the "false" "false" path). The indentation of the `if` statements displays the structure of the tests, but it is customary to display the structure even more clearly as

```
if ( condition-1 )
    statement-1
else if ( condition-2 )
    statement-2
else
    statement-3
```

As an example, the wind chill index is computed for a given air temperature in degrees Fahrenheit and wind speed in miles per hour from the formula

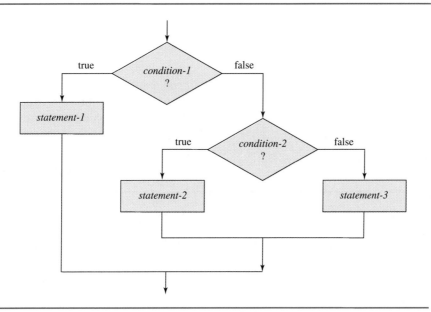

FIGURE 4.4 A flowchart for cascading if-else statements.

$$\text{Wind chill index} = \begin{cases} \text{temperature} & \text{wind} \leq 4 \text{ mph} \\[2ex] 91.4 - (10.45 + 6.69\sqrt{\text{wind}} \\ \quad - 0.447\text{wind}) \times \frac{91.4 - \text{temperature}}{22.0} & 4 \text{ mph} < \text{wind} \leq 45 \text{ mph} \\[2ex] 1.6 \times \text{temperature} - 55.0 & \text{wind} > 45 \text{ mph} \end{cases}$$

In Java this formula becomes

```
if (windSpeed <= 4)        //  little or no wind
   windChillIndex = temperature;
else if (windSpeed <= 45)   //  moderate wind
   windChillIndex =
      91.4 - (10.45 + 6.69 * Math.sqrt(windSpeed)
            - 0.447 * windSpeed) * (91.4 - temperature)/22.0;
else                        //  high wind
   windChillIndex = 1.6 * temperature - 55.0;
```

Nested if statements like this are useful and common, and you will often see them repeated several times, such as in

```
if ( condition-1 )
   statement-1
else if ( condition-2 )
   statement-2
else if ( condition-3 )
   statement-3
```

```
    . . .
else if ( condition-(i-1) )
    statement-(i-1)
else
    statement-i
```

The action here is summarized as follows: *condition-1, condition-2, condition-3*, and so on, are tested in sequence until one of them is found to be true; the corresponding statement is then executed. If none of the conditions are true, *statement-i* is executed.

QUICK EXERCISE 4.3

Write an `if` statement that computes the interest rate for an auto loan given the term of the loan (in months). Loans for a term of 24 months or less have a rate of 0.9 percent; 36-month loans carry a rate of 2.9 percent, 48-month loans a rate of 4.9 percent, and 60-month loans a rate of 6.9 percent.

QUICK EXERCISE 4.4

Suppose that a sales associate earns a monthly commission of 10 percent if monthly sales exceed $1000, 7 percent if sales exceed $500, but only 5 percent if sales are less than $500 for the month. Write an `if` statement to assign appropriate values to the variables `rate` and `pay`, given `monthly_sales`.

QUICK EXERCISE 4.5

Suppose the final grade cutoffs for a computer science course are based on a computed score: 90 to 100 is an A, 80 to 89 is a B, 60 to 79 is a C, 50 to 59 is a D, below 50 fails, or is an F. Write a nested `if` statement to write the final grade, given the variable `score`.

QUICK EXERCISE 4.6

The entry fee for the local art museum is calculated as follows: children under 5 years, free; adults 65 years and older, $1.50; all others, $2.50. Write an `if` statement to print the `entryFee` (of type `double`) based on the variable `ageOfEntrant` (of type `int`).

Another kind of nesting of if statements is shown in this example:

```
if ( condition-1 )
    if ( condition-2 )
        statement-1
    else
        statement-2
else
    statement-3
```

This example corresponds to the flowchart shown in Figure 4.5. Here *condition-1* is tested first. If it is true, the nested if (shown shaded) is executed. That is, *condition-2* is tested; if it is true, *statement-1* is executed, otherwise *statement-2* is executed. If *condition-1* is false, *statement-3* is executed. The result is that exactly one of the three statements is executed: *statement-1* is executed if *condition-1* and *condition-2* are both true (the "true" "true" path in the flowchart); *statement-2* is executed if *condition-1* is true and *condition-2* is false (the "true" "false" path); and *statement-3* is executed if *condition-1* is false, regardless of the truth of *condition-2* (the "false" path in the flowchart). Notice how the indentation of the if statements displays the structure of the tests.

Nested if statements can become quite complicated; therefore, you should write them with clear indentations of corresponding conditions and alternatives. Indentation alone is not sufficient, though. Consider what if statement might be written to correspond to the flowchart shown in Figure 4.6.

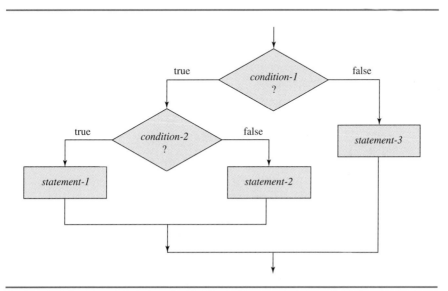

FIGURE 4.5   A flowchart for nested if-else statements.

QUICK EXERCISE 4.7	Write an `if` statement to calculate the maximum of three numbers. That is, given variables X, Y, and Z, assign to variable Max the maximum value among those three variables. You can assume X, Y, and Z contain three different numbers. What does your statement do if two of them are equal?

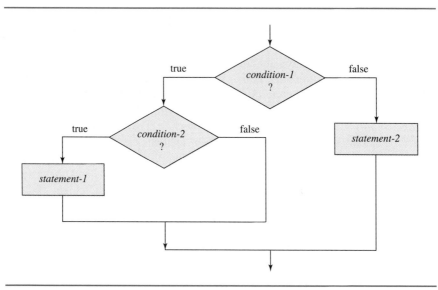

FIGURE 4.6   Flowchart for the *intended* meaning of code (1).

You might be tempted to write

```
if ( condition-1 )
   if ( condition-2 )
      statement-1                    (1)
else
   statement-2
```

The intent of the programmer is suggested by the indentation: *statement-1* should be executed if *condition-1* and *condition-2* are both true, *statement-2* should be executed if *condition-1* is false, and nothing at all should be done if *condition-1* is true and *condition-2* is false. But remember that white space is ignored by the compiler. Just because it looks right to a human doesn't mean the compiler will read it the same way. In fact, the rule is that *the `else` alternative is paired with the nearest unmatched `if` preceding it.* This rule means that the fragment will be interpreted as if it corresponded to the flowchart shown in Figure 4.7. Had the

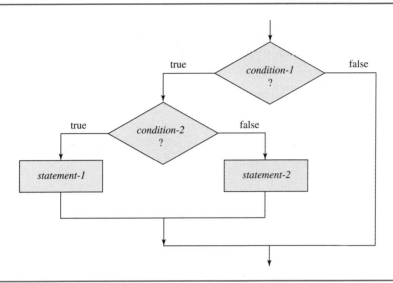

FIGURE 4.7   Flowchart for the *actual* meaning of code (1).

programmer intended this interpretation, the suggestive indentation would have
been

```
if ( condition-1 )
    if ( condition-2 )
        statement-1
    else
        statement-2
```

Again, to the compiler, the indentation is irrelevant, and the two forms shown
above are identical in meaning. This is known as a *dangling else* error. To get the   *dangling else*
desired effect (as shown in Figure 4.6), the programmer can enclose the "true"
part in a pair of braces:

```
if ( condition-1 ) {
    if ( condition-2 )
        statement-1
}
else
    statement-2
```

The best solution, however, is to reorganize the flow of the program to correspond
to the flowchart shown in Figure 4.8. The code becomes

```
if ( not condition-1 )
    statement-2
```

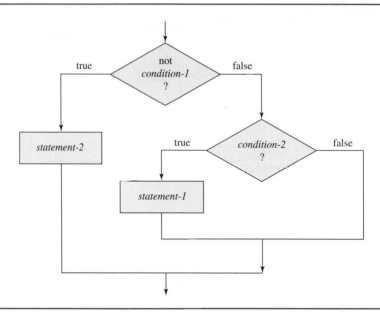

FIGURE 4.8   Reorganized code to avoid the dangling `else`.

```
else if ( condition-2 )
   statement-1
```

where *not condition-1* means the logical negation of *condition-1*. Thus, the intent of these statements is clear and unambiguous to both the computer *and* the person reading them.

For example, suppose that a clinic asks a first-time patient to either fill out an insurance form or pay in advance. On subsequent visits, the clinic asks nothing of a patient who has insurance, but asks uninsured patients to pay in advance.

The following program fragment is incorrect:

```
if (previousVisits > 0)
   if (noInsuranceOnFile)
      out.print("Please pay in advance.");           WRONG
else
   out.print("Please fill out insurance form or pay in advance.");
```

As explained above, the indentation has no effect on the logic of the code, and if the initial condition is false (i.e., if this is the patient's first visit), then nothing is printed. This code might be correctly written in a number of ways, but to obtain the best solution, we should negate the first condition, resulting in the code

```
if (previousVisits == 0)
   out.print("Please fill out insurance form or pay in advance.");
else if (noInsuranceOnFile)
   out.print("Please pay in advance.");
```

Notice how the expression `previousVisits == 0` is the negation of the formerly used `previousVisits > 0` (within the realm of nonnegative integers).

Dangling `else`	**Bug Alert 4.1**

Remember to match each `else` with the correct `if`. The rule is that an `else` is paired with the nearest unmatched `if` preceding it.

4.2

Constructing and Analyzing Boolean Expressions

> I said the thing which was not. (For they have no word in their language to express lying or falsehood.)
>
> ——Jonathan Swift
> *Gulliver's Travels*

> "Contrariwise," continued Tweedledee, "if it was so, it might be; and if it were so, it would be: but as it isn't, it ain't. That's logic."
>
> ——Lewis Carroll
> *Through the Looking-glass*

Conditions are called *Boolean expressions.*[3] Boolean expressions are formed in Java by comparing `int` and/or `double` values with *relational operators* such as `<=` (less than or equal to; see Table 4.1). The relational operators work the way you would expect on these data types (and also on the data types `float` and `long`, which we have not used). For example, the following conditions are all "true":

Boolean expressions relational operators

```
10 != 3
3 < 4.5
4 <= 4.0
(10 / 2) == (4 + 1)
```

---

[3]Boolean expressions are named for the British logician George Boole, 1815–1864. Therefore, it is appropriate to capitalize the word *Boolean* in conventional prose.

Mathematics	Java	English
$<$	$<$	Less than
$>$	$>$	Greater than
$\leq$	$<=$	Less than or equal to
$\geq$	$>=$	Greater than or equal to
$=$	$==$	Equal to
$\neq$	$!=$	Not equal to

TABLE 4.1   Relational operators in Java.

Notice that equality is tested using a double equals sign (==). Notice, too, that Java relaxes its usual type-pickiness when comparing an int and a double—the int is converted to a double prior to making the comparison. Parenthesized expressions are evaluated first, so the last expression above is equivalent to 5==5.

logical and
conjunction
logical inclusive
or
disjunction
logical negation
logical (Boolean)
operators

The relational operators return one of the two *Boolean values,* called true and false. In addition to the relational operators, which compare numbers and return Boolean values, there are several *Boolean operators* that combine Boolean values and return Boolean values. The most important of these are && (*logical and*, also called *conjunction*), || (*logical inclusive or*, also called *disjunction*), and ! (*logical negation*). For example, we can construct complicated conditions such as

```
(MINIMUM_WAGE <= wages) && (wages <= MAXIMUM_WAGE)
```

to express, in Java, the condition MINIMUM_WAGE $\leq$ wages $\leq$ MAXIMUM_WAGE.

The relational operators have their usual mathematical meaning. The logical operators need some explanation. The operator ! before a Boolean expression complements its value from true to false, and vice versa. The operator && combines two Boolean expressions, giving an expression that is true if both of the constituent expressions are true and false if either of the constituent expressions is false.

The operator || also combines two Boolean values, but it gives an expression that is true if *either* or *both* of its constituent values are true. This is not always what we mean when we use the word *or* in English; we often use *or* to exclude the possibility of both being true. For example, in Patrick Henry's famous remark "Give me liberty or give me death," it is unlikely that he wanted to include the possibility of *both* alternatives. The || operator in Java therefore is called the *inclusive or* because it includes the possibility of both being true. Java also provides an *exclusive or* operator ^, which is true when exactly one of its two constituents is true   (in other words, it is true if the two operands are different).

inclusive or
exclusive or

We've just seen an example of &&. The operator !   can be useful for avoiding the dangling else problem. As we said on page 109, the best way to avoid the problem is to use

```
if ( not condition-1 )
   statement-2
else if ( condition-2 )
   statement-1
```

where *not condition-1* is a condition that is the opposite of `condition-1`. We can now say exactly how to express this, using the Boolean complement operator:

```
if (! condition-1 )
   statement-2
else if ( condition-2 )
   statement-1
```

Combining Relational Operations   BUG ALERT 4.2

The expression

```
(MINIMUM_WAGE <= wages <= MAXIMUM_WAGE)
```

results in a compile-time error in Java. As stated at the bottom of Table 4.2, operators of the same precedence are evaluated left to right, so the above expression is taken to mean

```
((MINIMUM_WAGE <= wages) <= MAXIMUM_WAGE)
```

The value of the condition `(MINIMUM_WAGE <= wages)` is a Boolean expression, whereas the value of `MAXIMUM_WAGE` is an integer expression, and a Boolean cannot be compared to an integer. To combine relational operators to get the desired effect, you *must* use Boolean operators:

```
(MINIMUM_WAGE <= wages) && (wages <= MAXIMUM_WAGE)
```

Equal/Not Equal Comparisons with Type `double`   BUG ALERT 4.3

Recall from Bug Alert 3.5 (page 89) that numbers of type `double` are not always represented exactly in the computer. An important consequence of such inexact representation is that the relational operators `==` and `!=` may give unexpected results. For example, the relational expression `1.0/5.0 + 1.0/5.0 + 1.0/5.0 - 0.6 == 0.0` has the value `false`. Comparisons involving `double`s should always be done within a certain "tolerance." Pick a small value `epsilon` and, instead of comparing `x == y`, compare `Math.abs(x-y) < epsilon`; this tests if `x` and `y` are within `epsilon` of each other.

We can print `boolean` expressions to an `OutputBox` by using the methods `print` and `println`, as shown in Table 2.3 on page 43.

Often we wish to evaluate a Boolean expression and assign its value to a variable. Java has a primitive type `boolean` for this purpose, and we can declare a variable to be of type `boolean`. This technique often eliminates redundant computation, and sometimes it makes programs easier to read.

BUG ALERT 4.4

Equals Sign versus Double Equals Sign

Remember, a single equals sign = is used in an *assignment statement*, and a double equals sign == is a relational operator. A common error is to write

```
if (x=y)
  . . .
```

when you intended to write

```
if (x==y)
  . . .
```

Fortunately, the Java compiler usually gives an error message for the former code. However, in the rare case that `x` is a Boolean variable and `y` is a Boolean expression, the compiler will generate no error message!

QUICK EXERCISE 4.8

Write a Boolean expression for the desired qualities in the following personal ad: "Wanted for companionship: 25–40, nonsmoking, under 66 inches, under 140 pounds, good-looking, able to relocate." Use the Boolean variables `smoking`, `goodLooking`, and `ableToRelocate`, plus integer variables `age`, `height` (in inches), and `weight` (in pounds).

For example, suppose we want to test whether a student has "shown improvement" on exams or homework. By *shown improvement,* we mean "the grade on the third exam was higher than or equal to the grade on the second exam, and the grade of the second exam was higher than or equal to that of the first," and similarly for the homework. Suppose that the grades on the three exams are contained in the variables `ex1`, `ex2`, and `ex3`, and the grades on the three homeworks are contained in `hw1`, `hw2`, and `hw3`. One way to state the condition "exams improved" is

```
(ex1 <= ex2) && (ex2 <= ex3)
```

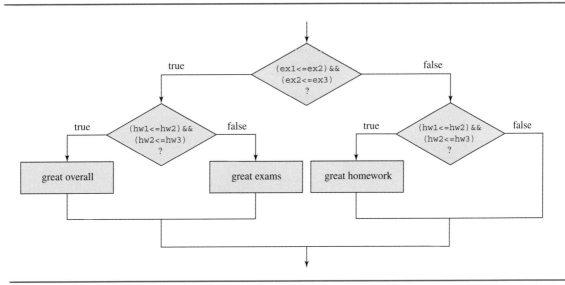

FIGURE 4.9   Flowchart for determining whether exams and homeworks improve.

The problem is to print a congratulatory message to the student, but that message will depend upon whether the student showed improvement in exams or in homeworks or in both. A flowchart for this problem is shown in Figure 4.9. Notice how the complicated expression for improving homeworks appears in two different diamonds, meaning that it will be repeated in our code in two different if statements. Using Boolean variables, we can avoid having to write this complicated condition more than once:

```
boolean exam_improved = (ex1 <= ex2) && (ex2 <= ex3);
boolean hwk_improved = (hw1 <= hw2) && (hw2 <= hw3);
if (exam_improved)
  if (hwk_improved)
    out.print("Great overall improvement!");
  else out.print("Great exam improvement!");
else if (hwk_improved)
  out.print("Great homework improvement!");
```

The modified flowchart is shown in Figure 4.10.

We discussed *precedence rules* of arithmetic operators in Chapter 3. These precedence rules need to be expanded to include Boolean operators (see Table 4.2). The Boolean operator ! has highest precedence, followed by ^, then &&, then ||. Notice that an expression without parentheses but having more than one operator

expanded precedence rules

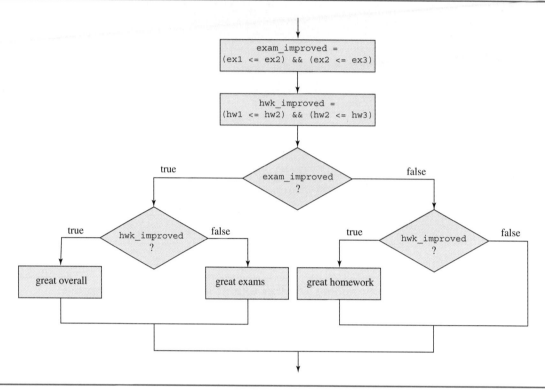

FIGURE 4.10   Improved flowchart for determining whether exams and homeworks improve.

of the same precedence is evaluated left to right. However, it's usually best to use parentheses. That way your intentions are clear.

**QUICK EXERCISE
4.9**

The following nested `if` statement was found in a piece of code written by a rather poor programmer. Rewrite it as a single assignment statement to the variable `result`.

```
if (x > 1.0)
  if ((x-1.0) > 1.0e-5)
    result = false;
  else
    result = true;
else
    result = true;
```

In the absence of parentheses, operators are evaluated in the following order:

1. !   - (unary)
2. * / %
3. + - (binary)
4. < <= > >=
5. == !=
6. ^
7. &&
8. ||

Operators within the same precedence level are evaluated left to right.

TABLE 4.2   Expanded precedence rules for arithmetic, relational, and Boolean operators in Java. Notice that the minus sign occurs twice: first as a *unary* operator (as in −3) and then as a *binary* operator (as in 5 − 3). See Appendix B for a more comprehensive description.

Sometimes rather complicated Boolean expressions are needed. Consider the following problem. Given a year, a month, and a day in that month, find the number of days from the beginning of the year to that day (the *day number*). It uses a fairly complicated sequence of conditionals, especially when leap years are taken into account:

```
 1    // Calculate dayNumber assuming all months have 31 days
 2    dayNumber = (month - 1) * 31 + day;
 3
 4    // Then correct for months beyond February
 5    if (month > 2) {
 6      // Assume non-leap year
 7      if ((month == 3) || (month == 4))
 8        dayNumber = dayNumber - 3;
 9      else if ((month == 5) || (month == 6))
10        dayNumber = dayNumber - 4;
11      else if ((month == 7) || (month == 8) || (month == 9))
12        dayNumber = dayNumber - 5;
13      else if ((month == 10) || (month == 11))
14        dayNumber = dayNumber - 6;
15      else if (month == 12)
16        dayNumber = dayNumber - 7;
17
18      if ((((year % 4) == 0) && ((year % 100) != 0))
19          || ((year % 400) == 0))
20        // Correct for leap year
21        dayNumber = dayNumber + 1;
22    }
```

Line 1 calculates the day number under the simplifying assumption that every month has 31 days. This approximation is then corrected in two ways. First, it is corrected for months beyond February by subtracting the number by which preceding months fall short of 31 days. The second correction in the program segment is for leap years, when February has 29 days instead of 28. In our calendar, a year is a leap year if it is divisible by 4, except that century years also need to be divisible by 400 to be leap years. (For example, 2000 was a leap year, but 1700, 1800, and 1900 were not leap years.) The Boolean expression

```
(((year % 4) == 0) && ((year % 100) != 0))
|| ((year % 400) == 0)
```

is true if either (or both) of the subexpressions

```
((year % 4) == 0) && ((year % 100) != 0)
```

or   ```(year % 400) == 0```

is true. The first of these is true if the year is divisible by 4 and is not a century year—a normal leap year. The second is true if the year is a century year divisible by 400. Thus the overall expression is true exactly when ```year``` is a leap year and false otherwise.

QUICK EXERCISE 4.10	Sketch the flowchart for the fragment of code beginning on page 115 that computes ```dayNumber```.

By the way, there is a remarkable formula (of unknown origin) that magically gives the correct values for adjusting months beyond February. Using this magic formula, and also utilizing a Boolean variable, we can rewrite the program as follows:

```
 1      boolean isLeapYear = ((year % 4) == 0)
 2                      && ((year % 100) != 0)
 3                      || ((year % 400) == 0);
 4
 5      // Calculate dayNumber assuming all months have 31 days
 6      dayNumber = (month - 1) * 31 + day;
 7
 8      // Correct for months beyond February
 9      if (month > 2) {
10        // Assume non-leap year
11        dayNumber = dayNumber - ((4 * month + 23) / 10);
12        if (isLeapYear)
13          // Correct for leap year
14          dayNumber = dayNumber + 1;
15      }
```

Of course, you can't usually rely on magic to simplify your ```if``` statements!

Comparing Objects

So far we have constructed Boolean expressions by making numerical comparisons and combining the results. Does it ever make sense to compare *objects*? Certainly it might make sense to try to determine if two objects are identical. For example, the following code will print "true":

```
1    OutputBox out = new OutputBox();
2    TrickMouse morte, sporte;
3    morte = new TrickMouse();
4    sporte = morte;
5    out.println(morte == sporte);
```

The assignment in line 3 returns a reference to a new `TrickMouse` object and assigns that reference to the variable `morte`. Subsequently in line 4 the contents of the variable `morte` are copied to the variable `sporte`. Consequently both `morte` and `sporte` refer to *exactly* the same object, so they are "equal." This is illustrated in Figure 4.11.

On the other hand, just because two objects look the same, they are not necessarily "equal." In essence, the comparison operator == tests whether two operands refer to exactly the same area of memory. In Figure 4.12, the variables

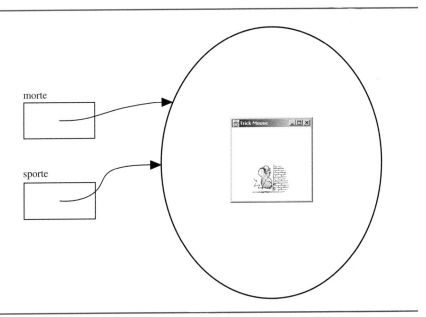

FIGURE 4.11 Two variables, each referring to the same object.

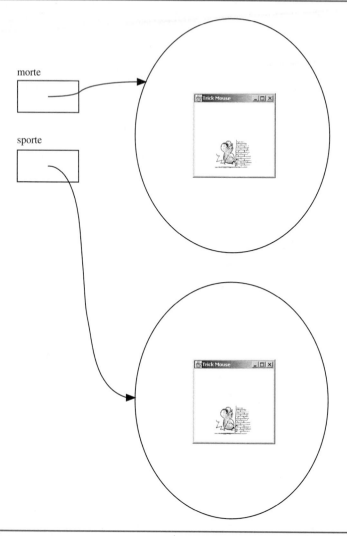

FIGURE 4.12 Two variables, referring to distinct (!=) but "equal" objects.

morte and sporte are not equal to each other, even though they refer to two TrickMouse objects that appear to be identical.

Nonetheless, it is sometimes useful to be able to compare two *distinct* object to see if they *contain equal data*. For example, we might want two TrickMouse objects to be considered "equal" if they are both doing the same thing—either both "speaking" or both "hitting the wall." To accomplish this, the TrickMouse class would have to offer an additional method:

```
boolean equals (TrickMouse other)
```

The `equals` method might be used as follows:

```
1    OutputBox out = new OutputBox();
2    TrickMouse morte = new TrickMouse(),
3             sporte = new TrickMouse();
4    morte.hitWall();
5    sporte.hitWall();
6    out.println( morte.equals(sporte) );
```

Clearly `morte` and `sporte` refer to distinct objects. However, each one is "speaking" the same phrase, so the `equals` method should return a `true` value. Notice the mechanism that is used: The `equals` message is sent to `morte` with a second object `sporte` supplied as an actual parameter. Within the `morte` object, work will be done to decide whether the `TrickMouse` that is supplied as a parameter is doing the same thing that `morte` is doing. Notice that there is a reflexive property here, so line 6 could also have been written `out.println( sporte.equals(morte) )`.

What about other kinds of comparisons between objects, such as "less than"? Such a comparison doesn't make much sense for objects like `TrickMouse`. But there *are* some objects for which it *would* make sense. For example, if there were a `Student` class that contained all of a student's academic records (home address, major, GPA, etc.), it might make sense to say that one `Student` is "less than" another by comparing their GPAs. Or perhaps the measure should be the number of credits earned. As before, the *meaning* of "less than" would be left to the programmer who writes the code. It would be poor programming practice to write a method with such a generic name as `lessThan` when there is no universal agreement as to what it would mean. Better names might be `hasHigherGPA` or `hasMoreCredits` or `isOlder`, so that the name of the method conveys some understanding of what the method actually does.

A conventional way of providing comparison methods for a class is to define a generalized method such as `boolean compareTo(Student other)` that returns −1 if the recipient object is "less than" the parameter object, 0 if they are equal, and +1 if the recipient is "greater than" the parameter. If there are many different kinds of comparisons, a second parameter is supplied giving an integer that tells which kind of comparison to make. Symbolic constants would typically be used so that the client doesn't need to remember which integers correspond to which comparisons. For example, we might define symbolic constants `GPA`, `CREDITS`, and `AGE`. So the following code would compare two students with respect to their ages:

```
Student a, b;
...
if ( a.compareTo(b, AGE) < 0 )
  out.println("Student a is younger than b");
```

4.3.1 Characters and Strings

Unicode

Characters were first discussed in Section 3.4.1. They are represented by numbers based on an international convention, called *Unicode*. Unicode assigns a number between 0 and 65,535 to almost every character in every major alphabet. The first 128 codes, from 0 to 127, are used for the English letters and punctuation as well as the decimal digits and the nonprinting characters mentioned earlier. These first 128 codes are inherited from a much older and very widely followed convention,

ASCII code

called *ASCII*, for *American Standard Code for Information Interchange*. We concern ourselves only with the characters in ASCII.

Table 4.3 gives the ASCII codes for the letters, digits, and the most common punctuation marks. (Again, for these characters, ASCII and Unicode are identical.)

Characters can be compared using all the same relational operators that apply to integers. The result of such a comparison is just the result of comparing the character's ASCII codes. Examining Table 4.3, we see that $'A' < 'Z'$, but $'Z' < 'a'$. We also note that the space character $' '$ is less than all letters, digits, and punctuation symbols.

Strings are particularly important objects in Java for which comparison operations are meaningful. Comparison of strings is done by comparing them character by character, left to right. The first character that differs dictates which string is less than the other. When strings of letters of the same case are compared,

lexicographic order

this corresponds to the ordinary dictionary order, also known as *lexicographic order*.

There are three subtleties that must be addressed:

1. What if one string is a prefix of the other (such as *wish* and *wishbone*)?
2. How do uppercase and lowercase characters compare?
3. How do special characters (such as %) compare?

The first question is easy to answer: The prefix is less than the longer string (just as in the dictionary). The second question is a matter of choice. In Java, there are methods provided that compare strings in either a *case-sensitive* or a *case-insensitive* mode. (In case-sensitive order, the ASCII order holds: Uppercase is always less than lowercase.) The third question is decided by the ASCII representation of the characters.

The additional comparison operations that Java provides for `Strings` are briefly documented in Table 4.4. All the methods shown there compare the receiver and the argument string using lexicographic order. This is the natural order for printing strings in many applications.

In detail, for lexicographic ordering, two `Strings`

s =	s_0	s_1	s_2	$\cdots$	s_{m-1}	
t =	t_0	t_1	t_2		$\cdots$	t_{n-1}

are compared as follows. First compare s_0 to t_0. If s_0 precedes t_0 in the alphabet (which can be determined by comparing them using <, which will compare their

Uppercase Letters		Lowercase Letters		Digits		Special Characters	
A	65	a	97	0	48	bell	7
B	66	b	98	1	49	tab	9
C	67	c	99	2	50	newline	10
D	68	d	100	3	51	space	32
E	69	e	101	4	52	!	33
F	70	f	102	5	53	"	34
G	71	g	103	6	54	#	35
H	72	h	104	7	55	$	36
I	73	i	105	8	56	%	37
J	74	j	106	9	57	&	38
K	75	k	107			'	39
L	76	l	108			(	40
M	77	m	109			)	41
N	78	n	110			*	42
O	79	o	111			+	43
P	80	p	112			,	44
Q	81	q	113			-	45
R	82	r	114			.	46
S	83	s	115			:	58
T	84	t	116			;	59
U	85	u	117			<	60
V	86	v	118			=	61
W	87	w	119			>	62
X	88	x	120			?	63
Y	89	y	121			@	64
Z	90	z	122			[	91
						\	92
						]	93
						^	94
						_	95
						{	123
						|	124
						}	125
						~	126

TABLE 4.3 ASCII codes for some characters.

ASCII codes), then s lexicographically precedes t (s < t). If t_0 precedes s_0, t < s; if $s_0 = t_0$, we still have no answer and need to repeat the process with s_1 and t_1, and so on. If we run out of characters in s before coming to a decision—that is, $s_i = t_i$ for all $i < m$—then either s is a prefix of t ($m < n$), in which case s < t, or the strings are equal ($m = n$). Similarly, if we run out of characters in t first and $n < m$, then t < s.

Note that the ordering given by compareTo depends directly on the ASCII codes of the characters and sometimes can be surprising. For example, Zorro

Example	Explanation
`int compareTo (String s)`	Compares two strings lexicographically, returning $< 0, == 0, > 0$ values.
`int compareToIgnoreCase (String s)`	Compares two strings lexicographically, ignoring case considerations.
`boolean equals (String s)`	Returns true if the strings are equal, false otherwise.
`boolean equalsIgnoreCase (String s)`	Returns true if the strings are equal, ignoring case; false otherwise.

TABLE 4.4   Comparison methods of Java's `String` class.

precedes abracadabra, because the ASCII code of Z is less than that of a. To ignore case when doing comparisons, which you normally want to do, you need to use compareToIgnoreCase.

QUICK EXERCISE 4.11

What values are returned by the following method calls?

```
"wish".compareTo("wishbone");
"wish you were here".compareTo("wishbone");
"wash".compareTo("Washington");
"wash".compareToIgnoreCase("Washington");
"wash and wear".compareTo("wash-and-wear");
```

4.4

switch **Statements**

The flowers that bloom in the spring,
Tra la,
Have nothing to do with the case.

—W. S. Gilbert
The Mikado

Multitudes, multitudes in the valley of decision!

—Bible
Joel 3:14

two-way branch
switch
statement
multiway
branching

While the `if` statement is used in Java to perform *two-way branching*, the `switch` *statement* is used to accomplish *multiway branching*. The multiway branch is a decision based on the value of an integer expression or variable. The general form is

```
switch ( expression ) {
    statement with case label
    statement with case label
    ...
    statement with case label
}
```

The value of *expression* determines at which *statement with case label* execution starts; each of these statements is labeled by either the keyword case (together with an integer constant) or the keyword default. Once begun, the execution continues, statement by statement, until either the end of the switch statement is reached or a break *statement* is encountered. In either case, the switch statement terminates, and the statement after it is executed. This is not as complicated as it may sound; a few examples will demonstrate the range of possibilities. Consider a program fragment to decide which of your three vehicles you should drive to the beach.

break statement

```
switch (numberOfPassengers) {
   case 0:  out.println("The Harley");
            break;
   case 1:  out.println("The Dune Buggy");
            break;
   default: out.println("The Humvee");
}
```

This switch statement will print one of three messages, depending on the value of numberOfPassengers: for 0 the Harley message, for 1 the Dune Buggy message, and for any other value for numberOfPassengers the Humvee message. Notice how each of the first two cases ends with a break statement. (This code fragment is meaningless for negative values of numberOfPassengers, even though it *does* print something.) The flowchart rendition of this code is shown in Figure 4.13.

There can be multiple case labels affiliated with a single statement in a switch statement. For example, consider the flowchart in Figure 4.14. The corresponding switch statement is

```
switch (age) {
   case 1:
   case 2:
   case 3:  out.println("Get a babysitter!");
            break;
   case 4:
   case 5:
   case 6:
   case 7:
   case 8:
   case 9:  out.println("Movies rated G would be okay.");
            break;
   case 10:
   case 11:
   case 12:
```

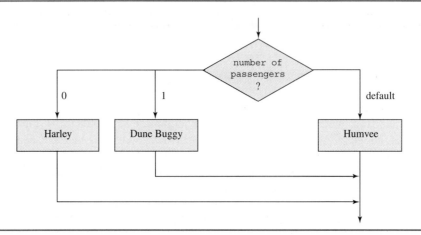

FIGURE 4.13   Flowchart for the vehicle choice code fragment.

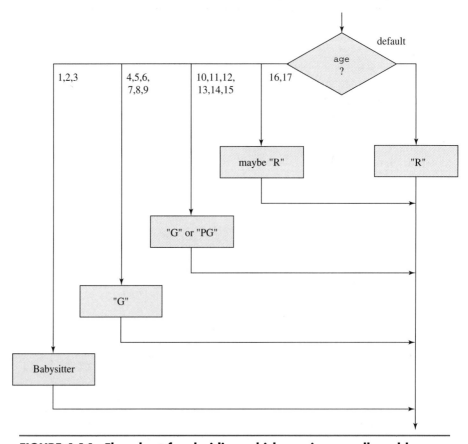

FIGURE 4.14   Flowchart for deciding which movies are allowable.

```
        case 13:
        case 14:
        case 15: out.println("Movies rated G or PG would be okay.");
                 break;
        case 16:
        case 17: out.println("Movies rated R might be okay.");
                 break;
        default: out.println("Movies rated R would be okay.")
    }
```

This switch statement will print one of the five messages, depending on the value of age: for age ≤ 3 the babysitter message, for 4 ≤ age ≤ 9 the G message, for 10 ≤ age ≤ 15 the G or PG message, and for 16 ≤ age ≤ 17 the "R might be okay" message; any other value of age will print the "R would be okay" message.

The controlling value for the switch needs to be an integer, but often symbolic constants are used in this context to make the intent of the code obvious. For example,

```
1    final int
2      SUNDAY=1,   MONDAY=2,  TUESDAY=3, WEDNESDAY=4,
3      THURSDAY=5, FRIDAY=6,  SATURDAY=7;
4
5    int d;
6    ...
7    switch (d) {
8      case SUNDAY:    out.print("Sunday");    break;
9      case MONDAY:    out.print("Monday");    break;
10     case TUESDAY:   out.print("Tuesday");   break;
11     case WEDNESDAY: out.print("Wednesday"); break;
12     case THURSDAY:  out.print("Thursday");  break;
13     case FRIDAY:    out.print("Friday");    break;
14     case SATURDAY:  out.print("Saturday");  break;
15   }
```

This switch statement will write the name of the day of the week specified by the variable d. Similarly,

```
1    switch (d) {
2      case MONDAY:
3      case WEDNESDAY:
4      case FRIDAY:
5        out.println("C.S. meets at 9:00 today.");
6        out.println("History meets at 10:00 today.");
7        out.println("Math meets at 2:00 today.");
8        break;
9      case TUESDAY:
10     case THURSDAY:
11       out.println("English meets at 9:00 today.");
12       out.println("Chemistry meets at 10:00 today.");
13       break;
14     case SUNDAY:
15     case SATURDAY:
16       out.println("Enjoy the weekend!");
17   }
```

writes the class schedule of the day.

Or, for instance, we can set correctly the value of the variable `numberOfDays` (representing the number of days elapsed since January 1) for a combination of `month` and `year`:

```
1    final int
2       JANUARY=1,   FEBRUARY=2,   MARCH=3,
3       APRIL=4,     MAY=5,        JUNE=6,
4       JULY=7,      AUGUST=8,     SEPTEMBER=9,
5       OCTOBER=10, NOVEMBER=11,  DECEMBER=12;
6
7    int m;
8    ...
9    switch (m) {
10      case FEBRUARY:
11        if ((((year % 4) == 0) && ((year % 100) != 0))
12            || ((year % 400) == 0))
13          numberOfDays = 29;
14        else
15          numberOfDays = 28;
16        break;
17      case APRIL:
18      case JUNE:
19      case SEPTEMBER:
20      case NOVEMBER: numberOfDays = 30; break;
21      case JANUARY:
22      case MARCH:
23      case MAY:
24      case JULY:
25      case AUGUST:
26      case OCTOBER:
27      case DECEMBER: numberOfDays = 31; break;
28    }
```

This example can be rewritten more concisely:

```
1    switch (m) {
2      case FEBRUARY:
3        if ((((year % 4) == 0) && ((year % 100) != 0))
4            || ((year % 400) == 0))
5          numberOfDays = 29;
6        else
7          numberOfDays = 28;
8        break;
9      case APRIL:
10      case JUNE:
11      case SEPTEMBER:
12      case NOVEMBER: numberOfDays = 30; break;
13      default: numberOfDays = 31;
14    }
```

For values of m in the range 1 through 12 (that is, JANUARY ...DECEMBER) these two versions are equivalent; if m is not in this range, however, the former statement does not set the value of numberOfDays, while the latter sets the value of numberOfDays to 31.

What if there is no case for the value of the controlling expression and no default either? Then nothing is done in the switch statement.

If every statement in a switch ends with a break, then the statement is equivalent to a cascade of if statements. That is, the statement

```
switch (expression ) {
   case value-1:  statements-1;  break;
   case value-2:  statements-2;  break;
   . . .
   case value-i:  statements-i;  break;
   default:  statements-(i+1)
}
```

is just a convenient way of writing

```
switchValue = expression;
if ( switchValue == value-1 )
   statements-1
else if( switchValue == value-2 )
   statements-2
. . .
else if( switchValue == value-i )
   statements-i
else
   statements-(i+1)
```

The purpose of the break statement is to terminate the execution of the switch statement in which it is embedded. In general, every case and the default should have break as its last statement. If you omit a break at the end of one of them, program execution just continues with the statements of the following case, which is usually not what you want. For example, the code

```
int i = 1;
switch (i) {                          DANGER
   case 0: out.print("0");
   case 1: out.print("1");
   case 2: out.print("2");
   case 3: out.print("3");
}                                     DANGER
out.println();
```

causes the output

```
123
```

since the code in cases 1, 2, and 3 is executed.

BUG ALERT 4.5	*Missing break*

Omitting a `break` statement in a `switch` can cause extra statements to be executed in the `case` with the missing `break`. Check `switch` statements carefully. This is a very common programming error!

QUICK EXERCISE 4.12	The following statement was intended to set `s` to the sign of `x`, that is, to `-1` if `x` is negative, to `0` if `x` is `0`, and to `1` if `x` is positive. What does it actually do?

```
switch (x) {
   case 0:  s = 0;                     Wrong
   default: if (x<0)
                s = -1;
            else
                s = 1;                  Wrong
}
```

4.5

Debugging Decision Making

> A problem worthy of attack
> Proves its worth by hitting back.
>
> —Piet Hein
> *Grooks*

To illustrate the process of debugging when a complicated case structure is involved, let's write an application to calculate a woman's panty hose size. Manufacturers of women's panty hose use a method similar to the following for determining a woman's size from her height and weight. First, compute

$$x = \lfloor \tfrac{1}{10}\text{height} - \tfrac{1}{50}\text{weight} - 2.4 \rfloor$$
$$y = \lfloor \tfrac{1}{4}\text{height} + \tfrac{1}{20}\text{weight} - 20.5 \rfloor$$

where $\lfloor x \rfloor$ is the largest integer less than or equal to x. Since we want x and y to be int values, we do not have to use the `Math.floor()` function (see Table 3.4), but can simply cast the expressions to `int`s. The required size of panty hose is then

	$y = 0$	$y = 1$	$y = 2$	$y = 3$
$x = 1$	A	B	C	D
$x = 0$			E	F

Combinations of x and y other than those given in the table do not correspond to any of the sizes manufactured. So, we need an application to read a woman's height and weight and tell her what size panty hose to buy. A flowchart for the program's logic is shown in Figure 4.15.

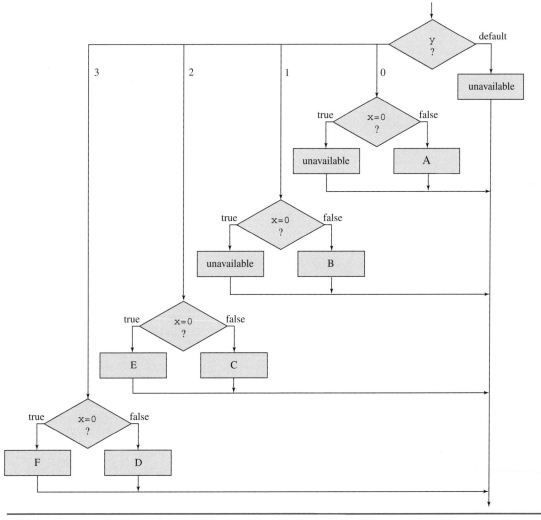

FIGURE 4.15 Flowchart for the panty hose computation.

Our output should look like this:

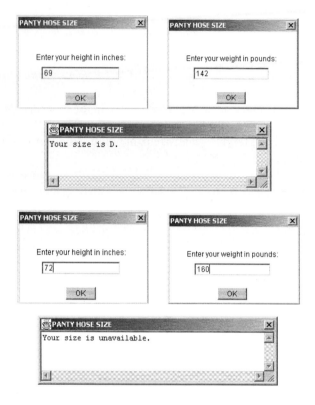

Here is our first attempt:

```
1   import CSLib.*;
2
3   public class Hose {
4     // Determine panty hose size.
5     // Author: Rebecca Kamin, September 12, 2000
6
7     public void compute () {
8       int height, // The woman's height...
9           weight; // ...and weight
10
11      InputBox in = new InputBox();
12      in.setTitle("PANTY HOSE SIZE");
13      in.setPrompt( "Enter your height in inches: ");
14      height = in.readInt();
15      in.setPrompt("Enter your weight in pounds: ");
16      weight = in.readInt();
17
18      int x = (int)(height/10.0 - weight/50.0 - 2.4);
19      int y = (int)(height/4.0 + weight/20.0 - 20.5);
```

Wrong

```
20
21          OutputBox out = new OutputBox();
22          out.setTitle("PANTY HOSE SIZE");
23          out.print("Your size is ");
24          switch (y) {
25            case 0: if (x == 0)
26                        out.print("unavailable");
27                    else
28                        out.print("A");
29            case 1: if (x == 0)
30                        out.print("unavailable");
31                    else
32                        out.print("B");
33            case 2: if (x == 0)
34                        out.print("E");
35                    else
36                        out.print("C");
37            case 3: if (x == 0)
38                        out.print("F");
39                    else
40                        out.print("D");
41            default: out.print("unavailable");
42          }
43          out.println(".");
44        }
45      }
```

Wrong *Wrong* *Wrong* *Wrong* *Wrong* *Wrong*

Notice the use of a cast (`int`) in lines 18 and 19. Recall from Section 3.6.3 on page 90 that these transform the `double` results of the expressions into `int` values so that they can be assigned to the `int` variables x and y. The Java compiler would complain if we attempted to assign a `double` to an `int` without such an explicit cast. When we execute the application, we get

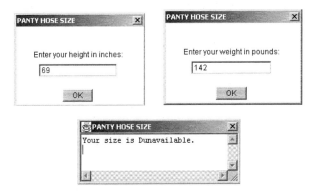

Close, but not close enough! The computer doesn't toss in extra characters in the output for no reason. Here, we observe that the output is the concatenation of two

possible outputs, which suggests pretty strongly that *both* output statements are being executed. A quick look reveals the error—one of the most common errors in Java: missing `break` statements. Fixing this, we have

```
1    import CSLib.*;
2
3    public class Hose {
4      // Determine panty hose size.
5      // Author: Rebecca Kamin, September 12, 2000
6
7      public void compute () {
8        int height, // The woman's height...
9            weight; // ...and weight
10
11        InputBox in = new InputBox();
12        in.setTitle("PANTY HOSE SIZE");
13        in.setPrompt( "Enter your height in inches: ");
14        height = in.readInt();
15        in.setPrompt("Enter your weight in pounds: ");
16        weight = in.readInt();
17
18        int x = (int)(height/10.0 - weight/50.0 - 2.4);
19        int y = (int)(height/4.0 + weight/20.0 - 20.5);
20
21        OutputBox out = new OutputBox();
22        out.setTitle("PANTY HOSE SIZE");
23        out.print("Your size is ");
24        switch (y) {
25          case 0: if (x == 0)
26                    out.print("unavailable");
27                  else
28                    out.print("A");
29                  break;
30          case 1: if (x == 0)
31                    out.print("unavailable");
32                  else
33                    out.print("B");
34                  break;
35          case 2: if (x == 0)
36                    out.print("E");
37                  else
38                    out.print("C");
39                  break;
40          case 3: if (x == 0)
41                    out.print("F");
42                  else
43                    out.print("D");
44                  break;
45          default: out.print("unavailable");
46        }
47        out.println(".");
48      }
49    }
```

which compiles. Execution gives

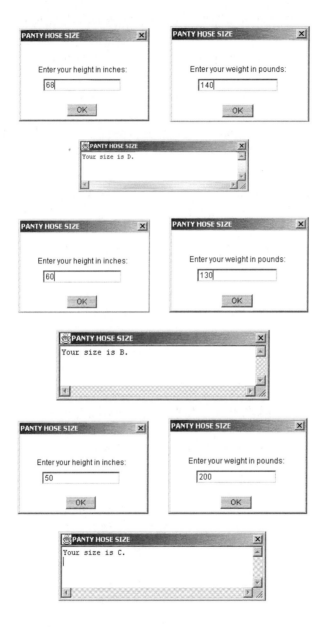

The result is suspicious because C is a small size but 200 pounds is a large woman.
To see what's going on, we add a debugging statement just before line 23 to tell
us the values of x and y:

```
out.println("x = " + x + ", y = " + y);
```

and we find

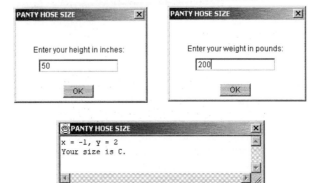

revealing that the values of x (and maybe y) can be negative. This possibility complicates the problem enormously, because it means there are many cases that we didn't take into account.

Having discovered the inadequacy of our approach, we decide to start over. First, we decide to separate the computation of the size from the output. Since the size will be A, B, C, D, E, F, or none at all, we define symbolic constants

```
final int
    NONE=0, A=1, B=2, C=3, D=4, E=5, F=6;
```

and use a variable, s, of type int to store the calculated size.

QUICK EXERCISE 4.13

The logic for the following case statement is a bit different from that shown in Figure 4.15. Sketch a flowchart for the final version.

```
int s = NONE;
switch (y) {
   case 0: if (x == 1) s = A; break;
   case 1: if (x == 1) s = B; break;
   case 2: switch (x) {
             case 0:  s = E; break;
             case 1:  s = C; break;
           }
           break;
   case 3: switch (x) {
             case 0:  s = F; break;
             case 1:  s = D; break;
           }
}
```

We are careful to initialize the value of s to NONE and to change its value *only* when both x and y have values that are acceptable. The desired output is now done with another switch, and the entire application is

```
1    import CSLib.*;
2
3    public class Hose {
4      // Determine panty hose size.
5      // Author: Rebecca Kamin, September 12, 2000
6
7      public void compute () {
8        final int
9          NONE=0, A=1, B=2, C=3, D=4, E=5, F=6;
10       int height, // The woman's height...
11           weight; // ...and weight
12
13       InputBox in = new InputBox();
14       in.setTitle("PANTY HOSE SIZE");
15       in.setPrompt("Enter your height in inches: ");
16       height = in.readInt();
17       in.setPrompt("Enter your weight in pounds: ");
18       weight = in.readInt();
19
20       int x = (int)(height/10.0 - weight/50.0 - 2.4);
21       int y = (int)(height/4.0 + weight/20.0 - 20.5);
22
23       int s = NONE;
24       switch (y) {
25         case 0: if (x == 1) s = A; break;
26         case 1: if (x == 1) s = B; break;
27         case 2: switch (x) {
28                   case 0:  s = E; break;
29                   case 1:  s = C; break;
30                 }
31                 break;
32         case 3: switch (x) {
33                   case 0:  s = F; break;
34                   case 1:  s = D; break;
35                 }
36       }
37
38       OutputBox out = new OutputBox();
39       out.setTitle("PANTY HOSE SIZE");
40       out.print("Your size is ");
41       switch (s) {
42         case A:    out.print("A"); break;
43         case B:    out.print("B"); break;
44         case C:    out.print("C"); break;
45         case D:    out.print("D"); break;
46         case E:    out.print("E"); break;
47         case F:    out.print("F"); break;
48         case NONE: out.print("unavailable");
49       }
50       out.println(".");
```

```
51       }
52     }
```

with the client:

```
1     public class HoseClient {
2       public static void main (String[] args) {
3         Hose h = new Hose();
4         h.compute();
5       }
6     }
```

It is easy to verify that the first `switch`, and hence the whole application, gives correct values in all cases.

4.6

More About Boolean Operators

The evaluation of the Boolean operators `&&` and `||` has an additional complication. The expression A `&&` B is evaluated as follows: first A is evaluated; if it is true, then B is evaluated and the result of the expression is true if B is true and false if not. However, if A is false, there is no need to evaluate B, since A `&&` B *must* be false regardless of the value of B, and so B *is not evaluated*. This allows us to write, for instance,

```
if ((x != 0) && (1/x > 100)) {
    ...
} else {
    ...
}
```

without fear that the evaluation of the condition will cause a division-by-zero error. The expression A `||` B is also evaluated only as far as necessary to determine its value: First A is evaluated; if it is false, then B is evaluated and the result of the expression is true if B is true and false if not. If A is true, there is no need to evaluate B, since A `&&` B *must* be true regardless of the value of B, and *short-circuit evaluation* so B *is not evaluated*. This is called *short-circuit evaluation*. Note that this does not apply to exclusive or (`^`); both of its arguments must be evaluated.

BUG ALERT 4.6   *Double Ampersands Mean "and," Double Bars Mean "or"*

Remember to use *two* ampersands for *and* and two vertical bars for *or*. A single ampersand (`&`) and a single vertical bar (`|`) are both legal operators in Java, with somewhat different meanings. So, if you write `&` or `|` when you mean `&&` or `||`, you will not get a syntax error, but the execution may not be what you wanted.

Often there is more than one way to write an expression in Java. As an illustration, let's write a Boolean expression that has the same value as *exclusive or*. Recall that exclusive or of A and B is true if either A or B is true but not both. The description in the last sentence is virtually the Boolean expression! We want

exclusive or

$$A \ || \ B \ \text{to be true} \qquad\qquad (4.1)$$

to guarantee that at least one of A or B is true; we want in addition

$$A \ \&\& \ B \ \text{to be false} \qquad\qquad (4.2)$$

to guarantee that A and B are not both true. This second condition is equivalent to wanting

!(A && B) to be true

so we can insist that both (4.1) and (4.2) are simultaneously satisfied by writing

(A || B) && !(A && B)

How can we be sure that this expression gives us what we want? The easiest way to show that a Boolean expression is correct is to construct a *truth table*. Truth tables are an organized way to analyze Boolean expressions by listing *all* the possible values of the Boolean variables, the results of any subexpressions, and the final results. In all cases, the table has a separate row for each distinct combination of truth values for the variables. In these cases, there are two variables, so each truth table has four rows, corresponding to the four combinations true/true, true/false, false/true, false/false. If there were *three* variables, then there would be eight rows. Table 4.5 contains four simple truth tables; the

truth table

Expression	A	B	Result
A && B	True	True	True
	True	False	False
	False	True	False
	False	False	False
A || B	True	True	True
	True	False	True
	False	True	True
	False	False	False
A ^ B	True	True	False
	True	False	True
	False	True	True
	False	False	False
!A	True		False
	False		True

TABLE 4.5 Boolean operators in Java.

truth table for the more complex expression (A || B) && !(A && B) is shown in Table 4.6. Examining Table 4.6, we find that the value of the expression (A || B) && !(A && B) is true when either A or B is true, but not both—precisely the effect we desire.

nor   Similarly, !(p||q) (the *nor* of p and q, which a person might read as "neither p nor q") is equivalent to !p && !q (which a person might read as "both not p and not q"). Both express that neither p nor q is true. Table 4.7 proves the equivalence (which is one variant of what is called DeMorgan's law) using truth tables.

**QUICK EXERCISE
4.14**

Using the Boolean variables p and q, write a Java Boolean expression that has the following values:

p	q	Value
True	True	False
True	False	True
False	True	True
False	False	True

The value of the expression is called the *nand* of p and q; together with the *nor* operation (page 138), the *nand* forms the basis of all computer circuitry.

**QUICK EXERCISE
4.15**

Show the equivalence of the following Boolean expressions using truth tables.
!(p && q)   and   (!p) || (!q)
This equivalence is another variant of DeMorgan's law.

A	B	A || B	A && B	!(A && B)	(A || B) && !(A && B)
True	True	True	True	False	False
True	False	True	False	True	True
False	True	True	False	True	True
False	False	False	False	True	False

TABLE 4.6   Truth table evaluation of the Boolean expression (A || B) && !(A && B) **to show that it is equivalent to the *exclusive or* of** A **and** B.

Input Values		Expression 1		Expression 2		
p	q	p || q	!(p || q)	!p	!q	!p && !q
True	True	True	False	False	False	False
True	False	True	False	False	True	False
False	True	True	False	True	False	False
False	False	False	True	True	True	True

TABLE 4.7 **The two expressions shown to be equivalent here (shaded in color) are the two sides of DeMorgan's law.**

Summary

The decision to take one of two alternative actions based on a true/false condition is implemented with an `if` statement:

```
if ( condition )
    statement    ←— The ''true'' part
else
    statement    ←— The ''false'' part
```

The condition following the keyword `if` is a Boolean expression. The statements may be any Java statement, including another `if` statement. If a compound statement is used, it is framed by braces { and }. Care should be taken to indent these statements logically. If the `else` alternative is not needed, it may be omitted.

Boolean expressions are formed by comparing values with *relational operators* <, >, <=, >=, ==, and != or by combining values with *Boolean operators* (&&, ||, ^, !). If objects are to be compared, then special Boolean methods (supplied by the corresponding class) must be used. Boolean expressions containing arithmetic, relational, and Boolean operators are evaluated using the precedence rules, summarized in Table 4.2. An organized way to examine the possible results of a Boolean expression is to make a *truth table* (see Table 4.6).

Characters are represented by numbers. The code for a given character is determined by an international convention, called *Unicode*. The English letters, as well as decimal digits and common English punctuation symbols, are assigned codes that are the same as in the older convention, called *ASCII*.

Strings are made up of characters and implemented by the class `String`. Strings are ordered according to the Unicode codes of their component characters. However, since uppercase characters come before lowercase characters, this is not the same as dictionary ordering. Strings can be compared lexicographically by the `String` methods `int compareTo(String s)` and `int compareToIgnoreCase(String s)`.

The `switch` statement provides a way to decide on alternative actions based on `int`-type expressions:

```
switch ( expression ) {
  case value: statements
```

```
        case value: statements
        . . .
        case value: statements
        default: statements
}
```

The statements of the possible cases can include any number of statements, even none. Statements usually are ended by a `break` statement, which causes execution of the `switch` to terminate. If a `break` is not present, the execution continues with the set of statements in the next case.

Exercises

1. Rewrite your application in Exercise 1 on page 93 to check that the shoe size is within the range of available sizes, 17 to 46, and to display an appropriate "error message" if not.

2. Show the equivalence of the following Boolean expressions, using truth tables.
   (a) `!(q || (p || p))` and `!(p || (p && q)) && !q`.
   (b) `(p || q) && (!(!p && !r))` and `p || !(!q || !r)`.
   (c) `(A || B) ^ (A && B)` and `A ^ B`.

3. Give values for integer variables x, y, and z such that each of the following expressions will yield true, if possible. Identify the expressions for which this is impossible.
   (a) `(x >= y) && (x >= z) && !(y >= z)`
   (b) `(x >= y) && (z >= x) && !(y >= z)`
   (c) `(x >= y) || (x >= z) && !(y >= z)`
   (d) `(x >= y) ^ (x >= z) && (z >= x)`
   (e) `(x >= y) ^ (x >= z) ^ (z >= x)`

4. The current rule (as of January 1, 2001) for Social Security contributions is this: 7.65 percent of your salary, up to $80,400, is taken as Social Security (FICA) tax, then 1.45 percent of everything above that is taken as Medicare tax. However, if you are self-employed, it is 15.3 percent up to $80,400, then 1.45 percent above that. Write a program that first asks the user whether he or she is self-employed and then asks for the annual salary, and calculates the FICA tax, the Medicare tax, and the total, for example,

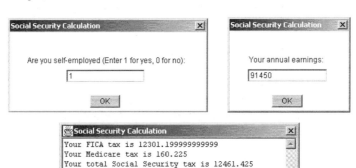

5. At wind chill indexes of −25 and below there is danger of freezing exposed flesh; at −75 and below there is *extreme* danger of freezing exposed flesh. Use the wind chill formula (page 103) to write an application that will print an appropriate warning.

6. Write an application to read an integer *n* between 0 and 100, and write *n* followed by the appropriate ordinal suffix (that is, *th*, *st*, *rd*, or *nd*). So if the user types "3" your program should output "3rd".

7. The following requirements for membership in the Congress of the United States are quoted from Article I of the Constitution of the United States:

> No Person shall be a Representative who shall not have attained to the Age of twenty five Years, and been seven Years a Citizen of the United States, and who shall not, when elected, be an Inhabitant of that State in which he shall be chosen.

> No Person shall be a Senator who shall not have attained to the Age of thirty Years, and been nine Years a Citizen of the United States, and who shall not, when elected, be an Inhabitant of that State for which he shall be chosen.

Using the `int` variables `age` and `lengthOfCitizenship`, write expressions to compute correct values for variables `eligibleForHouse` and `eligibleForSenate`, and use them to write a Java application to print the eligibility of a candidate for Congress. (Disregard state residency.) The output should look something like this:

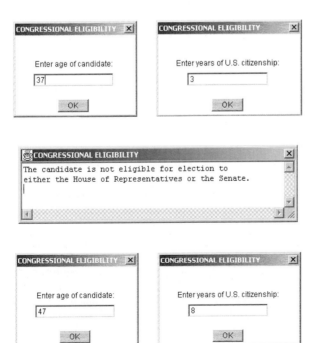

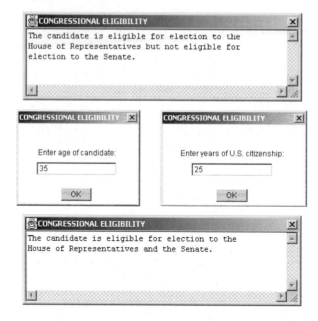

8. (a) The following formulas are used to calculate the handicap used to compensate weight lifters for differing body weights. The handicap is expressed in terms of the weight in kilograms:

$$40 \leq weight \leq 125, \quad handicap = 6.31926 - 0.262349 \times weight$$
$$+0.511550 \times 10^{-2} \times weight^2$$
$$-0.519738 \times 10^{-4} \times weight^3$$
$$+0.267626 \times 10^{-6} \times weight^4$$
$$-0.540132 \times 10^{-9} \times weight^5$$
$$-0.728875 \times 10^{-13} \times weight^6$$

$$125 < weight \leq 135, \quad handicap = 0.5208 - 0.0012(weight - 125)$$
$$135 < weight \leq 145, \quad handicap = 0.5088 - 0.0011(weight - 135)$$
$$145 < weight \leq 155, \quad handicap = 0.4978 - 0.0010(weight - 145)$$
$$155 < weight \leq 165, \quad handicap = 0.4878 - 0.0009(weight - 155)$$

Write an application to read in a body weight and calculate the handicap.

(b) The handicap described in part (a) is multiplied by the lifter's score

$$Score = squat + benchpress + deadlift$$

to calculate a handicapped score. Modify your application from part (a) to also read values for `squat`, `benchPress`, and `deadlift` (each in kilograms) and to calculate the lifter's handicapped score.

9. (a) The Center for Disease Control in Atlanta, Georgia, has computed various "recommended values" for a person's body mass index. The body mass index is a person's weight in kilograms divided by the square of his or her height in meters. For men, an index of 27.8 or more is considered high; for nonpregnant women the cutoff is 27.3. Write an application to read a person's `gender`, `height`, and `weight`; determine the `bodyMassIndex`; and print a message as to whether it is high. Your application should convert height from inches to meters (1 meter is

39.37 inches) and weight from pounds to kilograms (1 kilogram is 2.20 pounds). Your output should look like this:

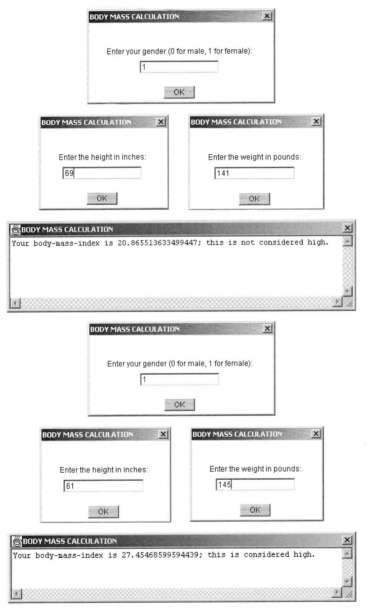

(b) The body mass index correlates with one's overall risk of developing heart disease.

$$\text{bodyMassIndex} \leq 25 \qquad \text{Risk is very low to low.}$$
$$25 < \text{bodyMassIndex} < 30 \qquad \text{Risk is low to moderate.}$$
$$30 \leq \text{bodyMassIndex} \qquad \text{Risk is moderate to very high.}$$

Modify your application so that it also prints a message describing the risk of heart disease.

10. The United Parcel Service (UPS) has the following limitations on the size and weight of packages accepted for shipment. A package cannot exceed 150 pounds or have a combined length plus girth (twice the width plus twice the depth) of over 130 inches. In addition, packages must not exceed 108 inches in length. The minimum charge for an "oversized" package (that is, package weighing less than 30 pounds but having a combined length plus girth of over 84 inches) is the same as for a package weighing 30 pounds. Write a program which reads as input the `weight`, `length`, `width`, and `depth` of a package to be shipped by UPS, and which prints whether the package can be shipped under the above restrictions. The output should indicate whether the package can be shipped at all and, if so, whether it is subject to the oversized minimum rate.

11. Postage rates are calculated (as of January 2001) according to the following rules:

Class	Rate
First class, domestic	$0.34 for the first ounce, $0.21 for each additional ounce
Postcards, domestic	$0.20
Book rate	$1.24 for the first pound, 2–7 pounds $0.43 per additional pound, $0.29 for each additional pound beyond 7 pounds

Define three symbolic integer constants for the three mail classes. Write a `switch` statement to determine the postage rate for sending an item given the `weight` in ounces (16 ounces = 1 pound) and the kind of mail `class` as an integer variable.

12. As part of a medical diagnosis system for a poison control center you have to prepare the `switch` statement to identify proper treatment for ingestion of various substances. The types of poison being considered are aspirin, alcohol, tobacco, chloroform, rat poison, strong acid, strong alkali, strychnine, and kerosene. Except for strong acids, strong alkalies, strychnine, and kerosene, the proper treatment is to administer fluid in large quantities, induce vomiting, and administer the universal antidote. For poisoning with strong acids, administer water and then milk of magnesia or baking soda solution; do not induce vomiting. For poisoning with strong alkalies, administer water and then vinegar or lemon juice; do not induce vomiting. For strychnine or kerosene ingestion, do not induce vomiting; get medical help immediately! Define nine symbolic integer constants for these nine poisons. Write the `switch` statement using an integer variable `PoisonType`; the statement should print the proper treatment.

13. Write an application to calculate the date following a given date. You will have to take into account leap years (see the `dayNumber` calculation on page 115). Your output should look something like this:

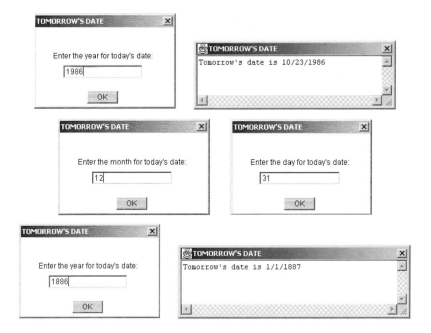

14. A certain medication for children is available in drops containing 1.23 grains of active ingredient per dropperful, in syrup containing 2.46 grains per teaspoon, and in chewable tablets containing 1.23 grains per tablet. The recommended dosage is 0.0931 grain of active ingredient per pound of body weight for children weighing from 7 to 110 pounds. Drops can be given in multiples of half dropperful, not exceeding 3 dropperful. Syrup can be given in multiples of quarter teaspoons up to 1 teaspoon and in multiples of half teaspoons for more than 1 teaspoon. Tablets cannot be broken and are not to be given to a child weighing less than 27 pounds. Partial dosages are rounded to the nearest permissible dose (for example, 0.65 teaspoon of syrup would become 0.75 teaspoon). Write an application to read a child's weight in pounds and print the correct dosage of the medication in terms of dropperful of drops, teaspoons of syrup, and tablets for that body weight. If more than one form of the medication is appropriate, give all possibilities. For example, your output might look like this:

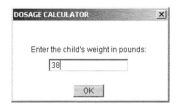

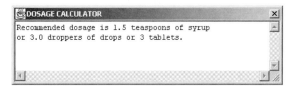

15. The children's game of Cootie is played with pencil, paper, and a die. The goal is to draw a complete picture of a "cootie" with a body, a head, two eyes, two antennae, six legs, and a tail:

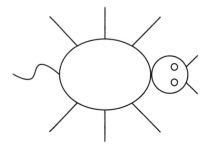

When the die is rolled, a 1 means the body may be drawn, 2 means the head may be drawn, 3 means a leg may be drawn, 4 means an antenna may be drawn, 5 means an eye may be drawn, and 6 means a tail may be drawn. The body must be drawn first; the head must be drawn before eyes or antennae.

(a) Assume Boolean variables `body`, `head`, and `tail` and `int` variables `eyes`, `antennae`, and `legs`. Write a Boolean expression that is true when the cootie is complete and false otherwise.

(b) Write a `switch` statement that changes the values of the variables appropriately, depending on the value of an `int` variable `toss`. For example, if `toss = 3`, you can increment `legs`, but only if `body` is *true* and `legs` < 6.

CHAPTER 5

CLASSES AND METHODS II: CLASSES WITH MULTIPLE METHODS

CHAPTER PREVIEW

Most classes have more than one method, as we see in classes we've used such as `String` and `OutputBox`. In this chapter, we see how such classes are defined. The major question that arises is, How can one method communicate with another? We see how to do this by using instance variables. Using multiple methods and instance variables allows for much better structuring of programs and moves us another step toward real object-oriented programming.

Objects are good.

—Aristotle
Ethics

Programs need to be correct and efficient. They also need to be well structured, so that they can be understood and modified ("maintained") by other programmers. Classes and methods are the major tools the Java programmer has for structuring programs. Most classes contain multiple methods, and such classes are most useful for structuring programs. We show how, and why, to create classes with multiple methods and how to using *instance variables* to permit communication among the various methods.

Building Classes with Multiple Methods

You may have noticed that Java's classes and our `CSLib` classes provide a variety of methods for your use. However, so far the classes that we've *written* have had only one method (such as `compute` or `convert`). We now see how we can build a class that provides a number of methods for our clients to use. As an example, we rewrite the `Hose` class from Section 4.5 so that it has three methods, described in Table 5.1.

Why would we want to do this? If we analyze the `compute` method, we see that there are really three "phases" that it goes through: the *input phase*, the *computing phase*, and the *output phase*. Combining all three into a single method is fine for a client that wants to behave exactly as our `HoseClient` does—reading the values of `height` and `weight` from an `InputBox`. But remember that what we're after is *maintainability*. Experience teaches the input and output are logically separable operations that often change over time. Breaking the class into the three methods of Table 5.1 allows the flexibility to be able to make this change more easily.

Looking back at the final version of `Hose` on page 135, we see that it is apparent that the `getData` method will contain lines 13 through 18, the `compute` method will contain lines 20 through 36, and the `display` method will contain lines 38 through 50. But one question must be answered: The `getData` method will assign values to `height` and `weight`, while the `compute` method must *use* those variables. Likewise, `compute` will assign to the variable s (the

Example	Explanation
`void getData()`	Reads and stores the height and weight data.
`void compute()`	Computes and stores the hose size.
`void display()`	Displays the results of the computation.

TABLE 5.1   Methods for the `Hose` **class.**

local variables

instance variables

computed size), while the `display` method must use it. The variables declared in methods—*local variables*—are not accessible from any other method, so they provide no way for one method to communicate information to another. Instead, the variables should be declared *outside* of the methods themselves, but *inside* the class definition. Such variables are called *instance variables*. In contrast to local variables, all methods of a class have access to the instance variables. So a typical class definition will look like

```
public class Classname {
  //  Author, date, explanation

    declarations of instance variables

    public void methodName1 ( parameters ) {
        declarations of local variables
        executable statements with relevant comments
    }

    public void methodName2 ( parameters ) {
        declarations of local variables
        executable statements with relevant comments
    }
    ...
}
```

Here is the new code for the `Hose` class and a client.

```
1    import CSLib.*;
2
3    public class Hose {
4       // Determine panty hose size.
5       // Author: Rebecca Kamin, September 12, 2000
6
7       final int
8         NONE=0, A=1, B=2, C=3, D=4, E=5, F=6;
9       int height, // The woman's height...
10          weight, // ...and weight
11          s;      // The computed size
12
13      // Obtain values for height and weight from user input.
14      public void getData () {
15         InputBox in = new InputBox("PANTY HOSE SIZE");
```

```
16      in.setPrompt("Enter your height in inches: ");
17      height = in.readInt();
18      in.setPrompt("Enter your weight in pounds: ");
19      weight = in.readInt();
20    }
21
22    // Compute size, s, from height and weight.
23    public void compute () {
24      int x = (int)(height/10.0 - weight/50.0 - 2.4);
25      int y = (int)(height/4.0 + weight/20.0 - 20.5);
26
27      s = NONE;
28      switch (y) {
29        case 0: if (x == 1) s = A; break;
30        case 1: if (x == 1) s = B; break;
31        case 2: switch (x) {
32                  case 0:  s = E; break;
33                  case 1:  s = C; break;
34                }
35                break;
36        case 3: switch (x) {
37                  case 0:  s = F; break;
38                  case 1:  s = D; break;
39                }
40      }
41    }
42
43    // Display the size in an OutputBox
44    public void display () {
45      OutputBox out = new OutputBox("PANTY HOSE SIZE");
46      out.print("Your size is ");
47      switch (s) {
48        case A:    out.print("A"); break;
49        case B:    out.print("B"); break;
50        case C:    out.print("C"); break;
51        case D:    out.print("D"); break;
52        case E:    out.print("E"); break;
53        case F:    out.print("F"); break;
54        case NONE: out.print("unavailable");
55      }
56      out.println(".");
57    }
58 }
```

```
1  public class HoseClient {
2    public static void main (String[] args) {
3      Hose h = new Hose();
4      h.getData();
5      h.compute();
6      h.display();
7    }
8  }
```

The UML diagram for this class is shown in Figure 5.1.

```
┌─────────────────────────┐
│          Hose           │
├─────────────────────────┤
│ height: int             │
│ weight: int             │
│ s: int                  │
├─────────────────────────┤
│ getData()               │
│ compute()               │
│ display()               │
└─────────────────────────┘
```

FIGURE 5.1   UML diagram for `Hose` **class.**

Comparing this code to the version of `Hose` on pages 134 and 135 we see a lot of similarity. We have made two changes: We pulled the declarations of the variables `height`, `width`, and `s` out of the `compute` method and to the beginning of the class, thereby making them instance variables. (The symbolic constants NONE, A, etc., have also been moved outside of the methods, for the same reason: so that all the methods can access them.) And we divided the `compute` method into three separate methods. The client just calls these three methods in sequence.

Note that several of the variables formerly in `compute` have remained local variables. The `getData` has local variable `in`: since this method has complete responsibility for inputting the data, there is no reason for any other method to know about the input box. Similarly, variables `x` and `y` are used only in the new version of `compute`, and `out` is only used in `display`. The fact that the three methods retained some local variables is an indication that they really were logically separable, and it gives us some confidence in our new structure.

QUICK EXERCISE 5.1	As we said before giving this example, the division into several methods makes it easier to make some kinds of changes to the class. Change the output so that when the size is unavailable, the program prints: `We're sorry, you need a custom size.`

5.2

Initialization of Instance Variables

Instance variable declarations can contain initializers, just as declarations of local variables do. However, unlike local variables, instance variables are automatically initialized even if their declarations contain no initializers. Specifically, integers and doubles are initialized to zero, characters are initialized to the character whose ASCII code is zero (a nonprinting character called the *null character*),   *null character* and boolean variables are initialized to `false`.

Thus, *Java always makes sure that every variable is initialized before it is used*, but it does it in two different ways: Instance variables are automatically initialized, as just explained; local variables must be initialized in the program, either within the declaration or by a subsequent assignment statement.

What about object types? Since there are so many different object types—and since programmers can define their own object types—there is no obvious default value to use for any given object type. But recall that variables that contain objects really contain *references* to those objects. There is a special kind of reference, called *null*, that doesn't point to anything; it is just a placeholder.   *null* Object-type variables are initialized to `null`. This value is rarely useful—you still need to allocate an actual object and assign it to the variable—but it is an actual value. In particular, you can test whether a reference is equal to null (x `==` null). Initializing to `null` is *not* the same as leaving the variable uninitialized—in the latter case, you have no idea *what* the variable might contain.

5.3

Scope of Variables

One question you might ask yourself is, What happens if an instance variable has the same name as a local variable, as in the following?

```
class C {
    int x;
    ...
    void f () {
      int x;
      ... x ...
    }
    ...
}
```

Probably it would be simplest if this just weren't allowed; the local variable in f would have to be renamed, perhaps to j, or i1, or something else. However, in reality there are so many variables that are used in real, full-sized programs that it would be a burden to impose this rule.

Instead, the principle followed is that declarations of instance and local variables that have the same name (i.e., same identifier) are distinct and unrelated. The coincidence of names is just an accident, just as in real life two people may be named John Smith, but they don't necessarily have anything else in common.

In particular, when the programmer of f chose the name i, she could just as well have chosen the name j or Mxyzptlk, just as long as it doesn't interfere with any other names used in f itself.

Following this principle, the only possible answer is, Within the body of f, references to i are to the local variable i of f; outside of f, references to i are to the instance variable. Local variables are just that—*local* to the method in which they are declared.

More generally, the issue is this: Given any use of an identifier, to what declaration does it refer?

variable scope   To answer this, the critical notion is that of *variable scope*. The scope of a variable—or, more properly, the scope of a *declaration* of a variable—is the part of the program in which a use of that variable refers to this declaration. Every use of a variable must be inside the scope of a declaration of that variable.

To give a foretaste of the rules defining the scope of variables, in the example above, the two declarations have the scope indicated here:

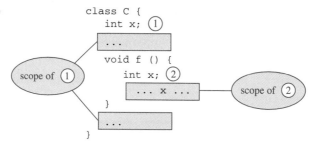

The "outer" x, the instance variable, has a scope that includes the entire class. However, that scope is interrupted by the body of f, because the declaration of f's local variable x hides, or *shadows*, that part of its scope.

From this example, we can see that the scope rules can be explained in terms of nested brackets. Note that every time there is a pair of nested brackets, and every time there is the first use of a variable, there can be new variables declared. This is even true for compound statements; for example, this is legal:

```
class C {
    int x;
    ...
    void f () {
        int x;
        ...
        if (...) {
            double z;
            ...
        } else {
            String z;
            ...
        }
        ...
    }
    ...
}
```

Every pair of braces encloses what is called a *block*, or *scope*, that is, an area   *block*
in which variables can be declared. In effect, the scope of a declaration extends
from that declaration to the end (closing brace) of the block in which it appears.
In addition, the heading of a `for` statement together with its body is considered
to be a block.

To be more specific, the scope rules are as follows:

1. The scope of an *instance variable* is the entire class body, meaning all its
   methods, except where it is shadowed by a declaration of the same identifier.
   (Instance variables can be declared anywhere within a class, as long as they
   are outside any method. Even if they are declared at the end of the class,
   their scope still covers the entire class.)
2. The scope of a *formal argument* in a method header is the entire method
   body.
3. The scope of a *local variable* in a method runs from the point just after the
   declaration to the end of the block in which it is declared. (Local variables
   need not all be declared at the beginning of a block; they can be declared
   anywhere within a block, as long as they are declared before they are used.)
4. It is not legal to declare a variable within a method using the same name as
   a variable in an enclosing block in that method. Nor is it legal to declare
   two instance variables with the same name.

For the example above, these rules give us this result:

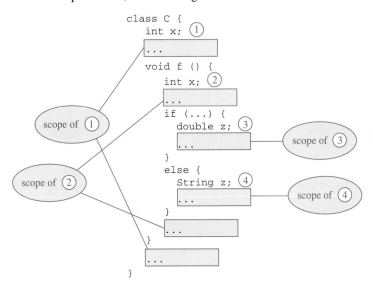

Note that, according to the last rule above, it would be illegal to rename
either of the variables z to x, even though it is okay for both of them to use
the same name (since neither block is contained within the other). We cannot
declare two instance variables with the same name, or two parameters with the
same name, or a parameter and a local variable with the same name, or two local
variables in the same or enclosing blocks with the same name.

The following are some examples of *illegal* declarations:

```
class C {
    int a;  ←| instance variable a |

    public void m1 (int b) {  ←| formal argument b |
       double b;  ←| clashes with formal argument b |
    }

    float a;  ←| clashes with instance variable a |

    public void m2 () {
       int c;  ←| local variable c |
       if (...) {
          double c;  ←| clashes with local variable c |
          ...
       }
    }
}
```

**QUICK EXERCISE
5.2**

What kind of error messages will the Java compiler give if you present it with the following program?

```
class D {
    int a;
    double x;

    public void m (int b) {
       String a;
       if (...) {
          int x;
          ...
       }
       else {
          double b;
          ...
       }
       char a;
       ...
    }
}
```

5.4

Class Constructors with Arguments

We have seen that objects are created using new, as in

```
OutputBox out = new OutputBox();
```

The form of the invocation of new is suggestive of calling a method with no arguments. In fact, that is exactly what is happening: A special kind of method called a *constructor* is called when an object is allocated. The purpose of the constructor is to initialize the instance variables of the object to values more useful than the defaults.

constructor

We will see in Chapter 7 how to define our own constructors. For now, we point out that, like other methods, constructors can have arguments. In fact, the OutputBox class has another constructor that takes a String argument and that sets the title to that argument. So instead of writing

```
OutputBox out = new OutputBox();
out.setTitle("A Title");
```

we can write

```
OutputBox out = new OutputBox("A Title");
```

Similarly, the InputBox and DrawingBox classes have constructors that takes a String argument to set the title. Hereafter, we will use these constructors rather than using setTitle, because it is more concise. We can still use setTitle if, for some reason, we want to *change* the title of an existing input or output box.

**QUICK EXERCISE
5.3**

A useful example of a class with constructor argument is Color in java.awt. The constructor Color (int r, int g, int b) constructs a color with the given "red/green/blue" components. The arguments are integers values between 0 and 255, inclusive. Write a program to draw a filled rectangle in a drawing box (use fillRect) after setting the color using setColor. (Don't forget to import java.awt.*.) Run the program at least six times using different values for the arguments.

5.5

A Clock **Class**

Finally, let's build a new class that incorporates many of the ideas that we've been discussing. The class, called Clock, will keep track of time as an hour and a minute. Various methods of the class will allow a client to create a new clock, to set the time, to display the time (in digital form in an OutputBox as well as analog form in a DrawingBox), and to compare two clocks. The methods of the Clock class are described in Table 5.2. The skeletal outline for the Clock class is as follows:

Example	Explanation
`void setup()`	Initializes the clock.
`void getData()`	Reads and stores the hour and minute data.
`String toString()`	Returns a "stringified" version of the time (suitable for printing).
`void setHour(int h)`	Sets the hour to h.
`void setMinute(int m)`	Sets the minute to m.
`int getHour()`	Returns the value of hour.
`int getMinute()`	Returns the value of minute.
`boolean priorTo(Clock c)`	Returns `true` if receiver< c.
`void display(DrawingBox d, int x, int y, int r)`	Draws the clock, with center at (x,y) and radius r, in the `DrawingBox` referred to by d.

TABLE 5.2   Methods for the `Clock` class.

```
1    public class Clock {
2
3        int hour,
4            minute;
5
6        public void setup () { ... }
7
8        public void getData () { ... }
9
10       public String toString () { ... }
11
12       public void setHour (int h) { ... }
13       public void setMinute (int m) { ... }
14
15       public int getHour () { ... }
16       public int getMinute () { ... }
17
18       public boolean priorTo (Clock c) { ... }
19
20       public void display (DrawingBox d, int x, int y, int r) { ... }
21   }
```

The first thing to notice is that there are four methods that return some value (i.e., they are not of type `void`). Two of these are easy to understand: `int getHour()` and `int getMinute()`; they return to the caller the value held in the `hour` and `minute` variables, respectively. But we haven't yet seen how a method can return a value.

To return a value, a method executes the statement

`return` *expression*;

where *expression* gives the value to return. The `return` statement can appear anywhere in the body of a method, and it always results in the immediate return from that method. This means that, for example, if you write inside a method

```
if (  condition  )
   return  x;
else
    statement;
```

then this is exactly the same as

```
if (  condition  )
   return  x;
statement;
```

In other words, the `else` is unnecessary because if the condition is true, then the method will return and the code after the `if` statement won't be executed anyway.

So the code for `getHour` is quite straightforward:

```
public int getHour () {
   return hour;
}
```

(From now on, to conserve space, we'll usually write one-statement methods on a single line.) The complete `Clock` class is

```
1   import CSLib.*;
2   import java.awt.*;
3
4   public class Clock {
5      // Maintain a clock.
6      // Author: Courtney Mickunas, November 21, 2000
7
8      int hour,
9          minute;
10
11     public void setup () {
12        hour = 12;
13        minute = 0;
14     }
15
16     // Obtain values for hour and minute from user input.
17     public void getData () {
18        InputBox in = new InputBox();
19        in.setPrompt("What is the hour?");
20        hour = in.readInt();
21        in.setPrompt("What is the minute?");
22        minute = in.readInt();
23     }
24
25     // Return the current time as a string.
26     public String toString() { return (hour + ":" + minute); }
27
28     public void setHour (int h) { hour = h; }
29     public void setMinute (int m) { minute = m; }
30
31     public int getHour () { return hour; }
32     public int getMinute () { return minute; }
33
34     // Compare the time of this clock to another.
```

```
35        // Return true if this time is less than
36        // the time of the other clock.
37        public boolean priorTo (Clock c) {
38          return (hour < c.getHour() ||
39                 hour == c.getHour() && minute < c.getMinute()
40                 );
41        }
42
43        // Draw a clock with radius r at (x,y) in the DrawingBox d
44        public void display (DrawingBox d, int x, int y, int r) {
45          double theta;      // angle from 12:00
46          int x1, y1;        // endpoint of a clock hand
47
48          // Draw the clock in black.
49          d.setColor(Color.black);
50          d.drawOval(x-r, y-r, 2*r, 2*r);
51
52          // Set the color to blue for the hands
53          d.setColor(Color.blue);
54          // Draw the minute hand.
55          theta = 2*Math.PI*minute/60.0;
56          x1 = x + (int)(r*Math.sin(theta));
57          y1 = y - (int)(r*Math.cos(theta));
58          d.drawLine(x, y, x1, y1);
59
60          // Draw the hour hand.
61          theta = 2*Math.PI*(hour+minute/60.0)/12.0;
62          x1 = x + (int)(r*.8*Math.sin(theta));
63          y1 = y - (int)(r*.8*Math.cos(theta));
64          d.drawLine(x, y, x1, y1);
65        }
66      }
```

The methods getHour and getMinute (lines 31 and 32) are written as described just above, with a single return statement. Likewise the method toString (lines 25 and 26) is written to return a String that is built by concatenating the hour, a colon, and the minute. This string is suitable for printing in an OutputBox.

The fourth method that returns a value is the priorTo method in lines 34 through 41. There are a number of things to notice. First, the values of the hour and minute of the receiver object are accessible through the instance variables hour and minute. But how do you obtain those same values from the second Clock object, the one that is supplied as an argument to the priorTo method? It's easy. You invoke the getHour and getMinute methods on that object. This is exactly what's done by the calls c.getHour() and c.getMinute() in the if statements.

The Clock class resembles the Hose class in a number of respects:

1. Declarations of instance variables occur in lines 8 and 9.
2. There is a separate input method, getData, and a separate output method, display, which play roles analogous to the routines in Hose of the same name.

QUICK EXERCISE
5.4

Convince yourself that the Boolean expression returned by the `priorTo` method does the correct thing. What should it return for two clocks that are set to identical times? What does it do?

On the other hand, instead of a single `compute` method that processes the data, here we have several methods, most of which merely look at or set the instance variables `hour` and `minute`. In effect, this class is being used primarily for the I/O routines (we discuss the `display` routine in detail shortly). However, either of these routines can be ignored: If a client chooses to use a different method of obtaining input, the instance variables of `Clock` can be set by calling the *settor* *methods*, `setHour` and `setMinute`; if it wants to use a different method of output, it can obtain the values of those instance variables by calling the *accessor* *methods*, `getHour` and `getMinute`. This gives us that much more flexibility to accommodate changes in the future.

settor methods

accessor methods

5.5.1 Drawing in the `Clock` **Class**

We now examine the `display` method in the `Clock` class (lines 43 through 65), which draws our clock with blue hands. This program illustrates the typical computations that must be done to draw complex pictures on a grid of pixels. For instance, if the value of `hour` is 5 and the value of `minute` is 30, the output will look like Figure 5.2. Examining the header for the `display` method (line 43), we see that the method takes a `DrawingBox` as its first argument. Presumably the client will have created a `DrawingBox`, and a reference to that `DrawingBox` will be provided as an argument to `display`. The second and

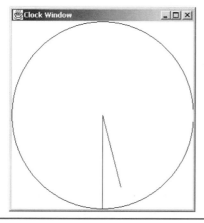

FIGURE 5.2 Sample graphical output for a clock.

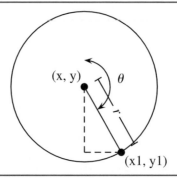

FIGURE 5.3   Geometry of the `Clock` **drawing.**

third arguments will give the (x, y) coordinates for the *center* of the clock, and the fourth argument will give the radius of the clock.

Drawing the clock circle is easy—we know its center and its radius, so we can easily compute the upper left corner for the rectangle that circumscribes the clock. (Recall from Table 2.4 on page 48 that the `drawOval` method requires as arguments the coordinates of the upper left corner, plus the width and height, of the circumscribing rectangle.) The upper left corner is at $(x - r, y - r)$, and the width and height are each $2 \times r$. In lines 49 and 50 first we set the drawing color to black, and, then we draw the circle. Since we are using the `Color` class, we must remember to import the `java.awt` package in line 2.

Before drawing the hands, we change the color to blue in line 53. To draw a hand of the clock, we must perform a bit of math. Recall that the `drawLine` operation can draw a line from a point (x, y) to a point $(x1, y1)$. Here the point (x, y) is the center of the clock, but we don't know what $(x1, y1)$ is—we need to calculate it from the hour or minute. We do this in two steps: Find the *angle* θ represented by the given hour or minute (see Figure 5.3), and then draw a line of length r from (x, y) in direction θ.

1. The angles from a point run from 0 to 360 degrees, which is the same as 0 to 2π radians (the measure used by the `Java Math` operations). The position of the minute hand is a certain fraction, namely $m/60$, of this amount. So, for the minute hand, θ is $2\pi(m/60)$, which explains line 55:

   ```
   theta = 2*Math.PI*minute/60.0;
   ```

   (`Math.PI` is the symbolic constant giving the `double` value closest to π.) Given these calculations, we need to draw a line of length r, at an angle θ (from vertical), starting at point (x, y), which we will do in step 2.

   For the hour hand, the calculation is a little more complicated, since it depends upon both the hour and the minute. Specifically, the fraction of 2π is $h/12 + m/(12 \times 60)$; that is, the `arc` between h and $h + 1$ (one-twelfth of the circle) is further divided into 60 parts, and the hour hand is moved m parts past h. This gives us line 61:

```
theta = 2*Math.PI*(hour + minutes/60.0)12.0;
```

Given this, we need to draw a line of length $0.8r$ (a bit shorter than the minute hand) at an angle θ (from vertical) starting at point (x, y).

2. The general problem we have now—and it is one that comes up quite often—is to draw a line of a given length at a given angle (relative to vertical) starting at a certain point. The problem is illustrated in Figure 5.3. Recall that $\sin\theta$ and $\cos\theta$ give the length and height, respectively, of a right triangle with angle θ and hypotenuse of length 1:

Thus, if the bottom point is (x, y), then the other end of the hypotenuse is at $(x + \cos\theta, y - \sin\theta)$ (we subtract because computer graphics coordinates are upside-down). Observe now that this picture scales linearly: If the hypotenuse has length r, then the lengths of the sides are $r\cos\theta$ and $r\sin\theta$. For the minute hand, this gives us lines 56 to 58:

```
x1 = x + (int)(r*Math.sin(theta));
y1 = y - (int)(r*Math.cos(theta));
d.drawLine(x, y, x1, y1);
```

For the hour hand, the only difference is that the length of the line is `r*.8` instead of `r`.

Here is a typical client for the `Clock` class.

```
1   import CSLib.*;
2
3   public class TwoClocks {
4       // Place two clocks in a DrawingBox, and compare them
5       // Author: Mary Angela McDermott, December 30, 2000
6
7       Clock c1,
8             c2;
9       DrawingBox d;
10      OutputBox out;
11
12      public void drawClocks () {
13          // Draw two clocks.
14
15          d = new DrawingBox();
16          d.setDrawableSize(300,300);
17
```

```
18        // Create and set the first clock.
19        c1 = new Clock();
20        c1.setup();
21        c1.getData();
22        c1.display(d,50,50,50);
23
24        // Create and set the second clock
25        c2 = new Clock();
26        c2.setup();
27        c2.getData();
28        c2.display(d,250,50,50);
29      }
30
31    public void compareClocks () {
32        // Compare the times of the two clocks.
33
34        out = new OutputBox("Comparison");
35        out.print(c1.toString() + " is ");
36        if (!c1.priorTo(c2)) out.print("not ");
37        out.print("prior to " + c2.toString());
38      }
39    }
```

This client has quite a bit of work to do. First it creates a DrawingBox and sets its drawable size. Then it creates the first of *two* Clock objects, sets that clock using input from getData, and displays it with a radius of 50 pixels, tucked in the upper left corner of the drawing area. Then the second clock is similarly created, set, and tucked in the upper right corner. Notice that to draw the clocks, in each case we must specify the (x, y) coordinates for the clock's center, plus the radius for the clock.

In the method compareClocks, the client compares the times of the clocks and prints a message in an OutputBox. The message uses the toString method to print the two clock times, and it prints either that c1's time "is prior to" or "is not prior to" c2's time. The only difference is whether the word not should be printed. You can see that in line 36 we determine that we *should* print the not if and only if the Boolean condition !c1.priorTo(c2) is true.

But there is something different about this client. It doesn't have a main method! In fact, it is simply a class itself. Therefore, TwoClocks expects to be used by yet another client—a client that will create an instance of TwoClocks, then invoke the drawClocks method, then invoke the compareClocks method. What we have is a class that

1. Is a class that expects to be used by a client
2. But is itself a client of the class Clock

A typical client of TwoClocks is

```
1    public class TwoClocksClient {
2
3      public static void main (String[] args) {
```

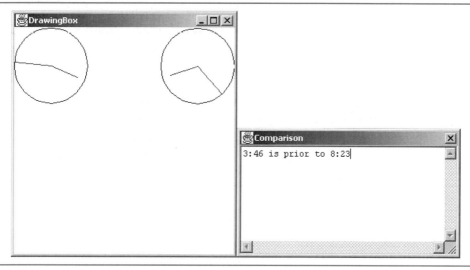

FIGURE 5.4 Output from the TwoClocks Client.

```
4          TwoClocks twins = new TwoClocks();
5          twins.drawClocks();
6          twins.compareClocks();
7      }
8  }
```

The output from all this consists of a DrawingBox *and* an OutputBox, shown
in Figure 5.4.

A UML diagram for this program is shown in Figure 5.5. The first thing to
notice is that the TwoClocks class has two instance variables shown. In UML
notation, an instance variable v of type T is shown as v:T.

This time, we also show *associations* between the classes involved. Asso-   *UML associations*
ciations are indicated by lines connecting classes and are often "annotated" with
text and "adorned" in various ways.

The association from TwoClocksClient to TwoClocks is annotated
"creates" and can be read "TwoClocksClient creates TwoClocks." The
open arrow adornment indicates that the class TwoClocksClient knows about
TwoClocks; but since there is not an arrow at the other end of the association,
TwoClocks does not know about TwoClocksClient. This is typically the
association that we have had between the (rather trivial) clients and the classes
that we've written. We often omit the client class and the "creates" association
in future UML diagrams, since it is not an important part of understanding the
program design.

The association that is annotated "uses" is read "TwoClocks uses Clock."
There are no arrows on the ends of the association, so we must rely on the solid arrow adornment to tell us the direction in which to read the "uses" annotation. The

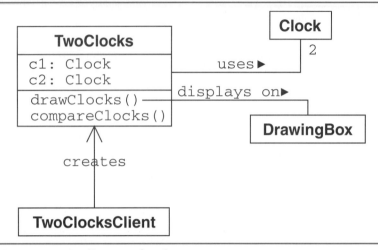

FIGURE 5.5   UML diagram for the `TwoClocks` **program.**

UML multiplicity   small digit "2" near the `Clock` end of the association is called a *multiplicity*, and it indicates that there will be *two* `Clock` objects associated with `TwoClocks`.

     The remaining association, given the solid arrow adornment, is read "`TwoClocks` displays on `DrawingBox`." This time, the `TwoClocks` end of the association is drawn near the `drawClocks` method, indicating that it is through that method that the association occurs.

     UML diagrams can show as much or as little detail as you would like about class relationships. We try to keep our UML diagrams as uncluttered as possible, while still conveying useful information about the structure of our programs.

QUICK EXERCISE 5.5

An unemployed programmer suggested that we could change `ClockClient`'s line 36 to

```
if (c2.priorTo(c1)) out.print("not ");
```

Should you hire this programmer?

QUICK EXERCISE 5.6

The multimethod `Hose` class that we wrote on page 150, whose methods are documented in Table 5.1, lacks accessor and settor methods for its instance variables `height`, `weight`, and `s`. Why might a client want such methods? Write these six methods.

Summary

Java programs are divided into *classes*. Class definitions have the form

```
public class  name {
     declarations of instance variables

     method definitions
}
```

The methods are the operations provided by the class.
Method definitions have the form

```
public  type or void  name  ( formal parameter list )  {
     local variable declarations
     statements
}
```

The *instance variables* are the variables that can be used in each of the methods. Variables declared inside the method can only be used in that method; these are called *local variables*.

A method is used within a program by a *message send*, also known as a *call statement*, consisting of an object, a period, the method name, and a parenthesized list of *arguments*, or *actual parameters*.

The mechanism used to specify the value to be returned by a method is the `return` statement:

```
return  value;
```

A method whose return type is `void` does not return a value. To return from such a method, you may use the statement

```
return;
```

Implicitly, every `void` method has a `return` at the very end, so that there is no need for an explicit return; the method returns when it "falls off the end."

Exercises

1. Modify the `Hose` class to report a choice of sizes in some cases, as follows: In `compute`, in addition to calculating y and x, calculate z as a double value equal to the value assigned to x *without* casting to `int`. Then report sizes according to this rule:

$y = 0, x = 1$:	s = A	
$y = 1, x = 1$:	s = B	
$y = 2$:	$0 \le z \le 0.8$:	E
	$0.8 < z \le 1.2$:	E *or* C
	$z > 1.2$:	C
$y = 3$:	$0 \le z \le 0.8$:	F
	$0.8 < z \le 1.2$:	F *or* D
	$z > 1.2$:	D

You must still separate the input, computation, and output into separate methods. The problem is to add the right instance variables so that `compute` will be able to communicate its findings to `display`.

Give the UML diagram for the new class.

2. In Chapter 4, we presented a class to calculate Social Security payments. Rewrite that class to have three methods—`getData`, `compute`, and `display`—and rewrite the client accordingly.

3. Exercise 14 in Chapter 4 required that you calculate the dosage of some medicines depending upon the child's weight. Divide that class into three methods, as in the previous exercise. As always, the major problem is to choose the instance variables needed to communicate the input values to the computation itself, and to communicate the results of the computation to the output method.

4. Exercise 15 in Chapter 4 describes the children's game of Cooties, in which different parts of the cootie's body are drawn, based on the throw of a die, until the cootie is complete. Write a class with the following methods:

```
void drawBody ()
void drawHead ()
void drawLeg ()
void drawAntenna ()
void drawEye ()
void drawTail ()
boolean gameOver ()
void display ()
```

The instance variables of the class should be used to store the number of each body part that has been added. The `draw` methods do not actually draw anything—that is done by `display`; they just add body parts. As discussed in the exercise, some calls to these methods should not result in adding anything, because they are in the wrong order; for example, none of the methods can add any body parts until `drawBody` has been called.

Give the UML diagram for the new class.

5. Modify the `Clock` class to produce its output in text form (using the `DrawingBox` method `drawString`). Only the body of the `display` method should be changed.

6. A `CashRegister` is an object with nine integer variables: `pennies`, `nickels`, `dimes`, `quarters`, `halfdollars`, `ones`, `fives`, `tens`, and `twenties`. Its operations are the nine operations to add coins or bills to the cash register, namely, `void addPennies (int p)`, `addNickels (int n)`, and so on. These operations can also remove coins or bills when negative arguments are provided. There is also the operation `int total ()` which returns the total amount of money in the cash register, in pennies. Write the `CashRegister` class.

7. Write a `Thermometer` class, with three operations: `void setTemp (int t)`, `void toggleScale ()`, and `void display ()`. The `setTemp` method sets the temperature to its argument (a number between 0 and 212). Initially, the temperature is interpreted on the Fahrenheit scale, but a call to `toggleScale` changes it to Centigrade; a subsequent call changes it back. The `display` method draws a thermometer in a drawing box, as a tall, thin rectangle with a small circle at the bottom,

with the circle and the correct portion of the rectangle in red. Show the temperature to the right of the top of the red portion of the thermometer, followed by the letter F or C, depending on the scale. When in Fahrenheit mode, the thermometer will show temperatures from 32 to 212; in Centigrade mode, it will show temperatures from 0 to 100. When the scale is toggled, the temperature should be recalculated so that the next time `display` is called it will show the correct number (although the height of the red part will not change).

8. The `Scoreboard` class represents a scoreboard giving the scores in a baseball game. It gives the inning and two scores, which it displays in a `DrawingBox` as

```
Inning   Home team   Visitors
   4          9          1
```

Its operations are

`void setup ()`	Create `DrawingBox` for display, and initialize.
`void homeTeamScores (int s)`	Add s to a home team's score.
`void visitorsScore (int s)`	add s to visiting team's score.
`void refresh ()`	Change the scoreboard to reflect the current score.

Note that `refresh` does *not* create a new `DrawingBox`; it just sends the `drawString` method to the one drawing box. The operations `homeTeamScores` and `visitorsScore` are to be called at the end of each team's at-bat, so that they should stricly alternate; if a team scored nothing in that inning, then use an argument of zero. The inning counter turns over after the visitors and home team have each reported their scores (it is traditional for the visitor to bat first).

The client is the class `BallGame`, with the single method `void playBall()`. It calls `setup` and then repeatedly uses an `InputBox` to ask the user for the next score for the visitors or home team, calling `visitorsScore` or `homeTeamScores` and `refresh` after each score is entered. It should play three innings (i.e., three at-bats for each side) and at the end display "Home team ahead," "Visitors ahead," or "Game tied." (Do not continue past three innings. To allow for a complete game, including the possibility of extra innings, requires the use of loops, which we cover in the next chapter; see Exercise 13 in Chapter 6.)

As in the `Clock` example, you should have a third class, `BallGameClient`, that contains just `main`; `main` creates a `BallGame` object and sends it the `playBall` message.
(a) Sketch the UML diagram for these classes.
(b) Write the code and test it.

9. In 10-pin (American-style) bowling, the object is to roll a ball toward a set of 10 pins and knock them all down. A bowler has 10 chances, called *frames*, with a maximum of two rolls in each frame (only one if the first roll knocks down all 10 pins). If all 10 pins are knocked down with one roll, it is called a *strike*; if it takes two rolls, it is a *spare*; and if there are pins remaining standing after two rolls, it is a *miss*. In this exercise, you will implement a `Bowler` class that will keep track of frames and the bowler's total score. We will use a simplified scoring scheme. (The next exercise gives the correct rules, which are far more complicated.) Specifically, the score will be simply the sum of the pins knocked down in 10 frames.

The `Bowler` class has three methods:

```
void roll (int pins)      Number of pins knocked down in one roll
int currentFrame ()       Number of current frame
int currentScore ()       Score obtained in last complete frame
```

You will need to have four instance variables: integers `frame`, `score`, and `lastRoll`, and boolean `middleOfFrame`. All the real work is done in the `roll` method, which must first decide if the roll represents a new frame (in which case that roll needs to be saved in `lastRoll` and `middleOfFrame` needs to be set to `true`).

The way that these four variables change when `roll` is called is best summarized in a table. (To fit the table on the page, we have abbreviated `frame` as `f`, `score` as `s`, `lastRoll` as `lr`, and `middleOfFrame` as `mod`.)

f	s	lr	mof	call roll (n)	f	s	lr	mof
f	s	0	false	$n = 10$	$f + 1$	$s + 10$	0	false
f	s	0	false	$n < 10$	f	s	n	true
f	s	m	true		$f + 1$	$s + m + n$	0	false

For example, the last line represents a bowler in the middle of a frame; the next roll, no matter what it is, will end the frame, with the score being incremented by the total of the two rolls.

The client, `BowlingGame`, should prompt the user for several rolls and report the frame and score after each one. As with the baseball-scoring exercise, we need to use iteration to run a complete game, so for now just have the bowler take a total of six rolls, whatever the result. Again, `BowlingGameClient` should consist of the single method `main`.

(a) Write the code for these classes, and test it.

(b) You may have noticed that some input sequences are illegal. For example, if the first roll is 3, then there remain only 7 pins, so the next roll cannot be larger than 7. Modify your code to detect and complain about any illegal entries.

10. The real rules of 10-pin bowling are more complicated because of how they reward strikes and spares. If the bowler makes a strike, then the 10 points for that strike are augmented by the total of the next two rolls, whatever they may be. For example, if a bowler rolls three strikes in a row, then the first frame adds 30 points to the score. Note that because of this rule the score in a frame may not be known until two more frames have been completed. If the bowler makes a spare, then the 10 points for that spare are augmented by the next roll, whatever it might be. For example, if a bowler bowls a spare and then a strike in the next frame, the frame with the spare is worth 20 points. If the bowler misses, the frame is worth just the total of the two rolls, no more. The tenth frame is special: If it is a strike, the player rolls exactly two more balls, and the total of the three rolls is added to the score (for a maximum of 30); if a spare, one more ball is thrown and again the total of the three rolls is added; if a miss, then the total of the two rolls is added and no third roll is taken.

Your task is to modify the `Bowler` class to follow these rules. A particularly complicating factor is that we may need to see one or two rolls *after* a frame before we can score that frame. So now the methods of the class are

```
void roll (int pins)        Number of pins knocked down in one roll
int lastFrameScored ()      Number of last frame for which a score is known
int lastCurrentScore ()     The score in that last frame
```

The instance variables we will use are `frame`, `score`, `held`, `roll1`, and `roll2`. And `held` is a number between 0 and 2 indicating how many rolls have not yet been counted in the score; those rolls are in turn recorded in `roll1` and `roll2`. For example, when the bowler bowls a strike, a 10 is placed in `roll1` and a 1 in `held`; after the next roll, whatever it is, that value will be placed in `roll2` and 2 in `held`, because the score in the frame with the strike cannot be calculated until one more ball is rolled.

The changes in these variables when `roll` is called can again be summarized in a table. If the variables have the values on the left before the call `roll` (n), they will have the values on the right afterward. (To fit the table on the page, we have abbreviated `frame` as f, `score` as s, `held` as h, `roll1` as r1, and `roll2` as r2.)

f	s	h	r1	r2		f	s	h	r1	r2
f	s	0	0	0		f	s	1	n	0
f	s	1	10	0		f	s	2	10	n
f	s	1	m	0	$m+n=10$	f	s	2	$10-n$	n
f	s	1	m	0	$m+n<10$	$f+1$	$s+m+n$	0	0	0
f	s	2	10	10	$n=10$	$f+1$	$s+30$	2	10	10
f	s	2	10	m	$m+n=10$	$f+1$	$s+20$	2	$10-n$	n
f	s	2	10	m	$m+n<10$	$f+2$	$s+10+2(m+n)$	0	0	0
f	s	2	m	p	$m+p=10$	$f+1$	$s+10+n$	1	n	0
10	s	2	10	10		11	$s+20+n$	0	0	0
10	s	2	m	m	$m+p=10$	11	$s+10+n$	0	0	0
11	s					11	s			

In interpreting these rules, they must be read from top to bottom, with the first rule that applies being used. For example, row 2 says what to do when there is one saved roll and it is a strike (10); row 3 says what to do when there is one saved roll and it is m; implicitly, row 3 applies only when m is less than 10.

The client class, `BowlingGame`, should be as in the previous exercise.

ITERATION

In this chapter we explore various mechanisms for the repetition of statements (iteration) and examine their use in detail. Special emphasis is placed on how to write a loop and ensure its correctness. We use iteration to allow users to enter a large amount of data. We use iteration in graphical programs to provide animation by repeatedly drawing frames of pictures.

"You are old, Father William," the young man said
"And your hair has become very white;
And yet you incessantly stand on your head—
Do you think, at your age, it is right?"

"In my youth," Father William replied to his son,
"I feared it might injure the brain;
But, now that I'm perfectly sure I have none,
Why, I do it again and again."

—Lewis Carroll
Alice's Adventures in Wonderland

We introduced the concept of iteration in Chapter 1 by using a simple `while` loop to move the mouse through a maze. In this chapter, you'll learn how to design your own loops.

6.1

`while` **Loops**

The kind of iterative statement that we mentioned in Chapter 1 is called a `while` loop, and it has the form

while statement

```
while ( condition )
    statement
```

It repeatedly executes *statement* (which can be either a series of statements surrounded by braces { } or a single statement without them). The *statement*, called the *body of the loop*, is repeated as long as *condition* is true. The entire `while` statement, together with its body, is a single Java statement. If we're careless in writing the loop and the condition never becomes false, the loop will continue to execute forever—an *infinite loop*.

body of the loop

infinite loop

Let's begin our study of while loops by expanding the program we wrote in Section 3.10 (page 68) to convert temperatures from Centigrade to Fahrenheit. Here is a Java program that, when executed, produces the table of equivalent Centigrade and Fahrenheit temperatures shown in Figure 6.2:

BUG ALERT 6.1	***Body of*** `while` ***Loop Consists of Single Statements***
	The body of a `while` loop must be a single statement. Consequently, if you want the body to consist of more than one statement, you must enclose them in braces to turn them into a compound statement.

```
1    import CSLib.*;
2
3    public class Temperature {
4      // Print a table of corresponding C/F temperatures.
5      // Author: M. Dennis Mickunas, June 9, 1996
6
7      public void tabulate () {
8        final double
9          LOW_TEMP = -10.0,
10         HIGH_TEMP = 10.0;
11       double
12         cent,  // The Centigrade temperature.
13         fahr;  // The Fahrenheit temperature.
14
15       OutputBox out = new OutputBox();
16       out.println("\tDEGREES C\tDEGREES F");
17
18       cent = LOW_TEMP;
19       while (cent <= HIGH_TEMP) {
20         fahr = (9.0/5.0) * cent + 32.0; // Convert C to F
21         out.println("\t" + cent + "\t\t" + fahr);
22         cent = cent + 1.0;   // Increment the Centigrade value.
23       }
24     }
25   }
```

As in the previous examples, the first line or lines import the package(s) that the program will use. Lines 8 through 10 contain the declarations of symbolic constants that will be used by the program. These are the starting and ending Fahrenheit temperatures that we wish to tabulate. Lines 11 through 14 declare, and comment, the variables to be manipulated by the program. There is only one method, `tabulate`, that is contained in lines 7 through 24.

The heart of the program is lines 15 through 23. The flowchart that corresponds to this code is shown in Figure 6.1. During the first iteration of the loop, the variable `cent` has the value `LOW_TEMP`. The compound statement in lines 19 through 23 is executed repeatedly as long as the value of `cent` does not exceed `HIGH_TEMP`. Since the value of `cent` initially is set to `LOW_TEMP` (which is -10.0) and the last statement in the sequence increases the value stored in `cent` by 1.0, eventually the value of `cent` will become bigger than `HIGH_TEMP` (which is 10.0) and the loop will terminate. Each time the statement in line 20

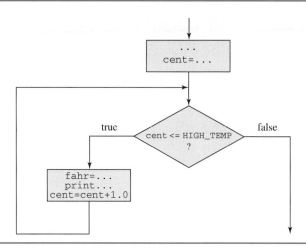

FIGURE 6.1   **Flowchart for the Table of Temperatures program.**

is executed, it calculates the Fahrenheit temperature corresponding to the current value of cent and puts that value in fahr. Finally, both values are printed by line 21. Recall from Chapter 3 that \t is an escape sequence representing the tab character, which aligns the output into neat columns.

Explain why the table produced as output, shown in Figure 6.2, has 21 lines of temperature equivalences instead of 20.	**QUICK EXERCISE** **6.1**

Modify the program so that it computes the table of equivalent temperatures for $$-10°F, \ -9°F, \ldots, 10°F$$ using the formula $$°C = (°F - 32) \times \tfrac{5}{9}$$	**QUICK EXERCISE** **6.2**

```
OutputBox                                                    ×
      DEGREES C        DEGREES F
      -10.0            14.0
       -9.0            15.8
       -8.0            17.6
       -7.0            19.4
       -6.0            21.2
       -5.0            23.0
       -4.0            24.8
       -3.0            26.6
       -2.0            28.4
       -1.0            30.2
        0.0            32.0
        1.0            33.8
        2.0            35.6
        3.0            37.4
        4.0            39.2
        5.0            41.0
        6.0            42.8
        7.0            44.6
        8.0            46.4
        9.0            48.2
       10.0            50.0
```

FIGURE 6.2 **A table of corresponding Fahrenheit and Centigrade temperatures from −10 to +10°C, obtained as output from the sample program.**

BUG ALERT 6.2

while Conditions and Type double

Recall from Bug Alert 4.3 (page 111) that equal/not equal comparisons with type `double` may be unreliable because of inexact representation. This means that you must be careful *not* to have the end condition of a `while` loop rely solely on an expression such as `(x != 0)` where `x` is of type `double`. In the unlucky event that `x` is inexactly represented, it may never be zero, and the loop will be an infinite loop.

As another example, suppose we want the computer to print the following children's song:

```
10 in a bed and the little one said,
     "Roll over, roll over."
They all rolled over and one fell out,
9 in a bed and the little one said,
     "Roll over, roll over."
They all rolled over and one fell out,
8 in a bed and the little one said,
 .
 .
 .
1 in a bed and the little one said,
     "Alone at last."
```

The first thing to do is to decide which pieces of the song are to be printed just once and which pieces are to be repeated. The pieces to be printed once go either before or after the loop; the ones that are repeated can be put inside the loop. The song can be divided into the first nine verses and the last verse. Each of the first nine has the form

```
-- in a bed and the little one said,
     "Roll over, roll over."
They all rolled over and one fell out,
```

where the `--` is replaced by the numbers 10, 9, etc. The last verse has only the two lines

```
1 in a bed and the little one said,
     "Alone at last."
```

We'll adopt the logic shown by the flowchart in Figure 6.3. This means that our program will be organized as

```
while ( more verses ) {
    print next verse
}
print last verse
```

We need one variable, which we call `numberInBed`, and a symbolic constant, `MAX_NUMBER_IN_BED`, to specify how many verses of the song are to be written. The program is

```
1   import CSLib.*;
2
3   public class TenInABed {
4      //  Print the nursery rhyme "Ten In a Bed."
5      //  Author: Leah S. Gordon, December 29, 1996
6
7      public void sing () {
8
9         final int MAX_NUMBER_IN_BED = 10;
10        int numberInBed;
11
12        OutputBox out = new OutputBox();
13        numberInBed = MAX_NUMBER_IN_BED;
14
15        while (numberInBed > 1) {
16           out.println(numberInBed + " in a bed and the little one said,");
17           out.println("     \"Roll over, roll over.\"");
18           out.println("They all rolled over and one fell out,");
19           numberInBed = numberInBed - 1;
20        }
21
22        out.println("1 in a bed and the little one said,");
23        out.println("     \"Alone at last.\"");
24     }
25  }
```

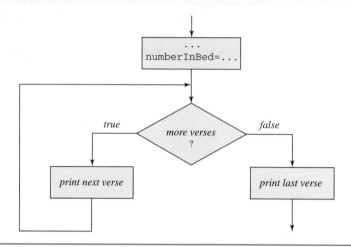

FIGURE 6.3   Flowchart for the Ten in a Bed program.

QUICK EXERCISE 6.3	Modify the program that prints "Ten in a Bed" to print the song "99 Bottles of Beer on the Wall."

```
99 bottles of beer on the wall,
99 bottles of beer,
If one of those bottles should happen to fall,
98 bottles of beer on the wall.

98 bottles of beer on the wall,
98 bottles of beer,
If one of those bottles should happen to fall,
97 bottles of beer on the wall.

. . .

1 bottle of beer on the wall,
1 bottle of beer,
If that one bottle should happen to fall,
No more bottles of beer on the wall!
```

for **Loops**

Let's look again at the loop used in the Centigrade/Fahrenheit table:

```
18      cent = LOW_TEMP;
19      while (cent <= HIGH_TEMP) {
20         fahr = (9.0/5.0) * cent + 32.0; // Convert C to F
21         out.println("\t" + cent + "\t\t" + fahr);
22         cent = cent + 1.0;    // Increment the Centigrade value.
23      }
```

This kind of iteration, in which we increment a variable each time through the loop, is so common that Java has a special form of looping mechanism that makes it easy to do exactly what is required—the *for statement*.

for statement

The for statement is written in the form

```
for ( statement1; condition; statement2 )
    statement3
```

and it causes *statement3*, called the body of the loop, to be executed repeatedly, as if we had written

```
statement1;
while ( condition ) {
    statement3;
    statement2;
}
```

Using a for statement, our temperature table loop can be rewritten as

```
18      for (cent = LOW_TEMP; cent <= HIGH_TEMP; cent = cent+1.0) {
19         fahr = (9.0/5.0) * cent + 32.0; // Convert C to F
20         out.println("\t" + cent + "\t\t" + fahr);
21      }
22      }
```

The advantages of doing it this way are its compactness and simplicity, and that all the computations governing the loop occur in the for statement, not spread throughout the loop. If we wanted to produce the table in reverse order, we could rewrite this as the for loop

```
for (cent = HIGH_TEMP; cent >= LOW_TEMP; cent = cent-1.0)
```

All the loops that we've seen so far in this chapter have this common characteristic—their bodies were executed some number of times as a variable *counted* the number of executions. For example, in the TenInABed loop, the variable numberInBed counted down, by 1s, from MAX_NUMBER_IN_BED down to 2. In the Temperature programs, the variable cent counted up, by 1s, from

iteration variable

index variable

LOW_TEMP to HIGH_TEMP. This variable is called the *iteration variable* or *index variable*. The for loop is designed to make it easier to write loops that use an index variable.

There is another twist that we can add to the for loop. If the loop index variable is not already used in the method either as a formal argument or as a local variable, then you are allowed to declare the type of the variable right in the for loop initialization statement:

```
for (double cent = HIGH_TEMP; cent >= LOW_TEMP; cent = cent-1.0)
```

This is a frequent programming practice with some interesting consequences. In this case, the scope of the index variable is the header and body of the for loop.

Generally, whenever we have such counting loops, the for statement is a natural programming choice.

QUICK EXERCISE 6.4

Modify the Quick Exercise 6.2 to use a for loop instead of a while loop.

Let's look briefly at another program that uses the for statement. This program reads a string from an InputBox and prints the reversed string in an OutputBox, illustrating how to extract individual characters from a string. So, given a string

$$s = \boxed{\quad s_0 \quad | \quad s_1 \quad | \quad s_2 \quad | \quad \cdots \quad | \quad s_{m-1} \quad}$$

we want to extract and print character s_{m-1}, then extract and print the previous character, and so on, until we extract and print character s_0.

The entire program is as follows:

```
1    import CSLib.*;
2
3    public class StringReverse {
4       // Print the reversal of a string
5       // Author: Stephanie Ries, October 9, 2000
6
7       String s;
8
9       public void getString () {
10         InputBox in = new InputBox();
11         s = in.readString();
12      }
13
14      public void reverse () {
15         OutputBox out = new OutputBox();
16         for (int i=s.length()-1; i>=0; i--) {
17            out.print(s.charAt(i));
18         }
19      }
20   }
```

with a client

```
1    public class StringReverseClient {
2
3      public static void main (String[] args) {
4        StringReverse sr = new StringReverse();
5        sr.getString();
6        sr.reverse();
7      }
8    }
```

What we have is a counting loop in lines 16 through 18, with a variable i, declared to be of type int, counting down by 1 from s.length()-1 to 0. Within the loop the variable i is used to extract the ith character of the string by calling the charAt function (see Table 3.6 on page 72).[1]

Multistatement for Loops

Bug Alert 6.3

When the body of a for loop consists of more than one statement, those statements must be surrounded by braces (to make them a compound statement).

6.3

do-while Loops

Java has an alternative to while loops for indefinite repetition. The *do-while* loop looks like this:

do-while statement

```
do
    statement
while ( condition );
```

It behaves just as its appearance suggests: *Statement* is executed again and again until *condition* is false. The difference between this and a while loop is that in a do-while loop the Boolean condition is checked *after* the body of the loop is executed, and as a consequence the body of the loop is *always* executed at least once.

---

[1]This program illustrates a convention that many programmers prefer to follow: Even though the body of the for loop contains only one statement, we choose to surround that single statement by braces. This is a precautionary move to allow for future expansion. If later we want to put a *second* statement inside the loop, such as a debugging print statement, as in the Hose program on page 133, we don't have to remember to put in the surrounding braces. Recall that a multistatement body *must* have surrounding braces.

To be precise, the statement

```
do
    statement
while ( condition );
```

is exactly the same as

```
    statement
while ( condition )
        statement;
```

where the same statement in the do-while loop body is copied before the while loop in addition to forming its body. Therefore, do-while is not absolutely necessary, but it is useful for those cases where the body of a loop needs to be executed at least once.

As an example, consider the following loop to count the number of digits in an int:

```
1    numberOfDigits = 0;
2    rest = number;
3    while (rest > 0) {
4      rest = rest / 10;
5      numberOfDigits++;
6    };
```

This loop provides correct output only for positive integers; it fails to work when number ≤ 0. We can correct this by changing the while condition to rest != 0, but this still fails for number $= 0$, which, by convention, has one digit. Instead of checking this case separately, it is easiest to make the loop work for *all* integer values by rewriting it as

```
1    numberOfDigits = 0;
2    rest = number;
3    do {
4      rest = rest / 10;
5      numberOfDigits++;
6    } while (rest != 0);
```

In this way the body of the loop always is executed at least once, even when number $= 0$. Notice also that the loop works correctly for negative values of number. For example, if number is initially -125, then rest takes on the values -125, then -12, then -1, then 0.

QUICK EXERCISE 6.5	Write an application reverseDigits that reads an integer and prints the number with its digits reversed. For example, if you input 120, your program should output 021.

When loops get even a little bit complicated, they become difficult to understand. You can attempt to follow the execution in your head, but it is easy to get lost. A possible result is the notorious "off-by-1" error, when a loop is executed either one time too few or one time too many. Here is a simple example. Suppose that you want to execute a loop exactly 1000 times. A for loop *should* be

```
for (int i=1; i<=1000; i++)
...
```

However, it would be very easy to write the comparison using < rather than <=. That would constitute an *off-by-1-error*—the loop would execute only 999 times.

Check Loop Conditions to Avoid **Off-by-1** Errors | BUG ALERT 6.4

You should carefully check both the initialization and the terminating conditions of loops to ensure that they do not run for too few or too many iterations.

6.4

Loop Invariants

An alternative to thinking through the entire execution of a program in detail is to realize that, at any point in the loop, there is *some* relationship among the program's variables that *always* holds whenever that point is reached. Usually, there is one point in the loop—most often the beginning—where this relationship is easiest to see. This relationship is called the *invariant* of the loop.

loop invariant

For example, the reason the previous loop worked is that the following relationship always holds when the loop body begins (no matter how many times the loop has already been executed): The number of digits in number is equal to numberOfDigits plus the number of digits in rest. It is obviously true when the loop first executes: rest = number and numberOfDigits = 0. Suppose that the loop has executed some number of times and rest is still not zero, so the loop begins to execute again. At this point the result is again clear: If rest is nonzero, the number of digits in rest/10 is exactly 1 less than the number of digits in rest, so if we divide it by 10 and increment numberOfDigits, the invariant still holds.

The point about invariants is that they allow us to focus on a single execution of the loop body and not think about what happens when the loop is iterated different numbers of times. Accordingly, we often include the invariant of the loop as a comment, as in:

```
1    numberOfDigits = 0;
2    rest = number;
3    do {
4      // number of digits in number is numberOfDigits
5      // plus the number of digits in rest
6      rest = rest / 10;
7      numberOfDigits++;
8    } while (rest != 0);
```

6.5

Reading Input in a Loop

In this section we examine a problem involving loop construction and show how to derive the appropriate loop structure. In our problem, we want to read test scores and compute the minimum, maximum, and average scores. Imagine someone at a computer entering a sequence of scores; after entering the last score, the person signals the end of the data by entering an "empty" field in the input dialog box. The dialog should look like this:

There are many questions to answer in writing this application. How do we calculate the average? The maximum? The minimum? What should the loop look like? Although these questions are interrelated, we can't answer all of them at once. The natural place to start is with the loop structure, so we will conceal the problems of how to compute the average, maximum, and minimum scores by lumping all this under the description "process the test score." The sequence of actions we want the program to take is

> Read a test score
> If end of input, stop the loop
> Process the test score
> Read a test score
> If end of input, stop the loop
> Process the test score
> Read a test score
> If end of input, stop the loop
>
> $\vdots$

These actions can be grouped either with the test as the first statement of a loop (that is, using a `while` loop) or with the test as the last statement of a loop (that is, using a `do-while` loop), as shown in Figure 6.4 (first two columns). The organization as a `while` loop is preferable here, because to use the `do-while` loop we need

```
read score
if ( not end of input )
   do {
      process score
      read score
   } while ( not end of input );
```

whereas using a `while` loop, we can write

```
read score
while ( not end of input ) {
   process score
   read score
}
```

This is more desirable because it is shorter and clearer. With the loop structure set, we can examine what the processing entails.

6.5.1   The Loop-and-a-Half

There is a difficult kind of looping problem that arises, sometimes called the *loop-and-a-half problem*. Let's reconsider the loop we used to read scores repeatedly in the example of the previous section. Examining Figure 6.4 (third column), we see that the loop can also be structured as a repetition of *read/test-for-end/process*. The difficulty is that the final execution must be only a "half execution," quitting in the middle when the *read score* returns the empty input. The logic is illustrated in Figure 6.5 We can do just that by using an `if` statement in the body of the loop to skip the final *process score* operation.

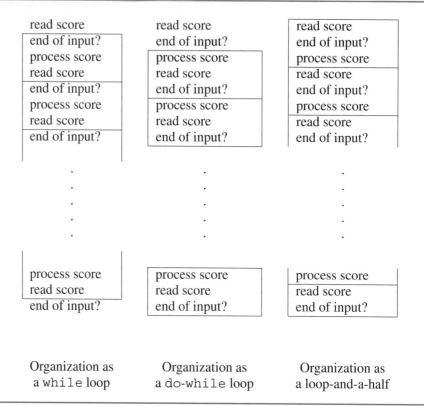

FIGURE 6.4   The three possible organizations of the loop for reading and processing scores.

```
while (true) {
    read score
    if ( end of input ) leave the loop
    process score
};
```

This style of `read/process` loop is advantageous when the `read` part is complex, because the code does not get reproduced in two places, both before and in the middle of the loop.

6.5.2 The `break` Statement in Loops

How can we accomplish the action in the foregoing code that asks to *leave the loop*? The `break` statement, which we introduced and used in the context of `switch` statements in Chapter 4, can be used to do this. When a `break` is

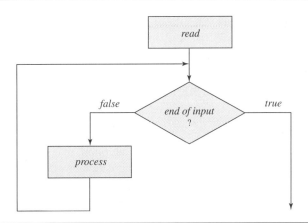

FIGURE 6.5   Flowchart for the loop-and-a-half problem.

encountered during the execution of a loop, the loop ends immediately, and execution continues with the statement following the loop. This applies for all three kinds of loops: `while` loops, `do-while` loops, and `for` loops. So the code that corresponds to Figure 6.5 is

```
while (true) {
    read score
    if ( end of input ) break;
    process score
}
```

6.5.3   Testing for End of Input

How do we test for the end-of-input condition? There are two common ways of doing this, depending on how the input is supplied to a program. When the input is obtained by reading a file, eventually you reach the *end of the file*, and a special signal is usually given for that occurrence. We'll take a closer look at file input in Chapter 15. However, when input is obtained interactively from a user, as with our `InputBox`, there is usually an agreement that the user will input some particular value to signal when the input is finished. The use of such a *sentinel* gives rise to *sentinel-controlled loops*. There are two common kinds of sentinel methods that are used.

end-of-file

sentinel-controlled loops

The first method is to use a special value to terminate the input. For example, if all the data in the input set consist of positive numbers, the user could enter −1 to terminate it. For example, here is some code that reads and processes input scores and also counts the number of legitimate scores entered:

```
int i = 0;
InputBox in = new InputBox();
in.setPrompt("Enter data, or -1 to terminate");

while ( true ) {
   score = in.readInt();
   if (score == -1) break;
   i++;
   process score
}
```

When the user enters -1, the loop ends. At that point, i is equal to the number of valid inputs. (Note that we do not need to create a new InputBox for each iteration of the loop. The one InputBox object will make itself appear each time it receives the readInt message.)

The second kind of sentinel is to use a method that provides an end-of-input signal. The InputBox class is designed to allow the user to indicate that there are no more data by entering the "empty" input value—when the user clicks "ok" without typing anything into the input field. The value returned by readInt is 0, by readDouble is 0.0, by readString is "", and by readChar is

null character   the character whose ASCII value is 0 (a nonprinting character called the *null character*). Most importantly, after this happens, an eoi (end-of-input) message sent to the InputBox will return true.

Thus, here is an alternative loop:

```
int i = 0;
InputBox in = new InputBox();
in.setPrompt("Enter data (empty input ends the data):");

while ( true ) {
   score = in.readInt();
   if ( in.eoi() ) break;
   i++;
   process score
}
```

A method such as eoi that answers a question about an object, returning either

predicate   true or false, is called a *predicate*. For the most part in this text, we'll use the eoi predicate to detect end of input, as in the foregoing loop.

QUICK EXERCISE 6.6

The loop-and-a-half problem discussed here in reference to I/O occurred in the ten-in-a-bed example of Section 6.1 (page 176). Recall that the first line of the last verse had to be placed after the loop, even though it is essentially the same as the first line of every other verse. Restructure the program using an infinite loop and the break statement so that the only line printed after the loop is the very last line.

6.5.4   The Scores **Program**

We return now to our original problem. To compute the average value of a series of scores, we will need to keep track of the number of scores entered and their sum. Therefore, the processing must include statements such as

```
numberOfScores++;                       // new score
sumOfScores = sumOfScores + score;   // update sum
```

We place a comment inside the loop, stating the loop invariant that the value of numberOfScores is the number of scores that have been read and their sum is the value of sumOfScores. For such an invariant to be true the first time through the loop, the initialization of the loop must include

```
int sumOfScores = 0,
    numberOfScores = 0;
```

The program so far looks like this:

```
1    int sumOfScores = 0;
2    int numberOfScores = 0;
3
4    InputBox in = new InputBox();
5    in.setPrompt("Enter score (empty input ends the data): ");
6
7    while (true) {
8      score = in.readInt();
9      if (in.eoi()) break;
10     numberOfScores++;                       // new score
11     sumOfScores = sumOfScores + score;   // update sum
12
13     // numberOfScores is the number of scores read
14     // so far and sumOfScores is their sum
15   }
```

Once the loop has ended, the average score is easily computed as

```
(double)sumOfScores / numberOfScores
```

We need the (double) cast so that the division used will not be integer division, because we want some precision in the average value.

   To add the computation of the maximum and minimum scores, we first decide what needs to be added to the loop invariant. Once written, the invariant will guide us in writing the Java statements. In addition to our invariant relationship between numberOfScores and sumOfScores, we want to have maxOfScores and minOfScores with the property that they are, respectively, the largest and the smallest of the scores that have been read. The complete invariant can be stated as

```
// numberOfScores is the number of scores read
// so far and sumOfScores is their sum; maxOfScores
// is the largest score and minOfScores is the smallest
// score read so far
```

To maintain the truth of this augmented invariant, we augment the loop to include the statements

```
if (maxOfScores < score)          // new largest score
   maxOfScores = score;
if (minOfScores > score)          // new smallest score
   minOfScores = score;
```

We also must ensure that maxOfScores and minOfScores are computed properly after the very first score is read. What should happen? Clearly, since only one score has been read, that score is both the minimum score so far and the maximum score so far. So we must make sure that the computation that compares that first score against the "previous" value of maxOfScores concludes that "this score is larger than the previous maxOfScores." This can be ensured by initializing maxOfScores to a value that will definitely be less than any score that might be read. Since we assume that all scores will be nonnegative, initializing maxOfScores to -1 will accomplish this. A similar argument can be made for minOfScores, leading to the conclusion that it should be initialized to 999 (higher than any possible score). These initializations occur in lines 11 and 12 in the following complete version of the program.

Finally, we must be careful to check that at least one score was entered; otherwise, the computation will result in an error, trying to divide by zero. (Why?) The resulting program with a typical client is as follows:

```
1    import CSLib.*;
2
3    public class Scores {
4       // Read scores and compute the minimum, maximum, and average
5       // scores.  Scores are read until the user enters the "empty"
6       // input value.
7       // Author: Arthur L. Reingold, October 31, 1994.
8
9       int sumOfScores = 0,
10          numberOfScores = 0,
11          maxOfScores = -1,     // phony max score
12          minOfScores = 999;    // phony min score
13
14      public void compute () {
15
16         int score;
17
18         InputBox in = new InputBox();
19         in.setPrompt("Enter score (empty input ends the data): ");
20
21         while (true) {
22            score = in.readInt();
23            if (in.eoi()) break;
24            numberOfScores++;                        // new score
25            sumOfScores = sumOfScores + score;   // update sum
```

```
26        if (maxOfScores < score)              // new largest score
27          maxOfScores = score;
28        if (minOfScores > score)              // new smallest score
29          minOfScores = score;
30
31        // numberOfScores is the number of scores read
32        // so far and sumOfScores is their sum; maxOfScores
33        // is the largest score and minOfScores is the smallest
34        // score read so far
35
36      }
37    }
38
39    public void print () {
40      OutputBox out = new OutputBox();
41      if (numberOfScores == 0)
42        out.println("No scores were entered.");
43      else if (numberOfScores == 1)
44        out.println("Only one score was entered.  It was "
45            + sumOfScores);
46      else {
47        out.println(numberOfScores + " scores were entered.");
48        out.println("The average score was "
49            + ((double)sumOfScores)/numberOfScores);
50        out.println("The maximum score was " + maxOfScores);
51        out.println("The minimum score was " + minOfScores);
52      }
53    }
54  }
```

```
1   public class ScoresClient {
2     public static void main (String[] args) {
3       Scores s = new Scores();
4       s.compute();
5       s.print();
6     }
7   }
```

<table>
<tr><td>

QUICK EXERCISE
6.7

</td></tr>
</table>

Suppose we rewrite the if statement in the Scores program as

```
if (maxOfScores < score)        // new largest score
    maxOfScores = score;
else if (minOfScores > score) // new smallest score
    minOfScores = score;
```

Does the code still work properly? Why or why not?

QUICK EXERCISE 6.8	Think about how to augment the `Scores` program to print the median of the scores. Can you do it with what you have learned so far in Java?

6.6

Debugging Loops

The *stock market problem* is to read in the values of a stock for a sequence of consecutive days and find the best pair of days to have bought and sold the stock to maximize profit. In this simplified version, only one buy and one sell are considered. In addition, "short selling" is not permitted; that is, you must buy before you sell. Suppose that the input is

followed by additional input of prices 18, 16, 17, 21, 15, 16, and end of input. The output should be

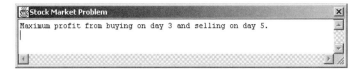

The solution to this problem is not entirely obvious. One idea is to buy on the day with the lowest price and sell on the day with the highest price, but then the sell day might precede the buy day! Another idea is to buy on the day with lowest price and sell at the highest price we can get after the buy day, but this is also wrong: In the preceding example this strategy would have us buy on day 6 and sell on day 7, for a profit of $1, when a profit of $5 is possible.

We can, however, make the following observation: Whatever day turns out to be the sell day, the correct buy day is the lowest-priced day that precedes it. This suggests the correct method: As you read the prices, keep track of the lowest price seen so far, call it `minPrice`, and the best possible profit so far, call it `profit`. Each time a new price is read, call it `priceToday`, calculate `priceToday - minPrice`; if it is greater than `profit`, it becomes the new value of `profit`. When all the prices have been read, `profit` contains the maximum possible profit.

This method makes no mention of the days themselves, just of the prices. Accordingly, we will develop the program in two stages, first writing a program to calculate the maximum profit according to the method just outlined and then extending that program to keep track of the buy and sell days. Such an approach often is useful when the basic algorithm is a little subtle; it can be tested in a simple program before adding bells and whistles. (The drawback is that we have to go to all the trouble of writing and debugging a program parts of which we know will have to be changed.)

So we first attempt to solve this simplified problem: Given inputs as above, calculate the maximum profit. The output for the inputs in the example will be

```
Maximum profit = 5 dollars
```

We assume that by now you've had plenty of experience correcting syntax errors, so we won't continue to show you how to do that. We'll build one method to do the output, and another to do the `read-process` loop. You should be able to recognize almost immediately that the `read-process` loop is really an instance of the loop-and-a-half phenomenon just discussed. Here's our first attempt.

```
1   import CSLib.*;
2
3   public class StockProfit {                    INCOMPLETE
4       // Determine best buy-sell period
5       // Author: Max Kamin, June 24, 1997
6
7       int profit = 0;         // best profit possible so far
8
9       public void compute () {
10          int minPrice = 9999999,    // lowest price so far
11              priceToday;            // last price input
12
13          InputBox in = new InputBox("Stock Market Problem");
14
15          while (true) {
16              // minPrice = minimum price seen before today.
17              // profit = maximum profit possible, if buy
18              //    and sell dates are before today.
19
20              // What is the next day's price?
```

```
21        in.setPrompt("Enter value of stock: ");
22        priceToday = in.readInt();              INCOMPLETE
23        if (in.eoi()) break;
24        // Is today a new minimum price?
25        if (priceToday < minPrice)
26          minPrice = priceToday;               INCOMPLETE
27        // Does a sell today maximize profit?
28        if (priceToday - minPrice > profit)
29            profit = priceToday - minPrice;
30      }
31    }
32
33    public void print () {                     INCOMPLETE
34      OutputBox out = new OutputBox("Stock Market Problem");
35      out.println("Maximum profit = " + profit + " dollars.");
36    }
37  }
```

We have an invariant stated in lines 16 through 18. The first time through the loop, this invariant must be vacuously true. Our initialization of minPrice to an unrealistic high price (in line 10) accomplishes that. The first price actually read will replace minPrice. Notice that profit is an instance variable (line 7), since it must be shared by both the compute and print methods. All other variables are local to compute.

An experienced programmer would sense immediately that the structure of this version can be improved. Take a look at the if statements in line 25 through 29. If the if condition in line 25 is true, then minPrice is set to be the same as priceToday; subsequently the if condition in line 28 could not possibly be true. So performing the test is useless. Consequently the if in lines 28 and 29 should be relegated to an else clause of the first if. Making that change, we have

```
15      while (true) {
16        // minPrice = minimum price seen before today.
17        // profit = maximum profit possible, if buy
18        //   and sell dates are before today.
19
20        // What is the next day's price?
21        in.setPrompt("Enter value of stock: ");
22        priceToday = in.readInt();
23        if (in.eoi()) break;
24
25        // Is today a new minimum price?
26        if (priceToday < minPrice)
27          minPrice = priceToday;
28        // else does a sell today maximize profit?
29        else if (priceToday - minPrice > profit)
30            profit = priceToday - minPrice;
31      }
```

Here is how this program executes on the preceding input data:

It looks like our strategy works, and we now can adapt our solution to the original problem. We continue to add features incrementally. First, let's add a variable to keep track of the current day, call it today, and use it to give the correct prompt:

```
1   import CSLib.*;
2
3   public class StockProfit {
4       // Determine best buy-sell period
5       // Author: Max Kamin, June 24, 1997
6
7       int profit = 0;          // best profit possible so far
8
9       public void compute () {
10          int minPrice = 9999999,    // lowest price so far
11              priceToday,            // last price input
12              today = 1;             // current day
13
14          InputBox in = new InputBox("Stock Market Problem");
15
16          while (true) {
17              // minPrice = minimum price seen before today.
18              // profit = maximum profit possible, if buy
19              //    and sell dates are before today.
20              // today = number of days read
21
22              // What is the next day's price?
23              in.setPrompt("Enter value of stock on day " +
24                           today + ": ");
25              priceToday = in.readInt();
26              today++;
27              if (in.eoi()) break;
28
29              // Is today a new minimum price?
30              if (priceToday < minPrice)
31                  minPrice = priceToday;
32              // else does a sell today maximize profit?
33              else if (priceToday - minPrice > profit)
34                  profit = priceToday - minPrice;
35          }
36      }
37
38      public void print () {
```

```
39        OutputBox out = new OutputBox("Stock Market Problem");
40        out.println("Maximum profit = " + profit + " dollars.");
41      }
42    }
```

To solve the original problem, we need to keep track not only of the best buy and sell days so far, but also of the day on which the minimum price was achieved. So add three new variables: a local variable `minDay` to keep the day on which `minPrice` was achieved, and instance variables `buyDay` and `sellDay`, the days on which the maximum profit could be obtained. It is not hard to see when we should update the values of these variables: Modify `minDay` whenever there is an assignment to `minPrice`; and assign to `buyDay` and `sellDay` whenever `profit` is changed.

```
1   import CSLib.*;
2
3   public class StockProfit {
4     // Determine best buy-sell period
5     // Author: Max Kamin, June 24, 1997
6
7     int profit = 0,        // best profit possible so far
8         buyDay = 0,        // best day to buy
9         sellDay = 0;       // best day to sell
10
11    public void compute () {
12      int minPrice = 9999999,    // lowest price so far
13          priceToday,            // last price input
14          today = 1,             // current day
15          minDay = 1;            // day of minPrice
16
17      InputBox in = new InputBox("Stock Market Problem");
18
19      while (true) {
20        // minPrice = minimum price seen before today.
21        // profit = maximum profit possible, if buy
22        //    and sell dates are before today.
23        // today = number of days read.
24        // minDay is the day on which minPrice was achieved.
25        // buyDay and sellDay are the best days to buy
26        //    and sell before today
27
28        // What is the next day's price?
29        in.setPrompt("Enter value of stock on day " +
30                     today + ": ");
31        priceToday = in.readInt();
32        today++;
33        if (in.eoi()) break;
34
35        // Is today a new minimum price?
36        if (priceToday < minPrice) {
37          minPrice = priceToday;
38          minDay = today;
39        }
40        // else does a sell today maximize profit?
```

WRONG (watermark repeated)

```
41        else if (priceToday - minPrice > profit) {
42            profit = priceToday - minPrice;        WRONG
43            buyDay = minDay;
44            sellDay = today;
45        }
46      }
47    }                                              WRONG
48
49    public void print () {
50      OutputBox out = new OutputBox("Stock Market Problem");
51      out.println("Maximum profit from buying on day "
52          + buyDay + " and selling on day " + sellDay + ".");
53    }
54  }
```

However, it doesn't give us quite the right answers. Given the input

followed by the rest of the input, we obtain

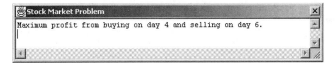

The correct buy and sell days are 3 and 5, so the numbers are off by just 1. We can see the problem by inspection: The variable today always contains the *next day's* number. It is initialized to 1, but is always incremented *immediately* after reading a price. For example, after reading the first price, it is incremented to 2. However, the assignments to minDay and sellDay are made on the assumption that today contains *today's* number. The solution is simple: Initialize today to 0. (In fact, we would have found this bug before now if we had taken the trouble to check the invariant carefully. When we first wrote "today is the number of days read," we should have noticed that it was actually 1 more than the number of days read.)

Well, it sounded simple, anyway. We see the problem with this solution as soon as we run the program:

Of course, now that `today` is initialized to 0, we should increment it *before* displaying the prompt. Changing that, we see this version works (almost) perfectly:

```
1    import CSLib.*;
2
3    public class StockProfit {
4      // Determine best buy-sell period
5      // Author: Max Kamin, June 24, 1997
6
7      int profit = 0,        // best profit possible so far
8          buyDay = 0,        // best day to buy
9          sellDay = 0;       // best day to sell
10
11     public void compute () {
12       int minPrice = 9999999,    // lowest price so far
13           priceToday,            // last price input
14           today = 0,             // current day
15           minDay = 0;                // day of minPrice
16
17       InputBox in = new InputBox("Stock Market Problem");
18
19       while (true) {
20         // minPrice = minimum price seen before today.
21         // profit = maximum profit possible, if buy
22         //    and sell dates are before today.
23         // today = number of days read.
24         // minDay is the day on which minPrice was achieved.
25         // buyDay and sellDay are the best days to buy
26         //    and sell before today
27
28         // What is the next day's price?
29         today++;
30         in.setPrompt("Enter value of stock on day " +
31                     today + ": ");
32         priceToday = in.readInt();
33         if (in.eoi()) break;
34
35         // Is today a new minimum price?
36         if (priceToday < minPrice) {
37           minPrice = priceToday;
38           minDay = today;
39         }
40         // else does a sell today maximize profit?
41         else if (priceToday - minPrice > profit) {
42           profit = priceToday - minPrice;
43           buyDay = minDay;
44           sellDay = today;
45         }
46       }
47     }
48
49     public void print () {
50       OutputBox out = new OutputBox("Stock Market Problem");
```

```
51          out.println("Maximum profit from buying on day "
52              + buyDay + " and selling on day " + sellDay + ".");
53     }
54   }
```

The only flaw in this code is the failure to handle an odd, but quite possible, case more gracefully: when *no* profit is possible. Notice what happens now:

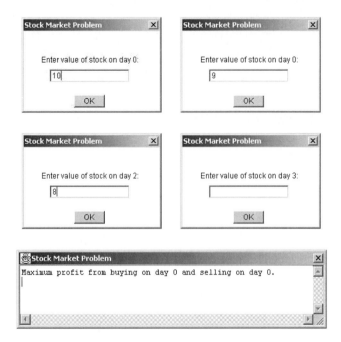

The original problem specification didn't say what to do in this case, but certainly advising to buy and sell on a nonexistent day can't be right! Making a small change to print an appropriate message in this case gives us our final solution:

```
1   import CSLib.*;
2
3   public class StockProfit {
4      // Determine best buy-sell period
5      // Author: Max Kamin, June 24, 1997
6
7      int profit = 0,      // best profit possible so far
8          buyDay = 0,      // best day to buy
9          sellDay = 0;     // best day to sell
10
11     public void compute () {
12        int minPrice = 9999999,   // lowest price so far
13            priceToday,           // last price input
14            profit = 0,           // best profit possible so far
15            today = 0,            // current day
```

```
16          minDay =0;              // day of minPrice
17
18      InputBox in = new InputBox("Stock Market Problem");
19
20      while (true) {
21        // minPrice = minimum price seen before today.
22        // profit = maximum profit possible, if buy
23        //    and sell dates are before today
24        // today = number of days read.
25        // minDay is the day on which minPrice was achieved.
26        // buyDay and sellDay are the best days to buy
27        //    and sell before today; or zero if no
28        //    profit was possible
29
30        // What is the next day's price?
31        today++;
32        in.setPrompt("Enter value of stock on day " +
33                    today + ": ");
34        priceToday = in.readInt();
35        if (in.eoi()) break;
36
37        // Is today a new minimum price?
38        if (priceToday < minPrice) {
39          minPrice = priceToday;
40          minDay = today;
41        }
42        // else does a sell today maximize profit?
43        else if (priceToday - minPrice > profit) {
44          profit = priceToday - minPrice;
45          buyDay = minDay;
46          sellDay = today;
47        }
48      }
49    }
50
51    public void print () {
52      OutputBox out = new OutputBox("Stock Market Problem");
53      if (buyDay == 0)
54        out.println("Try a different stock!");
55      else
56        out.println("Maximum profit from buying on day "
57          + buyDay + " and selling on day " + sellDay + ".");
58    }
59  }
```

For the input 10, 9, 8, this final solution provides the following advice:

6.7

More Drawing in Java

In addition to the methods that we've seen, our `DrawingBox` has a method for including an image at a given location. This assumes that the image is contained in a file as a GIF or JPEG image. Two steps are needed to display such an image: Create an `Image` object by reading in the file, and display the image. Reading from a file is easy for an application—one way is to pass to some method a string that spells out the complete path name for the file, such as `"C:/KMR/images/mouse.gif"`. But how can the Java graphics package display a GIF? The answer is that the GIF must be transformed to an `Image` object that is suited to the particular graphics software running on that particular machine.

The following is typical code that must be written to obtain a GIF image from a file, transform it to an `Image`, and display it in a `DrawingBox`:

```
1    import java.awt.*;
2    import CSLib.*;
3    ...
4    DrawingBox g = new DrawingBox();
5    ...
6    Toolkit tools = Toolkit.getDefaultToolkit();
7    Image mouse = tools.getImage("C:/KMR/images/mouse.gif");
8    g.drawImage(mouse, x, y);
```

When a Java program is running, information about that machine-specific and operating system–specific "graphics" object is kept in a Java `Toolkit` object. A `Toolkit` object has methods that are able to perform the transformation from a GIF to an `Image` that is suitable for the given system. To obtain the `Toolkit` object for the present program, you use the method `getDefaultToolkit()`, as in line 6 above. This is a class method, like those of Java's `Math` class (for example, `Math.sqrt` in Table 3.4 on page 70), and we'll learn more about them in Chapter 10. For now, you only need to know that it causes the variable `tools` to refer to the `Toolkit` object for the present program.

The `Toolkit` method that we'll use to read a GIF and transform it to an `Image` is called `getImage`, and it is used as in line 7 above. Notice that the complete path for the file is given (using Unix-style forward slashes) as a `String` argument, and the method returns a new `Image` object. Since the `Toolkit` and `Image` classes are part of the *java.awt* package, we must be sure to import   *java.awt* that package (as in line 1). Finally, the image is displayed with its upper left corner at location (x, y) by the `drawImage` method in line 8.

In Chapter 9, we will write a program based on the mouse-in-a-maze problem from Chapter 1. As a preview of that program, and as an example of drawing GIFs, the following program draws the maze and positions the mouse at its entrance. The program's output is shown in Figure 6.6.

FIGURE 6.6   Drawing in a program.

```
1    import CSLib.*;
2    import java.awt.*;
3
4    public class MouseMaze {
5      // Draw a maze
6      // Author: Diane M. Mickunas, November 9, 2000
7
8      DrawingBox g;
9      final int SIZE = 50;   // Width & length of a room in the maze
10     Image mouse;           // Image to be created from mouse.gif
11
12     public void setup () {
13       Toolkit tools = Toolkit.getDefaultToolkit();
14       mouse = tools.getImage("C:/KMR/images/mouse.gif");
15       g = new DrawingBox();
16       g.setDrawableSize(6*SIZE, 5*SIZE);
17     }
18
19     public void draw () {
20       g.drawLine(1*SIZE, 1*SIZE, 4*SIZE, 1*SIZE);   // top of maze
21       g.drawLine(1*SIZE, 1*SIZE, 1*SIZE, 2*SIZE);   // left side
22       g.drawLine(1*SIZE, 3*SIZE, 1*SIZE, 4*SIZE);
23       g.drawLine(1*SIZE, 4*SIZE, 5*SIZE, 4*SIZE);   // bottom
24       g.drawLine(5*SIZE, 1*SIZE, 5*SIZE, 4*SIZE);   // right side
25       g.drawLine(2*SIZE, 2*SIZE, 2*SIZE, 4*SIZE);   // various walls
26       g.drawLine(3*SIZE, 2*SIZE, 3*SIZE, 3*SIZE);   // various walls
27       g.drawLine(4*SIZE, 3*SIZE, 4*SIZE, 4*SIZE);   // various walls
28       g.drawLine(4*SIZE, 2*SIZE, 5*SIZE, 2*SIZE);   // various walls
29       g.drawImage(mouse, 5, (int)(2.5*SIZE));
30     }
31   }
```

with client

```
1    public class MouseMazeClient {
2      public static void main (String[] args) {
3        MouseMaze mm = new MouseMaze();
4        mm.setup();
5        mm.draw();
6      }
7    }
```

The symbolic constant SIZE and the variable mouse declared in the class are explained in the accompanying comments. We have a setup method in lines 12 through 17 that first obtains the present Toolkit (line 13) and then reads the GIF file and transforms it to an Image (line 14). In our call to setDrawableSize, we reason that the maze will be four rooms wide plus a room-size edge on either side; therefore the width of the DrawingBox should be 6 × SIZE. The maze will be three rooms high, plus a room-size edge on both the top and bottom; therefore the height of the DrawingBox should be 5 × SIZE. The actual drawing is done in the draw method, where we draw the lines of the maze using drawLine (lines 20 through 28) and then the mouse Image (line 29).

6.8

Iteration in Graphical Programs

In this section, we give a program, called Surprise, that illustrates how simple animation can be achieved in a program. It draws a circle that grows from a small dot to fill a DrawingBox and then shows a message in the middle. The "growing" of the circle is accomplished by a loop that draws larger and larger filled circles. The final result is shown in Figure 6.7. Using the fillOval method, the Surprise program is

```
1    import CSLib.*;
2    import java.awt.*;
3
4    public class Surprise {
5      // Surprise with an exploding balloon
6      // Author: Rachel McDermott, September 27, 1996
7
8      DrawingBox board;
9      int width, height,
10         dmax;      // The maximum-diameter circle
11
12     public void setup () {
13       board = new DrawingBox("Surpriser");
14
15       width = board.getDrawableWidth();
16       height = board.getDrawableHeight();
17       dmax = (int)Math.min(width, height);
18     }
```

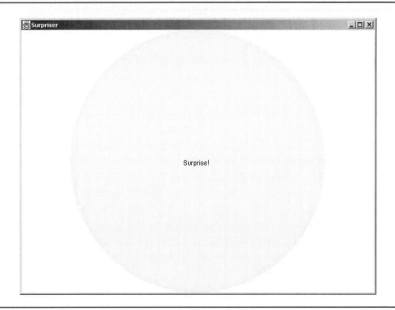

FIGURE 6.7 Drawing in a program.

```
19
20     public void draw (){
21        board.setColor(Color.yellow);
22        for (int diameter=0; diameter < dmax; diameter++) {
23          board.fillOval((width-diameter)/2, (height-diameter)/2,
24                         diameter, diameter);
25          Timer.pause(10);                    // sleep for 10 msec
26        }
27
28        board.setColor(Color.red);
29        board.drawString("Surprise!", (width-53)/2, (height+14)/2);
30     }
31   }
```

Since we will be using the Color class, we must import the java.awt package in line 2. In the setup method, we create a new DrawingBox, and in lines 15 through 17 we compute the maximum diameter of the balloon, using the getDrawableWidth and getDrawableHeight methods of the DrawingBox, together with the Math.min method.

The work of drawing a filled circle is done in the draw method, in lines 23 and 24. This action is repeated in a for loop, with diameter values that start at 0 and run as high as dmax-1. After each drawing of a filled circle, we use the CSLib class method Timer.pause to pause for 10 milliseconds. The CSLib class Timer has only one method, and it is documented in Table 6.1. Without this pause, the circles would be drawn so quickly that you would not be able to get any sense of "animation."

Example	Explanation
`void pause (long t)`	Pause for t milliseconds.

TABLE 6.1 Method of CSLib's `Timer` class.

Finally, in lines 28 and 29, the word *Surprise!* is "printed" in red in the middle of the large circle. The location of this text was determined by guessing that the "Surprise!" message is 53 pixels wide and 14 pixels high. In Chapter 13 we'll see how to determine those sizes algorithmically.

> **QUICK EXERCISE**
> **6.9**
>
> Modify the `Surprise` program so that after drawing the balloon, it pauses for 1 second and then erases the balloon from the outside inward. By drawing successively smaller and smaller unfilled circles in white (the color of the background), you can achieve the effect of *collapsing* the balloon.

We end this section with a program that will animate the advancement of the hands of the clock that we wrote in Chapter 5 (page 161). We draw a clock, just as before, after reading the value for hour and minute from InputBoxes. However, this time we raise another InputBox to ask how many minutes to advance the clock. Then we redraw the clock, advancing the minute by 1; we repeat this until we've advanced the proper number of minutes. The effect is that the clock's hands appear to sweep through the proper number of minutes. Then we repeat the process, raising the InputBox again to ask how many minutes to advance. Here's the program, with a client.

```
1   import CSLib.*;
2
3   public class Sweep {
4     // Maintain a Clock that can advance by sweeping.
5     // Author: Courtney Mickunas, November 21, 2000
6
7     Clock c;                  // Our own clock to manipulate.
8     DrawingBox d;             // ... in its own DrawingBox
9     final static int SIZE = 250;
10
11    public void setup () {
12      c = new Clock();
13      d = new DrawingBox("Ticking Clock");
14      d.setDrawableSize(SIZE, SIZE);
15      c.display(d, SIZE/2, SIZE/2, SIZE/2);
16    }
17
18    public void sweep () {
19      int advance = 0;        // How many minutes to advance.
```

```
20          InputBox in = new InputBox();
21
22          // Loop repeatedly, drawing the clock and reading input.
23          do {
24            // minute+advance is the desired final time
25            for (int i=1; i<=advance; i++) {
26              // Advance the time.
27              c.setMinute(c.getMinute()+1);
28
29              // Update the clock display.
30              d.clear();
31              c.display(d, SIZE/2, SIZE/2, SIZE/2);
32            }
33
34            in.setPrompt("Advance how many minutes?");
35            advance = in.readInt();
36          } while (!in.eoi());
37        }
38      }
```

with client

```
1     import CSLib.*;
2
3     public class SweepClient {
4       public static void main (String[] args) {
5         Sweep s = new Sweep();
6         s.setup();
7         s.sweep();
8       }
9     }
```

nested loop

This time there we have two loops—a do-while loop in lines 23 through 36 and a for loop in lines 25 through 32. We have what is called a *nested loop* structure, with one loop inside of another.

In each iteration of the for loop, we increment the Clock's time by 1 (in line 27) prior to drawing the new clock. Notice how we first obtain the current time using getMinute, then add 1 to that value, then use the resulting value as an argument to the setMinute method. Prior to drawing the new clock we need to erase the old one. For this we use the clear method (see Table 2.4 on page 48). Once we've finished with the for loop and the new time is shown on our clock, execution proceeds at the statements following the end of the for loop (line 32) where we ask for another increment for the time. If the user provides a valid integer, then the do-while loop repeats, executing the for loop again with a new value for advance. If the user does not provide an integer, then the eoi predicate is true, and the outer do-while loop ends; the sweep method then returns.

QUICK EXERCISE 6.10   Remove the clear call in line 30 of the Sweep class. What happens?

This program raises some interesting questions concerning the Clock class and how it behaves. For example, what happens if we ask to advance 65 minutes (starting at 12:00)? Does the time become 12:65, or 13:05, or 1:05? Does it matter? How can we find out? Whenever we use a predefined class, we must be aware of how it behaves under the circumstances that we'll present to it. Often the documentation for a class has insufficient detail to tell us everything we want to know, and we must experiment to discover certain behaviors.

1. Find out, by experimentation, what time the Clock records (according to the toString method) if we start at 12:00 and advance by 65 minutes.

2. Is there any danger of "integer overflow" (see Bug Alert 3.4 on page 88) with our version of Clock?

3. Suppose that you could type in integers instantaneously, and that Sweep would sweep through a 60-second advance in 1 second of real time. How long would it take before Sweep would cause Clock to fail with an integer overflow?

Summary

Iteration, the repetition of an action, is accomplished through several different types of loop structures in Java. The for statement is written

```
for ( statement1; condition; statement2 )
    statement3
```

and it causes *statement1* to be executed once and then *statement3*, the body of the loop, and *statement2* to be executed repeatedly as long as *condition* is true.
The while loop

```
while ( condition )
    statement
```

repeatedly executes *statement* (which can be a compound statement surrounded by braces, { and }) as long as *condition* is true. We must be careful in writing the loop to ensure that the *condition* eventually becomes false; otherwise, the loop will continue to execute forever—an infinite loop.

There are times when we purposely want to code an infinite loop. This is usually done only when the body of the loop is a compound statement and one of the enclosed statements can cause a break out of the loop, implementing a loop-and-a-half structure. One format is

```
while (true) {
    statement
    ... break ...
    statement
}
```

An alternative to `while` loops for indefinite repetition is available. The do-while loop

```
do
    statement
while ( condition );
```

behaves just as its appearance suggests: *Statement* is executed again and again until *condition* is `true`; the major difference between this and a `while` loop is that in a do-while loop the condition is checked *after* the body of the loop is executed, and as a consequence the body of the loop always is executed at least once.

Verifying that a loop gives the correct results is done by writing a *loop invariant*. The loop invariant is the set of relationships between the program variables at a particular point of the loop, where it should be stated in program comments. The correctness of the loop can be inferred from the loop invariant by verifying that the loop invariant is `true` the first time through the loop, that the loop invariant remains `true` from one iteration to the next, and hence that the loop terminates at the value we want.

By repeatedly drawing figures in a program while pausing briefly in between, it is possible to achieve an animation effect.

Exercises

1. Rewrite the temperature table program to convert from Fahrenheit temperature to kelvins (absolute temperature). The relationship between °F and K is

$$K = \tfrac{5}{9}(°F - 32) + 273.16$$

One kelvin (denoted by 1 K) is identical to 1° on the Centigrade scale, but a temperature of 0 K is equal to $-273.16°C$.

2. The sequence $0, 1, 1, 2, 3, 5, 8, \ldots$ of *Fibonacci numbers* is defined by the rule that each number is the sum of the previous two numbers. Write an application to print the first 20 Fibonacci numbers (using a symbolic constant `MAX_NUMBER = 20`).

3. There is a medieval puzzle about an old woman and a basket of eggs. On her way to market, a horseman knocks down the old woman, and all the eggs are broken. The horseman will pay for the eggs, but the woman does not remember the exact number she had, only that when she took the eggs in pairs, there was one left over; similarly, there was one left over when she took them three, four, five, or six at a time. When she took them seven at a time, however, she came out even. Write an application to determine the smallest number of eggs the woman could have had.

4. Modify the `reverseDigits` program from Quick Exercise 6.5 to ignore leading zeros, so that the reversal of `12000` is `21`.

5. Consider the following process. Start with any positive integer that is not a palindrome, say, 48. (A palindrome is something that reads the same both forward (left to right) and backward (right to left), such as the word *Mom* or the number 363.) Add 48 to its reversal, 84; we get $48 + 84 = 132$. Since 132 is not a palindrome, we add it to its reversal to get $132 + 231 = 363$ and we stop, having reached a palindrome.

(a) Write an application that reads an integer and applies the preceding process zero or more times until a palindrome results. Your application should count the number of times a number must be added to its reversal to reach a palindrome. Be sure the loop stops before an integer occurs that is too large for type `int` on your computer; for example, starting with 89 will require integers larger than $2^{31} - 1$ and so will be impossible on a 32-bit computer.

(b) Rewrite your program using the `BigInteger` class from `java.math`.

6. A number is *prime* if it is not divisible by any positive integer other than 1 and itself; 1 is not considered to be a prime. For example, 2, 5, 17, and 4,598,731 are primes, whereas 6 and 35 are not prime. Every integer 2, 3, 4, ... can be written as a product of powers of primes; for example,

$$
\begin{array}{llll}
 & 10 = 2^1 5^1 & 20 = 2^2 5^1 & 30 = 2^1 3^1 5^1 \\
 & 11 = 11^1 & 21 = 3^1 7^1 & 31 = 31^1 \\
2 = 2^1 & 12 = 2^2 3^1 & 22 = 2^1 11^1 & 32 = 2^5 \\
3 = 3^1 & 13 = 13^1 & 23 = 23^1 & 33 = 3^1 11^1 \\
4 = 2^2 & 14 = 2^1 7^1 & 24 = 2^3 3^1 & 34 = 2^1 17^1 \\
5 = 5^1 & 15 = 3^1 5^1 & 25 = 5^2 & 35 = 5^1 7^1 \\
6 = 2^1 3^1 & 16 = 2^4 & 26 = 2^1 13^1 & 36 = 2^2 3^2 \\
7 = 7^1 & 17 = 17^1 & 27 = 3^3 & 37 = 37^1 \\
8 = 2^3 & 18 = 2^1 3^2 & 28 = 2^2 7^1 & 38 = 2^1 19^1 \\
9 = 3^2 & 19 = 19^1 & 29 = 29^1 & 39 = 3^1 13^1
\end{array}
$$

The product of the prime powers equal to n is called the *prime factorization of n*. (Such prime factorizations play an important role in the design of secure encryption schemes for the transmission and storage of confidential data.) Write an application that reads an integer and prints its *prime factorization*. Your application should behave like this:

7. Given an approximation to the cube root of x, we get a better approximation by computing

$$
\text{Approximation} + \frac{1}{3}\left(\frac{x}{\text{approximation}^2} - \text{approximation}\right)
$$

Use this idea to write a method to calculate the cube root of x. Use 1.0 as the first approximation, and continue applying the given formula until the difference between successive approximations is less than a symbolic constant `ERROR = 1.0e-6`. (*Hint*: Use the `Math.abs` function.) (*Note:* This method is known as Newton's method for computing the cube root.)

8. Write an application to help do payroll calculations. Your application should read wages and compute and print the State of Illinois tax due (3 percent of wages); your application should continue reading wages until an end of input is encountered. At the end of input, the application should print the total of all wages paid and the total of all Illinois state taxes due. The output of the application should look like this:

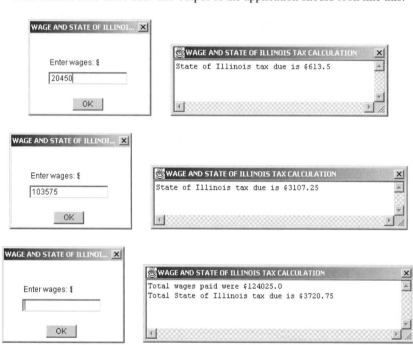

9. Write a program in which a ball bounces around within a DrawingBox. Initially, a small filled circle should be placed at a random location (x, y) within the DrawingBox, and the ball's direction of movement should be set to a random pair of doubles (δ_x, δ_y) in the range $0 < \delta_x < 1$ and $0 < \delta_y < 1$. In a loop, continually add (δ_x, δ_y) to (x, y) and redraw the circle at the new location. (To redraw the circle, first erase it by drawing over it in the background color; i.e., call setColor(getBackground()), then d.drawFillOval(...); then draw it at its new location by calling setColor(Color.black), and then calling d.drawFillOval(...) again.)

When the circle hits a side of the DrawingBox's window, change the direction as follows: If it hits the top or bottom, make it $(\delta_x, -\delta_y)$; if it hits either side, make it $(-\delta_x, \delta_y)$.

You may find that the ball moves too quickly for you to see it easily, so use Timer.pause to wait a few milliseconds between movements.

10. We were careful to set the size of the DrawingBox prior to drawing the mouse's maze in Figure 6.6. Draw the mouse's maze in a size proportional to the default size of the window. Recall that there are methods getHeight() and getWidth() that tell you the size of a DrawingBox. You need not change the size of the mouse; but

if you are ambitious, you can change its size by calling the `Image` instance method `getScaledInstance`:

```
Image scaledMouse =
    mouse.getScaledInstance(width, height, Image.SCALE_DEFAULT);
```

where `width` and `height` give the new size you would like the mouse to have. Now draw `scaledMouse` instead of drawing `mouse`.

11. Write a program to draw regular polygons. When the user inputs a positive integer n in an `InputBox`, the program draws an n-gon in its window. (The calculation of the points of the n-gon is similar to that for the position of the hands in the clock program, page 161.)

12. Mathematical curves can be drawn in drawing boxes by deciding on a range of x values and drawing dots at $(x, f(x))$ for various values of x within that range, with appropriate scaling to the size of the drawing box. For example, suppose we wish to draw a sine curve, with x values ranging from 0 to 10 rad in a drawing box of width w and height h. We will plot $(x, \sin x)$ for values of x from 0 to 10 in increments of 0.1 (using a loop, obviously). Each time we calculate a value of $\sin x$, we will place a dot (i.e., draw a filled circle) centered at point $(x(w/100), (h \sin x + h)/2)$. That is, we divide the x axis into 100 divisions and plot the points at those divisions. $\sin x$ is a number between -1 and 1. We convert this first to a number between $-h$ and $+h$, then to a number between 0 and $2h$, and finally to a number between 0 and h.

   (a) Write a class consisting of a single method, `void drawSineCurve (int x, double dx, int w, int h, int d)` that draws a sine curve between 0 and x in a drawing box of width w and height h. Also, `dx` is the value by which x should be incremented (0.1 in the example above), and d is the width of each dot, in pixels. Although you can calculate the number of iterations of the loop as `x/dx`, it is best to use a `while` loop and increment the iteration variable `x0` by `dx` until `x0` exceeds x. The client class should request five numbers from the user and pass these to the `drawSineCurve` method.

   (b) The more common method of drawing a mathematical curve is to draw lines between successive points, using `drawLine`. Thus, in our example above, we would draw lines from $(0, \sin 0)$ to $(0.1, \sin 0.1)$, $(0.1, \sin 0.1)$ to $(0.2, \sin 0.2)$, and so on, until we draw the final line from $(9.9, \sin 9.9)$ to $(10, \sin 10)$. Rewrite `drawSineCurve` using this method. A simple-minded way to do this would be to calculate $(x0, \sin x0)$ and $(x0 + dx, \sin (x0 + dx))$ at each iteration and draw a line between them. However, this would entail recalculating $(x0 + dx, \sin(x0 + dx))$ on the next iteration (i.e., after `x0` has been incremented by `dx`). You must avoid this recalculation by remembering the value of $\sin(x0 + dx)$ before going to the next iteration.

13. In Exercise 8 of Chapter 5, you wrote the `ScoreBoard` class to maintain and display scores in a baseball game. It had methods `setup`, `visitorsScore`, and `homeTeamScores`. Add method `boolean gameOver ()`. Method `gameOver` returns `true` when the inning is 9 or greater and one of the following conditions holds: The visitors have just finished their at-bat (so it is the middle of the inning), and the home team is ahead; or the home team has just finished its at-bat (so it is the end of the inning), and one of the teams is ahead. The client is the method `playBall` in class `BallGame`. It should continue asking for the visitors' and home team's scores alternately until the game ends, then declare a winner.

14. In Exercise 10 of Chapter 5, you wrote the `Bowler` class to maintain the score of a bowler in American-style 10-pin bowling. Add to it the method `boolean gameOver ()`, which is `true` when the frame is 11. Rewrite the client so that it continually prompts for the next roll until the game is over.

15. (a) Evaluate the expression

$$\sum_{i=1}^{10,000} \frac{1}{i}$$

with two different `for` loops. First use

```
for (int i = 1; i <= 10000; i++)
```
and then use
```
for (int i = 10000; i >= 1; i--)
```

(b) Explain why the values computed are not equal. Which is the more accurate value?

CHAPTER 7

CLASSES AND METHODS III: WORKING WITH OBJECTS

CHAPTER PREVIEW

Large programs are written by subdividing them into *classes*. With the `class` construct, the representation of a new type of object and the methods applicable to objects of that type can be specified. In this chapter, we discuss classes and their components—instance variables, constructors, and instance methods. We illustrate the class construct with several examples. We also discuss the concepts of *mutability* and *visibility*. Also included in this chapter is a discussion of *method overloading*.

You know my methods in such cases, Watson.

—Sir Arthur Conan Doyle
The Adventures of Sherlock Holmes.
"The Musgrave Ritual"

But here, unless I am mistaken, is our client.

—Sir Arthur Conan Doyle
His Last Bow. "Wisteria Lodge"

By now you are probably convinced that writing and debugging even a relatively small program are fraught with pitfalls and frustrations. Imagine how much more challenging it is to write large programs that do complicated things! Don't despair; the task of writing large programs can be made manageable by breaking the large problem into bite-size pieces, writing and debugging programs for these bite-size pieces, and then assembling the programs thus written into a single program. Encapsulation in Java, provided by the class mechanism, is an *extremely* powerful technique.

7.1

Object-Oriented Programming

Object-oriented programming (OOP) supports the view that programs are composed of objects that interact with one another. The fundamental view of an object is that it is composed of values, called *attributes* or *instance variables*, and *attributes* operations that it can perform on those values, called *instance methods*. *instance variables*

Objects are defined with a number of purposes in mind:

- An object *encapsulates* data values within a single entity.
- An object's behavior is often general enough to be *reused* in a variety of situations.
- An object often forms the basis from which other objects can be derived.

Rights of a Client

- To declare variables of the class type.
- To create instances of the class using the class constructors.
- To send messages to instances of the class by invoking the instance methods defined by the class.
- To know the public interface of the class (the names of instance methods, their number and types of parameters, and their return types).
- To know which instance methods alter (mutate) the instance.

Rights of a Class

- To define the public interface for the class.
- To hide all the details of implementation from the client.
- To protect "internal" data from access by the client.
- To change the implementation details *at any time*, provided that the public interface remains intact. (Or, to change the interface, with the concurrence of the client.)

FIGURE 7.1   Rights of clients and classes.

inheritance

This is accomplished by the OOP mechanism of *inheritance*, which we discuss in Chapter 12.

Objects and their clients each have certain rights and responsibilities. The rights are summarized in Figure 7.1.

Underlying all computation in Java is the idea that data are divided into individual chunks called *objects*. Messages requesting an action or value are sent to these objects. You have already used objects in a variety of ways.

For example, let's look at the `Temperature` program from Chapter 3:

```
1   import CSLib.*;
2
3   public class Temperature {
4       //  Convert temperature from Fahrenheit to Centigrade
5       //  Author: Robert Mickunas, March 26, 2001
6
7       public void compute () {
8           double temperature;  // The Fahrenheit temperature.
9           InputBox in;
10          OutputBox out;
11
12          in = new InputBox();
13          in.setPrompt("Please type the temperature (deg F): ");
14          temperature = in.readDouble();
15
16          out = new OutputBox();
17          out.print(temperature);
18          out.print(" deg F is ");
19          out.print((5.0 * (temperature - 32.0)) / 9.0);
```

```
20        out.println(" deg C");
21    }
22  }
```

The first action performed (line 12) is to create an object called in. Objects always reside in memory in an area called the *heap*; after line 12 we can picture the heap as shown in Figure 7.2*a*. In the next line, the program sends that object the message setPrompt, requesting that it write the given string in the InputBox, as shown in Figure 7.2*b*. In line 14, the in object receives the message readInt. It responds by displaying itself on the screen with the given prompt, waiting for the user to enter an integer; once the user types in the input and presses "ok," the InputBox erases itself from the screen. Subsequently the OutputBox, called out, is created and receives four messages, leaving the heap as shown in Figure 7.2*c*. (Note that the InputBox object still exists, even though it no longer appears on the screen. If we were to send it another readInt message, it would again show itself.)

heap

**QUICK EXERCISE
7.1**

Trace the Uppercase program from Chapter 3 (page 73), showing the objects and messages in each step, as in Figure 7.2.

**QUICK EXERCISE
7.2**

Sometimes it can be difficult to know exactly how an object responds to messages. For example, we've said that the InputBox does not show up on the screen until it receives the readInt message; but as far as we can tell by running the program, it shows up as soon as it is created, or perhaps when it receives the setPrompt message. Devise a test, or set of tests, to see when the InputBox actually shows itself on the screen. (*Hint*: Create two boxes and send them messages in different orders.) What about the OutputBox? Does it first display itself on the screen when it is created, when it receives a print message, or when it receives a println message? (*Hint*: Creating two OutputBoxes will not help here; try creating an OutputBox and an InputBox and interleaving message sends to both.)

We don't know what's inside the objects shown in Figure 7.2. However, they must contain some data, because otherwise they wouldn't be able to respond to messages sensibly. For example, the InputBox first receives the setPrompt message, but displays the prompt only when it receives the readInt message. How could it do this without remembering the prompt string? So a look inside the in object would reveal these data, as shown in Figure 7.2, plus probably some more. We won't show you everything in the object now because it's just a bit too complicated to understand at this point. (Since an OutputBox displays

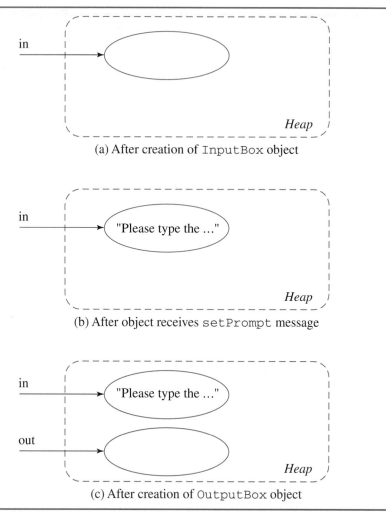

(a) After creation of `InputBox` object

(b) After object receives `setPrompt` message

(c) After creation of `OutputBox` object

FIGURE 7.2   The heap during execution of the Temperature program.

its output as soon as it receives a `print` message, it does not need to remember those strings.)

Different objects contain different data. However, the *kind* of data contained in an object is determined by the class of the object. Thus, any two `InputBox` objects will contain `String` values representing the prompts (at least, they will after they receive the `setPrompt` messages), but they will not necessarily be the same string.

Just as each object contains its own data, so also each responds to its own messages. And again, the set of messages to which an object can respond is determined by the *class* of the object. An `InputBox` object can respond to the setPrompt message, the readInt message, the readDouble message, and a variety of others; it cannot respond to a print or println message. The set of messages to which an object can respond, as determined by its class, is called the *protocol* or *interface* of that object (or class).

protocol

interface

As programmers, we need to know the interface of any objects we want to use. In fact, we must know not only the *names* of the messages and the number and types of arguments they take, but also exactly *what they do*. We should be able to find this information in the documentation of the class. On the other hand, we do not need to know exactly what local data are in an object. We can infer that an InputBox contains some String data, but we don't know, or care, what other data it contains.

To summarize, an object is a kind of container stored in the *heap*. It contains local data in its instance variables, and it responds to messages that are in its *protocol* or *interface*. A program that uses an object is called a *client* of the object. To write a client, we need to know the interface of that object, but we usually don't need to know what kind of data it contains.

Clocks Revisited

We are going to examine the Clock class from Chapter 5 (reproduced here) in a bit more detail, and we will modify it and add some more details to it.

```
1    import CSLib.*;
2    import java.awt.*;
3
4    public class Clock {
5       // Maintain a clock.
6       // Author: Courtney Mickunas, November 21, 2000
7
8       int hour,
9           minute;
10
11      public void setup () {
12         hour = 12;
13         minute = 0;
14      }
15
16      // Obtain values for hour and minute from user input.
17      public void getData () {
18         InputBox in = new InputBox();
19         in.setPrompt("What is the hour?");
20         hour = in.readInt();
21         in.setPrompt("What is the minute?");
22         minute = in.readInt();
23      }
```

```
24
25      // Return the current time as a string.
26      public String toString() { return (hour + ":" + minute); }
27
28      public void setHour (int h) { hour = h; }
29      public void setMinute (int m) { minute = m; }
30
31      public int getHour () { return hour; }
32      public int getMinute () { return minute; }
33
34      // Compare the time of this clock to another.
35      // Return true if this time is less than
36      // the time of the other clock.
37      public boolean priorTo (Clock c) {
38        return (hour < c.getHour() ||
39              hour == c.getHour() && minute < c.getMinute()
40              );
41      }
42
43      // Draw a clock with radius r at (x,y) in the DrawingBox d
44      public void display (DrawingBox d, int x, int y, int r) {
45        double theta;     // angle from 12:00
46        int x1, y1;       // end point of a clock hand
47
48        // Draw the clock in black.
49        d.setColor(Color.black);
50        d.drawOval(x-r, y-r, 2*r, 2*r);
51
52        // Set the color to blue for the hands
53        d.setColor(Color.blue);
54        // Draw the minute hand.
55        theta = 2*Math.PI*minute/60.0;
56        x1 = x + (int)(r*Math.sin(theta));
57        y1 = y - (int)(r*Math.cos(theta));
58        d.drawLine(x, y, x1, y1);
59
60        // Draw the hour hand.
61        theta = 2*Math.PI*(hour+minute/60.0)/12.0;
62        x1 = x + (int)(r*.8*Math.sin(theta));
63        y1 = y - (int)(r*.8*Math.cos(theta));
64        d.drawLine(x, y, x1, y1);
65      }
66    }
```

We said in Chapter 5 that a class definition has the form

```
public class Name {
    declarations of instance variables

    method definitions
}
```

But we know that a class has one or more constructors—remember that we are able to use the simple `InputBox()` constructor as well as the one that takes the title string as a parameter. Somewhere inside the class definition there must also be the definitions of constructors. Indeed, a class definition actually has the form

```
public class  name {
       declarations of instance variables

       constructor definitions

       method definitions
}
```

The *instance variables* say what kinds of local data the objects of that class contain. The *method definitions* give the interface of the class and say exactly what an object does when it receives each kind of message. (We use the term *message* to refer to the name of the method, and *method* to refer to its implementation, but the two terms are sometimes used interchangeably.) The *constructor* says how to initialize the instance variables of a brand new object.

instance variables

method definitions

constructor

7.3

Constructors

When a new `Clock` object is created, we need to assign some values to the instance variables. This is the job of the constructor. A constructor is called automatically whenever an object is created using `new`. In this case `setup` does exactly what the constructor should do, so now we'll *replace* `setup` by the `Clock` constructor.

```
public class Clock {
  // Maintain a clock.
  // Author: Courtney Mickunas, November 21, 2000

  int hour,
      minute;

  public Clock () {
    hour = 12;
    minute = 0;
  }
       ...              ←─ other methods
}
```

Notice the special form that the constructor takes—it looks like a regular instance method, but there is no return type specified and it has the same name as the class.

Initializing instance variables is just a matter of assigning to them, as with ordinary variables. Of course, when a constructor is called to initialize a new object, only the instance variables in that new object get modified; any previously created objects are unaffected by the assignment.

```
Clock c1 = new Clock();   // c1 set to 12:00
c1.setHour(8);
c1.setMinute(30);         // c1 set to 8:30
Clock c2 = new Clock();   // c2 set to 12:00;  c1 still 8:30
```

QUICK EXERCISE 7.3	Add a second hand to the clock. You will need to add another instance variable, change the constructor, add a new `setSecond` method, and change the `display` method.

7.3.1 Overloading Constructors

> Well, "slithy" means "lithe and slimy" . . . You see it's
> like a portmanteau—there are two meanings packed up
> into one word.
>
> —Lewis Carroll
> *Through the Looking-Glass*

A class can have more than one constructor. All the constructors have the same name—the name of the class—but differ in the number and/or types of the arguments. When a new object is created using `new`, this acts as a method call with arguments; the arguments provided by the client determine which constructor will be used.

For example, we could add the constructor that takes arguments for initializing the time, making our class:

```
public class Clock {
  // Maintain a clock.
  // Author: Courtney Mickunas, November 21, 2000

  int hour,
      minute;

  public Clock () {
    hour = 12;
    minute = 0;
  }

  public Clock (int h, int m) {
    hour = h;
    minute = m;
  }
      ...              ←──| other methods |
  }
```

Then a client could write

```
Clock c1 = new Clock(8, 20);
```

and it would be the same as writing

```
Clock c1 = new Clock();
c1.setHour(8);
c1.setMinute(20);
```

Add the new constructor just given. Then add a new constructor to be used to set the clock to an exact hour:

```
public Clock (int h) {
    hour = h;
    minute = 0;
}
```

Write a client that uses each of the new constructors.

**QUICK EXERCISE
7.4**

Leaving the new constructors you just added in the class, add another new constructor that sets the hour to 12 and the minute to its argument:

```
public Clock (int m) {
    hour = 12;
    minute = m;
}
```

What happens when you compile the class? Why?

**QUICK EXERCISE
7.5**

7.4

Overloading Methods

Methods can also be overloaded; that is, they can have different versions with a different number and/or types of arguments. This occurs with `OutputBox` since it has a variety of `print` methods, each taking a different type of parameter (`int`, `double`, `String`, `boolean`, etc.).

For another example, consider the `Clock`'s `display` method:

```
public void display (DrawingBox d, int x, int y, int r) { ... }
```

It displays the clock face with radius r and center (x, y) that are supplied by the caller. Suppose you wanted to define a method that draws the clock in the middle of the drawing window. You could define the method as follows:

```
5      // Draw a clock with radius r in the center of the DrawingBox
6      public void display (DrawingBox d, int r) {
7        int x, y;
8        x = d.getDrawableWidth()/2;
9        y = d.getDrawableHeight()/2;
10
11       double theta;     // angle from 12:00
12       int x1, y1;       // end point of a clock hand
13
14       // Draw the clock in black.
15       d.setColor(Color.black);
16       d.drawOval(x-r, y-r, 2*r, 2*r);
17
18       // Set the color to blue for the hands
19       d.setColor(Color.blue);
20       // Draw the minute hand.
21       theta = 2*Math.PI*minute/60.0;
22       x1 = x + (int)(r*Math.sin(theta));
23       y1 = y - (int)(r*Math.cos(theta));
24       d.drawLine(x, y, x1, y1);
25
26       // Draw the hour hand.
27       theta = 2*Math.PI*(hour+minute/60.0)/12.0;
28       x1 = x + (int)(r*.8*Math.sin(theta));
29       y1 = y - (int)(r*.8*Math.cos(theta));
30       d.drawLine(x, y, x1, y1);
31     }
```

This method

1. Computes x as d.getDrawableWidth()/2.
2. Computes y as d.getDrawableHeight()/2.
3. Then continues to do *exactly* what the old display does with (d, x, y, r).

We don't need to remove the old method. (In fact, we *shouldn't* remove the old method, since there might be existing clients who want to continue using the old method.) With both of them in the class, we can write

```
Clock c2 = new Clock(10, 15);
DisplayBox d = new DisplayBox();
c2.display(d, 150);
```

The result is shown in Figure 7.3.

As with the constructors, the definitions *must* differ in either the number or type of arguments, or the javac compiler will complain.

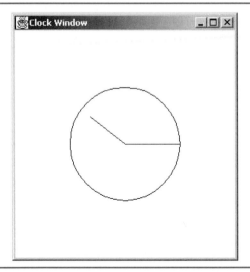

FIGURE 7.3 **A** Clock **object displayed in the middle of the** DrawingBox.

You can see how your Java compiler resolves overloading in specific cases by experiment. For example, consider this program, which tests what a compiler does for ambiguous overloading:

```
public class OverloadTest {

    int f(double x, int i) {return i;}

    int f(int i, double x) {return i;}

}
```

Write programs to determine how your compiler resolves the following overloading situations:

1. Method f has two definitions. In the first it has one argument, of type double; in the second it has two arguments, of types int and double. It is called with a single integer argument.
2. Method g has two definitions, both with two arguments. In one, both arguments are of type int, and in the other they are of type double. Here g is called with one integer and one double argument.

7.5

Methods Invoking Methods

Consider again the `display` methods of the `Clock` class. The new and old versions of `display` are very similar. In fact, the old version is more general than the new: Any client who sends a message

```
display(d, r);
```

could instead send

```
display(d, d.getDrawableWidth()/2, d.getDrawableHeight()/2, r);
```

thereby calling the old method instead, and it would have the same effect. So why do we need the new version at all? Why don't we insist that clients do the work required of the old method? The reason is that it would be more considerate of the clients to include both methods. The question is, How can we provide both methods without having to include nearly identical code in two places? The solution is to use the old version to implement the new one.

```
public void display(DrawingBox d, int r) {
  receiver-of-the-present-message.display(d,
                                d.getDrawableWidth()/2,
                                d.getDrawableHeight()/2,
                                r);
}
```

where *receiver-of-the-present-message* is the `Clock` object that received this call of `display(d,r)`. However, we have no way to *name* the receiver of a method within the body of that method. So how can we finish this code?

It turns out that, within the body of a method such as `display(d,r)`, another method of the same class [such as `display(d,x,y,r)`] can be called with the same receiver by calling that method *with no explicit receiver* at all. The method becomes

```
// Draw a clock with radius r in the center of the DrawingBox
public void display (DrawingBox d, int r) {
  display(d, d.getDrawableWidth()/2, d.getDrawableHeight()/2, r);
}
```

If `c` is a variable of type `Clock` and a client sends the `display(d,r)` message to `c` [that is, makes the call `c.display(d, r)`], then `display(DrawingBox d, int r)` will send the `display(d, d.getDrawableWidth()/2, d.getDrawableHeight()/2, r)` message to `c`.

7.5.1 An Improved Version of `Clock`

We should also correct some of the deficiencies of the `Clock` class. Recall that we can set a `Clock`'s time by invoking `void setHour(int h)` and `void setMinute(int m)`. In all versions of `Clock` so far, these methods simply set the `Clock`'s instance variables to the parameters:

```
public void setHour (int h) { hour = h; }
public void setMinute (int m) { minute = m; }
```

Consequently, we could set the time to foolish values such as $-57 : 63$. What we should have done is to set the hour so that it is between 1 and 12, and set the minute so that it is between 0 and 59. We really should have set the hour and the minute together, since they are obviously related. So we're going to change the Clock class to have a single method to set the time. Conceptually, we should have this:

```
public void set (int h, int m) {
   hour = h;
   minute = m;
}
```

But we also want to "correct" out-of-range values that might be supplied for h and m. A value such as $-57 : 63$ should be thought of as a clock that starts at 12:00 (represented as 12 hours and 0 minutes), then is turned back 57 hours, then is turned forward 63 minutes. As a result, we have a clock that is identical to one whose time is set to $4 : 03$. The easiest way to perform the needed computation is to convert the hours to minutes, thereby determining how many minutes to turn forward or backward. Then we note that turning 12 hours in either direction takes us back to where we started. So we convert the number to a value between $-(12 \times 60)$ and (12×60) by modulo ($\%$), then transform to a positive number (if necessary) by adding (12×60), and then separate into hours and minutes. So $-57 : 63$ corresponds to

$$
\begin{aligned}
-57{:}63 \quad &= -57 * 60 + 63 \text{ minutes} \\
&= -3420 + 63 \text{ minutes} \\
&= -3357 \text{ minutes} \\
&= -3357 \% (12 * 60) \text{ minutes} \\
&= -477 \text{ minutes} \\
&= -477 + (12 * 60) \text{ minutes} \\
&= 243 \text{ minutes} \\
&= 243/60 \text{ hours}, 243\%60 \text{ minutes} \\
&= 4 \text{ hours}, 3 \text{ minutes} \\
&= 4{:}03
\end{aligned}
$$

A further complication is that 0 hours should translate to 12 hours. So the proper computation is

```
public void set (int h, int m) {
   int totalMinutes = (h * 60 + m) % (12 * 60);
   // totalMinutes is between -(12 * 60) and (12 * 60)
   if (totalMinutes < 0) totalMinutes = totalMinutes + (12 * 60);
   hour = totalMinutes / 60;
   if (hour == 0) hour = 12;
   minute = totalMinutes % 60;
}
```

We should also rewrite both setHour and setMinute to work with out-of-range values. Remembering the little trick we used with display, we can simply have setHour and setMinute each call set:

QUICK EXERCISE 7.7	Write a simple program that prints a table showing that set works correctly for values of h ranging from −50 to +50 and values of m ranging from −100 to +100.

```
public void setHour (int h) { set(h, minute); }

public void setMinute (int m) { set(hour, m); }
```

We should also take care to have the constructors use set instead of assigning directly to hour and minute, and to correct input that is obtained by getData:

```
public Clock () {
    set(12,0);
}

public Clock (int hour, int minute) {
    set(hour, minute);
}

// Obtain values for hour and minute from user input.
public void getData () {
    InputBox in = new InputBox();
    in.setPrompt("What is the hour?");
    setHour(in.readInt());
    in.setPrompt("What is the minute?");
    setMinute(in.readInt());
}
```

Recall also the code for priorTo:

```
// Compare the time of this clock to another.
// Return true if this time is less than
// the time of the other clock.
public boolean priorTo (Clock c) {
    return (hour < c.getHour() ||
            hour == c.getHour() && minute < c.getMinute()
           );
}
```

Coding this required that we be able to look at the instance variables of c, so we used c.getHour() and c.getMinute(). It would be better if we could look at the instance variables of c directly. But—and this is crucial—we know how to see the instance variables only of the *receiver* of the message, and c is *not* the receiver. Rather, it is an argument that has type Clock; the receiver, as always, is implicit.

We already have used dot notation to send a message to an instance of a class. Dot notation also is used by methods of a class C to see the instance variables of objects of type C other than the receiver: name the object, followed by a period and then the name of the instance variable. Thus, the definition of priorTo would be more cleanly written as

```
// Compare the time of this clock to another.
// Return true if this time is less than
// the time of the other clock.
public boolean priorTo (Clock c) {
  return (hour < c.hour ||
          hour == c.hour && minute < c.minute
          );
}
```

Finally, look again at the display method that eventually does the drawing:

```
43      // Draw a clock with radius r at (x,y) in the DrawingBox d
44      public void display (DrawingBox d, int x, int y, int r) {
45         double theta;     // angle from 12:00
46         int x1, y1;       // end point of a clock hand
47
48         // Draw the clock in black.
49         d.setColor(Color.black);
50         d.drawOval(x-r, y-r, 2*r, 2*r);
51
52         // Set the color to blue for the hands
53         d.setColor(Color.blue);
54         // Draw the minute hand.
55         theta = 2*Math.PI*minute/60.0;
56         x1 = x + (int)(r*Math.sin(theta));
57         y1 = y - (int)(r*Math.cos(theta));
58         d.drawLine(x, y, x1, y1);
59
60         // Draw the hour hand.
61         theta = 2*Math.PI*(hour+minute/60.0)/12.0;
62         x1 = x + (int)(r*.8*Math.sin(theta));
63         y1 = y - (int)(r*.8*Math.cos(theta));
64         d.drawLine(x, y, x1, y1);
65      }
```

The code that draws the minute hand (lines 55 through 58) is very similar to the code that draws the hour hand (lines 61 through 64). We put this common code into a separate method (drawHand), and then we call drawHand with appropriate arguments.

```
// Draw a clock with radius r at (x,y) in the DrawingBox d
public void display (DrawingBox d, int x, int y, int r) {
  double theta;     // angle from 12:00
  int x1, y1;       // end point of a clock hand

  // Draw the clock in black.
  d.setColor(Color.black);
  d.drawOval(x-r, y-r, 2*r, 2*r);

  // Set the color to blue for the hands
  d.setColor(Color.blue);
  // Draw the minute hand.
  drawHand(d, x, y, r, minute/60.0, 1.0);
```

```
    // Draw the hour hand.
    drawHand(d, x, y, r, (hour+minute/60.0)/12.0, 0.8);
  }

  public void drawHand (DrawingBox d, int x, int y, int r,
                        double fraction, double scale) {
    int x1, y1;
    double theta = 2*Math.PI*fraction;
    x1 = x + (int)(r*scale*Math.sin(theta));
    y1 = y - (int)(r*scale*Math.cos(theta));
    d.drawLine(x, y, x1, y1);
  }
```

Although this doesn't save us either much space or much execution time in this case, it *does* isolate the complicated calculation, reducing the chance of our making an error in typing the code.

7.6

`this`

Odd as it may seem, an object can contain a reference to itself! Not only can it, but in fact every object automatically has available an instance variable called `this` that points to the object itself.

Even though you haven't declared it, you can use `this` as a variable in any of the class's methods. Normally, there is little point in doing so. There is no advantage to referring to an instance variable x as `this.x`, although it is quite legal to do so. Similarly, to send a message m to the receiver of the current message, you can write either `m(..args..)` or `this.m(..args..)`. In other words, `this.` is implicit in any reference to an instance variable or any method sent to the current receiver.

There are three cases when it is useful to refer to `this` explicitly, one minor and two major.

7.6.1 Avoiding Variable Name Collisions

The minor one is a common idiom when a method argument is being used simply to fill in the value of an instance variable, as occurs in our `set` method:

```
1    public void set (int h, int m) {
2       int totalMinutes = (h * 60 + m) % (12 * 60);
3       // totalMinutes is between -(12 * 60) and (12 * 60)
4       if (totalMinutes < 0) totalMinutes = totalMinutes + (12 * 60
5       hour = totalMinutes / 60;
6       if (hour == 0) hour = 12;
```

```
7       minute = totalMinutes % 60;
8   }
```

`this` can be used to distinguish an argument or local variable from an instance variable. If a method has an argument or local variable x and it also has an instance variable x, then `this.x` *always* refers to the instance variable. Thus, you will often see the above method written like this:

```
1   public void set (int hour, int minute) {
2       int totalMinutes = (hour * 60 + minute) % (12 * 60);
3       // totalMinutes is between -(12 * 60) and (12 * 60)
4       if (totalMinutes < 0) totalMinutes = totalMinutes + (12 * 60);
5       this.hour = totalMinutes / 60;
6       if (this.hour == 0) this.hour = 12;
7       this.minute = totalMinutes % 60;
8   }
```

In line 2, `hour` and `minute` are the arguments; in lines 5 through 7, `this.hour` and `this.minute` are the instance variables. This form is just a little bit clearer than the first, because the argument names indicate the purpose of each argument.

7.6.2 Passing the Receiver as an Argument

The second use of `this` as a variable arises in situations like the following. We have a method `boolean priorTo (Clock c)` to tell if the receiver's time is prior to c's. Let's consider how we might add the instance method `boolean after (Clock c)` to our class. This method should tell us whether the receiver represents a time later than c, the opposite of `priorTo`. We might try to code this as

```
public boolean after (Clock c) {
   return !priorTo(c);
}
```
Wrong

but this code will also return true if c is the *same time* as the receiver, which is not what it should do.

The correct code would do something like this:

```
public boolean after (Clock c) {
   return c.priorTo( receiver of this message);
}
```

The problem is that we again need to refer to the receiver of the message. The last time we were in this predicament (with `display` on page 226), we found that we could send a message *to the receiver of the current message* without explicitly naming the receiver. Here, we have no such easy solution, because we are passing the receiver of the current message as an argument, rather than sending a message to it.

 We can use `this` as if it were a variable referring to the receiver of the message:

```
public boolean after (Clock c) {
  return c.priorTo(this);
}
```

7.6.3 Chaining Constructors

You may have noticed that the two most recent `Clock` constructors are very similar:

```
public Clock () {
  set(12,0);
}

public Clock (int hour, int minute) {
  set(hour, minute);
}
```

So you might wonder whether we can eliminate some of the code duplication by having one call the other, as we did with the two versions of `display`. However, constructors are not invoked in the same way as other methods—they are invoked when a new object is created with `new`. Nonetheless, chaining constructors is something that is useful to do, and Java provides a special syntax for doing it.

From within one constructor, you can call another constructor by writing

> `this` (*arguments to the constructor*) ;

The usual strategy is to write one detailed constructor that has all possible parameters, then to write a number of additional constructors that take some subset of the parameters, and provide default values for the remaining ones. So our two constructors can be written

```
public Clock () {
  this(12,0);
}

public Clock (int hour, int minute) {
  set(hour, minute);
}
```

This doesn't buy us much in this particular case. But often there is a lot of duplicated code between constructors, and not only can this technique save some code, but also it can prevent careless errors by isolating all the working code in one constructor.

The UML class diagram for our expanded `Clock` class is

```
                          Clock

        hour: int
        minute: int

        Clock()
        Clock( :int, :int)
        setup( :int, :int)
        getdata()
        toString(): String
        setHour( :int)
        setMinute( :int)
        set( :int, :int)
        getHour(): int
        getMinute(): int
        priorTo( :Clock): boolean
        after( :Clock): boolean
        display( :DrawingBox, :int)
        display( :DrawingBox, :int, :int,:int)
```

A complete listing of the Clock class, with all its new methods, is as follows:

```
1   import CSLib.*;
2   import java.awt.*;
3
4   public class Clock {
5      // Maintain a clock.
6      // Author: Courtney Mickunas, November 21, 2000
7
8      int hour,
9          minute;
10
11     public Clock () {
12        this(12,0);
13     }
14
15     public Clock (int hour, int minute) {
16        set(hour, minute);
17     }
18
19     // Obtain values for hour and minute from user input.
20     public void getData () {
21        InputBox in = new InputBox();
22        in.setPrompt("What is the hour?");
23        setHour(in.readInt());
24        in.setPrompt("What is the minute?");
25        setMinute(in.readInt());
```

```
26        }
27
28        // Return the current time as a string.
29        public String toString () { return (hour + ":" + minute); }
30
31        public void setHour (int h) { set(h, minute); }
32        public void setMinute (int m) { set(hour, m); }
33
34        public void set (int hour, int minute) {
35          int totalMinutes = (hour * 60 + minute) % (12 * 60);
36          // totalMinutes is between -(12 * 60) and (12 * 60)
37          if (totalMinutes < 0) totalMinutes = totalMinutes + (12 * 60)
38          this.hour = totalMinutes / 60;
39          if (this.hour == 0) this.hour = 12;
40          this.minute = totalMinutes % 60;
41        }
42
43        public int getHour () { return hour; }
44        public int getMinute () { return minute; }
45
46        // Compare the time of this clock to another.
47        // Return true if this time is less than
48        // the time of the other clock.
49        public boolean priorTo (Clock c) {
50          return (hour < c.hour ||
51                  hour == c.hour && minute < c.minute
52                 );
53        }
54
55        public boolean after (Clock c) {
56          return c.priorTo(this);
57        }
58
59        // Draw a clock with radius r in the center of the DrawingBox
60        public void display (DrawingBox d, int r) {
61          display(d, d.getDrawableWidth()/2, d.getDrawableHeight()/2, r
62        }
63
64        // Draw a clock with radius r at (x,y) in the DrawingBox d
65        public void display (DrawingBox d, int x, int y, int r) {
66          double theta;      // angle from 12:00
67          int x1, y1;        // end point of a clock hand
68
69          // Draw the clock in black.
70          d.setColor(Color.black);
71          d.drawOval(x-r, y-r, 2*r, 2*r);
72
73          // Set the color to blue for the hands
74          d.setColor(Color.blue);
75          // Draw the minute hand.
76          drawHand(d, x, y, r, minute/60.0, 1.0);
77
78          // Draw the hour hand.
79          drawHand(d, x, y, r, (hour+minute/60.0)/12.0, 0.8);
```

```
80        }
81
82        public void drawHand (DrawingBox d, int x, int y, int r,
83                              double fraction, double scale) {
84           int x1, y1;
85           double theta = 2*Math.PI*fraction;
86           x1 = x + (int)(r*scale*Math.sin(theta));
87           y1 = y - (int)(r*scale*Math.cos(theta));
88           d.drawLine(x, y, x1, y1);
89        }
90     }
```

7.7

Visibility Qualifiers

From a client's point of view, an object is what engineers call a *black box*. It performs some useful functions, but its internal structure is completely unknown to its clients. This may sound like a bad thing, but quite the opposite is true. The ability to think of devices as black boxes is crucial to controlling the complexity of the machines that contain them. If an engineer had to know how every part of a machine worked in detail before being able to use it, nothing would ever get built! Furthermore, no part of a machine could be upgraded to a newer, better version, since the entire mechanism was built upon the knowledge that the original part had a certain internal structure.

Objects are the devices that make up our machines (i.e., programs). Each object provides services to clients in the form of messages that it can receive. Each "device" has an internal structure—the set of instance variables in each object and the implementations of the methods—which should be totally opaque to its clients. As long as the methods do what they're supposed to do, we do not care how they are implemented or what data the objects contain.

Unfortunately, this commonsense approach to building programs—what might be called the *information-hiding* approach—is too easily violated. One of the reasons we divide our programs into classes is so that the data of each can be protected from the other's methods. But we have failed to do so up to now. In fact, a client of Clock could actually write

information-hiding

```
1     Clock c = new Clock();
2     c.set(4, 30);
3     c.hour = 3;   // Shouldn't be allowed!!
4     c.display(d, 150);
```

In line 3, the client has done just what we said should not be done: directly accessed the instance variables of the object. For whatever reason, the client wasn't satisfied with using the clock as a black box—that is, just by sending it messages—but instead felt the need to look directly at the instance variables of the object. Just as with the mechanical device, we have lost the ability to *change* the Clock implementation. Now we must guarantee that, whatever we do, there is still an hour instance variable.

What should the client's programmer have done? First, she should have tried to live with the set of methods that the Clock class provides. In this case, writing c.set(3, 30) would have been just as good as writing c.hour = 3. Second, if that weren't possible, she should have negotiated with the owner of the class to add the methods she needed. Perhaps the owner would have pointed out the solution we just gave, or perhaps he would have written a new setHour method. In any case, he would have had an opportunity to provide a solution so that the client didn't have to violate the information-hiding principle.

visibility qualifiers

In Java, the writer of a class can *enforce* information hiding by using *visibility qualifiers* on instance variables. There are two such qualifiers: public and private (plus one more that we'll see in Chapter 12). They are used by placing them at the beginning of a variable declaration:

```
public int x;   //  Anyone with an object o of this class
                //  can access x by writing o.x
private int y;  //  No one can directly access y except
                //  the methods defined in this class
```

In general, public instance variables are those the clients of a class should be allowed to access, while the private ones are only for the methods of this class to see.

To enforce complete information hiding, *all instance variables should be declared* private.

QUICK EXERCISE 7.8 — Declare all the instance variables of Clock private. Which of the clients that we've used with Clock so far continue to work, and which do not?

In most of our programs, we have given no visibility modifiers on instance variables. We did this to avoid clutter and to have one fewer thing to explain, but it was a mistake. Instance variables without visibility modifiers have a visibility between public and private—they can be accessed by some classes but not all. Details are given in Chapter 12, but the bottom line is that this still allows too much access, so we should not be doing it. We should use private everywhere.

Everywhere? Then why have public instance variables at all? When a programmer is certain that the representation of a data item will not change, it is simpler, and makes life easier for the clients, to make the instance variables public. An example is the class Point, which is one of the classes provided by the Java system. Its purpose is to represent an (x, y) location in a graphical window, such as a DrawingBox. Here, the only sensible representation is the pair of integers giving the x and y coordinates of the point, in pixels, and there seems no reason to hide this from clients. Here, in simplified form, is the definition of `Point`:

```
public class Point {
    /** The x coordinate.  */
    public int x;

    /** The y coordinate. */
    public int y;

    public Point () { this(0, 0); }

    public Point (Point p) { this(p.x, p.y); }

    public Point (int x, int y) {
      this.x = x;
      this.y = y;
    }

    public double getX () { return x; }

    public double getY () { return y; }

    public Point getLocation () { return new Point(x, y); }

    public void setLocation (Point p) { setLocation(p.x, p.y); }

    public void setLocation (int x, int y) { move(x, y); }

    public void move (int x, int y) {
      this.x = x;
      this.y = y;
    }

    public boolean equals (Point pt) {
      return (x == pt.x) && (y == pt.y);
    }

    public String toString () {
      return "Point[x=" + x + ",y=" + y + "]";
    }
}
```

Notice that the class has three overloaded constructors that are chained using `this`, and that the `setLocation` method is also overloaded. The version of `equals` that we show is a simplified version of the actual method, but it illustrates the idea of comparing two `Point`s. Finally, the `toString` method allows us to print `Point` objects (usually for debugging purposes). When we use the `Point` class, the *x* coordinate of an instance p can be obtained by writing either `p.getX()` or `p.x`, and likewise for the *y* coordinate. We'll use the `Point` class in a number of upcoming graphical programs.

Methods can also have visibility qualifiers, and they mean the same thing as they do with instance variables:

QUICK EXERCISE 7.9	Add new `display` methods to the `Clock` class that take a `Point` argument, instead of an (x, y) pair of `int`s, to specify the center of the clock.

```
public void f () {   //  Anyone who has an object o of this
                     //  class can send it the message f
                     //  by writing o.f()
    ...
}

private void g () {  //  No one can send g to an object except
                     //    another method in this class
    ...
}
```

As before, unannotated methods have a visibility that is between public and private (again, see Chapter 12 for details). Recall the `drawHand` method that we added to `Clock` (page 229). It was never intended that `drawHand` be callable by clients—it was simply a "helper" method for our `display` method. In other words, `drawHand` should be declared `private`.

In UML diagrams, variables and methods that are private are shown with a leading minus sign, those that are public have a leading plus sign, and those that are unannotated have a blank prefix. So far we have not shown these symbols, but we will from here on.

7.8

Mutability

> What man that sees the ever-whirling wheel
> Of Change, the which all mortal things doth sway,
> But that thereby doth find, and plainly feel,
> How Mutability in them doth play
> Her cruel sports, to many men's decay?
>
> —E. Spenser
> *The Faerie Queene*

Often we want to transform an object from one state to another. For example, we may want to change the prompt in an `InputBox`, change the time held by a `Clock`, or change the capitalization of a `String`. In dealing with objects, there is often a choice between two ways of changing an object:

- **Mutation.** An object can be changed by assigning a new value to one or more of its instance variables. In the `Clock` class, when we say

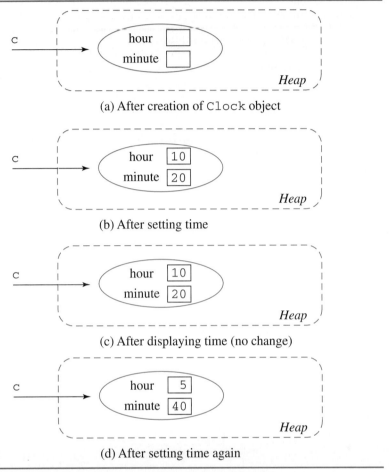

(a) After creation of Clock object

(b) After setting time

(c) After displaying time (no change)

(d) After setting time again

FIGURE 7.4 **The heap while executing mutating code.**

c.set(3, 10), the instance variables of c are altered. Thus, in executing the statements

```
1    d = new DrawingBox();
2    c = new Clock();
3    c.set(10,20);
4    c.display(d, 50, 50, 50);
5    c.set(5,40);
```

the sequence of states is as shown in Figure 7.4. c is the only Clock object ever created.

- **Nonmutation.** Instead of changing an object, we can create a new object similar to the original object, with just the required change. This requires that the methods within the class create new instances of that class. For example, the set method in Clock could be changed to

```
public Clock set_nonmut (int hour, int minute) {
   Clock c1 = new Clock();      // Create new object
   c1.set(hour, minute);        // Set its fields
   return c1;                   // Return new object
}
```

or more concisely,

```
public Clock set_nonmut (int hour, int minute) {
   return new Clock(hour, minute);
}
```

Note that the return type of this method (in either case) is Clock, not void.

As another example, suppose we want to include a method addHours that adds some number of hours to the time. Here are mutating (addHours_mut) and nonmutating (addHours_nonmut) versions:

```
public void addHours_mut (int i) {
   setHour(hour+i);
}

public Clock addHours_nonmut (int i) {
   return new Clock (hour+i, minute);
}
```

These methods do quite different things. To see how different, suppose the following lines occur in a program:

```
la_time = new Clock(8, 20);
chicago_time = la_time.addHours_mut(2);        Wrong
ny_time = chicago_time.addHours_mut(1);
```

If the idea is to create three clocks, representing times in three cities, then addHours_nonmut is the appropriate method to use, because it creates three clocks. If we use addHours_mut, it leaves only a single clock, and the application fails to work correctly.

It is not necessarily obvious whether to use mutating or nonmutating methods in a given situation. Mutating methods are usually a little easier to write and use, as in our small example, but they can make programs harder to understand. To see how, consider these four lines that might appear in the middle of a program:

```
c1.set(4, 30);
c2.set(5, 40);
c1.display(d, 50, 50, 50);
c2.display(d, 150, 50, 50);
```

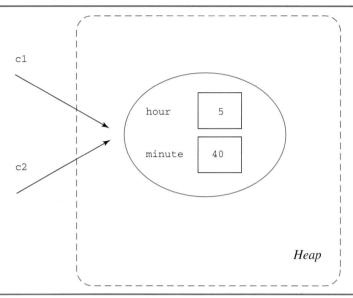

FIGURE 7.5   After assigning c1 **to** c2.

You would surely assume that the result would be the display of a 4:30 clock centered at $(50, 50)$ and of a 5:30 clock centered at $(150, 50)$. However, it is possible that *both* clocks will display 5:30. Can you see how this might happen?

One way it could happen is if the lines above were preceded by these:

```
Clock c1 = new Clock();
Clock c2 = c1;
```

After executing these two lines, the heap appears as in Figure 7.5.

Only objects are mutable. Primitive values like ints are not: When we write x+4 for integer variable x, we don't expect this operation to *change the contents* of x! Rather, a variable changes only when an assignment is made to it. With mutating operations, an object can change just by sending it a message.

Objects are not *necessarily* mutable. They are only mutable if the interface includes mutating methods. One example of a class with no mutating operations is String. For example, when we concatenate two strings by writing s1 + s2, neither of the strings s1 or s2 changes.

7.9

Design Decisions, Representation Independence, and Debugging

> Your glazing is new and your plumbing's strange,
> But otherwise I perceive no change;
>
> —Rudyard Kipling
> *A Truthful Song*

representation independence

implementation independence

In this section we explore a number of aspects of object-oriented programming. We see that by encapsulating the data for an object using the class construct, we can alter the representation of those data without affecting the class's previous behavior. Consequently, existing clients of that class will "perceive no change" in its behavior. This feature of OOP is called *representation independence* or *implementation independence*.

The Clock class that finally emerged (page 235) involves an association between the Clock class and the DrawingBox class. This association is established once a client sends a display message to a Clock object, supplying a DrawingBox object as an argument. This association is illustrated by the UML class diagram in Figure 7.6. Recall that such a diagram can be read "A Clock displays in a DrawingBox." The 0..1 multiplicity near the DrawingBox means that the Clock object may be associated with zero or one DrawingBox object. While a display message is being processed, there is an association with the one DrawingBox that was supplied as an argument; at other times, the association is with no DrawingBoxes. The 0..1 multiplicity near the Clock similarly indicates that during a display message a DrawingBox is associated with only *one* Clock, and the DrawingBox is not associated with any Clock at other times.

In using the Clock class, we may find that a given clock is *always* displayed in the same window. If that is the case, we might wish that we didn't always have to pass the DrawingBox in to display the clock. This is easily accomplished by providing the DrawingBox to the Clock's constructors and saving it in an instance variable. We don't want to demand that existing clients modify their code, so we *add* two new constructors that take a DrawingBox as an argument.

FIGURE 7.6   UML class diagram for the Clock-DrawingBox **association.**

We expect our new clients to send the `display` message *without* specifying a `DrawingBox`, so we must also write those methods. We can leverage our existing `display` methods, just as we did before. The code is identical to that on page 235, with the following additions:

```
1   import CSLib.*;
2   import java.awt.*;
3
4   public class Clock {
5      // Maintain a clock.
6      // Author: Courtney Mickunas, November 21, 2000
7
8      private int hour,
9                        minute;
10     private DrawingBox dbox;
11
12     public Clock (DrawingBox dbox) {
13        this(dbox, 12, 0);
14     }
15
16     public Clock (DrawingBox dbox, int hour, int minute) {
17        this.dbox = dbox;
18        set(hour, minute);
19     }

       ...

69     // Draw clock, radius r, in center of local DrawingBox
70     public void display (int r) {
71        display(dbox, r);
72     }
73
74     // Draw a clock with radius r at (x,y) in the local DrawingBox
75     public void display (int x, int y, int r) {
76        display(dbox, x, y, r);
77     }


79     // Draw clock, radius r, in center of supplied DrawingBox
80     public void display (DrawingBox d, int r) {
81        display(d, d.getDrawableWidth()/2,
82                d.getDrawableHeight()/2);
83     }
84
85     // Draw a clock with radius r at (x,y) in the DrawingBox d
86     public void display (DrawingBox d, int x, int y, int r) {

          ...
       }
     ...
    }
```

Notice that we have declared a private instance variable, dbox, in which we store the reference to the `DrawingBox` that is supplied to the new constructors. (We also made sure that our other instance variables are private.) The new specialized

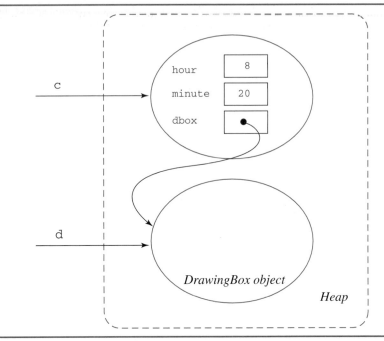

FIGURE 7.7   An object containing a reference to another object.

versions of display just call the old version with the private DrawingBox; the old version doesn't care whether the DrawingBox comes from the new display method or from an outside client.

A typical client for the current version of Clock looks like this:

```
1    import CSLib.*;
2
3    public class ClockClientNew {
4       public static void main (String[] args) {
5          DrawingBox d = new DrawingBox();
6          Clock c1 = new Clock(d, 8, 20);
7          c1.display(50);
8       }
9    }
```

Figure 7.7 shows the objects in existence after executing line 6. The UML class diagram (Figure 7.8) has changed just slightly. Now the association is established at the time a Clock object is created, and it persists throughout the lifetime of that object. Consequently a client might associate a single DrawingBox object with *many* Clocks; therefore the multiplicity for the Clock is 0..*.

Before the new version is released to the public, it is imperative to test it thoroughly. We already verified that it works with a new-style client (supplying a DrawingBox to the constructor), but we must also test it with a typical old-style client (supplying a DrawingBox to the display method):

FIGURE 7.8 UML class diagram for the `Clock-DrawingBox` **association.**

QUICK EXERCISE
7.10

Define a new `display` method that takes no arguments at all—it draws the largest clock possible in the middle of `dbox`.

```
1    import CSLib.*;
2
3    public class ClockClientOld {
4      public static void main (String[] args) {
5        Clock c1 = new Clock(5, 30);
6        DrawingBox d = new DrawingBox();
7        c1.display(d, 50);
8      }
9    }
```

We breathe a sigh of relief when the code passes this test as well! However, we know from experience that clients do not always read the documentation. So we ask what twisted uses a client might make of our new `Clock`. It doesn't take long to find a client that causes trouble:

```
1    import CSLib.*;
2
3    public class ClockClient {
4      public static void main (String[] args) {
5        Clock c1 = new Clock(5, 30);
6        c1.display(50);
7      }
8    }
```

This program leads to a run-time error:

```
java.lang.NullPointerException
        at Clock.display(Clock.java:81)
        at Clock.display(Clock.java:71)
        at ClockClient.main(ClockClient.java:6)
Exception in thread "main"
```

The error "null pointer exception" means that our program attempted to send a message to an object that has not yet been instantiated—it is still "null." The traceback information in the error message tells us the line numbers in `ClockClient` and `Clock` that allow us to trace the sequence of method calls. We find that the trace starts at line 6 in `ClockClient` (the trace needs to be read backward), then proceeds to line 71 of

```
69    // Draw clock, radius r, in center of local DrawingBox
70    public void display (int r) {
71      display(dbox, r);
72    }
```

and finally ends at line 82 of

```
79    // Draw clock, radius r, in center of supplied DrawingBox
80    public void display (DrawingBox d, int r) {
81      display(d, d.getDrawableWidth()/2,
82              d.getDrawableHeight()/2);
83    }
```

We could put debugging print statements in the vicinity of these method calls, for example,

```
    . . .

    OutputBox debug = new OutputBox("Debug Output");

    . . .

    // Draw clock, radius r, in center of local DrawingBox
    public void display (int r) {
      debug.println("Called display(int r) with r="+r);
      display(d, r);
    }

    . . .

    public void display (DrawingBox d, int r) {
      debug.println("Called display(DrawingBox d, int r) with"+
                " d="+d+
                " r="+r);
      display(d, d.getDrawableWidth()/2, d.getDrawableHeight()/2, r);
    }

    . . .
```

The output is

```
Debug Output                                              [X]
┌──────────────────────────────────────────────────────────┐
│ Called display(int r) with r=50                          ▲│
│ Called display(DrawingBox d, int r) with d=null r=50      │
│                                                           ▼│
│◄                                                         ►│
└──────────────────────────────────────────────────────────┘
```

and we quickly discover that dbox is null—that is, it has never been made to refer to a DrawingBox object. Of course, the reason is that the client misused our class—it used the display method that expected a DrawingBox to have been supplied to a constructor; however, the client used one of the *original* constructors that expect the DrawingBox to be supplied to display. No one ever supplied a DrawingBox to the Clock!

There are two ways to handle this dilemma. The less desirable way is to issue a stern warning that clients should not do things this way. The preferred way is to make our Clock class "robust" enough to handle this case. A junior programmer might suggest that we simply add constructor(s) to accommodate the kind of client who would do what we've just seen. Here they are:

```
20      public Clock () {
21         this(12, 0);
22      }
23
24      public Clock (int hour, int minute) {
25         d = new DrawingBox("Internal Clock");
26         d.setDrawableSize(300, 300);
27         set(hour, minute);
28      }
```

Unfortunately, we quickly discover that this gives syntax errors:

```
Clock.java:20: Clock() is already defined in Clock
    public Clock() {
          ^

Clock.java:24: Clock(int,int) is already defined in Clock
    public Clock (int hour, int minute) {
          ^

2 errors
```

Obviously, these two constructors have headings that are exactly the same as two of our other constructors—the ones that are used by our old-style clients. In fact, the only difference is that these new constructors create the private DrawingBox. So perhaps we can use these *instead of* the original constructors. We make that substitution and discover that, indeed, we are now able to handle the contrary client.

What we have done with these new constructors is to establish a *containment* relationship: When a class C has a local variable of class type D, then class C *contains* an object of class D. The new UML diagram is shown in Figure 7.9. The filled diamond is a particular kind of containment called a *composition* in the UML, and it shows that Clock contains a DrawingBox. This is sometimes referred to as the *has-a association*.[1]

containment

UML composition

has-a association

With this mechanism the client is no longer responsible for creating and handling the DrawingBox. When these new constructors are used, the heap

---

[1] The UML actually has two forms of containment: *composition* and *aggregation*, with aggregation being a weaker form of containment than composition. We will not make such a distinction and will use only composition.

FIGURE 7.9 UML class diagram for the `Clock-DrawingBox` **composition.**

looks exactly the same as in Figure 7.7 except that there is no reference to the `DrawingBox` from outside the `Clock` object.

Before we release this version, we must once again verify that it still works as expected for both old-style and new-style clients. Testing shows that there are no problems with the new-style clients. However, here is a simple old-style client:

```
1   import CSLib.*;
2
3   public class ClockClientOld {
4     public static void main (String[] args) {
5       Clock c1 = new Clock(5, 30);
6       DrawingBox d = new DrawingBox("My Clock");
7       d.setDrawableSize(300, 300);
8       c1.display(d, 50);
9     }
10  }
```

When we try this client, we get the unexpected output shown in Figure 7.10. Obviously an old-style client does not want our internal `DrawingBox` to show up at all! Luckily we have a way of fixing this. The `DrawingBox` class has yet another method that we have not yet used (or even told you about).

Name	Description
`void setVisible (boolean b)`	Makes the `DrawingBox` visible if b==true, invisible if b==false

The `setVisible` method is available for `OutputBox` as well. It seems that all we need to do is to make the `DrawingBox` invisible immediately after creating it in the constructor. With this, we have our final version of `Clock`:

```
1   import CSLib.*;
2   import java.awt.*;
3
4   public class Clock {
5     // Maintain a clock.
6     // Author: Courtney Mickunas, November 21, 2000
7
8     int hour,
```

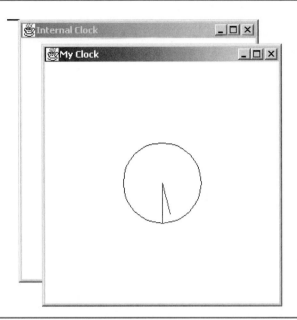

FIGURE 7.10 **Unexpected output from the** `Clock` **containing** `DrawingBox`**.**

```
9          minute;
10    DrawingBox d;
11
12    public Clock () {
13       this(12, 0);
14    }
15
16    public Clock (int hour, int minute) {
17       d = new DrawingBox("Internal Clock");
18       d.setDrawableSize(300, 300);
19       set(hour, minute);
20       d.setVisible(false);
21    }
22
23    public Clock (DrawingBox d) {
24       this(d, 12, 0);
25    }
26
27    public Clock (DrawingBox d, int hour, int minute) {
28       this.d = d;
```

```
29          set(hour, minute);
30      }
31
32      // Obtain values for hour and minute from user input.
33      public void getData () {
34          InputBox in = new InputBox();
35          in.setPrompt("What is the hour?");
36          setHour(in.readInt());
37          in.setPrompt("What is the minute?");
38          setMinute(in.readInt());
39      }
40
41      // Return the current time as a string.
42      public String toString() { return (hour + ":" + minute); }
43
44      public void setHour (int h) { set(h, minute); }
45      public void setMinute (int m) { set(hour, m); }
46
47      public void set (int hour, int minute) {
48          int totalMinutes = (hour * 60 + minute) % (12 * 60);
49          // totalMinutes is between -(12 * 60) and (12 * 60)
50          if (totalMinutes < 0)
51          totalMinutes = totalMinutes + (12 * 60);
52          this.hour = totalMinutes / 60;
53          if (this.hour == 0) this.hour = 12;
54          this.minute = totalMinutes % 60;
55      }
56
57      public int getHour () { return hour; }
58      public int getMinute () { return minute; }
59
60      // Compare the time of this clock to another.
61      // Return true if this time is less than
62      // the time of the other clock.
63      public boolean priorTo (Clock c) {
64          return (hour < c.hour ||
65                  hour == c.hour && minute < c.minute
66                  );
67      }
68
69      public boolean after (Clock c) {
70          return c.priorTo(this);
71      }
72
73      // Draw clock, radius r, in center of local DrawingBox
74      public void display (int r) {
75          display(d, r);
76      }
77
78      // Draw clock, radius r, at (x,y) in local DrawingBox
79      public void display (int x, int y, int r) {
80          display(d, x, y, r);
81      }
82
83      // Draw clock, radius r, in center of supplied DrawingBox
```

```
84    public void display (DrawingBox d, int r) {
85        display(d, d.getDrawableWidth()/2, d.getDrawableHeight()/2, r);
86    }
87
88    // Draw clock, radius r, at (x,y) in supplied DrawingBox
89    public void display (DrawingBox d, int x, int y, int r) {
90        double theta;    // angle from 12:00
91        int x1, y1;      // end point of a clock hand
92
93        d.setVisible(true);
94
95        // Draw the clock in black.
96        d.setColor(Color.black);
97        d.drawOval(x-r, y-r, 2*r, 2*r);
98
99        // Set the color to blue for the hands
100       d.setColor(Color.blue);
101       // Draw the minute hand.
102       drawHand(d, x, y, r, minute/60.0, 1.0);
103
104       // Draw the hour hand.
105       drawHand(d, x, y, r, (hour+minute/60.0)/12.0, 0.8);
106   }
107
108   private void drawHand (DrawingBox d, int x, int y, int r,
109                          double fraction, double scale) {
110       int x1, y1;
111       double theta = 2*Math.PI*fraction;
112       x1 = x + (int)(r*scale*Math.sin(theta));
113       y1 = y - (int)(r*scale*Math.cos(theta));
114       d.drawLine(x, y, x1, y1);
115   }
116 }
```

7.9.1 Representation Independence

The primary goal in producing a well-structured program is that it should be easy
to understand and modify. It should be easy to make common types of changes
in programs, such as altering the method of input or the format of output, without
producing unexpected errors in seemingly unrelated parts of the program.

Methods and classes are powerful structuring mechanisms. A method encapsulates the specific actions involved in producing a result; since it is common
to change the algorithm or other aspects of the method, this kind of isolation is
very helpful. A class encapsulates the representation of a type of data. Since
changes in data representation are also common, this encapsulation is also very
useful.

What exactly is meant by *encapsulation*? It means that all the the information about how a data item is represented is contained in the class. The objects of
the class are "black boxes" to their clients: They provide some services correctly
and efficiently, but *how* they do so is not known to the clients. Another term for

representation
independence

this is *representation independence*: The clients work because the *methods* of the class produce the correct results, regardless of how the objects of the class are represented.

To see the idea in a simple context, we will take our Clock class and make a simple change in its representation. Clients will be completely unaffected by the change.

Note that making instance variables *private* is critical to maintaining this representation independence. Changing representation *cannot* work if the instance variables of Clock objects are public. We are going to change how these variables are used, so clients that directly access them will no longer work the same way.

In our most recent version of Clock (page 248), as indeed in all our versions of Clock, we have represented a clock by two instance variables: hour and minute. The variable hour contains a number between 1 and 12, and minute contains a number between 0 and 59. For this exercise, we will change the representation in this way: The variable hour will contain a number between 0 and 11, with 0 being used in place of 12. The question is, How do we make this change while making sure all the methods work *exactly* the same as they do now?

For example, the accessor method getHour returns a number between 1 and 12 now, so it must continue to do so. If it just returns the instance variable hour, then this won't happen. This may seem puzzling, but there is no reason why getHour needs to return the hour instance variable directly. Instead, it can do something more complicated:

```
48      public int getHour () {
49         if (hour == 0)
50            return 12;
51         else
52            return hour;
53      }
```

Since minute contains exactly the same value as it did before, getMinute doesn't change at all.

The method that actually sets the values of the instance variables is set; it is called, directly or indirectly, by the constructors, the input routine getData, and the setHour and setMinute methods. So updating set will have the effect of updating all these methods.

Note that the meaning of the arguments of set does not, and cannot, change. Luckily, it so happens that 0 and 12 are already treated as meaning the same thing. That is, calling set(0, 15) and set(12, 15) gives the same result: The variable hour is set to 12, minute to 15. We want to change this so that, in both calls, hour will be set to zero. This change is simple: Just omit line 44 (shown commented out in this new version). In fact, the apparent pointlessness of line 44 is the original motivation for this change in representation:

```
39      public void set (int hour, int minute) {
40         int totalMinutes = (hour * 60 + minute) % (12 * 60);
41         // totalMinutes is between -(12 * 60) and (12 * 60)
```

```
42          if (totalMinutes < 0) totalMinutes = totalMinutes + (12 * 60);
43          this.hour = totalMinutes / 60;
44          // if (this.hour == 0) this.hour = 12;
45          this.minute = totalMinutes % 60;
46       }
```

Like getHour and getMinute, toString does little more than report the value of the instance variables. It needs a change similar to the change in getHour:

```
29       public String toString () {
30          if (hour == 0)
31             return ("12:" + minute);
32          else
33             return (hour + ":" + minute);
34       }
```

QUICK EXERCISE 7.11

We consulted with a local mathematics professor who assured us that with our latest version of Clock, we do not have to change any of our display methods at all. Why not?

What about priorTo? It looks fine, but actually does not quite work. Before the change in representation, 10:30 is considered "prior to" 12:15, because $10 < 12$, but now the opposite is true. Here is our new version of priorTo:

```
60       public boolean priorTo (Clock c) {
61          int oldhour = hour,
62             oldchour = c.hour;
63          if (oldhour == 0) oldhour = 12;
64          if (oldchour == 0) oldchour = 12;
65          return (oldhour < oldchour ||
66                oldhour == oldchour && minute < c.minute
67             );
68       }
```

Because we have managed to ensure that all methods return the same values as they did before, clients will see no difference between the new and old representations. This holds, of course, only if clients are forbidden to access the instance variables directly. That is why they must be declared private.

For a little more practice in changing representations, we can represent the time by a single number minute, between 0 and $12 * 60 - 1$. We can leave the constructors getData, setHour, and setMinute unchanged, as long as we change set. In fact, this produces a considerable simplification:

```
38       public void set (int h, int m) {
39          minute = (h * 60 + m) % (12 * 60);
40          // minute is between -(12 * 60) and (12 * 60)
41          if (minute < 0) minute = minute + (12 * 60);
42       }
```

The next methods we will look at are the accessors. In effect, the part of set that separated totalMinutes into minutes and hours is moved into these methods:

```
44      public int getHour () {
45        int hour = minute / 60;
46        if (hour == 0)
47          return 12;
48        else
49          return hour;
50      }
51
52      public int getMinute () { return (minute % 60); }
```

Once the remaining methods are fixed, the client will again see no change.

**QUICK EXERCISE
7.12**

Change the remaining methods in Clock to use the new representation. (*Hint*: It is easiest if you use getHour and getMinute where previously references to the instance variables hour and minute appeared.)

7.10

What Is main?

There is a small problem with our methodology. We write client programs that have the form

```
public class CClient {
    public static void main (String[] args) {
        C x = new C();
        x.method(...);
        ...
    }
}
```

We claim that when a program starts, main is invoked, and it in turn creates an object of type C, then invokes methods on that object. But if main is invoked, mustn't there be a receiver for the invocation? If so, then that receiver is an object of type CClient. But when was that object created? Who caused the CClient object to be created?

To put the question more broadly: If every method needs to be sent to a receiver, which is an object, how can the whole process begin? If there are no objects, then no methods can be invoked, and no objects can be created!

Well, as a matter of fact, not every method needs to have a receiver. Special methods called *static methods*, or *class methods*, have no receiver. They are not permitted to refer to any instance variables of the class; but, as a compensating advantage, they can be invoked when no objects of the class even exist. As is indicated by the keyword `static` in its header, `main` is such a method. Also `main` has the special distinction of being *the* method that is first invoked by the Java run-time system when an application begins. In our applications, `main`'s first and only action is to create an object (sometimes more than one), thereby invoking that class's constructor, and then to invoke methods on that object.

static methods
class methods

We will see in Chapter 10 that class methods are matched by an analogous facility for class *variables*. Both class methods and class variables can be quite useful, as we will see, but instance methods and instance variables are used far more often.

Summary

Java programs are divided into *classes*. Class definitions have the form

```
class  name  {
    declarations

    constructor definitions

    method definitions
}
```

Every object, or instance, of a class contains its own copies of the instance variables of the class. The constructors all have the same name as the class, and *no* return type; they are used to initialize the instance variables and are invoked automatically whenever an object of the class is created. The methods are the operations provided by the class.

Method definitions have the form

```
visibility-qualifier  type  name  ( formal parameter list)  {
    local variable declarations
    statements
}
```

where a *type* of `void` indicates a method that does not return anything. A method is used within a program by a *message send*, also known as a *call statement*, consisting of an object, a period, the method name, and a parenthesized list of *actual parameters*.

The *visibility-qualifier* is either `public` or `private`, or omitted entirely. Instance variables should normally be declared `private`.

The mechanism used to specify the value to be returned by a method is the `return` statement

```
return  value;
```

The name of a class is used as a type name in the rest of the program. *Clients* of the class can declare variables to contain references to objects of the class; the actual objects are usually allocated using new. Clients call methods of the class using *dot notation: object.method(arguments)*. This is called *sending a message*, and the *object* is called the *receiver of the message*.

Every object contains a variable called this which can be used to refer to the object itself.

Clients of a class cannot directly observe how that class represents its objects if the class's instance variables are private, as they always should be. The programmer of the class can change the instance variables at will, just ensuring that methods behave correctly. This, called *information hiding*, is an important principle to follow in designing classes.

Constructors can be *overloaded*, meaning that a class can have several of them, so long as each one has a different number or different types of arguments. When a constructor is called, Java will choose the correct one based on the number and types of the parameters provided to new. Methods can be overloaded similarly.

Bear in mind the distinction between *mutating* and *nonmutating* operations of a class. Mutating operations modify the instance variables of their receiver; nonmutating operations do not. Clients must be aware of which type of operation they are using. Usually mutating operations return void, while nonmutating operations return a value (possibly an object of the same class).

Classes are composed with one another in order to achieve certain desired behavior. Composition is either *association* (sometimes called *acquaintance*) or *containment* (sometimes called *aggregation*). In association, classes (and objects) are linked with one another in such a way that the objects remain visible to a client. In containment, an object of one class is constructed from objects of other classes, but only the composite object is visible to clients.

Exercises

1. Rewrite the Clock class to keep track of a 24-hour day.
   (a) Modify toString so that it returns the time with either "AM" or "PM" appended.
   (b) Add the method String toMilitaryTime (). This method returns the time in 24-hour (military) format (for example, 1345 hours instead of 1:45PM).
   (c) Add the method boolean isPM (). This method tells whether the receiver represents an afternoon time (noon or later) or a morning time.

2. Write a Clock client to print a daily schedule form in an OutputBox. The form should look like this:

```
 8:00AM   _____
 9:00AM   _____
10:00AM   _____
11:00AM   _____
12:00PM   _____
 1:00PM   _____
 2:00PM   _____
 3:00PM   _____
```

```
4:00PM  _____
5:00PM  _____
```

Your program should read the starting time, the ending time, and the interval between appointment lines.

3. Given a complex number $x + iy$, we can define the following operations:

- $|x + iy| = \sqrt{x^2 + y^2}$ is the *absolute value* operation.
- $s(x + iy) = sx + isy$, where s is a real number, is *scaling*.

Define a `Complex` class:

```
class Complex {
    private double x, y;  // represents number x + iy

    public Complex (double r, double i) {...}
    public double absoluteValue () {...}
    public Complex scale (double a) {...}
    public String toString () {...} // return the string "x + i y"
}
```

Fill in the definitions of the constructor and the three methods of this class. Then write a client to exercise this class as follows: Repeatedly read three numbers of type `double`, say, x, y, and s; create and print the complex number $x + iy$; print its absolute value; then create and print $s(x + iy)$. Continue until the user terminates the application.

4. Rewrite the `Clock` class to include seconds as well as minutes and hours. You need a third instance variable (`second`), an additional method [`public Clock addSeconds (int seconds)`], and revised constructors and other methods.

5. We did not include the following three operations in the `Complex` class of Exercise 3:

- The *complex conjugate* of $x + iy$ is $x - iy$.
- $(x + iy) + (x' + iy') = (x + x') + i(y + y')$ is *addition*.
- $(x + iy)(x' + iy') = (xx' - yy') + i(xy' + x'y)$ is *multiplication*. (Notice that scaling is just a special case, where $y = 0$.)

Add these new methods to the `Complex` class:
(a) `public Complex add (Complex c)`
(b) `public Complex multiply (Complex c)`
(c) `public Complex conjugate ()`
Modify the client you wrote in Exercise 3 to test these new methods. Now, each input cycle needs four numbers x, y, x', and y'; the complex numbers $x + iy$ and $x' + iy'$ should be created, the three new operations should be performed on them, and the results printed.

6. Add these new methods to `Clock`:
(a) `public boolean equals (Clock c)`. This method returns true if the receiver and `c` are the same, false otherwise.
(b) `public int subtractTimes (Clock c)`. This method returns the difference, in minutes, between the receiver and `c` (both presumed to occur on the same day).

7. The class `Rational` contains rational numbers (i.e., fractions) and has the usual arithmetic operations:

   (a) $\frac{n}{d} + \frac{n'}{d'} = \frac{nd' + n'd}{dd'}$

   (b) $-\frac{n}{d} = \frac{-n}{d}$

   (c) $\frac{n}{d} \times \frac{n'}{d'} = \frac{nn'}{dd'}$

   (d) $\frac{1}{n/d} = \frac{d}{n}$

   In addition, there should be a constructor that takes two integers n and d to the rational number n/d, and a method `floor` that returns the integer part of a rational number (namely, n/d, using integer division).

   Fill in this class definition:

   ```
   public class Rational {
   private int n, d;

       public Rational (int num, int den) {...}
       public Rational plus (Rational r) {...}
       public Rational negate () {...}
       public Rational minus (Rational r) {...}
       public Rational times (Rational r) {...}
       public Rational reciprocal () {...}
       public Rational divide (Rational r) {...}
       public int floor () {...}
   }
   ```

   Implement `minus`, using `negate` and `add`; implement `divide`, using `reciprocal` and `multiply`.

   Write a client similar to the one used in Exercise 5, where the inputs x, y, x', and y' represent the rational numbers x/y and x'/y'. Test `plus`, `minus`, `times`, and `divide`. (Be aware that the integers n and d tend to get very large, quickly exceeding the range of variables of type `int`. The result is that many examples will fail to work even when your code is correct.)

8. Rewrite the `Rational` class, using `BigIntegers`. Call this new class `BigRational`.

9. In Exercise 5 you represented a complex number using two real numbers: the real and imaginary parts of the complex number. There is a one-to-one correspondence between complex numbers and points on the plane; number $x + iy$ corresponds to point (x, y). An alternative representation, *polar representation*, identifies points by giving numbers r and θ (the *magnitude* and *argument*, respectively); (r, θ) represents the point that is at distance r from the origin along a line at angle θ from the x axis. The same operations that you defined in Exercise 5 can be defined using polar representation, with clients seeing no change in the observable behavior of the class.

   The absolute value and scaling operations are very simple: The absolute value of (r, θ) is r, and $a(r, \theta)$ is (ar, θ). The other operations are

   - $(r, \theta) \times (r', \theta') = (rr', \theta + \theta')$.

- $(r, \theta) + (r', \theta') =$

$$(\sqrt{(r \cos \theta + r' \cos \theta')^2 + (r \sin \theta + r' \sin \theta')^2},$$

$$\arctan(r \sin \theta + r' \sin \theta', r \cos \theta + r' \cos \theta'),$$

where $\arctan(y, x)$ gives the tangent of the angle from the positive x axis to the point (x, y).

- Conjugate of $(r, \theta) = (r, -\theta)$.

Implement the class `PolarComplex` with the same operations and types (including constructor) as `Complex`. Use the same client as Exercise 5, but change `Complex` to `PolarComplex`, and test that the results are exactly the same as for the class `Complex`.

10. As another example of objects containing other objects, we can create a class that draws clocks for Chicago, New York, and Paris. It should create a `DrawingBox` and place the clocks in the top left, top center, and top right of the `DrawingBox`. Below each clock it should display the name of the city.

11. In Exercise 10 of Chapter 5, you wrote a class to store the scores of a bowler in a bowling game. The class was called `Bowler`. Write a class `BowlingTourney` representing a competition between two bowlers. It should have a constructor and these methods:

`void nameBowlers (String b1, String b2)`	Gives names of competitors
`void roll (String b, int p)`	Gives the last roll for bowler named b
`String winner ()`	Gives winner, if both bowlers have finished their games

These methods should print error messages for all invalid inputs, including these cases: if the two bowlers' names are the same; if `roll` is called with a name that is not the name of either competitor; if `roll` is called with an invalid pin count; if `roll` is called after the bowler has finished her or his game; if `winner` is called when both bowlers have not finished.

Your client should repeatedly prompt for the bowler name and pin count and announce a winner when both games are over.

12. The class `Triangle` has a constructor with four arguments, giving a `DrawingBox` object in which a triangle is to be drawn and the three vertices of the triangle are

```
Triangle (DrawingBox b, Point p1, Point p2, Point p3)
```

It also has methods to change one vertex of the triangle and to change all vertices by the same amount:

`void changeVertex (int v, Point p)`	Replaces the vth vertex by p
`void move (Point p)`	Adds p.x to each x coordinate and p.y to each y coordinate; i.e., moves the triangle by p.

The constructor should draw the triangle in the drawing box, and the other two methods should immediately redraw it. They should do this by calling the private methods `erase` and `draw`:

`private void erase ()`	Draws the triangle in background color, effectively erasing it.
`private void draw ()`	Draws the triangle in foreground color.

That is, when `changeVertex` or `move` is called, it first calls `erase`, then makes the indicated change in the shape, then calls `draw`.

The client should initialize the drawing box and triangle and then repeatedly prompt the user to either change one vertex or move all vertices, and then prompt for the appropriate arguments.

13. Define `Circle` analogously to `Triangle` from Exercise 12. Its constructor arguments are the drawing box, center point, and radius (in pixels):

    ```
    Circle (DrawingBox b, Point p, int r)
    ```

    The other methods are variants of the `Triangle` methods. Each of these methods should immediately redraw the circle

`void changeCenter (Point p)`	Moves the circle to p.
`void changeRadius (int r)`	Replaces radius by r.
`void move (Point p)`	Moves the circle by p.

    as well as the private methods `erase` and `draw`.

14. Write a simple drawing program by repeatedly prompting the user to draw and adjust a new figure (triangle or circle) and by drawing these in the same drawing box. Draw the UML diagram for this program. One problem you will encounter is that adding and adjusting a new shape can cause pixels in existing shapes to disappear. This happens because when a shape is adjusted, the previous copy of that shape is erased; if there was some overlap between that shape and another shape (e.g., if two triangles share a side), the overlapping points will be erased. This problem cannot be solved with what we know about Java now, but we will solve it in Exercise 13 of Chapter 8.

ONE-DIMENSIONAL ARRAYS

In this chapter we introduce the *array*, a structure for storing large amounts of data. We discuss some of the many computations that become possible when a program can store large amounts of data. Among the most important of these are *searching* and *sorting*. We show how multiple images can be painted from an array, thereby accomplishing animation in programs.

Little boxes on the hill side, little boxes made of ticky
tacky.
Little boxes, little boxes, little boxes all the same.
There's a green one and a pink one and a blue one and a
yellow one.
And they're all made out of ticky tacky, and they all look
just the same.

—Malvina Reynolds
Little Boxes

An *array* is a sequence of variables of identical type. It can be used to store large   *array*
amounts of data without the need to declare many individual variables.

We show how to declare arrays and use them. The simplest kind of array
processing uses a `for` loop to look at each element in the array. We give a number
of examples of these types of loops.

We then give many examples of the use of arrays. One important use is to
sort lists of numbers, which is discussed in detail in Section 8.6. The important
operations of *sorting* an array and *searching* for an item in an array are explored
again, using the technique of *recursion*, in Chapter 14.

8.1

Array Basics

An *array* contains a fixed number, called its *length*, of variables of identical type.   *length*
An array is a specialized kind of object, and like any other object, an array must
be first declared and then allocated. A variable is declared to be an array in this
way:

```
int[] counts;
double[] scores;
String[] studentNames;
```
The brackets tell Java that the variable will be an array.[1]

Arrays are allocated using a variation on a feature we've used before: `new`.
We know how to allocate an object using `new`, of course. Arrays, however,

---

[1] An alternative form is to place the brackets after the variable name, as in `int counts[];`. This
is an old form, retained for compatibility with the programming languages C and C++; we will stick
with the newer form.

are different, because they require a notation to tell `new` how many variables to allocate. That notation is

> new *type* [*size*]

This expression allocates an array of length *size* with variables of type *type* and returns the array object. The array, like any object, is allocated in an area of *heap* memory called the *heap*.

Therefore, we can allocate typical arrays like this:

```
counts = new int[10];
scores = new double[15];
studentNames = new String[10];
```

The bracketed number is the length and says how many variables are in each array. We can picture the array `counts` like this:

Each box in this picture is an `int` variable. The numbers atop each box give that *subscript* variable's *subscript*, or *index*; an array of length 10 has subscripts from 0 to 9.
index   Similarly, the allocation of `scores` would create a sequence of 15 `double` variables, and the allocation of `studentNames` would create a sequence of 10 `String` objects.

Arrays can contain any type of value: primitive values or (references to) objects. When an array is first allocated, each element will be initialized to some value. For an array of primitive numerics (such as `int` or `double`), each element is initialized to zero; for an array of `boolean`s, each element is initialized to `false`. For an array of objects, each element is initialized to `null`.

The essential feature of arrays is the ability to use subscripts to obtain a
array subscripting specific variable. The notation for this *array subscripting* operation uses square brackets, as in

```
counts[0]    // the first variable in counts
counts[1]    // the second variable in counts
counts[9]    // the last variable in counts
counts[10]   // error!!
```

Each of these subscripted arrays, except the last, is an `int` variable and can be used in all the same ways that any `int` variable is used: on the left-hand side of an assignment statement, in an arithmetic expression, or as the argument of a method.

The problem with the last item is that `counts[10]` *does not exist*! Only 10 elements have been allocated for `counts`, designated 0 through 9. If you attempt to reference such a nonexistent array element, your program will crash horribly.

Here, for example, is a program to read in 10 integers and print them. It has the form of a class with two methods (`read10` and `print10`) and its client. Arrays can, of course, be instance variables in classes. Here we have one method to read the data into an array and another to print them.

```
1   import CSLib.*;
2
3   public class Simple {
4      // Simple:   read10 - reads 10 integers
5      //           print10 - prints 10 integers
6      // Author:   Maddie Kamin, Friday, April 13, 2001
7
8      int[] counts;
9
10     public Simple () {
11        counts = new int[10];
12     }
13
14     public void read10 () {
15        InputBox in = new InputBox();
16        in.setPrompt("Enter integer:");
17        counts[0]=in.readInt();
18        counts[1]=in.readInt();
19        counts[2]=in.readInt();
20        counts[3]=in.readInt();
21        counts[4]=in.readInt();
22        counts[5]=in.readInt();
23        counts[6]=in.readInt();
24        counts[7]=in.readInt();
25        counts[8]=in.readInt();
26        counts[9]=in.readInt();
27     }
28
29     public void print10 () {
30        OutputBox out = new OutputBox("Input");
31
32        out.print(counts[0] + " " + counts[1] + " "
33              + counts[2] + " " + counts[3] + " "
34              + counts[4] + " " + counts[5] + " "
35              + counts[6] + " " + counts[7] + " "
36              + counts[8] + " " + counts[9] + "\n");
37     }
38  }
```

```
1   public class SimpleClient {
2
3      public static void main (String[] args) {
4         Simple sim = new Simple();
5         sim.read10();
6         sim.print10();
7      }
8   }
```

Figure 8.1 gives a picture of the `Simple` object created by `SimpleClient`.

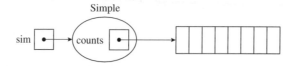

FIGURE 8.1   `Simple` **object created by** `SimpleClient`.

QUICK EXERCISE 8.1	Alter this program so that it prints the numbers in the reverse order from that in which they were read.

QUICK EXERCISE 8.2	Alter the program again, to print the *sum* of the numbers it has read.

The repetitive nature of the statements clearly indicates the need for a loop. We will rewrite this example using a loop, once we have gotten a little more practice with arrays.

It is of paramount importance in using arrays to understand that *array subscripts can be expressions*—they don't have to be constants. For example, if i is an integer variable, `counts[i]` refers to one of the variables in `counts`. If i = 0, it refers to `counts[0]`; if i = 1, it refers to `counts[1]`; and so on. Of course, values of i that are not in the range 0 to 9 must be avoided.

More complex expressions also can be used as subscripts. For instance, `counts[2*i]` refers to `counts[0]` if i is 0, `counts[2]` if i is 1, and so on. In this case, any value of i greater than 4 would result in an error. On the other hand, `counts[i/2]` is legal as long as i is between 0 and 19; it refers to `counts[0]` if i is 0 or 1, `counts[1]` if i is 2 or 3, and so on.

Arrays can be initialized by giving a list of all their elements, as in

```
int[] primes = {2, 3, 5, 7, 11, 13, 17, 19, 23, 29};
```

In this case, you need not allocate the array explicitly—Java will allocate and initialize an appropriate number of elements. This notation can be used only at the time an array is declared; it is illegal to write

```
int[] primes;
primes = {2, 3, 5, 7, 11, 13, 17, 19, 23, 29};
```
Wrong

You can use this feature to initialize an array of `Strings`. Here, for example, is a method that takes an integer as its argument and prints the name of the corresponding day of the week (with Sunday being day 1 of the week).

BUG ALERT 8.1

Arrays Are Subscripted from Zero

A source of confusion in using arrays in Java is subscripting from zero, which seems unnatural at first. Just remember that to create an array A of n variables of type T, use the declaration

```
T[] A;
...
A = new T[n];
```

or, more succinctly,

```
T[] A = new T[n];
```

Then keep in mind that the element A[n] does not exist—only A[0] through A[n-1] do. See also Bug Alert 8.4.

```
1   final String[] NAME = {
2         "Sunday", "Monday", "Tuesday", "Wednesday",
3         "Thursday", "Friday", "Saturday"};
4
5   public void printName (int day, OutputBox out) {
6      out.print(NAME[day-1]);
7      }
```

Since arrays are a kind of object, variables that are declared as arrays are really *references* to objects. The array NAME declared in the previous example is illustrated in Figure 8.2. An array of objects can be initialized to actual objects in the declaration by using object-valued expressions in the initializer. Thus, this declaration creates an array of four clocks, all set to 12:00:

```
Clock[] clockArray =
    {new Clock(), new Clock(), new Clock(), new Clock()};
```

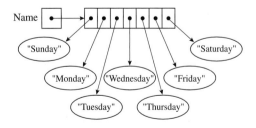

FIGURE 8.2 An array of strings.

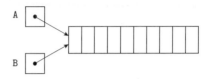

FIGURE 8.3   Two array variables pointing to the same array.

Just as two variables can point to the same object, so they can point to the same array. You can cause two variables to refer to the same array like this:

```
int[] A, B;
...
B = new int[10];
A = B;
```

alias   The result is depicted in Figure 8.3. Creating such *aliases* for an array usually is ill advised.

Bug Alert 8.2   *Array References Can Be Assigned, Arrays Can Be Copied*

Array names themselves are variables that refer to array objects. If A and B are arrays, writing

```
A = B;
```

causes both A and B to refer to the same array, as shown in Figure 8.3. On the other hand, if A and B are distinct arrays

```
int[] A = new int[10],
      B = new int[10];
```

then you can *copy* B to A; that is, you can copy the contents of each variable in B to the corresponding variable in A:

```
A[0] = B[0];
A[1] = B[1];
...
A[9] = B[9];
```

Before going on to examples, we make a point about a topic that we have not discussed in detail: *efficiency*. The ability to store large amounts of data means that, for the first time, we have the ability to do really time-consuming operations, so efficiency questions now become particularly interesting. The first computation in this book that is potentially very slow is *sorting*, which we discuss in Section 8.6. There is one important fact to bear in mind about arrays when considering the cost of computations involving them: Like arithmetic operations (addition, subtraction, comparisons, and so on), subscripting an array is an operation that takes time—not a lot, but if you do enough of it, it adds up. What all these operations have in common is this: They take a *constant* amount of time, no matter what the arguments are. This may be surprising, but it is true. A computer takes the same amount of time to add $1 + 1$ as it does to add 3,456,973 + 95,003,362, and it takes the same amount of time to access A[5498] as to access A[0]. (Of course, we can't say exactly how much time either operation will take, because computers vary. Array subscripting is likely to be several times slower than addition, but both take considerably less than 1 microsecond on a current PC.) That these operations take a fixed, constant amount of time is crucial in determining the overall efficiency of algorithms that involve arrays.

8.2

Simple Array-Processing Loops

The simplest kind of array processing uses a `for` loop to iterate over the subscripts of an array. To perform an operation on every element of an array A of length n, use the loop

```
for (int i=0; i<n; i++) {
   ... perform operation on A[i]
}
```

For example, this loop initializes the array `counts` to contain the numbers 0, 10, 20, and so on up to 90:

```
1    for (int i=0; i<10; i++) {
2       counts[i] = i*10;
3    }
```

As you know from Chapter 6, i is called the *index variable* of the loop. The first *index variable* time through the loop, i is 0, so the assignment in line 2 assigns 0 to counts[0]; the second time through, i is 1 and 10 is assigned to counts[1]; the third time, 20 is assigned to counts[2]; and so on. The last time through the loop, i is 9, so 90 is assigned to counts[9]. In the end, counts looks like this:

	0	1	2	3	4	5	6	7	8	9
counts	0	10	20	30	40	50	60	70	80	90

Just as objects can have instance variables, so, too, Java's arrays have an instance variable *length*, which is the number of elements in the array. Therefore, *length* the following code will print all elements of the array counts:

```
for (int i=0; i<counts.length; i++)
   out.println( counts[i] );
```

As another example, the code that follows is a more concise version of the program we gave earlier to read 10 numbers into counts and print them in order.

```
1   import CSLib.*;
2
3   public class Simple {
4     // Simple:  read10 - reads 10 integers
5     //          print10 - prints 10 integers
6     // Author:  Maddie Kamin, Friday, April 13, 2001
7
8     int[] counts;
9
10    public Simple () {
11        counts = new int[10];
12    }
13
14    public void read10 () {
15      InputBox in = new InputBox();
16      in.setPrompt("Enter integer:");
17
18      for (int i=0; i<10; i++)
19        counts[i]=in.readInt();
20    }
21
22    public void print10 () {
23      OutputBox out = new OutputBox("Input");
24
25      for (int i=0; i<10; i++)
26        out.print(counts[i] + " ");
27
28      out.println();
29    }
30  }
```

The loop in lines 18 and 20 executes counts[i]=in.readInt() 10 times, with i varying from 0 to 9. Similarly, the loop in lines 25 and 26 executes the output statement 10 times, with i varying from 0 to 9. At each iteration of the loop, the value of counts[i] is printed. Thus, in the first iteration, with i equal to 0, counts[0] is printed; in the second, with i equal to 1, counts[1] is printed; and so on.

Although an array cannot grow once it has been declared, you can accommodate a varying amount of data by making the array very large and filling only as much of it as you need. Suppose the set of inputs is of unknown size. The user will just keep entering input until it is done. Reading inputs was the subject of Section 6.5. Here is a loop to read a list of numbers into an array. The only restriction is that there be no more than 1000 numbers input. This limitation is encoded in the symbolic constant MAX_CLASS_SIZE.

```
InputBox in = new InputBox();
in.setPrompt("Enter data, or press OK to terminate");
final int MAX_CLASS_SIZE = 1000;
int size = 0;
int[] inputs = new int[MAX_CLASS_SIZE];
```

QUICK EXERCISE
8.3

Change the output from the previous program in these ways:

1. Print the numbers in reverse order, that is, counts[9], counts[8], ..., counts[0].
2. Print only the numbers with even-numbered indices, that is, counts[0], counts[2], ..., counts[8].
3. Print the entries counts[0], ..., counts[4] in order, then print the entries counts[9], ..., counts[5] in reverse. You will need to use two loops.

```
while (true) {
    inputs[size] = in.readInt();
    if (in.eoi()) break;
    size++;
}
```

When the user terminates the input process by entering an empty data item, the variable size contains the number of inputs entered.

QUICK EXERCISE
8.4

Change Simple to use this method of input, so that it can read and print any number of inputs (up to MAX_CLASS_SIZE).

8.3

Simple Computations on Numerical Data

One of the most important reasons to store data in an array is that it allows you to perform operations on the data that are difficult to perform if you can look at each datum only once. Reading and echoing inputs in reverse order is one example. Another is *sorting*, which we discuss in Section 8.6. In this section, we practice with some additional simple operations. Some of these operations were already done in earlier chapters without using arrays; we repeat these, using arrays, just for the practice. Other operations require arrays.

Suppose grades is an array of integers between 0 and 100, containing the exam grades of all students in a class. The integer variable size contains the number of scores in grades (which may be fewer than grades.length).

> **BUG ALERT 8.3**
>
> *Remember to Increment Index Variable in* `while` *Loop*
>
> When an array is processed by a `while` loop, you must initialize the index variable before the loop and increment it inside the loop. A common error in programming is to forget to increment the index variable.
>
> It is difficult to make this mistake when a `for` loop is used. This is one reason that a `for` loop is the preferred form, when it is applicable.

An instructor will be interested in a lot of different statistics about the class's performance. One of the first questions she is likely to ask is, What was the lowest score anyone got on the exam?

```
int min = 100;  // min grade is no more than 100!
for (int i=0; i<size; i++) {
  // min is worst grade among grades[0] .. grades[i-1]
  if (min > grades[i])
    min = grades[i];
}
```

It is easy to see that the invariant always holds: It holds vacuously when the loop begins, and the conditional statement clearly preserves it. When the loop ends, `i` is equal to `size`, so `min` is the worst grade among all the grades.

This loop only works for exams whose maximum grade is 100. The following loop is somewhat "cleaner" in that it does not rely on any preset maximum grade (it does assume that `size` is at least 1):

```
int min = grades[0];  // min grade is no more than grades[0]
for (int i=1; i<size; i++) {
  // min is worst grade among grades[0] .. grades[i-1]
  if (min > grades[i])
    min = grades[i];
}
```

In practice, the minimum is likely to be zero, since some students probably missed the exam. This loop finds the minimum nonzero grade:

```
int nzmin = 100;
for (int i=0; i<size; i++) {
  // nzmin is worst non-zero grade among grades[0] .. grades[i-1]
  if (nzmin > grades[i] && grades[i] > 0)
    nzmin = grades[i];
}
```

A statistic that is often of interest as a "measure of central tendency" is the *median*, the grade that divides the class exactly in half. That is, it is a grade such that exactly half the class falls below it and half above. Although this number is normally about the same as the average, it is much harder to calculate. The reader is urged to give this problem some thought. It turns out that the only way to find the median is, essentially, to sort the array and then see what value ends

QUICK EXERCISE
8.5

Write a single loop to calculate all the following: maximum and minimum grades, minimum nonzero grade, and number of zeros. For these calculations, you may assume a minimum possible grade of 0 and a maximum possible grade of 100.

QUICK EXERCISE
8.6

Add to the loop you just wrote the calculation of the average grade and the average of all the nonzero grades.

up in the middle. As mentioned earlier, sorting is a process that we will take up in Section 8.6 and again in Chapter 14.

Yet another thing the instructor might want to know is how the grades on the exam are distributed. We will draw a bar graph of the exam in Section 8.5. A simple version of this question is, How many students got an x on the exam? In fact, this is just a generalization of the problem of counting zeros. Another variant is, How many students got between x and y?

QUICK EXERCISE
8.7

Write a loop to test how many students got a 90 or above on the exam.

A seemingly similar problem is to answer the question, Did any student get a 90 on the exam? We could treat it similarly to the previous problem: Count the number of students who got a 90, and then see if that number is greater than zero. However, this loop structure is inefficient because, unlike our previous computation, this one does not require that we iterate over the entire array. The proper structure for this search process is a `while`: Keep iterating until *either* a 90 is found or we run out of students.

```
boolean found = false;
int i = 0;
while (i < size && !found) {
    // 90 does not occur among grades[0] .. grades[i-1]
    if (grades[i] == 90) found = true;
    i++;
}
```

As soon as a 90 is found, the loop is terminated, with `found` having value `true`; furthermore, `grades[i-1]` contains 90. If the loop ends because we have run out of students, then `found` will be `false`.

This loop can be simplified in two ways. First, increment i only when 90 is not found:

```
boolean found = false;
int i = 0;
while (i < size && !found) {
    // 90 does not occur among grades[0] .. grades[i-1]
    if (grades[i] == 90)
        found = true;
    else
        i++;
}
```

We come to the following interesting conclusion: When the loop terminates, grades[i] contains 90 if and only if i<size. That is, if we find 90 and terminate the loop early, i contains a valid subscript; otherwise, i is 1 too large to be a subscript of a student. This observation then leads to another: We can eliminate found all together and just use the value of i to determine if a 90 was found:

```
int i = 0;
while (i < size && grades[i] != 90) {
    // 90 does not occur among grades[0] .. grades[i-1]
    i++;
}
// 90 occurs in grades if and only if i < size
```

QUICK EXERCISE 8.8	Write a loop to determine whether any student got a grade between 80 and 89.

Searching for an item of data is among the most common operations in computer programs. It occurs when your doctor searches for your medical records, when you enter a string into a web search engine, and in numerous other applications. The method of searching we have employed is the simplest possible method. On the other hand, it is also the best possible method, unless we can impose some structure on the elements in the array. In practice, quite complex structuring methods, which are beyond the scope of this text, are used to facilitate the search process. We will look at this problem again in Chapter 14.

One advantage of reading data into an array is that it allows us to compare results from two different exams. Suppose we have grades on two exams in arrays grades1 and grades2. We know that the arrays contain the same number of valid grades, and that for each index i, grades1[i] and grades2[i] represent the grades for the same student on the two exams. When two arrays *parallel arrays* line up in this way, they are called *parallel arrays*; see Figure 8.4.

QUICK EXERCISE 8.9	Write a single loop that finds the average, maximum, and minimum nonzero grades on both exams (assuming all grades on both exams are between 0 and 100).

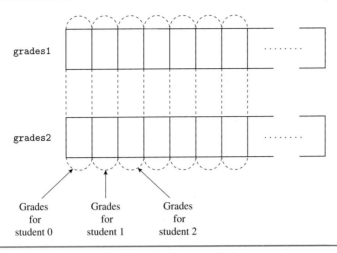

FIGURE 8.4 `grades1` and `grades2` **are parallel arrays.**

Let's first discuss how to read data into these two arrays. It can be done in two ways: Read both grades for each student before going on to the next student, or read all grades from the first exam and then all grades from the second exam. It is more common to maintain student grade information in a file of student "records," each record containing all the grades for a single student. Thus, we would read both scores for every student:

```
1   import CSLib.*;
2
3   public class Simple {
4      // Read and print grades
5      // Author: Michael McDermott, April 17, 2001
6
7      int size;
8      int[] grades1;
9      int[] grades2;
10     final int MAX_CLASS_SIZE = 1000;
11
12     public Simple () {
13        size = 0;
14        grades1 = new int[MAX_CLASS_SIZE];
15        grades2 = new int[MAX_CLASS_SIZE];
16     }
17
18     public void read () {
19        InputBox in = new InputBox();
20        while (true) {
21           in.setPrompt("First grade for this student:");
22           grades1[size] = in.readInt();
23
```

```
24              if (in.eoi()) break;
25
26              in.setPrompt("Second grade for this student:");
27              grades2[size] = in.readInt();
28              size++;
29           }
30       }
31
32       public void print() {
33           OutputBox out = new OutputBox("Input");
34
35           for (int i=0; i<size; i++) {
36               out.println(grades1[i] + " " + grades2[i]);
37           }
38           out.println();
39       }
40   }
```

QUICK EXERCISE
8.10

To read all the grades from exam 1 followed by all the grades from exam 2 requires two loops, one right after the other. Write these two loops. The grades on exam 1 will be immediately followed by a −1 to separate them from the grades on exam 2.

Having scores from two exams, the instructor might want to compare the performance of students on the exams. This loop counts the number of students whose grade improved from the first exam to the second:

```
int improved = 0;
for (int i=0; i < size; i++) {
    if (grades1[i] < grades2[i]) improved++;
}
```

QUICK EXERCISE
8.11

In a single loop, count the number of students whose grades improved, the number whose grades declined, and the number whose grades remained the same on the two exams.

QUICK EXERCISE
8.12

Modify your program from the previous exercise so that students who got a zero on either exam are not counted.

	QUICK EXERCISE
Write a loop to find the index of the most improved student.	**QUICK EXERCISE 8.13**

	QUICK EXERCISE
Write a loop to find the average improvement.	**QUICK EXERCISE 8.14**

8.4

Arrays of Objects

We start this section with a final version of the grade program we were working on in the last section. We add student names to the mix and write a complete program. This program reads the students' names and scores on two exams and prints a list giving the average score for each student. The input for each student is given in a succession of three InputBoxes in the form of a name (a String) and two integers.

The output is in two columns:

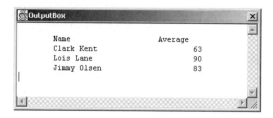

The client program is

```
1    public class GradeBookClient {
2
3      public static void main (String[] arg) {
4        final int MAX_CLASS_SIZE = 1000;
5        GradeBook gb = new GradeBook(MAX_CLASS_SIZE);
6        gb.read();
7        gb.printAvgs();
8      }
9    }
```

The class is called GradeBook, and it looks like this:

```
1    import CSLib.*;
2
3    public class GradeBook {
4      // A grade book of student grades.
5      // Author: D. Benjamin Gordon, August 25, 2000
6
7      private String[] names;
8      private int[] grades1,
9                    grades2;
10     private int size = 0;
11
12     public GradeBook(int number) {
13       names = new String[number];
14       grades1 = new int[number];
15       grades2 = new int[number];
16     }
17
18     public void read () {
19       // Read names and exam grades; size counts inputs
20       InputBox in = new InputBox();
21
22       while (true) {
23         in.setPrompt("Enter student name (null to terminate):");
24         names[size] = in.readString();
25
26         if (in.eoi()) break;
27
28         in.setPrompt("Enter first exam grade:");
29         grades1[size] = in.readInt();
```

```
30        in.setPrompt("Enter second exam grade:");
31        grades2[size] = in.readInt();
32        size++;
33      }
34    }
35
36    public void printAvgs () {
37      OutputBox out = new OutputBox();
38      out.println();
39      out.println("\tName                \tAverage");
40      for (int i=0; i<size; i++) {
41        out.println("\t" + names[i] + "\t\t\t" +
42                    (double)((grades1[i] + grades2[i])/2));
43      }
44    }
45  }
```

Notice that in this version, the maximum number of grades, indicated by the symbolic constant MAX_CLASS_SIZE, is passed into the GradeBook constructor, where it is used to allocate the various arrays. Note that the array of names contains strings, which are a kind of object. As we mentioned at the start of this chapter, arrays can be declared to contain any kind of data.

In fact, the parallel-array approach to this program does not seem to be the cleanest solution to our problem. A nicer structure for GradeBook would be to define a class of objects representing students—including their names and grades—and construct an array of those objects. The difference between this approach and the parallel-array approach is illustrated in Figure 8.5. With this new approach, the GradeBook class will contain an array of Student objects, as shown in the UML diagram of Figure 8.6.

The class Student is simple:

```
1   class Student {
2     private String name;
3     private int exam1, exam2;
4
5     public Student () {}
6     public void setName (String s) { name = s; }
7     public void setExam1 (int s) { exam1 = s; }
8     public void setExam2 (int s) { exam2 = s; }
9     public String getName () { return name; }
10    public int getExam1 () { return exam1; }
11    public int getExam2 () { return exam2; }
12    public int getAvg () { return (exam1+exam2)/2; }
13  }
```

The GradeBook class becomes

```
1   import CSLib.*;
2
3   public class GradeBook {
4
5     final int MAX_CLASS_SIZE = 1000;
```

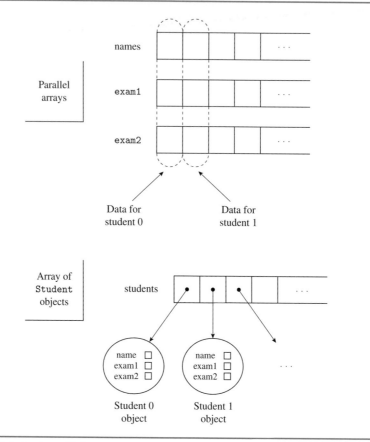

FIGURE 8.5 Parallel arrays versus array of Student **objects.**

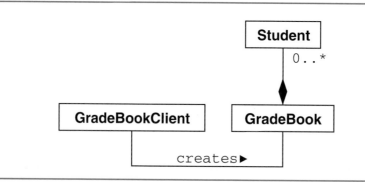

FIGURE 8.6 UML diagram for GradeBook **that uses an array of** Students.

```
6     Student[] students = new Student[MAX_CLASS_SIZE];
7     int size;
8
9     public int read () {
10        // Read names and exam grades; size counts inputs
11        String name;
12        int grade1, grade2;
13
14        InputBox in = new InputBox();
15        size = 0;
16
17        for (;;) {
18          in.setPrompt("Enter student name (null to terminate):");
19          name = in.readString();
20
21          if (in.eoi()) return size;
22
23          in.setPrompt("Enter first exam grade:");
24          grade1 = in.readInt();
25          in.setPrompt("Enter second exam grade:");
26          grade2 = in.readInt();
27          students[size] = new Student();
28          students[size].setName(name);
29          students[size].setExam1(grade1);
30          students[size].setExam2(grade2);
31          size++;
32        }
33
34        return size;
35     }
36
37     public void printAvgs () {
38        OutputBox out = new OutputBox();
39        out.println();
40        out.println("\tName                  \tAverage");
41        for (int i=0; i<size; i++) {
42          out.println("\t" + students[i].getName() +
43                          "\t\t\t" + students[i].getAvg());
```

8.4.1 Passing Arrays as Arguments

As one last point about arrays, we mention that they can be passed into methods as arguments, just as any other value can. Furthermore, when an array is passed as an argument to a method, any assignments made to that array inside the method will be retained when the method returns. In effect, passing an array as an argument creates an alias for that array. (Recall the earlier discussion on aliasing in Section 7.5.)

For example, following is yet another way to write the GradeBook class. In this version, the array of Student objects is declared and allocated *in the client*, who then passes it as an argument to the GradeBook methods. The modified UML diagram is shown in Figure 8.7.

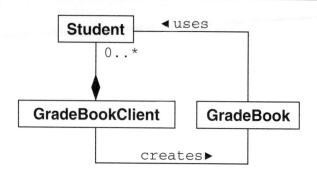

FIGURE 8.7   **UML diagram for** GradeBook **whose client uses an array of** Students.

```
1    import CSLib.*;
2
3    public class GradeBookClient {
4
5      public static void main (String[] args) {
6        final int MAX_CLASS_SIZE = 1000;
7        Student[] students = new Student[MAX_CLASS_SIZE];
8        int size;
9
10       GradeBook gb = new GradeBook();
11       size = gb.read(students);
12       gb.printAvgs(students, size);
13     }
14   }
15
```

Notice that in line 11, the read method returns an integer value, the number of students actually read. The read method does double duty: It reads the student information into the students array, and it reports back on the number of student records it has read.

The GradeBook class is mostly the same as before (page 279), but now it has no declaration of the students array, and the headers of its two methods have changed:

```
public int read (Student[] students)
public void printAvgs (Student[] students, int size) {
```

Aside from this, the only change in either method is that the return statement in read is changed to return size;.

The main point of this example, to repeat, is that when the students array is passed into read as an argument, what is really passed in is a pointer to the array, not an entirely new array. Therefore, assignments to that array in read affect the actual array, and are still there when the method returns to its caller.

This is the opposite of what happens with primitive values. Suppose we wanted to write a method readOneNumber that would just read a single integer value:

```
public void readOneNumber (int input) {
    InputBox in = new InputBox();
    input = in.readInt();
}
```

If the client had an integer variable s, it might call this new method by
readOneNumber(s); in the hope that the variable s would be set to the
number input by the user. In fact, this appears to be analogous to the way read
assigns values to the students array. However, attempting to communicate
this value back to the client by this method fails totally. After the return from the
call to read, the value of size in the client is zero; that is, it hasn't changed.

In programming parlance, arrays and objects are *passed by reference*—just
a pointer, or reference, to the array is passed—while primitive values are *passed
by value* — the contents of the variable are passed but not the variable itself, so
its contents cannot be changed in the called method.

pass by reference
pass by value

An Array of Objects Is Initially an Array of `Nulls`

Bug Alert 8.4

Each object in an array of objects must be separately instantiated. They are all
initially `null`.

8.5

Debugging Arrays

For our debugging exercise in this chapter, we solve a problem we suggested in
the last section: to find the distribution of grades on an exam. Specifically, given
a set of grades, we will produce a *histogram*, also called a *bar chart*, showing
how many students got scores in each of the intervals 0–9, 10–19, . . . ,90–100.
An example of our output is shown in Figure 8.15; this rather spartan output will
be spruced up in the exercises that follow.

Unlike the debugging sections of previous chapters, this one is an exercise
much more in program structure than in debugging program statements. When
an *algorithm* for a specific task is designed, the main goal is *efficiency*, although
simplicity is highly desirable. When a *program* is designed, the most important
goal is *maintainability*. Maintainability is the ability to modify the program to
accommodate future uses. It is impossible to write a program that can be easily
modified for any new use, but experience can teach you what changes are most
likely to occur and how to plan for those.

maintainability

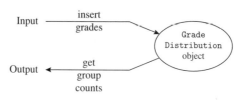

FIGURE 8.8 Structure of the histogram program.

For example, programs are often subject to modification in the way they obtain their input and produce their output. In our example, the program will get its inputs from an input box, but in other circumstances the input might come from a file; it will produce its output in the form of a bar graph, but a number of other output formats are possible. We want to design our histogram program in such a way that the basic calculations for maintaining the grade distribution are isolated, the input process communicates with those calculations in a simple way, and the output process gets the results of those calculations in a simple way. The basic outline of the program is shown in Figure 8.8.

The essential feature of this structure is that the grade distribution is calculated and stored in an object. The input and display routines are clients of this object. Since input and display routines may be changed independently, as much as possible they should communicate only through the grade distribution object, and not with each other.

In its role as an accumulator of data, the most important method of the distribution object is `void insertScore (int score)`, whereby the input routine can add a new score to the current set of scores. In its role as a reporter of the accumulated information, its most important method is `int groupCount (int group)`, whose argument is an integer between 0 and 9 (representing the ranges 0–9, 10–19, and so on). Additional methods are needed to initialize the object and to help the output routine to format the data properly.

Thus, the program will be structured in three classes (instead of our usual two classes): a client containing just a `main` routine, a class (which we call `GradeReport`) containing the heart of the computation (the methods `readScores` and `barGraph`), and a separate class `GradeDistribution` which is used by `GradeReport` to store the data as they are read. This structure is shown in the UML diagram of Figure 8.9. Separating the input and output methods in the `GradeReport` class emphasizes the independence of these operations.

The client class (which needs no debugging,[2] is

```
public class GradeClient {

    public static void main (String[] args) {
        GradeReport gr = new GradeReport();
        GradeDistribution distr = new GradeDistribution();

        gr.readScores(distr);
```

---

[2]In real life, programmers often make mistakes in even the simplest pieces of code, but for purposes of exposition, we will omit that part of the process.

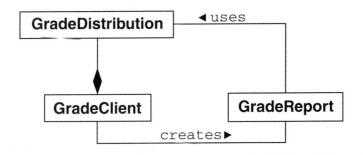

FIGURE 8.9 UML diagram for the histogram program.

```
        gr.barGraph(distr);
    }
}
```

The GradeReport class can be presented partially. We fill in the input routine, since it follows a pattern we have seen many times before.

```
import CSLib.*;

public class GradeReport {
  // Build and use a GradeDistribution
  // Author: Robert D. Klapper, November 16, 2000

  public void readScores (GradeDistribution distr) {
    InputBox in = new InputBox("Enter grade: ");
    while (true) {
      int g = in.readInt();
      if (in.eoi()) return;
      distr.insertGrade(g);
    }
  }

  public void barGraph (GradeDistribution distr) {

    // to be filled in ...
  }
}
```

As for the GradeDistribution class, we know very little about it as of yet:

```
    public class GradeDistribution {

      // instance variable declarations

      void insertGrade (int grade) { ... }

      int groupCount (int group) { ... }

      // other instance methods
    }
```

The basic idea is very simple: We will use an array of integers `counts` such that `counts[i]` will give the count of grades in the *i*th group, namely, $10i \ldots 10i + 9$. (We need to remember that group 9 is an exception, since it contains an extra value, 100.) What is particularly nice about this is that, given any grade, we can obtain its group by dividing by 10, using integer division.

This gives us our first version of `GradeDistribution`:

```java
public class GradeDistribution {
    // Keep track of a grade distribution.
    // Author: Rachel N. Reingold, January 31, 2001

    //   counts stores the count for each group.  That is,
    //   counts[0] is the number of grades between 0 and 9,
    //   counts[1] is the number of grades between 10 and 19, etc.
    private int[] counts;

    public GradeDistribution () {
        counts = new int[10];
    }

    // Report new grade to be added to distribution
    public void insertGrade (int g) {
        // Ignore grades that are out of range
        if (g < 0 || g > 100) return;
        int group = g / 10;
        if (group == 10) // i.e. grade = 100
            group = 9;
        counts[group]++;
    }

    // Return count for given group
    public int groupCount (int gp) {
        if (gp < 0 || gp > 10) return 0;
        return counts[gp];
    }

}
```

Our current purpose is to make sure that the `GradeDistribution` class is correct. Keep in mind that the only other code we've written up to now is the client and the input routine, both of which we have done many times now and feel quite confident about. The `GradeDistribution` class is something new. The output routine (`barGraph`) will be new also. So, to make debugging easier, we start with a simplified version of `barGraph`—hopefully, so simple that it can't be wrong—and this will let us test just `GradeDistribution`. Specifically, we will have `barGraph` just print out all the group counts in an output box:

```java
public void barGraph (GradeDistribution distr) {
    OutputBox out = new OutputBox("Debugging");
    for (int i=0; i<=9; i++)  // there are 9 groups
        out.println(distr.groupCount(i));
}
```

FIGURE 8.10 Output from version 1 of the histogram program.

The first version of the code is now complete and compiles correctly.[3] When run, it pops up an input window into which we can enter grades one at a time; when done, we enter nothing, which sets the end-of-input flag, as we have seen before. If the set of grades we enter is

    78 45 0 81 77 66 93 100 0 58 60

then the output will be as shown in Figure 8.10.

The `GradeDistribution` class seems to work fine. We turn our attention now to the output.

```
public void barGraph (GradeDistribution distr) {
    // With screen width w and height h, place bar     WRONG
    // for i(th) group at i*w/10 pixels from left, with
    // width w/10 and height h/20 times the count
    DrawingBox out = new DrawingBox("Grade Histogram");
    int w = out.getWidth(),
        h = out.getHeight();                           WRONG
    int barwidth = w/10;
    for (int i=0; i<10; i++) {
        int horizpos = i*barwidth,
            height = distr.groupCount(i)*h/20;          WRONG
        out.drawRect(horizpos, horizpos+barwidth, 0, height);
    }
}
```

The idea is simple enough: If the width of the output box is w, then it will be divided into 10 bars, each w/10 pixels wide. We assume that the count for each

---

[3]From now on, to save space and avert tedium, we will not show our syntax errors, although we still make them.

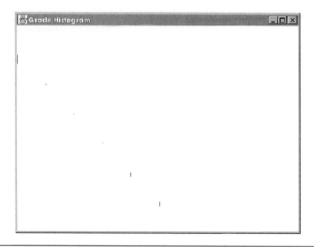

FIGURE 8.11   Output from version 2 of the histogram program.

group will be no more than 20, so we divide the height of the window into 20 parts; for each group, we find its count and multiply that by this quantity. Knowing the size and position of the bar for that group, we draw it using `drawRectangle`. For the inputs given above, the output is shown in Figure 8.11.

Obviously, this is no good. Actually, the main thing we did wrong is that we gave incorrect arguments to `drawRectangle`. We gave the two x coordinates followed by the two y coordinates. Sometimes, it's a good idea to read the documentation. As you can see on page 48, `drawRectangle`'s arguments are the (x, y) coordinate of the upper left corner, then the width and height of the rectangle. Changing that statement to

```
out.drawRect(horizpos, 0, barwidth, height);                    WRONG
```

produces the output shown in Figure 8.12, which is at least close enough to being correct that we can see what's wrong.

The problem with this version is also obvious: The bars are drawn from the top down instead of from the bottom up. Drawing from the bottom up is just a little unnatural, because instead of drawing from the baseline, we need to locate the upper left corner of the bar somewhere in the middle of the screen. But it is not really difficult: Just subtract the height of the bar from the maximum y value, which is the height of the window. This leads to our changing the output statement to

```
out.drawRect(horizpos, h-height, barwidth, height);             WRONG
```

which changes the output to that shown in Figure 8.13.

The strange thing about this output compared to the output in Figure 8.12 is that all the bars seem to be cut off. As a result, only the bars of height 2 show up at

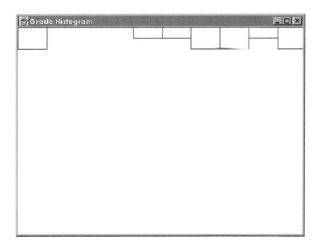

FIGURE 8.12 Output from version 3 of the histogram program.

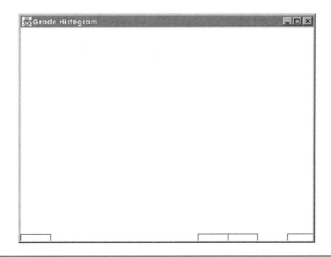

FIGURE 8.13 Output from version 4 of the histogram program.

all. To diagnose this problem, we first ought to rule out the possibility that our calculations of the locations and heights of the bars are incorrect. Simple as these calculations are, an error there is the most obvious cause of the problem. We add some output statements to the drawing code so we can look at the numbers directly:

```
public void barGraph (GradeDistribution distr) {
    // With screen width w and height h, place bar
    // for i(th) group at i*w/10 pixels from left, with
    // width w/10 and height h/20 times the count
    DrawingBox out = new DrawingBox("Grade Histogram");
    int w = out.getWidth(),
```

```
          h = out.getHeight();
       int barwidth = w/10;
    OutputBox debug = new OutputBox("Debugging");
    debug.println("Width, height: "+w+","+h);
    debug.println("(x,y) of upper-left corner, width, and height:");
       for (int i=0; i<10; i++) {
          int horizpos = i*barwidth,
             height = distr.groupCount(i)*h/20;
          out.drawRect(horizpos, h-height, barwidth, height);
    debug.println(""+horizpos+","+ (h-height)+
    ","+ barwidth+","+ height);
       }
    }
```

The output in the `debug` window is the following:

```
Width, height:
512,384
(x,y) of upper-left corner, width, and height:
0,346,51,38
51,384,51,0
102,384,51,0
153,384,51,0
204,365,51,19
255,365,51,19
306,346,51,38
357,346,51,38
408,365,51,19
459,346,51,38
```

These numbers look fine. The width of the window is 512, so we expect the bars to have width 51; that is, their starting *x* coordinates should be 0, 51, 102, etc. The height is 384, so the height of the bars should grow in increments of 19 (384/20); we can see this in two ways: The heights of the bars are 0, 19, and 38; and the upper left vertical positions of the bars are 384 (i.e., height of 0), 365 (384 − 19, height of 1), and 346 (384 − 38, height of 2). In short, it looks as if we calculated the positions correctly. Yet, for some reason, only the bars of height 2 are showing up.

In a situation like this, it helps to have a flash of inspiration; a good memory or a knowledgeable friend is also handy. Without any of the above, it would probably take us a long time to recognize the problem: We have used the *total* height and width of the window (including the borders) instead of the *drawable* height and width. If we change `getWidth` and `getHeight` to `getDrawableWidth` and `getDrawableHeight`, respectively, and run the above again, we get quite different numbers, especially for the vertical coordinates:

```
Width, height:
504,357
(x,y) of upper-left corner, width, and height:
0,322,50,35
50,357,50,0
100,357,50,0
150,357,50,0
200,340,50,17
250,340,50,17
300,322,50,35
```

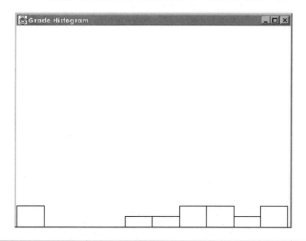

FIGURE 8.14 Output from version 6 of the histogram program.

```
350,322,50,35
400,340,50,17
450,322,50,35
```

Moreover, the output of the bar graph itself, shown in Figure 8.14, now looks quite reasonable.

Well, reasonable perhaps, but not perfect. As a matter of aesthetics, dividing the output window into 20 height divisions, regardless of the actual counts, is rather shortsighted. It relies on an assumption—that the maximum group count will always be 20—that is completely unjustified and should never have been made! Further, it is not difficult to remedy. Ideally, we would like to find the true maximum group count and divide up the output window accordingly. If the GradeDistribution class had a method maxCount that would tell us the maximum group count, then we could just change the calculation for height to

```
height = distr.groupCount(i)*h/distr.maxCount();
```

The effect of this change is shown in Figure 8.15. The maxCount method itself is very simple:

```
// Return maximum count of any group (this is
//   needed to calibrate sizes of graphs)
public int maxCount () {
  // size of maximum group
  int max = 0;
  for (int i=0; i<counts.length; i++)
    if (max < counts[i]) max = counts[i];
  return max;
}
```

At this point, the program is fine except for a rather serious issue of style. We said at the beginning of this section that our goal is to create a program that is *maintainable* in the sense of being capable of surviving under modifications. We

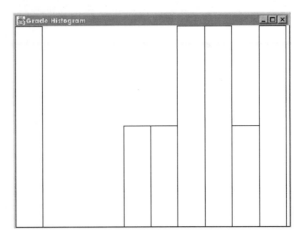

FIGURE 8.15   Output from version 7 of the histogram program.

have isolated the grade distribution calculation itself from the input and output, which have in turn been isolated from each other; input and output methods can be easily changed. But there is another obvious modification that we should allow for: changing the set of intervals. Currently, the intervals 0–9, 10–19, and so on are built into the `GradeDistribution` class and are assumed by the output routine. In a class with many students, it might be perfectly reasonable to have intervals of width 1, producing a graph showing the count for every grade. Or, we might have an exam in which the scores range in value from 0 to 20, and to get 10 groups we want to use intervals 0–1, 2–3, etc.

Here is our plan: The client of `GradeDistribution` will provide a description of the set of intervals when it first creates the `GradeDistribution` object. The latter will then classify grades into one of those intervals.

We first need to decide how to describe the set of intervals, which leads to a deeper question: What sets of intervals will be allowed? Abstractly, we are *partitioning* the set of grades—dividing it into a collection of smaller sets. There are a huge number of such partitions: For example, we could divide the set of grades into the even-numbered and odd-numbered grades, giving two large subsets. Such a division probably makes no sense for the applications we have in mind (why would an instructor care how many students got an odd-numbered grade as opposed to an even-numbered grade?), but it serves to illustrate the number of possibilities.

For our purposes, it seems likely that the only kinds of partitions we would care about are those that divide the set of grades into a relatively small number of sets of consecutive numbers. (In fact, we might even make a further restriction that all the intervals be of the same size. However, we would immediately run afoul of our primary example: Our tenth interval, 90–100, is larger than any of the other intervals.)

So we can describe the set of intervals with a single array of increasing integers. The array $\{a, b, c, \ldots\}$ represents the intervals a to $b - 1$, b to $c - 1$, and so on. a should be the lowest attainable score, and the last number in this array should be 1 greater than the highest attainable score. For example, the set of 10 intervals we have been using would be described by the array $\{0, 10, 20, 30, 40, 50, 60, 70, 80, 90, 101\}$.

We will supply this descriptive array when we create the GradeDistribution object. The size of this array affects the drawing of the bar graph, but only in a narrow way: It determines how wide each bar will be. To keep the barGraph method independent of the rest of the GradeReport class, we assume that the GradeDistribution class has one new method, int numGroups (), giving the number of groups.

With these modifications, the GradeReport class changes only slightly:

```
import CSLib.*;

public class GradeReport {
    // Build and use a GradeDistribution
    // Author: Robert D. Klapper, November 16, 2000

    public void readScores (GradeDistribution distr) {
        InputBox in = new InputBox("Enter grade: ");
        while (true) {
            int g = in.readInt();
            if (in.eoi()) return;
            distr.insertGrade(g);
        }
    }

    public void barGraph (GradeDistribution distr) {
        // With n groups and maximum count of m, and
        // screen width w and height h, place bar for
        // i(th) group at i*w/n pixels from left, with
        // width w/n and height h/m times the count
        DrawingBox out = new DrawingBox("Grade Histogram");
        int m = distr.maxCount(),
            n = distr.numGroups(),
            w = out.getDrawableWidth(),
            h = out.getDrawableHeight();
        int barwidth = w/n;
        for (int i=0; i<n; i++) {
            int horizpos = i*barwidth,
                height = distr.groupCount(i)*h/m;
            out.drawRect(horizpos, h-height, barwidth, height);
        }
    }
}
```

GradeDistribution changes much more significantly. In particular, the method of dividing a grade by 10 to find its interval no longer works. Instead, we need to search through the list of intervals to find the interval of each grade. Here is the new version of this class:

```
public class GradeDistribution {
  // Keep track of a grade distribution.
  // Author: Rachel N. Reingold, January 31, 2001

  // intervals stores beginning and ending of each
  //   group.  Groups are intervals[0]..intervals[1]-1,
  //   intervals[1]..intervals[2]-1, etc.
  //   Note that intervals.length is one more
  //   than the number of groups
  private int[] intervals;

  // counts stores the count for each group.  That is,
  //   counts[i] is the number of grades between
  //   intervals[i] and intervals[i+1]-1, inclusive.
  //   counts.length = intervals.length - 1
  private int[] counts;

  // Create distribution with given set of groups.
  // Argument is array to be copied into intervals.
  public GradeDistribution (int[] intervals) {
    this.intervals = new int[intervals.length];
    counts = new int[intervals.length-1];
    for (int i=0; i<intervals.length; i++)
      this.intervals[i] = intervals[i];
  }

  // Report new grade to be added to distribution
  public void insertGrade (int g) {
    // Ignore grades that are out of range
    if (g < intervals[0]) return;
    int i=0;
    while (i < counts.length && g >= intervals[i+1])
      i++;
    if (i == counts.length) return;
    else counts[i]++;
  }

  // Return number of groups
  public int numGroups () {
    return counts.length;
  }

  // Return count for given group
  public int groupCount (int gp) {
    if (gp < 0 || gp >= counts.length) return 0;
    return counts[gp];
  }

  // Return maximum count of any group (this is
  //   needed to calibrate sizes of graphs)
  public int maxCount () {
    // size of maximum group
    int max = 0;
```

```
    for (int i=0; i<counts.length; i++)
      if (max < counts[i]) max = counts[i];
    return max;
  }
}
```

We have paid a considerable cost in complexity as well as efficiency. As written, the output is exactly the same as illustrated in Figure 8.15. However, we have gained the ability to adjust the output easily. Changing the initialization of groups in the readAndReport method to

```
int[] groups = {0, 1, 26, 51, 76, 101};
```

produces the output shown in Figure 8.16.

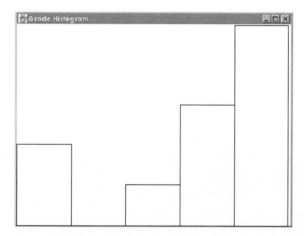

FIGURE 8.16 **Output from final version of the histogram program, with intervals 0–0, 1–25, 26–50, 51–75, and 76–100.**

8.6

Sorting and Searching

> "I weep for you," the Walrus said:
> "I deeply sympathize."
> With sobs and tears he sorted out
> Those of the largest size.
>
> —Lewis Carroll
> *Through the Looking-Glass, "The Walrus and the*
> *Carpenter"*

Two of the most frequently performed operations on arrays are *sorting* (placing the elements in a specified order) and *searching* (finding where, or if, a particular element occurs in an array). Each of these problems has been studied extensively to find efficient solutions; we discuss them further in Chapter 14. In this section we present simple, though not very efficient, methods for these operations.

8.6.1 Selection Sort

A simple method of sorting an array A of n elements is *selection sort*. It works like this:

- Find the smallest element among the elements A[0]...A[n-1]; suppose it is A[min].
- Move A[min] to position 0 and A[0] to position min (this is called *swapping*). At this point, A[0] contains the smallest element in the array, and the remaining elements are unsorted.
- Next, find the smallest element among A[1]...A[n-1] and swap it with A[1]. Now A[0] contains the smallest element, A[1] contains the second-smallest element, and A[2]...A[n-1] are unsorted.
- Proceed similarly for A[3], A[4], and so on.

For example, here is a trace of this method for a particular array A, containing elements 27, 12, 3, 18, 11, and 7:

Find the smallest element and place it at the front:

27	12	3	18	11	7

Find the next-smallest element and place it in the second position:

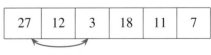

3	12	27	18	11	7

Do the same for the third element:

And the fourth:

Finally, the fifth:

A is now sorted:

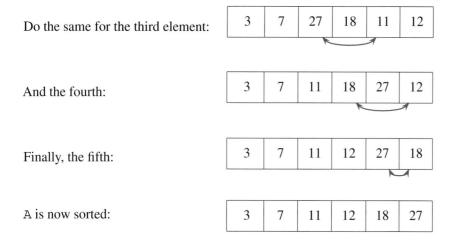

In summary, for each i from 0 to size-2 (where size is the number of elements in the array), find the smallest element among A[i]...A[size-1] and swap it with A[i].

```
1   public class SelectionSort {
2      // Sort an array of doubles
3      // Author: M. Dennis Mickunas, June 9, 2001
4
5      public void selectionSort (double[] A, int size) {
6         int i, j;
7         for (i=0; i<size; i++) {
8            // All elements in A[0]..A[i-1] are less than
9            // all elements in A[i]..A[size-1], and
10           // a[0]..A[i-1] is sorted.
11           int min = findMinimum(A, i, size);
12           swap(A, i, min);
13        }
14     }
```

The method findMinimum just iterates over all the elements from i to the end and finds the index of the smallest. Then swap interchanges two elements of A.

```
16     // Locate the smallest value in an array.
17     int findMinimum (double[] A, int i, int size) {
18        int j, min = i;
19        for (j=i+1; j<size; j++)
20           // A[min] <= all elements in A[i]..A[j-1]
21           if (A[j] < A[min]) min = j;
22        return min;
23     }
24
25     // Exchange A[i] and A[j]
26     void swap (double[] A, int i, int j) {
27        double temp = A[i];
28        A[i] = A[j];
29        A[j] = temp;
30     }
```

QUICK EXERCISE 8.16	The `swap` method looks more complicated than necessary. Explain why this version is wrong:

```
void swap (double[] A, int i, int j) {
  A[i] = A[j];
  A[j] = A[i];
}
```

BUG ALERT 8.5	It is tempting to write swap as

```
void swap (double x, double y) {
  double temp = x;
  x = y;
  y = temp;
}
```

and to call it with

```
swap (A[i], A[j]);
```

However, recall that the arguments to `swap` are passed *by value* (recall Section 8.9). So it is not possible to alter them within the swap method.

The `SelectionSort` class might be used by a client in this way:

```
1   import CSLib.*;
2
3   public class SelSortClient {
4
5     public static void main (String[] args) {
6       final int MAX_SIZE = 1000;
7       double[] input = new double[MAX_SIZE];
8       int size;
9
10      ArrayIO aio = new ArrayIO();
11      size = aio.read(input);
12
13      SelectionSort ss = new SelectionSort();
14      ss.selectionSort(input, size);
15
16      aio.print(input, size);
17    }
18  }
19
```

The `ArrayIO` class contains methods `read` and `print`, similar to the `read` and `printAvgs` methods of the `GradeBook` class on page 282, except that they read an array of doubles instead of `Student` objects, and instead of `printAvgs`, we have `print` to just print the array elements in sequence:

```
1    import CSLib.*;
2
3    public class ArrayIO {
4      // Read and print an array of doubles
5      // Author: D. Kamin, February 29, 2000
6
7      public int read (double[] A) {
8
9        InputBox in = new InputBox();
10       double num;
11
12       in.setPrompt("Enter double (null to terminate):");
13       int size = 0;
14
15       while (true) {
16         num = in.readDouble();
17         if (in.eoi()) return size;
18         A[size] = num;
19         size++;
20       }
21     }
22
23     public void print (double[] A, int size) {
24       OutputBox out = new OutputBox("Sorted output");
25       for (int i=0; i<size; i++) {
26         out.println(A[i]);
27       }
28     }
29   }
30
31
```

8.6.2 Insertion Sort

Another simple sorting method is *insertion sort*. Iterate over indices 1 to n-1. At the ith step, shift the elements A[0]...A[i] so that this part of the array is sorted. Note that when the ith iteration begins, elements A[0]...A[i-1] are already sorted, so the only shifting required is to insert A[i] into A[0]...A[i-1], moving some of those elements to the right to fit A[i] in.

For example, consider the array A again:

Sort the first two elements:

27	12	3	18	11	7

Move the third element so that the first three are sorted:

12	27	3	18	11	7

Move the fourth element so that the first four are sorted:

3	12	27	18	11	7

Move the fifth element so that the
first five are sorted:

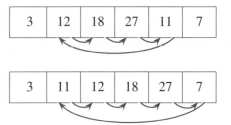

Move the sixth element so that all
six are sorted:

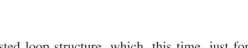

A is now sorted:

3	7	11	12	18	27

The method again has a nested loop structure, which, this time, just for the practice, we make explicit (instead of putting the inner loop into a separate method). The outer loop is the one we've been describing:

```
for (i=1; i<size; i++) {
    // Elements in A[0]..A[i-1] are sorted.
    insert A[i] into correct position in A[0]..A[i]
}
```

Inserting A[i] logically involves two steps: finding where it belongs—call this position j—and shifting the elements A[j]...A[i-1] over to the right. However, we can combine them into one process that works like this. In a loop, count index variable j *down* from i-1 to 0. At each iteration, if A[j] is greater than (the old value of) A[i], move it to the right and continue the loop. If A[j] is less than A[i], A[i] should be placed in position j+1 and the loop should be terminated. The complete method is as follows:

```
class InsertionSort {
    // Sort an array of doubles.
    // Author:  M. Dennis Mickunas, June 9, 2001

    public void insertionSort (double[] A, int size) {
        int i, j;
        for (i=1; i<size; i++) {
            // Elements in A[0]..A[i-1] are sorted.
            // Insert A[i] into correct position in A[0]..A[i]
            double Ai = A[i];
            j = i-1;
            while (j>=0 && A[j]>Ai) {
                // A[0]..A[i] sorted, but if j<i-1, A[j+1]
                // is a "gap"
                A[j+1] = A[j];
                j--;
            }
            // Note: Ai goes into A[j+1] even if j=-1
            A[j+1] = Ai;
        }
    }
}
```

8.6.3 Searching

We have said that these methods, though simple, are inefficient. We'll examine this claim shortly, but first we mention the problem of searching for an item in an array. The most obvious method is the one we presented on page 273: look at every element in the array until the element in question is found. This method is called *linear search*, or *sequential search*. We encapsulate it in a method that returns the index at which the element was found or, if not found, returns −1.

linear search

sequential search

```
1     // Locate key in an array of ints
2     int linearSearch (int[] A, int key) {
3        int i;
4        for (i=0; i<A.length; i++)
5           // key not in A[0]..A[i-1]
6           if (A[i] == key) return i;
7        // key not in A
8        return -1;
9     }
```

(One point before we proceed. For the sorting algorithms, we used an array of doubles, whereas here we have suddenly switched to an array of integers. Our reason is that searching for a specific double value in an array is unwise. Because double values are *approximate*—see Bug Alert 4.3—comparing two doubles for equality does not always give the correct result. For example, try the comparison 2.0==Math.sqrt(2.0)*Math.sqrt(2.0). One can, and should, compare approximate values with respect to a "fuzz factor." Pick a small value epsilon and, instead of comparing x == y, compare Math.abs(x-y) < epsilon; this tests if x and y are within epsilon of each other.)

8.6.4 Efficiency of Searching and Sorting

Let's look at the efficiency of some of these methods. We consider linear search first, because it's simplest. We analyze the efficiency first mathematically, then empirically.

By efficiency, we mean *speed*. But this already presents a problem: Different computers operate at different speeds. We can't say that such and such a method runs in 3.45 seconds, because even if the statement is true on one computer, it would be false on another. So, instead of attempting to say exactly how long it takes for the method to run, we will talk about how many operations it performs. In principle, we need to count every single operation: In the linear search loop, each iteration of the loop involves a comparison between i and A.length, an access to A[i], a comparison between that value and key, and an incrementing of i. (Technically, the incrementing of i happens one fewer time than the other operations, since it is not done for the first iteration; but if the array is long enough for the method to take a significant amount of time, this small difference won't matter.) Each of these operations takes time. However, each of these operations takes a *constant* amount of time, so for the purposes of analysis it is simplest to assume that all the time is taken up with just one of those operations, so we only have to count that one. We could pick any of those operations, but it is traditional in this field to count only *comparisons* of array elements (equality comparisons for searching and "less than" comparisons for sorting).

Consider linear search. Specifically, consider the case when `key` does not occur in A. How many comparisons does `linearSearch(A, key)` do before it returns `-1`? Exactly n, where n is the size of A. Its running time will be proportional to this number. In other words, there is a constant c such that the running time, which we'll call $T_{\text{linearSearch}}$, is

$$T_{\text{linearSearch}}(\text{A}, \text{key}) = cn$$

linear time   We say `linearSearch` runs in *linear time* in the length of the array.

We can find c for our particular computer by trying some examples. In fact, in principle, one example would suffice. Call `linearSearch` on an array of length, say, n, and suppose it takes s seconds; then $c = s/n$. However, there can be some variations, especially when n is small, so we do several experiments.

Array Size	**125,000**	**250,000**	**500,000**	**1,000,000**
Running time for linear search, in seconds	1	1	3	6

For arrays of sizes 125,000 and 250,000, the running times are too small to be measured accurately. Looking at the larger arrays, we see that our claim that the running time would be linear in the size of A has been verified. On this computer, $c \approx 0.000006$. In effect, this says it takes 6 microseconds per element to search in A.

Of course, searching for an element that *is* in the array is faster, since the search stops sooner. On average, it should only take about half as long. This is still linear time, with a different constant, namely, $c' = c/2$.

Sorting is a lot more time-consuming. Both selection sort and insertion sort perform a number of comparisons proportional to the *square* of the size of A. Consider selection sort. For each iteration `i`, it looks through all the elements from `i` to `n-1` to find the minimum element. There are `n-1` iterations. So the total number of comparisons is

$$
\begin{array}{ll}
n-1 & \text{(first iteration: find minimum among A[0]...A[n-1])} \\
+ \quad n-2 & \text{(second iteration: find minimum among A[1] ... A[n-1])} \\
+ \quad n-3 & \text{(third iteration: find minimum among A[2]...A[n-1])} \\
\quad \vdots & \\
+ \quad 1 & ((n-1)\text{st iteration: find minimum among A[n-2]...A[n-1])} \\
\hline
\end{array}
$$

$$(n-1)n/2 = n^2/2 - n/2$$

Since $n^2/2$ is much greater than $n/2$, we just say the number of comparisons—and therefore the running time—is proportional to n^2. That is, there is a constant c such that

$$T_{\text{selectionSort}}(\text{A}) = cn^2$$

Such an algorithm is said to be *quadratic* in the size of the array.

Again, we can determine c for a particular computer by experiment:

Array Size	**250**	**500**	**1000**	**2000**	**4000**
Running time for selection sort, in seconds	1	2	7	26	103

The difference between a quadratic algorithm and a linear one is substantial: Sorting an array of 1000 elements takes more time than searching in an array of 1 million elements! (Keep in mind, however, that we are sorting an array of doubles and searching in an array of integers; comparisons of doubles are considerably more expensive than comparisons of integers.)

We will not present the corresponding analysis for insertion sort. It is similar—like selection sort, its running time *normally* is proportional to the square of the size of the array—but it is also different in that its running time is *sometimes* much faster. That is, unlike selection sort, whose running time is the same for all arrays of a given length, insertion sort is sensitive to the contents of the array. For example, if the array is already sorted, insertion sort takes very little time. Its worst performance occurs when the array is initially sorted in reverse. An analysis more sophisticated than we can undertake here shows that, in some sense, insertion sort *usually* is quadratic.

These methods are adequate for small amounts of data, but *much* more efficient methods exist. In particular, if an array is sorted, it is possible to find an element in it in time proportional to $\log_2 n$ (the base-2 logarithm of n), a much smaller number than n (for example, $\log_2 1{,}000{,}000 \approx 20$). Sorting can be done in time proportional to $n \log_2 n$, which is much smaller number than n^2 (for $n = 1000$, $n^2 = 1{,}000{,}000$, while $n \log_2 n \approx 10{,}000$). These more efficient methods are presented in Chapter 14.

8.7

One-Dimensional Arrays and Graphics

In Chapter 6, we saw how to do primitive animation by repeatedly drawing in a `DrawingBox`. A similar technique can be used to do animation using GIFs. We simply read a sequence of GIFs into an array of `Images`.

Such a program is

```
1    import CSLib.*;
2    import java.awt.*;
3
```

```
4    public class Animate {
5
6      // Animate an applet with a sequence of GIFs
7      // Author: Norma D. Mickunas, May 9, 1996
8
9      final int NUMBER = 15;
10     int ticker = 0;
11     boolean started = false;
12     Image[] mouse = new Image[NUMBER];
13     int[] sleepTime = {1540,240,240,240,240,
14                        240,240,240,240,240,
15                        240,240,240,240,240};
16     DrawingBox g = new DrawingBox();
17
18     public void show () {
19
20       for (int i = 0; i < NUMBER; i++)
21         mouse[i] = Toolkit.getDefaultToolkit().
22                        getImage("images/T"+(i+1)+".gif");
23
24       ticker=0;
25       do {
26         g.drawImage(mouse[ticker], 70, 70);
27         Timer.pause(sleepTime[ticker]);
28         ticker = (ticker + 1) % NUMBER;
29       } while (true);
30     }
31   }
```

```
1    public class AnimateClient {
2
3      public static void main (String[] args) {
4        Animate anim = new Animate();
5        anim.show();
6      }
7    }
```

This program reads a sequence of 15 GIFs named T1.gif,...,T15.gif. These are images of a mouse running into a wall (see Figure 8.17).

By displaying them one after another, the mouse appears to run into the wall, then paint a mouse hole for itself to run through. In line 12, the array of Images is declared and created. The loop in lines 20 through 22 reads the 15 GIFs, just as we did in Section 6.12, but this time, we don't have a fixed string for the file name (such as T3.gif); rather, we form a new, slightly different string each time through the loop. You can see that the expression

```
"image/T" + (i+1) + ".gif"
```

forms the sequence of strings "image/T1.gif",...,"image/T15.gif". In the infinite loop of lines 24 through 29, the appropriate GIF images are repeatedly drawn using drawImage (again, as in Section 6.12).

One subtle point about this code is the insertion of pauses in the animation loop (line 27). We clearly need some delay in the loop, because without it the images would be displayed so quickly that we wouldn't see anything (try it). `Timer` is a class in `CSLib` whose (only) method is `pause`; its argument is an integer representing the number of milliseconds to pause. All it does is to wait for that much time before returning to its caller. We could give it a constant delay time, but instead we have used an array of integers, `sleepTime`, allowing us to vary the delay for each image. This array is almost constant, but contains a larger value for its first element than for all the others. The motive for this is to give the program some extra time to load the images before it begins the animation.

Summary

A *one-dimensional array* is a collection of variables. It is declared using the syntax

> *type* [] *array name* ;

and is allocated using `new`

> *array name* = new *type* [*size*] ;

Examples are

```
int [] answers = new int [100]; // 100 integers
char [] firstName = new char [20]; // 20 characters
String [] dayNames = new String [7]; // 7 references to Strings
```

Any of the variables in an array can be accessed by subscripting, as in `answers [15]` or `firstName [i]`. The valid subscripts of an array range from zero to the size of the array minus 1. Furthermore, the amount of time required to obtain an element of an array is very small and *constant*; that is, it does not depend on *which* element is referenced.

When an array is passed as an argument to a method, it behaves as an object, since a reference is passed. Therefore, the method can index the array and alter the contents of its elements.

Sorting and searching are two of the most common operations performed on large sets of data. *Linear search* looks for a value, or *key*, in an array by iterating over the entire array, looking at each element; it takes time proportional to the number of elements in the array, which is why it is called *linear* search. Selection sort sorts the elements of an array by repeatedly finding the minimum element in the nonsorted half of the array and moving it to the end of the sorted half. Insertion sort sorts an array by iterating over the nonsorted half of the array and inserting each element in the correct position in the sorted half. Both algorithms take time proportional to the square of the number of elements in the array, and they are therefore said to run in *quadratic* time. More efficient algorithms for these operations are described in Chapter 14.

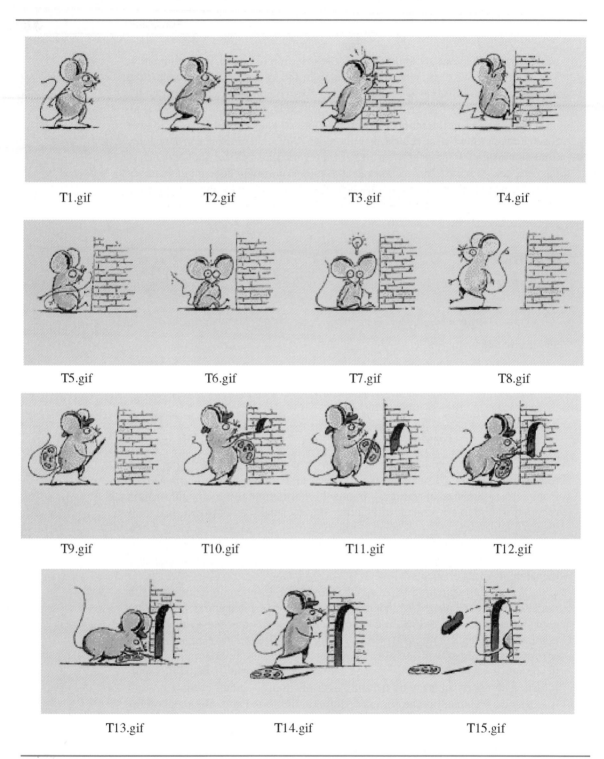

T1.gif T2.gif T3.gif T4.gif

T5.gif T6.gif T7.gif T8.gif

T9.gif T10.gif T11.gif T12.gif

T13.gif T14.gif T15.gif

FIGURE 8.17 Animation images.

Exercises

1. The *standard deviation* of a set of scores is a measure of how much the scores tend to clump near the mean. If everyone taking an exam gets nearly the same score, the standard deviation will be near zero, whereas if scores are spread evenly throughout a broad range, the standard deviation will be high. The standard deviation of a typical school exam graded on a 0 to 100 scale, with an average of 75, might be 10 to 15.

   The formula for computing the standard deviation of a set of scores $x_1, x_2, \ldots, x_n$, with a mean of $\bar{x} = (\sum_{i=1}^{n} x_i)/n$, is given by the formula

   $$s = \sqrt{\frac{\sum_{i=1}^{n}(x_i - \bar{x})^2}{n}}$$

   or, equivalently,

   $$s = \sqrt{\frac{\sum_{i=1}^{n} x_i^2}{n} - \bar{x}^2}$$

   Write a loop to calculate the standard deviation of a set of grades in an array `grades`, where `size` is the number of grades it contains.

2. An advantage of the last version of `GradeBook` (page 282) is that computations relating to student grades can be encapsulated in the `Student` class. For example, we can change the number of grades and the way in which the average is calculated. Make the following changes in that version of `GradeBook`, in sequence:
   (a) A better way to represent a student with several grades is to use a string for the student's name, as we already have, and an *array* for the grades. Make this change. For now, each student object contains an array of size 2.
   (b) In preparation for adding more grades per student, replace the methods `getExam1()` and `getExam2()` by a single method, `getExam(int which)`. The method `getExam(i)` will return the grade on exam i (i being, of course, either 1 or 2).
   (c) Add a method `numberOfGrades` to `Student`. The input loop in `read` should call this method to determine how many grades to read for each student.
   (d) Add two more exam grades for each student. Furthermore, drop each student's lowest grade. That is, let `getAvg` return the average of the three highest grades. If you have done the previous parts of this exercise correctly, this last change should be very simple.

3. Rewrite the minimum-nonzero-grade loop so that it does not depend upon any pre-determined maximum grade. This is actually much more difficult than it sounds. Replacing the assignment `min = 100` by `min = grades[0]` does not work, because `grades[0]` may be zero! In fact, you must start with a loop to find the first nonzero element in the array; after that, you can begin the `for` loop.

4. Write the following methods:
   (a) `int sum (int[] A, int size)` sums the elements `A[0]...A[size-1]`.
   (b) `int frequency (int[] A, int size, int p)` counts the number of occurrences of p among the values `A[0]...A[size-1]`.
   (c) `int max (int[] A, int size)` returns the maximum among the values `A[0]...A[size-1]`.

(d) `void insert (int[] A, int size, int p)` inserts p into A as the first element. The existing elements of A (`A[0]...A[size-1]`) are shifted over one position to the right; you can assume that A is large enough to hold this new element.

(e) `void insertInOrder (int[] A, int size, int p)` inserts p into A so as to leave A in numerical order, if it was in order originally. The elements of A greater than p are shifted one position to the right.

(f) `int find (int[] A, int size, int p)` returns the location at which p first occurs in A or `-1` if it does not occur at all.

5. A serious problem with our final histogram output (page 293) is that it has no labels. Each bar should have a label underneath it giving the range of scores that it includes. In order to retain the separation between the creation of the histogram and its display, the output routine should be able to query the `GradeDistribution` object to get the label for each bar. Add a method `String getLabel(int group)` to `GradeDistribution`, which returns a string representation of the numerical range of that group. Raise the bar graph and place the labels under each bar. You may assume that the bars are wide enough for the labels to fit underneath.

6. The method `linearSearchSorted` does the same thing as `linearSearch`, except that it assumes its array argument is sorted in ascending order. When a search key is *not* in the array, then the loop may be able to terminate sooner: Once an element is reached that is greater than the key, there is no need to look farther, because all the elements beyond that one will be even greater. Write `linearSearchSorted`.

7. There are some complications in the `Animate` program related to timing. To see why we cannot simplify it, try these variations:

(a) Remove the call to `Timer.pause`. What happens?

(b) Change the initialization of `sleepTime` so that all its elements are 240 (or, equivalently, change the call to `Timer.pause`, giving the constant 240 as its argument). What happens now?

(c) As a matter of fact, the entire approach of this program—reading the images into an array and then displaying them—is required by timing considerations. After all, we could just read each image from the file each time we want to display it. Make this change. What happens?

8. In Section 4.2 (page 116), we showed code that computes the number of days from the first of the given year to the given date. If all months had 31 days, this calculation would be simple, but because they don't, we had to use the "magic formula" `(4 * month + 23) / 10` as a correction factor. That this formula works is fortuitous, but it is hardly good style to depend on this kind of thing.

(a) A simple solution is to store the lengths of all the months in an array and then calculate the first day of the given month by adding the lengths of the months that precede it. All that is needed after that is to correct for leap years. Rewrite this code, using an array `monthLengths`, initialized to hold the lengths of the months.

(b) An even better solution is to define an array `daysPriorToThisMonth` that contains the total number of days in all months prior to the present month. Rewrite your code using this approach.

9. The *sieve of Eratosthenes* is a method of finding prime numbers by sifting out composite numbers. Start with

   2   3   4   5   6   7   8   9   10   11   12   13   14   15   16 $\cdots$ n

   Starting with 2, the first prime number, cross off every second number (except 2), leaving

   2   3   4̸   5   6̸   7   8̸   9   1̸0̸   11   1̸2̸   13   1̸4̸   15   1̸6̸ $\cdots$ n

   Then, starting from 3 (the next prime number), cross off every third number except 3, leaving

   2   3   4̸   5   6̸   7   8̸   9̸   1̸0̸   11   1̸2̸   13   1̸4̸   1̸5̸   1̸6̸ $\cdots$ n

   The italicized numbers are those that have already been found to be prime, and the ones in color are the multiples of the italicized numbers. At each step, find the smallest number p still in black—it is the next prime number—and italicize p and color every pth number after p. Continue this process until the smallest number in black exceeds $\sqrt{n}$; at that point all the italicized numbers are primes. Write an application to compute the prime numbers less than N (a symbolic constant) by the sieve of Eratosthenes, using an $(n + 1)$-element Boolean array `crossedOff[]` to represent the sequence. If `crossedOff[i]` is `true`, then i has been crossed off; if it is `false`, i has not yet been crossed off. (Elements `crossedOff[0]` and `crossedOff[1]` will just be ignored.)

10. Write a *self-reproducing* Java program. That is, the program should print an exact copy of itself [P. Bratley and J. Millo, "Self-Reproducing Programs," *Software—Practice and Experience* 2 (1972), pp. 397–400].

11. The most important feature of spreadsheet programs like Lotus 1–2–3® and Microsoft Excel® is that the value contained in one cell can be computed as a function of the values in other cells. If cell A1 contains the wholesale cost of a product, and A2 its retail cost, then you can enter the formula A2-A1, representing the profit on that item, into cell A3. It will be computed automatically when you enter the formula, and recalculated automatically whenever the contents of A1 or A2 change.

    One issue that arises in writing a spreadsheet program is what to do if there is a *circular* dependency among the items in the spreadsheet. Suppose the user inadvertently enters the formula A4+1 into cell A3 and A3+1 into cell A4. Such a mistake must be detected, so that the user can be warned, but how?

    We simplify the problem by having only a single row of cells instead of the usual grid of cells and, more importantly, by allowing each cell to depend on at most one other cell. Abstractly, we have a structure like this, where an arrow from cell i to cell j represents the fact that cell i is a function of cell j. For example, cell 3 contains a formula that refers to cell 6:

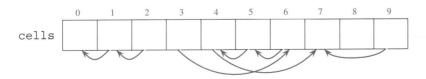

Your program should have as its input a sequence of n numbers (terminated by end of file) in the range $-1, \ldots, n-1$, giving the contents of the array cells. If cells[i] contains $j \geq 0$, it means that cell i is a function of cell j; if cells[i] contains -1, it means that cell i does not depend on any other cell. The dependencies just illustrated would be given as the 10 numbers

```
-1 0 1 6 7 4 5 -1 -1 7
```

To determine whether the set of dependences has a circularity, define an array of Booleans called visited and initialize it to all false. For each cell i, set visited[i] to true and then follow the arrows from i, setting visited[j] to true when an arrow leads to cell j. If an arrow ever leads to a cell k such that visited[k] is already true, there is a cycle. In that case, print a message indicating that cell k is in a cycle; otherwise, print a message indicating that there are no cycles.

12. The function int findMax (double[] A) finds the index in A at which it has its maximum value:

```
int findMax (double[] A) {
   int maxloc = 0;
   for (int i=1; i<A.length; i++)
      if (A[i] > A[maxloc]) maxloc = i;
   return maxloc;
}
```

Write a program that animates the findMax function. It should start by generating an array of 20 random numbers between 0 and 1 [use Math.random()]. Draw the array as a row of bars of varying height. At each iteration, the bar at maxloc should be colored in red (Color.red), while the bar at i should be gray (Color.gray). Show the array after each iteration of the loop, pausing for a brief interval after each iteration.

13. In exercise 14 of Chapter 7, you wrote a simple drawing program to draw triangles and circles in a drawing box. One problem with that program was that adjusting a new shape could cause parts of previous shapes to disappear. Since there was no memory of the previous shapes, there was no solution to this problem.

Revise that drawing program so that it keeps arrays of all the triangles and circles that have been drawn:

```
Triangle[] triangles = new Triangle[100];
Circle[] circles = new Circle[100];
```

When a new shape is added and adjusted, erase and redraw all the shapes. You can erase the entire drawing box by calling clear() and then send the draw message to each of the shapes in these two arrays. (You will need to make draw a public method in the Triangle and Circle classes.)

14. Starting from the previous exercise, you can extend your drawing program in a variety of ways now that you have all of the shapes stored in arrays. Extend the user's interface to allow the user to specify the shape they want to change (using an integer to specify it); this way, they can adjust any shape and not just the last one. Also give them the option of removing a shape (which means deleting it from the array).

CHAPTER 9

NESTED LOOPS AND TWO-DIMENSIONAL ARRAYS

CHAPTER PREVIEW

In this chapter we introduce *two-dimensional arrays*, which are used to represent grids of information, such as mathematical matrices and computer graphics. We show how computer graphics are generated using pixels. We also complete the mouse-in-a-maze example, using two-dimensional arrays to represent the maze.

Let all things be done decently and in order.

—Bible
I Corinthians 14:40

Two-dimensional arrays are used to represent mathematical matrices, images on a computer screen, the kinds of tables that one often sees in books or newspapers, and many other things. Just as one-dimensional arrays are often processed by loops, so two-dimensional arrays are often processed by *nested* loops. We look at these in detail in Section 9.1. We then introduce two-dimensional arrays, illustrating their use in several simple examples, as well as two larger examples: the mouse-in-a-maze, and the algorithms underlying graphical operations such as line and circle drawing.

two-dimensional arrays

9.1

Nested Loops

We've seen many examples of `while` and `for` loops. The calculations done in the body of the loop can be very complicated, including method calls. We have rarely seen loops that contain other loops; one example was the insertion sort algorithm on page 296. In this section, we will see numerous examples. Nested loops are frequently used in conjunction with two-dimensional arrays, which are the focus of the remainder of the chapter.

As we saw in treating one-dimensional arrays, `for` loops are often a bit easier to use than `while` loops for array processing. Similarly, nested `for` loops are the most common loop structure used in processing two-dimensional arrays.

The simplest structure for a nested `for` loop is as follows:

```
for (i=0; i<m; i++) {
    before inner loop
    for (j=0; j<n; j++) {
        body of inner loop
    }
    after inner loop
}
```

The *body* of the outer loop consists of the part before the inner loop, the inner loop, and the part after the inner loop. The inner loop is usually where the main computation is done. For each value of i between 0 and m-1, it is executed for all the values of j between 0 and n-1. Specifically, it is executed first for values i=0 and j=0; next for i=0, j=1; then i=0, j=2; and so on until i=0, j=n-1; then on to i=1, j=0; and so on until i=m-1, j=n-1. The easiest way to see this is to print the values of the loop indices. The loop

```
for (i=0; i<3; i++) {
    out.print("i= " + i + ": j =");
    for (j=0; j<4; j++) {
        out.print(" " + j);
    }
    out.println();
}
```

has the output shown in Figure 9.1.

Sometimes the extent of an inner nested loop will depend on the index value of the outer loop. One possible structure is illustrated by this loop, whose output is shown in Figure 9.2:

```
for (i=0; i<3; i++) {
    out.print("i= " + i + ": j =");
    for (j=0; j<=i; j++) {   // j ranges from 0 to i
        out.print(" " + j);
    }
    out.println();
}
```

Nested loop structures are nicely illustrated by printing output characters, such as asterisks, in the inner loop. For example, in the inner loop of the previous

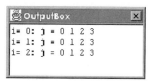

FIGURE 9.1   Output from simple nested loop.

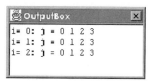

FIGURE 9.2   Output from second simple nested loop.

Change the header of the inner loop to `for (j=i; j<4; j++)`. What does it do?

example, instead of printing numbers, we might print an asterisk, skipping a line after the inner loop,

```
*
**
***
```

which gives a good sense of how often the inner loop is executing. For a more complicated example, in the following code, the inner loop executes most often when the outer loop index is either very small or very large.

```
for (int i = 1; i <= 9; i++) {
  for (int j = 0; j <= Math.abs(i-5); j++)
    out.print("*");
  out.println();
  }
```

It produces the output

```
*****
****
***
**
*
**
***
****
*****
```

The nested loop can be contained in other statements inside the loop. For example, this loop contains two inner loops, which are executed alternately:

```
for (int i = 1; i <= 10; i++) {
  if (i % 2 == 0) // i even
    for (int j = 1; j <= i/2; j++)
      out.print("*");
  else              // i odd
    for (int j = 1; j <= 5-i/2; j++)
      out.print("#");
  out.println();
  }
```

This loop produces the output

```
#####
*
####
**
###
***
##
****
#
*****
```

in which one triangle is interleaved with another, growing in the opposite direction.

<table>
<tr>
<td>QUICK EXERCISE
9.2</td>
<td>

Write a method that prints a triangle using asterisks:

```
*
**
***
****
*****
****
***
**
*
```

</td>
</tr>
</table>

<table>
<tr>
<td>QUICK EXERCISE
9.3</td>
<td>

Write a method that prints a "sawtooth" using asterisks:

```
*
**
***
****
*****
*
**
***
****
*****
*
**
***
****
*****
```

</td>
</tr>
</table>

Syntactic note: In our examples, we sometimes enclose the loop body in braces and sometimes don't; similarly for the true and false branches of a conditional statement. The rule is this: Braces are needed when the body of the loop or the branch of the conditional has more than one statement; otherwise,

> **QUICK EXERCISE 9.4**
>
> Write a loop to print an $n \times m$ array of asterisks, where n and m are variables.

they are optional. But the tricky part is to realize that a loop or `if` statement itself is considered a single statement, even if it contains multiple statements. For example, in

```
1    for (int i = ...) {
2      if (...) {
3        for (int j =  ...) {
4          out.print("*");
5        }
6      }
7      else {
8        for (int j = ...)
9          out.print("#");
10     }
11   }
```

the matching braces on lines 3 and 5 are optional, since the body of the loop is a single statement; in the similar loop in lines 8 and 9, the braces are omitted. More surprisingly, though, the matching braces in lines 2 and 6 are optional, because the entire true branch of the `if` consists of a *single* `for` loop, and likewise for the matching braces in lines 7 and 10. Thus, the loop could be written as

```
1    for (int i = ...) {
2      if (...)
3        for (int j =  ...)
4          out.print("*");
5      else            // i odd
6        for (int j = ...)
7          out.print("#");
8    }
```

But, in fact, even the one remaining pair of braces, on lines 1 and 8, is optional, since the body of the `for` loop consists of a *single* `if` statement, albeit a complicated one. Thus, we could write

```
1    for (int i = ...)
2      if (...)
3        for (int j =  ...)
4          out.print("*");
5      else            // i odd
6        for (int j = ...)
7          out.print("#");
```

Since the use of unnecessary braces can become tedious and even distracting, we sometimes follow ordinary programming practice by omitting them.

Now let's look at a harder example, with more useful output: a wind chill table that gives the equivalent wind chill index for temperatures ranging from 50°F down to −60°F and wind speeds ranging from 0 up to 50 miles per hour (mph). Since the wind chill index changes little with small changes in either temperature or wind speed, we want the temperatures to descend from 50 to −60°F in steps

TABLE OF WIND-CHILL INDICES												
degrees F:	50	40	30	20	10	0	-10	-20	-30	-40	-50	-60
0 mph:	50	40	30	20	10	0	-10	-20	-30	-40	-50	-60
5 mph:	48	37	27	16	6	-5	-15	-26	-36	-47	-58	-68
10 mph:	40	28	16	3	-9	-21	-34	-46	-58	-71	-83	-95
15 mph:	36	22	9	-5	-18	-32	-45	-59	-72	-86	-99	-113
20 mph:	32	18	4	-11	-25	-39	-53	-68	-82	-96	-111	-125
25 mph:	30	15	0	-15	-30	-45	-59	-74	-89	-104	-119	-134
30 mph:	28	13	-3	-18	-33	-49	-64	-79	-94	-110	-125	-140
35 mph:	27	11	-5	-20	-36	-51	-67	-83	-98	-114	-130	-145
40 mph:	26	10	-6	-22	-38	-54	-69	-85	-101	-117	-133	-149
45 mph:	25	9	-7	-23	-39	-55	-71	-87	-103	-119	-135	-151
50 mph:	25	9	-7	-23	-39	-55	-71	-87	-103	-119	-135	-151

FIGURE 9.3   The desired output from the application to produce a wind chill table.

of 10°F and the wind speeds to increase from 0 to 50 mph in steps of 5 mph. The output of the application should look like that shown in Figure 9.3. We have already written most of the code for computing the wind chill (page 103), so we can concentrate entirely on the necessary loop structure.

Here is the way to approach this type of loop construction. Write a list giving the sequence of actions that are to be done. For this example, it is apparent from Figure 9.3 that we want to do the following:

Print the heading line of the table
Print the first line of the table (0 mph wind chill indexes)
Print the second line of the table (5 mph wind chill indexes)
...
Print the eleventh line of the table (50 mph wind chill indexes)

The pattern here is that, after the title and heading line, we want to

Print the ith line of the table ($5 \times i$ mph wind chill indexes)

for $i = 0, 1, 2, \ldots, 10$. We can outline the application to be written as

print the heading line of the table
```
for (int i = 0; i <= 10; i++) {
```
    print the wind chill indexes for 5*i mph
    move to next output line
```
}
```

Now we need to apply a similar analysis to the process of printing a line of wind chill indexes for `5*i` mph, one for each temperature 50, 40, ..., −60°F. This amounts to

Print the label "$5 * i$ `mph:`" at the beginning of the line
Print the rounded wind chill factor for combination of $5 * i$ mph and 50°F
Print the rounded wind chill factor for combination of $5 * i$ mph and 40°F
...
Print the rounded wind chill factor for combination of $5 * i$ mph and −60°F

The pattern here is that, after printing the label at the left of the row, we print the *j*th wind chill index for the combination of $5 \times i$ mph and $10 \times j$°F for $j = 5, 4, \ldots, -6$. After the last one is printed, we want to move to the next output line by writing a new line. Therefore, the *i*th line of wind chill indexes is printed by

```
print label 5*i mph
for (int j = 5; j >= -6; j--) {
    print the rounded wind chill index of 5*i mph, 10*j degrees Fahrenheit
}
```

Nesting this inside the other loop gives us the outline

```
print the heading line of the table
for (int i = 0; i <= 10; i++) {
    print label 5*i mph
    for (int j = 5; j >= -6; j--) {
        print the rounded wind chill index of 5*i mph, 10*j degrees Fahrenheit
    }
    move to next output line
}
```

To print the heading line, we need to write the sequence of temperatures 50, 40, ..., −60°F across a line. This is done with a `for` loop almost identical to the preceding inner `for` loop:

```
for (int j = 5; j >= -6; j--) {
    print the column heading 10*j degrees Fahrenheit
}
move to next output line
```

Filling in the details of the printing of the various elements gives us the final application, in which we round a value using `Math.round` and cast it to an `int` for printing.

```
1    import CSLib.*;
2
3    public class WindChill {
4        // Produce a table of wind-chill indices
5        // Author: Haim Reingold, March 16, 1994
6
7        static final int
8            COLUMN_WIDTH = 5; //width of a column in the table
9
10       private double windChillIndex (
11               double temp,     // air temperature (deg F)
12               double speed) {  // wind speed (mph)
13           if (speed <= 4)          //  little or no wind
14               return temp;
15           else if (speed <= 45) //  moderate wind
16               return (91.4 - (10.45 + 6.69 * Math.sqrt(speed)
17                       - 0.447 * speed) * (91.4 - temp)/22.0);
18           else                     //  high wind
19               return (1.6 * temp - 55.0);
20       }
21
```

```
22      public void buildTable () {
23        OutputBox out
24        = new OutputBox("TABLE OF WIND-CHILL INDICES");
25
26        // write the column headings
27        out.print("degrees F:");
28        for (int j = 5; j >= -6; j--)
29          out.print(SFormat.sprintr(COLUMN_WIDTH, 10*j));
30        out.println();
31        out.println();
32
33        for (int i = 0; i <= 10; i++) {
34          out.print(SFormat.sprintr(COLUMN_WIDTH, 5*i));
35          out.print(" mph:"); // row label
36          for (int j = 5; j >= -6; j--)
37            out.print(SFormat.sprintr(COLUMN_WIDTH,
38                (int)Math.round(windChillIndex(10*j,5*i))));
39          out.println();
40        }
41      }
42    }
```

Notice that `windChillIndex` is a private method. It is used only as an auxiliary method from within the `buildTable` method.

This class also uses a new class in `CSLib` called `SFormat`. `SFormat` is used to help print data in neat columns, as we've done here. The `buildTable` method uses just one of the methods of `SFormat`, namely, `String sprintr(int w, int i)`, which returns a string containing the integer i in decimal, with enough spaces added to the beginning that its length is w. For example, `sprintr(8, 14)` returns a string containing six blanks, the character 1, and the character 4, as illustrated here:

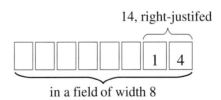

14, right-justifed

in a field of width 8

By using `sprintr` whenever we want to print an integer, we can assure that the output will occupy a certain number of columns, no matter how large or small the integer.

`SFormat` also contains operations to print doubles and other data types. The complete list is shown in Table 9.1. All the operations of `SFormat` are *static*, which means that they are invoked by writing `SFormat.method`, instead of the usual *object.method* (just as the `Math` methods are called by writing `Math.method`). Static methods, also called *class methods*, are explained in Chapter 10, which includes the implementation of `SFormat` as an example. Until then, just copy our syntax for calling methods of this class.

Name	Description
`String sprintr(int w,` `    int i)`	Returns a string of length w, consisting of the decimal representation of i, preceded by blanks
`String sprintr(int w,` `    String str)`	Returns a string of length w, consisting of string `str`, preceded by blanks
`String sprintr(int w,` `    int r, double d)`	Returns a string of length w, consisting of the decimal representation of d, with exactly r digits to the right of the decimal point, preceded by blanks

TABLE 9.1   Methods of the `SFormat` class.

9.2

Two-Dimensional Arrays

Two-dimensional arrays, in which data are arranged in a rectangle, are common in everyday life. For example, Table 9.2 shows the annual consumption of energy in the United States (in 10^{15} Btu) by source for the years 1989 through 1993. Such tables are often shown with column totals (in this case, these represent the total amount of energy from each source for the 5 years), row totals (total energy consumption for each year), and a grand total (total energy consumption for the entire 5-year period).

In this section, we present the fundamentals of working with two-dimensional arrays. We then give three examples: using a two-dimensional array to represent a crossword puzzle, showing the mouse from Chapter 1 mov-

	Coal	Natural Gas	Petroleum Products	Hydroelectric Power	Nuclear Power	Other	Total
1989	18.9	19.4	34.2	2.9	5.7	0.3	81.4
1990	19.1	19.3	33.6	3.0	6.2	0.2	81.4
1991	18.8	19.6	32.9	3.1	6.6	0.2	81.2
1992	18.9	20.3	33.5	2.8	6.7	0.2	82.4
1993	19.6	20.8	33.8	3.1	6.5	0.2	84.0
Total	95.3	99.4	168.0	14.9	31.7	1.1	410.4

TABLE 9.2   U.S. energy consumption, by source, 1989–1993, in quadrillions of Btu. [Source: _Statistical Abstract of the United States_, 114th ed. (Lanham, MD: Bernan Press, 1994).]

ing through a maze that is represented with a two-dimensional array, and drawing shapes on a computer screen.

9.2.1 Two-Dimensional Array Basics

Java provides a natural way of representing a table like Table 9.2—as a two-dimensional array. The declaration of an array `energyTable` with five rows and six columns

```
7      final int
8         NUM_SOURCES = 6,
9         NUM_YEARS = 5;
10
11     double[][]
12        energyTable = new double[NUM_YEARS][NUM_SOURCES];
```

creates a two-dimensional array of variables, as shown in Figure 9.4. The individual variables in this array are referenced using two numbers: a row number and a column number. The top row contains variables `energyTable[0][0]`, `energyTable[0][1]`,...,`energyTable[0][5]`; the second row `energyTable[1][0]`,..., `energyTable[1][5]`; and the last row has the variables `energyTable[4][0]`,...,`energyTable[4][5]`. As with one-dimensional arrays, all the elements of the two-dimensional array must be of the same type (`double` in this case, but we can make arrays of any type).

To illustrate the use of two-dimensional arrays, we present the program to read the 30 numbers contained in the middle of the array shown in Table 9.2 and print the totals shown in that table. As with one-dimensional arrays, the most

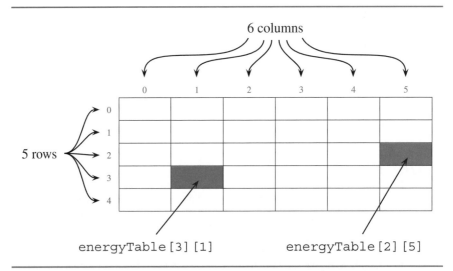

FIGURE 9.4 The two-dimensional array `energyTable`.

common method of processing two-dimensional arrays is to use a `for` loop. However, here you use nested `for` loops, in which the outer loop iterates over the rows (or columns) and the inner loop iterates over the columns (or rows). For example, here is a loop that reads the 30 numbers needed to fill `energyTable`, one row at a time:

```
24      int y, s;
25      for (y = 0; y < NUM_YEARS; y++)
26        for (s = 0; s < NUM_SOURCES; s++)
27          energyTable[y][s] = in.readDouble();
```

Don't Use Commas for Indexing Two-Dimensional Arrays   BUG ALERT 9.1

If you know another programming language or have seen matrices used in mathematics, you will probably want to write `energyTable[0, 0]`. This is wrong, and Java will give a compile-time error.

Let's trace this. Assume that the inputs are the numbers 18.9, 19.4, . . . , 0.3, 19.1, 19.3, . . . , 0.2; that is, the input data are given in row-by-row order. The outer `for` loop sets y to 0 and executes the inner `for` loop; it executes the input statement 6 times, with s ranging from 0 to 5. The effect is to read the first six inputs and place them in `energyTable[0][0]`, . . . , `energyTable[0][5]`. The outer `for` loop then increments y to 1 and again executes the inner `for` loop. It again executes the input statement 6 times, reading the next 6 inputs into `energyTable[1][0]`, . . . , `energyTable[1][5]`. This continues until, at the fifth iteration of the outer loop, y is 4 and the inner loop is executed for the last time, reading the last six inputs into `energyTable[4][0]`, . . . , `energyTable[4][5]`. After completion of this loop, the array is as shown in Figure 9.5.

	0	1	2	3	4	5
0	18.9	19.4	34.2	2.9	5.7	0.3
1	19.1	19.3	33.6	3.0	6.2	0.2
2	18.8	19.6	32.9	3.1	6.6	0.2
3	18.9	20.3	33.5	2.8	6.7	0.2
4	19.6	20.8	33.8	3.1	6.5	0.2

FIGURE 9.5 The array `energyTable`, after the input loop.

The next step in the program is to compute the annual totals, combining all energy sources for each year. That is, for each year y we want to add all the numbers `energyTable[y][s]` for all s. We store the annual totals in a one-dimensional array, called `yearTotals`. Since the totals will be computed in one method and printed in another (as we normally do), `yearTotals` is an instance variable:

```
14        double[] yearTotals = new double[NUM_YEARS];
```

We again use nested `for` loops to process `energyTable`:

```
34        for (y = 0; y < NUM_YEARS; y++) {
35          // Compute total for year y
36          yearTotals[y] = 0.0;
37          for (s = 0; s < NUM_SOURCES; s++)
38            yearTotals[y] =
39              yearTotals[y] + energyTable[y][s];
40        }
```

The totals for each source are computed similarly, and the grand total is computed by summing all the yearly totals (or, equivalently, the source totals). The only trick to printing the table, aside from getting the column headings to line up nicely, is being careful to print new lines in the right places. The final program given here produces the output shown in Figure 9.6.

```
1     import CSLib.*;
2
3     public class USenergy {
4        // Print a table of energy usage
5        // Author: Frieda F. Foster, May 23, 1996
6
7        final int
8          NUM_SOURCES = 6,
9          NUM_YEARS = 5;
10
11       double[][]
12          energyTable = new double[NUM_YEARS][NUM_SOURCES];
```

	Coal	Gas	Oil	Hydro	Nuclear	Other	Total
1989	18.9	19.4	34.2	2.9	5.7	0.3	81.4
1990	19.1	19.3	33.6	3.0	6.2	0.2	81.4
1991	18.8	19.6	32.9	3.1	6.6	0.2	81.2
1992	18.9	20.3	33.5	2.8	6.7	0.2	82.4
1993	19.6	20.8	33.8	3.1	6.5	0.2	84.0
Total	95.3	99.4	168.0	14.9	31.7	1.1	410.4

FIGURE 9.6   Output from the `energyTable` program.

```
13
14   double[] yearTotals = new double[NUM_YEARS];
15   double[] sourceTotals = new double[NUM_SOURCES];
16   double totalEnergy = 0.0;
17
18   final int
19     FIRST_YEAR = 1989;
20
21   public void readData () {
22     InputBox in = new InputBox();
23
24     int y, s;
25     for (y = 0; y < NUM_YEARS; y++)
26       for (s = 0; s < NUM_SOURCES; s++)
27         energyTable[y][s] = in.readDouble();
28   }
29
30   public void computeTotals () {
31     // Compute total energy use for each year
32     int y, s;
33
34     for (y = 0; y < NUM_YEARS; y++) {
35       // Compute total for year y
36       yearTotals[y] = 0.0;
37       for (s = 0; s < NUM_SOURCES; s++)
38         yearTotals[y] =
39           yearTotals[y] + energyTable[y][s];
40     }
41
42     // Compute total use of each source
43     for (s = 0; s < NUM_SOURCES; s++) {
44       // Compute total for source s
45       sourceTotals[s] = 0.0;
46       for (y = 0; y < NUM_YEARS; y++)
47         sourceTotals[s] =
48           sourceTotals[s] + energyTable[y][s];
49     }
50
51     // Compute total energy use
52     for (y = 0; y < NUM_YEARS; y++)
53       totalEnergy = totalEnergy + yearTotals[y];
54   }
55
56   public void printTable () {
57     OutputBox out = new OutputBox();
58     int y, s;
59
60     out.println("         "
61       + "  Coal"
62       + "    Gas"
63       + "    Oil"
64       + "  Hydro"
65       + "  Nuclear"
66       + " Other"
```

```
67              + "   Total");
68
69        for (y = 0; y < NUM_YEARS; y++) {
70          out.print(SFormat.sprintr(6, FIRST_YEAR+y));
71          for (s = 0; s < NUM_SOURCES; s++)
72            out.print(SFormat.sprintr(7, 1, energyTable[y][s]));
73          out.print(SFormat.sprintr(7, 1, yearTotals[y]));
74          out.println();
75        }
76        out.print(SFormat.sprintr(6, "Total"));
77        for (s = 0; s < NUM_SOURCES; s++)
78          out.print(SFormat.sprintr(7, 1, sourceTotals[s]));
79        out.print(SFormat.sprintr(7, 1, totalEnergy));
80        out.println();
81    }
82  }
```

9.2.2 Initializing Two-Dimensional Arrays

Two-dimensional arrays may be initialized by nesting one-dimensional array initializers inside a set of braces. For example, energyTable could be declared and initialized like this:

```
double[][] energyTable =
    {
      {18.9, 19.4, 34.2, 2.9, 5.7, 0.3},
      {19.1, 19.3, 33.6, 3.0, 6.2, 0.2},
      {18.8, 19.6, 32.9, 3.1, 6.6, 0.2},
      {18.9, 20.3, 33.5, 2.8, 6.7, 0.2},
      {19.6, 20.8, 33.8, 3.1, 6.5, 0.2}
    };
```

With such initialization, Java automatically allocates the proper number of array elements.

Don't forget that arrays have to be initialized, but here that involves two steps: allocating the array and initializing the elements of the array. The initializing declaration just shown does both. If, on the other hand, you write

```
double[][] EnergyTable;
```

it does neither: EnergyTable is not initialized. Or rather, it is uninitialized if it is a local variable; it is initialized to null if it is an instance variable or a class variable. Initializing the array variable itself is not the same as initializing the *elements* of the array. When you write

```
double[][] EnergyTable = new double[6][7];
```

the variable EnergyTable points to a two-dimensional array in the heap. The elements of that two-dimensional array are automatically initialized in the same way as is done for one-dimensional arrays: For arrays of numeric type, the elements are initialized to zero; for Boolean arrays, the elements are initialized to false; and for arrays of objects, the elements are initialized to null.

Arrays of objects can be initialized to actual objects in the declaration by using object-valued expressions in the initializer. Thus, this declaration creates a 2 × 3 array of clocks, all set to 12:00:

```
Clock[][] clockTable =
    {{new Clock(), new Clock(), new Clock()},
     {new Clock(), new Clock(), new Clock()}};
```

9.2.3 Two-Dimensional Arrays Are Arrays of Arrays

The correct way to think of two-dimensional arrays is that they are arrays whose elements are (references to) one-dimensional arrays. Therefore, when we write one-dimensional arrays

```
energyTable = new double[NUM_YEARS][NUM_SOURCES];
```

it is just a shorthand for

```
energyTable = new double[NUM_YEARS][];
for (int i=0; i<NUM_YEARS; i++)
   energyTable[i] = new double[NUM_SOURCES];
```

They are the same because, in either case, the array `energyTable` is actually stored in memory (in the heap, to be precise) as an array of references to other arrays. Here is what it looks like after initialization:

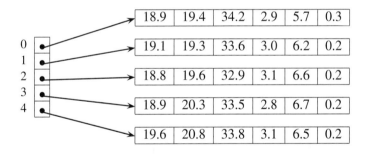

That two-dimensional arrays are really one-dimensional arrays of one-dimensional arrays has a number of implications. One is that the number of rows in a two-dimensional array A is `A.length` (`energyTable.length` is 5), and the number of columns in A is `A[0].length` (`energyTable[0].length` is 6). Therefore, we can write a function to enter values into a two-dimensional array:

```
1  void read2DArray (double[][] A) {
2     InputBox in = new InputBox();
3     in.setPrompt("Enter number:");
4     for (int row=0; row<A.length; row++)
5        for (int col=0; col<A[row].length; col++)
6           A[row][col]=in.readDouble();
7  }
```

The declaration of A as a formal parameter indicates that it is a two-dimensional array of doubles, without giving its dimensions. In line 3, A.length gives the size of the first dimension of A, that is, the number of rows in A. Since A[row] *itself* is a *singly dimensioned* array, A[row].length (in line 4) gives the size of the singly dimensioned array A[row]; that is, A[row].length gives the number of columns in A[row].

Another implication is that a two-dimensional array can be "ragged"; that is, it can have rows of different lengths. The statements

```
int[][] A = new int[5][];
for (int i=0; i<5; i++) {
  A[i] = new int[i+1];
}
```

produce an array shaped like this:

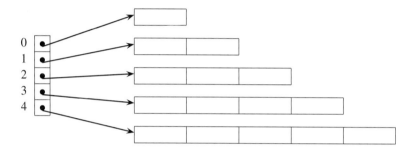

Such oddly shaped arrays can be useful in some applications, but we will not pursue this any further in this book.

Finally, we note that we can create three-dimensional arrays—arrays whose elements are references to two-dimensional arrays—and even higher-dimensional arrays. Again, we will not make use of this feature (but see Exercise 12 on page 360).

9.2.4   Returning Arrays from Methods

Like any other objects, arrays can be allocated and returned from methods. This awkward-looking syntax indicates that the method ident returns a two-dimensional array:

```
int[][] ident (int n)
```

Specifically, it produces an $n \times n$ identity matrix (all zeros except along the diagonal):

```
int[][] ident (int n) {
   int[][] M = new int[n][n];
   for (int i=0; i<n; i++)  // initialize to zeros
     for (int j=0; j<n; j++)
       M[i][j] = 0;
```

```
        for (int i=0; i<n; i++)  // set diagonal to ones
            M[i][i] = 1;
        return M;
    }
```

**QUICK EXERCISE
9.5**

Write a method to construct and return the following $n \times n$ integer arrays, where n is an argument to the method.

1. The matrix A that has value i+j in location A[i][j].
2. The matrix that has 0s around the outer border, 1s just inside that, 2s just inside that, and so on. For example, if $n = 5$, this matrix is

```
        0 0 0 0 0
        0 1 1 1 0
        0 1 2 1 0
        0 1 1 1 0
        0 0 0 0 0
```

9.3

Example: Crossword Puzzles

Many board games are played on grids, which are naturally represented as two-dimensional arrays. Chess and Go are well-known examples. Word games such as crossword puzzles and word search puzzles are also played on such grids. In this section, we give a representation of a crossword puzzle.

To simplify the example, we will write a class to represent a *single* crossword puzzle template, shown in Figure 9.8. Ideally, the puzzle would be reconfigurable, but we will leave this for the exercises. We will write a class whose objects represent configurations of this puzzle, beginning with the empty configuration shown in Figure 9.8. The class will provide a method to insert new words into the puzzle and to display the puzzle. These two methods are listed in Table 9.3.

As usual, we start slowly, with a class containing only the display method. The main question is how to represent the board. We will give the most obvious answer: Use a two-dimensional array of characters. Letters will represent themselves, unfilled squares will be represented by a blank character, and black squares will be represented by the character '#'. Thus, the following array represents the crossword puzzle shown in Figure 9.8 (but without any of the squares numbered):

Name	Description
void display (DrawingBox d)	Displays the current puzzle configuration
void addWord (int square, char dir, String word)	Inserts word in the puzzle at square number square in direction dir (a for across, d for down)

TABLE 9.3 Methods of the Crossword class.

```
private char[][] theBoard =
   {{' ', ' ', ' ', ' ', ' ', '#', ' ', ' ', ' ', ' ', ' ', ' '},
    {' ', '#', ' ', '#', ' ', '#', ' ', ' ', '#', ' ', ' '},
    {' ', ' ', ' ', ' ', ' ', ' ', '#', ' ', ' ', ' ', ' '},
    {' ', '#', '#', '#', ' ', ' ', '#', ' ', ' ', '#', ' ', ' '},
    {'#', ' ', ' ', ' ', ' ', ' ', ' ', ' ', ' ', ' ', ' ', '#'},
    {' ', '#', ' ', '#', ' ', ' ', '#', '#', ' ', '#', ' ', ' '},
    {' ', ' ', ' ', ' ', ' ', '#', ' ', ' ', ' ', ' ', ' '},
    {' ', '#', ' ', '#', ' ', ' ', '#', ' ', ' ', '#', ' ', ' '},
    {' ', ' ', ' ', ' ', ' ', ' ', '#', ' ', ' ', ' ', ' ', ' '}
   };
```

The display method is a classic doubly nested loop, with r ranging over the rows and c over the columns. sq_width and sq_height are the width and height, respectively, of each box:

```
for (int r=0; r<BOARD_HEIGHT; r++)
   for (int c=0; c<BOARD_WIDTH; c++) {
      if (theBoard[r][c] == '#')
         b.fillRect(c*sq_width, r*sq_height,
                         sq_width, sq_height);
      else {
         b.drawRect(c*sq_width, r*sq_height,
                         sq_width, sq_height);
         if (theBoard[r][c] != ' ')
            b.drawString(theBoard[r][c]+"",
                            (int)((c+0.45)*sq_width),
                            (int)((r+0.7)*sq_height));
      }
   }
```

If a square is black, it is drawn with fillRect; if it is nonblack, it is drawn at exactly the same size with drawRect; in the latter case, it may also contain a letter, which is drawn using drawString. The numbers 0.45 and 0.7 in the call to drawString were determined, by experiment, to place the letters in the center of the square.

The entire class is given in Figure 9.7. To see how the letters will appear, look ahead to Figure 9.10, but without the numbers. A client that simply creates a Crossword object and sends it the display message will produce the output shown in Figure 9.8, but without the numbers.

```
1   import CSLib.*;
2   import java.awt.*;
3
4   public class Crossword {
5     // Draw a 9x9 crossword puzzle
6     // Sherwin Kamin, Feb. 5, 2001
7
8     final static int BOARD_HEIGHT = 9,
9                      BOARD_WIDTH = 9;
10
11    private char[][] theBoard =
12      {{' ', ' ', ' ', ' ', ' ', '#', ' ', ' ', ' ', ' ', ' '},
13       {' ', '#', ' ', '#', ' ', '#', ' ', ' ', '#', ' ', ' '},
14       {' ', ' ', ' ', ' ', ' ', ' ', '#', ' ', ' ', ' ', ' '},
15       {' ', '#', '#', '#', ' ', ' ', '#', ' ', ' ', '#', ' ', ' '},
16       {'#', ' ', ' ', ' ', ' ', ' ', ' ', ' ', ' ', ' ', '#'},
17       {' ', '#', ' ', ' ', '#', ' ', ' ', '#', '#', '#', ' ', ' '},
18       {' ', ' ', ' ', ' ', '#', ' ', ' ', ' ', ' ', ' ', ' '},
19       {' ', '#', ' ', ' ', '#', ' ', ' ', '#', ' ', ' ', '#', ' ', ' '},
20       {' ', ' ', ' ', ' ', ' ', '#', ' ', ' ', ' ', ' ', ' '}
21      };
22
23    public void display (DrawingBox b) {
24      b.setDrawableSize(300,300);
25      int sq_height = 300/BOARD_HEIGHT,
26          sq_width = 300/BOARD_WIDTH;
27
28      for (int r=0; r<BOARD_HEIGHT; r++)
29        for (int c=0; c<BOARD_WIDTH; c++) {
30          if (theBoard[r][c] == '#')
31            b.fillRect(c*sq_width, r*sq_height,
32                       sq_width, sq_height);
33          else {
34            b.drawRect(c*sq_width, r*sq_height,
35                       sq_width, sq_height);
36            if (theBoard[r][c] != ' ')
37              b.drawString(theBoard[r][c]+"",
38                           (int)((c+0.45)*sq_width),
39                           (int)((r+0.7)*sq_height));
40          }
41        }
42    }
43
44  }
45
```

FIGURE 9.7 The preliminary version of the `Crossword` **class.**

Before we can insert words into the puzzle, we need to be able to label some of the squares with numbers. Our representation of the puzzle does not admit the inclusion of numbers, so we will have to do that separately. The way we've chosen to do this is to create a two-dimensional array `theNumbers` parallel to

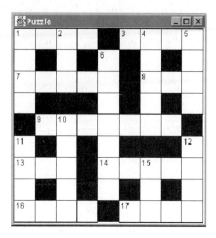

FIGURE 9.8   Blank crossword.

theBoard; each element theNumbers[r][c] either is zero, indicating that that square is unnumbered, or gives the square's number.

The final version of the Crossword class, shown in Figures 9.9 and 9.9, uses these two arrays to represent the puzzle. The display method is identical to the previous one except for the final if statement; again, the numbers 0.1 and 0.4 were determined experimentally to produce a good placement for the numbers. (Ideally, the numbers would be smaller than the actual entries in the puzzle, but again we do not know how to deal with fonts of different sizes.) Figure 9.8 shows the blank puzzle with these numbers.

Now, addWord is a little more difficult to write than display. Its arguments are the number of the square into which to place the new word, the direction (character 'a' for across, 'd' for down), and the word itself (as a string). The logic itself is not very complicated:

```
row, col = row and column of numbered square;
for (int i=0; i<word.length(); i++) {
    theBoard[row][col] = word.charAt(i);
    increment col by 1 if direction is down;
    otherwise, increment row by 1
}
```

Note that this is not a nested loop. We iterate over the word to be added, maintaining row and column numbers for the next character as we go.

What complicates the code is the need to check for erroneous words. We will see how this occurs in a moment, but first we will finish up the basic logic: First, to find the row and column of the given square number, we employ a method findSquare, which returns a Point. Method findSquare is a classic nested search loop, which terminates as soon as it finds the number in theNumbers. To return *two* numbers, it returns a Point; if it does not find the number in the puzzle, it returns null. Naturally, findSquare is a private method:

```java
import CSLib.*;
import java.awt.*;

public class Crossword {
    // Draw a 9x9 crossword puzzle, and allow words
    // to be entered into it
    // Sherwin Kamin, Feb. 5, 2001

    final static int BOARD_HEIGHT = 9,
                     BOARD_WIDTH = 9;

    private char[][] theBoard =
        {{' ', ' ', ' ', ' ', '#', ' ', ' ', ' ', ' '},
         {' ', '#', ' ', '#', ' ', '#', ' ', '#', ' '},
         {' ', ' ', ' ', ' ', ' ', '#', ' ', ' ', ' '},
         {' ', '#', '#', '#', ' ', '#', ' ', '#', ' '},
         {'#', ' ', ' ', ' ', ' ', ' ', ' ', ' ', '#'},
         {' ', '#', ' ', '#', ' ', '#', '#', '#', ' '},
         {' ', ' ', ' ', ' ', '#', ' ', ' ', ' ', ' '},
         {' ', '#', ' ', '#', ' ', '#', ' ', '#', ' '},
         {' ', ' ', ' ', ' ', '#', ' ', ' ', ' ', ' '}
        };

    private int[][] theNumbers =
        {{ 1,  0,  2,  0,  0,  3,  4,  0,  5},
         { 0,  0,  0,  0,  6,  0,  0,  0,  0},
         { 7,  0,  0,  0,  0,  0,  8,  0,  0},
         { 0,  0,  0,  0,  0,  0,  0,  0,  0},
         { 0,  9, 10,  0,  0,  0,  0,  0,  0},
         {11,  0,  0,  0,  0,  0,  0,  0, 12},
         {13,  0,  0,  0, 14,  0, 15,  0,  0},
         { 0,  0,  0,  0,  0,  0,  0,  0,  0},
         {16,  0,  0,  0,  0, 17,  0,  0,  0}};

    public void display (DrawingBox b) {
        b.setDrawableSize(300,300);
        int sq_height = 300/BOARD_HEIGHT,
            sq_width = 300/BOARD_WIDTH;

        for (int r=0; r<BOARD_HEIGHT; r++)
            for (int c=0; c<BOARD_WIDTH; c++) {
                if (theBoard[r][c] == '#')
                    b.fillRect(c*sq_width, r*sq_height,
                               sq_width, sq_height);
                else {
                    b.drawRect(c*sq_width, r*sq_height,
                               sq_width, sq_height);
                    if (theBoard[r][c] != ' ')
                        b.drawString(theBoard[r][c]+"",
                                     (int)((c+0.45)*sq_width),
                                     (int)((r+0.7)*sq_height));
                    if (theNumbers[r][c] != 0)
                        b.drawString(theNumbers[r][c]+"",
                                     (int)((c+0.1)*sq_width),
                                     (int)((r+0.4)*sq_height));
                }
            }
    }
}
```

333

FIGURE 9.9 Final version of the Crossword class.

```
60    public void addWord (int square, char dir, String word) {
61      Point p = findSquare(square);
62      if (p == null) {
63        new ErrorBox("No such word number: "+square);
64        return;
65      }
66      int row = p.x,
67          col = p.y;
68
69      int drow = 0,
70          dcol = 1;
71      if (dir == 'd') { drow = 1; dcol = 0; }
72
73      for (int i=0; i<word.length(); i++) {
74
75        if (col >= BOARD_WIDTH || row >= BOARD_HEIGHT) {
76          new ErrorBox("Word too long for board: "+word);
77          return;
78        }
79
80        // Square should be blank or match character
81        if (theBoard[row][col] == ' ' ||
82            theBoard[row][col] == word.charAt(i)) {
83          theBoard[row][col] = word.charAt(i);
84          row = row + drow;
85          col = col + dcol;
86        }
87        else // May be trying to write in black square
88          if (theBoard[row][col] == '#') {
89          new ErrorBox("Wrong length word: "+word);
90          return;
91        }
92        else {   // Must be non-matching character
93          new ErrorBox("Non-matching word: "+word);
94          return;
95        }
96      }
97
98      // Check if word filled spaces - if square after
99      // word is still on board, but not black, then trouble
100     if (col < BOARD_WIDTH && row < BOARD_HEIGHT
101         && theBoard[row][col] != '#') {
102       new ErrorBox("Non-filling word: "+word);
103       return;
104     }
105   }
106
107   private Point findSquare (int square) {
108     for (int i=0; i<BOARD_HEIGHT; i++)
109       for (int j=0; j<BOARD_WIDTH; j++) {
110         if (theNumbers[i][j] == square)
111           return new Point(i,j);
112       }
113     return null;
114   }
115
116 }
```

FIGURE 9.9 **Final version of the** Crossword **class (continued).**

```
107    private Point findSquare (int square) {
108       for (int i=0; i<BOARD_HEIGHT; i++)
109          for (int j=0; j<BOARD_WIDTH; j++) {
110             if (theNumbers[i][j] == square)
111                return new Point(i,j);
112          }
113       return null;
114    }
```

After returning from findSquare, if it did not return null, then it returned a Point p; the row and column of the numbered square are p.x and p.y, respectively. To simplify the part of the loop that says "*increment col by 1 if direction is down; otherwise, increment row by 1*," we define two variables, drow and dcol, the d standing for delta, meaning the change in the row or column number. For an across clue, these are 0 and 1, respectively; for a down clue, 1 and 0. Thus, in essence, addWord looks like this:

```
public void addWord (int square, char dir, String word) {
   Point p = findSquare(square);
   int row = p.x,
       col = p.y;

   int drow = 0,
       dcol = 1;
   if (dir == 'd') { drow = 1; dcol = 0; }

   for (int i=0; i<word.length(); i++) {
      theBoard[row][col] = word.charAt(i);
      row = row + drow;
      col = col + dcol;
   }
}
```

As occurs frequently in programming, error checking complicates matters significantly. In the final version of the Crossword class (Figure 9.9), the addWord method is about 3 times as long as the one we just gave.

All that is left to do is to add a client that prompts the user for words and fills in the puzzle. We leave this as an exercise. Figure 9.10 shows the board after several words have been entered.

QUICK EXERCISE 9.6

Another way to check for bad words is to place a column of black squares on the right edge of the puzzle and a row of black squares on the bottom edge. Thus, you would use a 10 × 10 array to represent a 9 × 9 puzzle. Make this change and simplify addWord as much as possible by taking advantage of the new representation.

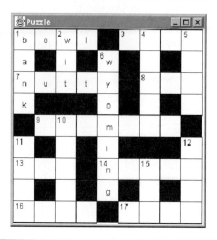

FIGURE 9.10   Partially completed crossword.

9.4

Mouse in a Maze Revisited

Let's revisit our mouse-in-a-maze problem. What makes this an appropriate moment to do so is that we now have a natural way to represent mazes. Since mazes are two-dimensional, it is sensible to represent them as two-dimensional arrays. What exactly does it mean for an object to "represent" a maze? It means that the object should respond to queries like `checkWall(dir, row, col)`, indicating whether there is a wall in the room at location (`row`, `col`) when looking in direction `dir`. We will follow the convention of representing directions by integers:

```
final int NORTH=0, EAST=1, SOUTH=2, WEST=3;
```

The public operations of the `Maze` class are given in Table 9.4.

There are countless ways to represent the maze. Even once we have decided to use two-dimensional arrays, there remain many alternatives (see Exercise 16). Our representation works like this: The locations in the maze are numbered by row and column, starting from $(1, 1)$ in the upper left to (h, w) in the lower right, where h and w are the height and width of the maze, respectively. We will assume an imaginary set of rooms on the upper and left sides of the maze; these have row or column number 0. This allows us to represent the walls by using two two-dimensional boolean arrays `eWall` and `sWall`. Array `eWall[r][c]` says whether there is a wall to the east of room (`r,c`). If we want to know whether there is a wall to the *west* of that room, we just look at `eWall[r][c-1]`, since having a wall to the west of room (`r,c`) is equivalent to having a wall to the east of room (`r,c-1`). Similarly, array `sWall` serves to store all the south walls of all the rooms and simultaneously all the north walls. Given this representation, the key method of the `Maze` class is defined like this:

Name	Description
`boolean checkWall (int dir, int row, int col)`	Returns `true` if room (row,col) has a wall in direction `dir`
`boolean checkWall (int dir, Point p)`	Overloading of `checkWall` in which the room location is given by a `Point` instead of two integers
`boolean outside (Point p)`	Returns `true` if point p is outside the maze
`Point getStartLocation ()`	Returns starting location of mouse (i.e., just outside of maze opening)
`int getStartDirection ()`	Returns starting direction of mouse (i.e., pointing at maze opening)
`Point getSize ()`	Returns height and width of maze

TABLE 9.4   Methods of the `Maze` class.

```
43      public boolean checkWall (int dir, int row, int col) {
44        switch (dir) {
45          case NORTH: return sWall[row-1][col];
46          case SOUTH: return sWall[row][col];
47          case EAST:  return eWall[row][col];
48          default:    return eWall[row][col-1];
49        }
50      }
```

The entire class is shown in Figure 9.11.

The process of moving a mouse through a maze and displaying its progress in a window, if done in proper object-oriented style, involves several classes. As much as possible, we want to "separate concerns," meaning, for example, that the representation of the maze should be separated from the logic used to navigate it, and both should be separated from the methods used to display the mouse and maze. Furthermore, there is a level of "control"—deciding when to move the mouse along—that is also logically separate. This leads us to employ five classes:

Maze. As we have seen, the `Maze` object is a kind of "map" of the maze.

Mouse. The mouse object implements the navigation algorithm (we use the wall-to-the-right method, as given in Chapter 1). It has to know its current location and direction and, of course, what maze it is in.

MazeDrawer. The maze and mouse objects need to be displayed on the computer screen. As we have observed before, the aesthetic decisions about this should be separated from the internal logic of the maze. The `MazeDrawer` object knows what maze it is drawing, of course, but it also knows what `DrawingBox` to put it in.

```
1    import java.awt.*;
2
3    class Maze {
4      // Representation of a maze object
5      // Author: Jamie Ries, October 5, 2000
6
7      final int NORTH=0, EAST=1, SOUTH=2, WEST=3;
8
9      // record the walls to the east
10     private boolean[][] eWall =
11         {{false ,false,false,false,false },
12          {true ,false,false,false,true },
13          {false,true ,true ,false,true },
14          {true ,true ,false,true ,true }};
15     // record the walls to the south
16     private boolean[][] sWall =
17         {{false,true ,true ,true ,false},
18          {false,false,false,false,true },
19          {false,false,false,false,false},
20          {false,true ,true ,true ,true }};
21     private int height = 3, width = 4;
22     private Point size = new Point(width, height);
23
24     // Where is the starting location?
25     public Point getStartLocation () {return new Point(0,2);}
26
27     // In which direction do you face to enter?
28     public int getStartDirection () {return EAST;}
29
30     public Point getSize() {return size;}
31
32     // Is a given position outside the maze?
33     public boolean outside (Point pos) {
34       return ((pos.x < 1)
35             || (pos.x > width)
36             || (pos.y < 1)
37             || (pos.y > height)
38           );
39     }
40
41     // Is there a wall to the 'dir' direction
42     // of location (row,col)?
43     public boolean checkWall (int dir, int row, int col) {
44       switch (dir) {
45         case NORTH: return sWall[row-1][col];
46         case SOUTH: return sWall[row][col];
47         case EAST:  return eWall[row][col];
48         default:    return eWall[row][col-1];
49       }
50     }
51
52     // Alternative version of checkWall
53     public boolean checkWall (int dir, Point location) {
54       return checkWall(dir, location.y, location.x);
55     }
56   }
```

FIGURE 9.11 The Maze class.

MouseDrawer. This object knows the mouse it is drawing—in particular, its location and direction—and the `DrawingBox` being used, as well as enough about the `MazeDrawer` to know where the maze's rooms are located on the screen.

MouseController. The `runMouse` method creates the objects listed above and then controls them. In this version of the program, it consists of a loop in which the mouse is repeatedly directed to make a move and then the maze and mouse are displayed, with a 1-second pause added between each move.

The overall structure of the five classes is shown in Figure 9.12. (Not shown is the trivial `MouseMazeClient` class, whose `main` method creates a `MouseController` object and sends it the `runMouse` message.)

The relationship between the mouse and maze objects is easily understood: The maze does not need to know that there is a mouse in it, but the mouse needs to know what maze it is in so it can move without attempting to walk through walls. The `MazeDrawer` object needs to know the maze it is displaying and the `DrawingBox` it is displaying it in. The `MouseDrawer` needs to know the mouse's location and direction and the `DrawingBox`; less obviously, it needs to enough about how the maze is displayed on the screen that it can tell where to put the mouse. Finally, the controller creates each of these objects and makes sure they know about each other (as much as necessary); it then tells the mouse to move and the mouse and maze to draw themselves.

We start with the `Mouse` class. In Table 9.5, we list the public methods of this class. In fact, this class is very much as we discussed in Chapter 1. Its most important method is `void makeMove()`. This method makes a single move, using the algorithm we presented in Chapter 1. The methods `tellLocation()` and `tellDirection()` are needed (only) by the mouse drawer. Finally, note that when a mouse is first created, it is passed a reference to the `Maze` it will be navigating; it needs to refer to this "map" in the `makeMove` method.

The `Mouse` class itself is shown in Figure 9.13. Examination of the `makeMove()` method (lines 29 to 44) shows that our original program in Chapter 1 was remarkably accurate. (Here, we need to define various private methods to perform such actions as `stepForward()` and `turnLeft()`.)

The `MouseDrawer` and `MazeDrawer` classes, given in Figure 9.14 and 9.15, respectively, are fairly simple. Each has a constructor in which it is given all the information it needs to draw its object, and each has `draw` as its only public method. Notice how the `draw` method of the mouse drawer consults the mouse to discover its location and direction.

Finally, the controller is given in Figure 9.16. As advertised, it creates a variety of objects, sometimes passing them into the constructors of other objects. There is one subtle point here that the reader may have noticed earlier as well: The `MouseDrawer` constructor takes the `MazeDrawer` object as an argument, but it does not save that reference; it just gets the two numbers it needs out of that object and saves them. Finally, the controller contains a loop that draws the maze and mouse, pauses for one second, moves the mouse, and then repeats.

Figure 9.17 is a screenshot of this program's graphical output.

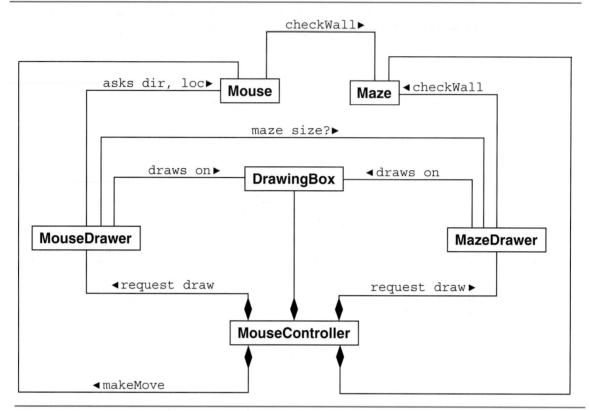

FIGURE 9.12 The UML diagram of the mouse-in-a-maze application.

Name	Description
Mouse (Maze m)	Creates a new mouse, placing it at the entrance to maze m
void makeMove ()	Moves one more step in the maze (or just stay still if already out of the maze)
Point tellLocation ()	Returns current location
int tellDirection ()	Returns current direction

TABLE 9.5 Methods of the Mouse class.

```
1    import CSLib.*;
2    import java.awt.*;
3
4    class Mouse {
5      // A mouse that can navigate a maze
6      // Author: Allan M. Mickunas, September 22, 1996
7
8      final int NORTH=0, EAST=1, SOUTH=2, WEST=3;
9
10     private Maze theMaze;
11     private boolean started = false; // true once the maze
12                                       // is entered.
13     private Point location; // The location of this Mouse
14     private int direction;  // The direction this Mouse is facing
15
16     public Point tellLocation () {return location;}
17
18     public int tellDirection () {return direction;}
19
20
21     public Mouse(Maze m) {
22       theMaze = m;
23       // Where do I start?
24       location = m.getStartLocation();
25       // In what direction do I face initially?
26       direction = m.getStartDirection();
27     }
28
29     public void makeMove() {
30       // Make one move, using wall-to-the-right
31       // algorithm from Chapter 1
32       if (started) {
33         if (!outside()) {
34           turnRight();
35           while (facingWall()) {
36             turnLeft();
37           }
38           stepForward();
39         }
40       } else {
41         stepForward();
42         started=true;
43       }
44     }
```

FIGURE 9.13 The Mouse class.

```
46    private boolean outside () {
47    // Am I outside the maze?
48      return theMaze.outside(location);
49    }
50
51    private boolean facingWall () {
52      return theMaze.checkWall(direction, location);
53    }
54
55    private void stepForward() {
56      switch (direction) {
57        case NORTH: location.y--; break;
58        case EAST:  location.x++; break;
59        case SOUTH: location.y++; break;
60        case WEST:  location.x--; break;
61      }
62    }
63
64    private void turnLeft() {
65      direction = (direction+3) % 4;
66    }
67
68    private void turnRight() {
69      direction = (direction+1) % 4;
70    }
71  }
```

FIGURE 9.13 The Mouse class (continued).

```
1    import CSLib.*;
2    import java.awt.*;
3
4    class MouseDrawer {
5      // Draw a mouse at proper location and orientation
6      // Author: Allan M. Mickunas, September 22, 1996
7
8      private Image[] mousegif = new Image[4];
9      private Mouse theMouse;
10     private DrawingBox d;
11     private int cellW, cellH;  // size of cells in this maze
12
13     public MouseDrawer (Mouse m, MazeDrawer md, DrawingBox d) {
14       theMouse = m;
15       this.d = d;
16       cellW = md.getCellW();
17       cellH = md.getCellH();
```

FIGURE 9.14 The MouseDrawer class.

```
19      // Get the four rodent images.
20      for (int i=0; i<4; i++) {
21        mousegif[i] = Toolkit.getDefaultToolkit().
22                           getImage("images/mouse"+i+".gif");
23      }
24    }
25
26
27    public void draw () {
28      // Draw the mouse
29      Point p = theMouse.tellLocation();
30      d.drawImage(mousegif[theMouse.tellDirection()],
31                  p.x*cellW+cellW/3,
32                  p.y*cellH+cellH/3);
33    }
34  }
35
36
```

FIGURE 9.14   The MouseDrawer **class (continued).**

```
1   import CSLib.*;
2   import java.awt.*;
3   import java.awt.event.*;
4
5   public class MazeDrawer {
6     // Draw a given maze in a given DrawingBox
7     // Author: Stephanie Ries, October 9, 2000
8
9     final int NORTH=0, EAST=1, SOUTH=2, WEST=3;
10
11    Maze theMaze;
12    DrawingBox d;
13    Point mazeSize;
14    int cellW, cellH;
15
16    public MazeDrawer (Maze theMaze, DrawingBox d) {
17
18      this.theMaze = theMaze;
19      this.d = d;
20
21      // Determine the size of a wall segment
22      mazeSize = theMaze.getSize();
23      cellW = d.getWidth() / (mazeSize.x + 2);
24      cellH = d.getHeight() / (mazeSize.y + 2);
25    }
```

FIGURE 9.15   The MazeDrawer **class.**

```
27      public int getCellW () {return cellW;}
28
29      public int getCellH () {return cellH;}
30
31      public void draw () {
32        d.clear();
33        // Draw the maze
34        for (int row = 1; row <= mazeSize.y + 1; row++)
35            for (int col = 1; col <= mazeSize.x; col++)
36                if (theMaze.checkWall(NORTH, row, col))
37                    d.drawLine( col*cellW, row*cellH,
38                               (col+1)*cellW, row*cellH);
39        for (int row = 1; row <= mazeSize.y; row++)
40            for (int col = 1; col <= mazeSize.x+1; col++)
41                if (theMaze.checkWall(WEST, row, col))
42                    d.drawLine( col*cellW, row*cellH,
43                               col*cellW, (row+1)*cellH);
44      }
45
46    }
```

FIGURE 9.15 The `MazeDrawer` class (continued).

```
1     import CSLib.*;
2
3     public class MouseController {
4       // Draw a mouse navigating a maze, using the
5       // "hug the wall to the right" algorithm
6       // Rebecca Kamin, Sept 12, 2000
7
8       public void runMouse () {
9         DrawingBox d = new DrawingBox("Mouse in maze");
10        Maze theMaze = new Maze();
11        MazeDrawer theMazeDrawer = new MazeDrawer(theMaze, d);
12        Mouse speedy = new Mouse(theMaze);
13        MouseDrawer speedyDrawer =
14                       new MouseDrawer(speedy, theMazeDrawer, d);
15
16        while (true) {
17          theMazeDrawer.draw();
18          speedyDrawer.draw();
19          Timer.pause(1000);
20          speedy.makeMove();
21        }
22      }
23    }
```

FIGURE 9.16 The `MouseController` class.

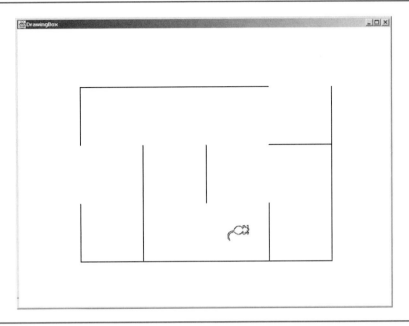

FIGURE 9.17   The mouse in a maze after the eighth move.

9.5

Drawing Pictures (*advanced*)

> Look here, upon this picture, and on this.
>
> ——William Shakespeare
> *Hamlet, III, iv*

Computer graphics is the study of methods of representing images and algorithms   *computer graphics*
for manipulating and displaying them. The most basic algorithms for display are
those for drawing lines and circles. In this section, we use a two-dimensional
array to represent the image to be displayed in a window on a computer screen or
on a printed page. We give a well-known algorithm, due to J. E. Bresenham, for
drawing lines and an algorithm for drawing circles. We illustrate these methods
by drawing these shapes in a `DrawingBox`.

We want to emphasize that, after this chapter, we will continue to use
`drawLine` and `drawOval` in the `DrawingBox` class to draw those shapes.
We are merely showing you algorithms that might be used to implement those
methods.

We have already explained, in Chapter 1 and again in Section 2.4, how
pictures displayed on a computer screen can be thought of as consisting of a grid
of small *pixels*. Figure 9.18 is copied from Chapter 2. The most obvious way to   *pixel*

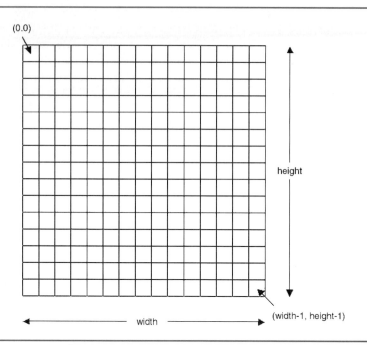

FIGURE 9.18   Each picture is made up of pixels.

frame buffer

store the screen's image is to use a two-dimensional array with one entry for each pixel, giving that pixel's color. This array is called a *frame buffer*. To change what appears on the screen, a program just has to write into the frame buffer; the new image will appear instantly (to human eyes).

resolution

The number of pixels in the frame buffer—the *resolution* of the display device—varies; 1000 × 1000 is the approximate resolution of present-day workstation screens. The number of available colors for each pixel also varies, from only two—black and white—to millions.

Given a system based on a frame buffer, as we've been describing, we will draw two simple shapes: lines and circles. For our examples, we use a two-color image, utilizing Java's predefined constants `Color.black` and `Color.white`. Moreover, we don't really write our information to a hardware frame buffer (since such low-level activities are highly machine-dependent). Rather, we write to a two-dimensional output-independent "software" frame buffer (called `SoftFrame`), which we draw into a `DrawingBox`. Since our purpose is illustrative, we will display the frame buffer at magnified size, so that we can more easily see what each drawing algorithm is doing.

We use a two-dimensional array to represent the soft frame buffer but hide the representation in `SoftFrame`. We want to provide just four public member methods—`clearSoftFrame`, `displaySoftFrame`, `drawLine`, and drawCircle—but we include some others for illustrative purposes. The drawHorizontalLine, drawVerticalLine, drawLongLine, and drawLine1 methods will be obsolete after drawLine is written; similarly, drawCircle1 is a preliminary version of drawCircle. And setPixel is a private instance method used to set pixels in the soft frame buffer (after bounds checking). The form for SoftFrame is

```
1   import CSLib.*;
2   import java.awt.*;
3
4   class SoftFrame {
5
6     // A Frame for drawing lines and circles.
7     // Author: Adrienne Baranowicz, December 2, 1999
8
9     private
10      Color[][] frameBuffer;
11      int width, height;
12
13    public SoftFrame (int w, int h) {
14      width = w;
15      height = h;
16      frameBuffer = new Color[height][width];
17    }
18
19    private void setPixel (int col, int row, Color c) {
20      if ((0 <= col && col < width)
21          && (0 <= row && row < height))
22        frameBuffer[row][col] = c;
23    }
24
25    public void clearSoftFrame () {
26      for (int col = 0; col < width; col++)
27        for (int row = 0; row < height; row++)
28          frameBuffer[row][col] = Color.white;
29    }
30
31    public void displaySoftFrame (String s) {
32      final int MAG = 4;  // Width & height of box used
33                          // to draw each pixel in the soft frame
34      DrawingBox d = new DrawingBox(s);
35      d.setDrawableSize(MAG*width, MAG*height);
36      for (int row = 0;
37               row < frameBuffer.length;
38               row++)
39        for (int col = 0;
40                 col < frameBuffer[row].length;
41                 col++) {
42          d.setColor(frameBuffer[row][col]);
43          d.fillRect(col*MAG, row*MAG, MAG, MAG);
44        }
45    }
```

. . . with additional instance methods:

```
public void drawHorizontalLine (int row) {...}
public void drawVerticalLine (int col) {...}
public void drawLongLine (double m, double b) {...}
public void drawLine1 (Point p1, Point p2) {...}
public void drawLine (Point p1, Point p2) {...}
public void drawCircle1 (Point p0, int r) {...}
public void drawCircle (Point p0, int r) {...}
```

These methods will draw lines and circles using a variety of algorithms. The `SoftFrame` constructor is supplied with the resolution of the picture, and it allocates a private array to hold the soft pixels. The method `displaySoftFrame` will later display the pixel array in a `DrawingBox`.

Position `frameBuffer[0][0]` represents the soft pixel in the upper left corner of the screen, `frameBuffer[width-1][0]` the upper right, `frameBuffer[0][height-1]` the lower left, and `frameBuffer[width-1][height-1]` the lower right.

Note that here the row number is the first array index and the column number is the second; `frameBuffer[r][c]` represents the pixel at column c, row r. In graphics the origin [point (0, 0)] is taken to be the pixel in the upper left corner, so that *higher* row numbers represent *lower* screen positions.

We use a resolution of 90×60 (that is, 90 pixels wide and 60 pixels high) for our soft frame buffer. We want to show some details that would be too small to observe in an actual graphical drawing. Therefore, we magnify our soft frame buffer so that one "soft pixel" translates into a square grid of 16 actual pixels.

As our first, rather trivial, examples, these `SoftFrame` methods draw horizontal and vertical lines, respectively, completely across the screen:

```
47    public void drawHorizontalLine (int row) {
48       for (int col = 0; col < width; col++)
49          setPixel(col, row, Color.black);
50    }
51
52    public void drawVerticalLine (int col) {
53       for (int row = 0; row < height; row++)
54          setPixel(col, row, Color.black);
55    }
```

Given such methods, the client

```
import CSLib.*;

public class DrawGrid {
   // Draw grid lines.

   final static int WIDTH = 90, HEIGHT = 60;

   public static void main (String[] args) {
      SoftFrame scr = new SoftFrame(WIDTH, HEIGHT);
      scr.clearSoftFrame();
      for (int r = 10; r < HEIGHT; r = r + 10)
         scr.drawHorizontalLine(r);
      for (int c = 10; c < WIDTH; c = c + 10)
```

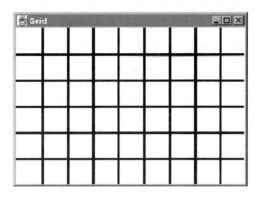

FIGURE 9.19   Drawing grid lines.

```
        scr.drawVerticalLine(c);
      scr.displaySoftFrame("Grid");
    }
  }
```

produces a checkerboard, as shown in Figure 9.19.

Drawing slanted lines is more challenging than drawing vertical or horizontal lines. A straight line can be described as the set of points (x, y) satisfying an equation of the form

$$y = mx + b$$

where m and b are real numbers; m is called the *slope*, and b is the *y intercept*. The larger the value of m, the more vertical the line: If $m = 0$, the line is perfectly horizontal; if $m = 1$, the line is slanted at a 45° angle; if m is much greater than 1, the line is nearly vertical. (It is impossible, however, to describe a perfectly vertical line with this equation, because that would require an infinite slope.)

Using this equation directly, we add the `drawLongLine` method to `SoftFrame`, to draw any nonvertical line across the screen:

```
public void drawLongLine (double m, double b) {
  for (int col = 0; col < width; col++) {
    int row = (int)Math.round(m*col + b);
    setPixel(col, row, Color.black);
  }
}
```

The slope m is a real number, so we do our calculations using doubles. These are converted to integers by casting the result of the Java function `Math.round()`.

Given this definition of `drawLongLine`, the client

```
import CSLib.*;

public class DrawBadLines {
  // Draw long lines badly.

  final static int WIDTH = 90, HEIGHT = 60;
```

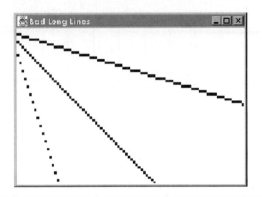

FIGURE 9.20   Drawing long lines.

```
public static void main (String[] args) {
   SoftFrame scr = new SoftFrame(WIDTH, HEIGHT);
   scr.clearSoftFrame();
   scr.drawLongLine(.3,2);
   scr.drawLongLine(1,5);
   scr.drawLongLine(3,10);
   scr.displaySoftFrame("Bad Long Lines");
  }
}
```

produces the picture shown in Figure 9.20.

This method has three problems. First, we normally don't want to draw a line across the screen; instead, we want to draw a line between two points. Second, this method is unable to draw vertical lines; there is no way to request it to do so, because we cannot make the first argument infinity.

The third and most subtle problem is that drawLongLine fails to draw all lines equally well. Notice the difference in the rendering of the top and middle lines compared to the third line. The first two, which are more nearly horizontal than the third (with slopes of 0.3 and 1, respectively), look fine with one pixel drawn in each column. The third, more vertical line (slope = 3) is drawn very weakly, with only 17 pixels to represent the entire line. (The second line has 55 pixels, though it is only about 50 percent longer than the third.) The reason for this is that drawLongLine draws at most one pixel per column, which makes sense only when $m \leq 1$. When $m > 1$, the line should be drawn with one pixel per *row*. To do this, we just reverse the roles of x and y, recasting the equation as

$$x = \frac{y - b}{m}$$

and iterating over the rows instead of the columns. Including all these improvements leads to our first complete line-drawing method, called drawLine1, shown in Figure 9.21. drawLine(p1, p2) draws a line between points p1 and p2. (swap is an auxiliary method used to simplify the code by ensuring that p1 is to the left of p2.)

```
64    private void swap (Point p1, Point p2) {
65      int x = p1.x,      y = p1.y;                   SLOW
66      p1.x = p2.x; p1.y = p2.y;
67      p2.x = x;      p2.y = y;
68    }
69
70    public void drawLine1 (Point p1, Point p2) {     SLOW
71      int row, col;
72
73      if (p1.x == p2.x) { // vertical line
74        if (p2.y < p1.y)
75          swap(p1, p2); // force p1.y <= p2.y        SLOW
76        for (row = p1.y; row <= p2.y; row++)
77          setPixel(p1.x, row, Color.black);
78      }
79      else {                                          SLOW
80        double m = (p2.y-p1.y)/(double)(p2.x-p1.x),
81               b = p1.y-m*p1.x;
82        if (Math.abs(m) < 1.0) {
83          if (p2.x < p1.x) // force p1 to left of p2  SLOW
84            swap(p1, p2);
85          for (col = p1.x; col <= p2.x; col++) {
86            row = (int)Math.round(m*col + b);
87            setPixel(col, row, Color.black);
88          }                                           SLOW
89        }
90        else { // Math.abs(m) >= 1.0
91          if (p2.y < p1.y) // force p1 above p2
92            swap(p1, p2);
93          for (row = p1.y; row <= p2.y; row++) {      SLOW
94            col = (int)Math.round ((row-b)/m);
95            setPixel(col, row, Color.black);
96          }
97        }                                             SLOW
98      }
99    }
```

FIGURE 9.21 The first general line-drawing method.

The client

```
import CSLib.*;
import java.awt.*;

public class DrawGoodLines {
  // Draw lines of varying length well.

  final static int WIDTH = 90, HEIGHT = 60;

  public static void main (String[] args) {
    SoftFrame scr = new SoftFrame(WIDTH, HEIGHT);
    scr.clearSoftFrame();
    scr.drawLine1(new Point(45,0), new Point(45,59));
    scr.drawLine1(new Point(0,30), new Point(89,30));
    scr.drawLine1(new Point(10,0), new Point(70,14));
    scr.drawLine1(new Point(50,20), new Point(55,50));
```

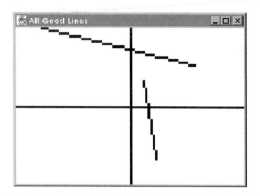

FIGURE 9.22   Drawing lines correctly.

```
        scr.displaySoftFrame("All Good Lines");
    }
}
```

produces the picture shown in Figure 9.22. `drawLine1` can draw partial lines and vertical lines, and it draws lines with slope greater than 1 as strongly as those with slope less than 1.

The method `drawLine1` is not a line-drawing method that would be used in real graphics applications. It draws lines quite well, but it's slow. Drawing a single pixel requires several floating-point arithmetic operations, which are considerably slower than integer operations. When a line contains hundreds or thousands of pixels (and a larger shape may contain hundreds of lines), the cost of these operations adds up. An algorithm called *Bresenham's algorithm* draws a line using only integer arithmetic operations.

Suppose we are drawing a line between points (x_0, y_0) and (x_n, y_n), such that $x_0 < x_n$ and $y_0 \leq y_n$ and the line has a slope $\Delta y / \Delta x$ (where $\Delta y = y_n - y_0$ and $\Delta x = x_n - x_0$) that is positive and less than or equal to 1. In drawing such a line, we iterate over the columns, drawing a pixel in each. Because the line is more nearly horizontal than vertical, we know that after we draw a pixel at position (x_i, y_i), the next pixel will be drawn at either $(x_i + 1, y_i)$ or $(x_i + 1, y_i + 1)$. In other words, the question at each iteration is whether to increment the y value. J. E. Bresenham discovered that this question could be answered by doing calculations involving only integer operations.

The proper y value to use for $x_{i+1} = x_i + 1$ is simply a matter of which value, y_i or $y_i + 1$, is closer to the actual value $y = mx_{i+1} + b$, that is, which of d_i and d_i' is smaller, where

$$d_i = y - y_i$$
$$d_i' = y_{i+1} - y$$

(Note that d_i and d_i' are both nonnegative.) Defining

$$p_i = \Delta x \, (d_i - d_i')$$

we can both assert that $d_i > d_i'$ if and only if p_i is positive and prove the following:

$$p_{i+1} = \Delta x \, (d_{i+1} - d_{i+1}')$$
$$= p_i + 2 \, \Delta y - 2 \, \Delta x \, (y_{i+1} - y_i) \tag{9.1}$$

In other words, we can calculate every value of p_i from the previous value, and the calculation uses only integer operations. Now we need only a starting value, and it can be shown that

$$p_0 = 2 \, \Delta y - \Delta x$$

This leads us to Bresenham's algorithm:

1. Draw (x_0, y_0) and calculate p_0.
2. Repeat for values of i from 1 to $\Delta x - 1$:
   (a) Calculate $x_{i+1} = x_i + 1$.
   (b) Calculate $y_{i+1} = y_i + 1$, if $p_i > 0$; and $y_{i+1} = y_i$, otherwise.
   (c) Draw a pixel at (x_{i+1}, y_{i+1}).
   (d) Use formula (9.1) to calculate p_{i+1}.

This code is given in Figure 9.23, but only for the case we've been discussing: $x_0 < x_n$, $y_0 \leq y_n$, and a line with positive slope less than or equal to 1. The code follows exactly the algorithm just given, except that in calculating the new value of p it uses the fact that, in formula (9.1), $y_{i+1} - y_i$ is either 0 or 1 (depending on whether $p_i > 0$) to simplify the computation.

Finally, we look at `drawCircle`. A circle is the set of points at a given distance r from a given point (x_0, y_0). Since the distance of a point (x, y) from

```
101    public void drawLine (Point p1, Point p2) {
102    // This version of drawLine works only if
103    // p1.x<p2.x, p1.y<p2.y, and the slope of
104    // the line is positive and <= 1
105       int dx = p2.x-p1.x;
106       int dy = p2.y-p1.y;
107       int p = 2*dy - dx;
108       int x = p1.x,
109           y = p1.y;
110       setPixel(x, y, Color.black);
111       for (x = p1.x+1; x <= p2.x; x++) {
112         if (p > 0) y++;
113         setPixel(x, y, Color.black);
114         if (p < 0)
115           p = p + 2*dy;
116         else
117           p = p + 2*(dy - dx);
118       }
119    }
```

FIGURE 9.23   Bresenham's algorithm for drawing lines (incomplete).

QUICK EXERCISE
9.7 Complete this final version of `drawLine` so that it can draw any line.

the center (x_0, y_0) is

$$\sqrt{(x - x_0)^2 + (y - y_0)^2}$$

we can define the circle as all points (x, y) satisfying the equation

$$(x - x_0)^2 + (y - y_0)^2 = r^2$$

Instead of using this equation directly, we can simplify the discussion by assuming that the center of the circle is at $(0, 0)$, which gives the equation

$$x^2 + y^2 = r^2$$

or

$$y = \sqrt{r^2 - x^2}$$

(where both the positive and negative roots correspond to points on the circle). When a pair (x, y) satisfying this equation is found, we just translate it to $(x_0 + x, y_0 + y)$ and draw a point there, as illustrated in Figure 9.24. This discussion leads directly to our first circle-drawing method, shown in Figure 9.25.

The client

```
import CSLib.*;
import java.awt.*;

public class DrawBadCircles {
   // Draw concentric circles badly.

   final static int WIDTH = 90, HEIGHT = 60;

   public static void main (String[] args) {
      SoftFrame scr = new SoftFrame(WIDTH, HEIGHT);
      scr.clearSoftFrame();
      Point center = new Point(WIDTH/2, HEIGHT/2);
      for (int r = 5; r < HEIGHT/2; r = r + 10)
         scr.drawCircle1(center, r);
      scr.displaySoftFrame("Bad Circles");
   }
}
```

produces the picture shown in Figure 9.26.

Like `drawLongLine`, `drawCircle1` draws circles poorly, because it favors the more horizontal parts of the circle (the top and bottom), drawing them much more strongly than the sides. It is also quite inefficient because of all the calls to `sqrt`, a time-consuming method.

Both the picture quality and the efficiency of this method can be improved by observing that it really is necessary to compute only one-eighth of the points

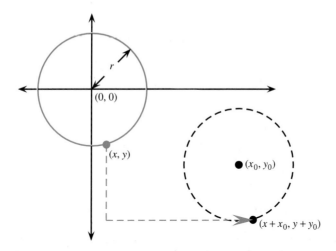

FIGURE 9.24 **Compute the circle relative to (0, 0) and then translate to (x_0, y_0).**

```
121     public void drawCircle1 (Point p0, int r) {
122       int r2 = r*r;
123       for (int x = -r; x <= r; x++) {
124         int y = (int)Math.round(Math.sqrt(r2 - x*x));
125         setPixel(p0.x+x, p0.y+y, Color.black);
126         setPixel(p0.x+x, p0.y-y, Color.black);
127       }
128     }
```

FIGURE 9.25 **The first version of** `drawCircle`.

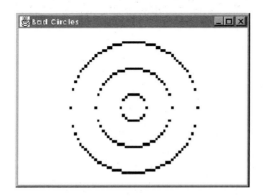

FIGURE 9.26 **Drawing circles—first try.**

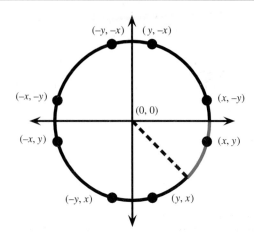

FIGURE 9.27   Computing one point on the circle gives seven others.

on the circle directly—those at angles between $0°$ and $45°$, the first *octant* of the circle—and symmetry can be used to find the rest. Figure 9.27 shows how. Given a circle centered at $(0, 0)$ and a point (x, y) in the first octant of the circle, we can immediately find seven other points in the other octants of the circle. The drawCircle method, shown in Figure 9.28, makes use of this observation. It iterates over rows, selecting columns in which to draw a pixel, until the column number equals or exceeds the row number, indicating that it has exhausted the first octant. Each time it finds a point to draw in the first octant, it draws the corresponding points in the other seven octants as well. Drawing the same circles we tried to draw in Figure 9.26 produces the much more satisfactory picture shown in Figure 9.29.

Bresenham has provided a more efficient algorithm for drawing circles, following the same idea as his line-drawing algorithm; see Exercise 14.

Summary

The bodies of loops can themselves contain loops; when they do, we say that the inner loop is *nested* in the outer loop. Such nested loops are often used in the processing of two-dimensional arrays.

A *two-dimensional array* is an array of arrays of variables in which a single variable is accessed by providing *two* indexes. A two-dimensional array declaration and initialization has the form

```
double[][] USenergy = new double[5][6];
Time[][] monthlyAppointments = new Time[31][16];
```

Two indexes must be provided to access an element: USenergy[year][type] and monthlyAppointments[14][3].

```
130    public void drawCircle (Point p0, int r) {
131      int r2 = r*r;
132      int y = 0;
133      int x = r;
134      do {
135        setPixel(p0.x+x, p0.y+y, Color.black);
136        setPixel(p0.x+y, p0.y+x, Color.black);
137        setPixel(p0.x-y, p0.y+x, Color.black);
138        setPixel(p0.x-x, p0.y+y, Color.black);
139        setPixel(p0.x-x, p0.y-y, Color.black);
140        setPixel(p0.x-y, p0.y-x, Color.black);
141        setPixel(p0.x+y, p0.y-x, Color.black);
142        setPixel(p0.x+x, p0.y-y, Color.black);
143        y++;
144        x = (int)Math.round(Math.sqrt(r2 - y*y));
145      }
146      while (y <= x);
147    }
```

FIGURE 9.28 A second version of drawCircle.

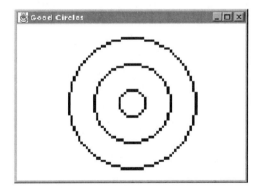

FIGURE 9.29 Drawing circles.

One use of two-dimensional arrays is to represent images on a computer screen. Bresenham has provided efficient algorithms, using only integer operations, for drawing lines and circles. Another use is to hold the "map" of the mouse's maze. For example, the two-dimensional Boolean array eWall says, for every room (given by its x and y coordinates), whether that room has a wall to its east.

Exercises

1. To assist a young friend learning to multiply, write an application to print the following multiplication table:

```
MULTIPLICATION TABLE

      1    2    3    4 ...    12

      2    4    6    8 ...    24

      3    6    9   12 ...    36

      .    .    .    .  ...    .

     12   24   36   48 ...   144
```

2. An $n \times n$ array is *symmetric* if `A[i][j] = A[j][i]` for all `i` and `j`. Write a Boolean-valued method whose argument is an integer array that returns `true` if the array is symmetric and `false` if not.

3. The *transpose* of a square matrix `m` is the matrix `t` such that `t[i][j] = m[j][i]` for all `j` and `i`. Write a method

   ```
   int[][] transpose (int[][] A)
   ```

   whose argument is a square matrix and which computes and returns its transpose. Print both the original array and its transpose.

4. In Exercise 3, instead of placing the transpose into a separate array, calculate the transpose *in place*; that is, change the argument to its transpose by rearranging its elements. This method should have type

   ```
   void transposeInPlace (int[][] A)
   ```

5. Pascal's triangle consists of rows of coefficients of $(a + b)^n$ for $n = 0, 1, 2, \ldots$. The triangle looks like this:

```
                          1
                      1       1
                   1      2       1
                1      3      3       1
             1      4      6      4       1
          1      5     10     10      5       1
                          .
                          .
                          .
```

   where the values from left to right in the nth row are

$$\binom{n}{i} = \frac{n!}{i!(n-i)!} \qquad i = 0, 1, 2, \ldots, n$$

   Write an application to print Pascal's triangle; the number of rows to be printed should be a symbolic constant. This is *not* an efficient method to produce Pascal's triangle— the point of the exercise is to construct the loops involved. (*Hint*: Use the `for` loop indexes as parameters to `SFormat.sprintr` to get the proper alignment of the values.)

6. Numerous representations of the crossword puzzle are possible. Change the representation we used in two different ways:

   (a) First, leaving `theBoard` as is, use a different representation for `theNumbers`: Instead of a parallel two-dimensional array, use an $n \times 2$ integer array, where n is the number of numbered squares. Row i of this array gives the row and column number in the puzzle of the square numbered i. For our example in Figure 9.9, the first part of the declaration would be

   ```
   int[][] theNumbers =
       {{1, 1}, {1, 3}, {1, 6}, {1, 7}, {1, 9},
        {2, 5},
        {3, 1}, {3, 7},
        ... };
   ```

   (b) Now change the representation for the entire puzzle to be a single two-dimensional array of `Square` objects. Each `Square` object contains its contents (as a character) and its number (if any).

7. (a) Fourteen different year calendars are possible—seven for January 1 falling on each day of the week in a nonleap year and seven more for a leap year. Print the 14 different calendars. (*Hint*: Use a triple-nested loop.)

   (b) Write an application to print a table indicating which of the 14 different calendars to use for each year from 1900 to 1999 (Gregorian).

8. Operations analogous to those used with ordinary numbers can be defined on matrices. For example, matrices can be added "componentwise," meaning that A+B is the matrix C such that for all `i` and `j`, `C[i][j] = A[i][j]+B[i][j]`. The *zero matrix* (the matrix containing all 0s) acts as the identity for matrix addition, just as zero is the identity for addition of numbers. Define two addition operations:

   ```
   void addMatrices (double[][] A, double[][] B, double[][] C)
   double[][] addMatrices (double[][] A, double[][] B)
   ```

   The first method adds A and B and places the result in C. The second allocates the result matrix in the heap and returns a reference to it.

   Matrix multiplication is more complicated. The product of A and B is the matrix C such that $C[i][j] = \sum_{k=0}^{n-1} A[i][k] \times B[k][j]$. (The identity matrix defined on page 328 is the identity for multiplication.) Define two versions of `multMatrices` analogous to the two versions of `addMatrices`.

9. A *magic square* is an $n \times n$ grid of the integers 1 through n^2 that sum to the same *magic square* value across rows, down columns, and along the two diagonals. An example is

8	1	6
3	5	7
4	9	2

   An old method for constructing magic squares of odd order was devised by de la Loubére. It involves placing the next number of the magic square diagonally up and to the right of the previous number, with the following caveats:

   (a) One row "up" from the top row lands you in the bottom row.

   (b) One column "right" from the rightmost column lands you in the leftmost column.

   (c) If the desired cell is already occupied, then instead place the next number below the previous one.

(d) Begin by placing the number 1 in the middle of the top row.

Write an application to read an odd integer and display a magic square of that order. (*The Mathematical Intelligencer*, vol. 14, no. 3, 1992, pp. 15–16.)

10. Conway's Game of Life is a simulation of a cellular automaton from one generation to the next. It is played out on a two-dimensional array of "cells." A cell is either "alive" (represented by a filled square) or "dead" (represented by an empty square). From one generation to the next, cells may die or come to life, according to the following rules. An empty square
    (a) comes to life (in the next generation) if three of its neighbors are alive (in the present generation);

    (b) otherwise, remains empty.

    A filled square
    (a) dies of loneliness if it has fewer than two neighbors;

    (b) dies of overcrowding if it has more than three neighbors;

    (c) otherwise, remains alive.

    Neighbor cells include the eight cells in the horizontal, vertical, and diagonal directions. A corner cell has only three neighbors, while other border cells have five neighbors.

    Write an application that plays out Conway's Game of Life on an 80 × 80 board, using * for a filled cell and "blank" for an empty cell. You should keep two copies of the array—one for the present generation and one for the succeeding generation.

    Try various initial patterns. Some interesting ones are

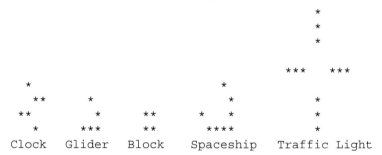

    [Conway's Game of Life was popularized by Martin Gardner's mathematical games column in the October 1970 and February 1971 issues of *Scientific American*. Also see William Poundstone, *The Recursive Universe* (Oxford: Oxford University Press, 1987).]

11. The American Bankers' Association font E–13B is used to print numbers on checks in magnetically readable ink. It is a simple font employing a 7 × 7 grid, as follows:

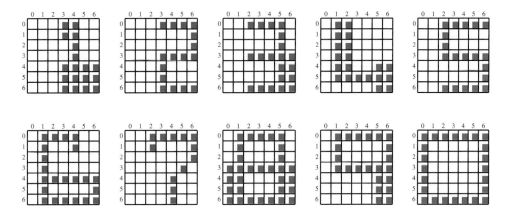

Write two methods:
(a) The `void printE13B (int digit)` prints `digit` (an integer between 0 and 9), using `Xs` for the filled-in boxes and leaving the others blank.
(b) The `int readE13B (boolean[][] grid)` has as its argument a 7×7 array of Booleans purporting to contain a character in the E–13B font, in the obvious way. The `readE13B` returns the corresponding digit, or -1 if `grid` contains none of the E–13B characters.

To solve this problem, employ a $10 \times 7 \times 7$ *three-dimensional* array

```
boolean[][][] E13B = {...};
```

Three-dimensional arrays work just as you would expect: `E13B[i][j][k]` gives the value of the `[j][k]` position in `E13B[i]`. Its initialization list has braces nested three deep. With this array correctly initialized, both methods are quite simple to program.

12. Add operations `drawBox` and `drawDisk` to the `SoftFrame` class. These calls draw *filled* shapes. The method `drawBox` is given three corners of a rectangle and draws the rectangle with the interior filled in in black. The method `drawDisk` has the same arguments as `drawCircle`, but it draws a circle filled in in black.

13. Use the line-drawing operations of the `SoftFrame` class and the `drawBox` method defined in Exercise 13 to draw a checkerboard.

14. Bresenham's circle-drawing algorithm has the same overall structure as his line-drawing algorithm. Suppose we are drawing the blue arc of the circle in Figure 9.27. Starting from the point $(r, 0)$, where r is the radius of the circle, the next point to draw is at either $(r, 1)$ or $(r - 1, 1)$. In general, in drawing this arc, if the last point drawn was (x_i, y_i), then the next point to draw is either $(x_i, y_i + 1)$ or $(x_i - 1, y_i - 1)$. We will compute quantities p_i that indicate by their sign which of the two points to draw next. We will not explain the justification for the following formulas; you may look in any book on computer graphics for more details.

We begin at point $(x_0, y_0) = (r, 0)$ and proceed to draw pixels at points (x_i, y_i), computed as follows for $i \geq 0$:

$$(x_{i+1}, y_{i+1}) = \begin{cases} (x_i, y_i + 1) & \text{if } p_i < 0 \\ (x_i - 1, y_i + 1) & \text{otherwise} \end{cases}$$

until we draw a point (x_i, y_i) such that $x_i = y_i$. The quantities p_i are computed as follows:

$$p_1 = 3 - 2r$$

$$p_{i+1} = \begin{cases} p_i + 4y_i + 6 & \text{if } p_i < 0 \\ p_i + 4(y_i - x_i) + 10 & \text{otherwise} \end{cases}$$

Being able to draw this arc is the key to drawing the circle. The tasks of drawing the other seven arcs and centering the circle at a point other than $(0, 0)$ are easily accomplished in the same way as we did them in `drawCircle`. Program Bresenham's circle-drawing algorithm and compare its performance to that of `drawCircle`.

15. There are numerous ways to represent the maze in the mouse-in-a-maze application. Change the `Maze` class—and *only* the `Maze` class—to use the following representations for the maze.

    (a) Use a two-dimensional array of integers, each integer a number between 0 and 15, with each bit of its binary representation representing a wall. The 1's bit is for north, the 2's bit for east, the 4's bit for south, and the 8's bit for west. For example, 5 (0101 in binary) is used to represent a room with walls only on its north and south sides. (To find the 2^i bit in the binary representation of a number, divide by 2^{i-1} and test if the quotient is even or odd.)

    (b) Use a two-dimensional array of strings, each string consisting of zero or more of the characters N, S, E, or W, each representing the presence of a wall on that side of a room.

    (c) Create a `Room` class whose instances describe the walls in a room, in any representation you choose. Then use a two-dimensional array of `Room` objects to represent the maze.

CLASSES AND METHODS IV: STATIC METHODS AND VARIABLES

CHAPTER PREVIEW

Large programs are written by subdividing them into *methods* to compartmentalize or *modularize* programming tasks. This chapter introduces class variables and class methods. *Class variables* have only one instance and are not contained in any object; *class methods* have no receiver and therefore can access only class variables. We give several examples that illustrate these features and the process of stepwise refinement. Also included in this chapter is a discussion of *method overloading* for class methods. Finally, we introduce Java *interfaces*, which specify the behavior of an object.

You know my methods in such cases, Watson.

—Sir Arthur Conan Doyle
The Adventures of Sherlock Holmes.
"The Musgrave Ritual"

We've already seen the advantages of using separate instance methods when building classes. We avoided duplication of code by using methods. We encapsulated code by using methods. We provided clients with a variety of possible object messages by using methods. However, when writing a client, we always used the form

```
class ClassnameClient {
//  Author, date, explanation
  public static void main (String[] args) {
      Classname variable = new  Classname();
      variable. method(...);
  }
}
```

The class *Classname* `Client` is a class but without instance methods. In fact, since we never create instances of the client class, there can be no objects to which we might send messages. Yet `main` looks very much like an instance method. The only difference is that its header is modified by the word `static`. Methods that are modified by the word `static` are called *class methods*. We'll see that we can define class methods in any class, and sometimes we need them instead of instance methods.

10.1

Class Variables and Class Methods

Instance variables and methods are associated with instances of a class. To invoke the instance method `f` associated with object `o`, we write `o.f(...)`; `o` is called the *receiver* of `f`, and `f` can refer to the instance variables of `o` directly. If `o` had a public instance variable `x`, then clients would refer to it by using the notation `o.x`.

class variables

Class variables are variables associated with a class, not with instances of the class. There is *one instance* of each class variable, not one instance per object. To create a class variable, add the keyword `static` to the variable's declaration.

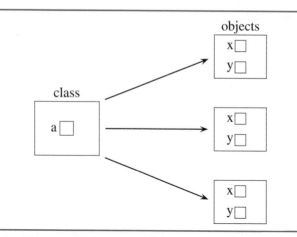

FIGURE 10.1   **Class with class variable a and instance variables x and y.**

The relationship between instance variables and class variables is illustrated in
class method   Figure 10.1. A *class method*, similarly, is a method associated not with an object
but instead with the class as a whole. A class method is not invoked by sending
it as a message to an object, and it has no receiver. The class method f in the
class C is invoked using the notation C.f(...). Because a class method has no
receiver, it cannot refer to instance variables. Like class variables, class methods
are created by adding the keyword static to the method definition.

     To understand the utility of class methods and class variables, consider this
programming scenario: In a client that uses the Clock class (page 248), the user
is allowed to select how Clock objects are printed—either using military time
or using civilian time. There might be a toString method for civilian time
and a separate toMilitaryTime method for military time (as in Exercise 1 on
page 256). We assume that the client would want the user to specify which format
is preferred, and the client would thereafter print using that format. The client
might permit the user to enter a command to toggle between the two formats. In
any case, the client program needs to remember which format is to be used from
that point onward (until the format is toggled again).

     How can the client remember the proper format? One possibility is for the
client to maintain a variable boolean useMilitaryTime. Then whenever
a Clock object, say now, is to be printed, the client would first check to see how
to do the printing and then call the proper method, like this:

```
if (useMilitaryTime)
    out.print(now.toMilitaryTime());
else
    out.print(now.toString());
```

However, this approach has a serious downside: Since Clock objects may be
stringified   *stringified*[1] in many places throughout a client, the variable useMilitaryTime

---

[1] *Stringify* is a word coined by computer programmers, meaning to turn into a string.

will have to be made available in all those places, possibly as an instance variable of the client, and perhaps as an additional argument to every method of the client that might want to stringify a Clock. This approach is prone to error; for example, there may be some obscure place in the client where stringification occurs, but where the programmer forgot to check the format desired.

Another approach is to make useMilitaryTime an instance variable of Clock, with a method to toggle it. Then we could have a *single* toString method that would return a string in the proper format. The client would be entirely relieved of the responsibility for checking which format is desired. The new version of toString would consult this Clock instance variable to decide how to print:

```
public class Clock {

    private boolean useMilitaryTime = false;
    ...

    public void toggleTimeFormat () {
      useMilitaryTime = !useMilitaryTime;
    }

    ...

    public String toString () {
      if (useMilitaryTime)
        // return string in military format
      else
        // return string in civilian format
    }
    ...
}
```

The client would then switch to military format by calling now.toggleTimeFormat(), and would obtain a stringified time by sending the toString message. However, this approach also has an important disadvantage: The client program needs to keep track of every Clock object in existence—Clock objects may have been created earlier and are now stored in variables and arrays in all different places—and the client program would need to send the toggleTimeFormat to every object. (Keep in mind that the user has specified that one or the other form, either military or civilian, be used for *all* stringification of Clock objects until further notice.)

We need a variable that can be changed once for all Clock objects—that is, it has only one instance—to which all objects have access. A class variable fits the bill perfectly. We can declare useMilitaryTime as a class variable in the Clock class, and toString can refer to it:

```
public class Clock {

    private static boolean useMilitaryTime = false;
    ...

    public static void toggleTimeFormat () {
```

```
        useMilitaryTime = !useMilitaryTime;
    }

    . . .

    public String toString () {
      if (useMilitaryTime)
        // return string in military format
      else
        // return string in civilian format
    }
    . . .
  }
```

Since the class variable does not belong to any particular object, we have made `toggleTimeFormat` a class method. Note that both it and `printTime` refer to `useMilitaryTime` by its unqualified name; they are not obliged to write `Clock.useMilitaryTime`.

With this solution, a client can switch to military time by writing

```
Clock.toggleTimeFormat();
```

This changes the one copy of `useMilitaryTime` that *all* instances of `toString` refer to. Thus, all `Clock` objects will now print in military format, no matter when or by whom they were created.

Class variables can be declared `public`. In that case, they can be accessed directly by clients, using the *class-name.variable-name* notation.[2]

QUICK EXERCISE 10.1	Implement this version of `Clock` and write a simple client for it. (You will need to write the military time formatting code.) Then modify the class and client by removing `toggleTimeFormat` and instead making `useMilitaryTime` a public class variable.

A point that bears repeating is that a class method is allowed to access class variables (and may invoke other class methods), but it is *not* allowed to access instance variables (and may not invoke instance methods). This makes sense, because the class method is called without reference to any particular instance; so if a class method wanted to invoke an instance method, there would be no instance to use! Similarly it makes no sense for a class method to have access to an instance variable.

---

[2]As we have said before, if a variable is declared using neither the `private` nor `public` keywords, it has a visibility somewhere between the two. This is explained further in Chapter 12.

Classes with No Instance Variables or Methods

Some classes contain only class variables and methods. Such classes have no objects of their own; accordingly, they have no constructors. They just provide a convenient way of packaging a collection of useful methods. We give two examples in this section.

One such class, that we have already used, is `Math`. It has the symbolic constants:

```
public static final double E = ...
public static final double PI = ...
```

The `final` indicates that their values cannot be changed. This class also has a large collection of methods, including `double sin (double a)`, `double sqrt (double a)`, and `int round (float a)`. All are public and static. These methods operate on built-in data types; there are no `Math` objects.

The second purely static class that we'll examine is the `SFormat` class from `CSLib`. We'll actually trace the development of a few of the static methods in that class. As you can see from Table 9.1 on page 321, `SFormat` has a number of overloaded methods. We already have used overloading for constructors and instance methods; it works the same way for class methods. As with instance methods, the various class methods that share a name need to have different numbers or types of arguments; that way, Java knows which method to use in any particular call.

Consider that you want to stringify values, of various types, right-justified in a string of a given size w. We will write the methods to do this. Rather than requiring us to use a different name for each type of argument [`String sprintrInt (int w, int i)`, `String sprintrDouble (int w, double d)`, etc.], Java allows us to call them all `sprintr`.[3]

It is easy to take a given `String`, `s`, and right-justify it in a field of width w—just attach a lot of blanks to the beginning and then take the trailing w characters:

```
String stringTooLong = "                    " + s;
String StringJustRight =
               stringTooLong.substring(stringTooLong.length()-w);
```

Recall from Table 3.6 on page 72 that the `String` method `substring`, when given a single integer argument `inx`, returns the suffix of the receiver from index `inx` to the end.

---

[3]You might think that we should call this method `toStringr`, but the name `sprint` was chosen in the spirit of similarly named methods from the C and C++ languages. The name `sprintr` means "print to a string, right-justified."

We can play the same game with an integer—concatenate a lot of blanks to the beginning of the integer (which in the process gets transformed to a string itself). Then we extract the suffix of the desired length.

```
String stringTooLong = "                                        " + i;
String StringJustRight =
                stringTooLong.substring(stringTooLong.length()-w);
```

A class for accomplishing this with `ints`, `Strings`, and `doubles` is

```
 1   public class SFormat {
 2
 3     // A class for formatting integers, strings, and decimals.
 4     // Author Marie Mickunas, August 2, 2001
 5
 6     private static String s;
 7     private static String BLANKS=
 8       "                                        ";
 9
10     public static String sprintr (int w, int i) {
11     // Stringify an integer right-justified
12     // in a field of width w
13       s=BLANKS+i;
14       return s.substring(s.length()-w);
15     }
16
17     public static String sprintr (int w, String str) {
18     // Right-justify a String in a field of width w
19       s=BLANKS+str;
20       return s.substring(s.length()-w);
21     }
22
23     public static String sprintr (int w, double d) {
24     // Stringify a double right-justified
25     // in a field of width w
26       s=BLANKS+d;
27       return s.substring(s.length()-w);
28     }
29   }
```

Calls such as `SFormat.sprintr(10, Math.PI)` will invoke the correct version of the method. Recall that we say that the name `sprintr` is *overloaded*, and this feature of Java—the ability to give multiple method definitions for a single name—is called *overloading*. We already have used overloading for constructors and for instance methods.

overloading

Notice that we declared the class symbolic constant `BLANKS` to be `private`, because we do not expect clients to access that constant.

10.2.1 Debugging `SFormat`

We might be quite content with the `SFormat` class until we try to print some computed decimals. For example, we would expect the following program to print `0.6`:

QUICK EXERCISE
10.2

Add a method called `void sprintzr (int w, int i)` to SFormat. It prints an integer right-justified in a field of width w, but with leading *zeros* instead of leading blanks.

```
1    import CSLib.*;
2    public class Test {
3
4        public static void main (String args[] ){
5        OutputBox out = new OutputBox();
6        out.println(SFormat.sprintr(3, 1.0/5.0+1.0/5.0+1.0/5.0));
7        }
8    }
```

Instead, it prints 001! Then we remember Bug Alert 3.5 on page 89—double-precision arithmetic is not always exact. If we try the same program with a field width of 18, we see that the actual value of 1.0/5.0+1.0/5.0+1.0/5.0 is 0.6000000000000001. Our version of sprintr is just extracting the trailing "001".

What we need is a version that has another argument telling how many places we want to print to the right of the decimal point: `void sprintr (int w, int r, double d)` prints d right-justified in a field of width w, with r places to the right of the decimal point. Let's analyze what we need to do. We want to produce *three* strings and then concatenate them: The first string is the integer part of d; the second string is the decimal point (.); the third string is the fractional part of d.

As for stringifying the integer part of d, we know that this portion should occupy a field of width w-r-1 (why?). This can be done by calling

   sprintr(w-r-1, *integer part of* d);

The integer part of d is given by (int)d.

Stringifying the fractional part takes a bit more thought. First we need to isolate the fractional part by subtracting the integer part (so, for example, 4.5678 becomes 0.5678). For this we'll need the Math.floor method (to obtain 4.0 from 4.5678). Then we need to "shift" the fraction left as many places as we wish to appear printed to the right of the decimal point. For example, if we want three places, then 0.5678 will become 567.8. Shifting n places left is done by multiplying by 10^n. Then we want to round the result and convert to an integer (so 567.8 becomes 568.0 and then 568). Then we just stringify the result. We remember that there are Math methods for obtaining a particular power of 10, and for obtaining the integer part of a decimal (floor). Putting all this together, we get the following:

```
public static String sprintr (int w, int r, double d) {
// Print a decimal with r decimal places to the right of
// the point in a field of width w.
   return sprintr(w-r-1, (int)d) + "." +
          sprintr(r, (int)Math.round(Math.pow(10.0,r)*
                              (d-Math.floor(d))));
}
```

We are very pleased when we see that sprintr(3,1,1./5.+1./5.+1./5.) produces "0.6". But our contentment is short-lived. We try sprintr (5,3,1.002) and find that it prints "1.   2". Hmmm—what we need is to stringify the fractional part with leading *zeros* instead of leading blanks. If you have been doing the Quick Exercises, you know how to do that! (You *have* been doing the Quick Exercises, haven't you? See Quick Exercise 10.2.)

QUICK EXERCISE
10.3

Fix String sprintr (int w, int r, double d) so that the fractional part is stringified with leading zeros.

Once again, we take a deep breath and hope that we've considered all contingencies. But it is not long before someone writes a program with the following call:

```
out.print( SFormat.sprintr(-3, i) );
```

What in the world was this programmer thinking? Apparently he has not even read the documentation, since a field width of −3 makes no sense at all. Oh well, we can't allow this to go unchecked, since it produces a run-time error (String index out of range). The quickest way to fix things is to ensure that we never call any of Java's methods with illegal arguments. In this case, we need to protect the calls to substring(int inx) to ensure that the argument inx is always between 0 and the length of the subject string. [There is in addition a hidden deficiency in our sprintr(int w, int i) and other methods—we attached only about 70 blanks, so there would be a problem if a user tried something like SFormat.sprintr(200, i).] If the user specifies a field width less than zero, we'll return the empty string. The largest string that sprintr can construct is the 70 blanks plus the print size of the integer, so that is what is returned if a very large field width is supplied by the user. We need to make these changes in all versions of sprintr that make a call to substring. We get

```
1   public class SFormat {
2
3     // A class for formatting integers, strings, and decimals.
4     // Author Marie Mickunas, August 2, 2001
5
6     private static String s;
7     private static String BLANKS=
8       "                                                                      ";
9
10    public static String sprintr (int w, int i) {
11    // Stringify an integer right-justified
12    // in a field of width w
13      if (w<=0) return "";
14      s=BLANKS+i;
15      return s.substring( Math.min(0, s.length()-w) );
16    }
```

```
17
18    public static String sprintr (int w, String str) {
19    // Right-justify a String in a field of width w
20       if (w<=0) return "";
21       s=BLANKS+str;
22       return s.substring( Math.min(0, s.length()-w) );
23    }
24
25    public static String sprintr (int w, double d) {
26    // Stringify a double right-justified
27    // in a field of width w
28       if (w<=0) return "";
29       s=BLANKS+d;
30       return s.substring( Math.min(0, s.length()-w) );
31    }
32
33    public static String sprintr (int w, int r, double d) {
34    // Stringify a decimal with r decimal places to the right of
35    // the point in a field of width w.
36       return sprintr(w-r-1, (int)d) + "."
37         + sprintzr(r, (int)Math.round(Math.pow(10.0, r)*
38                                          (d-Math.floor(d))));

    . . .
    }
```

You can see the test for too small a field width in line 13. The call to `Math.max` in line 15 ensures that the argument to `substring` is never negative, which is what would happen if a user supplied too large a value for `w`. (Recall that an argument of zero to `substring` returns the entire string.)

All this seems to work just fine. But we're just too conscientious a programmer to let it rest with this version. We know that many programmers will want to stringify a decimal with `r` decimal places to the right of the decimal point, but with *just enough* of a field width. Also, some will want to stringify a decimal with two decimal places, again with just enough space to hold the number. (This is for printing currency, so we can print things like "Hey deadbeat! You owe us $532.55, so pay up now!") We need two new methods:

```
String sprintr (int r, double d)
String sprintr (double d)
```

Write a `print` statement that prints the foregoing "deadbeat" warning.

**QUICK EXERCISE
10.4**

Before we begin coding the two new methods, we stop to think a bit. Overloading is great, but we have quite a few `sprintr` methods in our `SFormat` class by now. We should ask ourselves if these two new ones will conflict with any of the existing methods. Sure enough, although the `sprintr (double d)` version is new and different, there is already another one that will conflict with

sprintr (int r, double d), namely, sprintr (int w, double d).
There is no easy way around this dilemma—we cannot retain both versions. It
seems that the new one is more useful than the old one, so we'll remove the old
version and proceed to program our two new methods.

Assuming that we can program sprintr (int w, double d), we
can use that to implement sprintr (double d) as follows:

```
public static String sprintr (double d) {
    return sprintr(2, d);
}
```

Notice how one class method is able to call another—sprintr (double d)
calls sprintr (int r, double d). Since sprintr (int r, double d)
is a class method, there is no object to which the message is sent. Indeed,
sprintr (double d) doesn't have access to any objects, since it is a class
method.

It is natural to ask as well if the new sprintr (int r, double d)
can be crafted by using the existing sprintr (int w, int r, double d).
The answer is yes, but the solution is not immediately obvious.

QUICK EXERCISE **10.5**	Before reading further, see if you can discover the solution to writing sprintr (int r, double d) by using sprintr (int w, int r, double d). The answer is shown just below.

Here is the final version of SFormat:

```
1    public class SFormat {
2
3        // A class for formatting integers, strings, and decimals.
4        // Author Marie Mickunas, August 2, 2001
5
6        private static String s;
7        private static String BLANKS=
8          "
9
10       public static String sprintr (int w, int i) {
11       // Stringify an integer right-justified
12       // in a field of width w
13         if (w<=0) return "";
14         s=BLANKS+i;
15         return s.substring(Math.min(0, s.length()-w));
16       }
17
18       public static String sprintr (int w, String str) {
19       // Right-justify a String in a field of width w
20         if (w<=0) return "";
21         s=BLANKS+str;
22         return s.substring(Math.min(0, s.length()-w));
```

```
23        }
24
25        public static String sprintr (int w, int r, double d) {
26        // Stringify a decimal with r decimal places to the right of
27        // the point in a field of width w.
28           return sprintr(w-r-1, (int)d) + "."
29              + sprintzr(r, (int)Math.round(Math.pow(10.0, r)*
30                                  (d-Math.floor(d))));
31        }
32
33        public static String sprintr (int r, double d) {
34        // Like above, but fit fieldwidth to the number.
35           return (int)d + sprintr(r+1, r, d);
36        }
37
38        public static String sprintr (double d) {
39        // Like above, but 2 decimal places (as for currency).
40           return sprintr(2, d);
    ...
        public static String sprintzr (int w, int i) {...}
    }
```

You can see how we use `sprintr (int w, int r, double d)` to assist
in the implementation of `sprintr (int r, double d)`—lines 32 through
35. We use it to print the fractional part of d, including the decimal point. That
is, we ask for it to print r digits to the right of the decimal point in a field of
width `r+1`, where the +1 takes care of the decimal point. All we have to do is
to add to the front the stringified version of the integral part, given by `(int)d`;
the stringification occurs because we are concatenating `(int)d` to the `String`
result that is returned from the subsequent call to `sprintr`.

10.3

Modular Development and Debugging

> Teach us to number our days, that we may attain a wise
> heart.
>
> —Bible
> *Psalms* 90:12

In this section we use methods to develop a program for a nontrivial application.
You will see how a modular approach, in which you encapsulate program frag-
ments, allows you to build a complicated, interrelated collection of methods with
relative ease. The class that we write will have both instance methods and class
methods, as well as both instance variables and class variables.

The problem we want to solve is this: Given two dates, compute the number
of days elapsed from one date to the other. For example, from June 1, 1986, to

June 20, 1986, there were 19 days. From December 25, 1983, to March 1, 1984, there were 67 days. John F. Kennedy was inaugurated on January 20, 1961, and assassinated on November 22, 1963, having been president of the United States for 1036 days. Although most people are aware of the basic rules by which the calendar works, the exact calculations are not obvious, and there are real applications for such a program, including the calculation of interest compounded daily and the prediction of such phenomena as eclipses.

The main part of the job will lie in defining the class `Date`. `Date` has both instance methods and class methods.

10.3.1   The `Date` Class

Before we can start developing the program, we must ensure that we understand all the conditions to be satisfied. We will insist that the program work for any two dates from at least 1000 AD through 2199 AD, and therein lies a subtle difficulty.

The calendar in use today in most countries is the new style, or Gregorian, calendar, designed by a commission assembled by Pope Gregory XIII. The calendar is based on a 365-day year, divided into 12 months of lengths 31, 28, 31, 30, 31, 30, 31, 31, 30, 31, 30, and 31 days in normal years and 366 days in leap years, with the extra day added to make the second month 29 days long. A year is a leap year if it is divisible by 4 and is not a century year (multiple of 100) or if it is divisible by 400. The Gregorian calendar differs from its predecessor, the old-style, or Julian, calendar only in that the Julian calendar did not include the century rule for leap years—all century years were leap years.

Julius Caesar instituted the Julian calendar in 45 BC on the first of January, 709 years after the founding of Rome; it was a modification of the ancient Egyptian calendar. Since every fourth year was a leap year, a cycle of 4 years contained $4 \times 365 + 1 = 1461$ days, giving an average length of year of $1461/4 = 365.25$ days. This is about 11 minutes, 14 seconds more than the actual length of the solar year, and over the centuries the calendar started to slip with respect to the solar year. By the 16th century, the date of the true vernal equinox had shifted from around March 21 to around March 11. If this error were not corrected, eventually Easter, whose date depends on the vernal equinox, would be in the summer. Pope Gregory instituted only a minor change in the calendar—century years not divisible by 400 would no longer be leap years, giving an average length of year of $(400 \times 365 + 97)/400 = 365.2425$ days. However, he also corrected the accumulated 10-day error in the calendar by proclaiming that Thursday, October 4, 1582, the last date in the (old-style) Julian calendar, would be followed by Friday, October 15, the first day of the new-style (Gregorian) calendar. Catholic countries followed his rule, but Protestant and Orthodox countries resisted. Spain, Portugal, and Italy adopted it immediately, as did the Catholic states in Germany. The Protestant parts of Germany waited until 1700, Great Britain and its American colonies waited until 1752, Russia adopted the new calendar only after the revolution in 1918, Bulgaria adopted it in 1920, and Turkey in 1928.

With this summary of the development of the calendar, we now face the heart of the problem: How are we to compute, say, the number of days George

Washington lived—he was born February 11, 1732, on the Julian calendar and died on December 14, 1799, on the Gregorian calendar. Should we convert dates from one calendar to the other? If so, how do we do it?

What we'll do is simply to reckon all dates from 1000 AD to the present according to the Gregorian calendar. That is, rather than say that George Washington was born on February 11, 1732 (Julian), we'll consider his birthday to be February 22, 1732 (Gregorian), for the purposes of our calculations. It is an interesting exercise to convert dates from one calendar to the other. (See Exercise 15 at the end of this chapter.)

Before undertaking the actual calculation of elapsed days, we consider what kinds of methods a client might want in a class that provides date manipulation.

We discovered that symbolic constants are useful, and this would be a good time to show a variety of symbolic constants that the Date class might provide:

```
1   // Class variables (all symbolic constants)
2
3   public final static String[]
4      DAY_NAME = {"Sun", "Mon", "Tue", "Wed",
5                  "Thu", "Fri", "Sat"},
6      MONTH_NAME = {"",
7       "January",   "February", "March",    "April",
8       "May",       "June",     "July",     "August",
9       "September", "October",  "November", "December"};
10
11  public final static int
12     SUNDAY=0,   MONDAY=1, TUESDAY=2, WEDNESDAY=3,
13     THURSDAY=4, FRIDAY=5, SATURDAY=6;
14
15  public final static int
16     JANUARY=1,    FEBRUARY=2, MARCH=3,     APRIL=4,
17     MAY=5,        JUNE=6,     JULY=7,      AUGUST=8,
18     SEPTEMBER=9, OCTOBER=10, NOVEMBER=11, DECEMBER=12;
```

Notice that DAY_NAME and MONTH_NAME are arrays of type String; but because their definitions are declared final, they cannot later be altered. For that reason, the array elements must be given their values using array initialization (see Section 8.4 on page 266).

Now let's consider what class methods might be useful to a client. As we think about how to write them, we will discover other methods needed as part of the task. Those methods, in turn, will lead to others, and so on. This is called a *top-down approach* because we see the problem from the top in outline form and successively refine the outline by looking at each section in greater detail, at each subsection in greater detail, at each sub-subsection in greater detail, and so on until we reach the bottom of the pyramid, where further refinement is not needed; this process is called *stepwise refinement*. Following this approach suggests a logical order in which to begin writing the necessary parts. Eventually all (or most of) the constituent parts will become apparent. At that point we can begin writing them—the needs of debugging the individual parts dictate the order in which we write them.

top-down approach

stepwise refinement

First, a client might want to know if a given month/day/year is legal. As we begin to write this method, we quickly realize that we must be able to tell how many days are in a given month (to determine, for example, that June 31 is illegal); therefore, we need a class method to do this, say, int lastDayOfMonth (int month, int year). If we *assume* that we can write lastDayOfMonth, then we can proceed to write dateIsLegal.

```
1    public static boolean dateIsLegal (int m, int d, int y) {
2    // Determine whether month m, day d, year y
3    // is a legal date on the Gregorian calendar;
4    // date must be on or after Jan 1, 1 AD.
5
6       return
7          (1 <= y) &&                          // year is okay
8          (1 <= m) && (m <= 12) &&    // month is okay
9          (1 <= d) &&                          // day is...
10         (d <= lastDayOfMonth(m, y));    //         ...okay
11      }
```

Next we proceed to write lastDayOfMonth. This is used by dateIsLegal, but it might be something a client would want to invoke, so we make it public. Again we realize that we need another method, boolean leapYear (int year), which will allow us to compute the last day of February. If we assume that we can write leapYear, then we can write lastDayOfMonth:

```
1    public static int lastDayOfMonth (int m, int y) {
2    // Returns the number of days in month m of
3    // year y on the Gregorian calendar
4
5       switch (m) {
6         case 2: if (leapYear(y))
7                     return 29;
8                 else
9                     return 28;
10        case 4:
11        case 6:
12        case 9:
13        case 11: return 30;
14        default: return 31;
15      }
16     }
```

Finally, we can write leapYear, which we also make public:

```
1    public static boolean leapYear (int y) {
2    // Returns true if y is a leap year
3    // according to the Gregorian calendar
4
5       // y must be a multiple of 4 and NOT a century
6       // year or must be a century year divisible by 400
7
8       return (((y % 4) == 0) && ((y % 100) != 0))
9              || ((y % 400) == 0);
10     }
```

We'd like to start debugging the three methods we've just written before we start writing something new. The ability to debug sections of code separately is an advantage of modular programming. So far we have the class Date with three class methods; we now build a main static method in an application class that does nothing but read a date and echo it back.

```
1    import CSLib.*;
2
3    public class TestDate {
4
5      public void test () {
6        int month, day, year;
7        InputBox in = new InputBox();
8        in.setPrompt("Enter month: ");
9        month = in.readInt();
10       in.setPrompt("Enter day: ");
11       day = in.readInt();
12       in.setPrompt("Enter year: ");
13       year = in.readInt();
14
15       OutputBox out = new OutputBox();
16       out.print("The date "
17             + month + "/" + day + "/" + year);
18       if (!Date.dateIsLegal(month, day, year))
19         out.println(" is not legal.");
20       else
21         out.println("is legal");
22     }
23   }
```

Here is the client:

```
1    public class TestDateClient {
2      public static void main (String[] args) {
3        TestDate td = new TestDate();
4        td.test();
5      }
6    }
```

This debugging technique may seem like a waste of time—why not just continue to develop the program? Experienced programmers realize that the few minutes used for such a test can save hours of trouble later. It is far easier to pin down a problem when you have only a handful of methods than after you've developed a great many methods.

After testing a number of dates, both legal and illegal, we convince ourselves that our work is okay up to this point.

Once we are satisfied that all the foregoing methods are correct, we are ready to continue developing our class. Let's consider what instance variables might be contained in objects of the Date class and then determine what the constructors will be. Clearly a Date object must contain instance variables to keep the month, day, and year:

```
1    // Instance variables
2
3    private int
4       m, // the month of this instance of Date
5       d, // the day of this instance of Date
6       y; // the year of this instance of Date
```

This leads to the definition of two constructors: One will allow the client to create an "empty" Date (and we have to supply a way to fill in the instance variables later), and the other will allow the client to create a specific Date.

```
1    // Constructors
2
3    public Date () {}
4
5    public Date (int month, int day, int year) {
6       m=month; d=day; y=year;
7    }
```

A client who has created an instance of a Date may wish to have *instance methods* for leapYear, lastDayOfMonth, and dateIsLegal. Rather than duplicate the logic we used when writing those class methods, we can simply have the instance methods call the class methods.

```
1    public boolean dateIsLegal () {
2    // Determine whether this instance's month, day, year
3    // is a legal date on the Gregorian calendar;
4    // date must be on or after Jan 1, 1 AD.
5       return dateIsLegal(m, d, y);
6    }
7
8    public int lastDayOfMonth () {
9    // Returns the number of days in this instance's
10   // month and year on the Gregorian calendar
11      return lastDayOfMonth(m, y);
12   }
13
14   public boolean leapYear () {
15   // Returns true if this instance's year is a leap year
16   // according to the Gregorian calendar
17      return leapYear(y);
18   }
```

Notice that the instance methods access the instance variables, passing them as explicit arguments to the class methods. Notice also the interplay between an *instance method* such as leapYear and the corresponding *class method*. The method name is overloaded, but the argument lists are different, so Java can tell which method a client means to use. The instance method is allowed to use the class method by calling it directly. However, the class method is not able to do the same thing—call the instance method directly. Often you'll want to make your classes general in this way, including both class methods and instance methods that do the same thing. That way, you offer clients some choice in how they wish to do things.

For the client to be able to fill in an empty `Date`, let's provide an *instance* method, `void readDate ()`. This method will use an `InputBox` to read the month, day, and year into a `Date` instance. To make it robust, we'll refuse to accept an illegal date from the user. If the user enters an illegal date, we'll issue a complaint and ask again for the date components.

```
1    public void readDate () {
2       InputBox in = new InputBox();
3       while (true) {
4          in.setPrompt("Enter month: ");
5          m = in.readInt();
6          in.setPrompt("Enter day: ");
7          d = in.readInt();
8          in.setPrompt("Enter year: ");
9          y = in.readInt();
10         if (dateIsLegal(m, d, y)) return;
11         ErrorBox e = new ErrorBox("Not a valid date, try again.");
12      }
13   }
```

In line 11, we see another `CSLib` class that we can use—`ErrorBox`. This class presents an error message; it halts the program until the user closes the box. The constructor takes the error message as an argument, and there are no public methods that the user can call.

Continuing with our philosophy of offering clients some generality, we also provide a class method `getDate`.

```
1    public static Date getDate () {
2       Date d = new Date();
3       d.readDate();
4       return d;
5    }
```

This class method may seem rather strange to you. It is contained in the class `Date`; it *creates* an object of type `Date`; it invokes the *instance method* `readDate` *on that newly created object*; and then it returns that filled-in `Date` object as its return value. So here we have a *class method* invoking an *instance method!* There is no contradiction with what we said earlier—a class method cannot *directly* invoke an instance method. However, a class method can first *create* an instance and *then* send messages to that instance! Thus, the client can read a `Date` in two different ways: using the instance method `getDate`

```
Date d;            // Declare a Date.
d = new Date();   // Now create it.
d.readDate();     // Now read it.
```

or using the class method `getDate`

```
Date d;                    // Declare a Date.
d = Date.getDate();        // Now create it and read it.
```

Now let's return to the original problem. To compute the number of days between two dates, it is convenient to convert a Gregorian date to an *absolute date*, which we define as the number of days elapsed from some arbitrary starting point, absolute date 0. In this way, every day after that starting point is represented by a unique positive integer, and computing the number of days between two given dates will require only subtracting one absolute date from the other.

A natural choice for absolute date 0 is the day before January 1, 1 AD This date is a Sunday; therefore day-of-the-week calculations are easily made by computing *absolute date* %7. So, it's settled: The absolute date associated with any given day is the number of days since the day before January 1, 1 AD.

How can we convert from Gregorian dates to absolute dates? For a given date, say, George Washington's birthday—February 22, 1732—we would calculate as follows. The years $1, 2, 3, \ldots, 1731$ contain $1731 \times 365 = 631,815$ days, ignoring leap years. Since every fourth year (ignoring century nonleap years) is a leap year, the years $1, 2, 3, \ldots, 1731$ contain $1731/4 = 432$ leap days. Thus the years $1, 2, 3, \ldots, 1731$ contain $631,815 + 432 = 632,247$ days. But we must subtract the century leap days wrongly included; for year n, we must subtract $n/100$, since $n/100$ is the number of century years that have passed. However, we've just subtracted *all* the century years, including those that are multiples of 400; these *are* leap years, so we add them back. Thus we have found that there are

```
1731*365 + 1731/4 - 1731/100 + 1731/400
```

or $632,234$ days from January 1, 1 AD (which is absolute date 1) through December 31, 1731 AD. Since February 22 is the 53d day of 1732, the absolute date is $632,234 + 53 = 632,287$.

We write an instance method, `absolute`, to compute the absolute date of a given `Date` instance. To write the `absolute` method, we need a method for the day number calculation; for a day d in year y, the day number of d is the number of days from the first day of year y up to and including d; see page 115. Let's make this an instance method.

```
1    public int dayNumber () {
2    // Calculate the day number in the year of this instance
3    // on the Gregorian calendar
4
5        // Calculate day number assuming all months have 31 days
6        int number = (m - 1) * 31 + d;
7
8        // Correct for months beyond February
9        if (m > 2) {
10         number = number - ((4 * m + 23) / 10);
11         if (leapYear())
12            number = number + 1;
13       };
14
```

```
15        return number;
16     }
```

The calculation of the absolute date from the Gregorian date is a matter of adding together the number of days in that year prior to that date and the number of days in years prior to that year:

```
1      public int absolute () {
2      // Calculate the absolute date of this instance's date
3      // according to the Gregorian calendar.
4
5        return
6          dayNumber()            // days this year
7            + 365*(y-1)          // days in prior years
8            + (y-1)/4            // \
9            - (y-1)/100          // leap years
10           + (y-1)/400;         // /
11     }
```

Finally, we'll need a way to stringify a Date (so we can print it). We casually type the following:

```
public static String toString () {
// Stringify the present date                Wrong
   return (m + "/" + d + "/" + y);
}
```

But, when we try to compile it, we get the error message

```
Date.java:Can't make a static reference to nonstatic
         variable m in class Date.
return (m + "/" + d + "/" + y);
        ^

1 error
```

Of course, our mistake was in using the static modifier with toString, thereby making it a class method. Class methods cannot access instance variables. We meant for toString to be an instance method, which is allowed to access the instance variables. The correct version of toString is

```
1      public String toString () {
2      // Stringify the present date
3        return (m + "/" + d + "/" + y);
4      }
```

Our Date class now looks like this:

```
1    import CSLib.*;
2
3    public class Date {
4
5    // Class variables (all symbolic constants)
```

```
 6
 7    public final static String[]
 8      DAY_NAME = {"Sun", "Mon", "Tue", "Wed",
 9                   "Thu", "Fri", "Sat"},
10      MONTH_NAME = {"",
11       "January",   "February", "March",     "April",
12       "May",       "June",     "July",      "August",
13       "September", "October",  "November", "December"};
14
15    public final static int
16      SUNDAY=0,   MONDAY=1, TUESDAY=2, WEDNESDAY=3,
17      THURSDAY=4, FRIDAY=5, SATURDAY=6;
18
19    public final static int
20      JANUARY=1,    FEBRUARY=2, MARCH=3,      APRIL=4,
21      MAY=5,        JUNE=6,     JULY=7,       AUGUST=8,
22      SEPTEMBER=9, OCTOBER=10, NOVEMBER=11, DECEMBER=12;
23
24  // Class methods
25
26    public static boolean dateIsLegal (int m, int d, int y) {
27    // Determine whether month m, day d, year y
28    // is a legal date on the Gregorian calendar;
29    // date must be on or after Jan 1, 1 AD.
30
31      return
32        (1 <= y) &&                 // year is okay
33        (1 <= m) && (m <= 12) &&    // month is okay
34        (1 <= d) &&                 // day is...
35        (d <= lastDayOfMonth(m, y));   //       ...okay
36    }
37
38    public static int lastDayOfMonth (int m, int y) {
39    // Returns the number of days in month m of
40    // year y on the Gregorian calendar
41
42      switch (m) {
43        case 2: if (leapYear(y))
44                  return 29;
45                else
46                  return 28;
47        case 4:
48        case 6:
49        case 9:
50        case 11: return 30;
51        default: return 31;
52      }
53    }
54
55    public static boolean leapYear (int y) {
56    // Returns true if y is a leap year
57    // according to the Gregorian calendar
58
59      // y must be a multiple of 4 and NOT a century
```

```
60        // year or must be a century year divisible by 400
61
62        return (((y % 4) == 0) && ((y % 100) != 0))
63             || ((y % 400) == 0);
64     }
65
66   public static int dayOfWeek (int m, int d, int y) {
67   // Tell which day of the week is m/d/y
68      return new Date(m,d,y).absolute()%7;
69   }
70
71   public static Date getDate () {
72      Date d = new Date();
73      d.readDate();
74      return d;
75   }
76
77 // Instance variables
78
79   private int
80      m, // the month of this instance of Date
81      d, // the day of this instance of Date
82      y; // the year of this instance of Date
83
84 // Constructors
85
86   public Date () {}
87
88   public Date (int month, int day, int year) {
89      m=month; d=day; y=year;
90   }
91
92 // Instance methods
93
94   public boolean dateIsLegal () {
95   // Determine whether this instance's month, day, year
96   // is a legal date on the Gregorian calendar;
97   // date must be on or after Jan 1, 1 AD.
98      return dateIsLegal(m, d, y);
99   }
100
101   public int lastDayOfMonth () {
102   // Returns the number of days in this instance's
103   // month and year on the Gregorian calendar
104      return lastDayOfMonth(m, y);
105   }
106
107   public boolean leapYear () {
108   // Returns true if this instance's year is a leap year
109   // according to the Gregorian calendar
110      return leapYear(y);
111   }
112
113   public void readDate () {
```

```
114        InputBox in = new InputBox();
115        while (true) {
116          in.setPrompt("Enter month: ");
117          m = in.readInt();
118          in.setPrompt("Enter day: ");
119          d = in.readInt();
120          in.setPrompt("Enter year: ");
121          y = in.readInt();
122          if (dateIsLegal(m, d, y)) return;
123          ErrorBox e = new ErrorBox("Not a valid date, try again.");
124        }
125      }
126
127      public int absolute () {
128      // Calculate the absolute date of this instance's date
129      // according to the Gregorian calendar.
130
131        return
132          dayNumber()                  // days this year
133            + 365*(y-1)                // days in prior years
134            + (y-1)/4                  // \
135            - (y-1)/100                // leap years
136            + (y-1)/400;               // /
137      }
138
139      public int dayNumber () {
140      // Calculate the day number in the year of this instance
141      // on the Gregorian calendar
142
143        // Calculate day number assuming all months have 31 days
144        int number = (m - 1) * 31 + d;
145
146        // Correct for months beyond February
147        if (m > 2) {
148          number = number - ((4 * m + 23) / 10);
149          if (leapYear())
150            number = number + 1;
151        };
152
153        return number;
154      }
155
156      public String toString () {
157      // Stringify the present date
158        return (m + "/" + d + "/" + y);
159      }
160
161      public int dayOfWeek () {
162      // Tell which day of the week this Date is.
163        return absolute()%7;
164      }
165    }
```

We can test the new instance method `absolute` with the following test and client:

```
1   import CSLib.*;
2
3   public class TestDate {
4     public void test () {
5       Date d = Date.getDate();
6       OutputBox out = new OutputBox();
7       out.print("The date entered was " +
8                 d.toString() +
9                 " = absolute date " + d.absolute());
10    }
11  }
```

```
1   public class TestDateClient {
2     public static void main (String[] args) {
3       TestDate td = new TestDate();
4       td.test();
5     }
6   }
```

Satisfied that all this machinery works, we finally can write the main application we wanted all along—one that reads in two Gregorian dates and computes the number of days elapsed between them:

```
1   import CSLib.*;
2
3   public class SpanDates {
4     public void span () {
5       Date d1, d2;
6       int a1, a2;
7
8       d1 = Date.getDate();
9       a1 = d1.absolute();
10
11      d2 = Date.getDate();
12      a2 = d2.absolute();
13
14      OutputBox out = new OutputBox();
15      out.println("There are " + (a2-a1) + " days from " +
16                  d1.toString() + " to " + d2.toString());
17    }
18  }
```

```
1   public class SpanDatesClient {
2     public static void main (String args[]) {
3       SpanDates sd = new SpanDates();
4       sd.span();
5     }
6   }
```

Run the SpanDates program and answer the following questions:

1. How many days old are you?
2. How many days until you graduate?
3. How many days until you retire (on your 65th birthday)?
4. How many days did George Washington live?

10.4

Interfaces

Let's consider again the mouse-in-a-maze program from Section 6.12. Our Mouse class was hard-coded so that makeMove used a right-hand-on-the-wall algorithm. There are many other algorithms that might have been used, including left-hand-on-the-wall. We could have programmed our Mouse so that its constructor received as an argument an object that encapsulated the move algorithm, call this an object of type MouseAlgorithm. The only requirement for the MouseAlgorithm object is that it have a method, call it makeAlgorithmicMove. Then the makeMove method in the Mouse could simply invoke the makeAlgorithmicMove method of the MouseAlgorithm. The trick is that our MouseMazeClient could provide any number of different implementation of the MouseAlgorithm class to cause our Mouse to behave in different ways. The classes Maze, MazeDrawer, and MouseDrawer are exactly as before. The UML diagram for these classes is shown in Figure 10.2. The UML equivalent of a Java interface is indicated by italicizing the class name; the *implements association* is indicated by a dashed line with a closed, unfilled arrowhead at the abstract class end.

*UML implements
association*

Here's the modified code for Mouse:

```
1    import java.awt.*;
2
3    class Mouse {
4      // A mouse that can navigate a maze
5      // Author: Allan M. Mickunas, September 22, 1996
6
7      final int NORTH=0, EAST=1, SOUTH=2, WEST=3;
8
9      private Maze theMaze;
10     private Point location; // The location of this Mouse
11     private int direction;  // The direction this Mouse is facing
12     private MouseAlgorithm ma;
13
14     public Point tellLocation () {return location;}
15
16     public int tellDirection () {return direction;}
17
18     public Mouse (Maze m, MouseAlgorithm ma) {
19       this.ma = ma;
```

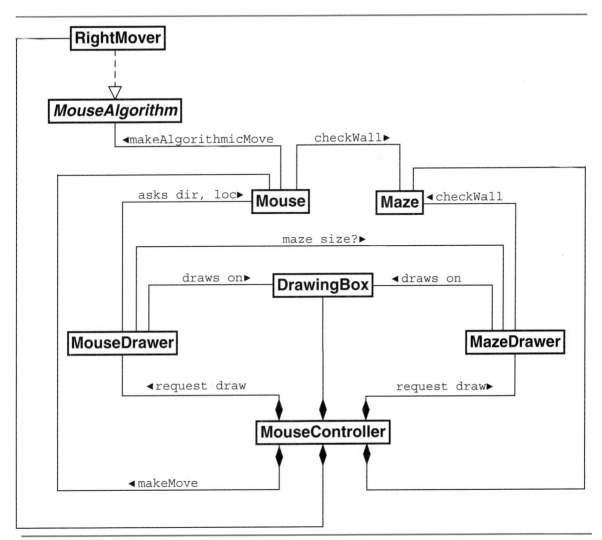

FIGURE 10.2 A UML class diagram for the `MouseMazeGUI` **program.**

```
20      // Where do I start?
21      location = m.getStartLocation();
22      // In what direction do I face initially?
23      direction = m.getStartDirection();
24      theMaze = m;
25    }
26
```

```
27        public void makeMove () {
28           ma.makeAlgorithmicMove(this);
29        }
30
31        public boolean outside () {
32        // Am I outside the maze?
33           return theMaze.outside(location);
34        }
35
36        public boolean facingWall () {
37           return theMaze.checkWall(direction, location);
38        }
39
40        public void stepForward () {
41           switch (direction) {
42             case NORTH: location.y--; break;
43             case EAST:  location.x++; break;
44             case SOUTH: location.y++; break;
45             case WEST:  location.x--; break;
46           }
47        }
48
49        public void turnLeft () {
50           direction = (direction+3) % 4;
51        }
52
53        public void turnRight () {
54           direction = (direction+1) % 4;
55        }
56     }
```

Notice how a `MouseAlgorithm` is passed into the constructor and saved in a private instance variable. Then within the `makeMove` method, we invoke `makeAlgorithmicMove` on that instance variable. We must pass `this` to `makeAlgorithmicMove` so that it can call back to methods `outside`, `facingWall`, `stepForward`, `turnLeft`, and `turnRight`; in addition, we need to make those methods `public` so that the `MouseAlgorithm` object can call them.

The only requirement imposed by `MouseAlgorithm` is that it have a method with the header

```
public void makeAlgorithmicMove (Mouse aMouse)
```

Yet, we'd like to provide a number of different implementations that have this interface.

interface declaration   It turns out that this is so common and so useful that Java has a more convenient way of specifying it, using an interface declaration. *Interface declarations* are just like classes except that they use the word `interface` instead of `class` and are restricted to containing method declarations without bodies, and symbolic constant definitions:

```
interface interface_name {
 definitions of symbolic constants, and declarations of
 abstract methods
 }
```

Furthermore, classes that contain concrete definitions of these methods indicate this by writing `implements` *interface_name* in their headers:

```
public class classname implements interface_name {
...
}
```

This serves as a contract whereby the class declares that it intends to implement every method in the interface.

So we can write `MouseAlgorithm` as an interface:

```
1  public interface MouseAlgorithm {
2    public void makeAlgorithmicMove (Mouse m);
3  }
```

We can implement this interface with a class, say `RightMover`, as follows:

```
1  public class RightMover implements MouseAlgorithm {
2    private boolean started = false;
3
4    public void makeAlgorithmicMove (Mouse iAm) {
5      if (started) {
6        if (!iAm.outside()) {
7          iAm.turnRight();
8          while (iAm.facingWall()) {
9            iAm.turnLeft();
10         }
11         iAm.stepForward();
12       }
13     } else {
14       iAm.stepForward();
15       started=true;
16     }
17   }
18 }
```

Notice that the `makeAlgorithmicMove` method uses the various (now public) methods of the `Mouse` instance that it passed as an argument, and implements the right-hand-on-the-wall algorithm. If our client creates a `Mouse` via `new Mouse(aMaze, new RightMover())`, then that `Mouse` will use the right-hand-on-the-wall algorithm. On the other hand, we might define:

```
1  public class LeftMover implements MouseAlgorithm {
2    private boolean started = false;
3
4    public void makeAlgorithmicMove (Mouse iAm) {
5      if (started) {
6        if (!iAm.outside()) {
7          iAm.turnLeft();
8          while (iAm.facingWall()) {
9            iAm.turnRight();
10         }
11         iAm.stepForward();
12       }
13     } else {
14       iAm.stepForward();
15       started=true;
```

```
16          }
17        }
18      }
```

A client that creates a Mouse via new Mouse(aMaze, new LeftMover()) will have a Mouse that uses the left-hand-on-the-wall algorithm!

A key point is that in each case, the client would be passing as an argument to the Mouse constructor *an instance of a MouseAlgorithm*, which is exactly what is expected by the Mouse constructor. However, the methods in the two classes, RightMover and LeftMover, could implement radically different ways of traversing a maze!

Here's the MouseMazeController that ties everything together, and asks the user to indicate what kind of mouse is desired.

```
1   import CSLib.*;
2
3   public class MouseMazeController {
4     // Draw a mouse navigating a maze, using a choice of algorithms
5     // Rebecca Kamin, Sept 12, 2000
6
7     public void runMouse () {
8       DrawingBox d = new DrawingBox("Mouse in maze");
9       Maze theMaze = new Maze();
10      MazeDrawer theMazeDrawer = new MazeDrawer(theMaze, d);
11      Mouse speedy;
12
13      InputBox in = new InputBox();
14      in.setPrompt(
15        "Type 1 for a left-mover, otherwise you get a right-mover");
16      if (in.readInt() == 1)
17        speedy = new Mouse(theMaze, new LeftMover());
18      else
19        speedy = new Mouse(theMaze, new RightMover());
20
21      MouseDrawer speedyDrawer =
22                    new MouseDrawer(speedy, theMazeDrawer, d);
23
24      while (true) {
25        theMazeDrawer.draw();
26        speedyDrawer.draw();
27        Timer.pause(1000);
28        speedy.makeMove();
29      }
30    }
31  }
```

Finally, here's the trivial client that creates the MouseMazeController:

```
1   public class MouseMazeClient {
2
3     public static void main (String[] args) {
4       MouseMazeController mmc = new MouseMazeController();
5       mmc.runMouse();
6     }
7   }
```

Why bother to distinguish interfaces in this way? One reason, as we have seen, is that an interface can be implemented by many different classes. Another is that *a class can implement more than one interface.* Therefore, if interface I1 requires function f1, interface I2 requires function f2, and class C defines both f1 and f2 (with the required types, of course), then C can be declared to implement both interfaces.

```
class C implements I1, I2 {
...
}
```

Like class definitions, interfaces are placed in separate files, with the .java extension. Packages contain interfaces as well as classes, and the naming conventions described previously for classes in packages also apply to interfaces.

We should emphasize that an interface might require that its implementer(s) provide more than one method. For example, we can imagine extending our maze program so that it begins to look like an adventure game—if the mouse enters a room with a cat, then a fight will ensue! So we might postulate a method in the MouseAlgorithm class, say void fight (Mouse aMouse), that would perform some fighting algorithm. Or if the mouse enters a room with a treasure, we might require a method boolean hasKey () to tell if the mouse has a key to open the treasure. Such an interface would then be

```
public interface MouseAlgorithm {

    public void makeAlgorithmicMove (Mouse aMouse);
    public void fight (Mouse aMouse);
    public boolean hasKey ();
}
```

10.4.1 Defining Uniform Constants

Another use for interfaces is to give definitions of symbolic constants used in several classes. In the mouse-in-a-maze program, we had three different classes that used symbolic constants NORTH, EAST, SOUTH, and WEST, assigning them values 0, 1, 2, and 3, respectively. Keeping such symbolic constants in sync between two or more classes may sound easy, but it can be difficult when there are many constants and many classes. The problem can be alleviated by placing all the constant definitions in one interface and including that interface in every class that needs to use those constants. Thus, we could have an interface

```
public interface Direction {
    int NORTH=0, EAST=1, SOUTH=2, WEST=3;
}
```

and then modify the headers of the classes that need to use those constants:

```
public class Mouse implements Direction {
    ...
}

public class Maze implements Direction {
    ...
}

public class MazeDrawer implements Direction {
    ...
}
```

When defined in an interface, all symbolic constants are assumed to be public, static, and final, so the corresponding keywords can and should be omitted.

The key point to remember is that if a class implements an interface, then it is obliged to provide definitions for each method mentioned in the interface.

Summary

Either a variable or a method of a class can be declared `static`, which makes it a *class variable* or *class method*. The class attribute means that the variable or method exists for the benefit of the class itself, even if no objects of the class have been declared or allocated. Class variables are referenced using the class name and dot notation; likewise, class methods are invoked using the class name and dot notation.

An interface is a class that includes only declarations of methods and definitions of symbolic constants. Its syntax is

```
public interface interface_name {
    definitions of symbolic constants
    declarations of headers for required methods
}
```

An interface can be implemented by any number of classes, and a class can implement more than one interface. A class states that it implements interfaces $I_1, I_2, \ldots, I_n$—that is, defines the methods declared in all those interfaces—by placing the clause `implements   $I_1, I_2, \ldots, I_n$` in its header.

Exercises

1. Encapsulate the central calculation of the Social Security tax program (on page 99) with a class method that returns a value of type `double`; and modify the program to use this class method.

2. Write a class method that computes the exclusive or (see Table 4.6 on page 138).

3. Given the time of day in terms of the variables `hour`, `minute`, `second`, and `dayHalf` (that is, AM or PM), write a class method called `fractionOfDay` to calculate and return the fraction of the day (type `double`) that has elapsed. For example,

```
fractionOfDay(12, 0, 0, AM)
```

would return 0.0,

```
fractionOfDay(12, 0, 0, PM)
```

would return 0.5, and

```
fractionOfDay(11, 59, 59, PM)
```

would return 0.999988426.

4. Write a static method `triangle` that takes three `double` values and returns true if the three values are the sides of a triangle and false if not. For three lengths to form a triangle, the sum of any two lengths must exceed the third length.

5. Write a static method called `majority` having three Boolean parameters. The value returned should be true if any two of the arguments are true and should be false otherwise.

6. Extend the class `SFormat` to include overloaded methods to stringify values *centered* in a field of width w:

```
private static String sprintc (int w, String s) {...}
private static String sprintc (int w, int i) {...}
private static String sprintc (int w, double d) {...}
```

7. Extend the class `SFormat` to include overloaded methods to stringify `int` and `double` values right-justified (like `sprintr`), but with leading zeros.

8. (a) Write a class method to compute the day of the week:

```
public static int dayOfWeek (int m, int d, int y)
```

   Remember that Sunday is day 0.

   (b) Write `dayOfWeek` again, this time as an instance method. Use the class method to assist you.

9. (a) Fourteen different year calendars are possible—seven for January 1 falling on each day of the week in a nonleap year and seven more for a leap year. Print the 14 different calendars. (*Hint*: Use a triple-nested loop.)

   (b) Write an application to print a table indicating which of the 14 different calendars to use for each year from 1900 to 1999.

10. Write a method to return the number of days left in a year. The arguments to the method should be the month, day, and year.

11. Modify the method `toString` so that it produces a string like

```
Sunday, August 31, 1986
```

(Note the inclusion of the day of the week.)

12. The seasons of the year are defined as

   Fall: September 21–December 20
   Winter: December 21–March 20
   Spring: March 21–June 20
   Summer: June 21–September 20

Write a method that returns the season, given the month and day. Use the symbolic constants

```
public final static int FALL=0, WINTER=1, SPRING=2, SUMMER=3;
```

13. Daylight savings time moves the clock ahead one hour in the spring and back one hour in the fall. As of 1987, daylight savings time begins on the first Sunday in April and ends on the last Sunday in October. Write a method `daysOfDaylightSavings` that computes the number of days of daylight savings time in a given year, which is a parameter of the method.

14. Modify the `Date` class as follows.
    (a) Write a method

    ```
    public int xdayOnOrBefore (int absoluteDate, int x)
    ```

    to return the absolute date of the x day of the week (Sunday and so on) that falls in the seven-day period ending on absolute date `absoluteDate`.
    (b) Explain how to use your method in part (a) to compute the absolute date of the x day prior to a given absolute date, following a given absolute date, nearest to a given absolute date, and on or after a given absolute date.
    (c) Use your method in part (a) to write a method

    ```
    public int nthXday (int n, int x, int month, int year)
    ```

    that determines the absolute date of the nth x day in a given month in a given year. Your method should count backward from the end of the month when n < 0.

15. Write a class `JulianDate` that implements everything the `Date` class does, except that it uses the Julian calendar. Include in the `JulianDate` class constructor `JulianDate (Date gd)` that takes a Gregorian date as an argument and constructs its Julian equivalent.

16. The signs of the zodiac are the 12 equal parts of the celestial sphere, each 30° wide, bearing the name of a constellation for which they were originally named:

    Aries: March 21–April 19
    Taurus: April 20–May 20
    Gemini: May 21–June 21
    Cancer: June 22–July 22
    Leo: July 23–August 22
    Virgo: August 23–September 22
    Libra: September 23–October 23
    Scorpio: October 24–November 21
    Sagittarius: November 22–December 21
    Capricorn: December 22–January 19
    Aquarius: January 20–February 18
    Pisces: February 19–March 20

    (a) Write a program to determine a zodiac sign, given the month and the day. Use the symbolic constants

    ```
    public static final int
        ARIES=0, TAURUS=1, GEMINI=2, CANCER=3,
        LEO=4, VIRGO=5, LIBRA=6, SCORPIO=7,
        SAGITTARIUS=8, CAPRICORN=9, AQUARIUS=10, PISCES=11;
    ```

    (b) Try to find GIF or JPEG images representing the signs of the zodiac. Extend your answer to part (a) and write a program that displays the correct image alongside the name of the sign in a `DrawingBox`.

The Java AWT Part I: Mouse Events (Optional)

In this chapter we introduce *event-driven programming*. We show how a Java program can respond to *mouse events*, including mouse clicks and mouse movements, by implementing a particular *listener interface*. We further show how mouse events can be used to build highly interactive programs.

Good things come in small packages.

—Folk saying

This chapter describes some parts of the Java distribution that are not part of the Java language itself. These classes and mechanisms, called the Java *Abstract Windowing Toolkit*, or *AWT*, are simply conventions used by Java programmers and supported by the basic Java run-time libraries. In principle, you could rewrite these libraries using an entirely different approach to handling events. In fact, the approach incorporated in earlier versions of Java's basic libraries, and still described in some books, is quite different.

Abstract Windowing Toolkit

Consequently, this chapter (and subsequently Chapter 13) is labeled *optional*. Very little in these optional chapters has to do with fundamental *computer science*. It does not even have to do with Java per se. Nonetheless, you cannot be a *complete* Java programmer without understanding the AWT. So even if you skip these chapters for now, you'll certainly want to come back to them later. We will go into much greater detail on the AWT in Chapter 13. Here, our purpose is to introduce one feature of the AWT: responding to mouse clicks.

11.1

Mouse Events

One very important use of interfaces in Java occurs in the Java *Abstract Windowing Toolkit* or *AWT*, and it involves defining methods that respond to various *events*. An event is some occurrence outside the program to which the program must respond, such as a user pressing a key on the keyboard. There is some method that first detects the event; we call that method the *event manager*. Suppose we are writing a new class that wants to know when an event occurs. It sends a message to the manager saying, "Please inform me when an event occurs." But *how* does the manager "inform" the object? All it can do is to send the object a message, and it can only do that if it knows what object is making the request. So the object really has to say, "Please inform me when an event occurs, and here is a reference to me." The "reference to me" is, of course, `this` (see Section 7.6 on page 230).

events

event manager

In the case of mouse events, the "manager" is some window object, such as a `DrawingBox`; call it w. Our object wants to know when a user clicks

Name	Description
void mouseClicked (MouseEvent e)	Called when a mouse button is clicked.
void mousePressed (MouseEvent e)	Called when a mouse button is pressed.
void mouseReleased (MouseEvent e)	Called when a mouse button is released.
void mouseEntered (MouseEvent e)	Called when the mouse enters a component area.
void mouseExited (MouseEvent e)	Called when the mouse leaves a component area.

TABLE 11.1   Methods defined in the `MouseListener` interface.

in the window, so that it can take an appropriate action, such as sending some drawing messages to the window. It registers its interest in knowing about mouse clicks by sending the message w.addMouseListener(this). After that, w will remember the object, and whenever the mouse is clicked, it will send the mouseClicked message to the object.

Given that the object has declared itself to be a "mouse listener," there are other messages that the manager might send to the object: mousePressed, mouseReleased, mouseEntered, and mouseExited. In all, these are precisely the methods that are defined in Java's MouseListener interface. In other words, the object must implement the MouseListener interface. The methods specified by the MouseListener interface are summarized in Table 11.1.

So to create an object that can respond to mouse clicks, you write a class of the form

```
import java.awt.event.*;
...

public class classname implements MouseListener {
    ...
        // in an initialization method, such as a constructor
        manager.addMouseListener(this);
    ...
    public void mouseClicked (MouseEvent e) {
        // Take appropriate action for mouse click event
        // (x,y) location of mouse given by e.getX() and e.getY()
        ...
    }

    public void mousePressed (MouseEvent e) { ... }
    public void mouseReleased (MouseEvent e) { ... }
    public void mouseEntered (MouseEvent e) { ... }
    public void mouseExited (MouseEvent e) { ... }
}
```

To summarize, you must do the following:

1. Import the java.awt.event package (along with any other packages you may need, such as CSLib). The MouseListener interface is part of the java.awt.event package.
2. In the class header, add the words implements MouseListener.

3. Send the addMouseListener message to the mouse event manager. No mouse clicks will be intercepted until this call is made, so it should be done in some method that is called early, such as the constructor.

4. Define the methods mouseClicked, mousePressed, mouseReleased, mouseEntered, and mouseExited, as shown above. All five methods must be defined, with their headers exactly as shown. If you are interested only in mouse clicks, you can define the other methods trivially:

```
public void mousePressed (MouseEvent e) { }
```

The empty body means that the method won't do anything, but it still must be defined. Within mouseClicked, the argument e, of type MouseEvent, can be used to find the location at which the mouse was clicked by calling e.getX() and e.getY().

As our first example, we'll write a version of the Clock class, called ClickableClock, that responds to mouse clicks by advancing the time by 5 minutes. The UML diagram for this program is seen in Figure 11.1. We could have simply anchored the tail of the "implements" association (the dashed

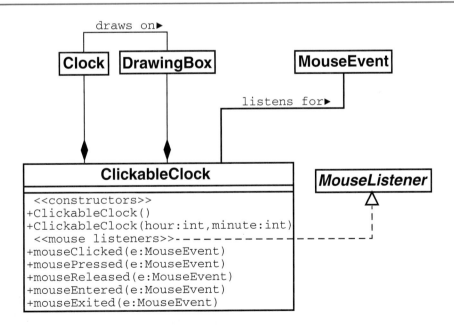

FIGURE 11.1   UML diagram for the ClickableClock **program.**

line) at the edge of `ClickableClock`. But here we can provide just a little more information—we group the methods of `ClickableClock`, and anchor the tail of the "implements" association near the method(s) that actually implement the interface methods. It often makes sense to group the methods of a class—constructors, accessors, etc., including those methods that provide the implementation for an interface. Such groups of methods can be separated by a *UML stereotype*—merely a descriptive word enclosed in guillemets ($\ll \gg$).

UML stereotype

```
1    import CSLib.*;
2    import java.awt.*;
3    import java.awt.event.*;
4
5    public class ClickableClock implements MouseListener {
6       // Maintain a clock.
7       // Author: Courtney Mickunas, November 21, 2000
8
9       private DrawingBox d;
10      private Clock myClock;
11      private final int WIDTH = 300,
12                        HEIGHT = 320,
13                        RADIUS = Math.min(WIDTH, HEIGHT)/2,
14                        INCREMENT = 5;
15
16      public ClickableClock () {
17         this(12, 0);
18      }
19
20      public ClickableClock (int hour, int minute) {
21         d = new DrawingBox("ClickableClock Window");
22         d.setDrawableSize(WIDTH, HEIGHT);
23         myClock = new Clock(d, hour, minute);
24         myClock.display(RADIUS);
25         d.addMouseListener(this);
26      }
27
28      public void mouseClicked (MouseEvent e) {
29         setMinute(getMinute()+INCREMENT);
30         d.clear();
31         myClock.display(RADIUS);
32      }
33
34      public void mousePressed (MouseEvent e) { }
35      public void mouseReleased (MouseEvent e) { }
36      public void mouseEntered (MouseEvent e) { }
37      public void mouseExited (MouseEvent e) { }
38
39      public void getData () { myClock.getData(); }
40      public String toString() { return myClock.toString(); }
41      public void setHour (int h) { myClock.setHour(h); }
42      public void setMinute (int m) { myClock.setMinute(m); }
43      public void set (int h, int m) { myClock.set(h, m); }
44      public int getHour () { return myClock.getHour(); }
45      public int getMinute () { return myClock.getMinute(); }
46      public boolean priorTo (Clock c) { return myClock.priorTo(c); }
```

```
47      public boolean after (Clock c) { return c.priorTo(myClock); }
48    }
```

A DrawingBox is a mouse manager in the sense that it is always informed when the mouse is clicked inside its window, so it can in turn inform other objects. The client simply creates a ClickableClock object:

```
public class ClickableClockClient {
  public static void main (String[] args) {
    ClickableClock c = new ClickableClock();
  }
}
```

Let's look at some of the details of ClickableClock. First, a ClickableClock has private objects Clock and DrawingBox that are created by its constructor. Recall that a Clock (on page 248) has a lot of versatility; however, we'll use it in a restricted way, supplying the DrawingBox to its constructor (in line 23). We want a ClickableClock to have almost all the functionality of a regular Clock, so we must define methods such as setHour and getHour. When a client calls one of these methods, we should simply call the corresponding method in our private Clock. So we define all these methods as *conduit methods* in lines 39 through 47. There are some methods that we do not want a client to have available, such as the various display methods—we will always display our private Clock in our private DrawingBox, and we will update that display every time a mouse click occurs. In addition, we want a client to be able to compare the time in our ClickableClock with that of any other Clock, so the priorTo and after methods are somewhat specialized. (We'll see in Chapter 12 how to make these methods much more generalized, allowing comparisons between two ClickableClocks as well.)

conduit methods

The part that responds to mouse clicks is mouseClicked, in lines 28 through 32. This method increments the clock and redisplays it (after first clearing the DrawingBox area). Notice that we use our private Clock's display method; we have no display methods for ClickableClock.

| **QUICK EXERCISE 11.1** |
| Modify the ClickableClock so that it advances by 5 minutes whenever the cursor enters or leaves the window. |

To take this just a little further, we can use the location of the mouse to control how much to advance the time. This version advances the time by 5 minutes if the mouse is clicked in the upper half of the window, and by 10 minutes if the mouse is clicked in the lower half. The only change is in the mouseClicked method:

```
28      public void mouseClicked (MouseEvent e) {
29        if (e.getY() < HEIGHT/2)
```

```
30              setMinute(getMinute()+INCREMENT);
31          else
32              setMinute(getMinute()+2*INCREMENT);
33          d.clear();
34          myClock.display(RADIUS);
35          }
```

The method `int getY()` is one of the methods of the `MouseEvent` class, and it tells us the *y* coordinate at which the mouse event occurred. There is similarly a `getX()` method in `MouseEvent`.

QUICK EXERCISE **11.2**	Modify the last version of `ClickableClock` so that it divides the window into quadrants and increments the clock by 1, 5, 10, or 60 minutes depending upon whether the mouse was clicked in the northwest, northeast, southwest, or southeast quadrant, respectively.

The idea of "events" covers many other types of occurrences, such as keyboard clicks and actions on widgets such as buttons and menus. The details vary in each case, and we leave them for Chapter 12. However, to finish the story about mouse events, we should say how to catch two other events not covered above: mouse moving and mouse dragging (moving with a button depressed).

The Java event model divides mouse events into two groups: the *mouse* events such as mouse clicking, which were covered above, and the *mouse motion* events, such as moving and dragging. The latter class of events is handled similarly to what we have seen, but the details differ. What is required for mouse motion events is that the object register its interest with a manager by calling the method `addMouseMotionListener`, and the object must be prepared to receive messages defined in the `MouseMotionListener` interface; that is, the object must implement the `MouseMotionListener` interface, which involves defining *two* methods.

```
import java.awt.event.*;
...

public class classname implements MouseMotionListener {
    ...
        // in an initialization method, such as a constructor
        manager.addMouseMotionListener(this);
    ...
    public void mouseMoved (MouseEvent e) {
        // Take appropriate action for mouse motion event
        // (x,y) location of mouse given by e.getX() and e.getY()
        ...
    }

    public void mouseDragged (MouseEvent e) { ... }
}
```

The method mouseMoved will be called each time the mouse makes any sufficiently large movement. (And mouseDragged will be called instead of mouseMoved if a button is depressed.) The meaning of *sufficiently large* depends upon the system you are using, but it is certainly quite small — a millimeter of movement is more than enough to trigger a mouse motion event. The mouse motion events thus share one feature that distinguishes them from mouse events: Mouse motion events tend to occur much more frequently. You can click a mouse button, causing mouseClicked to be called, perhaps 5 times in 1 second; you can move the mouse fast enough in the same period of time to have mouseMoved be called perhaps 100 times.

Modify the ClickableClock so that it advances by 1 minute whenever the mouse moves.

**QUICK EXERCISE
11.3**

Last, if you want your object to catch all seven mouse events, write

```
import java.awt.event.*;
...

public class classname implements MouseListener,
                                   MouseMotionListener {
    ...
        // in an initialization method, such as a constructor
        manager.addMouseListener(this);
        manager.addMouseMotionListener(this);
    ...
        public void mouseMoved (MouseEvent e) { ... }
        public void mouseDragged (MouseEvent e) { ... }
        public void mouseClicked (MouseEvent e) { ... }
        public void mousePressed (MouseEvent e) { ... }
        public void mouseReleased (MouseEvent e) { ... }
        public void mouseEntered (MouseEvent e) { ... }
        public void mouseExited (MouseEvent e) { ... }
}
```

11.2

Objects in GUI Programs

In this section, we create a graphical program that you should find amusing. We are going to put a pair of animated eyes in the corner of our program, and they will follow the cursor as it moves around the DrawingBox. Each eye will be a black circular pupil that rolls along the inside perimeter of a larger pink circle. Figure 11.2 is a snapshot, but you have to see it in action to appreciate it.

FIGURE 11.2   Snapshot of the TwoEyes **program.**

There are two important aspects to this program. For one thing, it responds to mouse movements, something we have seen how to do using mouse listeners and mouse motion listeners. For another, we will structure the program using three classes: In addition to the usual client class, the Eyes class (see Figure 11.4) will encapsulate the position and drawing of eyes, and the TwoEyes class (see Figure 11.3) will create a DrawingBox object, and create and manipulate the Eyes objects. The two pairs of eyes shown in Figure 11.2 are each objects of this class. This division of labor results in much cleaner code than we would obtain if we had only the TwoEyes class itself; the benefits of this structure are explored further in Exercise 1. A UML diagram for this program is shown in Figure 11.5.

In the TwoEyes client, the separate class Eyes has a method gaze which takes a DrawingBox object as an argument and draws the pair of eyes. In line 10, the program declares an instance variable called cursor which will contain the location of the mouse (more below); the cursor is initialized to appear as if it is initially in the middle of the DrawingBox. Then the program declares two instance variables of type Eyes. In the TwoEyes constructor, it registers itself as a MouseMotionListener, then sets its size (to make sure it looks okay), and then creates two Eyes objects; the arguments tell those objects where they are placed on the screen. The mouseMoved method just sets the cursor to the

```
1    import CSLib.*;
2    import java.awt.*;
3    import java.awt.event.*;
4
5    public class TwoEyes implements MouseMotionListener {
6
7      // Animated eyes that follow the cursor.
8      // Author: Caitlin Little, December 27, 1996
9
10     private final int WIDTH = 700,
11                       HEIGHT = 600;
12     private Point cursor = new Point(WIDTH/2, HEIGHT/2);
13     private Eyes e1, e2;
14     private DrawingBox d;
15
16     public TwoEyes () {
17       d = new DrawingBox();
18       // Register the Listener.
19       d.addMouseMotionListener(this);
20       d.setDrawableSize(WIDTH, HEIGHT);
21       e1 = new Eyes(new Point(Eyes.EYE_RADIUS*2+2,
22                               Eyes.EYE_RADIUS+2));
23       e2 = new Eyes(new Point(WIDTH-Eyes.EYE_RADIUS*2-2,
24                               Eyes.EYE_RADIUS+2));
25       e1.gaze(d, cursor);
26       e2.gaze(d, cursor);
27     }
28
29     public void mouseMoved (MouseEvent e) {
30       cursor = e.getPoint();
31       e1.gaze(d, cursor);
32       e2.gaze(d, cursor);
33     }
34
35     public void mouseDragged (MouseEvent e) {}
36   }
```

FIGURE 11.3 The TwoEyes **class.**

mouse location and calls the gaze method for the two eyes. The mouse location for a particular MouseEvent can be obtained by using the method getPoint as in line 30. All the actual work of drawing the eyes is done in the Eyes class.

We have also included a mouseDragged method, as required by the MouseMotionListener interface; however, it does nothing, since we are not interested in responding to mouse drags.

The cursor is an object of type Point; it is initialized at the time of its declaration, but it has no useful value until the mouse moves into the

```
1    import CSLib.*;
2    import java.awt.*;
3    import java.awt.event.*;
4    import java.applet.*;
5
6    public class Eyes {
7
8      // Animated eyes that follow the cursor.
9      // Author: Caitlin Little, December 27, 1996
10
11     private Point left, right, leftPupil, rightPupil;
12     public static final int
13       EYE_RADIUS = 30,
14       PUPIL_RADIUS = 10;
15
16     // create a pair of eyes, centered at Point c
17     public Eyes (Point c) {
18       // Determine center of each eyeball
19       left = new Point(c.x-EYE_RADIUS-1, c.y);
20       right = new Point(c.x+EYE_RADIUS+1, c.y);
21     }
22
23     public void gaze (DrawingBox d, Point cursor) {
24
25       // Draw the pink eyes
26       d.setColor(Color.pink);
27       fillCircle(d, left, EYE_RADIUS);
28       fillCircle(d, right, EYE_RADIUS);
29
30       // Draw the pupils
31       d.setColor(Color.black);
32       leftPupil = compute(cursor, left);
33       fillCircle(d, leftPupil, PUPIL_RADIUS);
34       rightPupil = compute(cursor, right);
35       fillCircle(d, rightPupil, PUPIL_RADIUS);
36     }
37
38     private void fillCircle (DrawingBox d, Point p, int radius) {
39       d.fillOval(p.x-radius, p.y-radius, 2*radius, 2*radius);
40     }
41
42     private Point compute (Point cursor, Point eye) {
43     // Compute the location of the pupil, given the
44     // locations of the eye and the cursor.
45       double d = Math.sqrt((cursor.x-eye.x)*(cursor.x-eye.x)
46                          + (cursor.y-eye.y)*(cursor.y-eye.y));
47       int r = EYE_RADIUS - PUPIL_RADIUS;
48       return new Point(eye.x + (int)((cursor.x-eye.x)*r/d),
49                        eye.y + (int)((cursor.y-eye.y)*r/d));
50     }
51   }
```

FIGURE 11.4 The Eyes class.

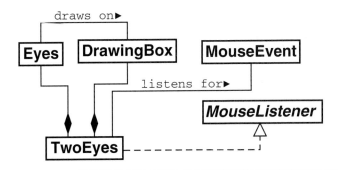

FIGURE 11.5 **UML diagram for the** TwoEyes **program.**

DrawingBox's drawing area. (We also use Points as arguments to the Eyes constructor, one Point each for the locations of the left eye and the right eye.) When the mouse moves into, or moves within, the program's window, mouseMoved is called; it sets cursor to the location of the mouse and then sends the gaze message to each eye, giving the DrawingBox object and the location of the mouse.

What would happen if we did not initialize the cursor in line 12 of the TwoEyes program?

QUICK EXERCISE 11.4

The Eyes class is shown in Figure 11.4. It is quite simple, once you understand the little bit of geometry required to figure out where the pupils in each eye should be, given the location of the eye and the mouse. Notice that there are only two public methods, the ones used by the client, TwoEyes; namely, the constructor and gaze. The other two methods, fillCircle and compute, are auxiliary methods used by the public methods but not intended for use by clients, so they are private.

In Figure 11.6, we see that the center of the eye is at Point e [with coordinates $(e.x, e.y)$], and the cursor is at Point c. Therefore, the distance between the center of the eye and the cursor is

$$d = \sqrt{(c.x - e.x)^2 + (c.y - e.y)^2}$$

We also know that r is the radius of the eye. So, by using similar triangles, we see that the center of the pupil is at $(p.x, p.y)$, where

$$p.x = e.x + (c.x - e.x) \times r/d$$

and

$$p.y = e.y + (c.y - e.y) \times r/d$$

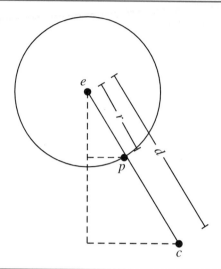

FIGURE 11.6 Geometry of the Eyes program.

Actually, we want the pupil to have its center not on the circumference of the eye, but rather just inside. This is accomplished by using EYE_RADIUS - PUPIL_RADIUS as the value for r.

In lines 11 through 14 we create the Points that are the centers of the two eyes, and we define the constants EYE_RADIUS and PUPIL_RADIUS. In lines 42 through 50, we have encapsulated the geometric computation that computes the position of a pupil, given the position of the cursor and the position of the center of the eye. Rather than draw our filled circles by the verbose fillOval method, we have written a utility method fillCircle (lines 38 through 40) that takes as parameters the center of the circle and its radius and performs the

utility method   necessary calculations to supply fillOval with its arguments. Such a *utility method* often makes the remaining code much easier to read and understand. In fact, our gaze method (lines 23 through 36) is quite straightforward, simply drawing two pink eyes (knowing their centers and radii) and two black pupils (computing their centers, and knowing their radii).

11.3

Debugging Classes

As our debugging example for this chapter, we're going to write a program that mimics a simple draw program. This program pops up a window in which lines can be drawn by clicking on the left mouse button. Specifically, each time the

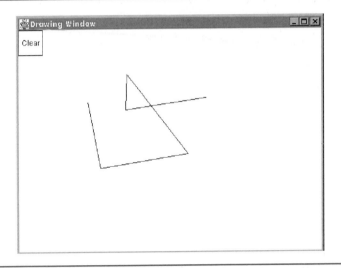

FIGURE 11.7 Running the Draw program.

mouse is clicked, a line is drawn from the location of that mouse click to the previous mouse click location. In addition, there is a "button" in the upper left corner labeled *Clear*; clicking the mouse while within that button causes the window to be cleared so the user can start over. Figure 11.7 shows how the window looks in the middle of running the program.

As we saw in Section 11.3, our program, called Draw, will have to implement the MouseListener interface. This means it has to have the words implements MouseListener in its header, and a call to addMouseListener, and it has to include definitions for mouseClicked, mouseEntered, etc. From the description of the problem, it is clear that we will have to remember the location of the *last* mouse click. The usual action when the mouse is clicked is simple: Draw a line from the current mouse location to the previous (saved) mouse location, *and* change the previous location to the current location. The only subtlety here is that we have to decide what to do for the very first mouse click, since we want to be sure not to draw a line for that one. Our solution is to set the previous location to −1 and test for it before drawing a line.

Here is our first attempt. We haven't implemented the Clear button, but that is intentional; we'll get the basic functionality working first, and then we'll add the "bells and whistles."

```
1    import CSLib.*;
2    import java.awt.event.*;                          WRONG
3
4    public class Draw implements MouseListener {
5      // Draw lines where mouse is clicked
6
7      public Draw () {                                 WRONG
8        int last_x = -1, last_y;
```

```
 9        DrawingBox d = new DrawingBox ("Drawing Window");
10        d.setSize(300, 300);                                WRONG
11        d.addMouseListener(this);
12      }
13
14      public void mouseClicked (MouseEvent e) {
15        if (last_x != -1)                                   WRONG
16          d.drawLine(last_x, last_y, e.getX(), e.getY());
17        last_x = e.getX();
18        last_y = e.getY();
19      }
20    }                                                       WRONG
```

Compiling this version produces quite a long list of errors:

```
Draw.java:4: Draw should be declared abstract;
it does not define mousePressed(java.awt.event.MouseEvent) in Draw
public class Draw implements MouseListener {
       ^

Draw.java:15: cannot resolve symbol
symbol  : variable last_x
location: class Draw
    if (last_x != -1)
        ^

Draw.java:16: cannot resolve symbol
symbol  : variable last_x
location: class Draw
        d.drawLine(last_x, last_y, e.getX(), e.getY());
                   ^

Draw.java:16: cannot resolve symbol
symbol  : variable last_y
location: class Draw
        d.drawLine(last_x, last_y, e.getX(), e.getY());
                           ^

Draw.java:16: cannot resolve symbol
symbol  : variable d
location: class Draw
        d.drawLine(last_x, last_y, e.getX(), e.getY());
        ^

Draw.java:17: cannot resolve symbol
symbol  : variable last_x
location: class Draw
    last_x = e.getX();
    ^

Draw.java:18: cannot resolve symbol
symbol  : variable last_y
location: class Draw
    last_y = e.getY();
    ^

7 errors
```

The error on line 4 occurs because we forgot to define all the methods required for mouse listeners, since mouseClicked is the only one we need. We need to add definitions for the other methods, even if they're trivial definitions.

The errors in lines 16 through 18 were all made because we made the variables last_x, last_y, and d local to the constructor instead of making them instance variables. Since mouseClicked needs to access them, they cannot be local to the constructor.

With these errors repaired, we get this version of the code, which compiles without errors:

```
1   import CSLib.*;
2   import java.awt.event.*;
3
4   public class Draw implements MouseListener {
5       // Draw lines where mouse is clicked
6
7       int last_x = -1, last_y;
8       DrawingBox d = new DrawingBox ("Drawing Window");
9
10      public Draw () {
11          d.setSize(300, 300);
12          d.addMouseListener(this);
13      }
14
15      public void mouseClicked (MouseEvent e) {
16          if (last_x != -1)
17              d.drawLine(last_x, last_y, e.getX(), e.getY());
18          last_x = e.getX();
19          last_y = e.getY();
20      }
21      public void mousePressed (MouseEvent e) {}
22      public void mouseReleased (MouseEvent e) {}
23      public void mouseEntered (MouseEvent e) {}
24      public void mouseExited (MouseEvent e) {}
25  }
```

This works fine, as far as it goes. Now we need to add the Clear button.

We will again take this slowly. The first step is to draw the button, and then we'll think about making it work. Our first attempt is to add these two lines at the end of the constructor:

```
d.drawRectangle(0, 0, 20, 20);
d.drawString("Clear", 0, 10);
```

However, this doesn't look very good, as shown in Figure 11.8. We could do better if we had a clear idea of how big the text was, but here we'll just use trial and error. After a few tries, we end up using

```
d.drawRectangle(0, 0, 40, 40);
d.drawString("Clear", 6, 25);
```

This looks fine (as shown in Figure 11.7), but it doesn't do anything. If we click the mouse within the area of the Clear button, a line will be drawn to it just as it would to any other point. So our next job is to add the "clear" functionality to our drawing program. The main idea is that when we detect a mouse click—that

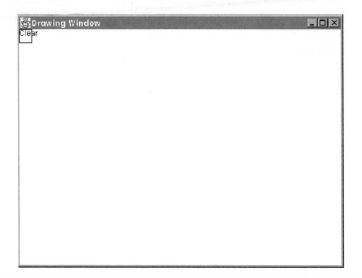

FIGURE 11.8 A badly drawn Clear button.

is, when `mouseClicked` is called—we can check whether the location of the mouse was within the Clear button's area, and perform the appropriate action, which is to clear the screen.

Our next step, then, is to change `mouseClicked` to check for clicks within the Clear button:

```
17    public void mouseClicked (MouseEvent e) {
18      int x = e.getX(), y = e.getY();
19      if (x <= 40 && y <= 40)
20        d.clear();
21      else if (last_x != -1)
22        d.drawLine(last_x, last_y, x, y);
23      last_x = x;
24      last_y = y;
25    }
```

The idea is very simple: If the mouse click was within the area of the Clear button, we clear the drawing window; otherwise, we draw the line (unless this is the first mouse click).

Can you see the error here? The `clear` method clears the *entire* window, including the Clear button itself! The remedy is simple: Redraw the Clear button after clearing the screen. Since the same button-drawing code is now used twice, we'll define a method to do that, and our new code becomes

```
1    import CSLib.*;
2    import java.awt.event.*;              ALMOST RIGHT
3
4    public class Draw implements MouseListener {
5      // Draw lines where mouse is clicked
```

```
6
7       int last_x = -1, last_y;          ALMOST  RIGHT
8       DrawingBox d = new DrawingBox ("Drawing Window");
9
10      public Draw () {
11         d.setSize(300, 300);
12         d.addMouseListener(this);       ALMOST  RIGHT
13         drawClearButton();
14      }
15
16      private void drawClearButton () { ALMOST  RIGHT
17         d.drawRectangle(0, 0, 40, 40);
18         d.drawString("Clear", 6, 25);
19      }
20
21      public void mouseClicked (MouseEvent e) { RIGHT
22         int x = e.getX(), y = e.getY();
23         if (x <= 40 && y <= 40) {
24            d.clear();
25            drawClearButton();           ALMOST  RIGHT
26         }
27         else if (last_x != -1)
28            d.drawLine(last_x, last_y, x, y);
29         last_x = x;
30         last_y = y;                     ALMOST  RIGHT
31      }
32      public void mousePressed (MouseEvent e) {}
33      public void mouseReleased (MouseEvent e) {}
34      public void mouseEntered (MouseEvent e) {}
35      public void mouseExited (MouseEvent e) {}  RIGHT
36   }
```

We're almost done, but Figure 11.9 shows what happens now in three successive clicks of the window.

The problem is that, in the last lines of mouseClicked, last_x and last_y are set to the location of the mouse click, even if it was within the Clear button. The solution is shown in the mouseClicked method of the final version of the code:

```
1    import CSLib.*;
2    import java.awt.event.*;
3
4    public class Draw implements MouseListener {
5       // Draw lines where mouse is clicked
6
7       int last_x = -1, last_y;
8       DrawingBox d = new DrawingBox ("Drawing Window");
9
10      public Draw () {
11
12         d.setSize(300, 300);
13         d.addMouseListener(this);
14         drawClearButton();
15      }
16
```

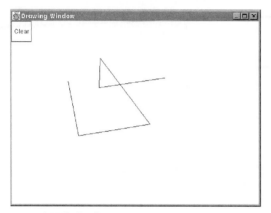

(a) While drawing

(b) Just after clearing

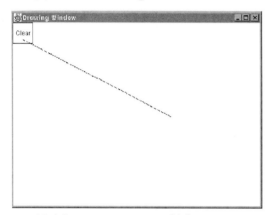

(c) After next mouse click

FIGURE 11.9   The next-to-last implementation doesn't work.

```
17      private void drawClearButton () {
18        d.drawRectangle(0, 0, 40, 40);
19        d.drawString("Clear", 6, 25);
20      }
21
22      public void mouseClicked (MouseEvent e) {
23        int x = e.getX(), y = e.getY();
24        if (x <= 40 && y <= 40) {
25          d.clear();
26          drawClearButton();
27          last_x = -1;
28          return;
29        }
30        if (last_x != -1)
31          d.drawLine(last_x, last_y, x, y);
32        last_x = x;
33        last_y = y;
34      }
```

```
35      public void mousePressed (MouseEvent e) {}
36      public void mouseReleased (MouseEvent e) {}
37      public void mouseEntered (MouseEvent e) {}
38      public void mouseExited (MouseEvent e) {}
39    }
```

Add a button just below the Clear button, labeled Skip, which causes a new line to be started at the next mouse click, without clearing the DrawingBox.	**QUICK EXERCISE** **11.5**

Add a button just below the Skip button, labeled Close, which causes a new line to be drawn between the first and last points in the last set of line segments.	**QUICK EXERCISE** **11.6**

Summary

An *event* is an outside occurrence to which an object needs to respond. The mouse triggers a MouseEvent or a MouseMotionEvent and causes one of the methods mouseMoved, mousePressed, mouseReleased, mouseEntered, mouseExited, mouseClicked, or mouseDragged to be called.

To create an object that can respond to mouse events, you write a class of the form

```
import java.awt.event.*;
...

public class classname implements MouseListener {
    ...
        // in an initialization method, such as a constructor
        manager.addMouseListener(this);
    ...
    public void mouseClicked (MouseEvent e) { ... }
    public void mousePressed (MouseEvent e) { ... }
    public void mouseReleased (MouseEvent e) { ... }
    public void mouseEntered (MouseEvent e) { ... }
    public void mouseExited (MouseEvent e) { ... }
}
```

All five methods must be defined to complete the implementation of MouseListener; otherwise, your Java compiler will complain.

To create an object that can respond to mouse motion events, you write a class of the form

```
import java.awt.event.*;
...

public class classname implements MouseMotionListener {
```

Name	Description
Point getPoint()	Return the x, y position of the event.
int getX()	Return the horizontal x position of the event.
int getY()	Return the vertical y position of the event.

TABLE 11.2   Methods of the `MouseEvent` **class.**

```
      ...
      // in an initialization method, such as a constructor
      manager.addMouseMotionListener(this);
      ...
   public void mouseMoved (MouseEvent e) { ... }
   public void mouseDragged (MouseEvent e) { ... }
}
```

Both methods must be defined to complete the implementation of `MouseMotionListener`; otherwise, your Java compiler will complain.

A class can respond to both mouse events and mouse motion events by implementing both `MouseListener` and `MouseMotionListener` and by defining all seven of the required methods.

The `MouseEvent` class is defined in the `java.awt.event` package, and it has three important methods that tell about the event, shown in Table 11.2.

Exercises

1. The beauty of having `Eyes` as a separate class is that it is easy to create new eyes and different kinds of eyes.
   (a) Add eyes in the other two corners of the application window.
   (b) Modify the application so that the eyes change only when the mouse is clicked.
   (c) Define a class `ShyEyes` that is like `Eyes` except that its pupils always turn *away* from the cursor. Define your application to contain both `Eyes` and `ShyEyes`.
   (d) Modify the `Eyes` application so that the eyes "sleep" when the mouse is outside the application and "awaken" when it moves inside the application. You can draw a sleeping eye by drawing a horizontal diameter instead of the pupil.
   (e) Modify the `Eyes` application further so that when the cursor is inside the application area, the eyes sleep when you press on the mouse button and awaken when you release it.

2. Write a method

```
   void drawPolygon (DrawingBox d, Point[] points)
```

that connects all the points in an array of points by lines (including connecting the last point to the first). To test it, write a program in which the user designates the vertices of the polygon by mouse clicks; each time the mouse is clicked, the polygon is redrawn with the new point included as the last point.

3. Recall that Conway's Game of Life was described in Exercise 10 on page 360.
   (a) Program Conway's Game of Life as a graphical application. Consider the top row to be adjacent to the bottom row (as if the game board were rolled over to form a cylinder), and the left column adjacent to the right column (as if the cylinder were rolled around to form a doughnut). Permit the selection of an initial pattern by clicking with the mouse. Code your mouse listener so that the game begins when the user clicks on a designated area of the DrawingBox (such as near the edge, or in a Start button that disappears once the game begins).
   (b) Keep track of the age of each cell, and display different-aged cells in different colors.

4. Write a tic-tac-toe playing application. You click with the mouse in a square to make a move, alternating between X and O. The game should continue like this until X or O wins or all spaces are filled, at which time an appropriate message should be displayed, written across the playing board.

5. Modify the mouse maze-walking program from Chapter 9 so that the MouseMazeClient is a MouseListener. The client should make a move every time the mouse is clicked in the DrawingBox.

6. In computerized drawing programs, one places a shape on the screen and then can perform various operations, such as moving, resizing, and rotating. Define the Rectangle class to represent rectangles and perform those operations:

```
class Rectangle {
private int
   x1, y1,      // one corner
   x2, y2;      // the opposing corner

public Rectangle (int X1, int Y1,    // (X1, Y1) is one corner
                  int X2, int Y2)    // (X2, Y2) is opposite corner
   {...}

   public void move (int deltax, int deltay) {
      // Move this rectangle deltax in the x direction,
      // deltay in the y direction
      ...
   }

   public void reshape (int x, int y, int newx, int newy) {
      // (x, y) is one of the four corners.  It is to be moved
      // to (newx, newy), leaving the opposite corner stationary
      ...
   }

   public void rotate () {
      // Rotate rectangle 90 degrees, leaving center fixed
      ...
   }

   public void display (DrawingBox d) {
      // Draw the rectangle in the DrawingBox
      ...
   }
}
```

Integers are used here instead of floating-point numbers because the points represent positions on the screen, viewed as a grid.

Write an application to test this class. It should start with a square drawn in the middle of the application's window. There should be buttons indicating whether to move, reshape, or rotate; indicating which corner to move in a reshape action; and indicating the direction to move the entire rectangle or the selected corner.

7. Write an application similar to the one in Exercise 6 on page 419, but using the mouse to indicate how to move or reshape the rectangle. This application should have just one button, the Rotate button, and it should start, as before, with a square drawn in the middle of the window. The square is rotated by pressing the rotate button, and the square is moved or resized by giving two mouse clicks, as follows. Assume the mouse clicks are at points p and q, respectively. If p is "near" one of the rectangle's corners, then this is a reshape operation, and q is the new location of that corner. Otherwise, if p is "near" one of the rectangle's sides, then this is also a reshape operation, but one that moves that entire line, either vertically or horizontally. If the line is a horizontal line, then q's y coordinate is the y coordinate to which that line should be moved; if it is a vertical line, q's x coordinate gives the x coordinate. If p is not near a corner or a line but is inside the rectangle, then this is a move operation: q gives the location to which the rectangle should be moved; specifically, the rectangle should be moved so that q is in the same relative location with respect to the rectangle as p was before the move. Finally, if p is outside the rectangle, the mouse clicks should be ignored.

8. A somewhat more difficult version of Exercise 7 is to use "clicking and dragging" to effect the moves and reshapes. That is, to move a corner of the rectangle, you should click *and hold* the mouse key, move the mouse to the desired new location of the corner, and release it. This should work similarly for reshaping on a side and for moving. Furthermore, you should show the rectangle changing shape and moving as the mouse is dragged. You will have to declare your application to be both a `MouseMotionListener` and a `MouseListener`:

```
class RectangleDrawing
        implements MouseMotionListener,MouseListener {
```

which means you will have to define all seven methods listed on page 405. However, only `mousePressed`, `mouseReleased`, and `mouseDragged` are of interest; the rest can be defined with empty bodies.

12 INHERITANCE AND EXCEPTIONS

CHAPTER PREVIEW

In this chapter we show how to organize predefined classes using Java *packages* and how access to methods and variables is controlled within and among packages. We discuss the important object-oriented technique of *inheritance*, which permits us to refine and extend existing classes. Finally, we discuss Java's *exception* facility and show how programmer-defined exceptions are created.

Damnosa hereditas.
(Ruinous inheritance.)

—Gaius
Institutes, ii:163

In this chapter, we complete our study of the Java language by explaining three features: *packages*, *inheritance* (and abstract classes), and *exceptions*. Packages were introduced and partially described in Chapter 2, because it is difficult to do anything without using them; but we give a more complete explanation here. Inheritance and exceptions have not been previously discussed, but are important language features. Furthermore, it is virtually impossible to use the classes provided with the Java compiler—the so-called application programming interface, or API—without understanding these features.

With this chapter, we will have covered almost all the Java language. The appendixes list those language features that, because we consider them either uninteresting details or too advanced for an introductory programming book, we have omitted.

12.1

Packages

Java's *application programmer interface (API)* is the name given to all the classes provided to programmers along with the Java compiler. Dozens of classes are in the API, and it continues to grow with each new version of the compiler. We have seen parts of it in earlier chapters, such as the `Math` class and, if you read Chapter 11, the `MouseEvent` class. *API*

All these predefined classes create an organizational problem. To solve this problem, Java places these classes in different *directories* (or *folders*) on your computer system. The classes in each directory form a *package*. The concatenation of the directory names (starting from a certain root directory) forms the *package name*. Some useful Java system package names are given in Table 12.1. For example, `java.applet` is the package of classes in directory `applet` of directory `java`. The location of the `java` directory itself varies on different platforms, but the `javac` and `java` programs know where it is. *directory* *folder* *package* *package name*

If you wish to use a class in a certain package (e.g., class `Math` in the package `java.lang`), you can write out the *fully qualified name* like this: *fully qualified name*

423

Package Name	Contents
java.applet	Classes for implementing applets
java.awt	Classes for graphics, windows, and GUIs
java.awt.event	Classes that support the AWT event-handling model
java.awt.image	Classes for image processing
java.awt.peer	Interface definitions for platform-independent GUIs
java.io	Classes for input and output
java.lang	Basic language classes (such as Math)
java.net	Classes for networking
java.util	Useful auxiliary classes such as Date

TABLE 12.1   Some useful predefined packages in Java.

```
x = java.lang.Math.sqrt(3);
```

However, that's rather inconvenient. Java provides a way to specify that you wish to use the classes in a particular package without having to use their fully qualified names. The *import statement* is used for this purpose. We have seen it many times. Its syntax is

import statement

```
import  package_name.*;
```

It allows all the classes in the package to be used without qualifying their names. A variant is

```
import  package_name.class_name;
```

which allows the use of the unqualified name of that one class. For example, the following code

```
java.util.Date d = new java.util.Date();
java.awt.Point p = new java.awt.Point(1,2);
java.awt.Button b = new java.awt.Button();
```

can be abbreviated

```
import java.util.Date;
import java.awt.*;
...
Date d = new Date();
Point p = new Point(1,2);
Button b = new Button();
```

Java always assumes that the classes in java.lang are available. Thus, it's as if you have the statement import java.lang.*; at the beginning of every program.

What about the classes that *you* define? We haven't specified that any of our classes should be part of a particular package. All the files that you place in one directory belong to the same, unnamed package. To cause a class to be placed in a particular named package, it is necessary not only to store the file in the appropriate directory but also to compile the class with a *package statement*, telling Java that the class is part of a specific package:

package statement

```
package package_name;
```
This must be the very first noncomment line in the source file. For example, the file `Math.java` begins with the line `package java.lang;`.

You can put different Java files in different packages even if they are in the same directory, by including `package` statements with different names. Thus, when we said earlier that the classes in each directory form a package, we weren't speaking the perfect truth. In fact, they can form several packages. (The converse does not hold: Classes in different directories cannot be part of the same package.)

12.1.1 Packages and Visibility Rules

For the most part, the only difference between a class in one package or another is the name used to refer to the classes in the two packages. However, another difference relates to the visibility of names.

Consider the case of instance variables. As you know, public instance variables of a class `C` are accessible to any method of any other class. (An example of a class with public variables is `Point`, in package `java.awt`.) Private instance variables are visible only to the methods of `C` itself. What if a variable is declared as neither public nor private? Then it has *package visibility*: It is visible in methods defined in other classes *in the same package* as `C` and not in any others. The same applies to static variables and instance and static methods.

package visibility

The visibility of classes follows an analogous rule. A class declared public is visible to all classes, and a class not declared public is visible to the classes in its own package. A class cannot be declared `private`.[1]

The Java distribution includes the source code of many of the classes in the API. Much is to be learned about Java from perusing these source files; ask your local guru where to find them. Also, the on-line documentation, available at `java.sun.com`, is organized by packages.

QUICK EXERCISE 12.1

Experiment with the package visibility rules by writing two classes, A and B. Put them in the same directory. Put the statement `package A;` at the beginning of `A.java`, and `package B;` at the beginning of `B.java`. Give A three instance variables, with visibility `public`, `private`, and package (i.e., no modifier), respectively, and then add a method to B that refers to each of these variables. Explain what happens.

---

[1]With one exception, noted in Appendix A.

12.2

Inheritance

inheritance
derived class
subclass
specialization
base class
superclass
parent class
inherited

One of the most important and highly touted features of Java—indeed, of all object-oriented languages—is *inheritance*. In Java, inheritance involves defining a new class (called a *derived class* or *subclass*) as a *specialization* of an already existing class (called the *base class* or *superclass* or *parent class*). The variables and methods of the superclass become part of the subclass; they are *inherited* by the subclass. The subclass may define additional variables and methods, and may even redefine the inherited ones. Inheritance supports the reuse of code, because it can provide varying functinality without having to create multiple copies of nearly identical classes. Moreover, inheritance in Java implies that whenever a program requires the use of the original superclass, the subclass can be substituted instead.

If you want to define a class C as a subclass of a class B, the form is

```
class C extends B {  // C is a subclass of B
   ...
}
```

The body of C follows the usual syntax. The new part is the `extends` B in the class header. With C a subclass of B, the objects of C contain all the instance variables of objects of B as well as the instance variables declared in C, and the objects respond to all the instance methods defined in B as well as those defined in C. This is illustrated, using UML syntax, in Figure 12.1. In UML, an unfilled solid arrow indicates subclassing.

As an example, recall the `Clock` class introduced in Section 7.15 (page 248). For the sake of brevity, we offer here a version that includes only `advanceMinutes` (a mutating operation to advance the time by a certain number of minutes) and `toString`:

```
1
2   public class Clock {
3      // Maintain a simple clock.
4      // Author: Courtney Mickunas, November 21, 2000
5
6      private int hour, minute;
7
8      public Clock () {
9         hour = 12;  minute = 0;
10      }
11
12      public Clock (int h, int m) {
13         hour = h;  minute = m;
14      }
15
16      // Convert clock to printable format
17      public String toString () {
```

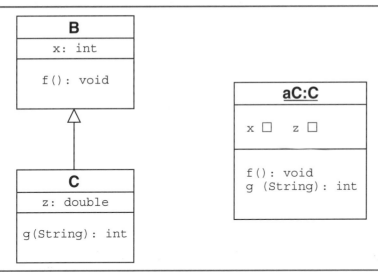

FIGURE 12.1 The effect of inheritance. The unfilled closed-head arrow is UML notation for inheritance. A typical c object is shown on the right.

```
18        String result = hour + ":";
19        if (minute < 10) result = result + "0";
20        return (result + minute);
21     }
22
23     public void advanceMinutes (int m) {
24        int totalMinutes = (hour * 60 + m) % (12 * 60);
25        // totalMinutes is between -(12 * 60) and (12 * 60)
26        if (totalMinutes < 0) totalMinutes = totalMinutes + (12 * 60);
27        hour = totalMinutes / 60;
28        if (hour == 0) hour = 12;
29        minute = totalMinutes % 60;
30     }
31  }
```

Suppose we want a class representing more exact time, counting seconds as well as minutes and hours. We may want to retain our current definition—not every client wants to have such exact time—while providing a new class, PreciseClock. But PreciseClock is mostly the same as Clock, merely having a new instance variable, second, and a new instance method, void advanceSeconds(int) (and possibly a new constructor). We don't want to replicate all of Clock when we write PreciseClock; we want merely to add the details. This is accomplished with inheritance:

```
1   public class PreciseClock extends Clock {
2       // Clock with a second hand
3       // Janet Kamin, August 12, 2001
4
```

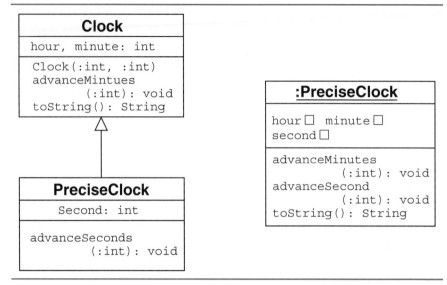

FIGURE 12.2 `PreciseClock` **inheriting from** `Clock`. **A typical** `PreciseClock` **object is shown on the right.**

```
5        private int second;
6
7        public PreciseClock () {
8          second = 0;
9        }
10
11       public void advanceSeconds (int s) {
12         int advMinutes = s / 60;
13         second = second + s % 60;
14         if (second < 0) {
15           advMinutes--;
16           second = second + 60;
17         }
18         else if (second >= 60) {
19           advMinutes++;
20           second = second - 60;
21         }
22         advanceMinutes(advMinutes);
23       }
24     }
```

Objects of this new `PreciseClock` class have instance variables `hour`, `minute`, and `second` and instance methods `advanceMinutes`, `toString`, and `advanceSeconds`, as shown in Figure 12.2. The program

```
1      import CSLib.*;
2
3      public class ClockClient {
4        public static void main (String[] args) {
5          OutputBox out = new OutputBox();
```

```
6       Clock lunchtime = new Clock();
7       PreciseClock takeoff = new PreciseClock();
8       takeoff.advanceSeconds(334);
9       out.println(lunchtime.toString());
10      out.println(takeoff.toString());
11    }
12  }
```

has this output:

```
12:00
12:05
```

The method advanceSeconds increments the instance variable second, determines by how many minutes (if any) the time is being advanced, and then calls advanceMinutes. Because PreciseClock objects inherit the instance methods of Clock, they can respond to advanceMinutes. That is, when a PreciseClock object receives an advanceSeconds message, it ultimately sends itself an advanceMinutes message.

Note that toString does for PreciseClock objects exactly what it did for Clock objects: stringifies the hour and minute hands of the clock. It does not automatically adjust itself to print the second hand. We will see how to do that in the next section.

As this example shows, when C is a subclass of B, we can think of C objects as specialized, or more "refined," versions of B objects. In particular, since C objects can respond to all the messages that B objects can (if not more), we can always use a C object wherever we can use a B object.

For this reason, the relationship between a class and its superclass is sometimes referred as an *"is-a" association* (as in "a C *is a* B"). By contrast, when an object contains an instance variable that refers to an object of another class, it is called a *"has-a" association*.

"is-a" association

"has-a" association

A class can have any number of subclasses, and those subclasses can in turn have further subclasses, creating an *inheritance hierarchy*. A class in the hierarchy inherits the variables and methods of all the classes above it in the hierarchy. We refer to a class C and all the classes that inherit from it (its subclasses, its subclasses' subclasses, and so on) as C*'s hierarchy*. The classes in C's hierarchy, except for C itself, are C's *descendants*. The classes above C—its superclass, its superclass's superclass, etc.—are C's *ancestors*.

inheritance hierarchy

descendants

ancestors

This is illustrated in Figure 12.3.

12.2.1 Inheritance and Visibility Rules

For variables and methods of a class, there is always the question of *visibility*— who can refer to those variables and methods? We have long used public and private, and in the last section we learned about package visibility. Inheritance complicates matters.

To see why, consider the PreciseClock class again. Suppose we want to define void preciseToString () to show the second in addition

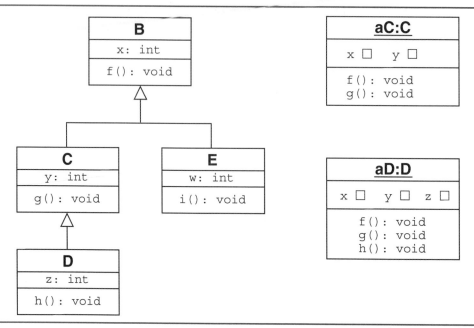

FIGURE 12.3   **In an inheritance hierarchy, a class inherits variables and methods from all its ancestors. Typical objects of classes** c **and** d **are shown on the right.**

to the minute and hour. This seems straightforward enough. Just add to PreciseClock:

```
public String preciseToString () {
    String result = hour + ":";
    if (minute < 10) result = result + "0";
    result = result + minute + ":";
    if (second < 10) result = result + "0";
    return (result + second);
}
```

But we will now get a compile-time error from javac, for a fairly obvious reason: Variables hour and minute are private!

Let's review the visibility rules we know: Private variables and methods of a class cannot be accessed by any other classes. Public variables and methods can be accessed by anyone. Variables and methods having package visibility can be accessed by classes in the same package but not by classes in a different package.

These rules apply to subclasses as well as clients. In particular, private variables and methods cannot be accessed by a class's subclasses; public variables and methods can be. Variables and methods having package visibility can be accessed by a class's subclasses only if those subclasses are in the same package as the class.

So, what do we do about the preciseToString method? We could make the hour and minute variables public, but that would violate our usual rule about hiding the representations of objects. Giving them package visibility has the same problem: These variables were made private to protect them from access by any other methods, even those in the same package. It is not as bad as letting everyone access them, but it isn't good either.

To solve this problem, Java provides another visibility modifier: *protected*. A member (a variable or a method) with protected visibility can be referenced by a class's subclasses or by clients in its package, but not by clients in any other package.

protected

Therefore, when there is the possibility that a class will have subclasses, it is best to use `protected`. Inherited protected variables and methods are considered to be protected members of the subclass (visible to further subclasses but hidden from clients), and inherited public variables and methods are considered to be public members of the subclass (visible to everyone).

The solution to our `preciseToString` problem, then, is to change the declarations of the instance variables of the `Clock` class to give them protected visibility:

```
6       protected int hour, minute;
```

After that, the definition of `preciseToString` given above works fine. This change—making the `private` instance variables `protected`—has no effect on existing clients of `Clock` and does not allow them access to `hour` and `minute`, but it does allow `PreciseClock` (and any other classes in `Clock`'s hierarchy) access to these variables.

12.2.2 Redefining Methods in Subclasses

Aside from adding new variables and methods, a subclass can *redefine*, or *override*, inherited methods. This is an extremely important feature of inheritance.

override

As a simple example, `PreciseClock` can redefine `toString` instead of having to define another method with a different name:

```
1    public class PreciseClock extends Clock {
2        // Clock with a second hand
3        // Janet Kamin, August 20, 2001
4
5        private int second;
6
7        public PreciseClock () {
8            second = 0;
9        }
10
11       // Convert clock to printable format
12       public String toString () {
13           String result = hour + ":";
14           if (minute < 10) result = result + "0";
15           result = result + minute + ":";
16           if (second < 10) result = result + "0";
17           return (result + second);
18       }
```

```
19
20      public void advanceSeconds (int s) {
21        int advMinutes = s / 60;
22        second = second + s % 60;
23        if (second < 0) {
24          advMinutes--;
25          second = second + 60;
26        }
27        else if (second >= 60) {
28          advMinutes++;
29          second = second - 60;
30        }
31        advanceMinutes(advMinutes);
32      }
33    }
```

PreciseClock objects now have three instance variables (as before), but only three methods: advanceMinutes, advanceSeconds, and toString. The UML diagram for this pair of classes is shown in Figure 12.4. The client code

```
public static void main (String[] args) {
  OutputBox out = new OutputBox();
  Clock lunchtime = new Clock();
  PreciseClock takeoff = new PreciseClock();
  takeoff.advanceSeconds(334);
  out.println(lunchtime.toString());
  out.println(takeoff.toString());
}
```

produces the output

```
12:00
12:05:34
```

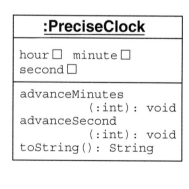

FIGURE 12.4 PreciseClock **inheriting from** Clock, **overriding** toString.

BUG ALERT 12.1

Overriding vs. Overloading

Although often confused, these two concepts are entirely different. A method is *overloaded* if it has multiple definitions that are distinguished by having different numbers or types of arguments. It is *overridden* when a subclass gives a different definition, with the same number and types of arguments.

Suppose we defined `toString` in `PreciseClock` like this:

```
public String toString (boolean printSeconds) {
    if (printSeconds)
        ... // return string with hours,
            // minutes, and seconds
    else
        ... // return string with only
            // hours and minutes
}
```

Sending the `toString` message with no arguments—`takeoff.toString()`—will call the inherited version of `toString`. The no-argument version of `toString` was not overridden at all; instead, a completely new method was defined.

QUICK EXERCISE 12.2

Define another subclass of `Clock` called `MilitaryClock`, which keeps hours in the range 0–23 instead of 1–12. Only the `advanceMinutes` method needs to be overridden.

12.2.3 Inheritance and Visibility, Again

We hate to bring this up again, but there is just one more slight complication related to visibility that arises with inheritance. If C is a subclass of B, there are two kinds of circumstances in which a C method m might want to look at members of B objects: when m is a client of B in the ordinary sense (e.g., if it declares variables of type B) and when m wants to look at the inherited members of its receiver. These two cases are illustrated here:

```
class B {
  int x;
  void f () { ... }
}

class C extends B {
  void m (B b) {
    ... x ... f() ...      // looking at the members of m's receiver
    ... b.x ... b.f() ...  // looking at the members of another B object
  }
}
```

The difficulty we had with `PreciseClock` above occurred when it wanted to reference the members of its receiver. It is not clear that granting this kind of access—which we did by declaring the `Clock` variables `protected`—should imply the other kind of access.

Thus, in discussing visibility rules in the presence of inheritance, we must distinguish between two ways of accessing a member: *client access* and *receiver access*. A method has *client access* to a member of another class if it can directly access the member using dot notation; in the example above, m needs to have client access to x and f in order for `b.x` and `b.f()` to be legal. A method has *receiver access* to a member of another class (which can only be itself or an ancestor class) if it can access that member just by giving its name (in unqualified form); in the example above, m has receiver access to x and f.

In everything we have seen so far, either a method has both kinds of access to a member, or it has neither. However, there is one exception to this: When a member of a class B is `protected`, any subclass of B defined in a different package from B has only receiver access to that member. In the example above, all the references to x and f in m are legal if C is in the same package as B; if C is in a different package, then the references to `b.x` and `b.f()` are illegal.

The effects of all these combinations are summarized in Table 12.2.

12.2.4   Constructors

When an object of a subclass is created, Java naturally wants to call a constructor of that class. However, it also wants to call a constructor for the superclass to initialize the instance variables declared in that superclass. The general rule is that the superclass's constructor is executed first, followed by that of the subclass. In general, given a class hierarchy

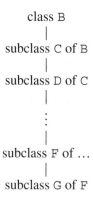

class B

subclass C of B

subclass D of C

⋮

subclass F of ...

subclass G of F

if a new G object is created, the constructors will be called in the order B, C, ..., G. This way, each class in the hierarchy is responsible for initializing instance variables declared at that level.

This is just what happened in `PreciseClock` above. The zero-argument constructor of `Clock` was called automatically, initializing the hour and minute to 12 and 0, respectively. Then the constructor of `PreciseClock` set the second to 0.

The only question is, If a superclass has a constructor with arguments but no zero-argument constructor, where will it get the arguments for its constructor?

Visibility	`public`	Default	`protected`	`private`
Client in the same package	C	C	C	None
Client in a different package	C	None	None	None
Subclass in the same package	C & R	C & R	C & R	None
Subclass in a different package	C & R	None	R	None

TABLE 12.2 Access provided by visibility modifiers (R is receiver access; C is client access).

The answer is that the subclass must explicitly call the superclass's constructor with arguments. However, to do this, it must use a syntax that is different from anything we've seen so far:

```
class C extends B {
   ...
  public C (...) {
    super ( B's constructor arguments) ;
     ...
  }
   ...
}
```

The call to *super(...)* *must be the first statement* in the body of C's constructor. If the programmer does not put an explicit call to `super(...)` as the
first statement in the body of the subclass's constructor, then Java automatically
inserts a call to `super()` there. (If the superclass has no zero-argument constructor, Java supplies a default constructor that does nothing but call *its* superclass's
zero-argument constructor.)

super(...)

Suppose we want to add a three-argument constructor for `PreciseClock`
in which the client supplies the hour, minute, and second. We write it as follows:

```
11    public PreciseClock (int h, int m, int s) {
12      super(h, m);
13      second = s;
14    }
```

The hour and minute are set by the superclass constructor `Clock (int h,
int m)`, and the second by the subclass constructor. The call `super(h, m)` at
the beginning of the `PreciseClock` constructor allows the `Clock` constructor
to do this initialization.

Define the two-argument constructor for `PreciseClock` that does nothing but
invoke the two-argument `Clock` constructor.

**QUICK EXERCISE
12.3**

Do Not Assign Superclass Object to Subclass Variable

If C is a subclass of B, then it is legal to write

```
B aB = new C();
```

However, it is not legal to write

```
C aC = new B();
```

The problem is that this makes it look as if the object referred to by aC is capable of responding to all of C's messages. But since C may add new messages not defined in B, a B object cannot respond to them. At some point during the execution of the program, someone might send a message defined in C to aC, with dire consequences.

The fundamental idea is that objects in subclasses have all the capabilities (i.e., methods) defined in the superclass, plus possibly more. Thus, it is safe to use a subclass object wherever a superclass object might be used, but not vice versa.

12.2.5   Dynamic Binding

We stated in the previous discussion that a PreciseClock object *is* a Clock object. This is not actually true, but it is very close to being true: A PreciseClock object can be used anywhere that a Clock object can be. For example, this declaration and assignment are perfectly legal:

```
Clock dawn;
dawn = new PreciseClock(3, 45, 30);
```

A Clock variable can contain a reference to a PreciseClock object. More generally, a C variable can contain a reference to any object of any class in C's hierarchy of subclasses.

Now consider the method call

```
... dawn.toString() ...
```

There are two definitions of toString, one for Clock objects and one for PreciseClock objects. The definition of dawn is a bit of both: It is declared to have type Clock, but it actually contains a reference to an object of type PreciseClock. So which version of printClock is invoked? The answer is: the definition in PreciseClock. This is the method associated with the object actually contained in dawn.

In the programs we've seen until now, whenever a message is sent in a Java program, it is possible to determine, without running the program, which instance method will be invoked. Even when a method is overloaded, this property continues to hold. It may be complicated and require a deep understanding of the Java compiler, but in principle, every time a message is sent, the exact method that will be invoked can be determined *at compile time*. This property is known *static binding* as the *static binding* of methods.

However, when a method is overridden by a subclass, this property is violated. If a method is overridden, then when that message is sent to an object of that class or any subclass of it, the call is *dynamically bound*. This means that the method actually invoked depends on the class of its receiver. Because the instance method has been redefined in subclasses, this can make a difference. Sending the `toString` message to `dawn` illustrates this.

dynamically bound

Most languages use static binding for all method calls, in part because static binding is somewhat more efficient than dynamic binding and in part because programs are easier to read when one can always determine what method is referred to in any call. Object-oriented languages, however, use dynamic method binding with inheritance. This controlled use of dynamic binding is an important feature of object-oriented languages.

As a further example of dynamic binding, consider this version of `Clock`, where we have added a `print` method:

```
1    import CSLib.*;
2
3    public class Clock {
4        // Maintain a simple clock.
5        // Author: Courtney Mickunas, November 21, 2000
6
7        protected int hour, minute;
8
9        public Clock () {
10           hour = 12;  minute = 0;
11       }
12
13       public Clock (int h, int m) {
14           hour = h;  minute = m;
15       }
16
17       // Convert clock to printable format
18       public String toString () {
19           String result = hour + ":";
20           if (minute < 10) result = result + "0";
21           return (result + minute);
22       }
23
24       public void print (OutputBox out) {
25           out.println(toString());
26       }
27
28       public void advanceMinutes (int m) {
29           int totalMinutes = (hour * 60 + m) % (12 * 60);
30           // totalMinutes is between -(12 * 60) and (12 * 60)
31           if (totalMinutes < 0) totalMinutes = totalMinutes + (12 * 60);
32           hour = totalMinutes / 60;
33           if (hour == 0) hour = 12;
34           minute = totalMinutes % 60;
35       }
36   }
```

The `print` method just prints the stringified version of the object in an output window.

Making no changes to `PreciseClock`, consider what the following client will print:

```
import CSLib.*;

public class ClockClient {
  public static void main (String[] args) {
    OutputBox out = new OutputBox();
    Clock lunchtime = new Clock();
    PreciseClock takeoff = new PreciseClock(1, 30, 44);
    lunchtime.print(out);
    takeoff.print(out);
  }
}
```

It is important in understanding inheritance (in particular, dynamic binding) to see why this client has the output

```
12:00
1:30:44
```

Even though `print` has just one definition, which is inherited by `PreciseClock`, it still invokes the "correct" version of `toString` when its receiver is a `PreciseClock` object. In the body of `print`, the `toString` message is sent to the receiver, `this`. Although `this` nominally has the type `Clock`, what matters when a message is sent to an object is the *actual, current* type of the object, in this case, `PreciseClock`.

Indeed, it is possible for a variable to refer to different types of objects at different times during the execution of the program. For example, we would get the same effect from this client as from the one just shown:

```
import CSLib.*;

public class ClockClient {
  public static void main (String[] args) {
    OutputBox out = new OutputBox();
    Clock lunchtime = new Clock();
    lunchtime.print(out);
    lunchtime = new PreciseClock(1, 30, 44);
    lunchtime.print(out);
  }
}
```

12.2.6 super

We have already seen one use of the keyword `super`, namely, when we want to invoke the superclass's constructor. Another use occurs when we want to invoke a method from a superclass in case we have overridden that method.

As an example, look at the definitions of `toString` in `Clock`

```
public String toString () {
    String result = hour + ":";
    if (minute < 10) result = result + "0";
    return (result + minute);
}
```

and `PreciseClock`

```
public String toString () {
    String result = hour + ":";
    if (minute < 10) result = result + "0";
    result = result + minute + ":";
    if (second < 10) result = result + "0";
    return (result + second);
}
```

These methods have a great deal in common. In fact, the method in `PreciseClock` is pretty much just the method in `Clock` followed by the addition of the seconds. We would like to be able to define `toString` in `PreciseClock` by saying, "Invoke the `toString` from `Clock`, and then add the seconds." The problem is, we can't say this in the most obvious way:

```
public void toString () {
    String result = toString();   // call toString in Clock
    return (result + ":" + second);
}
```

The call to `toString` on line 2, which is shorthand for `this.toString()`, just invokes this same method again, leading to an infinite loop! The way to do this is to send the `toString` message to `super`. And `super` is not a different object from `this`; it is just `this` viewed (temporarily) as a `Clock` object instead of a `PreciseClock` object. Together with the additional code to ensure that the second part takes exactly two spaces, this leads to the correct version of `toString` in `PreciseClock`:

```
public String toString () {
    String result = super.toString() + ":";
    if (second < 10) result = result + "0";
    return (result + second);
}
```

12.2.7 Abstract Methods and Abstract Classes

It is sometimes useful to have classes that have no objects of their own but exist only so that their subclasses can inherit from them. Such a class might define a general class of some type of object but lack some crucial methods without which its objects cannot do anything useful; subclasses are supposed to supply those methods. Such a class is called an *abstract class*. The missing methods are *abstract class* called *abstract methods*. We will use this feature in this section to help write a *abstract methods* mouse-in-a-maze program that allows for the definition of different types of mice using different navigation strategies.

In Chapter 9 (page 340), we wrote an application that animated the mouse-in-a-maze from Chapter 1.[2] We had six classes in that application: one representing the maze; one, the mouse; a drawer class for each of them; the animation controller; and a simple client. In that version, the mouse's movements were animated by drawing successive positions of the mouse with a 1-second delay:

```
1   import CSLib.*;
2
3   public class MouseController {
4       // Draw a mouse navigating a maze, using the
5       // "hug the wall to the right" algorithm
6       // Rebecca Kamin, Sept 12, 2000
7
8       public void runMouse () {
9           DrawingBox d = new DrawingBox("Mouse in maze");
10          Maze theMaze = new Maze();
11          MazeDrawer theMazeDrawer = new MazeDrawer(theMaze, d);
12          Mouse speedy = new Mouse(theMaze);
13          MouseDrawer speedyDrawer =
14                      new MouseDrawer(speedy, theMazeDrawer, d);
15
16          while (true) {
17              theMazeDrawer.draw();
18              speedyDrawer.draw();
19              Timer.pause(1000);
20              speedy.makeMove();
21          }
22      }
23  }
```

As we have noted before, the importance of program structure lies in the ease with which the program can be modified for new purposes. We have spoken, for example, of structuring the program in such a way as to allow for input and output to be modified; indeed, that is exactly why we used the "drawer" classes for this application. Another obvious change that we might want to make here—this is something we mentioned as far back as Chapter 1—is to use a different algorithm for traversing the maze.

Suppose, then, that we want to change this program to use the straight-ahead-if-possible algorithm: Always go straight ahead if possible; if not, then turn right until it is possible to go straight. (Do you think this is a good strategy?)

If we look at the six classes, we can see that only the Mouse class needs to be changed (which is a good indication that our structure was sound). The Mouse class looks like this:

---

[2] You need not have read Chapter 8 to follow this example. The only use of the material from that chapter (namely, two-dimensional arrays) is encapsulated in the Maze class, which we will not touch here.

```
public class Mouse {
    private instance variables

    public Point tellLocation () ...
    public int tellDirection () ...
    public Mouse(Maze m) ...
    public void makeMove() ...
    private boolean outside () ...
    private boolean facingWall () ...
    private void stepForward() ...
    private void turnLeft() ...
    private void turnRight() ...
}
```

By replacing the makeMove method with this one

```
public void makeMove () {
// Use "walk-straight-ahead-if-possible" algorithm
  if (started) {
    if (!outside()) {
      while (facingWall()) {
        turnRight();
      }
      stepForward();
    }
  } else {
    stepForward();
    started=true;
  }
}
```

we immediately get the new behavior.

Run this new mouse through our maze. Does it use a good strategy, after all?	**QUICK EXERCISE** **12.4**

In one sense, we should be pretty proud of ourselves. The change we made was very "clean." It affected only the one method that it clearly *had* to affect. You would be surprised at how often a change like this will trigger changes in a wide variety of seemingly unrelated places, especially in programs that are not object-oriented.

But the result is far from perfect. Suppose that we want to have *both* kinds of mice at our disposal, either because we keep changing our mind or, perhaps, because we want to allow the user to choose the strategy. In other words, rather than throw out the earlier version of Mouse and replace it by the new one, we want to keep both versions. The first thing we need to do is to give them different names, say, RightMouse and StraightMouse. Then we need to change the controller appropriately. This is all quite easy to do.

**QUICK EXERCISE
12.5**

Make this change: The first version of `Mouse` should be renamed `RightMouse`; the animation controller should be changed to use this name and should itself be renamed to `RightMouseController`. Make similar changes for `StraightMouse`.

Okay, now we have the two classes existing simultaneously, but we shouldn't be proud of our work anymore. What we have done is to create two classes, each about 60 lines long and each *nearly identical* except for one method. Not only have we wasted space and time, but in the long run we will find that we have a maintenance nightmare, for this reason: Any modification to the mice will have to be done twice, once for `RightMouse` and again, identically, for `StraightMouse`. Each time we add a new type of mouse, we add to the maintenance burden.

Here is where inheritance comes to the rescue. We can create a single `Mouse` class that has all the methods and variables except `makeMove`, and then two separate subclasses consisting of just the `makeMove` method. With this modification, the `Mouse` class is

```
1   import java.awt.Point;
2
3   class Mouse implements Direction {
4     // A mouse that can navigate a maze
5     // Author: Allan M. Mickunas, September 22, 1996
6
7     protected Maze theMaze;
8     protected boolean started = false; // true once the maze
9                                         // is entered.
10    protected Point location; // The location of this Mouse
11    protected int direction;  // The direction Mouse is facing
12
13    public Point tellLocation () {return location;}
14
15    public int tellDirection () {return direction;}
16
17    public Mouse (Maze m) {
18      theMaze = m;
19      // Where do I start?
20      location = m.getStartLocation();
21      // In what direction do I face initially?
22      direction = m.getStartDirection();
23    }
24
25    protected boolean outside () {
26    // Am I outside the maze?
27      return theMaze.outside(location);
28    }
29
30    protected boolean facingWall () {
31      return theMaze.checkWall(direction, location);
32    }
```

```
33
34      protected void stepForward () {
35        switch (direction) {
36          case NORTH: location.y--; break;
37          case EAST:  location.x++; break;
38          case SOUTH: location.y++; break;
39          case WEST:  location.x--; break;
40        }
41      }
42
43      protected void turnLeft() {
44        direction = (direction+3) % 4;
45      }
46
47      protected void turnRight() {
48        direction = (direction+1) % 4;
49      }
50    }
```

The RightMouse class is

```
1     public class RightMouse extends Mouse {
2       // A mouse that can navigate a maze, using the
3       // "wall-to-the-right" algorithm
4       // Author: Allan M. Mickunas, September 22, 1996
5
6       public RightMouse (Maze m) {
7         super(m);
8       }
9
10      public void makeMove () {
11      // Use "wall-to-the-right" algorithm
12        if (started) {
13          if (!outside()) {
14            turnRight();
15            while (facingWall()) {
16              turnLeft();
17            }
18            stepForward();
19          }
20        } else {
21          stepForward();
22          started=true;
23        }
24      }
25    }
26
```

and the StraightMouse class is

```
1     public class StraightMouse extends Mouse {
2       // A mouse that can navigate a maze, using the
3       // "walk-straight-ahead-if-possible" algorithm
4       // Author: Allan M. Mickunas, September 22, 1996
```

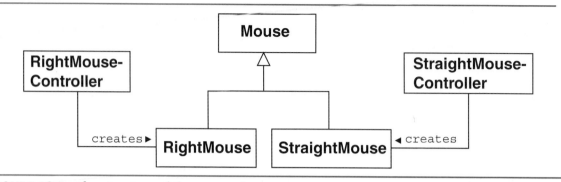

FIGURE 12.5 **The structure of the** Mouse **classes.**

```
5
6     public StraightMouse (Maze m) {
7       super(m);
8     }
9
10    public void makeMove () {
11    // Use "walk-straight-ahead-if-possible" algorithm
12      if (started) {
13        if (!outside()) {
14          while (facingWall()) {
15            turnRight();
16          }
17          stepForward();
18        }
19      } else {
20        stepForward();
21        started=true;
22      }
23    }
24  }
25
```

The Mouse class is just the same as before except for two things:
The makeMove method has been deleted, and the private variables have
become protected variables. The clients RightMouseController and
StraightMouseController are completely unchanged. We have now succeeded in structuring the mice so as to make it as easy as possible to add new mice
with new strategies. The UML diagram for these classes is seen in Figure 12.5.

QUICK EXERCISE 12.6	Write LeftMouse, using the wall-to-the-left algorithm. Then write LeftMouseController.

Well, to be picky, we do have one problem remaining: Although we have avoided duplicating code for different mice, we have duplicated code in the controllers! All our animation controllers are identical except for one line, where the type of the mouse is given. If we want to have just one controller, then we need to allow the user to select a strategy, and then the controller can create either a `RightMouse` or a `StraightMouse` and run it through the maze; nothing else needs to change.

Here is our first attempt, which is awfully close to being correct, but needs one subtle, but important, change:

```
1   import CSLib.*;
2
3   public class MouseController {
4     // Draw a mouse navigating a maze, using the
5     // "hug the wall to the right" algorithm
6     // Rebecca Kamin, Sept 12, 2000
7
8     public void runMouse () {
9       DrawingBox d = new DrawingBox("Mouse in maze");
10      Maze theMaze = new Maze();
11      MazeDrawer theMazeDrawer = new MazeDrawer(theMaze, d);
12
13      InputBox mouseChoice = new InputBox();
14      mouseChoice.setPrompt(
15        "Choose RightMouse (0) or StraightMouse (1)");
16      int choice = mouseChoice.readInt();
17
18      Mouse speedy;
19      if (choice == 0)
20        speedy = new RightMouse(theMaze);
21      else
22        speedy = new StraightMouse(theMaze);
23
24      MouseDrawer speedyDrawer =
25          new MouseDrawer(speedy, theMazeDrawer, d);
26
27      while (true) {
28        theMazeDrawer.draw();
29        speedyDrawer.draw();
30        Timer.pause(1000);
31        speedy.makeMove();
32      }
33    }
34  }
```

When we compile this class, we get the following error:

```
MouseController.java:30: Method makeMove() not found in class Mouse.
       speedy.makeMove();
```

We can't really argue with this: The Mouse class doesn't contain a `makeMove` method. True, each of its subclasses contains such a method, but the Java compiler doesn't look that closely. *When a variable is declared to have a particular object type C, and a message is sent to that variable, then C, or some ancestor of C, must define a method with that name.*

There is an easy solution to this: Put a trivial definition of `makeMove` in the `Mouse` class:

```
public void makeMove () {
   // do nothing - this is just to appease the compiler
}
```

Since each subclass will override this definition with a real definition, there is no harm in adding this method. However, this "solution" ignores an important fact about the `Mouse` class: *It has no objects.* That is, we never create a `Mouse` object, only a `RightMouse` or `StraightMouse` object. The `Mouse` class exists only so that these specific kinds of mice can inherit its code. A class that should never be instantiated, but only used as a superclass for other classes, is called an *abstract class*; its subclasses that are intended to be instantiated are called *concrete classes*.

abstract class
concrete classes

Java provides a way to state explicitly that a class is abstract, by declaring it as such in its header. Using this method has one important advantage over our last attempt: The compiler will make sure that a user never tries to create an object of an abstract class.

When a class is declared to be abstract, it can include methods that are themselves given without definitions, which are called *abstract methods*. These are again declared as such in their headers, and instead of an empty body, as we used above, they have no body at all, just a semicolon:

```
abstract  modifiers  return-type  method-name (parameters) ;
```

All this brings us to the final version of `Mouse`, shown in Figure 12.7. Our last version of the Controller now compiles and runs correctly. This is now a rather nice structure for this application, if we do say so ourselves. The UML chart is shown in Figure 12.6. The final versions of `Mouse`, `RightMouse`, `LeftMouse`, and `MouseController` are given in Figures 12.7 to 12.10.

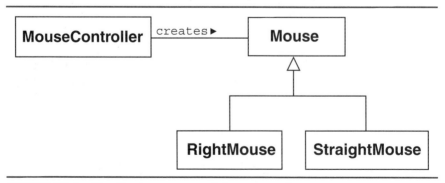

FIGURE 12.6 The final structure of the `Mouse` classes.

```
1   import java.awt.*;
2
3   abstract class Mouse implements Direction {
4     // A mouse that can navigate a maze
5     // Author: Allan M. Mickunas, September 22, 1996
6
7     protected Maze theMaze;
8     protected boolean started = false; // true once the maze
9                                        // is entered.
10    protected Point location; // The location of this Mouse
11    protected int direction;  // The direction Mouse is facing
12
13    public Point tellLocation () {return location;}
14
15    public int tellDirection () {return direction;}
16
17    public Mouse (Maze m) {
18      theMaze = m;
19      // Where do I start?
20      location = m.getStartLocation();
21      // In what direction do I face initially?
22      direction = m.getStartDirection();
23    }
24
25    abstract void makeMove () ;
26
27    protected boolean outside () {
28    // Am I outside the maze?
29      return theMaze.outside(location);
30    }
31
32    protected boolean facingWall () {
33      return theMaze.checkWall(direction, location);
34    }
35
36    protected void stepForward () {
37      switch (direction) {
38        case NORTH: location.y--; break;
39        case EAST:  location.x++; break;
40        case SOUTH: location.y++; break;
41        case WEST:  location.x--; break;
42      }
43    }
44
45    protected void turnLeft() {
46      direction = (direction+3) % 4;
47    }
48
49    protected void turnRight() {
50      direction = (direction+1) % 4;
51    }
52  }
53
```

FIGURE 12.7 Final version of the Mouse **class.**

```
1    import java.awt.*;
2
3    public class RightMouse extends Mouse {
4      // A mouse that can navigate a maze, using the
5      // "wall-to-the-right" algorithm
6      // Author: Allan M. Mickunas, September 22, 1996
7
8      public RightMouse (Maze m) {
9        super(m);
10     }
11
12     public void makeMove () {
13       if (started) {
14         if (!outside()) {
15           turnRight();
16           while (facingWall()) {
17             turnLeft();
18           }
19           stepForward();
20         }
21       } else {
22         stepForward();
23         started=true;
24       }
25     }
26   }
27
```

FIGURE 12.8   Final version of the `RightMouse` class.

QUICK EXERCISE 12.7	Add the `LeftMouse` to this menagerie, modifying the client to allow for a choice among the three types of mice.

12.2.8 The `Object` Class

We note that all other classes are considered descendants of one special class, called `Object`, in package `java.lang`. A class that is defined with no super-class, by definition, is a subclass of `Object`. It is legal but redundant to add `extends Object` to the header of such a class.

12.2.9 Interfaces

We have already discussed *interfaces* in detail in Chapter 9. We mention them again here only to point out that they bear a strong resemblance to abstract classes. In fact, an interface is very much like an abstract class containing only abstract methods and definitions of constants. However, there is one important difference: A class may implement multiple interfaces, whereas it can have only one superclass.

```
1   import java.awt.*;
2
3   public class StraightMouse extends Mouse {
4     // A mouse that can navigate a maze, using the
5     // "walk-straight-ahead-if-possible" algorithm
6     // Author: Allan M. Mickunas, September 22, 1996
7
8     public StraightMouse (Maze m) {
9       super(m);
10    }
11
12    public void makeMove () {
13      if (started) {
14        if (!outside()) {
15          while (facingWall()) {
16            turnRight();
17          }
18          stepForward();
19        }
20      } else {
21        stepForward();
22        started=true;
23      }
24    }
25  }
```

FIGURE 12.9 Final version of the StraightMouse class.

12.3

Exceptions

I would to God they would either conform, or be more wise, and not be catched!

—Samuel Pepys
Diary, 7 Aug. 1664

An *exception* is something that is not supposed to happen, but might happen   *exception*
anyway. Exceptions are an unfortunate but unavoidable fact of life in computer
programming. For example, whenever you do division, there is the possibility that
the denominator is zero; when you reference an array, the subscript might be out of
bounds. Of course, such exceptions can be avoided just by writing your programs
correctly. Other kinds of exceptions can't be avoided so easily: Whenever you
attempt to read a file (we will see how to do this in Chapter 15), there is a possibility
that the file does not exist; when you make a network connection, it may suddenly
disconnect; even when you attempt to create a new object, there is a chance that
the computer has run out of memory and can't do it.

```
1    import CSLib.*;
2
3    public class MouseController {
4      // Draw a mouse navigating a maze, using the
5      // "hug the wall to the right" algorithm
6      // Rebecca Kamin, Sept 12, 2000
7
8      public void runMouse () {
9        DrawingBox d = new DrawingBox("Mouse in maze");
10       Maze theMaze = new Maze();
11       MazeDrawer theMazeDrawer = new MazeDrawer(theMaze, d);
12
13       InputBox mouseChoice = new InputBox();
14       mouseChoice.setPrompt("Choose RightMouse (0) or StraightMouse (1)");
15       int choice = mouseChoice.readInt();
16
17       Mouse speedy;
18       if (choice == 0)
19         speedy = new RightMouse(theMaze);
20       else
21         speedy = new StraightMouse(theMaze);
22
23       MouseDrawer speedyDrawer =
24                    new MouseDrawer(speedy, theMazeDrawer, d);
25
26       while (true) {
27         theMazeDrawer.draw();
28         speedyDrawer.draw();
29         Timer.pause(1000);
30         speedy.makeMove();
31       }
32     }
33   }
```

FIGURE 12.10   Final version of the MouseController **class.**

Exceptions present a challenge to the programmer. They can occur in so many situations that a conscientious attempt to deal with all of them (such as you would want to make if you were writing an industrial-strength application) can overwhelm the programming process. On the other hand, the failure to deal with exceptions is probably the main cause of computer crashes.

From a programming point of view, the basic difficulty of dealing with exceptions arises from this observation: *The place where an exception occurs may not be the best place to recover from it.* Consider, for example, a method

```
void m (double[] A, int i) { ... A[i] ... }
```

Suppose that when m evaluates A[i], i is negative. This is an example of an exception. Now m could check to make sure that the value of i is in bounds. That would be annoying, but the deeper problem is that once it discovered that i was negative, m wouldn't know what to do about it! The origin of the problem lies not in m, but rather in the method that called m, because that method should not have passed m bad arguments. m should return to its caller an indication that the arguments were erroneous, so that the caller could do something to recover (such as get a better value of i and call m again). Of course, the caller might be in the same predicament itself: It passed a bad argument to m because it received bad arguments from *its* caller. Somewhere up the "call chain" is a method that ought to take responsibility for this error. Perhaps it needs to get some new input from the user and start the process again, or perhaps it needs to try a different way of calculating the answer it wants, or perhaps it just needs to halt the program and give up. The point is that we need a way for a method to signal to its caller that an error has occurred, tell it what the error was, and allow it to take appropriate action. This is just what the exception mechanism of Java provides.

It is worth noting that many programming languages do not have this feature, because it is not strictly necessary. The situation described above can be handled by ordinary method call and return. For example, the method m could be changed to return an error indication such as −1. This kind of solution has been used in many, many programs. However, when used conscientiously, this approach is extremely tedious and can often *double* the size of the program just with error-checking code. The inevitable result is that it is often applied carelessly and some exceptions are not handled. The designers of Java and many other languages have therefore chosen to add this feature to ease the programmer's burden.

So, what is the exception-handling mechanism? It consists of three parts:

1. A mechanism for creating special *exception classes* (whose instances we will refer to as *exception objects*). *(exception classes, exception objects)*

2. A new statement, *throw e*, used to signal the occurrence of an exception and return control to the calling method. Here, *e* is an expression that evaluates to an exception object. Executing this statement is called *throwing* the exception object. *(throw e)*

3. Another new statement, *try/catch*, that allows the calling method to "catch" the thrown exception object and take appropriate action. *(try/catch)*

We will start our discussion with the last item, the `try/catch` statement. Java includes numerous exception classes in the API, and many built-in operations and methods throw exceptions. Just as we did with classes, we will first see how to *use* the built-exceptions, then learn how to construct and throw our own exceptions.

Table 12.3 lists some of the more common exceptions, giving their class names and the circumstances under which they occur.

An example is array overflow. Specifically, there is a class `ArrayIndexOutOfBoundsException`, and whenever a program attempts to subscript an array with an invalid index, the Java system creates an `ArrayIndexOutOfBoundsException` object and throws it. Normally, this is fatal: The program will halt and display an error message. However, you can

Exception Class	Cause of Exception
ArithmeticException	Various arithmetic errors, such as division by zero
ArrayIndexOutOfBoundsException	Evaluating A[i] when i < 0 or i ≥ A.length
NegativeArraySizeException	Attempting to allocate an array using a negative size
NullPointerException	Evaluating e.x or calling e.m(..) when e has not been properly initialized (i.e., contains null)

TABLE 12.3   Some common exceptions in Java.

catch this error if you want to. Suppose you have a method m

```
void  m () {
    ... body of m ...
}
```

The body of m may call other methods as well as doing its own calculations. If you are concerned that an out-of-bounds exception might occur *at any time* during the execution of m—either in m itself or in one of the methods that it calls—you

try/catch statement

can use the try/catch statement:

```
void  m () {
    try     {
        ... body of m ...
    }
    catch (ArrayIndexOutOfBoundsException ae) {
        ... code to recover from error ...
    }
}
```

This does exactly as the previous version of m did, namely, execute the body of m, except that if the out-of-bounds exception occurs during execution of the body, then the method in which the error occurred immediately stops and returns

catch block

control to the *catch block* in m (meaning the catch line and the associated code). The occurrence of the subscripting error may be deep in the call chain—perhaps m called n which called p, and p is where the error happened. Immediately p will halt and return to n, which will immediately return to m, which will go directly to the catch block. In short, wherever the error occurred, there will be an immediate return, through all the methods that were called in between, to m, and, more specifically, to the catch block in m.

The header of the catch block—its first line—looks like a method header with no return type. The parenthesized part consists of a class name and a variable name, just like a method header with one argument. Like a method, the body of the catch block can refer to that variable. What can it do with it? Remember that it is an object of the named exception class, so the question is, What methods are defined in the ArrayIndexOutOfBoundsException class? A look at the Java documentation shows that this class has a constructor (which we don't need to know, since we aren't the ones who need to throw this exception) and one method:

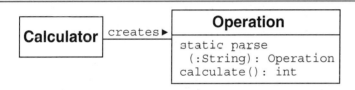

FIGURE 12.11 UML for the two main classes of the calculator.

```
String getMessage ()
```

In fact, all exception classes define this method. Each exception object can respond to this message by returning a string descriptive of the error that occurred. Thus, our catch block might be

```
catch (ArrayIndexOutOfBoundsException ae) {
    new ErrorBox("Error: "+ae.getMessage());
}
```

12.3.1 Example: Simple Calculator

A calculator may occasionally be called upon to perform an operation that makes no sense, such as dividing by zero, but it should not crash with an error. In this section, we write a very simple calculator that is able to recover cleanly from such errors (actually division by zero is the only error of that type). It accepts from the user inputs of the form *integer operator integer*, where the integers are positive; the *operator* is +, -, *, or /; and there are no spaces.

We first give a version of this program that does not catch exceptions. Its UML diagram is given in Figure 12.11. The code for the main loop of the calculator (reading inputs as above, printing results, and then reading inputs again, ad infinitum), as well as the simple client, is given in Figure 12.12. It makes use of the class `Operation`, shown in Figure 12.13, whose objects contain two integers and an operator. `Operation` has two main methods: `calculate` performs the operation on the two integers and returns the result; its structure is a `switch` statement on the operator. And `parse` is a static method that interprets the user's input string, breaking it into an integer, an operator symbol, and an integer, and then places these values into an `Operation` object, which it then returns.

This code contains nothing really new. Note that in `Operation`, all methods are private (even the constructor) except `parse` and `calculate`, since these are the only two methods that clients should use.

The problem with this code is as we described above: If the user inputs 4/0, the calculator will terminate with an exception, instead of giving an error message and continuing.

```
1    import CSLib.*;
2
3    public class Calculator {
4      // Read string giving arithmetic expression and calculate
5      // Robert Klapper, Nov. 16, 1997
6
7      void calcloop () {
8        InputBox in = new InputBox("Calculator");
9        OutputBox out = new OutputBox("Calculator output");
10
11       while (true) {
12         String s = in.readString();
13         if (in.eoi()) return;
14         Operation op = Operation.parse(s);
15         int res = op.calculate();
16         out.println(s + " = " + res);
17       }
18     }
19
20   }
```

```
1    public class CalculatorClient {
2
3      //  Read string giving arithmetic expression and calculate
4
5      public static void main (String[] args) {
6        new Calculator().calcloop();
7      }
8    }
```

FIGURE 12.12   Main loop of the calculator, without error recovery, and client.

> **QUICK EXERCISE 12.8**   Consider how you would solve this problem without using Java's exception mechanism.

To recover cleanly from bad input (i.e., division by zero), we can put the call to calculate into a try block. This code is shown in Figure 12.14. When it is executed, if the user inputs a division by zero, it produces an ErrorBox with an error message; after the user dismisses the ErrorBox, the program continues.

We note that there are a variety of other kinds of invalid inputs that could cause trouble from which we make no attempt to recover. We will return to this in a little while.

> **QUICK EXERCISE 12.9**   Two kinds of errors are bad integers and bad operator symbols. Try these two inputs and report what happens: 40+x   50&43.

```
1    public class Operation {
2
3      // Objects represent the operands and operator of an
4      //  arithmetic expression.
5      // Rachel Reingold,  Jan. 31, 2000
6
7      private int opnd1, opnd2;
8      private char optr; // must be +, -, /, or *
9
10     private Operation (int opnd1, int opnd2, char optr) {
11       this.opnd1 = opnd1;
12       this.opnd2 = opnd2;
13       this.optr = optr;
14     }
15
16     static Operation parse (String s) {
17       // s should have form "integer op integer"
18       // Divide into three parts and return Operation object
19
20       int i = getInteger(s, 0);
21       int opnd1 = Integer.parseInt(inputfrag);
22
23       char optr = s.charAt(i);
24
25       i = getInteger(s, i+1);
26       int opnd2 = Integer.parseInt(inputfrag);
27
28       return new Operation(opnd1, opnd2, optr);
29     }
30
31     private static String inputfrag;
32
33     private static int getInteger (String s, int loc) {
34       int endloc = loc;
35       do { endloc++; }
36       while (endloc < s.length() && isDigit(s.charAt(endloc))) ;
37       inputfrag = s.substring(loc, endloc);
38       return endloc;
39     }
40
41     private static boolean isDigit (char c) {
42       return ('0' <= c && c <= '9');
43     }
44
45     int calculate () {
46       switch (optr) {
47         case '+': return opnd1+opnd2;
48         case '-': return opnd1-opnd2;
49         case '/': return opnd1/opnd2;
50         case '*': return opnd1*opnd2;
51       }
52       return 0;   // shouldn't happen!
53     }
54   }
```

FIGURE 12.13 Operation **class, with** parse **and** calculate.

```
1    import CSLib.*;
2
3    public class Calculator {
4
5      // Read string giving arithmetic expression and calculate
6      // Robert Klapper, Nov. 16, 1997
7
8      void calcloop () {
9        InputBox in = new InputBox("Calculator");
10       OutputBox out = new OutputBox("Calculator output");
11
12       while (true) {
13         String s = in.readString();
14         if (in.eoi()) return;
15         Operation op = Operation.parse(s);
16         try { int res = op.calculate();
17             out.println(s + " = " + res);
18           }
19         catch (ArithmeticException ae) {
20             new ErrorBox ("Error: " + ae.getMessage());
21           }
22       }
23     }
24   }
```

FIGURE 12.14   Main loop of the calculator, with error recovery.

We have now seen the basics of the try/catch statement, which we summarize:

- If a method m is concerned that an exception, say someException, might occur during its execution, it can place the suspect code in a try/catch statement:

  ```
  try {
      code that might throw  SomeException
  }
  catch (SomeException se) {
      code to recover from error
  }
  ```

  Note that the try statement need not include the entire body of m. The try/catch statement can occur anywhere that a statement can occur. The body of the try statement may consist of just one statement, and there may be several try statements in m's body.
- Now, suppose the body of the try statement in m contains a call to n, and the body of n calls p. Assume also that neither n nor p contains try statements.

- A `SomeException` occurs in p. A `SomeException` object is created, initialized, and thrown.
- There is an immediate return from p to n. Since n does not have a `try` statement (the case where it does is discussed below), it immediately returns to m.
- Execution resumes in m in the catch block for `SomeException`. The exception object `se` can be queried for information about the error by sending it the `getMessage` message (or any other messages that the `SomeException` class has defined).

QUICK EXERCISE 12.10

Write methods that throw each of the exceptions listed in Table 12.3. You will know when you've succeeded because the program will terminate with an error message giving the name of the exception. It is easy to see how to produce each type of exception, except that the simplest attempts don't always work. For example, if you place the expression `1/0` in the middle of a method, it probably will *not* cause an `ArithmeticException`, because the *compiler* will recognize it and eliminate it from the code. On the other hand, if you read x from the user and then calculate `1/x`, then a zero input from the user will definitely produce the exception.

Once you are able to *produce* each of these errors, modify these four programs so that they *catch* the error and recover in some way (such as by prompting the user for another input).

In the following sections we elaborate on this basic mechanism, and then we show how to create and throw your own exceptions.

12.3.2 Control Flow through Exceptions

One question we left open in the above discussion is this: Suppose a method called from within a `try` statement has a `try` statement itself and catches the same exception. To be concrete, our methods m, n, and p might look like this.[3]

```
void m () {
    ...
    try { ... n() ... }
    catch (ArrayIndexOutOfBoundsException ae) {
        ...
    }
    ...
}
```

---

[3]These methods may, and probably will, be in different classes, and even in different packages, despite the way we have placed them together in this example.

```
void n () {
    ...
    try { ... p() ... }
    catch (ArrayIndexOutOfBoundsException ae) {
        ...
    }
    ...
}


void p () { ... A[i] ... }
```

Now, m calls n from its `try` statement, and then n calls p from its `try` statement, and then p gets into trouble and throws an `ArrayIndexOutOfBoundsException`. Who will handle it, n's catch block, m's catch block, or both? The answer is n's catch block.

When an exception is thrown, control returns from that method and from its calling method, and so on, just until control gets to a method that made its call from within a `try` statement that contains a catch block for that exception. In other words, it returns to the most recent call that is able to handle the exception. In that case, what about the catch block in m? It is not executed. In fact, since n handles the error, m will never even know that it occurred.

There is one exception to this rule: In its catch block, n may decide that it wants to "pass the buck" to m, because it is incapable of recovering from the error. In this case, n's catch block can "rethrow" the exception by executing a `throw` statement. Control will then flow back to m's catch block, as if n had not caught the error:

```
void n () {
    ...
    try { ... p() ... }
    catch (ArrayIndexOutOfBoundsException ae) {
        if (able to handle error) {
            handle it
        }
        else throw ae;
    }
    ...
}
```

Thus, when p throws the error, controls flows to n's catch block. If n executes the `throw` statement, the process continues, with control returning to the most recent call that can handle this exception (namely, m).

QUICK EXERCISE **12.11**	Take one of the programs you wrote for Quick Exercise 12.10 and insert an extra method in between the code that produces the exception and the code that handles it; that method should simply rethrow the exception.

12.3.3 Uncaught Exceptions and the `finally` Clause

The `ArrayIndexOutOfBoundsException` is just one of many exceptions in Java (see Table 12.3). Suppose we have a `try` statement, like the ones above, that handles the `ArrayIndexOutOfBoundsException`. Suppose that during execution of this statement's body, some method throws a `NullPointerException`. Control returns from the offending method in search of a catch block for `NullPointerException`. When it gets back to the `try` statement that handles `ArrayIndexOutOfBoundsExceptions`, it treats it just as if this weren't a `try` statement at all: It just immediately returns to that method's caller and keeps looking for a `NullPointerException` handler.

For example, suppose we have

```
void m () {
    ...
    try { ... n() ... }
    catch (ArrayIndexOutOfBoundsException ae) { ... }
    ...
}

void n () {
    ...
    try { ... p() ... }
    catch (NullPointerException npe) { ... }
    ...
}

void p () { ... A[i] ... anObject.v ... }
```

Now m calls n which calls p. Depending upon the circumstances, p may throw an `ArrayIndexOutOfBoundsException`, if i is an invalid index, or a `NullPointerException`, if anObject was not properly initialized. (Hopefully it will throw neither.) If it throws a `NullPointerException`, then n will catch it and handle it; as before, m never even knows an exception has occurred. If p throws an `ArrayIndexOutOfBoundsException`, then control returns briefly to n, finds that n cannot handle this type of exception, and continues its search, returning to m, which can and does handle it. There is one more case to consider: Suppose the `catch` block in n contains a `throw` statement. If p throws a `NullPointerException`, then n's catch block will be executed until it executes the `throw` statement. As before, it will stop and control will return to m, in search of a catch block that can handle this exception. Since m cannot handle a `NullPointerException`, control will immediately return to m's caller and the search will continue. Hopefully, there is an appropriate catch block somewhere farther up the call chain.

A problem can arise from the fact that returns through `try` statements are too "immediate." When p throws an `ArrayIndexOutOfBoundsException`, the return through n to m's catch block does not give n a chance to regain control even for an instant. The problem is that n may need to do some "cleaning up" before it returns. Maybe, before it calls p, n opens a window on the screen, with the intention of closing it after p returns. When p returns by throwing an exception that n doesn't handle, n never gets the opportunity to close the window. (Of course, the caller of n knows nothing about this window and cannot close it, so the window will remain on the screen indefinitely.)

finally The Java try statement includes an optional *finally* clause to cope with this problem:

```
try { ... }
catch (SomeException se) { ... }
finally { ... }
```

The statements in the finally clause will always be executed, no matter how the body of the try statement terminates. Thus, if n is

```
void n () {
    ...
    try {
        ...    open window ... p() ...
    }
    catch (SomeException se) { ... }
    finally {
        ...    close window ...
    }
    ...
}
```

the window will get closed no matter what: If the try block executes without provoking any exceptions, the finally clause will be executed after the body of the try statement is done; if p throws SomeException, so that control passes from the call to p directly to the catch block, the finally clause will be executed after the catch block finishes; if p throws SomeException and then the catch block decides to rethrow it, the finally clause will be executed before the return to the caller; and if p throws SomeOtherException that this try statement cannot handle, then the finally clause will be executed before control passes out of n in search of a handler.

QUICK EXERCISE 12.12

Again try this using one of the programs you wrote for Quick Exercise 12.10. Pop up a DrawingBox, call a method that throws an exception, and then close the DrawingBox by sending the close message. Then do the same thing but place the close call in the finally clause. (Because execution is likely to go by quickly, you won't be able to see the difference between the two versions unless you place some delays in the code using Timer.pause(1000).)

12.3.4 Handling Multiple Exceptions

The general form of the `try/catch` statement is

```
try {   body of statement }
catch ( ExceptionClass1   name1) { ... }
catch ( ExceptionClass2   name2) { ... }
...
catch ( ExceptionClassn   namen) { ... }
finally { ... }
```

where n can be any number greater than zero, and the `finally` clause is optional. The semantics of this statement is as follows: The body is executed. If at any time during its execution an exception is thrown—and if it is not caught by another method first—control returns to this statement. Whatever the body was doing is halted. If the thrown exception object has any of the types `ExceptionClass1`, ..., `ExceptionClassn`, then that catch block is executed. If it finishes without rethrowing the exception, then the `finally` clause is executed and control flows to the next statement; if it executes a `throw` statement, then the `finally` clause is executed, control returns to the calling method, and the search for a handler for that exception continues.

This general form allows us to catch more than one type of error:

```
void m () {
    ...
    try { ... n() ... }
    catch (ArrayIndexOutOfBoundsException ae) { ... }
    catch (NullPointerException npe) { ... }
    ...
}

void n () { ... A[i] ... anObject.v ... }
```

> **QUICK EXERCISE 12.13**
>
> Place all your exception-generating methods into one class and call each of them from one `try` block, with `catch` blocks for each type of exception.

12.3.5 The `Exception` Hierarchy

A `try` statement can indiscriminately catch all errors by using the special exception class `Exception`:

```
try { ... }
catch (Exception e) {
    ... handle any kind of exception ...
}
```

This raises the question: What if we have a catch block for `Exception` *and* one for `ArrayIndexOutOfBoundsException`?

```
try { ... }
catch (ArrayIndexOutOfBounds ae) { ... }
catch (Exception e) { ...   }
```

If an `ArrayIndexOutOfBoundsException` is thrown, which handler is executed? In fact, this raises a question about `Exception` itself: How can an `Exception` handler catch an `ArrayIndexOutOfBoundsException` at all, given that `Exception` is not the type of an `ArrayIndexOutOfBoundsException` object?

The exception mechanism uses inheritance to classify exceptions. All the exception classes are in a single inheritance hierarchy, whose root class is `Exception`.[4] If a catch block names an exception class, then it will catch any error object created by a class in that class's hierarchy.

The rule for catch blocks is simple: Go through the catch blocks in order until a clause is found that catches that exception, and execute that one. In the example above, the first catch block—the one for `ArrayIndexOutOfBoundsException`—is the one that is executed. What if we had written that statement as follows?

```
try { ... }
catch (Exception e) { ...   }
catch (ArrayIndexOutOfBounds ae) { ... }
```

Clearly, this makes no sense in that the second catch block will never be executed. Since every exception object is in the `Exception` hierarchy, the first catch clause will always be the one executed. In fact, the Java compiler will produce an error message in this case, complaining that the second catch block can never be reached.

RunTimeException

unchecked exceptions

`Exception` has one special subclass called *RunTimeException*.[5] Any exceptions that are in the `RunTimeException` hierarchy have the distinction that they do not *have* to be caught; they are called *unchecked exceptions*. `ArrayIndexOutOfBoundsException` and `NullPointerException` are unchecked exceptions. That is why we have been able to avoid handling these exceptions throughout this book.

checked exceptions

mandatory exceptions

All exceptions that are in the `Exception` hierarchy but not in the `RunTimeException` hierarchy *must* be either handled or "declared." (We will see what *declared* means in Section 12.3.7.) These are called *checked exceptions*, or *mandatory exceptions*. It so happens that most of the exceptions in those parts of Java that we have studied—in particularly, the `java.lang` package—are in the `RunTimeException` class, which makes them unchecked exceptions. The `java.awt` and `java.io` packages have numerous examples of checked exceptions, but we have not studied these packages yet. Exceptions that programmers define themselves are usually checked. So we will go on to the next aspect of the exception mechanism: creating our own exception classes.

---

[4]Actually, `Exception` has a superclass `Throwable`, whose objects can also be thrown and caught, but we will not have occasion to look any more closely at this technicality.

[5]Rather oddly, since all exceptions occur at run time.

12.3.6 Creating and Throwing Exceptions

It is often convenient to create your own types of exceptions, representing circumstances that you consider exceptional in your own program but that might not otherwise be exceptional. For example, your program may request input from the user which must be, say, an integer between 0 and 100. If you use the `readInt` method in `InputBox`, any integer will be acceptable. The `readInt` method sees nothing wrong with integers outside of the 0–100 range; this is an error in your program but not in the world at large. In this case, you might find it advantageous to create an `InvalidIntegerException` class, so that you can use the `try/catch` statement to handle this situation.

Creating exceptions is extremely simple: Just define a class in the `Exception` hierarchy:

```
class InvalidIntegerException extends Exception {
    ...
}
```

Since `Exception` itself is defined in `java.lang`, you do not even have to add an `import` statement. It is merely by convention that names of exception classes are given the suffix `Exception`; it is not a requirement of the language.

Exception classes are like any other classes, their location in the `Exception` hierarchy being their only distinguishing characteristic. They can have variables and methods and can be as complicated as you like. In practice, however, they are usually small, containing only the instance variables needed to hold a description of the exception and only the methods needed to access those variables.

The `Exception` class itself has only one method, which is, of course, inherited by all classes in its hierarchy, namely,

```
String getMessage ()
```

which returns a string descriptive of the exception. `Exception` also defines a null constructor and a one-argument constructor, `Exception(String)`, which allows the client to place the descriptive message into the object. By convention, you should also supply a constructor with a `String` argument. Thus, most exception classes are as simple as this:

```
class InvalidIntegerException extends Exception {

    InvalidIntegerException (String s) {
        super(s);
    }

    InvalidIntegerException () {
        this("");
    }
}
```

You can create more specialized exceptions with equal ease:

```
class IntegerTooBigException extends InvalidIntegerException {
    ...
}

class IntegerTooSmallException extends InvalidIntegerException {
    ...
}
```

Then elsewhere in the program you have the choice of catching all invalid inputs in one block

```
try { ... getUserInput() ... }
catch (InvalidIntegerException iie) { ... }
```

or catching them separately

```
try { ... getUserInput() ... }
catch (IntegerTooBigException itbe) { ... }
catch (IntegerTooSmallException itse) { ... }
```

12.3.7 Declaring Exceptions in Method Headers

Having defined your own exception class, you can now create and throw objects of this class. You again use the `throw` statement

```
throw   expr;
```

where *expr* evaluates to an object of an exception class. The method that reads user inputs might throw the exception for some other method to handle:

```
int getUserInput () {                               Incorrect
    InputBox in = new InputBox();
    int i = in.readInt();
    if (i < 0 || i > 100)
        throw new InvalidIntegerException("Bad user input");
    return i;                                       Incorrect
}
```

However, there is a problem. Although correct in principle, the `getUserInput` message has an error that will require a bit of work to explain.

Exceptions that are not in the `RunTimeException` hierarchy, such as `InvalidIntegerException`, are, as we have mentioned before, *checked exceptions*: They *must* be either handled or declared. We know what it means to handle them: When you call a method that can throw such an exception, you do so inside a `try` statement that has a catch block for that exception. (It is not necessary for the catch block to do anything significant—it can even have an empty body—but it has to be there.) We now want to explain what "declaring" an exception means.

We start with a question: If Java insists that checked exceptions be handled, how does it know whether a particular method might throw a particular exception? It can look inside the body of the method for a `throw` statement, but that is unreliable for two reasons: The `throw` statement may just give an expression that evaluates to an exception object, providing no way to know, at compile time, what specific type of exception it might be; and, furthermore, the method might not itself *initiate* the throwing of the exception, but might just have that exception pass through it in search of a handler, as in

```
void m () {
    ...
    try { ... n() ... }
    catch (InvalidIntegerException iie) { ... }
    ...
}

void n () {
    ... p() ...
}

void p () {
    ... throw new InvalidIntegerException(); ...
}
```

The Java compiler cannot figure out that a call to n can throw an exception. Instead, the Java programmer is required to *declare* that a method may throw an exception. She does this by putting a throws clause in the method header:

```
void n () throws InvalidIntegerException {
    ... p() ...
}

void p () throws InvalidIntegerException {
    ... throw new InvalidIntegerException(); ...
}
```

p must declare that it may throw the exception, even though it is obvious from its body. (The throws clause does not say that p *always* throws this exception, only that it *might* throw it.) And n must declare that it can throw the exception, even though it only does so indirectly; it does *not* have to actually catch and rethrow the exception: The body of n does not change at all. As for m, nothing changes, not even its header; it does not throw this exception, it just *handles* it, so it does not put the throws clause in its header.

To return to the example that opened this section, we need to add a throws clause to make that method legal:

```
int getUserInput () throws InvalidIntegerException {
    InputBox in = new InputBox();
    int i = in.readInt();
    if (i < 0 || i > 100)
        throw new InvalidIntegerException("Bad user input");
    return i;
}
```

To reiterate: A method that may terminate by throwing a checked exception (whether it throws the exception itself or just lets it pass through) must declare that possibility with a throws clause in its method header. A method that calls another method containing a throws clause must, in turn, either handle the exception or declare, with a throws clause, that this exception may pass through it looking for a handler.

As a last point: If a method can produce more than one type of checked exception, it includes all of them in its throws clause, separated by commas.

12.3.8   The Calculator Example Continued

As we observed in discussing the calculator example the last time, there are several errors that might occur in a user's input from which we do not recover. These will not necessarily manifest themselves as arithmetic errors, but may cause some other problems. For example, if you give an input x+y, the method Integer.parseInt will be called with argument x, which does not look like an integer; that method will throw the NumberFormatException. Another possibility is that the user does not enter a valid operator; as written now (page 455), the calculate method just returns zero, but it should return an error.

So there are two corrections we should make: When we call Integer.parseInt in parse, we should look out for a NumberFormatException. When we call calculate, we should throw an exception so that the input loop can print an appropriate message. First, let's take care of the number problem. This is simple; just add a new catch block to the input loop:

```
import CSLib.*;

public class Calculator {
    // Read string giving arithmetic expression and calculate
    // Robert Klapper, Nov. 16, 1997

    void calcloop () {
        InputBox in = new InputBox("Calculator");
        OutputBox out = new OutputBox("Calculator output");

        while (true) {
            String s = in.readString();
            if (in.eoi()) return;
            try { Operation op = Operation.parse(s);
                  int res = op.calculate();
                  out.println(s + " = " + res);
            }
            catch (ArithmeticException ae) {
                new ErrorBox ("Error: " + ae.getMessage());
            }
            catch (NumberFormatException nfe) {
                new ErrorBox ("Input Format Error:"+ nfe.getMessage());
            }
        }
    }
}
```

The code now recovers cleanly from an erroneous input such as x+y. But if we give it as an input 4#2, it will return zero. Again, we could simply return a value from `calculate` that would indicate that there was an error, but what value could it be? Any integer could conceivably be the result of an arithmetic operation, including zero. The right thing to do here is to throw an exception, but which one? We will make up our own. Since the basic problem here is a parsing problem (invalid input), we will call the new class `ParseException`:

```
public class ParseException extends Exception {

    // Objects represent errors in parsing, such as
    // non-numbers or non-operators.

    ParseException (String s) {
        super("Parsing error: " + s);
    }

    ParseException () {
        super("");
    }

}
```

We change `calculate` to raise this exception instead of just returning zero

```
int calculate () throws ParseException {
    switch (optr) {
        case '+': return opnd1+opnd2;
        case '-': return opnd1-opnd2;
        case '/': return opnd1/opnd2;
        case '*': return opnd1*opnd2;
    }
    throw new ParseException("Bad operator");
}
```

and the input loop to catch it:

```
import CSLib.*;

public class Calculator {

    // Read string giving arithmetic expression and calculate
    // Robert Klapper, Nov. 16, 1997

    void calcloop () {
        InputBox in = new InputBox("Calculator");
        OutputBox out = new OutputBox("Calculator output");

        while (true) {
            String s = in.readString();
            if (in.eoi()) return;
            try {
                Operation op = Operation.parse(s);
                int res= op.calculate();
```

```
                    out.println(s + " = " + res);
            }
         catch (ArithmeticException ae) {
           new ErrorBox ("Error: " + ae.getMessage());
         }
         catch (NumberFormatException nfe) {
           new ErrorBox ("Error: " + nfe.getMessage());
         }
         catch (ParseException pe) {
           new ErrorBox (pe.getMessage());
         }
       }
     }
   }
```

QUICK EXERCISE 12.14	We haven't actually caught all parsing errors. See what happens when you input just 4+. Fix the code so that it recovers from this error.

Summary

The concatenation of the directory names (starting from a certain root directory) forms a *package name*. If you wish to use a class in a certain package, you can write out the *fully qualified name*, or you can use an `import` statement to identify the package, with one of two variants:

```
import  package_name.class_name;
import  package_name.*;
```

Inheritance allows a programmer to customize a class for a specific application without modifying that class at all. A new class is defined that inherits from the first class and adds or redefines its instance methods as necessary.

A class C is said to be subclass of B (or, equivalently, B is a superclass of C) if the declaration of C has the form

```
class C extends B {  // C is a subclass of B
   ...
}
```

Now, objects of class C can be used wherever objects of class B are expected; for example, a message defined in B can be sent to a C object, and a C object can be assigned to a variable of type B. The principle of dynamic binding dictates that the type of the receiver of a message determines which method should be invoked.

The visibility modifier `protected` can be used instead of `public` or `private`. Members declared after this keyword are visible to other classes in the same package and to subclasses defined in other packages but not to its clients in other packages. The effects of these combinations are summarized in Table 12.2.

The syntax for invoking the constructor of a superclass is

```
class C extends B {
    ...
    public C (...) {
        super ( B's constructor arguments) ;
        ...
    }
    ...
}
```

The modifier `abstract` in a class's header tells Java that the class can have no objects of its own (although its subclasses can). The method modifier `abstract` tells Java that the method is expected to be defined in a subclass. The syntax is

visibility_modifier `abstract` *return_type method_name* *(parameters)* ;

Whenever a class includes an abstract method, Java insists that the class itself be declared `abstract`. Such an abstract class *cannot be instantiated* by a client.

Java's exception-handling mechanism consists of three parts:

1. A mechanism for creating *exception classes*.
2. The `throw e` statement, used to signal the occurrence of an exception and return control to the calling method. Here, `e` is an expression that evaluates to an exception object. Executing this statement is called "throwing" the exception object.
3. The `try/catch` statement, that allows the calling method to "catch" the thrown exception object and take appropriate action.

The form for a `try/catch` statement is

```
try {
    ... code that might throw SomeException ...
}
catch (SomeException se) {
    ...code to recover from error ...
}
finally {
    ... cleanup code ...
}
```

The code in the `finally` clause will be executed whether an exception occurred or not.

An exception can be created by defining a subclass of `Exception`, providing simple constructors.

```
class InvalidIntegerException extends Exception {
    InvalidIntegerException (String s) {
        super(s);
```

```
        }

        InvalidIntegerException () {
            this ("");
        }
    }
```

Such an exception can be thrown by the statement

```
    throw new InvalidIntegerException();
```

If a method wants to throw such an exception, the method header must declare that the exception might be thrown. An example is:

```
    int getUserInput () throws InvalidIntegerException {
        InputBox in = new InputBox();
        int i = in.readInt();
        if (i < 0 || i > 100)
            throw new InvalidIntegerException("Bad user inut");
        return i;
    }
```

Exercises

1. Any class, C, that contains a single instance of some class B, can often be rewritten to be a subclass of B instead. Early in this book we saw many examples of a class that contains a single instance of some other class. Rewrite some of them to use subclassing instead.

   (a) The WarningMouse class that from Chapter 2 contained a TrickMouse. Rewrite the WarningMouse so that it is a subclass of TrickMouse.

   (b) The Rectangle class from Chapter 2 contained a DrawingBox. Rewrite Rectangle so that it is a subclass of DrawingBox.

   (c) The Surprise class from Chapter 6 contained a DrawingBox. Rewrite Surprise so that it is a subclass of DrawingBox. Change the setup method to be a Surprise constructor.

   (d) The Crossword class from Chapter 9 was passed a DrawingBox by its client. Rewrite Crossword so that it is a subclass of DrawingBox, and change the client accordingly.

   (e) The MouseController class from Chapter 10 contained a DrawingBox. Rewrite MouseController so that it is a subclass of DrawingBox, adding a constructor to do the setup. Redraw the UML class diagram for this collection of classes.

   (f) The ClickableClock class from Chapter 11 contained a DrawingBox. Rewrite ClickableClock so that it is a subclass of DrawingBox.

   (g) The TwoEyes class from Chapter 11 contained a DrawingBox. Rewrite TwoEyes so that it is a subclass of DrawingBox.

   (h) The Draw class from Chapter 11 contained a DrawingBox. Rewrite Draw so that it is a subclass of DrawingBox.

   (i) Rewrite your code for the "Eyes" Exercise 1 of Chapter 11 so that your application is a subclass of DrawingBox.

   (j) Rewrite your code for the "Game of Life" Exercise 3 of Chapter 11 so that your application is a subclass of DrawingBox.

(k) Rewrite your code for the "Tic-tac-toe" Exercise 4 of Chapter 11 so that your application is a subclass of `DrawingBox`.

(l) Rewrite your code for the clickable `MouseMazeClient` Exercise 5 of Chapter 11 so that your application is a subclass of `DrawingBox`.

(m) Rewrite your code for the drawing Exercises 6, 7, and 8 of Chapter 11 so that your applications are subclasses of `DrawingBox`.

2. Add an instance method to the `Mouse` class—`public void makeRecordMove()`—which simply invokes the method `makeMove()` and then records the new location and direction for the mouse. Use a large array to record the configurations for the mouse. The client of `Mouse` (namely, `MouseController`) should be changed to invoke the instance method `makeRecordMove()` instead of `makeMove()`. When the mouse has completed its navigation, the client should print a summary of the mouse's moves. (You need to provide yet another instance method of `Mouse` to accomplish this.)

3. Now that the base `Mouse` class can monitor its subclasses (acting like a good "parent" to its "children"), we can allow the superclass to intervene when something bad happens. That is, you should modify `makeRecordMove` so that it can prevent the mouse from running in circles. First, define a new protected method, `void backup()`. Now, when `makeMove()` returns to `makeRecordMove()` with a new configuration (location *and* direction) *that the mouse has already experienced*, `makeRecordMove()` should refuse that suggestion and invoke *another* method—`makeAlternativeMove (int attempt)`—which will choose a different move. The `makeRecordMove()` similarly may reject *that* suggestion and ask `makeAlternativeMove(int attempt)` for another. If, after three tries, `makeAlternativeMove(int attempt)` is unable to find a suitable move, then `makeRecordMove()` should cause the mouse to back up.

13 JAVA AWT PART II (OPTIONAL)

CHAPTER PREVIEW

Java is a fine programming language, yet it is not for that alone that it has generated so much excitement, but for its potential role in animating the World Wide Web. In this chapter we discuss the meaning of that role, and we begin to show how you can animate your own small part of the web by writing applets in Java. We first introduce Java graphical components, including text fields, buttons, and labels, and we show how Java programs can be made to react to users' actions upon those components. By doing this, we will no longer have to rely on the CSLib package to write graphical programs. We further show how the Java applications that we've written can be run from within web browsers.

The fundamental things apply,
As time goes by.

—Herman Huupfeld
"As Time Goes By"

Suit the action to the word, the word to the action.

—William Shakespeare
Hamlet

The Java system comes with certain predefined methods such as `Math.sqrt (double d)`. The classes and methods provided with the Java compiler (or any compiler for any language) are called the *application programming interface* (*API*). The API is provided to make it easier to program applications and applets. The Java API consists of a large collection of classes (several hundred), each with many methods. All are organized into *packages*. The Java API includes more than 36 packages, at last count. They contain classes and methods for everything from generating random numbers to loading sound files to accessing Internet sites. However, we use only a small number of the packages. In fact, in the main part of this book we use only four: `java.applet`, `java.awt`, `java.awt.event`, and `java.lang`.

application programming interface

packages

13.1

The Java AWT

We have seen how `java.awt` and `java.awt.event` appeared in the `import` statements in some of our applications. Those `import` statements were included so that all the classes in those packages would be available to our application.

There is a reason why we did not explicitly import the `java.lang` packages. This is the only package that is automatically imported in every Java program; saying `import java.lang.*` would be redundant. This package contains classes such as `Math` and `String`, which are so basic that everyone will use them frequently.

473

The java.awt and java.awt.event packages are another matter. We have often used the Point class from java.awt, but other than that we have used these classes very little. The java.awt.event package was used only in the optional Chapter 11. We'll use many more of their classes in this chapter.

abstract
windowing toolkit

The acronym awt stands for *abstract windowing toolkit*. The classes in this package are used to create all sorts of stuff that one normally associates with

graphical user
interfaces

graphical user interfaces (*GUIs*): buttons, menus, text areas, scroll bars, and so on. Each of these items, called *components*, has an associated class. The package

components

java.awt.event contains classes that allow us to interact with the graphical components.

There are two important components that we have already seen indirectly, the Frame and the Dialog components. Our CSLib's DrawingBox and OutputBox are really variants of Frame, while our InputBox and ErrorBox are variants of Dialog. Frame and Dialog are special Java components that are sometimes referred to as the *windows* in a GUI.

Until now, we have relied on the DrawingBox class from the CSLib package for writing graphical programs. However, real Java graphical programs require much more powerful packages and classes. The class that we will use in place of our DrawingBox is Java's Frame class.

A Frame is merely a window with a title bar and a border. A typical Java GUI application will create and display one or more Frames, often arranging other components inside these Frames. A Frame is initially not visible; your program must make it visible by sending the setVisible(true) message to it. The Frame class is a subclass of java.awt's Window class, which in

Container

turn is a subclass of the *Container* class; the Container class is capable of having other components added to it via the add method. One component that can be added to a Frame is the Button component. The Button has a label and can be "clicked on" by the user, appearing to depress and pop back.

For example, you can create and place a pair of buttons in a frame as follows:

```
1    Frame f = new Frame("Two Buttons Frame");
2    Button redButton = new Button("Red");
3    Button blueButton = new Button("Blue");
4    f.add(redButton);
5    f.add(blueButton);
6    f.setVisible(true);
```

In line 1 we create a Frame, passing a string to the constructor for the title of the Frame (just as with CSLib's DrawingBox and others). In lines 2 and 3 we create two Buttons; the string argument gives the label that will appear on the Button. Then we add the Buttons to the Frame and make the Frame visible.

There's actually a bit more that we have to do to get a properly working program, but fundamentally the above code is correct. But how exactly are components added to a Container? Are they stacked one on top of the other? Or are they arranged in random locations within the Frame? Clearly not. The answer is that there is a *LayoutManager* object that governs how components are arranged within a Container. The Container class has a method setLayout(LayoutManager) that allows the programmer to specify a particular LayoutManager. The one that we'll use for now is the easiest to understand, the *FlowLayout manager.*

LayoutManager

FlowLayout manager

The FlowLayout manager arranges added components in a line from left to right, flowing to the next line as needed. Of course, just as we saw with DrawingBox and OutputBox, we can set the size of a Container by using the setSize (int width, int height) method. Indeed, if we fail to set the size of a Container, then it shows up as a very small window—too small to show its contained components. (Containers are resizable, so the user can increase the size by using the mouse and thereby bring the contained components into view.) So here's the same code, with the Frame size set and with a layout manager specified:

```
1    import java.awt.*;
2
3    public class TwoButtons {
4       Frame f;
5       Button redButton, blueButton;
6
7       public TwoButtons () {
8          f = new Frame("Two Buttons Frame");
9          redButton = new Button("Red");
10         blueButton = new Button("Blue");
11         f.setLayout(new FlowLayout());
12         f.add(redButton);
13         f.add(blueButton);
14         f.setSize(100, 50);
15         f.setVisible(true);
16      }
17   }
```

Running this program results in the following output.

Our guess for the size of the Frame wasn't very good. But there is an elegant way to adjust the size of a container to be just large enough to

BUG ALERT 13.2	***Be Sure to Make the Frame Visible.***
	A Frame is not visible until it receives the setVisible(true) message.

preferred size   accommodate its contained components. Every component has a *preferred size*.
pack()   By sending to a Container the *pack()* message, it will be resized to be just
large enough to hold all its components set to their preferred sizes. In addition to
methods for setting and getting a Component's actual size, there are methods
setPreferredSize(...) and getPreferredSize(...) for manipulating a Component's preferred size. For a Button, the default preferred size
is just large enough to contain the Button's label. Some components have a preferred size that is initially set to zero. Here's a complete application incorporating
these concepts.

```
1   import java.awt.*;
2
3   public class TwoButtons {
4       Frame f;
5       Button redButton, blueButton;
6
7       public TwoButtons () {
8           f = new Frame("Two Buttons Frame");
9           redButton = new Button("Red");
10          blueButton = new Button("Blue");
11          f.setLayout(new FlowLayout());
12          f.add(redButton);
13          f.add(blueButton);
14          f.pack();
15          f.setVisible(true);
16      }
17  }
```

Running this program results in the following output.

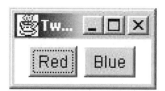

If you click on either of the buttons, they appear to "depress" as buttons normally
do, but of course, no action is taken. We must program them to perform some
sort of action. We'll see how to do that just a bit later in this chapter.

A class diagram is shown in Figure 13.1. It shows that the TwoButtons
class *contains* one Frame and two Button instances. However, it does not
show all the details that we know about these and other classes. For example, the

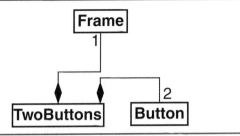

FIGURE 13.1 A UML class diagram for the `TwoButtons` **program.**

methods are not explicitly shown, nor are the superclasses (such as `Component` and `Container`) shown. A good UML diagram should show only the classes and associations that are important to understanding things; extraneous classes and relationships just clutter the diagram.

13.1.1 Using Inheritance

Notice that in the `TwoButtons` program, the client creates an instance of the `TwoButtons` class, which in turn creates an instance of a `Frame`. By using inheritance, we can cause the `TwoButtons` class *itself* to *be* the frame. So the client can create an instance of a `TwoButtons`, which would itself be a `Frame`. Thereafter, the `TwoButtons` constructor would add components to *itself*. The effect is that the client no longer has to worry about creating a separate `Frame`. Rather, the `TwoButtons` class has all the characteristics that are desired. This code has the same effect as the previous version:

```
1   import java.awt.*;
2
3   public class TwoButtons extends Frame {
4     Button redButton, blueButton;
5
6     public TwoButtons () {
7       super("Two Buttons Frame");
8       redButton = new Button("Red");
9       blueButton = new Button("Blue");
10      setLayout(new FlowLayout());
11      add(redButton);
12      add(blueButton);
13      pack();
14      setVisible(true);
15    }
16  }
```

In line 3 we see that class `TwoButtons` extends class `Frame`. In line 7 we see the use of `super` to set the superclass `Frame`'s title (see Section 12.2.4 on

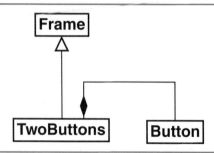

FIGURE 13.2   A UML class diagram for the alternative TwoButtons
program.

page 434). Throughout the body of the constructor, where we previously sent messages to an instantiated frame f, we now send the messages to the TwoButtons object itself. Another way of viewing this is that the TwoButtons instance sends messages to this implicitly. It is often confusing to the novice to see the TwoButtons constructor sending messages to the instance that it is constructing! However, this mechanism is used often in Java. A new object already exists when a constructor is entered; it is referenced by this.

The UML class diagram for our new TwoButtons program is shown in Figure 13.2. This time, TwoButtons is a subclass of Frame, and as such, TwoButtons contains Buttons.

QUICK EXERCISE 13.1	The two buttons in these classes are labeled Red and Blue but are colored in the default color. Modify both versions of TwoButtons to draw the buttons in red and blue, respectively. You will need to consult the documentation for Button (Table 13.1).

13.1.2   Other Simple Components

Label
TextField
TextArea

Besides the Button, there are three other Java components that are very simple and easy to use: the *Label*, the *TextField*, and the *TextArea*. A Label component contains some text that can be set using either the constructor or the method setLabel (String s). A TextField is a box into which a user can type text. It is editable in simple ways (backspace, delete, etc.). The text can be retrieved using String getText (), and it can be set using setText (String s). Finally, the TextArea component is a multiline scrollable and editable text area. It is the basis for the OutputBox in the CSLib package. Text is appended to a TextArea by using the method append (String s); text can be inserted by using the method

Name	Description
Button ()	Constructs a new button.
Button (String l)	Constructs a new button with label l.
String getLabel ()	Gets the label for this button.
void setLabel (String l)	Sets the label of this button to l.
void addActionListener (ActionListener l)	Makes l a listener for action events from this button.

TABLE 13.1 Some methods of the Button class. Other methods are inherited from Component. addActionListener is explained in Section 13.2.

Name	Description
static int CENTER	Indicates that the label should be centered.
static int LEFT	Indicates that the label should be left-justified.
static int RIGHT	Indicates that the label should be right-justified.
Label ()	Constructs a new label.
Label (String s)	Constructs a new label with s as the text, left-justified.
Label (String s, int align)	Constructs a new label with s as the text, with the specified alignment.
String getText ()	Gets the text that for this label.
setText (String t)	Sets the text for this label to t.

TABLE 13.2 Some constants and methods of the Label class. Other methods are inherited from Component.

insert (String s, int position) and can be replaced by using the method replaceRange (String s, int start, int end). These four simple kinds of components are summarized in Tables 13.1, 13.2, 13.3, and 13.4. Each class represents a kind of component of a GUI. Like the Button, the Label, TextField, and TextArea have preferred sizes that are just large enough to accommodate them. Each of these GUI components is a subclass of the Component class; the important inherited methods are summarized in Table 13.5.

**QUICK EXERCISE
13.2**

To see what these components look like on your computer, create a class ComponentDemo that is like TwoButtons but instead of buttons includes a label, a text field, and a text area.

Name	Description
`TextField ()`	Constructs a new text field.
`TextField (int c)`	Constructs a new empty text field with c columns.
`TextField (String s)`	Constructs a new text field with s as the text.
`void addActionListener (ActionListener l)`	Makes l a listener for action events from this text field.
`void setColumns (int c)`	Sets the number of columns to c.
`String getText ()`	Gets the text that is in this text field.

TABLE 13.3   Some methods of the `TextField` class. Other methods are inherited from `Component`. `addActionListener` is explained in Section 13.2.

Name	Description
`TextArea ()`	Constructs a new text area.
`TextArea (int r, int c)`	Constructs a new empty text area with r rows and c columns.
`TextArea (String s)`	Constructs a new text area with s as the text.
`TextArea (String s, int r, int c)`	Constructs a new text area with r rows and c columns and with s as the text.
`void addActionListener (ActionListener l)`	Makes l a listener for action events from this text area.
`void append (String s)`	Appends s to the text in this text area.
`int getColumns ()`	Gets the number of columns in this text area.
`int getRows ()`	Gets the number of rows in this text area.
`void insert (String s, int p)`	Inserts s at position p in this text area.
`voiid replaceRanges (String s, int start, int end)`	Replaces text between positions start and end with s.
`void setColumns (int c)`	Sets the number of columns to c.
`void setRows (int r)`	Sets the number of rows to r.

TABLE 13.4   Some methods of the `TextArea` class. Other methods are inherited from `Component`. `addActionListener` is explained in Section 13.2.

Name	Description
`void addMouseListener` `        (MouseListener l)`	Makes l a listener for mouse events from this component.
`void addMouseMotionListener` `        (MouseMotionListener l)`	Makes l a listener for mouse motion events from this component.
`Color getBackground ()`	Gets the background color of this component.
`Font getFont ()`	Gets the font of this component.
`FontMetrics` `    getFontMetrics (Font f)`	Gets the font metrics for the font f.
`Color getForeground ()`	Gets the foreground color for this component.
`Graphics getGraphics ()`	Gets the graphics context for this component.
`int getHeight ()`	Gets the height of this component.
`Dimension getMinimumSize ()`	Gets the minimum size of this component.
`Dimension getPreferredSize ()`	Gets the preferred size of this component.
`Dimension getSize ()`	Gets the size of this component.
`int getWidth ()`	Gets the width of this component.
`void paint (Graphics g)`	Paints this component.
`void paintAll (Graphics g)`	Paints this component and its subcomponents.
`void repaint ()`	Requests a repaint of this component.
`void setAlignment (int align)`	Sets the alignment for the label text.
`void setFont (Font f)`	Sets the font of this component.
`void setForeground (Color c)`	Sets the foreground of this component.
`void setSize (int w, int h)`	Sets the size of this component.
`void setSize (Dimension d)`	Alternate version of setSize.
`void setVisible (boolean b)`	Shows or hides this component depending on b.
`String toString ()`	Stringifies this component.
`void update (Graphics g)`	Updates this component (clear it and paint it).

TABLE 13.5 Some methods of the `Component` class. These methods are discussed in this chapter.

13.2

The Java AWT Event Model

Components should do more than just take up space in your program's window. Clicking on a button or typing in a text field should cause something to happen. This is where the package `java.awt.event` comes in; its classes define various types of events, such as the event of a user clicking on a button. The various reactive components work very similarly to the mouse events that we saw in Chapter 11. The major difference is that the mouse is not affiliated with any on-screen artifact, whereas buttons, text fields, and other reactive components do have on-screen artifacts.

In order to include a reactive component, such as a `Button`, in programs, the basic steps are as follows:

1. In the class heading, the program declares itself to implement the `ActionListener` interface.

2. Typically in the constructor, once the `Button` has been created, `this` object registers itself as being interested in listening for events from the `Button` by sending the add `ActionListener` message to the button.

3. The one method of the `ActionListener` interface (namely, `actionPerformed`) is defined. The `ActionEvent` argument can be used to find out more about the event. The method `actionPerformed` is invoked when the event (a button press) occurs. The `ActionListener` interface is shown in Table 13.6.

These steps are summarized in Figure 13.3.

Once again, a UML class diagram is useful for illustrating the associations between classes. The UML diagram for the skeletal code of Figure 13.3 is shown in Figure 13.4. The UML generalization and composition associations are just as they were for the second version of `TwoButtons`. But this time we include additional information about Java events. We see that `Button` has a "generates" association with `ActionEvents`; the `ActionEvents` in turn are "listened for" by the `classname`. Finally, in order for `classname` to be able to fulfill its role as an event listener, it must implement the Java interface `ActionListener`. UML notation for a Java interface is indicated by italicizing the interface name;

Method	Purpose
`void actionPerformed (ActionEvent e)`	Called when any action event occurs

TABLE 13.6 The `ActionListener` interface. Action events are generated by buttons and text fields.

```
public class classname extends Frame implements ActionListener {
  ...
  Button buttonname;  // or TextField
  ...

  public classname () {
    ...
    buttonname = new Button("button label");
    ...
    add(buttonname);
    ...
    buttonname.addActionListener(this);
    ...
  }

  ...

  public void actionPerformed (ActionEvent e) {
    ... what to do when buttonname is pushed ...
  }
}
```

FIGURE 13.3 Outline of a program with one reactive component, a button. (Other types of reactive components are similar. Programs with more than one reactive component are discussed later in this chapter.)

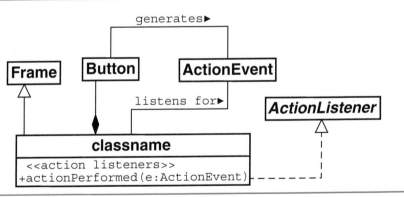

FIGURE 13.4 A UML class diagram for a program with a Button.

the *implements association* is indicated by a dashed line with a closed, unfilled   *UML implements*
arrowhead at the abstract class end. We could have just anchored the tail of   *association*
this "implements" association at the edge of classname. But here we can
provide just a little more information—we group the methods of classname and

anchor the tail of the "implements" association near the method(s) that actually implement(s) the interface methods. This is an example where it makes sense to group the methods of a class—constructors, accessors, etc., including those methods that provide the implementation for an interface. That group of methods can be separated by a *UML stereotype*, which is a descriptive word enclosed in guillemets ≪ ≫.

UML stereotype

Let's give a simple example. We'll flesh out the outline of Figure 13.3. The text in the button will be a stringified integer, and each click of the button will increment the integer:

```
1    import java.awt.*;
2    import java.awt.event.*;
3
4    public class ButtonInt extends Frame
5                           implements ActionListener {
6
7        Button intButton;
8        int count = 0;          // our counter
9
10       public ButtonInt () {
11           super("Button Counter");
12           intButton = new Button("" + count);
13           setLayout(new FlowLayout());
14           add(intButton);
15           intButton.addActionListener(this);
16           pack();
17           setVisible(true);
18       }
19
20       public void actionPerformed (ActionEvent e) {
21           count++;
22           intButton.setLabel("" + count);
23       }
24   }
```

Whenever the `Button intButton` is pressed, the `actionPerformed` method is called. It increments `count`, changes the label of `intButton`, and asks that the frame be repainted. The output after the button has been pressed three times is

Actually, this same idea works for `TextFields` and `Buttons` but needs to be modified slightly for some other components. For example, some components are registered as `ItemListeners` instead of `ActionListeners`, using the method `addItemListener` instead of `addActionListener`. We will

cross this bridge when we get to it. Another complicating factor is that a program may contain more than one reactive component, and `actionPerformed` needs to know which one to react to; we will deal with this issue shortly.

Write a class `ButtonToggle` that has a single button whose label switches between `On` and `Off` each time it is clicked.

13.3

A Temperature Conversion GUI

Our next example shows the use of text fields. Recall the temperature conversion program from Section 3.10 on page 68. Let's rewrite that program to take its input from a `TextField`, and to produce its output in a `Label`, with each component placed in the `Frame`.

Our program, called `TempConversion`, creates a `TextField` in which to enter a number; that number is interpreted as a number of degrees on the Fahrenheit scale, and its equivalent on the Centigrade scale is displayed. The program is shown in Figure 13.5, and a snapshot of the program's output is shown in Figure 13.6.

The first few lines are just as in the prototype in Figure 13.3. We have the usual `import` statements, the `extends Frame` clause, the `implements ActionListener` clause, the constructor, and the required method `actionPerformed`.

Notice how, in lines 9 and 10, we have declared the objects `tFahr` and `lCent`. The reason for the strange-looking names is that we have used a convention for naming variables that refer to components, in which the first letter tells something about the nature of the component. In these cases, the leading `t` tells us that `tFahr` refers to a `TextField` component, and the leading `l` tells us that `lCent` refers to a `Label` component. As with other naming conventions, this is merely a suggestion that sometimes helps us remember what a variable means. You might imagine that, without some sort of naming convention, we might use the name `labelCent` on one day, `outputCent` on another, and `centMessage` on yet another. In graphical programs, variables that refer to components (such as `lCent` and `tFahr`) are usually instance variables, so that they can be initialized by the constructor and accessed by listeners and other methods.

Other familiar parts of the program are seen in lines 14 through 27, where the frame details are handled (setting the title via the `super` constructor, setting

```
1    import java.awt.*;
2    import java.awt.event.*;
3
4    public class Temperature extends Frame
5                          implements ActionListener {
6      // Convert from Fahrenheit to Centigrade
7      // Author: Jennifer Mickunas, August 23, 1996
8
9      TextField tFahr;
10     Label lCent;
11
12     public Temperature () {
13
14     // Set the title and the layout manager
15       super("Temperature Conversion");
16       setLayout(new FlowLayout());
17
18     // Create the TextField and the Label
19       tFahr = new TextField(10);
20       lCent = new Label("I'll tell you what that is in degrees C");
21
22     // Lay out the three Components
23       add(new Label("Please type the temperature (deg F): "));
24       add(tFahr);
25       add(lCent);
26       pack();
27       setVisible(true);
28
29     // Register the Component Listener
30       tFahr.addActionListener(this);
31     }
32
33     // Respond to Action Event: typing in the tFahr TextField
34     public void actionPerformed (ActionEvent e) {
35       double fahr=0.0,
36              cent=0.0;
37       fahr = Integer.parseInt(tFahr.getText());
38       cent = 5.0 * (fahr - 32) / 9.0;
39       lCent.setText(fahr + " deg F is " + cent + " deg C");
40       pack();
41     }
42   }
```

FIGURE 13.5   A GUI temperature conversion program.

the layout manager, packing the frame, and making the frame visible) and where the TextField and two Labels are created and added to the frame; these can be seen in Figure 13.6. (As we mentioned before, TextFields are used to allow users to enter text. In doing so, users can employ the standard methods of

FIGURE 13.6 Output from the temperature conversion program.

editing with which anyone who has filled in a form on a web page is familiar: selecting text by clicking and dragging, replacing text by selecting it and typing the next text, deleting characters using the Backspace and Delete keys, and so on. All these actions are handled by the TextField class.)

The remaining lines of the program relate to the actions of reading from the TextField and displaying the converted temperature, and they mirror the three steps outlined for a Button.

- In the class declaration (lines 4 and 5), the program declares itself to be an ActionListener.
- In line 30, the program registers the TextField tFahr as the component it is interested in "listening to." (The argument this refers to the Temperature object itself and says that this object will listen for the events.)
- Starting on line 33, the program defines the method actionPerformed, to be called when the user presses the Enter key. (We'll examine the class ActionEvent shortly; we do not need to use it in this program.) That method gets the String that was entered and calls method int Integer.parseInt (String s) to convert it to an int. The method then performs the conversion to Centigrade, and finally changes the label lCent to a new string. Because lCent has already been added to the frame, this new label value shows up immediately. The purpose of the pack call in line 40 is to resize the frame to just the right size to accommodate the Centigrade temperature.

Integer is another of Java's predefined classes, meant primarily for working with integers *as objects* rather than as primitive ints. It essentially "wraps" an int in a class structure, so that it can be treated as an object. The Integer class has a number of instance methods and class methods, summarized in Table 13.7. Here we have used just the class method parseInt.

Run the Temperature program. Try out a number of actions with the program. Does everything work as you would expect?	**QUICK EXERCISE** **13.4**

Name	Description
`Integer (int v)`	Constructs an `Integer` with value v.
`Integer (String s)`	Constructs an `Integer` with value given by the string s. It is an error if s has any noninteger characters, including blanks.
`int compareTo (Integer b)`	Compares this `Integer` to b, returning -1, 0, or +1 for less than, equal to, or greater than result.
`int intValue ()`	Returns the `int` value of this `Integer`.
`static int parseInt (String s)`	Parses s, returning the `int` it represents. Equivalent to `new Integer(s).intValue()`.
`String toString ()`	Stringifies this `Integer`.

TABLE 13.7   **Some methods of the `Integer` class.**

13.3.1 Closing the Window

You may have noticed (especially if you have done the Quick Exercises) that when you run the `Temperature` program, not all the standard widgets on the frame work. The iconify and maximize buttons work fine, as do their counterparts in the drop-down menu. However, neither the "close window" button nor the "close" menu item does what you expect. The reason for this is that the Java *WindowEvents* implementation of `Frame` is capable of *generating* various *WindowEvents* such as the closing of the window and the iconification of the window. (See Table 13.8.) Some of these events cause a change in the appearance of the window, such as iconification/deiconification. But others cause no special change in the window's appearance and have no other associated action—it is necessary for the programmer to provide listeners if there is to be any action taken.

So if we want our `Temperature` program to listen for the window closing *WindowListener* event, we must implement the *WindowListener* interface and its seven required methods. These are summarized in Table 13.9. Of course, we could do this

Name	Description
`static int WINDOW_ACTIVATED`	The window has been made the user's active window.
`static int WINDOW_CLOSED`	The window has been closed.
`static int WINDOW_CLOSING`	The window is being closed.
`static int WINDOW_DEACTIVATED`	The window is no longer the user's active window.
`static int WINDOW_DEICONIFIED`	The window has been deiconified.
`static int WINDOW_ICONIFIED`	The window has been minimized.
`static int WINDOW_OPENED`	The window has been made visible for the first time.

TABLE 13.8   **Some constants of the `WindowEvent` class.**

Method	Purpose
void windowOpened (WindowEvent e)	Called when a window is opened
void windowClosing (WindowEvent e)	Called when a window is being closed
void windowClosed (WindowEvent e)	Called when a window has been closed
void windowIconified (WindowEvent e)	Called when a window is iconified
void windowDeiconified (WindowEvent e)	Called when a window is deiconified
void windowActivated (WindowEvent e)	Called when a window is activated
void windowDeactivated (WindowEvent e)	Called when a window is deactivated

TABLE 13.9   The `WindowListener` interface. Window events are generated by mouse actions on a `Window` object.

directly in class `Temperature` itself. But writing code for closing a window is done so often that we usually define a new class, say `ClosableFrame`, that extends Java's `Frame`. Then instead of `Temperature` extending `Frame`, we have it extend `ClosableFrame`. The action that we usually want to define is `windowClosing`, within which we just terminate the program. A version of `ClosableFrame` is shown in Figure 13.8.

The UML diagram for `ClosableFrame` and window events (Figure 13.7) closely resembles that of Figure 13.4 where we diagrammed `Button` action events. However, this time the source of the event is not a created component, but the `Window` superclass of `ClosableFrame`.

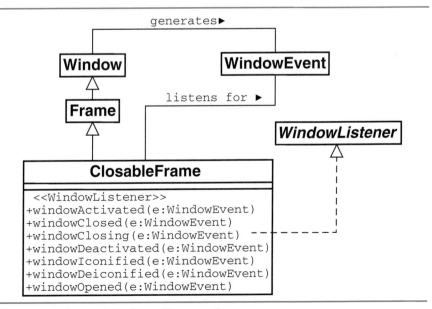

FIGURE 13.7   A UML class diagram for `ClosableFrame`.

```
1    import java.awt.*;
2    import java.awt.event.*;
3
4    public class ClosableFrame extends Frame implements WindowListener {
5
6       public ClosableFrame () {
7          this("");
8       }
9
10      public ClosableFrame (String title) {
11         super(title);
12         addWindowListener(this);
13      }
14
15      public void windowClosing (WindowEvent e) {
16         dispose();
17         System.exit(0);
18      }
19      public void windowActivated (WindowEvent e) {}
20      public void windowClosed (WindowEvent e) {}
21      public void windowOpened (WindowEvent e) {}
22      public void windowDeactivated (WindowEvent e) {}
23      public void windowDeiconified (WindowEvent e) {}
24      public void windowIconified (WindowEvent e) {}
25
26   }
```

FIGURE 13.8   The `ClosableFrame` class.

Notice in line 4 that the new class extends `Frame` and implements the `WindowListener` interface. The main constructor in lines 10 through 13 invokes the `Frame`'s constructor and then registers `this` instance as a listener for window events. In lines 15 through 18 we implement the one method that will be called when the user attempts to close the window; this method calls `dispose()`, which cleans up the resources used by the `Frame` and then terminates the program via a call to `System.exit(0)`. The remaining `WindowListeners` are defined as do-nothing methods in lines 19 through 24.

Included in CSLib is a version of `ClosableFrame`. In all of our remaining programs that would extend `Frame`, we'll extend `ClosableFrame` instead.

QUICK EXERCISE **13.5**	Change the header in our `Temperature` program to extend `ClosableFrame` instead of `Frame`, and verify that the program terminates when you click on the window-close widget. Be sure to import `CSLib.*`.

Using Conditionals with Reactive Components

Let's extend the Fahrenheit to Centigrade temperature conversion program that we wrote earlier. This time, we will write the program so that it can convert temperatures in either direction. Instead of one input TextField, we will have two. Depending on which one the user utilizes for input, the program will compute the appropriate converted temperature and display it in the *other* TextField (using setText—see Table 13.3). The program is

```
1   import CSLib.*;
2   import java.awt.*;
3   import java.awt.event.*;
4
5   public class Temperature extends ClosableFrame
6                   implements ActionListener {
7
8     // Convert temperature from/to Fahrenheit/Centigrade
9     // Author: Peter Baranowicz, September 10, 2000 \
10
11    TextField tFahr = new TextField(9),
12              tCent = new TextField(9);
13
14    public Temperature () {
15      super("Two Way Conversion");
16
17      // Lay out the Components.
18      setLayout(new FlowLayout());
19      add(new Label("Fahrenheit"));
20      add(tFahr);
21      add(new Label("Centigrade"));
22      add(tCent);
23      pack();
24      setVisible(true);
25
26      // Register Component Listeners
27      tFahr.addActionListener(this);
28      tCent.addActionListener(this);
29    }
30
31    public void actionPerformed (ActionEvent e) {
32      // Respond to Action Events:
33      //      1. tFahr TextField
34      //      2. tCent TextField
35      double fahr, cent;
36
37      if (e.getSource()==tFahr) {
38        fahr = Double.parseDouble(tFahr.getText());
39        cent = 5.0 * (fahr - 32.0) / 9.0;
40        tCent.setText(cent + "");
41      }
42      else {
```

```
43        cent = Double.parseDouble(tCent.getText());
44        fahr = 9.0 * cent / 5.0 + 32.0;
45        tFahr.setText(fahr + "");
46      }
47    }
48  }
```

In lines 11 and 12, we declared the *two* TextFields that we use. We use the same mechanism as before for creating a TextField, except that we now do it along with the declaration of the variables. In the Temperature constructor, we arrange for a flow layout manager, set up the window with the two labeled TextFields (and affiliated Labels), and register them *both* by calling addActionListener.

Now we must handle *two* possible ActionEvents: data input (i.e., the user typing the Enter key) in the tFahr TextField and data input in the tCent TextField, but there can be only one definition of the method actionPerformed. To distinguish the two events, we use an if-else statement in the actionPerformed method (lines 37 and 42). The argument e of actionPerformed identifies the object that caused the event. The method call e.getSource() in line 37 identifies the particular component in which the event occurred. Thus, we can tell if the user typed the Enter key in the tFahr field by the test e.getSource() == tFahr; in that case, we fill in tCent. Otherwise, the user entered a number in tCent, and we need to fill in tFahr. The only methods of interest in class ActionEvent are those inherited from class EventObject, summarized in Table 13.10.

Another extension to this program will permit the user to type a decimal number in the TextField, so we need to receive a double instead of an int. Recall that the Integer class has a method parseInt; the Double class has a similar method, called parseDouble. The Double class is summarized in Table 13.11. Finally, the appropriate conversion is computed in line 39, and the *other* TextField is filled out in line 40. Thus TextFields can be used both to receive input [as in tFahr.getText()] and to display output

Name	Description
public Object getSource ()	Returns the object on which the event initially occurred.
String toString ()	Stringifies the event object.

TABLE 13.10 Methods of the EventObject **class.** ActionEvent **is a subclass of** EventObject.

Name	Description
`Double (double v)`	Constructs an `Double` with value v.
`Double (String s)`	Constructs an `Double` with value given by the string s. It is an error if s has any non-decimal characters, including blanks.
`int compareTo (Double b)`	Compares this `Double` to b, returning -1, 0, or +1 for less than, equal to, or greater than result.
`double doubleValue ()`	Returns the `double` value of this `Double`.
`double parseDouble (String s)`	Parses s, returning the `double` it represents. Equivalent to new `Double(s).doubleValue()`.
`String toString ()`	Stringifies this `Double`.

TABLE 13.11 Some methods of the `Double` class.

[as in `tCent.setText(cent + "")`]. Notice that, in line 40, we did not write `tCent.setText(cent)` because `setText` requires that it be given a `String`, not a `double`. The easiest way to "convert" the `double` to a `String` is by concatenating it with the "empty string." The code in the `else` alternative is the counterpart of that in the `then` alternative.

Try changing line 40 in the `Temperature` program to `tCent.setText(cent);`. What happens?	**QUICK EXERCISE 13.6**

13.4.1 More Components

Now that we know how to handle multiple events, let's spread our wings a bit and build a program that uses some more components. Another useful component that Java provides is a *Checkbox*. A `Checkbox` always has a label, and the user clicks on it to "select" it. The general form for declaring and adding a `Checkbox` is

Checkbox

```
Checkbox choice = new Checkbox("label");
...
add(choice);
```

Checkboxes typically are used to select one or more items. For example, if you were ordering a car, you might check "power brakes" and "power steering" but omit "air conditioning."

```
Checkbox powerBrakes = new Checkbox("Power Brakes");
Checkbox powerSteering = new Checkbox("Power Steering");
Checkbox airConditioning = new Checkbox("Air Conditioning");
```

```
. . .
add(powerBrakes);
add(powerSteering);
add(airConditioning);
```

which would look like this:

A `Checkbox` is a reactive component, like a `TextField`: The program may need to react when the user clicks on it. However, a `Checkbox` is registered in a slightly different way than a `TextField`; the idea is the same but the details—mainly, type and method names—differ a bit. Specifically, the program is declared with `implements ItemListener` (instead of `ActionListener`), the `Checkbox` is registered by calling `addItemListener` (instead of

itemState
Changed

`addActionListener`), and the event is handled by method *itemState Changed* (instead of `actionPerformed`). Just as `actionPerformed` has an argument of type `ActionEvent`, `itemStateChanged` has an argument of type `ItemEvent` that can be used to distinguish among different `Checkbox` components. That is, within `itemStateChanged (ItemEvent e)`, we can use `e.getSource()` to tell which item event triggered the state change, just as we distinguished among multiple `Textfield ActionEvents` in the temperature conversion program. The classes `Checkbox` and `ItemEvent` are summarized in Tables 13.12 and 13.13, and the `ItemListener` interface is summarized in Table 13.14.

radio buttons

Often, we want only one of a group of `Checkboxes` to be selected at any one time; such groups of `Checkboxes` are called *radio buttons* (because they behave as the pushbuttons on a radio do). In Java, we use a `CheckboxGroup` for this purpose. When we create a `Checkbox`, we can tell Java to include it as part of a `CheckboxGroup`; we must also tell whether the `Checkbox` should be *selected* (`true`) or not (`false`). For example, when ordering a car, you might choose "hardtop" or "convertible," but not both. To add `Checkboxes` for these choices while making "hardtop" the selected member of a `CheckboxGroup`, we would write

```
CheckboxGroup bodyStyle = new CheckboxGroup();
Checkbox hardtop =
        new Checkbox("Hardtop", bodyStyle, true);
Checkbox convertible =
        new Checkbox("Convertible", bodyStyle, false);
. . .
add(hardtop);
add(convertible);
```

If the user selects one `Checkbox` in a `CheckboxGroup`, the previously selected `Checkbox` will be unselected. Java provides a method for finding out which

Name	Description
`Checkbox ()`	Creates a new check box with no label.
`Checkbox (String l)`	Creates a new check box with label l.
`Checkbox (String l, boolean state)`	Creates a new check box with label l; selected if `state == true`.
`Checkbox (String l, CheckboxGroup g, boolean state)`	Creates a new check box as part of check box group g, with label l; selected if `state == true`.
`void addItemListener (ItemListener l)`	Makes l a listener for item events from this check box.
`String getLabel ()`	Gets the label of this check box.
`boolean getState ()`	Gets the state of this check box.
`void setLabel (String l)`	Sets the label of this check box.
`void setState (boolean state)`	Sets the state of this check box.

TABLE 13.12 Some methods of the `Checkbox` class.

Name	Description
`static int DESELECTED`	Indicates that the item was deselected.
`static int SELECTED`	Indicates that the item was selected.
`int getStateChange ()`	Returns the type of state change.

TABLE 13.13 Some constants and methods of the `ItemEvent` class. (Other methods are inherited from `EventObject`.)

Method	Purpose
`void itemStateChanged (ItemEvent e)`	Called when any item event occurs

TABLE 13.14 The `ItemListener` interface. Item events are generated by checkboxes.

Checkbox in a group is selected:

   Checkbox *CheckboxGroup*`.getSelectedCheckbox()`

The class `CheckboxGroup` is summarized in Table 13.15.

   Let's rewrite the body mass program from Exercise 9 on page 142. This time, we will have a `TextField` for height, a `TextField` for weight, and radio buttons to select male or female. The complete program is as follows:

Name	Description
CheckboxGroup ()	Creates a new check box group.
Checkbox getSelectedCheckbox ()	Returns the curretly selected check box in this check box group.
void setSelectedCheckbox (Checkbox box)	Sets box as the selected check box in this check box group.
String toString ()	Stringifies this check box group.

TABLE 13.15 Some methods of the `CheckboxGroup` **class.**

```
1   import CSLib.*;
2   import java.awt.*;
3   import java.awt.event.*;
4
5   public class BodyMass extends ClosableFrame
6                    implements ItemListener, ActionListener {
7
8      // Determine Body-Mass-Index and Obesity
9      // Author: Deborah Mickunas, October 13, 1996
10
11        // Declare Components
12        TextField tHeight, tWeight;
13        Label lIndex, lHigh;
14        CheckboxGroup gender;
15        Checkbox maleCheck, femaleCheck;
16
17     public BodyMass () {
18        super("Body Mass Program");
19
20        // Allocate components.
21        tHeight = new TextField(5);
22        tWeight = new TextField(5);
23        lIndex = new Label("What is your body-mass-index?      ");
24        lHigh = new Label("Is this considered high or not?");
25        gender = new CheckboxGroup();
26        maleCheck = new Checkbox("Male", gender, true);
27        femaleCheck = new Checkbox("Female", gender, false);
28
29        // Arrange Components
30        setLayout(new FlowLayout());
31        add(maleCheck);
32        add(femaleCheck);
33        add(new Label("Height (in meters):"));
34        add(tHeight);
35        add(new Label("Weight (in kilograms):"));
36        add(tWeight);
37        add(lIndex);
38        add(lHigh);
39
40        setSize(250,200);
41        setVisible(true);
42
```

```
43      // Register Component Listeners
44      tHeight.addActionListener(this);
45      tWeight.addActionListener(this);
46      maleCheck.addItemListener(this);
47      femaleCheck.addItemListener(this);
48    }
49
50    public void itemStateChanged (ItemEvent e) {
51      // Respond to Item Events:
52      //        1. femaleCheck Checkbox
53      //        2. maleCheck Checkbox
54      compute();
55    }
56
57    public void actionPerformed (ActionEvent e) {
58      // Respond to Action Events:
59      //        1. tHeight TextField
60      //        2. tWeight TextField
61      compute();
62    }
63
64    private void compute () {
65      double height = new Double(tHeight.getText()).doubleValue();
66      double weight = new Double(tWeight.getText()).doubleValue();
67      double bodyMassIndex = weight / (height * height);
68      boolean female =
69                  (gender.getSelectedCheckbox() == femaleCheck);
70
71      lIndex.setText("Your body-mass-index is " + bodyMassIndex);
72      if ((bodyMassIndex > 27.8) ||
73        female && (bodyMassIndex > 27.3))
74          lHigh.setText("This is considered high.");
75      else
76          lHigh.setText("This is not considered high.");
77    }
78  }
```

Since this program contains both TextFields and Checkboxes, it declares itself to implement both the ActionListener and ItemListener interfaces (lines 5 and 6).

Notice how the two Checkboxes are created as part of the gender CheckboxGroup (lines 25 through 27) with the maleCheck Checkbox initially selected. Our code registers this program as the Listener for all four of the Components (lines 44 through 47).

Within the itemStateChanged method (lines 50 through 55), we *could* check to see which Checkbox triggered the ItemEvent in the same way that we checked for TextField events. However, the only thing that we really need to do is to call the private method compute, where all of the real work is done. Likewise, in the actionPerformed method (lines 57 through 62), we just call the private compute method.

Within `compute`, we first read the input from both the `tHeight` and the `tWeight` `TextField`, and we compute `bodyMassIndex` (lines 65 through 67). Then we determine which of the `gender` `Checkboxes` is selected in lines 68 through 69. We could have used the style

```
if (gender.getSelectedCheckbox() == femaleCheck)
    female = true;
else
    female = false;
```

However, we used the style of directly assigning to the Boolean variable the result of evaluating a Boolean expression.

Finally, we display the results in two `Label` Components in lines 71 through 76. Once the program is underway, the screen might appear as shown in Figure 13.9. Notice that rather than using `pack()`, we set the `Frame` size explicitly to 250 × 200 pixels.

Notice that in line 71 the `double` variable `bodyMassIndex` is concatenated to a string, so `setText` is given the `String` that it expects. When we first start up the program, we need to display *something* in the two `Labels` `lIndex` and `lHigh`. When they are declared and created, we specify that they should

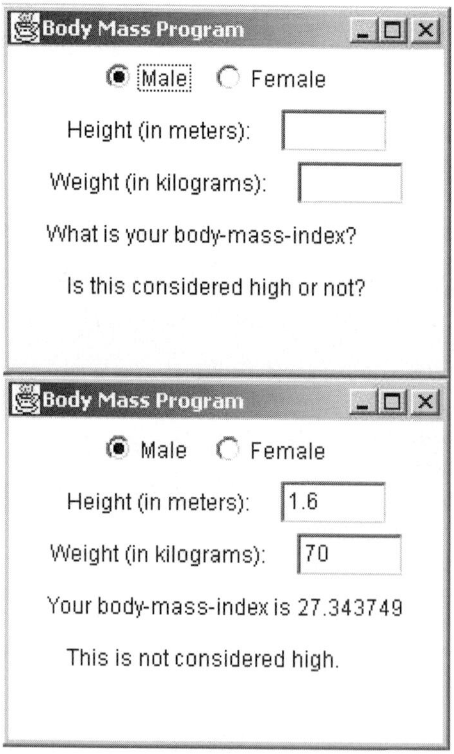

FIGURE 13.9 Typical output from the `BodyMass` program.

initially display some meaningful messages; more precisely, "What is your body mass index?" and "Is this high or not?" These labels are then changed, in `itemStateChanged` and `actionPerformed`, to show the results.

**QUICK EXERCISE
13.7**

What would the output of the `BodyMass` program look like if we had not explicitly set the frame size to 250 × 200? What would it have looked like if, instead, we had done a `pack()`?

**QUICK EXERCISE
13.8**

In the `BodyMass` program, what happens if you enter zero for the height (or just click on a radio button with blanks in the height field)? How might you change the program to have better behavior in such circumstances?

13.5

Drawing in a Frame

In previous chapters we used the `CSLib` class `DrawingBox` to draw pictures and GIFs. Now we will see how you can draw directly in a frame. The Java API provides methods to draw lines, circles, rectangles, and text in a frame and to include GIF and JPEG images, very much as we did with the `DrawingBox`.

To draw in a `Frame`, you override the `Frame`'s `paint` method:

```
public void paint (Graphics g)
```

The `Graphics` object g is created by the Java run-time system, not by you, and it is used for drawing operations. To use it, you must consider the `Frame` to be a grid, with point (0, 0) at the upper left and some point with positive coordinates (x, y), depending upon the size of the frame, at the lower right. This is almost identical to the `DrawingBox` coordinate system with which you are already familiar.[1]

The `Graphics` class provides many of the same drawing methods that are provided in the `DrawingBox` class, including almost all those shown in Table 2.4 on page 48. (The methods `setDrawableSize`, `getDrawableWidth`, and

---

[1]The difference is that we wrote the `DrawingBox` class in `CSLib` so that pixel (0, 0) is in the upper left of the *drawing area*. By contrast, a `Frame` places its (0, 0) pixel in the upper left of the *title bar*.

```
import java.awt.*;

public class MyDrawing extends ClosableFrame {
...
public MyDrawing () {
...
}
...
public void paint (Graphics g) {
...
g.drawLine(...);
...
g.drawImage(...);
...
}
...
}
```

FIGURE 13.10   Typical drawing code.

getDrawableHeight are DrawingBox methods that are not defined for
Frames.)

The method paint will be called by the Java run-time system whenever
the frame needs to be drawn, such as when it is moved or resized or deiconified or
uncovered. You need to do all the drawing for a Frame from within the paint
method. So the typical way of drawing in a Frame is shown in Figure 13.10.

QUICK EXERCISE
13.9
Write a program to draw the biggest oval possible in a Frame, using the method
drawOval(0,0, getWidth(), getHeight()).

As our first example in this section, we will write a program that has a button
and also draws graphics in a frame. It will also allow us to make an important
point about how "painting" works. This program is called RandomCircles. It
consists of a single button, labeled Circle, which when pushed, causes a circle,
of randomly chosen size and location, to be drawn in the frame (using height 300
and width 300).

Placing the button in the frame and defining the actionPerformed
method are done just as we did earlier. One new feature is the use of random
numbers. The function Math.random(), with no arguments, returns a random
double in the range of 0.0 to 1.0. Thus, if SIZE is the size of the frame (which,
as we said, is 300), then these two statements choose a random location for the
center of a circle:

```
27        x = (int) (SIZE * Math.random());
28        y = (int) (SIZE * Math.random());
```

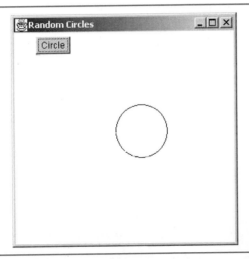

FIGURE 13.11   A screen dump of the `RandomCircles` program.

Similarly, we can generate a random diameter. Except for the odd-looking definition of `actionPerformed`, the program is a straightforward combination of the features introduced earlier. A screen dump of the program is shown in Figure 13.11.

```
1   import CSLib.*;
2   import java.awt.*;
3   import java.awt.event.*;
4
5   public class RandomCircles extends ClosableFrame
6                               implements ActionListener {
7     // Draw some random circles.
8     // Author: Elaine M. Baranowicz, October 29, 1996
9
10    private Button circleButton;
11    private static final int SIZE = 300;
12
13    public RandomCircles () {
14      super("Random Circles");
15      circleButton = new Button("Circle");
16      setLayout(new FlowLayout());
17      add(circleButton);
18      circleButton.addActionListener(this);
19      setVisible(true);
20      setSize(SIZE,SIZE);
21    }
22
23    public void paint (Graphics g) {
24      int diameter, radius, x, y;
25
26      // Generate a random center for the circle.
27      x = (int) (SIZE * Math.random());
```

BUG ALERT 13.3	*Painting, Repainting, and Updating*

One of the most confusing aspects of the Java AWT is the way frames are updated. The paint method should include all of the drawing that needs to be done. The Java run-time system automatically redraws most, but not all, components in the frame. However, when something occurs that requires the frame to be repainted, you should always call repaint instead of paint. The repaint method, in turn, calls update, which clears the frame, and then paints it.

```
28          y = (int) (SIZE * Math.random());
29
30          // now randomly compute the diameter
31          diameter = (int) (300 * Math.random());
32          radius = (int)(diameter/2);
33
34          g.drawOval(x-radius, y-radius, diameter, diameter);
35      }
36
37      public void actionPerformed (ActionEvent event) {
38          repaint();
39      }
40  }
```

In this program, the actionPerformed method does not really do anything itself; it just indicates that paint should be called again to generate a new circle. It would be natural just to have it call paint, but there is a problem: paint has an argument, which is a Graphics object, and actionPerformed does not know what to supply for that argument. So Java provides a function repaint, with no arguments, which in turn calls paint with the appropriate argument.

If you were to enter and run this program, you might be surprised to discover that, no matter how many times you pushed the Circle button, only one circle appears in the frame. It is a different circle each time but still only one. The reason is that repaint *clears the frame* before it calls paint. To prevent this, add the following function definition to the program:

```
41      public void update (Graphics g) {
42          paint(g);
43      }
```

This works because repaint actually calls the function update, which in turns clears the frame and calls paint. By overriding the superclass's version and giving our own definition of update, which omits the frame-clearing code and just calls paint, we prevent that clearing behavior from occurring.

In any case, with this one new function definition, each time we push the button, a new circle is added to the frame. Figure 13.12 is a screen dump after pushing the Circle button four times. (It shows five circles: the one drawn when the program started and the four drawn when the button was pushed.) Another thing that you might notice about the RandomCircles program is that when

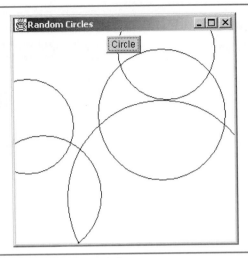

FIGURE 13.12 **A screen dump of the new** `RandomCircles` **program with** `update` **redefined.**

a circle is drawn on top of the button, the button immediately pops to the top of the view. So apparently the `repaint` method also redraws all the components of the frame—buttons, textboxes, etc.

It is sometimes the case that we want to draw in an isolated section of the frame, without obstructing buttons, text boxes, and other components. The Java AWT provides a component for just such a task, the `Canvas`. But before we examine the use of the `Canvas` class, it might be helpful to understand the inheritance relationships among all the components that we have seen, and some that we have yet to see.

13.6 The AWT Component Hierarchy

Some subclasses of the `Component` class are shown in Figure 13.13. As you can see from the diagram, the `Component` class is "abstract"—indicated in the UML by an italicized name—so your program cannot create `Component` objects directly. Rather, it must create one of the concrete subclass objects. There are two kinds of subclasses for `Component`: `Container` classes and *noncontainer* classes. Obviously, the `Container` classes can contain other components; that is, a `Container` has affiliated with it a layout manager, and defines the `add` method. Even though the `Container` class is not abstract, it initially has no associated layout manager, so you should not use `Container` directly. You should use one of `Container`'s subclasses.

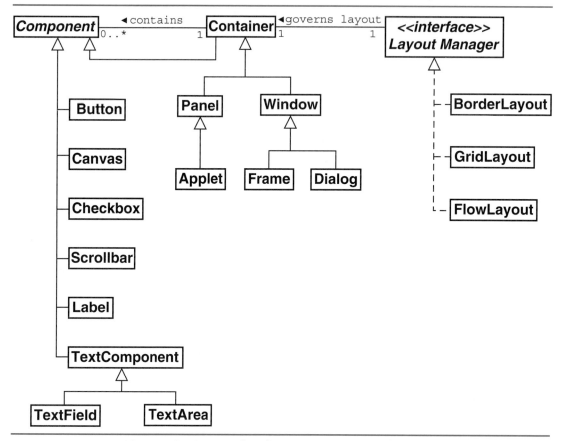

FIGURE 13.13 **UML for the AWT** Component **class inheritance hierarchy.**

The Panel class is used when we want to reserve a rectangular component into which we will place other components. Since Panel is itself a Component, it can be added to Containers, just as other Components are. Later in this chapter we will see how the Panel can be used effectively to arrange components just the way we want them. The Applet class has additional methods that allow it to be used in web pages. Later in this chapter we will also see how to build Applets.

The Window class is used when we want a *top-level* Container, that is, a new pop-up window. Windows are very much like Panels except that they pop up on their own and cannot be added to Containers. Windows have no borders and no title/menu bar; the Frame subclass adds borders and a title bar to the Window class. The Dialog subclass likewise adds to the Window a title bar and a border, but it has some features that distinguish it from a Frame which make it suitable for short user input.

The remaining subclasses of Component are simple graphical artifacts, some of which we have already used—Button, Checkbox, Label, and TextField. We will see how to use the Scrollbar in Section 13.9.

The Canvas **Class**

It should now be clear where the Canvas class fits into this scheme. We sometimes want to reserve a region of a frame for drawing. Buttons, check boxes, and the like are inappropriate for this task. Windows might be ideal, except that they are "top-level" and cannot be added to containers. The Panel class might work, but since it is a container, it offers much greater functionality than we need. It is the Canvas class that does just what we want. It can be added to a container, and it has the methods paint, update, and repaint that we have used for drawing. Moreover, a Canvas has its own coordinate system, and it has no borders that "clip off" its drawings (as happens with a Frame—see Quick Exercise 13.9).

As an example of using a Canvas, we will redo the Clock program from Section 7.15 on page 248. This time, the Clock class will extend Canvas, so it should define a paint method from which it will draw itself. We'll simplify the old version of Clock a bit. The various display methods and multiple constructors that take a DrawingBox from outside now make no sense, since we'll always be drawing directly into the Clock itself, which is a Canvas. More correctly, we'll be drawing on the the Graphics that is supplied to the paint method. Our display (DrawingBox d, int x, int y, int r) method must be changed to paint (Graphics d), with the computation of x, y, and r done just inside paint. Here's the new Clock code:

```
1   import CSLib.*;
2   import java.awt.*;
3
4   public class Clock extends Canvas {
5      // Maintain a clock.
6      // Author: Courtney Mickunas, November 21, 2000
7
8      int hour,
9          minute;
10
11     public Clock () {
12        this(12,0);
13     }
14
15     public Clock (int hour, int minute) {
16        set(hour, minute);
17     }
18
19     // Return the current time as a string.
20     public String toString () { return (hour + ":" + minute); }
21
22     public void setHour (int h) { set(h, minute); }
23     public void setMinute (int m) { set(hour, m); }
24
```

```
25      public void set (int hour, int minute) {
26         int totalMinutes = (hour * 60 + minute) % (12 * 60);
27         // totalMinutes is between -(12 * 60) and (12 * 60)
28         if (totalMinutes < 0) totalMinutes = totalMinutes + (12 * 60)
29         this.hour = totalMinutes / 60;
30         if (this.hour == 0) this.hour = 12;
31         this.minute = totalMinutes % 60;
32      }
33
34      public int getHour () { return hour; }
35      public int getMinute () { return minute; }
36
37      // Compare the time of this clock to another.
38      // Return true if this time is less than
39      // the time of the other clock.
40      public boolean priorTo (Clock c) {
41         return (hour < c.hour ||
42                  hour == c.hour && minute < c.minute
43                 );
44      }
45
46      public boolean after (Clock c) {
47         return c.priorTo(this);
48      }
49
50      // Draw a clock in this Canvas.
51      public void paint (Graphics d) {
52         int w = getWidth()-1,
53             h = getHeight()-1;
54         int x = w/2,
55             y = h/2;                  // center at (x,y)
56         int r = Math.min(x, y);   // radius
57
58         // Draw the clock in black.
59         d.setColor(Color.black);
60         d.drawOval(x-r, y-r, 2*r, 2*r);
61
62         // Set the color to blue for the hands
63         d.setColor(Color.blue);
64         // Draw the minute hand.
65         drawHand(d, x, y, r, minute/60.0);
66
67         // Draw the hour hand.
68         drawHand(d, x, y, (int)(r*0.8), (hour+minute/60.0)/12.0);
69      }
70
71      private void drawHand (Graphics d, int x, int y,
72                             int r, double fraction) {
73         int x1, y1;       // end point of a clock hand
74         double theta;     // angle from 12:00
75
76         theta = 2*Math.PI*fraction;
77         x1 = x + (int)(r*Math.sin(theta));
78         y1 = y - (int)(r*Math.cos(theta));
```

```
79          d.drawLine(x, y, x1, y1);
80        }
81      }
```

Notice that Clock is a subclass of Canvas (line 4), and the new version of paint does as we said—it computes the width and height of the Canvas and uses those values to compute the size and location of the clock.

A client that uses this new Clock class might look like this:

```
1    import CSLib.*;
2    import java.awt.*;
3    import java.awt.event.*;
4
5    public class ClockWithButtons extends ClosableFrame
6                    implements ActionListener {
7
8      // Display an analog clock
9      // Author: Lynn D. Mickunas, November 18, 2000
10
11      Clock c = new Clock();
12      Button
13        bHour = new Button("Advance Hour"),
14        bMinute = new Button("Advance Minute");
15
16      public ClockWithButtons () {
17        setLayout(new FlowLayout());
18        add(bHour); add(bMinute); add(c);
19        bHour.addActionListener(this);
20        bMinute.addActionListener(this);
21        c.setSize(300, 300);
22        c.setBackground(Color.pink);
23        pack();
24        setVisible(true);
25      }
26
27      public void actionPerformed (ActionEvent e) {
28        int hour = c.getHour(),
29            minute = c.getMinute();
30        if (e.getSource() == bHour)
31          hour++;
32        else
33          minute++;
34        c.set(hour,minute);
35        c.repaint();
36      }
37    }
```

This client places within its frame two buttons and a Clock object, using the flow layout manager, then performs the normal pack and setVisible actions (lines 16 through 25). There are some interesting things to notice about the new Clock. The client is able to set the size of the Clock directly as well as its background color (lines 21 and 22). More correctly, it is setting those attributes in the superclass Component—remember that Clock is a subclass of Canvas, which is a subclass of Component, which has the setSize and

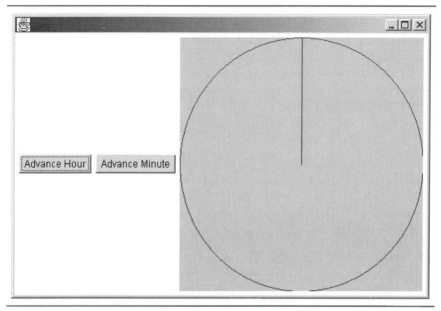

FIGURE 13.14 Snapshot of the `Clock` **program.**

`setBackground` methods. As usual, the client listens for button pushes, using `actionPerformed`, incrementing either `hour` or `minute`, as appropriate. Then in line 34 we tell the `Clock` object to set its time differently, and in line 35 we ask the `Clock` to repaint itself. A sample screen shot is shown in Figure 13.14.

Java's AWT run-time system keeps track of just when any component requires repainting, such as when it has been covered and then uncovered by some other window, or when its frame has been deiconified. What the run-time system does is to repaint all components that it thinks might need repainting. That is why every paintable component—`Canvas` in this case—must have a `paint(Graphics)` method. But Java is not always aware of the need to repaint a component. In this case, we can change the recorded time for our `Clock`, but that certainly does not give Java any clue that a repaint is in order. That is why we must explicitly ask for it in line 35.

The nuances of painting and repainting are often difficult to understand. For example, you might think that in line 35 we could have instead written

```
repaint();
```

thereby asking that the entire frame be repainted, and expecting that all its contained components would be repainted as well. Unfortunately, only *some* contained components get repainted in such circumstances (the *lightweight* components), and our `Clock` is not lightweight (since it is a subclass of `Canvas`, which is not "lightweight"). So that is why we must explicitly ask for the `Clock` to be repainted. On the other hand, when a frame is repainted after deiconification, all contained components *do* get repainted, whether lightweight or not.

The Java run-time system is very precise about what needs repainting. Replace line 35 of the `ClockClient` by `repaint()`. Notice how even after pushing the buttons, the `Clock` does not get repainted. What happens if you iconify and then deiconify the frame? What happens if you click on the hour button, then completely cover the clock with some other window, and then uncover it? What happens if you click on the hour button, then *partially* cover and uncover the clock?

Don't Paint, Repaint!

It is important that rather than call `paint` directly, your methods call `repaint` when they think the display needs to be repainted. This permits the Java run-time system to decide if that portion of the display *really* needs to be painted or not.

13.8

Designing the Screen Layout

Before going on to the major graphical program of this section, we will introduce the screen layout capabilities of Java by revisiting the `BodyMass` program from Section 13.4.1 (page 497). We have not yet discussed alternative ways of arranging components as they are added to a container. We have been careful to choose a size for each frame so that it looks fine, but if you attempt to resize the frame area, the appearance may not be pleasing. For example, if you run the `BodyMass` program on page 497 and drag on the right side to widen the frame, you might get something resembling Figure 13.15.

This occurs because, when we add components to the frame, they are laid out left to right as room permits and placed on a new line only when required. This is a consequence of the *layout manager*, which governs how components *layout manager* are arranged when they are `added` to a frame. In our `BodyMass` program, we were using the default layout manager, which for a `Frame` is the `FlowLayout` manager.

The Java API defines several layout manager classes. To change the layout manager used by a graphical frame, send the message

        setLayout(*layout-manager-object*) ;

to the frame. In the two programs of this section, we will use three layout managers:

FlowLayout. If the frame's layout manager is set to be an object of this class

        setLayout(new FlowLayout());

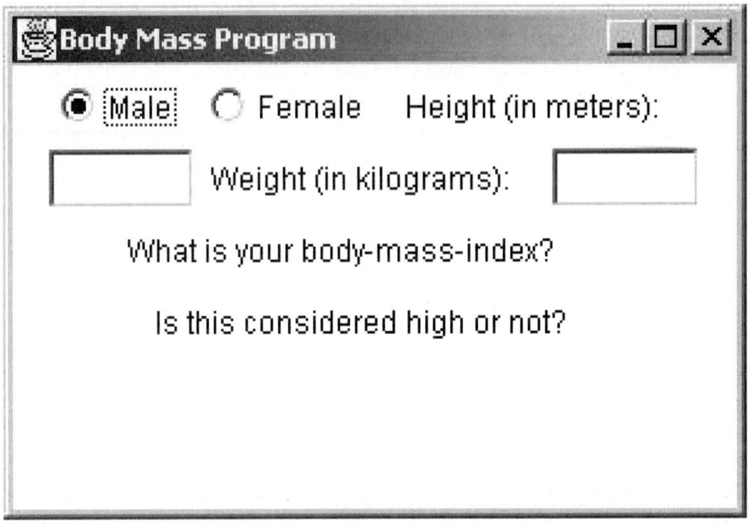

FIGURE 13.15   Poor layout for the `BodyMass` program.

then the frame will arrange the components according to the order in which they were added (by `add`), going left to right and top to bottom. This is the default layout, so the call to `setLayout` is not necessary (but is harmless).

`GridLayout`. With a `GridLayout` object as its layout manager, the frame will arrange itself into a grid of fixed size and will place objects into the grid in the order in which they were added (by `add`), going left to right and top to bottom. For example,

```
setLayout(new GridLayout(3, 5));
```

divides the frame into a grid with three rows and five columns. It is an error to add more than 15 components, but if fewer are added, the leftover places in the grid will be left empty. All cells of the grid have the same dimensions.

`BorderLayout`. When this type of layout is used

```
setLayout(new BorderLayout());
```

the frame is divided into north, south, east, west, and center areas, as shown in Figure 13.16. Components are added to the frame with a special two-argument `add` method. For example,

```
add("North", new Label("The Title"));
```

adds `The Title` to the top of the window, centered. It is an error to add two components to the same position in the window.

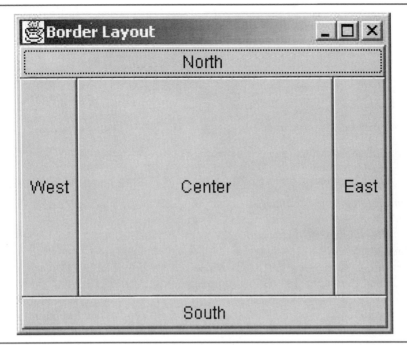

FIGURE 13.16 The BorderLayout **manager.**

For example, using GridLayout, one might arrange a list of labels in the frame using these lines:

```
setLayout(new GridLayout(3, 2));
add(new Label("Roger Ebert"));
add(new Label("Two thumbs up!"));
add(new Label("Janet Maslin"));
add(new Label("Hated it!"));
add(new Label("Rex Reed"));
add(new Label("I can't decide."));
```

The advantage of using GridLayout instead of the default FlowLayout is that the labels always will line up in two columns, no matter how the frame is resized.

However, used alone like this, the layout managers rarely give good results. Usually, different parts of the frame need to be organized differently. To achieve this, you can use *container classes*, in particular, the class Panel, to lay out *container classes* various rectangular portions of a frame. (Neither the Window class nor the Frame class can be used to carve out a portion of a larger frame. Windows pop up a new window of their own, and Frames have a surrounding border.) Panel objects are *components that contain other components*. A Panel has its own layout manager, and components are added to it just as they are added to Frames. Then the Panel is treated as a single component that is added to yet other containers, according to *those* container's layout managers. Therefore, it is typical to see code like this to build a GUI frame:

```
Panel p1 = new Panel();
  p1.setLayout(new GridLayout(2, 1));
  p1.add(component₁ );
  p1.add(component₂ );
Panel p2 = new Panel();
  p2.setLayout(...);
  p2.add(component₃);
  ...
setLayout(new BorderLayout());
add("North", p1);
add("Center", p2);
```

Even more complex arrangements can be specified by placing `Panels` inside other `Panels`.

Now we rewrite the `BodyMass` program from Section 13.4.1. We will improve the layout of the program so that the male/female radio buttons will both be on line 1, the `tHeight` `Label` and corresponding `TextField` will be on line 2, the `tWeight` `Label` and corresponding `TextField` will be on line 3, the "What is your body mass index?" `Label` will be on line 4, and the "Is this considered high or not?" `Label` will be on line 5. The key point is that the arrangement will remain this way no matter how the overall frame may be resized. Obviously, each of these five lines should be a separate component of a grid layout with one column and five rows. Moreover, each of the first three should be "encapsulated" in a `Panel` using a flow layout. The new `BodyMass` program follows:

```
1   import CSLib.*;
2   import java.awt.*;
3   import java.awt.event.*;
4
5   public class BodyMass extends ClosableFrame
6                 implements ItemListener, ActionListener {
7
8     // Determine Body-Mass-Index and Obesity
9     // Author: Deborah Mickunas, October 13, 1996
10
11      // Declare and allocate Components
12      TextField
13        tHeight = new TextField(5),
14        tWeight = new TextField(5);
15      Label
16        lIndex = new Label("What is your body-mass-index?    "),
17        lHigh = new Label("Is this considered high or not?");
18      CheckboxGroup
19        gender = new CheckboxGroup();
20      Checkbox
21        maleCheck = new Checkbox("Male", gender, true),
22        femaleCheck = new Checkbox("Female", gender, false);
23      Panel
24        p1 = new Panel(),  // line 1
```

```
25      p2 = new Panel(), // line 2
26      p3 = new Panel(); // line 3
27
28   public BodyMass () {
29     super("Body Mass Program");
30
31   // Set Label properties
32     lIndex.setAlignment(Label.CENTER);
33     lIndex.setFont(new Font("Helvetica", Font.PLAIN, 14));
34     lIndex.setForeground(Color.blue);
35
36     lHigh.setAlignment(Label.CENTER);
37     lHigh.setFont(new Font("Helvetica", Font.BOLD, 18));
38     lHigh.setForeground(Color.red);
39
40   // Arrange Components
41     setLayout(new GridLayout(5,1));
42     p1.add(maleCheck);
43     p1.add(femaleCheck);
44     add(p1);
45     p2.add(new Label("Height (in meters):"));
46     p2.add(tHeight);
47     add(p2);
48     p3.add(new Label("Weight (in kilograms):"));
49     p3.add(tWeight);
50     add(p3);
51     add(lIndex);
52     add(lHigh);
53
54     pack();
55     setVisible(true);
56
57   // Register Component Listeners
58     tHeight.addActionListener(this);
59     tWeight.addActionListener(this);
60     maleCheck.addItemListener(this);
61     femaleCheck.addItemListener(this);
62   }
63
64   public void itemStateChanged (ItemEvent e) {
65     // Respond to Item Events:
66     //      1. femaleCheck Checkbox
67     //      2. maleCheck Checkbox
68     compute();
69   }
70
71   public void actionPerformed (ActionEvent e) {
72     // Respond to Action Events:
73     //      1. tHeight TextField
74     //      2. tWeight TextField
75     compute();
76   }
77
78   private void compute () {
```

```
79          double height =
80                  new Double(tHeight.getText()).doubleValue();
81          double weight =
82                  new Double(tWeight.getText()).doubleValue();
83          double bodyMassIndex = weight / (height * height);
84          boolean female =
85                  (gender.getSelectedCheckbox() == femaleCheck);
86
87          lIndex.setText("Your body-mass-index is " + bodyMassIndex);
88          if ((bodyMassIndex > 27.8) ||
89              female && (bodyMassIndex > 27.3))
90                  lHigh.setText("This is considered high.");
91          else
92                  lHigh.setText("This is not considered high.");
93          pack();
94      }
95  }
```

There are a number of parts that are different from the earlier program. First, we have used a different technique for allocating the various components—we allocate them right along with their declarations (lines 11 through 26). We have seen this technique before, and the choice of whether we use this technique or the one where allocation is done in the constructor is a matter of style. As part of component declaration/allocation, we instantiate three `Panels`, p1, p2, and p3, which will hold the components of the top three lines of our frame (lines 23 through 26).

There is some difference from the original `BodyMass` program in lines 40 through 52. We add the appropriate components to each of our new `Panels`, and we add each of those `Panels` in turn to the `Frame`. Since those `Panels` have not had layout managers specified for them, they each use the default `FlowLayout` manager. The layout manager for the `Frame` is set to a `GridLayout` with one column and five rows (line 41), so our five components—three panels and two labels—are added in the proper order.

Another difference occurs in lines 31 through 38, where we specify various properties of the two messages `lIndex` and `lHigh`. Notice that, in lines 32 and 36, we set the alignment of the labels using a symbolic constant of the `Label` class, `Label.CENTER`. We have also changed the fonts and colors of the labels. Changing colors is nothing new, but changing fonts (lines 33 and 37) is. Those *font family* two lines can be explained easily. *Helvetica* is the name of a *font family* or *typeface* *typeface*, which includes characters with a common "look" in various sizes and styles (such as italic and bold). In line 33, we ask for the plain style of Helvetica *point* in size 10 (called 10 points, a *point* being a length used by typographers, equal to approximately $\frac{1}{72}$ inch). In line 37, we ask for the bold style in 20-point size. The `Font` class is summarized in Table 13.16. The start-up screen is shown in Figure 13.17.

Finally, there are two additional subtle changes that we have made. Instead of setting the frame's size to a particular dimension, we just `pack()` it in line 54. This causes each component of the frame to be packed to its preferred size—each text field, label, and check box. Then, working outward, the panels are set to *their* preferred sizes—in each case just big enough to "flow out" the contained

Name	Description
`static int BOLD`	The bold style.
`static int ITALIC`	The italic style.
`static int PLAIN`	The plain style.
`Font (String name, int style, int size)`	Creates a new font with the given name, style, and size.
`String getFamily ()`	Returns the family name for this font.
`int getStyle ()`	Returns the style for this font.
`String getFontName ()`	Returns the face name for this font.
`String getName ()`	Returns the name for this font.
`int getSize ()`	Returns the size for this font.
`boolean isBold ()`	Indicates whether this font is bold.
`boolean isItalic ()`	Indicates whether this font is italic.
`boolean isPlain ()`	Indicates whether this font is plain.
`String toString ()`	Stringifies this font.

TABLE 13.16   Some constants and methods of the `Font` class.

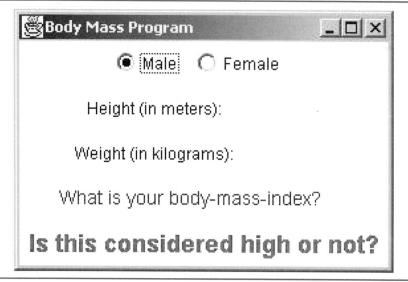

FIGURE 13.17   The final body mass applet, resized.

components. Finally, the full frame is set to *its* preferred size—just tall enough for the five components and just wide enough for the widest line! Perfect sizing! In addition, we can do a `pack()` anytime a recomputation is performed—in `compute()`—so that if a message gets much bigger or much smaller, the frame adjusts itself.

QUICK EXERCISE 13.11	Run the new `BodyMass` program with a variety of inputs, and notice how the frame resizes itself appropriately.

13.9

A Calendar Program

Scrollbar

Let's write a program to display a monthly calendar. We use the layout techniques of this chapter, together with a new component—the `Scrollbar`. The program will begin by displaying the present month, but we will allow the user to select any month from January 1000 to December 2199 by moving the scrollbar from side to side. When our program runs, the screen will look like Figure 13.18. (We moved the display to show January 1900.)

You cannot tell by the gray scale picture, but the "January 1900" banner is red on a yellow background, and the body of the calendar is blue on gray. By examining the desired screen appearance, you should be able to deduce what kinds of `Panels` and layouts we use. The names that we give to the various components are as follows:

1. `banner` contains the name of the month and the year.
2. `select` contains the `Scrollbar`.

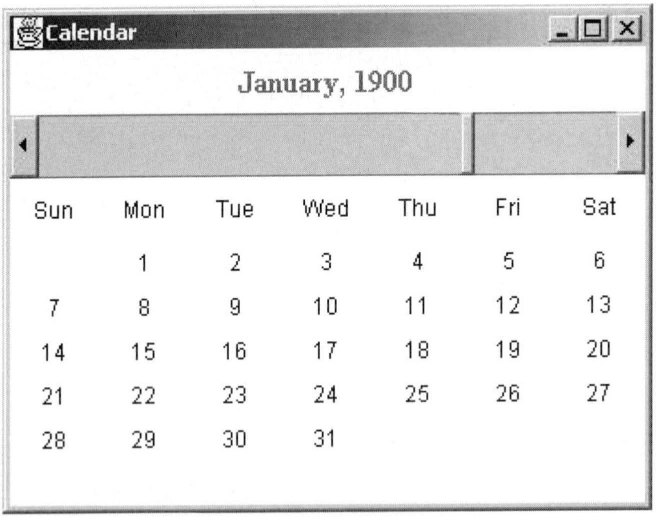

FIGURE 13.18   Output of the `Calendar` program.

3. days is a Panel containing the days of the week.

4. pBody is a Panel containing the body of the calendar.

Before reading further, see if you can figure out our layout plan.

Here is the plan. We use the BorderLayout manager (the one with "North", "South", "East", "West" and "Center" panels, shown in Figure 13.16). For our calendar, the "North" strip will contain the banner, the select, and the days components; the "Center" portion will contain the body of the calendar. The remaining border positions will not be used, so they will have zero size. The "North" strip is another Panel with a 3 × 1 GridLayout; within this Panel, the banner component will be on line 1, the select component on line 2, and the days component on line 3. The days component is yet another Panel with a 1 × 7 GridLayout, each cell containing a Label telling the day of the week. In the "Center" position we place a Panel that uses a 6 × 7 GridLayout, putting a Label into each cell.

Why couldn't we use a 4 × 1 grid layout for our calendar, with the four rows containing the banner, the select, the days, and the pBody components?	**QUICK EXERCISE** **13.12**

Before we continue, it is necessary to understand how the Scrollbar component works. The leftmost position of the Scrollbar corresponds to some integer value, and the rightmost to a larger integer value. When instantiating a Scrollbar, the programmer must specify these extreme values as well as the desired initial position of the "bubble," the desired direction of the scroll bar (Scrollbar.HORIZONTAL or Scrollbar.VERTICAL), and the thickness of the bubble. During program execution, the user can cause the Scrollbar's bubble to move toward one end or the other in three ways:

1. Clicking on either "end button" causes the bubble to move one "unit" in that direction.

2. Clicking in the area between an end button and the bubble causes the bubble to move 10 units in that direction.

3. Clicking and dragging on the bubble can cause it to move to any position.

These operations trigger events that the Scrollbar's Adjustment-Listener must interpret using the method adjustmentValueChanged. The interface AdjustmentListener is summarized in Table 13.17. Therefore, the Scrollbar is a complex but very powerful graphical interface component that allows the user to select an integer in a predefined range. The methods of the Scrollbar are summarized in Table 13.18.

We use the Scrollbar to select a month between January 1000 and December 2199. Since there are 12*1200 months in the range of interest, we

Method	Purpose
void adjustmentValueChanged (AdjustmentEvent e)	Called when any adjustment event occurs

TABLE 13.17 The `AdjustmentListener` **interface. Adjustment events are generated by scrollbars.**

Name	Description
static int HORIZONTAL	Indicates a horizontal scrollbar.
static int VERTICAL	Indicates a vertical scrollbar.
Scrollbar ()	Creates a new vertical scrollbar.
Scrollbar (int orient)	Creates a new scrollbar with orient orientation.
Scrollbar (int orient, int value, int visible, int min, int max)	Creates a new scrollbar with orient orientation, value for its initial value, visible for the size of the bubble, and given min and max values.
void addAdjustmentListener (AdjustmentListener l)	Makes l a listener for this scrollbar's adjustment events.
int getBlockIncrement ()	Returns the block increment value.
int getMaximum ()	Returns the maximum value.
int getMinimum ()	Returns the minimum value.
int getOrientation ()	Returns the orientation.
int getUnitIncrement ()	Returns the unit increment.
int getValue ()	Returns the current value of this scrollbar.
int getVisibleAmount ()	Returns the size of the bubble.
void setBlockIncrement (int i)	Sets the block increment to i.
void setMaximum (int i)	Sets the maximum value to i.
void setMinimum (int i)	Sets the minimum value to i.
void setOrientation (int i)	Sets the orientation to i.
void setUnitIncrement (int i)	Sets the unit increment to i.
void setValue (int i)	Sets the current value to i.
void setVisibleAmount (int i)	Sets the bubble size to i.
String toString ()	Stringifies this scrollbar.

TABLE 13.18   Some constants and methods of the `Scrollbar` class.

have our `Scrollbar` run through the values 0 to 13399, and we obtain the `Scrollbar` value in the variable `tallyMonth`. Thus, `tallyMonth=0` corresponds to `month=1` and `year=1000`, while `tallyMonth=13399` corresponds to `month=12` and `year=2199`. The conversion from `tallyMonth` to `month` and `year` is quite easy:

$$year = tallyMonth/12$$
$$month = tallyMonth - 12 \times year + 1$$
$$year = year + 1000$$

Here is the complete code for the `Calendar` program:

```java
import CSLib.*;
import java.awt.*;
import java.awt.event.*;
import java.util.*;

public class GUICalendar extends ClosableFrame
                    implements AdjustmentListener {

  // A Calendar, valid from 1/1/1000 to 12/31/2199
  // Author: Mark J. Mickunas, January 20, 1996

  Label banner;        // Month, year banner -- line 1
  Scrollbar select;    // Scrollbar -- line 2
  Panel days,          // days of week -- line 3
       pHead,          // contains lines 1, 2, 3 -- in "North" of frame
       pBody;          // contains body -- in "Center" of frame

  int tallyMonth;      // in the range 0..13399

  Label[][] lDate = new Label[6][7];


  public GUICalendar () {
    super("Calendar");

  // Find out today's date.
    Calendar calendar = new GregorianCalendar();
    int month = calendar.get(Calendar.MONTH);// 0 through 11 !!!
    int year = calendar.get(Calendar.YEAR);

    tallyMonth = (year-1000)*12 + month;

  // Allocate and lay out the components
    banner = new Label();
    banner.setAlignment(Label.CENTER);
    banner.setBackground(Color.yellow);
    banner.setFont(new Font("TimesRoman",Font.BOLD, 16));
    banner.setForeground(Color.red);

    select = new Scrollbar(
                  Scrollbar.HORIZONTAL, // orientation
                  tallyMonth,           // initial value
                  1,                    // slider width
                  0,                    // minimum value
                  1200*12);             // maximum value

    days = new Panel();
    days.setLayout(new GridLayout(1,7));
    for (int i = 0; i<7; i++) {
      Panel p = new Panel();
      p.add(new Label(MyDate.DAY_NAME[i], Label.CENTER));
      days.add(p);
    }
```

```
55      pHead = new Panel();
56      pHead.setLayout(new GridLayout(3,1));
57      pHead.add(banner);
58      pHead.add(select);
59      pHead.add(days);
60
61      pBody = new Panel();
62      pBody.setLayout(new GridLayout(6,7));
63      for (int i=0; i<6; i++)
64        for (int j=0; j<7; j++) {
65          lDate[i][j] = new Label("",Label.CENTER);
66          lDate[i][j].setForeground(Color.blue);
67          pBody.add(lDate[i][j]);
68        }
69
70      setLayout(new BorderLayout());
71      add("North",pHead);
72      add("Center",pBody);
73
74    // Register this applet as the scrollbar listener.
75      select.addAdjustmentListener(this);
76      compute();
77      pack();
78      setVisible(true);
79    }
80
81    public void compute() {
82    // Given tallyMonth, set the banner appropriately
83    // and fill in the calendar body.
84
85    // Compute month/year from the scrollbar position
86    // and repaint the calendar body appropriately
87      int year = tallyMonth/12;
88      int month = tallyMonth - 12*year + 1;
89      year = year + 1000;
90
91      banner.setText (MyDate.MONTH_NAME[month] + ", " + year);
92
93    // Blank out the calendar
94      for (int i=0; i<7; i++)
95        for (int j=0; j<6; j++)
96          lDate[j][i].setText("");
97
98    // Day of the week for day 1 of the month
99      int firstOfMonth = MyDate.dayOfWeek(month, 1, year);
100
101   // The first label to be filled is lDaye[0][firstOfMonth]
102     int x = firstOfMonth;
103     int y = 0;
104
105   // Run through all days in the month
106     for (int i = 1;
107          i <= MyDate.lastDayOfMonth(month, year);
108          i++) {
```

```
109
110        lDate[y][x].setText(""+i);
111        x++;
112
113     // Is it time to move to the next line?
114        if (x==7) {
115           y++;
116           x = 0;
117        }
118     }
119     repaint();
120   }
121
122   public void adjustmentValueChanged (AdjustmentEvent e) {
123   // Handle the scrollbar events
124      tallyMonth = e.getValue();
125      compute();
126   }
127 }
```

First, the constructor (lines 23 through 79) is where the work of setting up the frame layout takes place. In the constructor, we

1. Determine the `month, year` for today's date (lines 26 through 29).
2. Compute `tallyMonth` (line 31) for the scrollbar.
3. Instantiate the `banner Label`, and set its alignment, font, and foreground color (lines 34 through 38).
4. Instantiate the `select Scrollbar`, setting its initial value to `tallyMonth` (lines 40 through 45).
5. Lay out everything appropriately (lines 55 through 72).
6. Register `AdjustmentListener`(s) for the `select Scrollbar` (line 75).
7. Call `compute()` to initially set the `banner Label` and the calendar body (line 76).

Within the constructor, we can compute today's date by using the class `GregorianCalendar` in Java's `java.util` package (lines 26 through 29). The only methods and constants that we use are from `GregorianCalendar`'s superclass, `Calendar`; these are summarized in Table 13.19. We see that `GregorianCalendar` numbers months from 0 through 11, whereas our `Date` class uses 1 through 12, so we must be aware of this when we write our code.

The `compute` method itself must

1. Construct the month/year string from the value of `tallyMonth` (lines 85 through 91).
2. Update the `banner Label` (line 91).
3. Set the 42 individual day labels to blank (lines 93 through 96).
4. Determine the first day of the week to fill in, or equivalently, how many labels to skip on the first line (lines 99).

Symbolic Constant	Purpose
`static int DAY_OF_MONTH`	Field number for day of the month.
`static int MONTH`	Field number for month.
`static int YEAR`	Field number for the year.

Method	Purpose
`int get (int field)`	Returns the value for a specified field.

TABLE 13.19 A few constants and methods of Java's `Calendar` class.

5. Place the numerals 1, 2, ... *last day of the month* in successive labels (lines 101 through 118).
6. Call `repaint()` to draw the body of the calendar (line 119).

The reason why we encapsulate the `compute` code in a single method is that it is called from two places—first from the `Calendar`'s constructor and subsequently every time the scrollbar changes.

The only event of interest is activity within the `select` scrollbar, which is handled by the `adjustmentValueChanged` method:

```
122    public void adjustmentValueChanged (AdjustmentEvent e) {
123    // Handle the scrollbar events
124      tallyMonth = e.getValue();
125      compute();
126    }
```

For such a `Scrollbar` event we must obtain the integer value for the `Scrollbar`'s bubble (line 124) and then call `compute()` to redraw the calendar body.

13.10

Java and the Web

Most readers of this book are familiar with the World Wide Web. You use it whenever you use a *web browser*, such as Netscape Communicator, Microsoft's Internet Explorer. Browsers allow you to view *home pages* (also called *web pages*) set up by other users on other computers that are on the web. These home pages contain text and images and, less frequently, sound and animation. The computer that provides the home page is called a *server* (or *http server*, for *hypertext transport protocol server*); your computer is the *client* (although, at the

home pages
web pages

server
client

same time, it may be a server for other clients). Each home page has an address, giving the server it is on and its location on that server. This address is called a *uniform resource locator* (*URL*).

Home pages are written in a computer language called *hypertext markup language* (*HTML*), a language very different from Java. HTML pages are typed into a file, as Java programs are. They are not compiled, but when a computer on the web requests an HTML document, it receives the text in the file and uses it to create the image that the browser displays. In Section 13.10.1, we provide a quick HTML primer, enough for you to create a simple home page with text and images.

uniform resource locator

hypertext markup language

For the most part, when you view a web page in a browser, it is static—that is, it does not move much. There are limited exceptions, but something as dynamic as, for example, a video game could not be written as an HTML document. Simply put, HTML documents cannot exploit the computing power of the client. Java applets can overcome this limitation of web pages. Later in this chapter, we show how to write applets and include them in your own web pages.

13.10.1 HTML

Books—large ones!—have been written about how to write web pages in HTML. We will show you how to write simple HTML documents with some text and pictures. If you are interested in learning more, consult one of those large books or just look at the HTML "source" for pages as you surf; all web browsers provide a way to do this.

The simplest web page is one that has only text. Here is an example:

```
1   <HTML>
2   <HEAD>
3   <TITLE> My first home page </TITLE>
4   </HEAD>
5   <BODY>
6
7   My name is Napoleon I, Emperor of France.
8   I'm just learning HTML, so please be patient.
9   Soon, I will have the greatest home page in the
10  entire civilized world.
11
12  </BODY>
13  </HTML>
```

Figure 13.19 is a shot from Microsoft's Internet Explorer showing how it looks. There are several points to take from this web page. First, the entire document is surrounded by lines containing <HTML> and </HTML>. Words placed like this within angle brackets are called *tags*. Many tags come in pairs, indicating the beginning and end of some part of the HTML document. The <HTML> / </HTML> pair surrounds the entire document. Within this pair, the <HEAD> / </HEAD> pair encloses a <TITLE> / </TITLE> pair, which encloses the title; the browser places this title at the top of its window. The <BODY> /

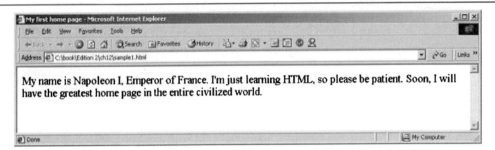

FIGURE 13.19   A screen dump showing the HTML document on page 523 in Internet Explorer.

</BODY> pair encloses the rest of the document. Each HTML page should consist of a head followed by a body. (As you can see in the example, tags do not have to go on a separate line.)

There are various ways to give the body of your home page some structure. The simplest mechanism is to use *headings* and *paragraphs*. The paragraph tag <P> simply leaves space in a document, corresponding to the start of a new paragraph; it has no closing tag. There are several heading tags, <H1>, ..., <H6>, corresponding to different heading levels. Tag H1 is for the biggest headings (like chapter titles) and H6 for the smallest (such as subsection titles). In practice, some headings may come out the same size. This HTML document shows the use of headings and paragraphs, as well as the <CENTER> tag pair to center the heading.

```
1    <HTML>
2    <HEAD>
3    <TITLE> Emperor Napoleon's Home Page </TITLE>
4    </HEAD>
5    <BODY>
6
7    <CENTER><H1>Napoleon I</H1></CENTER>
8
9    <P>
10   My name is Napoleon I, Emperor of France.
11   I am a famous general and have conquered many countries.
12   I'm most proud of my work at Austerlitz, and have always
13   felt that my generalship at Waterloo has been underestimated.
14
15   <P>
16   In my spare time, I like to do origami
17   and spend quiet evenings at home with my wife Josephine.
18   </BODY>
19   </HTML>
```

Figure 13.20 is a screen dump of this web page. (Note that the large H1 title is in the *body* of the HTML document; the title portion of the web page simply provides the text displayed as the title of the window.)

Many HTML tags include *attributes*, written as a name, an equals sign, and a value (which is usually a string in quotes). Pictures—*GIF* or *JPEG*[2] images

GIF

---

[2]GIF stands for *graphics interchange format*; JPEG stands for *joint photographic experts group*.

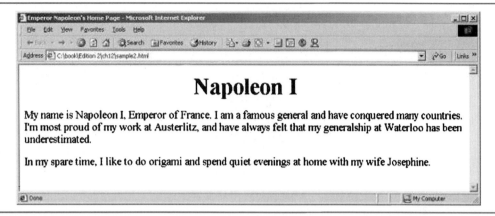

FIGURE 13.20   A screen dump showing the HTML document on page 524 in Internet Explorer.

stored in their own files—can be included in web pages by using the IMG tag   *JPEG*
with the SRC attribute. It is common practice to store all images in a subdirectory,
simply as a matter of organization. This web page (whose screen dump is shown
in Figure 13.21) assumes that the files me.jpg and grayline.gif are stored
in the directory images, a subdirectory of the one that contains the HTML page.[3]

```
1    <HTML>
2    <HEAD>
3    <TITLE> Emperor Napoleon's Home Page </TITLE>
4    </HEAD>
5    <BODY>
6
7    <CENTER>
8    <IMG SRC="images/me.jpg">
9    <H1>Napoleon I</H1>
10   </CENTER>
11
12   <P>
13   <IMG SRC="images/greyline.gif">
14
15   <P>
16   My name is Napoleon I, Emperor of France.
17   I am a famous general and have conquered many countries.
18   I am most proud of my work at Austerlitz, and have always
19   felt that my generalship at Waterloo has been underestimated.
20
21   <P>
22   In my spare time, I like to do origami
```

---

[3]You can find lots of small images like these by surfing the net. When an image shows up in the web page you are viewing, your browser will allow you to save your own copy of it; check the documentation for the browser.

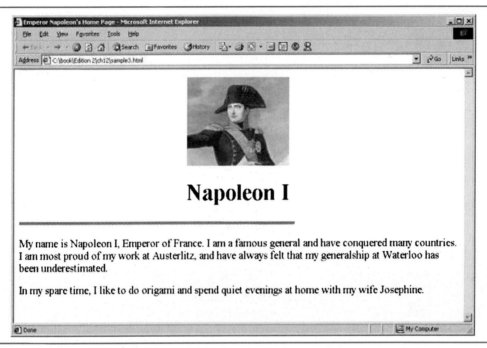

FIGURE 13.21   A screen dump showing the HTML document on page 525 in Internet Explorer.

```
23   and spend quiet evenings at home with my wife Josephine.
24   </BODY>
25   </HTML>
```

A key feature—really, *the* key feature—of HTML pages is their ability to link to other HTML pages (as well as non-HTML files). Usually, links are highlighted in some way, and clicking on them causes the browser to load the linked page. To include a link, use the <A> / </A> tag pair. The HREF attribute gives the address of the page you wish to link to, and the text (or image) within the <A> / </A> pair is the link. The following HTML document (screen dump in Figure 13.22) contains one link to another page in this directory and one link to a page on another server.

```
1    <HTML>
2    <HEAD>
3    <TITLE> Emperor Napoleon's Home Page </TITLE>
4    </HEAD>
5    <BODY>
6
7    <CENTER>
8    <IMG SRC="images/me.jpg">
9    <H1>Napoleon I</H1>
10   </CENTER>
11
```

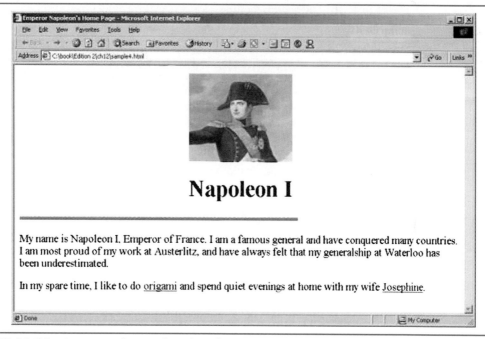

FIGURE 13.22   A screen dump showing the HTML document on page 526 in Internet Explorer.

```
12    <P>
13    <IMG SRC="images/greyline.gif">
14
15    <P>
16    My name is Napoleon I, Emperor of France.
17    I am a famous general and have conquered many countries.
18    I am most proud of my work at Austerlitz, and have always
19    felt that my generalship at Waterloo has been underestimated.
20
21    <P>
22    In my spare time, I like to do
23    <A HREF=
24    "http://www.yahoo.com/Recreation/Hobbies_and_Crafts/Origami/">
25    origami</A>
26    and spend quiet evenings at home with my wife
27    <A HREF="jojo.html">Josephine</A>.
28    </BODY>
29    </HTML>
```

You can create your own simple home page using just the HTML features we presented. For it really to be a web page, you must place it on an http server with an appropriate name and in an appropriate directory; ask your system administrator how to do this.

The features we have covered allow the creation of only "static" web pages. You may have seen active-looking web pages—for example, those with animated

GIFs or forms and search facilities—but HTML provides very limited facilities for such active pages. The purpose of Java is to remedy this.

13.10.2 Applets and the APPLET Tag

Imagine you would like to provide a simple video game on the Internet. You are willing to do all the work and provide the game for free. In fact, you will provide it to anyone who can access your home page. But how? You might provide it as an executable file; but then users have to download and store it and then exit their browsers to run it. Furthermore, many will be unwilling to try it for fear of viruses. The best solution would be to provide it as part of your home page, but there is no way to write the game in HTML.

Here is where Java comes in. It can be used to write *applets*—computer programs that run within a window of your home page set aside for the applet. The browser can guarantee that the applet cannot store unwanted data on your machine and does not carry a virus. With an applet (or several!) running in your home page, it is truly an *active* page.

Fortunately, all the programs that we have written so far can be transformed to applets! More precisely, we can write a "shell" applet that allocates an instance of any of the programs we have written so far. Once your applet shell is written and compiled into a .class file, you must write some HTML to include it in your web page. In your web page you use the <APPLET> tag to open a window for the applet and start it up.

```
<APPLET CODE=" filename.class",
        WIDTH= integer,
        HEIGHT= integer>
</APPLET>
```

The <APPLET> tag gives the name of the class file as the CODE attribute, and the size of the applet's window as the WIDTH and HEIGHT attributes. The HTML page in Figure 13.23 includes the BodyMass program as an applet, which we will now explain. Notice that the Java program must specify the full file name for the program's .class file, enclosed in double quotes. The size of the applet is set to 0×0 in line 33 because we do not place anything explicitly in the browser window; we just run the BodyMass program, which pops up its own frame.

The Java shell for an applet always has a particular form, as follows:

```
1    import java.applet.*;
2    public class BodyMassApplet extends Applet {
3
4      public void init () {
5        new BodyMass();
6      }
7    }
```

As you can see, the applet shell is almost trivial. As always, it defines a new class having the same name as the file. The class is a subclass of Applet, which is a class defined in the java.awt package; the Applet class is summarized in Table 13.20. Consequently, lines 1 and 3 appear as you would expect. The real

```
 1   <HTML>
 2   <HEAD>
 3   <TITLE> Emperor Napoleon's Home Page </TITLE>
 4   </HEAD>
 5   <BODY>
 6
 7   <CENTER>
 8   <IMG SRC="images/me.jpg">
 9   <H1>Napoleon I</H1>
10   </CENTER>
11
12   <P>
13   <IMG SRC="images/greyline.gif">
14
15   <P>
16   My name is Napoleon I, Emperor of France.
17   I am a famous general and have conquered many countries.
18   I am most proud of my work at Austerlitz, and have always
19   felt that my generalship at Waterloo has been underestimated.
20
21   <P>
22   In my spare time, I like to do
23   <A HREF=
24   "http://www.yahoo.com/Recreation/Hobbies_and_Crafts/Origami/">
25   origami</A>
26   and spend quiet evenings at home with my wife
27   <A HREF="jojo.html">Josephine</A>.
28
29   <P>
30   Also, I am just learning to write applets!
31   Here is my first effort;  I hope you like it:
32
33   <APPLET CODE="BodyMassApplet.class" WIDTH=0 HEIGHT=0>
34   </APPLET>
35
36   </BODY>
37   </HTML>
```

FIGURE 13.23 An HTML document with an embedded applet.

difference is that the `init` method is used instead of the `main` method, Within this `init` method, we just allocate the desired `Frame` subclass — `BodyMass` in this case.

Sometimes you want to transform a program completely into an applet, drawing in the *applet's* field rather than in a separate pop-up frame. Our graphical programs can be easily transformed as follows:

1. Set the size that you want the applet to be in your HTML file.
2. Add the `import java.applet.*;` statement.
3. Change `extends Frame` (or `extends ClosableFrame`) to `extends Applet`.

Name	Description
URL getCodeBase ()	Returns the base URL from where this applet was loaded.
Image getImage (URL url)	Returns an image from the given URL.
void init ()	Called by the browser to inform this applet that it has been loaded.
void start ()	Called by the browser to inform this applet that it should start its execution.
void stop ()	Called by the browser to inform this applet that it should stop its execution.

TABLE 13.20   Some methods of the Applet class.

4. Change the constructor heading to `public void init()`.
5. Eliminate any code that is meaningless in an applet, such as setting the title, packing, and resizing. (These are meaningless because there is no title in the applet portion of a browser, and the HTML specifies a fixed size for the applet.)

So if we change line 33 in Napoleon's HTML file to

```
33     <APPLET CODE="BodyMass.class" WIDTH=200 HEIGHT=200>
```

and make the above changes to BodyMass, turning it into an applet, we get the results shown in Figure 13.24. The modified code is as follows:

```
1    import CSLib.*;
2    import java.applet.*;
3    import java.awt.*;
4    import java.awt.event.*;
5
6    public class BodyMass extends Applet
7                    implements ActionListener, ItemListener {
8
9      // Determine Body-Mass-Index and Obesity
10     // Author: Deborah Mickunas, October 13, 1996
11
12       // Declare Components
13       TextField tHeight, tWeight;
14       Label lIndex, lHigh;
15       CheckboxGroup gender;
16       Checkbox maleCheck, femaleCheck;
17
18     public void init () {
19
20         // Allocate components.
21         tHeight = new TextField(5);
22         tWeight = new TextField(5);
23         lIndex = new Label("What is your body-mass-index?     ");
24         lHigh = new Label("Is this considered high or not?");
25         gender = new CheckboxGroup();
26         maleCheck = new Checkbox("Male", gender, true);
```

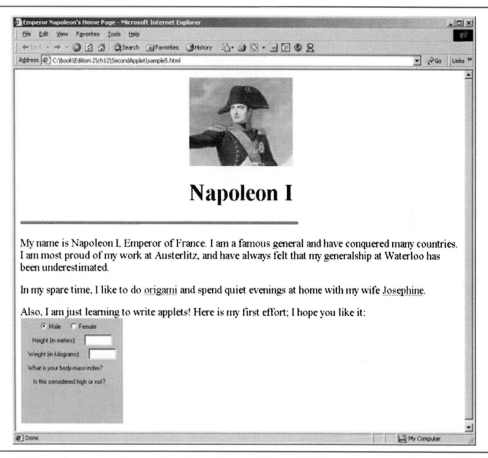

FIGURE 13.24   A screen dump showing the modified HTML document with an embedded applet.

```
27          femaleCheck = new Checkbox("Female", gender, false);
28
29          // Arrange Components
30          setLayout(new FlowLayout());
31          add(maleCheck);
32          add(femaleCheck);
33          add(new Label("Height (in meters):"));
34          add(tHeight);
35          add(new Label("Weight (in kilograms):"));
36          add(tWeight);
37          add(lIndex);
38          add(lHigh);
39
40          setSize(250,200);
41          setVisible(true);
42
43          // Register Component Listeners
44          tHeight.addActionListener(this);
```

```
45        tWeight.addActionListener(this);
46        maleCheck.addItemListener(this);
47        femaleCheck.addItemListener(this);
48     }
49
50     public void itemStateChanged (ItemEvent e) {
51        // Respond to Item Events:
52        //       1. femaleCheck Checkbox
53        //       2. maleCheck Checkbox
54        compute();
55     }
56
57     public void actionPerformed (ActionEvent e) {
58        // Respond to Action Events:
59        //       1. tHeight TextField
60        //       2. tWeight TextField
61        compute();
62     }
63
64     private void compute () {
65        double height =
66              new Double(tHeight.getText()).doubleValue();
67        double weight =
68              new Double(tWeight.getText()).doubleValue();
69        double bodyMassIndex = weight / (height * height);
70        boolean female =
71              (gender.getSelectedCheckbox() == femaleCheck);
72
73        lIndex.setText("Your body-mass-index is " + bodyMassIndex);
74        if ((bodyMassIndex > 27.8) ||
75           female && (bodyMassIndex > 27.3))
76           lHigh.setText("This is considered high.");
77        else
78           lHigh.setText("This is not considered high.");
79     }
80  }
```

Summary

Web pages are written in hypertext markup language, or HTML. HTML documents contain *tags*, some in opening and closing pairs, which allow the insertion of headings and pictures. Applets are included in web pages by using the APPLET tag

```
<APPLET CODE=" filename.class",
        WIDTH= integer,
        HEIGHT= integer>
</APPLET>
```

The essential parts of a Java applet are

```
import java.applet.*;

public class Classname extends Applet {

   public void init() {
      ...
   }
}
```

Unlike an application, an applet does not contain a `main` method. Its class header must include the words `extends Applet`.

In a graphical program, you can add components such as buttons and text fields. You can make the applet respond to events like button presses by "registering" the component. This is done by calling the `addActionListener` method and defining the `actionPerformed` method (thereby implementing the `ActionListener` interface).

You can draw simple shapes, and include images from files, in a subclass of `Canvas` or `Container` by defining the `paint` method. The Java run-time system passes to it a `Graphics` object. `Graphics` methods like `drawLine`, `fillRect`, and `drawImage` are used to display pictures in the `Canvas` or `Container`.

To change the color of components, use `setBackground` and `setForeground`. To change the color of pictures drawn with `Graphics` methods, use `setColor`.

Quite a few books have more complete details on Java components; the definitive and most up-to-date list is the one at the Sun Microsystems, Inc., web site:

```
http://www.javasoft.com
```

From that home page, you can locate the documentation for Java 2 (version 1.3 as of this writing) of the Java API, which is most current at the time of this writing and is the version that we use in this book.

The `TextField` component can be used for both input [using `getText()`] and output [using `setText()`]. A `Checkbox` component causes an event to be triggered when the user "selects" it by clicking on it with the mouse. `Checkboxes` may be grouped into a `CheckboxGroup`, in which case only one may be selected at any one time. Such grouped `Checkboxes` are called *radio buttons*. A `Button` component triggers an event when the user clicks on it with the mouse.

`Checkboxes` are registered as reactive components slightly differently from `TextFieldss` and `Buttons`. They are registered using `addItemListener`, and the events they generate are handled in `itemStateChanged`.

A layout manager governs the manner in which components are arranged on the screen. The default layout manager is the `FlowLayout` manager, which arranges components from left to right and top to bottom. Another layout manager is the `GridLayout` manager, which arranges components in an $n \times m$ rectangular grid. Yet a third layout manager, the `BorderLayout` manager, allows the placement of components at north, south, east, west, and center locations.

Exercises

1. Modify the `Temperature` program so that it gets a temperature in degrees Fahrenheit and displays the equivalent Centigrade *and* Kelvin temperatures.

2. In Section 3.22 on page 86, you wrote a program to calculate the price of a coffee order. Turn this application into a graphical program with appropriately labeled text fields for input.

3. Reprogram the `BodyMass` program so that the message "This is not considered high" is displayed in blue, 16-point Helvetica type, while the message "This is considered high" is displayed in red, 40-point bold Helvetica type. Be sure to resize the window when you increase this message size.

4. Modify our `CalendarApplet` so that today's date is enclosed in a rectangle.

5. Modify our `CalendarApplet` so that the first row of the calendar body ("Sun Mon ... Sat") is displayed in magenta, bold, 16-point Helvetica font.

6. Many electronic devices use seven-segment displays to show numbers. These displays consist of seven straight lines as shown here (with labels added for reference):

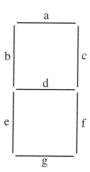

   Zero is drawn with segments a, b, c, e, f, and g; 1 is usually drawn with lines c and f; 2 with lines a, c, d, e, and g; and so on. Write a program with a text field for input of a number between 0 and 9 which draws the seven-segment version of that number.

7. In Exercise 7 on page 141 you wrote an application to compute whether a person is eligible for candidacy for Congress, given the person's age and years of citizenship. Rewrite this as a graphical program, using two `TextFields` for input.

8. In Exercise 11 on page 144 you wrote a switch statement to compute the postage rate for an item, given the weight of the item and the mail class. Write a graphical program to compute and display the postage rate. Use a `TextField` to input the weight, and use three grouped radio buttons to select the class of mail.

9. Write a program to display various red, green, and blue (RGB) combinations. Write a program that reads three values, each between 0 and 255, representing the red, green, and blue components, and displays a filled rectangle in that color. Use text fields for input. Include six buttons, labeled `Less red`, `More red`, `Less green`, and so on. When one of these buttons is pushed, the value in the corresponding `TextField` is incremented or decremented by 10, and the new color is displayed.

10. Recall from Chapter 2 that colors are objects of class `Color`, whose constructors include a three-argument constructor in which three integers between 0 and 255 supply the red, green, and blue components of the color. A color can be made redder by increasing the red component, and likewise for green and blue. It can be darkened by reducing all three values and lightened by increasing them.

   Define a program `ColorTest` that contains integer variables `red`, `green`, and `blue`, in the range 0 to 255, for the red, green, and blue values of a color.

It has methods to modify these variables individually, as well as to modify them all (i.e., to change the brightness of the combined color). In addition, it has methods getColor, getRedComponent, getGreenComponent, and getBlueComponent. Each of these returns a Color object. For example, getRedComponent returns the color with RGB components (red, 0, 0).The method getColor returns the color with RGB components (red, green, blue).

Your program should have buttons for changing the three hues (red, green, and blue) by a fixed percentage and for changing the brightness. Another button, labeled increase or decrease, indicates in which direction the other buttons operate; clicking on it toggles it. For example, if the direction button says increase, then clicking on the Red button will increase the amount of red shown; clicking on the direction button changes its label to decrease, so that clicking on the Red button decreases the amount of red. The program should display boxes showing the red, green, and blue components and the combined color, side by side (use setBackground and drawFillRect); each time one of the buttons is pressed, these colors need to be changed.

11. Write a program to display a color bar. You should have two check boxes, labeled Color 1 and Color 2, respectively, and three text fields, labeled Red, Green, and Blue. The user enters two colors by first clicking on the Color 1 box and then entering integers (in the range 0 to 255) in the text fields, and then clicking on the Color 2 box and entering integers in the text fields. Given these two colors, say (r_1, g_1, b_1) and (r_2, g_2, b_2), show a bar of colors consisting of 10 narrow strips of color, with the leftmost strip containing color 1 and the rightmost strip containing color 2, and the eight strips in between containing shades between those two colors. Specifically, if $\delta_r = r_2 - r_1$, and similarly for δ_g and δ_b, then the color strips should contain (r_1, g_1, b_1) (color 1), $(r_1 + \delta_r/9, g_1 + \delta_g/9, b_1 + \delta_b/9)$, $(r_1 + 2\delta_r/9, g_1 + 2\delta_g/9, b_1 + 2\delta_b/9)$, and so on.

12. In exercise 12 in Chapter 6, you wrote an application to draw a sine curve in a drawing box. Modify this application in three ways:
    (a) Add three text fields to replace the input windows prompting for the x range (two doubles) and the x increment (one double). Each time a new number is entered and the user types the enter key, the graph should be redrawn.
    (b) Add a check box from which the user can choose a sine, cosine, or tangent, curve. If more than one curve is selected, draw all the curves at once. If one of the number inputs is changed, all the selected curves should be redrawn.
    (c) Revise the program from part b to use radio buttons instead of check boxes, so that only one curve at a time can be selected.

13. Modify the RandomCircles program from Section 13.5 on page 502 to draw circles filled with a specified color. Use the idea of the ColorTest program (Exercise 10 on page 534) to let the user specify a color. Specifically, the program should have six buttons: Circle, More (which toggles to Less and back), Red, Green, Blue, and Bright. The Circle button places a random circle in the program, filled with the current color. Whenever any of the other buttons is pressed, this indicates a change in the color, and all the circles should be redrawn in the new color. Implement the program by defining a Circle class with constructor Circle(Point loc, int radius) and method draw(Graphics g, Color c), and have the program store an array of Circle objects.

RECURSION

Recursion is a programming technique in which a method calls itself. It is an advanced technique that, once grasped, can lead to solutions to problems that would be difficult to write without it. Among our examples are `quicksort`, perhaps the best all-around sorting method known, and Gaussian elimination, a method for solving systems of linear equations. We introduce a data structure, the *linked list*, that stores values (as an array does) but has the useful property of being able to grow dynamically. It is particularly natural to use recursion when writing methods on linked lists; our largest example of this is `mergesort`, another very efficient sorting method. We give programs for drawing two types of *fractal* curves, designs whose description is inherently recursive.

Recursion is the mechanism of having a method invoke itself or, in other words, having a message send itself as a further message. Recursion is a fundamental technique in programming, and in this chapter we analyze the technique in detail.

14.1

Introduction to Recursion

The most basic technique in solving any problem is to divide it into smaller subproblems. Those subproblems may in turn be divided into even smaller subproblems, continuing until you get to a problem small enough to be solved directly. We do this when we create a collection of classes and methods that together solve a programming problem; each class or method is the solution of a subproblem. Some of these subproblems are easy enough that we don't need to define any more methods but can solve them directly.

When we solve computational problems, often the subproblems are very similar in structure to the original problem. We can think of the subproblems as just being simpler versions of the same problem. Here are some examples:

- *Sorting an array.* Consider the insertion sort method (page 296), in which the elements are successively inserted into the sorted part of the array, thereby increasing the size of the sorted "subarray" until it encompasses the entire array. One way to think of this method is this: To sort an array *A*, first sort all of *A* except the last element, then insert the last element in the correct order. The subproblem "sort all of *A* except the last element" is similar to the original problem, but easier because we are being asked to sort a slighty smaller array. Of course, if A is so small that it has no subarrays, we can sort it directly; in fact, if A has only one element, then we can "sort" it by doing nothing! This leads to a very concise description of the insertion sort method, where $sort(A, n)$ means "sort the elements of A from 0 to n."

$$sort(A, n) = \begin{cases} \text{insert } A[n] \text{ in } sort(A, n - 1), \text{ if } n > 0 \\ \text{do nothing, if } n = 0 \end{cases}$$

We can actually use this description *directly* in Java, creating a version of insertion sort that follows it closely (as we will do on page 549). Even if we stick with our earlier version, it is worthwhile to have such a concise description of the algorithm. Furthermore, the idea of using recursion will lead us to the discovery—actually, a fairly simple discovery, once we understand recursion—of much more efficient sorting algorithms.

- *Solving a set of simultaneous equations.* Given a set of n equations in n unknowns

$$
\begin{array}{ccccccccc}
a_{11}x_1 & + & a_{12}x_2 & + & \cdots & + & a_{1,n}x_n & = & b_1 \\
a_{21}x_1 & + & a_{22}x_2 & + & \cdots & + & a_{2,n}x_n & = & b_2 \\
\cdots & \cdots & \cdots & \cdots & & \cdots & \cdots & \cdots & \cdots \\
a_{n,1}x_1 & + & a_{n,2}x_2 & + & \cdots & + & a_{n,n}x_n & = & b_n
\end{array}
$$

there is a well-known method to solve this system for the values of $x_1, \ldots, x_n$: Use the last equation to express x_n in terms of the other unknowns

$$x_n = \frac{b_n - a_{n,1}x_1 - \cdots - a_{n,n-1}x_{n-1}}{a_{n,n}}$$

and then *eliminate* x_n by replacing every occurrence of it in the remaining equations by the expression on the right-hand side. The result, after simplification, is a system of $n - 1$ equations in $n - 1$ unknowns. This is a problem similar to the original in structure, but smaller, so we should be able to solve it using the same general idea. If we have a system that has just one equation in one unknown ($ax = b$), it can be solved directly ($x = b/a$) and there is no need to solve any subproblems. Again, this allows us to write a concise description of this classic algorithm. As we will see in Section 14.5.4, we can implement this method directly in Java. Even if we choose not to, it is good to have this description, which is far clearer and more direct than the usual description of the method, which involves several nested loops.

- *Binomial coefficients.* The binomial coefficient $\dbinom{m}{n}$, read "m choose n," is the number of subsets of size n possessed by a set S of size m. For example, $\dbinom{12}{5}$ is the number of ways of choosing a starting lineup in a basketball game from a total roster of 12 players. The problem of calculating $\binom{m}{n}$ can be broken into two similar subproblems in this way: Choose an element $x \in S$ (it doesn't matter which one). Every n–element subset of S either contains x or does not. In other words, it is either an $(n - 1)$–element subset of $S - \{x\}$ with x added, or an n-element subset of $S - \{x\}$. Thus, we can find $\binom{m}{n}$ by summing $\binom{m - 1}{n - 1}$ and $\binom{m - 1}{n}$. Both subproblems are similar to the original, but they are simpler because the sets in question are smaller. When the sets get really small, we don't need to consider any subproblems at all: for example, every set has exactly one subset of size 0 (namely, the empty set), and a set of size 0 has no subsets of size greater than 0. Thus, we can immediately solve the problems $\binom{m}{0}$ (always equal to 1, no matter what m is) and $\binom{0}{n}$ (always equal to 0, as long as $n > 0$).

In each of these cases, a problem could be solved by dividing it into one or two similar, but easier, subproblems. An algorithm expressed in this way is called a *recursive algorithm*.

recursive algorithm

Having expressed an algorithm recursively, a Java programmer has a choice: Either copy this description of the algorithm directly into Java, or write a different, perhaps nonrecursive, implementation of the algorithm. Recursive algorithms are sometimes avoided because they are said to be inefficient. Indeed, they are sometimes less efficient than nonrecursive implementations, but they are sometimes *more* efficient. We will see examples of both in this chapter.

In any case, recursive algorithms are often simpler and more concise than nonrecursive ones. It is always worthwhile to have a clear and concise description of an algorithm, even if, in the end, you decide to implement a different, more efficient version. That is why an understanding of recursion is an essential tool in any programmer's repertoire.

14.2

A First Example

It is important to realize that recursively described algorithms *can be* implemented in Java (and most other programming languages) directly. In other words, a method can *call itself* with different arguments, to solve a (presumably, smaller) subproblem.

As an example, consider the problem of counting the number of digits in the decimal representation of an integer. We last discussed this problem in Section 6.6

(page 182), where we wrote the loop in this method:

```
int numberOfDigits (int n) {
   int numDigits = 0;
   int rest = n;
   do {
      // The number of digits in n is numDigits
      // plus the number of digits in rest
      rest = rest / 10;
      numDigits++;
   }
   while (rest != 0);
   return numDigits;
}
```

At that time, we didn't know how to think recursively. If we had, we might have begun by writing this definition of the function named digits:

$$\text{digits}(n) = \begin{cases} 1 & \text{if } -9 \leq n \leq 9 \\ 1 + \text{digits}(n/10) & \text{otherwise} \end{cases}$$

For example, we can compute the number of digits in 321 as

$$\begin{aligned}
\text{digits}(321) &= 1 + \text{digits}(321/10) = 1 + \text{digits}(32) \\
&= 1 + [1 + \text{digits}(32/10)] = 1 + [1 + \text{digits}(3)] \\
&= 1 + [1 + (1)] \\
&= 3
\end{aligned}$$

This definition can be turned directly into an elegant Java method:

```
1   int numberOfDigits (int n) {
2      if (( -10 < n) && (n < 10))
3         return 1;
4      else
5         return 1+numberOfDigits(n/10);
6   }
```

Like all recursive definitions, this *appears* to be circular. We all know that circular definitions are unacceptable because they lead nowhere, but the "circularity" here is not really a circle. Rather, it is a downward *spiral* that eventually terminates. The number of digits is defined by reference to the number of digits in a smaller value, which is defined in terms of the number of digits in a still smaller value, which eventually is defined in terms of the number of digits in a one-digit number. Because a one-digit number obviously has one digit, we can retrace our way outward on the spiral to compute the number of digits; that is what we just did.

Which definition is more efficient, the loop from Chapter 5 or the recursive definition we just gave? In a broad sense, they both use the same *algorithm*— divide by 10 until there is nothing left—so their speeds should be comparable. Indeed, their running times are nearly indistinguishable. In some other languages, and in some implementations of Java, the recursive version would be slower, because making method calls is usually slower than iterating a loop. On the other hand, the recursive version was really easy to write.

In this chapter, we will see many examples of recursion. We find that the use of recursion sometimes can yield solutions to problems that would be very difficult to find if we knew how to write only iterative algorithms (algorithms that use loops).

Time the two versions of the digits function on your computer. They each run far too fast to see any difference if you call them just once. You need to write a loop in your `main` program that calls them multiple times—perhaps 1 million times or more—in order to see the difference. You should take into account the cost of the 1 million method calls themselves by running your program with 1 million calls to a method that does nothing at all. For example, if calling the do-nothing method 1 million times takes 10 seconds, calling the nonrecursive version of digits takes 20 seconds, and calling the recursive version takes 25 seconds, then we calculate that the recursive version is 50 percent slower than the nonrecursive one (15 seconds versus 10 seconds).

14.3

Divide and Conquer

The way to think about recursion is this: If you want to compute $f(x)$, but you can't compute it directly, *assume* you can compute $f(y)$ for any value y smaller than x; then use the value of $f(y)$ to find the value of $f(x)$. This analysis will show how to use a recursive call in your Java method.

You are not quite done. There must be some values of x for which $f(x)$ can be calculated directly—if $f(x)$ *always* involved calling $f(y)$ for some y, the function would make recursive calls forever and never return—so you have to determine what those are and account for them in your function. These are called the *base cases*.

base cases

As an example of expressing a computation of $f(x)$ in terms of $f(y)$ for values of y less than x, suppose we want a method that will compute an integer raised to an integer power. That is, we will define the function `int power(int k, int n)`, which computes k^n. Thinking recursively, we ask this fundamental question:

> Given that we want to compute `power(k, n)`, for what values $k1 \leq k$ and $n1 \leq n$ can the value of `power(k1, n1)` help?

For example, would it help to know power(k-1, n), or power(k, n-1), or power(k-1, n-1)? In fact, power(k, n-1) helps: if we have power(k, n-1), which we know to equal k^{n-1}, we can calculate power(k, n) = k^n by multiplying by k. Thus, we arrive at a simple recursive function:

```
static int power(int k, int n) {
    // Raise k to the power n
    return k*power(k, n-1);
}
```
NEEDS BASE CASES

As the shading indicates, this function won't work as is—it just leads to the function calling itself over and over without end—because we need to handle the base case. Again, the base case is a value, or set of values, for k and n such that the result of the call can be computed directly, with no recursive calls. For power, if n = 0, then the result is always 1; this is a sensible base case, because each recursive call decreases n by 1, so eventually power will call itself with n equal to 0. This leads to a correct recursive definition:

```
static int power(int k, int n) {
    // Raise k to the power n
    if (n==0)
        return 1;
    else
        return k*power(k, n-1);
}
```

The algorithm we just developed essentially is the same one you would probably use if you were to write power iteratively. However, a virtue of recursion is that it can sometimes lead you to efficient algorithms that would be very hard to write using loops. As an example, we can give a much more efficient method for calculating power, based on a different way of answering the question above. We asked if, in calculating power(k, n), it would be helpful to know a value such as power(k, n-1)? But it turns out that it can be helpful to know the value of power for even smaller arguments: It helps to know the value of power(k, n/2) = $k^{n/2}$ if n is even, because $k^n = (k^{n/2})^2$; likewise, $k^n = (k^{(n-1)/2})^2 \times k$ if n is odd. By using the same base case as in the first version of power, this leads directly to the Java method

```
1   static int power (int k, int n) {
2   // Raise k to the power n.
3     if (n == 0)
4       return 1;
5     else {
6       int t = power(k, n/2);
7       if ((n % 2) == 0)
8         return t*t;
9       else
10        return k*t*t;
11    }
12  }
```

(Note that the expression $n/2$ is integer division, so it calculates $n/2$ if n is even and $(n - 1)/2$ if n is odd, which is just what we want.)

Why is this more efficient than the first version? Instead of recursively solving a slightly smaller instance of the same problem—k^{n-1}—this method recursively solves a problem that is *one-half the size* of the original—$k^{n/2}$. Such an algorithm is called a *divide-and-conquer* algorithm. If we use the number of multiplications as a measure of efficiency, we find that the first version of power uses n multiplications to calculate k^n, whereas the second version uses approximately $\log n$ multiplications, a much smaller number. [You can see this more clearly after reading the next section; see Exercise 1(d) on page 600.]

divide-and-conquer

It is important to understand that recursive methods are not always more efficient than iterative ones. On the contrary, a recursive method using the same algorithm as an iterative method almost always will be somewhat *slower* than the iterative method. Depending upon the Java compiler, the first version of power might well be two or three times slower than the obvious iterative version. They would both do the same number of multiplications (n multiplications to calculate k^n), but recursion involves computational overhead, especially the method calls, that makes it more expensive. On the other hand, it is unlikely that we would ever have found the second version of power if we didn't know how to use recursion, and it is much more efficient than even the iterative version, because it actually does fewer multiplications.

QUICK EXERCISE 14.2

As in Quick Exercise 14.1, compare the running times of the two recursive versions of power. One problem you will find is that you cannot supply very large arguments to this method without causing an integer overflow. You have several options to deal with this: (1) As in Quick Exercise 14.1, call the method in a loop and then subtract out the cost of the loop. (2) Use 1 as the first argument; then the second argument can be as big as you like without causing an overflow. (3) Ignore the overflow; for this exercise, you don't care about getting the correct answer, just calculating the running time.

14.4

Under the Hood

We have emphasized that it is best to write recursive methods without thinking about how the recursive calls are handled. (Our mantra has been "*assume* the recursive call returns the correct result and just use it.") Nonetheless, it is natural to wonder how this all works, especially because it seems so circular.

The mechanism of recursion actually involves nothing beyond what we have already learned, but it is worthwhile to review it with an eye toward understanding this new use.

We have mentioned how method calls are *nested*. If method f calls method g, then when g is done, the program returns to f and continues executing from just after the call to g.

Before g returns to *f*, it might call method h, which might call yet another method, and so on. Thus, at any moment there may be several unfinished method calls. The method called most recently executes, while the others wait for the methods they called to return so they can continue. We can visualize this "stack" of methods as sheets of paper in a pile: when a method is called, a new sheet is added, and when it returns, that sheet is discarded:

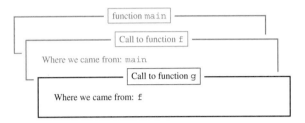

We can get a more accurate view by placing on each piece of paper the values of the parameters and local variables. Suppose we make the call power(7, 5), using the second version of power—the divide-and-conquer version—from somewhere in main:

```
main () {
    .
    .
    .
    int x = power(7, 5);
    .
    .
    .
}
```

On a piece of paper, write the lines

Call to method power
Where we came from: main
Value supplied for k: 7
Value supplied for n: 5
Value of t: as yet uninitialized

Here n is compared to 0; because the value of n on the top piece of paper is 5, the else clause (lines 6 through 10) is executed. The first action in the else clause is to set t to power(7, 2), which causes a recursive call, so the stack of papers now looks like this:

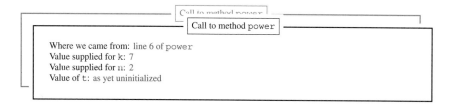

Again, n is compared to 0; because the value of n on the top piece of paper is 2, the `else` clause is executed. The first action in the `else` clause is to set t to `power(7,1)`, which causes a recursive call, so the stack of papers now looks like this:

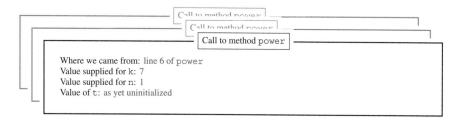

Yet again, n is compared to 0; because the value of n on the top piece of paper is 1, the `else` clause is executed. The first action in the `else` clause is to set t to `power(7,0)`, which causes a recursive call, so the stack of papers now looks like this:

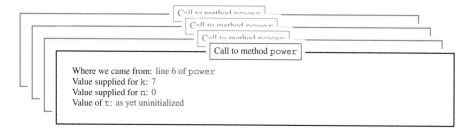

Now the value of n on the top piece of paper *is* 0, so `power` returns the value 1 from line 4; this causes the top piece of paper to be removed from the stack and t to be set to the value returned, namely, 1. The stack now is

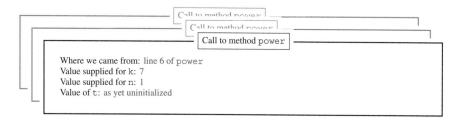

We continue with the execution of `power`, line 7. Because the value of n on the top piece of paper is 1, n % 2 is 1, and we return the value k*t*t = 7 from the `else` clause (line 8), leaving the stack

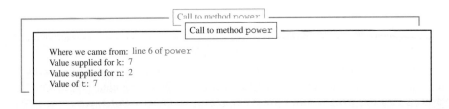

Call to method power

Call to method power

Where we came from: line 6 of power
Value supplied for k: 7
Value supplied for n: 2
Value of t: 7

We continue with the execution of `power`, line 7. Because the value of n on the top piece of paper is 2, n % 2 is 0, and we return the value t*t = 49 from the `else` clause (line 10), leaving this:

Call to method power

Where we came from: main
Value supplied for k: 7
Value supplied for n: 5
Value of t: 49

Again we continue with the execution of `power`, line 7. Because the value of n on the top piece of paper is 5, n % 2 is 1, and we return the value k*t*t = 16,807 from the `else` clause (line 10), ending the call to `power` from `main`. Whenever you are uncertain about what is happening in a recursive computation, simulate it with pieces of paper. This is the only surefire way to see the actions occurring. Try it for `power(2,14)`.

14.5

Processing Arrays Recursively

In this section, we further explore arrays and recursion by developing recursive versions of `selectionSort` and `insertionSort`. We further develop `quickSort`—perhaps the best all-around sorting method known.

The basic idea of writing a recursive method, as expounded in the previous section, is to *assume* the method works for smaller values. For arrays, a "smaller" value means a shorter array. In many cases, it is not necessary actually to construct *subarray* a smaller array. Instead, you can use a subarray. A *subarray* of an array A is a contiguous set of elements of A. It can be represented by two subscripts signifying the lower and upper bounds of the subarray.

For example, consider finding the sum of the elements of the subarray of A given by `lo` and `hi`, that is, the elements `A[lo]`, `A[lo+1]`,..., `A[hi]`. Assume that `sum` will correctly compute the sum of any smaller subarray, such as `A[lo+1]` ... `A[hi]`. How can we use that value to find the sum of `A[lo]` ... `A[hi]`? Easy, add `A[lo]` to it.

```
static double sum (double[] A, int lo, int hi) {
   return A[lo] + sum(A, lo+1, hi);
}
```

What is an appropriate base case? If `hi < lo`, the subarray has zero elements:

```
static double sum (double[] A, int lo, int hi) {
  if (hi < lo)
    return 0.0;
  else
    return A[lo] + sum(A, lo+1, hi);
}
```

Now that we can sum any subarray of A, we can easily sum all of A: This is the same as summing the subarray from 0 to `A.length-1`.

The idea of using subarrays is illustrated by each of the sorting algorithms in this section.

QUICK EXERCISE 14.3

(1) Write `product` to calculate the product of all the numbers in an array.
(2) Write `String concat (String[] words, int lo, int hi)`, which concatenates the strings in `words[lo]` ...`words[hi]` into one long string.
(3) Write `Point sum (Point[] pts, int lo, int hi)` to sum the points (that is, sum the x values and sum the y values) in `pts[lo]` ...`pts[hi]`.

14.5.1 Selection Sort

Selection sort was described in Section 8.6 (page 296). As we discussed, it follows a natural scheme for sorting items by hand. You may wish to review the iterative version of `selectionSort` before continuing here.

Selection sort can be written using subarrays. Suppose we are to sort the subarray of A from `lo` to `hi`. We first look at the entire subarray. After placing the smallest element in `A[lo]`, we ignore that position and proceed to sort the subarray `A[lo+1]` ...`A[hi]`. Because that is a smaller subarray, we can assume it gets sorted correctly, so now the entire subarray from `lo` to `hi` is sorted. The base case is the one-element subarray, that is, the case when `lo = hi`.

This discussion suggests the following simple recursive definition of `selectionSort`. We define the method `findMinimum` so that it locates the smallest element in a subarray.[1]

```
 1                                        int lo, int hi) {
 2      // Recursive selection sort
 3      // Author: Ruth N. Reingold,  April 22, 1995
 4
 5      // A[0]..A[lo-1] contain the smallest values in A,
 6      // in ascending order.
 7      if (lo < hi) { // subarray has more than one element
 8        swap(A, lo, findMinimum(A, lo, hi));
 9        selectionSort(A, lo+1, hi);
10      }
11    }
12
```

We will explain momentarily why we have made this method private.

The method `int findMinimum (double[] A, int lo, int hi)` returns the location of the smallest value in the subarray `A[lo]` ... `A[hi]`. It is itself recursive: The smallest element in the subarray `A[lo]` ... `A[hi]` is either `A[lo]` or the smallest element in the subarray `A[lo+1]` ... `A[hi]`, depending on which is smaller.

```
 1    private static int findMinimum (double[] A, int lo, int hi) {
 2      if (lo == hi)
 3        return lo;
 4      else {
 5        int locationOfMin = findMinimum(A, lo+1, hi);
 6        if (A[lo] < A[locationOfMin])
 7          return lo;
 8        else
 9          return locationOfMin;
10      }
11    }
```

The sequence of arrays displayed on page 296 gives an exact trace of the call `selectionSort(A, 0, 5)`, when A is the array pictured there.

Clients should be able to call a one-argument version of `selectionSort`, because they do not care whether it is implemented using subarrays or iteration. That is why we have made the preceding "helper" functions private. We can provide a one-argument function for clients to call; with Java's overloading, we can give it the same name as the three-argument function:

```
 1    public static void selectionSort (double[] A) {
 2      selectionSort(A, 0, A.length-1);
 3    }
```

Because this recursive method uses the same algorithm as the iterative version of Chapter 8, it runs more slowly. On one computer, the iterative version sorts

---

[1]It is not necessary to make it static, but if a method makes no mention of any instance variables, it may as well be.

a 5000-element array in 69 seconds, when the recursive version takes 180 seconds. Our main purpose here was to demonstrate how straightforward it can be to write recursive functions on arrays.

Run this sorting method on two arrays of 5000 elements: one initially in ascending order (i.e., sorted) and the other initially sorted in descending order. How long does each take? Do they take the same amount of time? Why or why not?

14.5.2 Insertion Sort

Insertion sort also was discussed in Section 8.6. It is based on another natural method of sorting by hand. Again, you may wish to review that section before proceeding.

The recursive structure of insertion sort perhaps is even simpler than that of selection sort. As usual, we wonder how solving a smaller problem can help us solve the problem at hand. Specifically, how can the (assumed) ability to sort arrays of length $n - 1$ be used to sort an array of length n? The answer is really simple: Sort the array of length $n - 1$ and then insert the nth element in the proper place in that sorted array. In terms of subarrays, this says that to sort subarray A[0] ... A[hi] (here we need only subarrays whose lower bound is zero), sort A[0]...A[hi-1] and then insert A[hi] into that subarray. The method insertInOrder(A, hi, x) inserts x into subarray A[0] ... A[hi-1] (using location A[hi] to allow for the extra element). Insertion sort looks like this:

```
1    private static void insertionSort (double[] A, int hi) {
2        // Sort  A[0] ... A[hi]
3        if (hi > 0) {
4            insertionSort(A, hi-1);
5            insertInOrder(A, hi, A[hi]);
6        }
7    }
```

The method insertInOrder moves an element into a subarray. Its recursive structure also is simple. To insert x into subarray A[0]...A[hi-1], do one of two things: If x ≥ A[hi-1], just place x into A[hi]; if x ≤ A[hi-1], move A[hi-1] into A[hi] and insert x into subarray A[0]...A[hi-2]:

```
1    private static void insertInOrder (double[] A,
2                            int hi, double x) {
3        // Insert x into A[0]...A[hi-1], filling in
4        // A[hi] in the process.
5        // A[0]...A[hi-1] are sorted.
6        if (hi == 0 || A[hi-1] <= x)
```

```
7          A[hi] = x;
8        else {
9          A[hi] = A[hi-1];
10           insertInOrder(A, hi-1, x);
11         }
12       }
```

Again, we provide clients with a one-argument version of `insertionSort`:

```
1      public static void insertionSort (double[] A) {
2        insertionSort(A, A.length-1);
3      }
```

QUICK EXERCISE 14.5

Run this sorting method on the same two arrays of 5000 elements as in Quick Exercise 14.4: one initially in ascending order (i.e., sorted) and the other initially sorted in descending order. How long does each take? Do they take the same amount of time? Why or why not?

14.5.3 Quicksort

quicksort

The use of recursion sometimes can lead to more efficient algorithms that would be difficult to write, or even to imagine, without it. *Quicksort*[2] is an elegant and ingenious sorting method, perhaps the best all-around method known. Like our efficient version of the `power` method, quicksort is a divide-and-conquer algorithm, in that it recursively sorts a subarray that is (roughly) one-half the size of the original array. Although, in theory, it can run as slowly as selection sort, in practice it almost always runs much faster.

Quicksort makes clever use of the subarray concept. To sort A, first move all the smaller elements of A into the bottom half and all the larger elements into the top half, so that every element in the bottom half is less than every element in the top half. Then sort the two halves recursively, and the entire array will be sorted. More specifically, given that A is of size `size`, do the following steps:

1. *Partition* A into its smaller elements and its larger ones, placing the smaller ones in positions A[0] ... A[m-1] for some m (not necessarily in order), the larger ones in positions A[m+1] ... A[size-1] (not necessarily in order), and the "middle" element in A[m]. Thus, the array A

5	27	12	3	18	11	7	19

---

[2]It is traditional in computer science to write *quicksort* as a single word.

might be partitioned as

5	7	3	11	12	27	18	19

with m = 4.

2. *Recursively sort* A[0] ... A[m-1]. In our example, A becomes

3	5	7	11	12	27	18	19

3. *Recursively sort* A[m+1] ... A[size-1]. In our example, A becomes

3	5	7	11	12	18	19	27

The overall structure of the quickSort method, then, is

```
static int partition (double[] A, int lo, int hi) {
    // Choose middle element among A[lo] ... A[hi],
    // and move other elements so that A[lo] ... A[m-1]
    // are all less than A[m] and A[m+1] ... A[hi] are
    // all greater than A[m]
    //
    // m is returned to the caller

         ⋮

}

static void quickSort (double[] A, int lo, int hi) {
    int m;

    if (hi > lo+1) { // there are at least 3 elements,
                     // so sort recursively
        m = partition(A, lo, hi);
        quickSort(A, lo, m-1);
        quickSort(A, m+1, hi);
    }
    else // 0, 1, or 2 elements, so sort directly
        if (hi == lo+1 && A[lo] > A[hi])
            swap(A, lo, hi);
}
```

The base case in this recursion occurs when the subarray A[lo] ... A[hi] contains zero elements (lo = hi+1), one elements (lo = hi), or two elements (lo = hi-1). If the subarray contains no elements, we ignore it. If it contains one element, it is already sorted and there is nothing to do. If it contains two elements and they are out of order, they need to be swapped.

As usual, we will provide clients with a one-argument version of the function:

```
static void quickSort (double[] A) {
  quickSort(A, 0, A.length-1);
}
```

The `quickSort` method itself is done, but the hard part remains—writing `partition`. Really there are two problems here, choosing the middle element *pivot* in the subarray and doing the partitioning. For the middle, or *pivot*, element, we want to find the *median* of the subarray `A[lo]` ... `A[hi]`—the element `A[j]` such that exactly one-half of the elements in the subarray are less than it and one-half are greater. Then, the recursive calls in `quickSort` will sort subarrays one-half as long as the original array, which gives the greatest efficiency.

Unfortunately, we can't do this. There is no simple way to find the median element among `A[lo]` ... `A[hi]` except to sort them and choose the element in the middle, which is what we're trying to do in the first place. Instead, we have to *guess* at the median element and hope for the best. In practice, a good way of choosing the pivot—that is, of guessing the median of the subarray—is to take the median of three of its elements, specifically `A[lo+1]`, `A[(lo+hi)/2]`, and `A[hi]`. This is the method we use. (See Exercise 10(b) at the end of this chapter for a further discussion of this issue.)

Having made our choice, for better or worse, we begin the partitioning process. We hope we have chosen the median of the subarray, so that the partitioning process will divide the subarray exactly in half, but there is no way to be sure. Only when the partitioning process is done can we know how many elements are less than the pivot and how many are greater. The dividing line between these is the index we call m.

Suppose our subarray looks like this at the start:

From the three highlighted elements we select the median, `A[hi]`, to be our pivot element. Swapping it with `A[lo]`, we can begin the partitioning process.

Again, we have no way of knowing how many elements are less than the pivot and how many are greater. We will shuffle around the elements in `A[lo+1]` ... `A[hi]` so that all the elements less than the pivot (`A[lo]`) appear to the left of all the elements greater than the pivot:

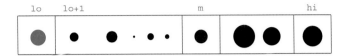

Only when the partitioning is done do we see where the dividing line between the small elements and the large ones is. The integer we call m is the largest subscript that contains a value less than the pivot. In this example, we got a decent split, but not a perfect one: The pivot element was a bit larger than the median, so the left partition is larger than the right partition. Because we know A[lo] is greater than the small elements and less than the large ones, we can swap it with A[m]:

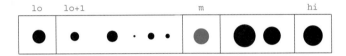

The partition has now done its job. Sorting A[lo] ... A[m-1] and A[m+1] ... A[hi] will leave us with a sorted array.

We now describe how the partition process works. The quickSort method calls a three-argument version of partition, passing it to the array and to the low and high bounds of the subarray; partition returns the location m where the array was split. There is a four-argument version of partition

```
int partition (double A[], int lo, int hi, double pivot)
```

that does the real work. The three-argument version

```
static int partition (double[] A, int lo, int hi) {
    // Choose middle element among A[lo] ... A[hi],
    // and move other elements so that A[lo] ... A[m-1]
    // are all less than A[m] and A[m+1] ... A[hi] are
    // all greater than A[m]
    //
    // m is returned to the caller
    swap(A, lo, medianLocation(A, lo+1, hi, (lo+hi)/2));
    int m = partition(A, lo+1, hi, A[lo]);
    swap(A, lo, m);
    return m;
}
```

moves the pivot element into A[lo], calls the four-argument partition to shuffle the elements in the subarray A[lo+1] ... A[hi], and then swaps A[lo] and A[m]. (The method medianLocation finds the middle elements among A[lo+1], A[(lo+hi)/2], and A[hi]; it will be shown on page 556.)

The four-argument version of partition is given a subarray and the pivot element and does the main partitioning work, shuffling the elements in the subarray so that the elements less than the pivot precede the elements greater than the pivot. The method is based on a clever use of subarrays. As usual, we *assume* that `partition` will work on any smaller subarray, and we ask ourselves how we can use that capability to partition the subarray `A[lo] ... A[hi]`.

For example, *assume* that we can partition `A[lo+1] ... A[hi]`. Does that help? Indeed it does. If `A[lo] < pivot`, it is all we need! Therefore, part of the `partition` method is

```
static int partition (double[] A,
                      int lo, int hi,
                      double pivot) {
  if (A[lo] <= pivot) // A[lo] in correct half
    return partition(A, lo+1, hi, pivot);
  ...
}
```

What if `A[lo] > pivot`? In that case, we know that `A[lo]` belongs in the upper half of the subarray, so we swap it with `A[hi]`. We have no idea where the new value of `A[lo]` belongs, because we haven't looked at it; but we do know that the new value of `A[hi]` belongs where it is, so we need not look at it any more. In other words, we can finish the job by partitioning the subarray `A[lo] ... A[hi-1]`. This is a smaller subarray, so we *assume* that `partition` can handle it. So `partition` now looks like this:

```
static int partition (double[] A,
                      int lo, int hi,
                      double pivot) {
  if (A[lo] <= pivot) // A[lo] in correct half
    return partition(A, lo+1, hi, pivot);
  else {              // A[lo] in wrong half
    swap(A, lo, hi);
    return partition(A, lo, hi-1, pivot);
  }
}
```

The appropriate base case here is the one-element subarray (`lo=hi`). When we see a one-element subarray, however, we have to decide whether it is a small element or a large element. If it is small (less than `pivot`), then it is at the middle point (the point referred to as m earlier); otherwise, it is just above the middle point. This observation gives us the final version of this method:

```
static int partition (double[] A,
                      int lo, int hi,
                      double pivot) {
  if (hi == lo)
    if (A[lo] < pivot)
      return lo;
    else
      return lo-1;
  else if (A[lo] <= pivot) // A[lo] in correct half
    return partition(A, lo+1, hi, pivot);
  else {                   // A[lo] in wrong half
    swap(A, lo, hi);
    return partition(A, lo, hi-1, pivot);
  }
}
```

Let us illustrate this process. We use a six-element subarray:

The three-argument version of partition is called. It chooses the third element in the subarray (that is, A[(lo+hi)/2]) as the pivot, swaps it into A[lo], and calls the four-argument version. The situation, as we are about to begin the partitioning process, is as follows:

At each step of the process, we place a box around the subarray being partitioned in that call; the circles outside of that box, aside from the pivot element shown in color, already are in the correct half of the subarray. Because A[lo] is greater than the pivot, we swap it with A[hi]

and call partition recursively with a smaller subarray:

Because A[lo] is smaller than pivot, it already is in the correct half; so we simply call partition recursively, with a smaller subarray:

With A[lo] greater than pivot, we again swap

and call partition recursively:

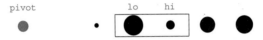

Again, A[lo] is greater than pivot, so we swap

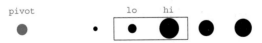

and call `partition` recursively:

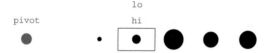

With `lo` and `hi` equal, the partitioning process is finished. Because `A[lo]` is less than the pivot, `lo` is returned as the dividing line between the two halves.

The quicksort algorithm now is complete. The method `medianLocation` finds the subscript of the median of three values in an array, given their subscripts. The final version is as follows:

```
1   static int medianLocation (double[] A,
2                                   int i, int j, int k) {
3     if (A[i] <= A[j])
4       if (A[j] <= A[k])
5         return j;
6       else if (A[i] <= A[k])
7         return k;
8       else
9         return i;
10    else // A[j] < A[i]
11      if (A[i] <= A[k])
12        return i;
13      else if (A[j] <= A[k])
14        return k;
15      else
16        return j;
17  }
18
19  static int partition (double[] A,
20                            int lo, int hi,
21                            double pivot) {
22    if (hi == lo)
23      if (A[lo] < pivot)
24        return lo;
25      else
26        return lo-1;
27    else if (A[lo] <= pivot) // A[lo] in correct half
28      return partition(A, lo+1, hi, pivot);
29    else {                    // A[lo] in wrong half
30      swap(A, lo, hi);
31      return partition(A, lo, hi-1, pivot);
32    }
33  }
34
35  static int partition (double[] A, int lo, int hi) {
36    // Choose middle element among A[lo] ... A[hi],
37    // and move other elements so that A[lo] ... A[m-1]
38    // are all less than A[m] and A[m+1] ... A[hi] are
39    // all greater than A[m]
40    //
41    // m is returned to the caller
```

```
42      swap(A, lo, medianLocation(A, lo+1, hi, (lo+hi)/2));
43      int m = partition(A, lo+1, hi, A[lo]);
44      swap(A, lo, m);
45      return m;
46    }
47
48    static void quickSort (double[] A, int lo, int hi) {
49      int m;
50
51      if (hi > lo+1) { // there are at least 3 elements,
52                       // so sort recursively
53        m = partition(A, lo, hi);
54        quickSort(A, lo, m-1);
55        quickSort(A, m+1, hi);
56      }
57      else // 0, 1, or 2 elements, so sort directly
58        if (hi == lo+1 && A[lo] > A[hi])
59          swap(A, lo, hi);
60    }
61
62    static void quickSort (double[] A) {
63      quickSort(A, 0, A.length-1);
64    }
```

The running time of quickSort in the best case is $T_{\text{quickSort}}(A) = cn \log n$. This case occurs when the division of the array is exactly "in half" each time.

On the other hand, if we are unlucky and the partitioning elements turn out very poorly—in the worst case, the second-smallest or second-largest element in the subarray—then the division of the subarrays is not in half at all. Instead, A[lo] and A[lo+1] contain the smallest values in the subarray, and subarray A[lo+2]...A[hi] has to be sorted recursively (or A[hi-1] and A[hi] contain the largest values, and A[lo]...A[hi-2] has to be sorted recursively). Far from dividing the array in half, the partitioning process has produced a subarray two items shorter than the one it was handed. An analysis similar to the analysis of selection sort (Section 8.6) tells us the cost of quicksort in this case will be $T_{\text{quickSort}}(A) = cn^2$.

In practice, it is not easy to contrive examples on which quicksort will show its worst-case performance. We ran the iterative version of selection sort on a 5000-element array on one computer, and it ran for 69 seconds (keep in mind that selection sort will run in the same amount of time for every 5000-element array, so there is no need to do the experiment more than once). On various arrays of the same size—for example, an array that already was sorted, one that was sorted in descending order, one that was generated randomly, and several others—the running time for quickSort ranged from a low of 2 seconds to a high of 6 seconds. So when we say quicksort is faster than selection sort, we're not kidding!

Most important, if we consider the *average* performance over all possible arrangements of n values in an array, quickSort's running time is $T_{\text{quickSort}}(A) = cn \log n$. Both selection sort and insertion sort have average running times of cn^2—a dramatic difference.

Run `quickSort` on the same two arrays of 5000 elements that we used for selection sort and insertion sort: one initially in ascending order (i.e., sorted) and the other initially sorted in descending order. How long does each take? Do they take the same amount of time? Why or why not? (On a fast computer, this algorithm may run too fast to get any reasonable timings; if so, increase the sizes of the arrays until the sorting time is at least 5 seconds.)

Another "obvious" divide-and-conquer method for sorting works like this: To sort A, recursively sort the first half of A and then the second half of A; then "merge" the two sorted halves. Although this merging process seems intuitively simple, it is actually a bit tricky when using arrays. We will discuss this method, called *merge sort*, in Section 14.6.4, after we have introduced a new method for storing large lists of data.

14.5.4   Solving Linear Systems

Our next example is one of the most basic of all mathematical computations on a computer—the solution of a system of simultaneous linear equations. This problem demonstrates the use of subarrays of two-dimensional arrays, exactly analogous to our uses of subarrays of one-dimensional arrays earlier in this chapter. It also is a lovely example of the use of recursion.

We are presented with a set of equations in the variables, or *unknowns*, $x_1, \ldots, x_n$:

$$
\begin{array}{ccccccc}
a_{11}x_1 & + & a_{12}x_2 & + & \cdots & + & a_{1,n}x_n & = & b_1 \\
a_{21}x_1 & + & a_{22}x_2 & + & \cdots & + & a_{2,n}x_n & = & b_2 \\
\cdots & \cdots & \cdots & \cdots & & \cdots & \cdots & \cdots & \cdots \\
a_{n,1}x_1 & + & a_{n,2}x_2 & + & \cdots & + & a_{n,n}x_n & = & b_n
\end{array}
$$

and we need to find values for the unknowns that will satisfy all n equations simultaneously.

Gaussian elimination   The method known as *Gaussian elimination*, with its numerous variants, is the basic method used in solving such systems. It is a recursive method, which we can derive by asking our usual question: *Assuming* that we are able to solve smaller systems—say, those consisting of $n - 1$ equations in $n - 1$ unknowns— how can we use that capability to solve the n-equation system? There is a simple answer to this question: We can *eliminate* variable x_n by expressing it in terms of the remaining variables

$$
x_n = \frac{b_n - a_{n,1}x_1 - \cdots - a_{n,n-1}x_{n-1})}{a_{n,n}} \tag{14.1}
$$

(if $a_{n,n}$ is not zero) and then substituting this into the other equations. For example, the first equation becomes

$$a_{11}x_1 + \cdots + a_{1,n-1}x_{n-1} + \frac{a_{1,n}(b_n - a_{n,1}x_1 - \cdots)}{a_{n,n}} = b_1$$

which we can write as

$$\left(a_{11} - \frac{a_{1,n}a_{n,1}}{a_{n,n}}\right)x_1 + \cdots + \left(a_{1,n-1} - \frac{a_{1,n}a_{n,n-1}}{a_{n,n}}\right)x_{n-1} = b_1 - \frac{a_{1,n}b_n}{a_{n,n}}$$

Eliminating x_n from each of the other equations in this way, we end up with $n - 1$ equations in the variables $x_1, \ldots, x_{n-1}$. Solving this system, which we assume we can do recursively, yields values for those variables, and we can use Equation (14.1) to find the value of x_n, solving the original system.

We need to show that the base case can be solved, but that is easy. The system of one equation in one unknown

$$ax = b$$

has the solution $x = b/a$ if $a \neq 0$.

So we might express this algorithm as

```
solve (system E of n equations in n unknowns)  {
   if (n == 1)
      // system is ax = b
      return (b/a) ;
   else {
      eliminate last equation, yielding system E';
      solve(E'), yielding x₁, ..., xₙ₋₁;
      xₙ = value obtained from equation (14.1);
      return (x₁, ..., xₙ₋₁, xₙ);
   }
}
```

The representation of the basic system of n equations is simple. We use a two-dimensional array containing the values a_{ij} and a one-dimensional array containing the values b_i:

```
double [] []  A = new double [n] [n] ;
double []     B = new double [n] ;
```

As for returning the vector of values, we pass in an array X to hold these values. It will be filled in by `solve`.

However, because indexing of arrays is from zero, from now on we will rename the unknowns $x_0, \ldots, x_{n-1}$, so that our system becomes

$$
\begin{aligned}
a_{00}x_0 &+ a_{01}x_1 &+ \cdots + &\; a_{0,n-1}x_{n-1} &= b_0 \\
a_{10}x_0 &+ a_{11}x_1 &+ \cdots + &\; a_{1,n-1}x_{n-1} &= b_1 \\
&\cdots \\
a_{n-1,0}x_0 &+ a_{n-1,1}x_1 &+ \cdots + &\; a_{n-1,n-1}x_{n-1} &= b_{n-1}
\end{aligned}
$$

It still is a system of *n* equations in *n* unknowns, so the method suggested earlier still applies.

The key observation here is that we can place the coefficients of the smaller system of equations in the upper left portion of A. When `solve` is called, we need to tell it which subarray of A (and B) contains the system it has to solve. When `solve` is called from outside, the subarray, of course, is the entire array. In the first recursive call, it is the subarray whose lower right limit is `A[n-2][n-2]`, with right-hand sides of the equations given by `B[0]` ... `B[n-2]`. In the next recursive call, the lower right limit is `A[n-3][n-3]` and the right-hand sides are `B[0]` ... `B[n-3]`. Thus, the recursive calls see smaller and smaller parts of the upper left portion of A. In the final recursive call, `solve` will be asked to solve a system whose upper and lower limits meet; that is, the only coefficient is `A[0][0]`.

Here, then, is `solve`, along with the auxiliary method `computeXi`, which performs the computation given in Equation (14.1); `eliminate` will be given subsequently.

```
 1    static void computeXi (
 2                double[][] A,  // Using A[0][0]..A[i-1][i-1]
 3                double[] B,    // and B[i],
 4                double[] X,    // and X[0]..X[i-1], compute
 5                int i          // X[i] using equation (11.1)
 6                ) {
 7      double t = B[i];
 8      for (int j=0; j<i; j++)
 9        t = t - A[i][j]*X[j];
10      X[i] = t/A[i][i];
11    }
12
13    static void solve (
14                double[][] A,  // Solve system with coeffic-
15                               // ients in A[0][0]..A[i][i],
16                double[] B,    // and right-hand sides B[0]..B[i]
17                double[] X,    // Place solutions in X[0]..X[i]
18                int i
19                ) {
20      if (i == 0) // one-equation system - solve directly
21        X[0] = B[0]/A[0][0];
22      else {
23        eliminate(A, B, i);  // eliminate Xi;  new system is
24                             // in A[0][0]..A[i-1][i-1]
25                             // and B[0]..B[i-1]
26        solve(A, B, X, i-1);   // Fill in X[0]...X[i-1]
27        computeXi(A, B, X, i); // calculate X[i] from A, B,
28                               // and X[0]...X[i-1]
29      }
30    }
```

The method `eliminate` alters the values in `A[0][0]` ... `A[i][i]` and `B[0]` ... `B[i]` to represent the smaller system. Because it needs to modify each value in each row of the submatrix, a doubly nested loop structure is the clear choice.

```
1    static void eliminate (double[][] A,
2                           double[] B, int i) {
3      // Eliminate variable xi from system whose
4      // coefficients are in  A[0][0]..A[i][i],
5      // with right-hand sides B[0]..B[i]
6      double m;
7
8      for (int j=0; j<i; j++) {
9        m = A[j][i] / A[i][i];
10       B[j] = B[j] - m*B[i];
11       for (int k=0; k<i; k++)
12         A[j][k] = A[j][k] - m*A[i][k];
13     }
14   }
15
```

The method `solve` works fine for many examples. For example, if n = 3, we provide the following values for A and B (we leave it to the reader to write the input loops):

$$
A:\quad
\begin{array}{ccc}
1.0 & 1.0 & 1.0 \\
1.0 & 2.0 & 2.0 \\
1.0 & 1.0 & 2.0
\end{array}
\qquad
B:\quad
\begin{array}{c}
1.0 \\
1.0 \\
2.0
\end{array}
$$

Here `solve` will find the solution X = 1 −1 1.

However, `solve` can also fail. Given this input

$$
A:\quad
\begin{array}{ccc}
1.0 & 2.0 & 2.0 \\
2.0 & 4.0 & 4.0 \\
1.0 & 1.0 & 2.0
\end{array}
\qquad
B:\quad
\begin{array}{c}
1.0 \\
2.0 \\
2.0
\end{array}
$$

the program produces this odd-looking output:

```
Solution vector is: -1.#IND -1.#IND -1.#IND
```

The term `-1.#IND` means "negative indefinite," indicating something's wrong. However, the *program* hasn't really failed here. This system has no solution—or rather, no unique solution—because the equations just don't contain enough information. Because the second equation is obtained from the first by multiplying both sides by 2, it adds no information, and what we really have is *two* equations in three unknowns. That is not enough to give a definite answer.

On the other hand, here we give the same equations as in the first example above, only in a different order:

$$
A:\quad
\begin{array}{ccc}
1.0 & 1.0 & 2.0 \\
1.0 & 2.0 & 2.0 \\
1.0 & 1.0 & 1.0
\end{array}
\qquad
B:\quad
\begin{array}{c}
2.0 \\
1.0 \\
1.0
\end{array}
$$

Here solve again produces the -1.#IND output. This is distressing. Changing the order of the equations in a system doesn't change the solution. What has gone wrong?

We see the problem by printing out intermediate values. If, at the end of eliminate, we print the two-dimensional array A, the last example produces

```
-1 -1 2
-1  0 2
 1  1 1

-1.#INF -1 2
-1  0 2
 1  1 1

Solution vector is: -1.#IND -1.#IND -1.#IND
```

The first array printed is A after one step of elimination. The important part of A at that point is the 2×2 array in the upper left, because this gives the coefficients in the smaller system of equations. Here we see exactly what caused the problem: A[1][1], representing the coefficient of variable x_1, which we need to eliminate from this system, is zero. Remember that the elimination process works only if the coefficient $a_{n-1,n-1}$ of x_{n-1} is not zero. Therefore, even though we started with a system in which the coefficient of x_2 was not zero, the elimination process produced a system in which the coefficient of x_1 was zero, and the attempt to solve the smaller system recursively failed.

This can be fixed easily. Although $a_{n-1,n-1}$ might be zero, at least one of the coefficients $a_{i,n-1}$ of x_{n-1} in one of the equations must be nonzero. Otherwise, there is no useful information about x_{n-1} in the entire system, and therefore no unique value for it. Furthermore, changing the order of the equations in the system won't change the order of the results. These considerations lead us to the following solution: If $a_{n-1,n-1}$ is zero, find an i such that $a_{i,n-1}$ is nonzero; then swap row i and row $n-1$, as well as the values b_i and b_{n-1}, and proceed as before. This method is known as *partial pivoting*. We add a method partialPivot (with its auxiliary method swapRows) and then put a call to partialPivot in solve.

partial pivoting

```
 1    static void swapRows (
 2                  double[][] A, int w, int j, int i
 3                  ) {
 4       double temp;
 5       // Swap first w+1 elements of rows j and i of A
 6       for (int k=0; k<=w; k++) {
 7          temp = A[j][k];
 8          A[j][k] = A[i][k];
 9          A[i][k] = temp;
10       }
11    }
12
```

```
13    static void partialPivot (
14                  double[][] A, double[] B, int i
15                  ) {
16      // Swap rows so that A[i][i] is non-zero
17      int j = i-1;
18      while ((j >= 0) && (A[j][i] == 0))
19        // Find row with non-zero first element
20        j--;
21      if (j == -1) {
22        new ErrorBox("Pivoting failed:  system unsolvable");
23        Timer.pause(3000);  // let user read message
24        System.exit(1);
25      }
26      swapRows(A, i, j, i);
27      swap(B, j, i);
28    }
29
30    static void solve (
31            double[][] A, // Solve system whose coeffic-
32                          // ients are in A[0][0]..A[i][i],
33            double[] B, // and right-hand sides B[0]..B[i]
34            double[] X, // Place solutions in X[0]..X[i]
35            int i) {
36      if (i == 0) // one-equation system - solve directly
37        X[0] = B[0]/A[0][0];
38      else {
39        if (A[i][i] == 0)
40          partialPivot(A, B, i); // swap rows so A[i][i]!=0
41        eliminate(A, B, i);   // eliminate Xi; new system
42                              // is in A[0][0]..A[i-1][i-1]
43                              // and B[0]..B[i-1]
44        solve(A, B, X, i-1);   // Fill in X[0]...X[i-1]
45        computeXi(A, B, X, i);// calculate X[i] from A, B,
46                              // and X[0]...X[i-1]
47      }
48    }
```

This version of `solve` produces the same answer for both arrangements of the system given previously.

The time complexity of Gaussian elimination is not hard to calculate. On an $n \times n$ matrix, the first step is the elimination of variable x_{n-1}; this requires that a simple constant-time calculation be performed for each element in the $(n-1) \times (n-1)$ submatrix, a total time proportional to n^2. The next step is to recursively solve an $(n-1) \times (n-1)$ matrix. On return from the recursive call, the time to compute x_{n-1} is proportional to n, so we won't count that. Overall, then, the time to solve an $n \times n$ matrix is proportional to $c_1 \times n^2 + c_2 \times (n-1)^2 + \cdots + c_n$, which is proportional to n^3. Pivoting involves only an additional amount of work that is proportional to n in each call and so will not alter this result.

14.6

Recursive Functions on Lists

I've got a little list—I've got a little list

—W. S. Gilbert
The Mikado

The list could surely go on, and there is nothing more
wonderful than a list, instrument of wondrous
hypotyposis.

—Umberto Eco
The Name of the Rose

Most real-life computer programs store lots of information while they're running. Often, they can't even predict how much they'll have to store. Your text editor, for example, doesn't know how much you're going to type until you finish typing it.

That's the biggest shortcoming of what we've covered so far in this book: There has been no way to store an unknown amount of data. We can create a large array and use only part of it, but that wastes memory. If we wanted to be sure the array is big enough for every run of the program, we would have to make it really big, and then only a small fraction of it would be needed most of the time.

In this chapter we introduce a technique to solve this problem. The technique allows us to store as many data items as we want by dynamically creating objects to store them. The technique is to introduce a type of data structure called a *linked list*, or just *list*.

14.6.1   Linked Structures

Data used in computer programs can have a complex structure in which some data items are related to other data items. Consider, for example, how you might represent a family tree, or a map of airline routes, or a strand of DNA. Often, the most appropriate representation is as a collection of objects that point to one another, that is, contain references to one another. Such *linked structures* are illustrated in the figures on this and the next several pages.

linked structure   Our ability to construct such structures is based on the fact that *objects of class T can contain variables of type T*. Thus, the declaration of the data member m here is perfectly legal:

```
public class T {
   private T m;
   ...
}
```

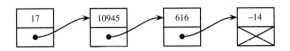

FIGURE 14.1 **Representing the list 17, 10945, 616, −14.**

Remember that m really is just a *reference* to an object of type T. So when we create a T object, it contains a reference to an object of type T, which may contain a reference to an object of type T, which may contain . . . . But this sequence must end somewhere, namely, with an object that contains the reference null.

We can illustrate the situation by using arrows, or *pointers*, as we have before when showing references to objects. A list of integers constructed as a linked structure is shown in Figure 14.1; the big X in the last object means that the reference in that object contains null. Such a structure is called a *linearly linked list*, or simply a *linked list*.

Linked lists are used very frequently in computer programming. The individual objects in a linked list are called *cells*. The first cell in a list (the one containing 17 in Figure 14.1) is called the *head* of the list; the remainder of the list is its *tail*.

There are other kinds of linked structures that are often used in programming. There can be a link from the last cell back to the head of the list. Such a structure is called a *circularly linked list*.

pointers

linearly linked list

cell
head
tail

circularly linked list

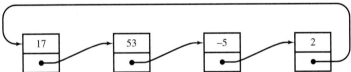

There can be two links per cell, one pointing to the next cell and one pointing to the previous one. Such a structure is called a *doubly linked list*.

doubly linked list

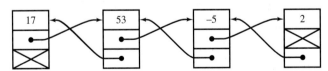

We can combine the two foregoing structures into a *circular doubly linked list*.

circular doubly linked list

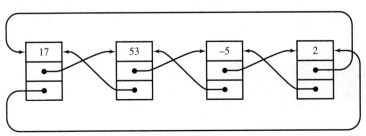

A single *root cell* can have one or more links pointing to *children*, each of which has links pointing to its children, and so on. Such a structure is called a *tree*. A cell that has no children is called a *leaf* of the tree.

tree
leaf

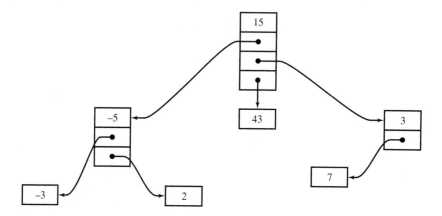

A cell can have one or more links, each pointing to any other cell. Such a structure is called a *graph*.

graph

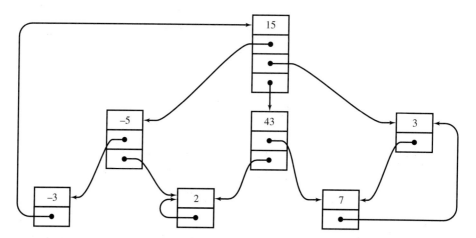

In this book we present only linearly linked lists, which, for brevity, we call simply *lists*. We show how to define classes whose objects are list cells, and we describe applications for operations such as inserting elements into a list.

The list of integers shown in Figure 14.1 is constructed using the aforementioned idea of a reference within an instance. Given the class

```
1   class IntList {
2       private int value;
3       private IntList tail;
4
5       public IntList (int v, IntList next) {
```

```
6           value = v; tail = next;
7           }
8
9       public int getValue () { return value; }
10
11      public IntList getTail () { return tail; }
12  }
```

the list in Figure 14.1 can be constructed using the code

```
1           IntList cell4 = new IntList(-14, null);
2           IntList cell3 = new IntList(616, cell4);
3           IntList cell2 = new IntList(10945, cell3);
4           IntList cell1 = new IntList(17, cell2);
```

Here, `cell1` refers to the head of the list. Notice how we constructed the cells in reverse order. Stop for a moment and consider why we had to do it this way.

We also see clearly the importance of the `null` reference. Without it, there would be no way to create the first cell—what arguments could we pass to the constructor?

We need not have a variable referring to each cell in the list. These statements construct the same list using a single variable, `list`, which refers to the head of the list:

```
1           IntList list = new IntList(-14, null);
2           list = new IntList(616, list);
3           list = new IntList(10945, list);
4           list = new IntList(17, list);
```

A trace of these statements is shown in Figure 14.2. Even better coding is

```
1           IntList list = new IntList(17,
2                             new IntList(616,
3                                new IntList(10945,
4                                   new IntList(-14, null))));
```

14.6.2 Constructing Lists from Input

We need the `IntList` class not merely to construct four-element lists but also to construct unpredictably large lists. A simple example is an application that reads in a list of numbers from the user—as many as the user wants—stores them in a list, and then prints the list in reverse order. (This is simpler than reading them in, storing them, and printing them in the order in which they were entered; that application will come later.)

Given that the `IntList` class allows us to store the numbers as we read them, there are two parts to solving this problem:

1. Read the numbers and store them in a list, in reverse order.
2. Print the list.

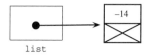

(*a*) After statement 1.

(*b*) After statement 2.

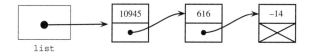

(*c*) After statement 3.

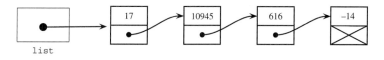

(*d*) After statement 4.

FIGURE 14.2   Building the list 17, 10945, 616, –14.

Suppose the user's input is the sequence of numbers 2, 3, 5, 7, 11, 13, 17, 19, 23, 29, 31, and 37, followed by the empty input (end-of-input indicator). Our application will construct the list

and then print it, producing the output

           37, 31, 29, 23, 19, 17, 13, 11, 7, 5, 3, 2

The outline of our application, then, is

```
public class PrintReversed {

  void print (IntList list) { ... }

  IntList readReverseList () { ... }
}

public class PrintReversedClient {

  public static void main (String args[]) {
      PrintReversed pr = new PrintReversed();
      IntList theList = pr.readReverseList();
      pr.print(theList);
  }
}
```

and we need to write the client method `readReverseList`, which constructs the list just shown and returns a reference to its head (the leftmost cell), and `print`, which prints the elements of a list.

The method `readReverseList` reads numbers from the user and keeps doing so until the user types an end-of-file character. For each number read, `readReverseList` creates a new `IntList` object using new and puts that number into it. Then `readReverseList` puts the entry into the list it has been constructing. And `print` just iterates over the list and prints every element.

```
1    IntList readReverseList () {
2        int inputval;
3        IntList front = null;
4
5        InputBox in = new InputBox();
6
7        while (true) {
8          inputval = in.readInt();
9          if (in.eoi()) break;
10          front = new IntList(inputval, front);
11        }
12
13        return front;
14    }
15
16    void print (IntList list) {
17        OutputBox out = new OutputBox();
18        while (list != null) {
19          out.print(list.getValue()+" ");
20          list = list.getTail();
21        }
22        out.println();
23    }
```

Let's follow this application for a few steps, assuming the user's input consists of the numbers 2, 3, ..., 37. Initially, `front` is `null`:

Because there is input remaining, we read it and create a new `IntList` object. That object contains the integer just read and the value of `front`

and a reference to it is assigned to `front`:

There is more input, so we read the next number, 3, and again construct an `IntList` object containing that number and the contents of `front`

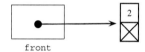

and assign to `front` a reference to the object just created:

This continues until the last number, 37, has been read:

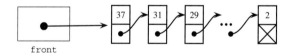

Then `readReverseList` is done, and it returns a reference to the head of the list, which is contained in `front`.

QUICK EXERCISE 14.7   Write a loop to sum the elements in a list.

14.6.3 Using Recursion in the `IntList` Class

By exploiting our ability to send messages to any of the cells in a list, we can perform many operations on lists using recursion in a very natural way.

The instance method `int length ()` computes the length of a list. In writing code for instance methods, a good policy is to place yourself in the position of an object. In writing `length`, your thinking might go like this:

> I have an integer called `value` and a list reference called `tail`. To compute my length, I need to find the length of the list that my `tail` refers to—which I can do by sending it the `length` message—and add 1 to the result. If my `tail` field is null, then I am the only item in the list, so I should just return 1.

This leads directly to the following code:

```
1    public int length () {
2      if (tail == null)
3        return 1;
4      else
5        return 1 + tail.length();
6    }
```

Taking the "object-oriented" view, in which we place ourselves in the position of an object receiving the `length` message, led us to a simple and correct version of the method.

Let's try it again with `toString`, which returns a string representation of a list (specifically, the numbers in the list separated by commas):

> To convert myself to a string means converting `value` to a string, concatenating ", ", and then concatenating the string version of the rest of the list—that is, the list referred to by `tail`—which I can do by sending it the `toString` message. However, if my `tail` field is `null`, then I am the last item in the list, and I merely convert `value` to a string.

```
1    public String toString () {
2      String myValue = Integer.toString(value);
3      if (tail == null)
4        return myValue;
5      else
6        return myValue + ", " + tail.toString();
7    }
```

Another useful operation returns a reference to the *n*th cell in a list. Following Java convention, we will assume the list cells are numbered from 0, so for a list of length ℓ, the legal arguments to `nth` are $0, \ldots, \ell - 1$. For any other argument, `nth` returns `null`. Here is how you might think this through:

> I have received the message `nth(n)`, asking me to return the nth cell in this list. If n = 0, I should return the head of the list; namely, myself, or `this`. If n > 0,

I need to get a cell out of the tail of this list, but instead of cell n, I should request cell n − 1. For example, suppose n = 1—that is, the message requested the second cell in the list which is exactly the cell my tail will return if I send it the message nth(0). In other words, the second cell in the list is the same as the first cell in the tail of the list. Similarly, the third cell in the list is the same as the second cell in the tail, so if n = 2, I should send the message nth(1) to my tail. In general, if cell n was requested, I should request cell n − 1 from my tail.

This reasoning leads directly to this solution:

```
1    public IntList nth (int n) {
2      if (n == 0)
3        return this;
4      else if (tail == null)
5        return null;
6      else
7        return tail.nth(n-1);
8    }
```

> **QUICK EXERCISE 14.8**
>
> In Quick Exercise 14.7, you wrote a method to sum the elements of a list. Write this method recursively.

In Chapter 7, we introduced the notion of mutating and non-mutating methods. With respect to lists, we will say a method is *mutating* if it alters any of the cells (either the value or the link) in its receiver or in any other list that it receives as an argument. Otherwise, the method is *nonmutating*.

This distinction is important for programming the methods in IntList. Mutating and nonmutating versions of the same operation can differ significantly in their complexity and efficiency. However, the basic approach to recursive programming does not change. Because we find the mutating operations usually are somewhat easier to write, we will confine ourselves to such operations in this subsection; Section 14.6.4 contains several examples of nonmutating list operations.

For example, consider void addToEnd_mut (int n), which adds a new cell, containing n, at the end of its receiver. Because it is going to change its receiver, rather than construct and return a new list, there is no need for it to return a reference to its result. So its return type is void. We add the _mut at the end of its name to remind us that it is a mutating operation.

As usual in writing any member method, you need to place yourself in the position of an object (i.e., the list cell) receiving an addToEnd_mut message, with argument n. There are two possibilities. The first is that you are a cell *not* at the end of the list:

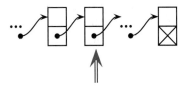

You can tell that you're not at the end, because your `tail` is not `null`. In this case, there is nothing to do but send the `addToEnd_mut` message along to the next entry.

Eventually, the message will reach the last cell, which is the only one that can do anything about it. This brings us to the second possibility—that you are the last cell in the list:

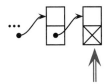

You know you're the last cell because your `tail` field is `null`. You need to do two things now: create a new cell containing n and set your `tail` field to refer to it.

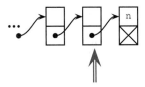

The code for `addToEnd_mut` is

```
1    public void addToEndM (int n) {
2      if (tail != null)
3        // we're a cell in the middle of the list
4        tail.addToEndM(n);
5      else // we're the last cell
6        tail = new IntList(n, null);
7    }
```

Let's examine this in detail. Suppose `list1` is an `IntList` variable initialized by

```
IntList list1 = new IntList(10, new IntList(20, null));
```

as shown in Figure 14.3a. Figure 14.3 traces the call `list1.addToEnd_mut(30)`.

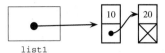

(*a*) Initial value of list1.

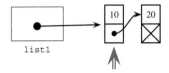

(*b*) After `list.addToEnd_mut(30)`.

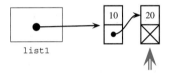

(*c*) After `tail.addToEnd_mut(30)`.

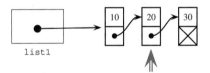

(*d*) After `tail = new IntList(30, null)`.

FIGURE 14.3 Tracing the `addToEnd_mut` method.

1. When it is sent to `list1`, the `addToEnd_mut` message recognizes that the reference `list1.tail` is not null, so it sends the `addToEnd_mut` message to `tail`, leading to Figure 14.3c.

2. When `list1.tail`, receiving the `addToEnd_mut` message, sees that its `tail` field *is* null, it creates a new `IntList` object, containing 30 and `null`, and modifies its own `tail` field to refer to that object.

QUICK EXERCISE
14.9

Write the mutating operation `void addAfterNth_mut (int n, int x)` that adds `x` as the (n+1)st element of the receiver (counting from zero). If the receiver has fewer than n-1 elements, this method does nothing.

As another example, `IntList addInorder_mut (int n)` adds the integer n to its receiver in a position that keeps the list in numerical order, assuming it was so to begin with. If you consistently use `addInorder_mut` to build your list, the list always will be in numerical order. It also returns the new reference to the head of the list; this is necessary because the new cell containing *n* may go at the front of the list (if *n* is less than the element at the head of the list). However, most of the time, the receiver of the message will continue to be the head of the list.

Here is the definition of `addInorder_mut`; its explanation follows.

```
public IntList addInorderM (int n) {
    if (n < value)
        return new IntList (n, this);
    else if (n == value)
        return this;
    else if (tail == null) {
        tail = new IntList(n, null);
        return this;
    }
    else {
        tail = tail.addInorderM(n);
        return this;
    }
}
```

Consider a cell in the middle of a numerically ordered list that receives the `addInorder_mut (n)` message. Its actions will depend not only on whether it is in the middle or at the end of the list but also on how its value—call it *p*—compares with *n*. There are four cases, in total, to consider:

1. If *p* is greater than *n*,

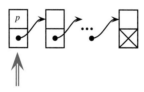

Line 3 allocates a new cell to hold *n*, places it at the front of the list

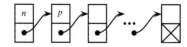

and returns a reference to it.

2. If *p* equals *n*, we need to make a choice about what the method is supposed to do. There are two alternatives: Insert a new cell with value *n* or simply ignore the request. We choose the latter course; line 5 reflects this decision.

3. If p is less than n but the receiver's `tail` field is `null`, then

Here we should end up with the list

and should return a reference to the cell containing p; this is accomplished by statements 7 and 8.

4. If p is less than n and `tail` is not `null`,

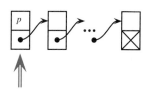

For this case, the receiver passes the message on to its `tail` and then sets `tail` to whatever is returned by that call (line 11). It returns a reference to itself (line 12) as the result.

QUICK EXERCISE 14.10	Write the mutating operation `IntList addNth_mut (int n, int x)` that makes x the nth element of the receiver (counting from zero). If the list has fewer than n − 1 elements, this method does nothing and returns the receiver. Note that if argument n is zero, x is added as the new head of the list, which is why the resulting list must be returned from this method.

14.6.4 Sorting Lists

In this section, we present a very efficient divide-and-conquer sorting algorithm, called *merge sort*. It can be used to sort arrays as well as lists (see Exercise 16), but because of the way it uses memory, quicksort generally is preferable for sorting arrays. For lists, merge sort is an excellent alternative.

Before we get to merge sort itself, we need two list operations that we will write in nonmutating form. That is, these will return brand new lists and not alter their receivers in any way.

The first operation, `merge`, merges two sorted lists into a single sorted result. Suppose we have the lists

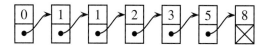

and

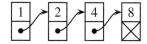

We want to produce this list:

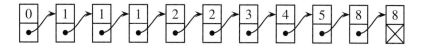

We will write `merge` as a nonmutating instance method of `IntList` (this is the first time we've added a method to the `IntList` class). One of the lists to be merged will be the receiver, and the other will be the argument, so `merge` will have the header

```
IntList merge (IntList L)
```

It will create a new list, altering neither the receiver nor the argument. Here, placing yourself in the position of the receiver, you can reason as follows:

> If my value is less than `L`'s value, then my value will be at the head of the new list, so I should create a new cell containing it and "proceed recursively"; that is, send the `merge` method to my tail, with `L` as its argument. The list that is returned will be the tail of the result, and the final result will be obtained by putting the new cell at its front. If `L`'s value is less than mine, the new cell should contain `L`'s value, and I should send the `merge` method back to myself, with the tail of `L` as the argument. Again, whatever is returned will be the tail of the result, and the result will be obtained by putting the new cell at its front. I need to consider two base cases: If `L` is null, then it has no value to compare, but in that case the result of the merge is just me. If mine is the smaller value, so I want to send the `merge` message to my tail, I need to be sure that my tail isn't null; if it is, then `L` would be the result of merging it with `L`.

This leads to the definition

```
1    IntList merge (IntList L) {
2        if (L == null)
```

```
3          return this;
4       if (value < L.value)
5          if (tail == null)
6             return new IntList(value, L);
7          else
8             return new IntList(value, tail.merge(L));
9          else
10            return new IntList(L.value, merge(L.tail));
11      }
```

Now let's consider the opposite of merging: splitting a list into two pieces with one piece consisting of the first, third, fifth, ... elements of the original list and the other piece consisting of the second, fourth, sixth, ... elements of the original list. Both lists must keep the items in the same relative order as in the original list. Therefore, we want the list

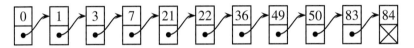

to be split into two parts:

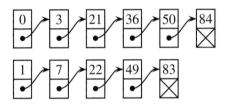

Expressing such a split recursively depends on the following idea. The original list is to be split into the first, third, fifth, ... elements and the second, fourth, sixth, ... elements. When we remove the first item from the original list, what was the second element on the original list becomes the first element on the foreshortened list, what was the third element of the original list becomes the second element of the foreshortened list, and so on. That means that if we split the foreshortened list, the roles of even-indexed and odd-indexed positions become interchanged!

Because this is an instance method, the list to be split is this. Let's assume it's split into the two lists L1 and L2. Then L1, which is to be the odd-indexed items from this, should consist of the first item from this, followed by the *even-indexed* items from the foreshortened this (because those were the other odd-indexed elements of the original this). Similarly, L2, which is to be the even-indexed items from this, should contain the *odd-indexed* items from the foreshortened this (because those were the even-indexed elements of the original this). We return these component lists as a pair of IntLists, defining a new class for this purpose:

```
1    class IntListPair {
2      public IntList x, y;
3
4      public IntListPair (IntList x, IntList y) {
5        this.x=x; this.y=y;}
6    }
```

IntListPair is one of those rare classes that contain public instance variables. It is precisely analogous to the Point class, but contains pairs of lists instead of pairs of integers.

The definition of split is

```
1    IntListPair split () {
2      if (tail == null)
3        return new IntListPair(this, null);
4      else {
5        IntListPair p = tail.split();
6        return new IntListPair(new IntList(value, p.y),
7                               p.x);
8      }
9    }
```

We can now present merge sort, a very simple and very efficient sorting method. The idea is just this easy: To sort a list L, split L into two halves, sort each half (recursively!), and then merge the sorted results. The bases are the zero-element and one-element lists. The idea is illustrated in Figure 14.4.

```
1    public static IntList mergeSort (IntList L) {
2    // Sort L by recursively splitting and merging.
3
4      if ((L == null) || (L.getTail() == null))
5        return L;              // Zero or one item
6      else {                   // Two or more items
7        // Split it in two parts...
8        IntListPair p = L.split();
9        // ...then sort and merge the two parts
10       return mergeSort(p.x).merge(mergeSort(p.y));
11     }
12   }
```

The mergeSort is a well-known example of the divide-and-conquer algorithm. The cost of the merge sort as the number of items n gets large is

$$T_{\text{mergeSort}}(A) = cn \log n$$

Note that merge sort *always* has this performance, whereas the generally excellent quicksort sometimes can have quadratic performance. However, we must add that using linked lists entails somewhat greater overhead than using arrays, so that merge sort generally will not be as fast as quicksort in practice. In a 5000-element list, our version of mergeSort ran in 12 seconds, slower than quickSort but still far better than selectionSort.

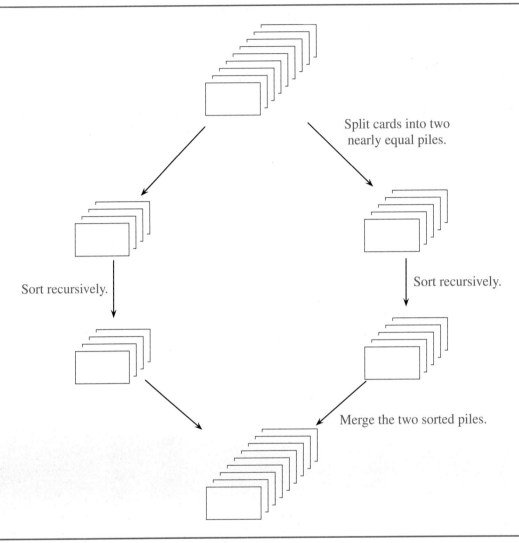

Split cards into two
nearly equal piles.

Sort recursively.

Sort recursively.

Merge the two sorted piles.

FIGURE 14.4   Schematic representation of merge sort.

14.7

Dynamic Programming

We presented the essentials of a recursive definition of the binomial coefficients at the start of this chapter. A complete definition based on our observations would be

$$\binom{m}{n} = \begin{cases} \binom{m-1}{n} + \binom{m-1}{n-1} & \text{if } m, n > 0 \\ 1 & \text{if } n = 0 \\ 0 & \text{if } n > 0, m = 0 \end{cases}$$

We can translate this directly into Java:

```
5    static int choose (int m, int n) {
6        if (n == 0)
7            return 1;
8        else if (m == 0)
9            return 0;
10        else
11            return choose(m-1, n) + choose(m-1, n-1);
12    }
```

This definition is correct but very slow. Calculating choose(30, 15) (= 155,117,520) on our computer takes 130 seconds. Using an iterative version is unlikely to save us much time in Java, but more importantly it is difficult to think of one! Nor is there an obvious divide-and-conquer method. What to do?

A close look at the choose method shows why it is so slow: It repeatedly *recomputes* the same binomial coefficients. For example, choose(30, 15) leads to calls to choose(29, 15) and choose(29, 14); choose(29, 15) in turn leads to calls to choose(28, 15) and choose(28, 14), while choose(29, 14) leads to calls to choose (28, 14) and choose(28, 13). This is illustrated in Figure 14.5, where each calculation of choose(*m*, *n*) is shown with the two calls that it makes— choose(*m*, *n* − 1) and choose(*m* − 1, *n* − 1)—below it.

The point to notice is that choose(28, 14) is called, and computed in its entirety, twice! (This implies, of course, that every subcomputation of that computation is called twice.) Following this reasoning further would reveal

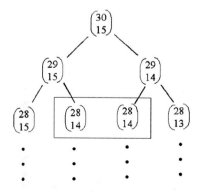

FIGURE 14.5 The "call tree" for choose(30, 15). **Notice that** choose(28, 14) **is computed twice.**

many more repeated calls. In fact, in computing choose(30, 15), the call choose(0, 2) is made 142,422,675 times!

This analysis suggests a simple solution: Every time choose(m, n) is called, when it completes its calculation, it should store its result in a table. The next time choose(m, n) is called, it just takes the value out of the table—no recursive calls, nor any computation at all, are required. This method is known as *tabulation*, or *caching*; the term *dynamic programming* is used for a similar concept, although usually in an iterative context.

tabulation

caching

dynamic

programming

The cache in this case has a simple structure: a two-dimensional array of size $(m + 1) \times (n + 1)$. [We use this size because we want to store the results for calls of choose(x, y) where x can range from 0 to m and y can range from 0 to n.] One question arises: How do we know when choose is being called with some arguments for the first time? We initialize the cache to contain -1 everywhere; since choose(m, n) is always nonnegative, when we look into the cache and see -1, we know that this is the first time this value is being computed. The public version of choose initializes the cache and calls the private version, chooseCache. And chooseCache does exactly the same calculation is before, except that it always records its answer in the cache and checks the cache before doing any calculation. (Note that chooseCache calls *itself* recursively; calling choose would defeat the entire method. Can you see why?)

```
static int[][] cache;

private static int chooseCache (int m, int n) {
    if (cache[m][n] == -1) {
        int ans;
        if (n == 0)
            ans = 1;
        else if (m == 0)
            ans = 0;
        else
            ans = chooseCache(m-1, n) + chooseCache(m-1, n-1);
        cache[m][n] = ans;
    }
    return cache[m][n];
}

public static int choose (int m, int n) {
    cache = new int[m+1][n+1];
    for (int i=0; i<m+1; i++)
        for (int j=0; j<n+1; j++)
            cache[i][j] = -1;
    return chooseCache(m, n);
}
```

For the call choose(30, 15), which took 130 seconds using the non-caching version, the running time of the caching version is too small to measure.

The lesson of this section is that even when a recursive definition of a function is horrendously slow, it may be possible to optimize it without finding an entirely new algorithm.

The definition of the binomial coefficients can be changed easily to calculate the *cost*—that is, number of addition operations—of naively calculating them. The recursion is simple: Depending on the values of m and n, the cost of calculating $\binom{m}{n}$ is either the cost of $\binom{m-1}{n}$ plus the cost of $\binom{m-1}{n-1}$ plus 1, or it is 0:

$$\text{cost}(m, n) = \begin{cases} 1 + \text{cost}(m - 1, n) + \text{cost}(m - 1, n - 1) & \text{if } m, n > 0 \\ 0 & \text{otherwise} \end{cases}$$

Write a method to calculate cost with and without using caching.

14.8

Recursive Drawings

Interesting examples of recursion come from functions that draw certain intricate, recursively defined curves. These curves are called *fractal*, or *self-similar*, because they have a structure that is repeated at every scale.

fractal
self-similar

14.8.1 Example: Sierpiński Curves

Figure 14.6 shows the first four curves in the sequence of *Sierpiński curves*: curves of orders 2 to 4 formed by taking four copies of the previous curve and "pasting" them together, as shown in Figure 14.7. We want to write a program that draws such curves.

The recursive structure of the Sierpiński curve is shown in Figure 14.7: To draw the Sierpiński curve of order i, draw four curves of order $i - 1$, erase the edges in the middle (the darker lines in Figure 14.7), and draw new edges connecting the four curves (the dashed lines in Figure 14.7). We will see how to erase lines shortly.[3]

The Sierpiński curve of order i is easy to draw once the geometry of the curve is understood. Figure 14.8 shows the geometry for the order 1 case, and Figure 14.9 shows the geometry for the other cases ($n > 1$). For the latter, ℓ is the length of the side of a curve of order $n - 1$, which we will have to calculate. We also will have to calculate the points a, b, c, and so forth. For example, a is $(\ell - 1, \ell)$, b is $(\ell, \ell - 1)$, and c is $(\ell + 2, \ell - 1)$.

Note that we only use points with integer coefficients. The result is that the curves get bigger as their order increases, so that eventually they will not fit in

---

[3]A more elegant recursive formulation, which allows the entire curve to be drawn without erasures and without lifting the pen from the page, is possible (S. N. Kamin and E. M. Reingold, *Programming with Class: A C++ Introduction to Computer Science*, McGraw-Hill, New York, 1996).

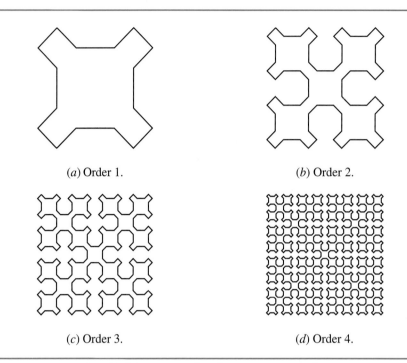

(*a*) Order 1.   (*b*) Order 2.

(*c*) Order 3.   (*d*) Order 4.

FIGURE 14.6   Sierpiński curves of orders 1, 2, 3, and 4.

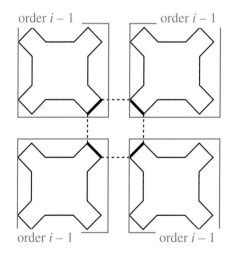

**FIGURE 14.7   The recursive structure of the Sierpiński curve of order *i*.
The dashed lines must be added and the adjacent bold
lines deleted to form the order *i* curve from four order
i − 1 curves.**

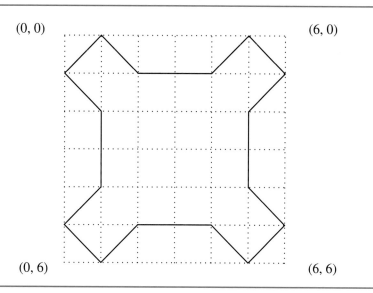

(0, 0)   (6, 0)

(0, 6)   (6, 6)

FIGURE 14.8 Geometry of the Sierpiński curve of order 1.

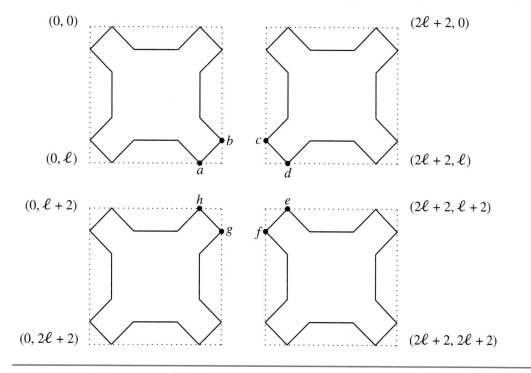

(0, 0)   (2ℓ + 2, 0)

(0, ℓ)   (2ℓ + 2, ℓ)

(0, ℓ + 2)   (2ℓ + 2, ℓ + 2)

(0, 2ℓ + 2)   (2ℓ + 2, 2ℓ + 2)

FIGURE 14.9 Geometry of Sierpiński curve of order i. Here, ℓ is the length of the side of a curve of order i − 1.

the drawing window. This is a problem we ignore for now; it is easy to solve anyway.

In drawing the curve of order n, we need to draw the curves of order $n - 1$ at various locations. Therefore, we provide the drawing function with two arguments: the order of the curve and the position at which to draw it. For the latter, we will give the upper left (northwest) corner of the curve [for example, $(0, 0)$ for the curve in Figure 14.8].

The function void sierp(int ord, Point nw) does the drawing just as we described. It uses a few auxiliary functions. First, the class PointOps includes two operations on points (of which only add is used in sierp):

```
1    import java.awt.*;
2
3    class PointOps {
4
5      static Point add (Point p, int dx, int dy) {
6        return new Point (p.x+dx, p.y+dy);
7      }
8
9      static Point scale (Point p, double s) {
10       return new Point ((int)(p.x*s), (int)(p.y*s));
11     }
12   }
```

To simplify drawing the curve of order 1, we declare the variables origin and lastpoint and the method drawTo:

```
39     Point origin, lastpoint;  // used to simplify drawing
40
41     void drawTo (int x, int y) {
42       Point newpt = PointOps.add(origin, x, y);
43       drawLine(lastpoint, newpt);
44       lastpoint = newpt;
45     }
```

This way, we can draw the curve in terms of the coordinates in Figure 14.8. The method call to curvesize (n) returns the length of the side of a curve of order n (the quantity ℓ in Figure 14.9).

```
64     void sierp (int ord, Point nw) {
65       // draw Sierpinski curve of order ord, with
66       // northwest point at nw
67       if (ord == 1) {
68         origin = nw;
69         lastpoint = PointOps.add(nw, 1, 0);
70         drawTo(2,1); drawTo(4,1); drawTo(5,0);
71         drawTo(6,1); drawTo(5,2); drawTo(5,4);
72         drawTo(6,5); drawTo(5,6); drawTo(4,5);
73         drawTo(2,5); drawTo(1,6); drawTo(0,5);
74         drawTo(1,4); drawTo(1,2); drawTo(0,1);
75         drawTo(1,0);
76       } else {
77         int size = curvesize(ord-1);
78         sierp(ord-1, nw);
```

```
79      sierp(ord-1, PointOps.add(nw, size+2, 0));
80      sierp(ord-1, PointOps.add(nw, 0, size+2));
81      sierp(ord-1, PointOps.add(nw, size+2, size+2));
82      Point a = PointOps.add(nw, size-1, size),
83            b = PointOps.add(a, 1, -1),
84            c = PointOps.add(b, 2, 0),
85            d = PointOps.add(c, 1, 1),
86            e = PointOps.add(d, 0, 2),
87            f = PointOps.add(e, -1, 1),
88            g = PointOps.add(f, -2, 0),
89            h = PointOps.add(g, -1, -1);
90      undraw(a,b); undraw(c,d);
91      undraw(e,f); undraw(g,h);
92      drawLine(b,c); drawLine(d,e);
93      drawLine(f,g); drawLine(h,a);
94    }
95  }
```

The method `undraw` erases a line by drawing over it in the background color:

```
47      void undraw (Point p1, Point p2) {
48        theWindow.setColor(background);
49        drawLine(p1, p2);
50        theWindow.setColor(Color.black);
51      }
```

The scaling works like this. The `draw` method in `Sierpinski` calculates `scaleFactor` as a function of the size of the window and the order of the curve. It also knows the upper left point that it can draw into [this is not (0, 0), because we want to leave a little room on the sides of the curve, for aesthetic reasons]; this is in the variable `nwOfWindow`. The `drawLine` method scales the points and adds this offset before drawing a line:

Here is the complete program. Figure 14.10 shows the result of drawing the Sierpiński curve of order 4 (in a 300 × 300 window).

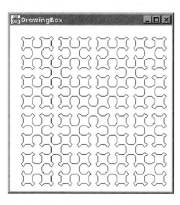

FIGURE 14.10 Output of the Sierpiński applet.

```
1   import CSLib.*;
2   import java.awt.*;
3
4   public class SierpinskiClient {
5
6
7     public static void main (String[] args) {
8       InputBox in = new InputBox();
9       in.setPrompt("Desired Order:");
10      int order = in.readInt();
11      DrawingBox out = new DrawingBox();
12      out.setDrawableSize(300, 300);
13      Sierpinski waclaw = new Sierpinski(new Point(20,20),
14                            out.getBackground());
15      waclaw.setOrder(order);
16      waclaw.draw(out, out.getDrawableWidth(),
17                       out.getDrawableHeight());
18    }
19  }
```

```
1   import CSLib.*;
2   import java.awt.*;
3
4   class Sierpinski {
5
6     // Draw Sierpinski curves
7     // Author: R. H. Kamin, June 30, 1997
8
9     int order;
10    DrawingBox theWindow;
11    double scaleFactor;
12    Point nwOfWindow;  // drawing area starts here
13    Color background;
14    int windowSize;    // minimum of height and width
15
16    Sierpinski (Point p, Color c) {
17      nwOfWindow = p;
18      background = c;
19      order = 1;
20    }
21
22    void setOrder (int o) {
23      // Negative or zero order leads to infinite loop
24      order = Math.max(o, 1);
25    }
26
27    int curvesize (int ord) {
28      return Power.power(2, ord+2) - 2;
29    }
30
31    public void draw (DrawingBox b, int w, int h) {
32      theWindow = b;
33      windowSize = Math.min(w-nwOfWindow.x,
34                            h-nwOfWindow.y) - 10;
35      scaleFactor = (windowSize*1.0) / curvesize(order);
```

```
36          sierp(order, new Point(0,0));
37     }
38
39     Point origin, lastpoint;  // used to simplify drawing
40
41     void drawTo (int x, int y) {
42       Point newpt = PointOps.add(origin, x, y);
43       drawLine(lastpoint, newpt);
44       lastpoint = newpt;
45     }
46
47     void undraw (Point p1, Point p2) {
48       theWindow.setColor(background);
49       drawLine(p1, p2);
50       theWindow.setColor(Color.black);
51     }
52
53     void drawLine (Point p1, Point p2) {
54       Point
55         p1s = PointOps.add(
56                   PointOps.scale(p1, scaleFactor),
57                   nwOfWindow.x, nwOfWindow.y),
58         p2s = PointOps.add(
59                   PointOps.scale(p2, scaleFactor),
60                   nwOfWindow.x, nwOfWindow.y);
61       theWindow.drawLine(p1s.x, p1s.y, p2s.x, p2s.y);
62     }
63
64     void sierp (int ord, Point nw) {
65       // draw Sierpinski curve of order ord, with
66       // northwest point at nw
67       if (ord == 1) {
68         origin = nw;
69         lastpoint = PointOps.add(nw, 1, 0);
70         drawTo(2,1); drawTo(4,1); drawTo(5,0);
71         drawTo(6,1); drawTo(5,2); drawTo(5,4);
72         drawTo(6,5); drawTo(5,6); drawTo(4,5);
73         drawTo(2,5); drawTo(1,6); drawTo(0,5);
74         drawTo(1,4); drawTo(1,2); drawTo(0,1);
75         drawTo(1,0);
76       } else {
77         int size = curvesize(ord-1);
78         sierp(ord-1, nw);
79         sierp(ord-1, PointOps.add(nw, size+2, 0));
80         sierp(ord-1, PointOps.add(nw, 0, size+2));
81         sierp(ord-1, PointOps.add(nw, size+2, size+2));
82         Point a = PointOps.add(nw, size-1, size),
83               b = PointOps.add(a, 1, -1),
84               c = PointOps.add(b, 2, 0),
85               d = PointOps.add(c, 1, 1),
86               e = PointOps.add(d, 0, 2),
87               f = PointOps.add(e, -1, 1),
88               g = PointOps.add(f, -2, 0),
89               h = PointOps.add(g, -1, -1);
90         undraw(a,b); undraw(c,d);
```

```
91          undraw(e,f); undraw(g,h);
92          drawLine(b,c); drawLine(d,e);
93          drawLine(f,g); drawLine(h,a);
94        }
95      }
96    }
```

14.8.2 Example: Hilbert Curves

Our second curve-drawing example employs the so-called Hilbert curves, the first four of which are shown in Figure 14.11. Each curve of order 2 and higher is formed by four copies of the previous curve, just as in the Sierpiński curves. However, here the constituent curves of order $i - 1$ are rotated and reflected as they combine to form the curve of order i. Figure 14.12 shows how four copies of the basic pattern are combined to form the curve of next-higher order.

We'll write a class Hilbert that incorporates a method hilbert to draw the curve, just as Sierpinski contained a method sierp. HilbertCurve will differ from SierpinskiCurve only in that it will have an instance variable of type Hilbert, instead of Sierpinski, to which it will send the draw message.

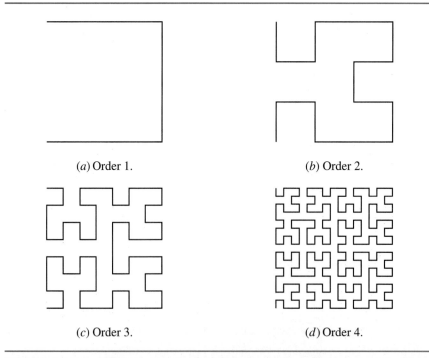

(a) Order 1.   (b) Order 2.

(c) Order 3.   (d) Order 4.

FIGURE 14.11   Hilbert curves of orders 1, 2, 3, and 4, shown reduced in size from the description in the text.

FIGURE 14.12 Recursive structure of the Hilbert curve of order *i*. Each of the four quadrants contains a Hilbert curve of order *i* − 1 in the orientation shown. Quadrant A contains the mirror image of a curve of order *i* − 1 rotated 90° counterclockwise; quadrants B and C contain curves of order *i* − 1; quadrant D contains the mirror image of a curve of order *i* − 1 rotated 90° clockwise. The dotted lines connect the four curves.

There is another difference between the `hilbert` and `sierp` methods. Whereas `sierp` drew the curve as it went along, `hilbert` will store a list of points, which it will subsequently connect with lines. For this purpose, it will use the predefined Java class *Polygon*. `Polygon` is little more than a list of `Points`. *Polygon* Indeed, we could easily write it ourselves, but since it is already provided in the `java.awt` package, we may as well use it. A listing of some of its methods is given in Table 14.1. Note that `addPoint(Point p)` is a mutating operation, analogous to our `addToEnd_mut` (page 572). Once we have all the points in the curve in a list, we can draw them one at a time.

The difficult part of this problem lies in defining the `hilbert` method in such a way that it can draw a Hilbert curve of any order *in any orientation*. Specifically, we need to be able to draw a curve rotated by 90° and to draw it *reflected* (draw its left-to-right mirror image). To see this, examine Figure 14.11*b* and *c*. The upper left part of Figure 14.11*c* appears to be *b* rotated 90° clockwise, but this is not quite right: If we want to start drawing both curves at (0, 0) (the

Name	Description
`int npoints`	Number of points in the polygon
`int[] xpoints`	*x* coordinates of points in the polygon
`int[] ypoints`	*y* coordinates of points in the polygon. `xpoints` and `ypoints` are parallel arrays of length `npoints`.
`void addPoint(int x, int y)`	Add point (x, y) at end of receiver
`boolean contains(Point p)`	Determines whether p falls inside the polygon

TABLE 14.1 Some methods and public instance variables of the `Polygon` class.

northwest corner), then to get the upper left portion of Figure 14.11c we need to first reflect Figure 14.11b and then rotate it counterclockwise.

To illustrate, we draw the various copies of Figure 14.11b with a circle where we wish to start drawing and a square where we want to end. Then, in composing Figure 14.11c from four copies of b, we will want to be sure that the square of one copy matches up with the circle of the next. For example, we want to start drawing both Figure 14.11b and Figure 14.11c at the upper left. So Figure 14.11b is the curve

To fit it in as the upper left part of Figure 14.11c, we first reflect and then rotate it counterclockwise:

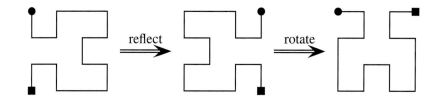

Using Figure 14.11b, unchanged, as the upper right and lower right parts of Figure 14.11c allows the circles and squares to match up correctly:

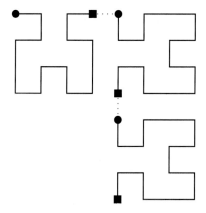

The final copy of Figure 14.11b is obtained by reflecting and rotating 90° clockwise:

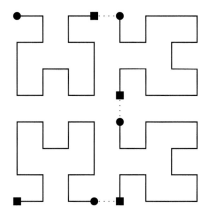

So, the overall method of drawing a Hilbert curve of order n is this. Starting with an "appropriately oriented" Hilbert curve C of order $n - 1$,

> Draw the mirror image of C, rotated 90° counterclockwise.
> Connect to the next copy of C by going "east."
> Draw a copy of C.
> Connect to the next copy of C by going "south."
> Draw a copy of C.
> Connect to the next copy of C by going "west."
> Draw the mirror image of C, rotated 90° clockwise.

The reason for all the quotes is that since Hilbert curves are drawn at different orientations, "east" does not always mean east, "south" may mean north, and so on.

Here, then, is the really clever part. We tell the `hilbert` function about the orientation we want it to use by giving a complete set of four compass directions in the following way. Assume that we are standing on the applet facing north, so that east is to our right, south is behind us, and west is to our left and that, in this orientation, the curve we are to draw will have its open end to our left. Assume further that we have a method to draw the curve of lower order C, also with the open side of the curve to our left. We can describe the drawing of the larger curve as follows:

> Draw the mirror image of C, rotated 90° counterclockwise.
> Connect to the next copy of C by going `right`.
> Draw a copy of C.
> Connect to the next copy of C by going `behind`.
> Draw a copy of C.
> Connect to the next copy of C by going `left`.
> Draw the mirror image of C, rotated 90° clockwise.

The trick is that `right`, `left`, and `behind` are arguments to `hilbert`. For example, if we are facing in direction `facing`, with `left` to our left, `right`

to our right, and `behind` behind us

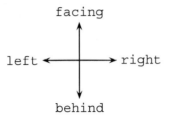

then we can tell `hilbert` to draw a curve reflected and rotated 90° counter-clockwise by giving it the directions

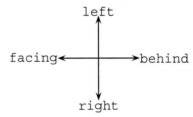

Therefore, we make the heading of `hilbert` be

```
66    void hilbert (
67        int i,      // order of Hilbert curve to be drawn
68        int facing, // the compass direction we are facing
69        int right,  // the compass direction to our right
70        int behind, // the compass direction at our back
71        int left){  // the compass direction to our left
72    // Collect the coordinates of successive points on
73    // the Hilbert curve of order i, starting at location
74    // lastpoint, oriented as specifed by "local" compass
```

With `Hilbert` having this structure, we specify that the drawing be the mirror image and rotated 90° counterclockwise from our current orientation (i.e., quadrant A of Figure 14.12) by switching around the directions. We'll be facing what is currently `left`, to our right will be what is currently `behind`, behind us will be what is currently `right`, and to our left will be what is currently `facing`. Therefore, to draw a Hilbert curve of order $i - 1$ in such an orientation, we call

```
Hilbert(i-1, left, behind, right, facing);
```

Now we move to the `right` (to quadrant B of Figure 14.12) and draw a Hilbert curve of order $i - 1$ in our present orientation with

```
Hilbert(i-1, facing, right, behind, left);
```

and we move in the direction `behind` (to quadrant C of Figure 14.12) and draw the same thing again. Finally, we move to our `left` (to quadrant D of Figure 14.12) and draw the mirror image of the Hilbert curve of order $i - 1$, rotated 90° clockwise

```
Hilbert(i-1, right, facing, left, behind);
```
which corresponds to

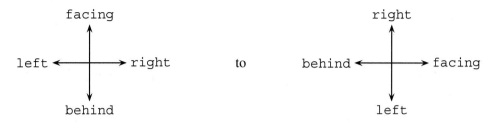

This is tricky, so study it carefully.

The method `hilbert` therefore is

```
66    void hilbert (
67        int i,       // order of Hilbert curve to be drawn
68        int facing,  // the compass direction we are facing
69        int right,   // the compass direction to our right
70        int behind,  // the compass direction at our back
71        int left){   // the compass direction to our left
72    // Collect the coordinates of successive points on
73    // the Hilbert curve of order i, starting at location
74    // lastpoint, oriented as specifed by "local" compass
75
76        if (i == 0)
77            poly.addPoint(lastpoint.x, lastpoint.y);
78        else {
79            hilbert(i-1, left, behind, right, facing);
80            move(right);
81            hilbert(i-1, facing, right, behind, left);
82            move(behind);
83            hilbert(i-1, facing, right, behind, left);
84            move(left);
85            hilbert(i-1, right, facing, left, behind);
86        }
87    }
```

where the method `move` properly adjusts the values of the `Point` variable `lastpoint` as we move in one direction or another. Notice that the recursion in the method `Hilbert` bottoms out when we call for drawing a zeroth-order curve—we can think of a zeroth-order Hilbert curve as being simply a vertex of the curve whose coordinates are to be added to `Polygon`.

Finally, we define a method `hilbert (int i)` to supply the initial call to `hilbert` with the actual compass points for the various directions and to initialize `lastpoint`.[4]

---

[4]Notice that the initial value of `lastpoint` is obtained by *copying* `nwOfWindow` (this is what the `Point` constructor we've called does). It would be an error simply to do the assignment `lastpoint = nwOfWindow`; it would draw the curve correctly the first time but not the next. This is because `move` is a mutating operation, and if we did the assignment, then `lastpoint` and `nwOfWindow` would be the same object, so that `nwOfWindow` would be changed.

The entire `Hilbert` program is

```
1   import CSLib.*;
2
3   class HilbertClient {
4
5     static InputBox in;
6     static Hilbert david;
7     static int order;
8
9     public static void main (String[] args) {
10      in = new InputBox();
11      in.setPrompt("Desired Order:");
12      david = new Hilbert();
13      order = in.readInt();
14      david.hilbert(order);
15      DrawingBox out = new DrawingBox(
16                      "Hilbert curve of order " + order);
17      david.draw(order, out);
18    }
19  }
```

```
1   import java.awt.*;
2   import CSLib.*;
3
4   class Hilbert {
5
6     // Draw Hilbert curves
7     // Author: Kathryn Mickunas, May 23, 1996
8
9     int order;
10    Point nwOfWindow;      // drawing area starts here
11    Polygon poly;
12    int offset;
13
14    Hilbert () {
15      nwOfWindow = new Point(0,0);
16      poly = new Polygon();
17    }
18
19    int curvesize (int ord) {
20      return Power.power(2, ord) - 1;
21    }
22
23    public void draw (int order, DrawingBox b) {
24      b.clearRect(0,0,b.getDrawableWidth(),
25                    b.getDrawableHeight());
26      int windowSize =
27            Math.min(b.getDrawableWidth()-nwOfWindow.x,
28                    b.getDrawableHeight()-nwOfWindow.y) - 10;
29      int scaleFactor =
```

```
30         (int)((windowSize*1.0) / curvesize(order));
31      drawPolyline(b, scaleFactor, poly.xpoints, poly.ypoints,
32                             poly.npoints);
33    }
34
35    void drawPolyline(DrawingBox b, int sf,
36                      int[] xpts, int[] ypts, int npts) {
37      for (int i=0; i<npts-1; i++) {
38        drawLine(b, sf, xpts[i], ypts[i], xpts[i+1], ypts[i+1]);
39      }
40    }
41
42    void drawLine(DrawingBox b, int sf,
43                  int x1, int y1, int x2, int y2) {
44      b.drawLine(sf*x1, sf*y1, sf*x2, sf*y2);
45    }
46
47    static final int NORTH=0, EAST=1, SOUTH=2, WEST=3;
48
49    Point lastpoint;
50
51    void move (int d) {
52    // Move one unit in direction d from point lastpoint.
53
54      switch (d) {
55        case NORTH:lastpoint.y = lastpoint.y-1;
56                  break;
57        case EAST: lastpoint.x = lastpoint.x+1;
58                  break;
59        case SOUTH:lastpoint.y = lastpoint.y+1;
60                  break;
61        case WEST: lastpoint.x = lastpoint.x-1;
62                  break;
63      }
64    }
65
66    void hilbert (
67        int i,       // order of Hilbert curve to be drawn
68        int facing,  // the compass direction we are facing
69        int right,   // the compass direction to our right
70        int behind,  // the compass direction at our back
71        int left){   // the compass direction to our left
72    // Collect the coordinates of successive points on
73    // the Hilbert curve of order i, starting at location
74    // lastpoint, oriented as specifed by "local" compass
75
76      if (i == 0)
77        poly.addPoint(lastpoint.x, lastpoint.y);
78      else {
79        hilbert(i-1, left, behind, right, facing);
80        move(right);
81        hilbert(i-1, facing, right, behind, left);
82        move(behind);
83        hilbert(i-1, facing, right, behind, left);
```

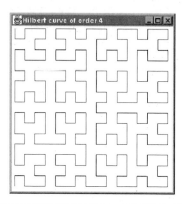

FIGURE 14.13   Output of the Hilbert program.

```
84              move(left);
85              hilbert(i-1, right, facing, left, behind);
86          }
87      }
88
89      void hilbert (int i) {
90      // Draw a Hilbert curve of order i.
91          lastpoint = new Point(nwOfWindow);
92          hilbert(i, NORTH, EAST, SOUTH, WEST);
93      }
94
95  }
```

As we said, the client itself (the `HilbertCurveClient` class) is nearly identical to `SierpinskiClient`; one minor difference is that `Hilbert` does not need to know the background color of the drawing box because it does not need to erase any lines.

`Hilbert`'s draw method is very similar to that of `Sierpinski`. Just as before, this method must compute `scaleFactor`, which is the size of the window divided by the width of the Hilbert curve of order `order` (which is $2^{\text{order}} - 1$). However, because `hilbert` draws the curve in one continuous line, it uses this value a little differently. This quantity represents the number of pixels in a line of "unit" length, so the `move` method simply uses this value instead of 1.

The output for the fourth-order curve is shown in Figure 14.13.

Summary

A method is *recursive* if, as part of its action, it calls itself. The recursive version of a computation often is simpler and more elegant than the iterative form. Recursion is a powerful tool; it can make difficult programming jobs more manageable.

To simulate a recursive method to check its execution, use a stack of papers with all relevant information written on the papers. This relevant information consists of the place from which the method was called, the values of any parameters, and the values of any local variables.

Keep in mind the following distinctions concerning parameters, class variables, and local variables for recursive methods:

1. Parameters communicate information from one level to the next in the recursion.
2. Local variables are invisible from one level to the next—each level has its own copies of local variables. Different levels of recursion do not have access to the values of or the ability to modify the local variables of other levels of recursion.
3. Class variables establish communication among all levels of recursion simultaneously.

The single most important paradigm in the design of algorithms is the *divide-and-conquer principle*. This paradigm is the backbone of many of the most efficient algorithms. The principle is to break a problem into smaller subproblems of the same type, solve those subproblems recursively, and meld the solutions found for the individual subproblems into a solution for the entire problem.

Three popular methods for sorting the contents of an array are selection sort, insertion sort, and quicksort. *Selection sort* and *insertion sort* have quadratic time complexity, although insertion sort runs much faster when the array is already partially sorted. *Quicksort* is quadratic in the worst case, but on average it has $n \log n$ time complexity; in practice, it has excellent efficiency.

Two-dimensional arrays are used to represent matrices in mathematical calculations. An example is the solution of a system of linear equations, which can be done by the method of Gaussian elimination.

Linked data structures are those made up of objects that contain references to other objects of the same type. Examples are linked lists, doubly linked lists, and trees. The recursive nature of these data structures makes it natural to write recursive methods to manipulate them.

Tabulation, or *caching*, is a method of speeding up methods by storing the results of method calls in a table and then looking them up rather than recomputing them. In some cases, this method can dramatically improve the performance of the method.

Self-similar curves are drawings that have a naturally recursive definition. The very elegant programs that draw these curves would be much more complex without the use of recursion.

Exercises

1. Answer these questions concerning the two recursive versions of power:
   (a) In the first version, we could have used $n = 1$ as the base case, instead of $n = 0$:
   ```
   if (n==1)
       return k;
   else ...
   ```
   Show that the case $n = 1$ is handled correctly by the version we gave, but the case $n = 0$ would not be handled correctly if we made this change.

(b) What happens if we make the preceding change (using $n = 1$ as the base case) in the second version?

(c) What happens in each of these functions if n is negative?

(d) The second version is purported to be much more efficient than the first. Produce a table showing (i) how many multiplications and (ii) how many calls to power need to be performed by each version of power for $k = 3$ and $n = 0, 1, 2, 4, 8, 16, 32,$ and 64.

2. An example of the elegance of recursive definitions comes from a problem in everyday life: making change.
   (a) Develop a recursive definition for the number of ways to make change for n dollars, assuming that pennies, nickels, dimes, quarters, half dollars, \$1 bills, and \$5 bills are available.
   (b) Use your definition as the basis of a program to compute the number of ways to make change for a specified amount.
   (c) Modify your program in part (b) to list *all* the ways of making change instead of just computing the number of ways.

3. Suppose that you are in charge of a softball league with 16 teams. During the 15-week season, each team must play each other team exactly once. Write a recursive application that will print an appropriate 15-week schedule.

4. Ackermann's function $A(m, n)$ is defined for nonnegative integers by the recurrence

$$A(m, n) = \begin{cases} n + 1 & \text{if } m = 0 \\ A(m - 1, 1) & \text{if } m > 0, n = 0 \\ A(m - 1, A(m, n - 1)) & \text{if } m > 0, n > 0 \end{cases}$$

Write a program to compute this function. Be warned that the value of $A(m, n)$ grows super-rapidly!

5. One of the most famous of all recursive definitions is that of the *Fibonacci function*:

$$\text{fib}(n) = \begin{cases} \text{fib}(n - 1) + \text{fib}(n - 2) & \text{if } n \geq 2 \\ n & \text{otherwise} \end{cases}$$

Implemented directly, it is extremely slow. A simple cache, consisting of an array of n integers, can speed it up tremendously. Implement the Fibonacci function directly and using a cache, compare the speeds of the two implementations.

6. Write a Java method to calculate the nth number in the Newman-Conway sequence defined by $P(1) = P(2) = 1$ and for $n \geq 3$, $P(n) = P(P(n-1)) + P(n - P(n-1))$.

7. Collections of objects are usually sorted by comparing only parts of those objects. For example, suppose we define the class Appointment

```
class Appointment {
  private Clock appointmentTime;
  private String description;
  public
    . . .
}
```

where `Clock` is the class defined in Figure 5.7 on page 137. Two `Appointment` objects will be compared by comparing the `Clock` objects they contain. Now suppose

```
Appointment[] Schedule;
```

contains a sequence of appointments, but it is given in the order in which the appointments were made, not in their chronological order. Rewrite `selectionSort` with prototype

```
void selectionSort (Appointment[] sched, int lo, int hi)
```

and then do likewise for `insertionSort` and `quickSort`. In each case, the only movement of data should be the swapping of array elements.

8. All the sample arrays used in this section contained distinct elements, but all the algorithms can sort arrays that contain duplicate elements. The duplicates are simply bunched together, as you would expect, so that

10	3	1	3	5	10

when sorted, becomes

1	3	3	5	10	10

The question arises of whether the relative positions of duplicate elements are preserved in the sorted array. That is, if we mark the duplicate elements

10_1	3_1	1	3_2	5	10_2

does the sorting process retain the order

1	3_1	3_2	5	10_1	10_2

or reverse it

1	3_2	3_1	5	10_2	10_1

or sometimes one and sometimes the other? This may not be significant when sorting arrays of numbers, but when we are sorting appointments, as in Exercise 7, the original order tells us which appointment was made first. In case of a scheduling conflict, this information can be useful.

A sorting algorithm that retains the original order of duplicate elements is called *stable*. Determine whether each of the three sorting algorithms studied in this section is stable; and either explain why it is or give an example showing that it is not.

9. Quicksort is not especially fast in sorting small arrays. It might be improved if it were modified to

```
if (hi-lo < size)
   insertionSort( ...);
else {
   ... // as above
   }
```

where `size` needs to be determined by experimentation. Make this modification, comparing the times with the original version of `quickSort` on several sets of test data and different values of `size`. Is there any value of `size` on which this version consistently beats the original?

To go a little further, we can leave the individual subarrays of length `size` unsorted until the end. The array will be filled with these subarrays, which are internally unsorted but correctly ordered among themselves. In such a case, insertion sort runs very well. So change `quickSort` to

```
if (hi-lo < size)
   ;        // do nothing
else {
   ... // as above
   }
```

and call `insertionSort` after calling `quickSort`. Compare the running times of this version to those of the previous versions.

10. Comparisons of sorting methods based on contrived examples cannot necessarily be relied on to predict the efficiency of these algorithms in practice. Another way to do the comparison is to generate arrays randomly.

In this exercise we will construct such arrays and use them to explore the efficiency of our sorting methods, especially `quickSort`. If you place the line

```
import java.util.Random;
```

at the beginning of your program, you can instantiate a new Random object via

```
Random rand = new Random();
```

and then you can call the method `double rand.nextDouble()`. It returns a different double number x, in the range $0 \le x < 1$, each time it is called. Furthermore, the sequence of numbers it returns is *pseudorandom*, meaning it has no apparent pattern. Therefore, an array of n random numbers can be produced by a loop like this:

```
double[] A = new double[n];
for (int i=0; i<n; i++) A[i] = rand.nextDouble();
```

(a) Use such a randomly generated array to compare the three sorting methods. Letting n be 1000 will be enough to show the differences. Although we cannot predict exactly what sequence of random numbers you will get, you are almost sure to see these results: Selection sort will be the slowest, insertion sort somewhat faster, and quicksort by far the fastest of the three.

(b) We can use such random arrays to explore an important aspect of quicksort, the choice of the pivot element in partition. Recall that, in choosing a pivot element, the goal is to approximate the median element of the subarray A[lo] ...A[hi]. We chose the median of A[lo+1], A[(lo+hi)/2], and A[hi]. We use the random array to explore other possibilities.

Set n large enough that sorting the array with quickSort takes about 20 seconds (probably somewhere between 30,000 and 50,000 elements) and try the following methods of choosing the pivot element:

- A[lo]. This would have been a very poor choice for our contrived examples (why?), but it should work fairly well for random data.
- The middle element among A[lo], A[hi], and A[(lo+hi)/2]. This is almost identical to the guess we used, but you will be surprised at how poorly it performs on an array that is in strictly decreasing order. Look at the partitions obtained for this array to see why it runs so slowly.
- A randomly chosen element. You can generate a random integer in the range lo...hi using this assignment:

  ```
  int randomInt = lo +
  (int)(rand.nextDouble()*(hi-lo+1));
  ```

  Then rand.nextDouble() generates a number x such that $0 \le x < 1$. If, for example, lo = 0 and hi = 10, the number on the right-hand side will be $0 + 11x$, which is a number in the range $0 \le 11x < 11$. When it is assigned to randomInt, it will be truncated to an integer between 0 and 10, as required.

11. Write a client readForwardList using addToEnd_mut. It should read a list of numbers (like readReversedList on page 570) but in such a way that toString() lists them in the order in which they were read.

12. Program a mutating version of remove that removes an element from the receiver.

    ```
    IntList removeM (int n)
    ```

    Make sure that you can handle the case in which the item being removed is the *first* one on the list. As before, if the receiver is a one-element list containing n, return the null reference.

13. Program the mutating operation IntList removeNthM (int i), which removes the ith cell from its receiver and returns the new head of the list. The latter normally will be the same as the current head, but when removeNthM is called with argument 1, the new head will be the second cell in the list. If i is greater than the length of the receiver, do nothing.

14. Use removeNthM to solve the *Josephus problem*, named for the Jewish historian of the Roman-Jewish War of the first century. The story goes that 10 Jews were trapped in a cave by Roman soldiers, and they determined to commit suicide rather than surrender. They decided to do so in an unusual way: They all stood in a circle, and with one man chosen to begin, every other man committed suicide. The question is, Which was the last man to die?

We want you to solve this problem in a more general setting. For given positive integers m and n, construct a list of the numbers from 1 to n. Then, starting from 1, remove every mth item; if this takes you past the end of the list, then consider the list to be a circle and continue from the beginning. For example, if n is 10 and m is 6, you start with the list

```
1 2 3 4 5 6 7 8 9 10
```

Eliminate element 1, leaving

```
2 3 4 5 6 7 8 9 10
```

then count off 6 and eliminate element 7:

```
2 3 4 5 6 8 9 10
```

then count off 6 from there, looping around to the front, and eliminate element 4:

```
2 3 5 6 8 9 10
```

Continue in this way, eliminating 2, then 10, and so on. Continue in this way until only one man is left, and print his number.

15. Define the following nonmutating instance methods.
    (a) `IntList copy ()` simply creates a fresh copy of a list identical to the receiver of the message.
    (b) `IntList extractPositive ()` returns a list consisting of just the positive integers occurring in the receiver (in the same order as they occur there). If the receiver contains no positive numbers, then the `null` reference is returned.
    (c) `IntList remove(int n)` returns a list identical to the receiver, except that all occurrences of n, if any, are removed. If the receiver has no occurrences of n, then an exact copy is returned. If the receiver has just one cell, and it contains n, then the `null` reference is returned.

16. Merge sort can be used with arrays. Its general structure is

```
void mergeSort (double[] A, int lo, int hi) {
  if ((hi-lo) < 2)
    <sort the array directly>
  else {
    mergeSort(A, lo, (lo+hi)/2);
    mergeSort(A, (lo+hi)/2+1, hi);
    <merge the two sorted halves of A>
    }
  }
```

However, the difficulty lies in the last line. There is no easy way to merge two halves of A into a sorted whole. It is fairly simple, on the other hand, to merge the two halves into a separate array, which then can be copied back into A. Write the method

```
double [] merge (double[] A,
                 int lo, int middle, int hi)
```

which merges sorted subarrays `A[lo]` ... `A[middle]` and `A[middle+1]` ... `A[hi]` into a new array that is allocated on the heap and returned as the value of the `merge` method. Use this to finish `mergeSort` and check its running time on a 10,000-element array.

17. Suppose you fold a piece of paper in half, then fold it in half again, and so on for some number of folds. (The folds are parallel to one another.) If you unfold and flatten the paper, the pattern of folds will be ∨ after one fold, ∧∨∨ after two folds, ∧∧∨∨∧∨∨ after three folds, and so on. (Try it!) The pattern for $n + 1$ folds is obtained from the pattern for n folds as follows. Take the *reflected* pattern for n folds, add the fold ∨ at the end, and then add the original pattern for n folds. *Reflected* means upside down and in reverse order. (Again, try it!) Using 1 for ∨ and 0 for ∧, write a recursive method to produce the pattern for n.

18. The following sequence of curves is called the *Sierpiński gasket*; see "Four Encounters with Sierpiński Gasket," by Ian Stewart, *The Mathematical Intelligencer* 17, no. 1 (January 1995), pages 52–64, for details.

Write an applet to draw members of this sequence of curves.

TEXT PROCESSING AND FILE INPUT/OUTPUT

CHAPTER PREVIEW

We explain the `java.io` package, which is the API for file handling. We introduce a variant of Java's `String` class, the `StringBuffer` class, which is mutable. We show how files can be read and written, and how to handle exceptions that occur when doing so. Finally, we show how console input and output can be performed.

Most programs read from, and write to, files. From a language point of view, file-handling operations are not a part of the Java language itself, but are provided in a collection of classes in the Java API. Specifically, the `java.io` package is provided for this purpose.

The structure of the `java.io` package is quite complex and uses many of the advanced features of the Java language, including inheritance and exceptions. It also makes heavy use of *wrapper classes*—not a new language feature, but a common pattern for structuring classes. We start this chapter with a discussion of the `StringBuffer` class, which is in `java.lang` but is particularly useful in conjunction with files. We next discuss the notion of wrapper classes and then buffered I/O, and we finally dive into the `java.io` package.

15.1

The Classes `String` and `StringBuffer`

The Java compiler provides a number of methods for performing operations on `String`s, and we already have used a few of them, namely, `substring`, concatenation (+), `length`, and `charAt`. (Remember, the first character in a `String` is numbered 0.)

The `String` class is immutable. A string, once created, cannot be changed, although new strings can be created. Java also provides a mutable class, called *StringBuffer*. It has some of the same operations as `String` and includes mutating operations such as

StringBuffer

```
public void setCharAt (int index, char ch)
```

which changes the character at position `index` to `ch`. Some of the methods for the `StringBuffer` class are summarized in Table 15.1.

Java provides a way of converting back and forth between `String` and `StringBuffer`: There is a `StringBuffer` constructor that takes a `String`

Method	Meaning
`int length ()`	Returns the present length
`char charAt (int index)`	Retrieves the character at `index`
`StringBuffer delete (int index)`	Deletes the character at `index`
`StringBuffer delete (int start, int end)`	Deletes the characters from position `start` to `end`.
`StringBuffer replace (int start, int end, String s)`	Replaces the characters from position `start` to `end` by the string `s`.
`String substring (int begin, int end)`	Returns string consisting of characters in receiver from `begin` to `end`
`String substring (int begin)`	Returns the substring from `begin` to the end of the string
`void setCharAt (int index, char ch)`	Replaces the character at `index` with `ch`
`StringBuffer insert (int index, String s)`	Inserts the string `s` at `index`
`StringBuffer insert (int index, char ch)`	Inserts the character `ch` at `index`
`StringBuffer append (String s)`	Appends the string `s`
`StringBuffer append (char ch)`	Appends the character `ch`
`String toString ()`	Converts to a string.

TABLE 15.1   Some instance methods of `StringBuffer`.

as an argument, and there is a `String` constructor that takes a `StringBuffer` as an argument. Therefore, the following code fragment will print `Hello, Tailor!`:

```
OutputBox out = new OutputBox();
String s="Hello, Sailor!";
StringBuffer sb = new StringBuffer(s);
sb.setCharAt(7, 'T');
out.println(sb);
```

Although `println` is not overloaded with a `StringBuffer` argument, we can print without an explicit conversion since `StringBuffer` *does* have a `toString` method. One of the few circumstances in which Java will perform an implicit conversion occurs when a `String` is required and an object has a `toString` method.

An important feature of `StringBuffer` is that its objects can grow dynamically as required. Methods are available for appending to a `StringBuffer` and for inserting in the middle of a `StringBuffer`. Note that they return a value of type `StringBuffer`, instead of returning `void`, as is more common for mutating operations. This is done just for convenience; the `StringBuffer` returned, in fact, is just the receiver itself.

15.2

Sequential Files

All our applications so far have taken their input from an `InputBox` and produced output to an `OutputBox` or `DrawingBox`. However, often we need to take input from a *file* stored on our disk. Java has a package of predefined classes *file* that assist us in doing this, the `java.io` package. Computer programmers use many different kinds of files: word processing and other document files; raw data files, such as satellite data files; graphical data files; streams of audio and video data; Java `class` files; and so forth.

We like to think of such files as being composed of either characters or integers.[1] In this section, we consider only files composed of characters. It is convenient to think of such files as composed of multiple *lines*, each one ending with an end-of-line character. You can imagine that we could write an application that would read a line of such a file and print that line, repeating until the end of file is encountered. Likewise, you can imagine that we might write an application that would *create* such a file.

The Java classes that support file input are in the `java.io` package, and they include `FileReader`, which allows us to "open" a file for reading, and `BufferedReader`, which is a *wrapper class* that provides additional methods *wrapper class* that treat the file as a stream of characters; `BufferedReader` also increases the efficiency of reading and allows line-oriented reading. We say that a class `W` *wraps* a class `Y` if:

1. `Y` is a concrete (not abstract) class.
2. `W`'s constructor takes `Y` as an argument, storing a local copy of `Y`.
3. `W` reimplements all of `Y`'s methods.

The notion of wrappers is used heavily in `java.io`. It is not a new language feature, but refers to a way of extending the capabilities of a class. Normally, if a class `C` needs to be enhanced with additional or modified methods, we create a subclass of `C` that overrides `C`'s methods as necessary. An alternative approach is to define a class that contains a `C` object (in an instance variable) and defines all the methods of `C`, either by "delegating" them to the `C` object or by redefining them. Such a class is called a wrapper class for `C`. Thus, if `C` contains methods `void f ()` and `int g (String s)`, the simplest possible wrapper class would look like this:

```
class CWrapper {
    C aC;

    CWrapper (C aC) { this.aC = aC; }
```

---

[1]As we discussed in Chapter 3, there is not really a lot of difference between characters and numbers, but there are some differences. For example, characters always correspond to nonnegative integers, which turns out to be important, as we will soon see.

```
void f () { aC.f(); }

int g (String s) { return aC.g(s); }
}
```

This class just provides an exact copy of the functionality of C (like a subclass that adds no variables or methods). Actual wrapper classes make some modifications in the methods of C, either adding new methods or redefining C's methods.

To describe the relation between a subclass and a superclass, we used the term *is-a*. Similarly, the relation between a wrapper class and the class it wraps could be termed *has-a*. The decision of when to use an *is-a* relation (inheritance) or a *has-a* relation (wrapping) is a subtle one for which no general rule can be given. However, note that a single class can only be a subclass of one other class, but a wrapper can wrap a class and, at the same time, can be a subclass of another class. So, in a sense, wrapping gives us another way to reuse code that can be employed in addition to subclassing.

15.2.1   Input

The relationships between the input classes that we'll use are shown in Figure 15.1. Although we show BufferedReader wrapping Reader, we know (from the foregoing requirements) that it cannot directly wrap the abstract class Reader; rather, it must wrap one of the concrete subclasses of Reader. For example, we'll see that it is useful for BufferedReader to wrap FileReader. The close and read methods of BufferedReader are merely conduits to the superclass close and read methods, while BufferedReader adds a new readLine method. The important methods of FileReader and BufferedReader are summarized in Tables 15.2 and 15.3.

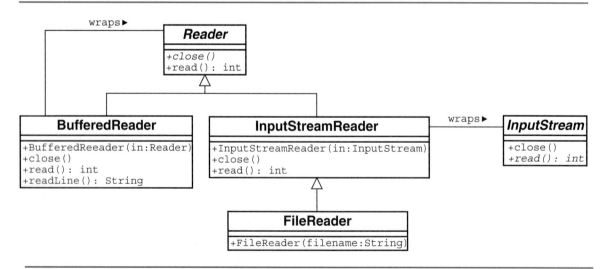

FIGURE 15.1   A UML class diagram for some Java input classes.

Name	Description
FileReader (String filename)	Creates a new file reader from filename

TABLE 15.2 **The constructor of the** FileReader **class. Operations** read **and** close **are inherited from** InputStreamReader.

Name	Description
BufferedReader (Reader in)	Creates a new buffered reader from the reader in
void close ()	Closes the stream
int read ()	Reads a single character
int read (char[] cbuf, int off, int len)	Reads len characters (or until end-of-file) into cbuf[off] and subsequent locations
String readLine ()	Returns a line of text

TABLE 15.3 **Methods of the** BufferedReader **class. All nonconstructor methods throw** IOException.

BUG ALERT 15.1

FileNotFoundException must be caught for FileReader

If the FileReader constructor is unable to locate the file specified by its argument, then it throws a FileNotFoundException. This exception must be either caught or thrown by any program that uses FileReader.

BUG ALERT 15.2

IOException must be caught for BufferedReader

Every method of BufferedReader except the constructor throws IOException. Therefore, if you use any such method, your program must either catch IOException or declare that it throws IOException.

A file with the name *filename* might be made available for reading by

```
FileReader fr = new FileReader(filename);
```

However, reading (using read) from such a FileReader would likely be quite inefficient. Each call to read returns a single character. But the underlying device might require that blocks of, say, 512 bytes be read. So each single-byte read would induce a read of a block of bytes. It would be more efficient to read 512 bytes at a time from FileReader and then to pick out the bytes one at a time. This is called *buffering* the read. FileReader indeed has a read   *buffering* method that is capable of reading a block of 512 (or more) bytes. But we certainly don't want to write a program to do the buffering work. Luckily, there is already a wrapper class that does this for us: `BufferedReader`. So the usual way of making a *filename* available for reading is to wrap a `FileReader` with a `BufferedReader`:

```
BufferedReader br
   = new BufferedReader(
             new FileReader(filename));
```

`BufferedReader` provide a basic method `int read()` for reading a single character, but it utilizes `FileReader`'s more efficient block reads. The `read()` method returns an int instead of a char because it returns −1 when the end of file is encountered. `BufferedReader` also provides a method, `String readLine ()`, that reads an entire line (ending with the end of line); `readLine()` returns `null` when the end of file is encountered.

As an example of performing input, the following program prints a file to an `OutputBox`:

```
1    import CSLib.*;
2    import java.io.*;
3
4    public class Copy {
5       // Copy a file to an OutputBox
6       // Author: Angela McDermott, September 1, 1996
7
8       public Copy (String filename) throws IOException {
9          // open local file given by filename
10         br = new BufferedReader(new FileReader(filename));
11      }
12
13      public void copy () throws IOException {
14         OutputBox out = new OutputBox();
15         int i;
16         while (true) {
17            i = br.read();
18            if (i==-1) return;
19            out.print((char)i);
20         }
21      }
22   }
```

Notice how the `read` returns an `int` (line 20); end of file is indicated by a return value of −1 (tested in line 21). If end of file was not encountered, then before using the value returned by `read`, we must cast it to a `char` (as in line 22).

QUICK EXERCISE 15.1	Write a client for `Copy`, called `CopyClient`, that reads the file name from an `InputBox`. Test it by having it copy itself to the `OutputBox`.

15.2.2 Output

Output is supported by `FileWriter` and `BufferedWriter`, with methods for writing a single character, an array of characters, or a string and for writing the end of line. In addition, because we often want to convert integers, Booleans, doubles, strings, and the like to characters and write those characters, a convenience wrapper class is provided by Java, `PrintWriter`. The relationships between the output classes that we'll use are shown in Figure 15.2. The important methods are summarized in Tables 15.4, 15.5, and 15.6. A file with the name *filename* is made available for printing by

```
PrintWriter pr
  = new PrintWriter(
        new BufferedWriter(
            new FileWriter(filename)));
```

The `PrintWriter` class has overloaded methods for converting all the primitive types to strings; these methods are void `print(...)` and void `println(...)`, which are what we've been using with `OutputBox` all along.

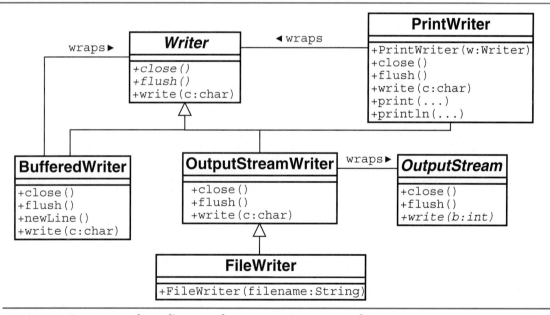

FIGURE 15.2 A UML class diagram for some Java output classes.

Name	Description
FileWriter (String filename)	Creates a new file writer from `filename`

TABLE 15.4 The constructor of the `FileWriter` class.

Name	Description
`BufferedWriter (Writer out)`	Creates a new buffered writer from the writer `out`
`void close ()`	Closes the stream
`void flush ()`	Flushes the stream
`void newLine ()`	Writes a line separator
`void write (char c)`	Writes the character `c`
`void write (char[] cbuf, int off, int len)`	Writes `cbuf [off]` ... `cbuf [off+len-1]`

TABLE 15.5 Methods of the `BufferedWriter` class. All nonconstructor methods throw `IOException`.

Name	Description
`PrintWriter (Writer out)`	Creates a new print writer from the writer `out`
`void close ()`	Closes the stream
`void flush ()`	Flushes the stream
`void write (char c)`	Writes the character `c`
`void write (char[] cbuf, int off, int len)`	Writes `cbuf [off]` ... `cbuf [off+len-1]`
`void print (item type)`	Prints the `item` according to its *type*
`void println (item type)`	Prints the `item` according to its *type*, followed by a line separator

TABLE 15.6 Methods of the `PrintWriter` class. All nonconstructor methods throw `IOException`.

BUG ALERT 15.3	*FileNotFoundException must be caught for FileWriter*

If the `FileWriter` constructor is unable to locate the file specified by its argument, then it throws a `FileNotFoundException`. This exception must be either caught or thrown by any program that uses `FileWriter`.

BUG ALERT 15.4	*IOException must be caught for BufferedWriter and PrintWriter.*

Every method of `BufferedWriter` and `PrintWriter` except the constructor throws `IOException`. Therefore, if you use any such method, your program must either catch `IOException` or declare that it throws `IOException`.

15.2.3   Console Output

All our textual output so far has been done by printing to an OutputBox. Java provides a comparable window into which you can print and println just as we have with OutputBox. This window is called the *Java console*; there is a variable System.out that refers to this object. So instead of writing

Java console
System.out

```
OutputBox out = new OutputBox();
...
out.println("A message");
```

you can write

```
System.out.println("A message");
```

This works for any of the primitive types as well as any object that has a toString method. It is also possible for an application to receive input from the Java console. That is, the console is both an InputStream and a PrintWriter object.[2] However, it is very inconvenient to use the Java console for input, since you can read only characters (and lines) from System.in. If you write a program that wants the user to type a decimal, such as 35.5, then your program must do all the work of reading the characters, checking for errors, and converting the characters to a double. You have now mastered enough of Java to write such programs, but we won't have the opportunity to do that in the remainder of this book. However, later in this chapter, we *will* show you how to read lines of characters from System.in.

There is only one console window available. On batch systems (such as command-line Unix or DOS) the console window is the same window in which you type commands such as javac Hello.java. If you are using an integrated development environment or a browser, then there is a menu command that will allow you to make the Java console visible.

Debugging File I/O

Let's write an application that simply reads an existing file and prints the lines of the file (to System.out) while numbering them from 1. First, we will want to use *command-line arguments* in this application. Here is how they work: When we had a client, say, AppClient, we ran that client by typing

command-line arguments

```
java AppClient
```

---

[2]This is not quite true. System.out is of type PrintStream, which is obsolete, but which cannot be eliminated because to do so would break a lot of existing Java code. However, for our purposes, we can treat the Java console *as if* it were a PrintWriter.

We can supply additional name(s) by typing

```
java Appclient name1 name2 ...
```

How can our application know about the additional name(s)? Recall that every application has a static method

```
public static void main (String[] args)
```

Although we haven't used it so far, the parameter `args` contains those additional names. Although we have called them *names*, each can be any sequence of characters without blanks; that is, blanks separate the successive names.

We suppose that the name of the file will be supplied as an additional command-line argument when we run the application. So, if the application is named `Cat.java` and we wish to list the file `stuff`, we type

```
javac Cat.java CatClient.java
java CatClient stuff
```

We'll capture that string and pass it into the constructor for our class. Here's our first attempt at the application

```
1   import java.io.*;
2
3   public class Cat {
4      // Read and echo a text file, numbering the lines
5      // Author: Angela McDermott, September 1, 1996
6
7      private BufferedReader br;
8
9      public Cat (String filename) {
10        // open local file given by filename
11        br = new BufferedReader(new FileReader(filename));
12     }
13
14     public void readAndEcho () {
15        String s = "";
16        for (int line = 1; ; line++) {
17           s = br.readLine();
18           if (s == null) return;   // if end-of-file
19           System.out.println(line + "\t" + s);
20        }
21     }
22  }
```

with the client

```
1   public class CatClient {
2
3      public static void main (String[] args) {
4         Cat c = new Cat(args[1]);
5         c.readAndEcho();
6      }
7   }
```

In line 4 of the client, we obtain the command-line argument from args [1] and, using that, construct the Cat instance. In the Cat constructor, we create a new FileReader and then the BufferedReader. Notice the degenerate for loop starting at line 16. It initializes line and increments it each time, but there is no exit test! The way that we expect this loop to terminate is via a return that is executed when we read an end of file (indicated when readLine returns null).

When we attempt to compile this program, we get some errors indicating that there are exceptions we failed to handle:

```
Cat.java:11: unreported exception java.io.FileNotFoundException;
must be caught or declared to be thrown
      br = new BufferedReader(new FileReader(filename));
                                   ^

Cat.java:17: unreported exception java.io.IOException;
must be caught or declared to be thrown
        s = br.readLine();
              ^

2 errors
```

The first error indicates that the constructor FileReader might throw the exception FileNotFoundException. This certainly is reasonable, so we need to use a try-catch statement when invoking this constructor. (You may want to review Section 12.3 on exceptions.) Likewise, the readLine method might encounter trouble and throw an IOException. IOException has a number of subclasses, some of which are illustrated in Figure 15.3. Our next attempt is as follows:

```
 1    import java.io.*;
 2
 3    public class Cat {
 4       // Read and echo a text file, numbering the lines
 5       // Author: Angela McDermott, September 1, 1996
 6
 7         private FileReader fr;
 8         private BufferedReader br;
 9
10       public Cat (String filename) {
11          // open local file given by filename
12          try {
13            fr = new FileReader(filename);
14          }
15          catch (FileNotFoundException e) {
16            System.out.println("File Not Found: " + filename);
17            System.exit(-1);
18          }
19
20          br = new BufferedReader(fr);
21       }
22
23       public void readAndEcho () {
24          String s = "";
25          for (int line = 1; ; line++) {
```

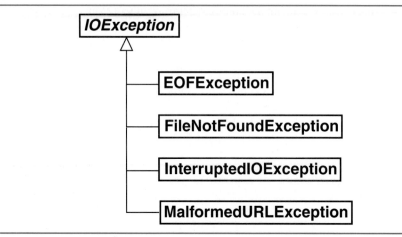

FIGURE 15.3   The `IOException` **inheritance hierarchy.**

```
26              try {
27                s = br.readLine();
28              }
29              catch (IOException ioe) {
30                System.out.println("Error Reading File");
31                System.exit(-1);
32              }
33              if (s == null) return;   // if end-of-file
34              System.out.println(line + "\t" + s);
35            }
36          }
37        }
```

with the client

```
1    public class CatClient {
2      public static void main (String[] args) {          Wrong
3        Cat c = new Cat(args[1]);
4        c.readAndEcho();
5      }
6    }
```

Notice that we now create the `BufferedReader` in two stages (lines 12 through 20), and we display an appropriate error message if the file cannot be found. If that happens, we also use the Java method `System.exit` to terminate the program abnormally (line 17). Similarly, we use a try-catch statement around the `readLine` method call (lines 26 through 32). This time the program compiles, and we execute it by

```
java CatClient stuff
```

but executing it gives a run-time error:

```
java.lang.ArrayIndexOutOfBoundsException
        at CatClient.main(CatClient.java:3)
Exception in thread "main"
```

It might take a bit of pondering to realize that the third component on the command line is provided in `args[0]`, not `args[1]`. So, after we change the one use of `args[1]` to `args[0]` in our client (line 3), the program finally works as intended.

Compile the code for `Cat` and `CatClient`, and verify that it works by running `java CatClient CatClient`.

**QUICK EXERCISE
15.2**

15.4

A Mail-Merge Application

In a mail-merge application, the user provides a template of a letter, with *merge fields* at specific places, and a list of items to be used to fill the merge fields, such as the recipient's name. The application generates personalized copies of the letter. Our application uses two files for input: a file containing the template, with the percent sign % used to indicate the merge fields; and a file containing the data items, each terminated by a pound sign #. Each file has the same base name, but the template file has the suffix `.template` and the data item file has the suffix `.list`. Suppose we have a file `mailing.template` that contains

```
%

Dear %,

You may have already won TEN MILLION DOLLARS.

%, I know you would just love to have all this wonderful
money, so SEND IN THE ENTRY FORM, now!

Your pal,

Edna McWoman
```

and a file `mailing.list` that contains

```
Joseph Shmoe
10 Wasta Way
Makesme, IL#
Joseph#
Joe#
Joan Simone
1001 Outta Place
Okeydo, KY#
Joanie#
Joan#
```

We execute our application, `MailMerge`, via

```
javac MailMerge.java
java MailMerge mailing
```

This will read the input files `mailing.template` and `mailing.list` and produce all its output in the file `mailing.out`.

In the foregoing example, the letter has three merge fields, and the data file contains data for two persons, yielding the following output:

```
Joseph Shmoe
10 Wasta Way
Makesme, IL

Dear Joseph,

You may have already won TEN MILLION DOLLARS.

Joe, I know you would just love to have all this wonderful
money, so SEND IN THE ENTRY FORM, now!

Your pal,

Edna McWoman


-----------------------------------
Joan Simone
1001 Outta Place
Okeydo, KY

Dear Joanie,

You may have already won TEN MILLION DOLLARS.

Joan, I know you would just love to have all this wonderful
money, so SEND IN THE ENTRY FORM, now!

Your pal,

Edna McWoman


-----------------------------------
```

Suppose there were n merge fields in the letter. The data file will contain p sequences of characters (possibly including new lines), each terminated by a pound sign; we refer to all these as *fields*. The fields are used to replace the merge fields in the letter, yielding *p/n* customized letters. The fields probably include an address, but they also may include other information, such as a name to use in the salutation. (The letter cannot contain any %s except those to indicate merge fields nor two successive %s, and the fields cannot contain #s, but see Exercise 11 at the end of this chapter.)

One point should be noted carefully here. Within a field, all characters *up to* the ending # must be read, including new lines. However, the # *and the new line following it* are not included in the field.

Here is the code:

```
 1   import java.io.*;
 2
 3   public class MailMerge {
 4      // A Mail Merge Application
 5      // Author: Mary Angela McDermott, December 30, 1996
 6
 7      BufferedReader template, mailList;
 8      PrintWriter out;
 9
10      public void openFiles (String fn) throws IOException {
11
12         template = new BufferedReader(
13                     new FileReader(fn + ".template"));
14         mailList = new BufferedReader(
15                     new FileReader(fn + ".list"));
16
17         out = new PrintWriter(
18                  new BufferedWriter(
19                     new FileWriter(fn + ".out")));
20      }
21
22      private StringBuffer readUpto (BufferedReader br,
23                                     char delim)
24                                     throws IOException {
25
26         StringBuffer sb = new StringBuffer();
27         int inputchar;
28
29         while (true) {
30            inputchar = br.read();
31            if (inputchar == -1 || inputchar == delim) return sb;
32            sb.append((char)inputchar);
33         }
34      }
35
36      private StringBuffer[] st = new StringBuffer[10];
37
38      private int readTemplate() throws IOException {
39         int n;
40
41         // Read the first portion of template (which may
42         // be empty, if there is a % as the first character).
43         st[0] = readUpto(template, '%');
44         // Read the remaining portions of template.
```

```
45       for (n=1; n<10; n++) {
46          st[n] = readUpto(template, '%');
47          if (st[n].length() == 0) return n;
48       }
49       return n;
50    }
51
52    public void merge () throws IOException {
53       StringBuffer sm;
54
55       int n = readTemplate();
56
57       // Read the first field
58       sm = readUpto(mailList, '#');
59
60       while (true) {
61          // If no more fields
62          if (sm.length() == 0) return;
63
64          // Interleave template portions with fields.
65          out.print(st[0]);
66          for (int i=1; i<n; i++) {
67             mailList.read();  // get past newline
68             out.print(sm);       // print field
69             out.print(st[i]); // print next template portion
70             sm = readUpto(mailList, '#');
71          }
72          out.println("--------------------------------");
73       }
74    }
75
76    public void closeFiles () {
77       out.close();
78    }
79 }
```

with a typical client

```
1  import java.io.*;
2
3  public class MailMergeClient {
4     public static void main (String[] args) throws IOException {
5        MailMerge mm = new MailMerge();
6        mm.openFiles (args[0]);
7        mm.merge();
8        mm.closeFiles();
9     }
10 }
```

We defined three public methods in the MailMerge class—openFiles to open the input and output files, merge to perform the merge, and closeFiles to close the files.

The openFiles method (lines 10 through 20) is quite straightforward. Notice that we composed the BufferedReader/FileReader constructors and the PrintWriter/BufferedWriter/FileWriter constructors in single statements (lines 12 through 19). How can we do this without taking care of the `FileNotFoundExceptions` that troubled us in our `Cat` application? The answer is that we "pass the buck" in this application, indicating that `openFiles` throws `IOException`. We use `IOException` because the `FileWriter` constructor can throw an `IOException` (if, e.g., there is no permission to create the file, or there is no room on the device, etc.). Since `IOException` is a superclass of `FileNotFoundException`, it suffices to throw just `IOException` rather than both `FileNotFoundException` and `IOException`.

To do the input of both the `template` file and the `list` file, we define a method, `readUpTo`, that reads characters from a `BufferedReader` up to a certain character, called the *delimiter* (lines 22 through 34). Notice how we use a `StringBuffer` to accumulate characters up to but not including the delimiter. Notice, again, the cast to the `char` that we want (line 32). Note that if the remaining input does not contain the delimiter, then a call to `readUpto` will read all the remaining input, terminating when the value -1 is returned by `read()` in line 30, indicating that the end of file has been reached. We also note that the `read` in line 30 of `readUpto` can cause `IOException` to be thrown; so we state that `readUpto` throws `IOException`.

The reading of the `template` file is encapsulated in a private method `readTemplate` (lines 38 through 50), forming strings out of the portions that are separated by merge fields (indicated by `%`). We assume that no more than nine merge fields are in the template (yielding 10 strings). We begin by reading the first field (line 43). Every time we begin a new iteration of the ensuing "infinite loop," we will have read ahead to the first of the next group of fields. If that first field is blank (line 47), then we return from `readTemplate`. Eventually, `readTemplate` returns the number of template phrases that were read. The phrases are stored in the private instance variables `st[0]` through `st[n-1]`.

In the `merge` method (lines 52 through 74) we begin by reading the `template` file. Then we print the various template portions, reading and interleaving the fields as we go (lines 64 through 71). When the final template portion has been printed, we print a cut line of dashes (to separate the various letters on the output file).

The only thing to notice about the client is that either it must enclose the method calls `openFiles` and `merge` in `try-catch` blocks (since those methods may throw `IOExceptions`), or the client must itself throw `IOException`, as is done in line 4.

15.5

A Database Application

In this section, we develop an application to search a collection of audio compact disks (CDs). We suppose that a *database* of CDs is stored in a file, say, `MyCDs`, spelling out

1. The title
2. The artist

3. The year of publication

4. A "call" number

5. A rating

record

field

Each CD in our collection will have one line containing the preceding information. Each such line is termed a *record* of the database. Each component (title, artist, etc.) is called a *field* of the record. The fields on each line are separated by the characters : :. The very first line of the database contains the number of records in the database.

Our application will ask the user to enter a string to match against the title or a string to match against the artist. The user can specify whether uppercase and lowercase matter (i.e., the match be either case-sensitive or case-insensitive). Also, the user can specify that the match be found anywhere in the field or only at the beginning (a prefix match). By definition, if no match string is specified for a field, then that empty string matches any value in that field. Our program will show us all matching records, one after the other.

In this program, we'll use the Java console both for output and for input. This will not be very difficult, since the input will always be a string, so no conversion is required. Here's a sample database.

```
5
The Complete Recordings::Robert Johnson::1996::Columbia C2K 64916::good
Founder of the Delta Blues::Charlie Patton::1995::Yazoo 2010::great
Hide Away::Freddy King::1993::Rhino R2 71510::pure Freddy
Sufferin' Mind::Guitar Slim::1991::Specialty SPCD-7007-2::my favorite
West Side Soul::Magic Sam::1967::Delmark DD-615::nothing better
```

Here's a typical session. We have shown the user's responses (corresponding to System.in) in color.

```
Enter part of artist's name:
Enter part of title: the
Case matters (y,n)? y
Match prefix only (y,n)? y
Sorry, there were no matches for your query.
Try again? y
Enter part of artist's name:
Enter part of title: the
Case matters (y,n)? y
Match prefix only (y,n)? n
Result: Charlie Patton, Founder of the Delta Blues
   Yazoo 2010, 1995, rated great.
Do you want to see the next match? y
No more matches for this query.
Try again? y
Enter part of artist's name:
Enter part of title: the
Case matters (y,n)? n
Match prefix only (y,n)? n
Result: Robert Johnson, The Complete Recordings
   Columbia C2K 64916, 1996, rated good.
Do you want to see the next match? y
```

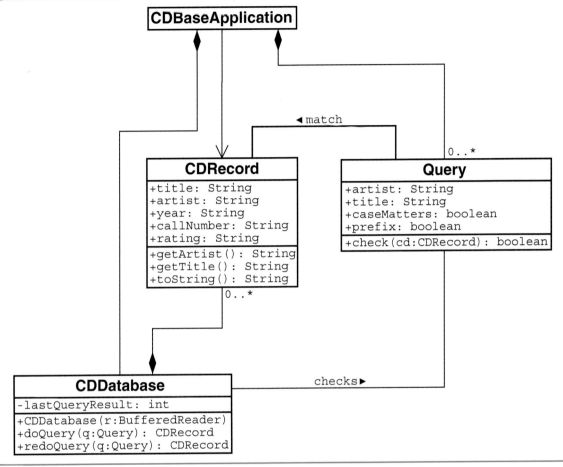

FIGURE 15.4 A UML class diagram for the `CDDatabase` **program.**

```
Result: Charlie Patton, Founder of the Delta Blues
   Yazoo 2010, 1995, rated great.
Do you want to see the next match? y
No more matches for this query.
Try again? n
```

This application consists of four classes, related as shown in the UML diagram in Figure 15.4.

CDRecord. The objects of this class represent individual CDs. When the application begins, it creates as many `CDRecord` objects as there are CDs in the database.

CDDatabase. This is the collection of all the CDs in the database. This also includes operations to find the next CD in the database that satisfies a given query.

Query. This represents a query, that is, an artist name, a record name, and Boolean values that indicate whether the matches are prefix matches and whether they are case-sensitive matches.

CDBaseApplication. This class contains the main query loop, which reads the query from the user, as shown previously.

Our first order of business, then, is to define the class that will describe a record in our CD collection. We need to provide accessor methods to retrieve the artist and title fields, along with a method to print a complete record in a suitable format. And finally we want to be able to read an individual record from our BufferedReader file. So our complete CDRecord class is as follows:

```java
import java.io.*;

public class CDRecord {
    // CD Database Search
    // Author: Samuel N. Kamin, June 1, 1996

    String title, artist, year, callNumber, rating;

    public CDRecord () {}

    public static CDRecord getRecord (BufferedReader r)
                                    throws IOException {
        String input = input = r.readLine();
        CDRecord cd = new CDRecord();
        int fieldStart = 0,
            fieldEnd;

        fieldEnd = input.indexOf("::", fieldStart);
        cd.title = input.substring(fieldStart, fieldEnd);
        fieldStart = fieldEnd+2;
        fieldEnd = input.indexOf("::", fieldStart);
        cd.artist = input.substring(fieldStart, fieldEnd);
        fieldStart = fieldEnd+2;
        fieldEnd = input.indexOf("::", fieldStart);
        cd.year = input.substring(fieldStart, fieldEnd);
        fieldStart = fieldEnd+2;
        fieldEnd = input.indexOf("::", fieldStart);
        cd.callNumber = input.substring(fieldStart, fieldEnd);
        fieldStart = fieldEnd+2;
        cd.rating = input.substring(fieldStart);
        return cd;
    }

    public String getArtist () { return artist; }

    public String getTitle () { return title; }

    public String toString () {
        return (artist + ", " + title + "\n  " + callNumber
                + ", " + year + ", rated " + rating + ".");
    }
}
```

Therefore, to read the next record, we simply perform a `readLine()` (line 13) and then split up the resulting string by searching for occurrences of `::`. The `String` method `int indexOf (String s, int start)` searches the receiver of the message for `s`, starting at position `start` in the receiver. If a match is found, `indexOf` returns the index in the receiver of the first character of the match; or if the string `s` cannot be found, it returns -1. The instance method `substring` is used to extract the fields once their boundaries are found.

Now that we have a `CDRecord` class, we need a `CDDatabase` class. Fundamentally, this is an array of `CDRecords`. We also need a constructor, which will read the entire database, record by record, from a `BufferedReader`; and we need to keep track of where we are in the database while queries are being performed.

```
1   import java.io.*;
2
3   public class CDDatabase {
4     // CD Database Search
5     // Author: Samuel N. Kamin, June 1, 1996
6
7     private CDRecord[] cds;
8     private int lastQueryResult = -1;
9
10    public CDDatabase (BufferedReader r) throws IOException {
11      String line = "";
12      line = r.readLine();
13      int dblength = Integer.parseInt(line);
14      cds = new CDRecord[dblength];
15      for (int i=0; i<dblength; i++)
16        cds[i] = CDRecord.getRecord(r);
17    }
18
19    public CDRecord doQuery (Query q) {
20      return checkCDs(0, q);
21    }
22
23    public CDRecord redoQuery (Query q) {
24      if (lastQueryResult == -1) // Last query failed
25        return null;
26      return checkCDs(lastQueryResult+1, q);
27    }
28
29    private CDRecord checkCDs (int start, Query q) {
30      for (int i=start; i<cds.length; i++)
31        if (q.check(cds[i])) {
32          lastQueryResult = i;
33          return cds[i];
34        }
35      // Matching record not found
36      lastQueryResult = -1;
37      return null;
38    }
39  }
```

As mentioned before, the first line of the database file is an integer telling how many records are in the file. This integer is read in lines 12 and 13, using the Integer.parseInt class method that we saw in Table 13.7. Then we allocate the proper number of CDRecords in the array, and we read each one, using the class method CDRecord.getRecord(r).

The methods doQuery and redoQuery both use the private helper method checkCDs, but they start at different records—doQuery starting at the first record and redoQuery starting just after the last successful match. We have yet to see what a Query looks like, but we assume that we can send the boolean check (CDRecord cdr) message to a Query to see if the given record satisfies the query. The instance variable lastQueryResult remembers the array index of the record that most recently satisfied a query (line 32), with −1 indicating an unsuccessful match (line 36).

Let's now look at the Query class. We know that it will have an instance method boolean check (CDRecord cdr), which will check whether the given CDRecord satisfies the query. But the query itself must be constructed; and there are methods to do this:

```
1   class Query {
2     // Query a CD Database
3     // Author: Samuel N. Kamin, June 1, 1996
4
5     String artist, title;
6     boolean
7       caseMatters, // if true, consider case when matching
8       prefix; // if true, match only when provided string
9               // is prefix of actual artist or title
10
11    public Query () {
12      artist = "";
13      title = "";
14      caseMatters = false; // case doesn't matter
15      prefix = false;       // match anywhere
16    }
17
18    public void setArtist (String a) { artist = a; }
19    public void setTitle (String t) { title = t; }
20    void setCase (boolean b) { caseMatters = b; }
21    void setPrefix (boolean b) { prefix = b; }
22
23    public boolean check (CDRecord cd) {
24      return (matches(artist, cd.getArtist()) &&
25              matches(title, cd.getTitle()));
26    }
27
28    private boolean matches (String pat, String str) {
29      // Determines whether pat occurs within str.
30      // caseMatters and prefix are consulted to determine
31      // how to match.
32
33      if (!caseMatters) {
34        pat = pat.toLowerCase();
```

```
35          str = str.toLowerCase();
36       }
37       if (prefix) return str.startsWith(pat);
38       return (str.indexOf(pat) != -1);
39    }
40  }
```

Most of the query setup methods are quite simple. The methods `setArtist` and `setTitle` simply remember the strings that will match against those fields. The `setCase` and `setPrefix` methods record whether the match should be case-sensitive and prefix-only. The method `boolean check (CDRecord cd)` does the matching to which we alluded earlier. It must attempt to match the string `artist` to the artist field of the `cd` and the string `title` to the title field. The actual work is done by the method `boolean matches (String pat, String str)`, which returns `true` if `pat` occurs in `str` and `false` otherwise. The check anchors the match to be a prefix-only match if appropriate and matches without regard to case, if appropriate.

We can now put all this together into an application. The constructor opens the database file `MyCDs` and creates a `CDDatabase`. The client then invokes a method (`queryLoop`) that repeatedly prompts the user to

1. Enter part of an artist's name.
2. Enter part of a title.
3. Indicate whether case matters.
4. Indicate whether the match should be prefix-only.

The `queryLoop` method then will report the results of the query. If a match was found on the previous query, the application will ask if the user wants to see the next match.

```
1   import CSLib.*;
2   import java.io.*;
3
4   public class CDBaseApplication {
5      // CD Database Search
6      // Author: Samuel N. Kamin, June 1, 1996
7
8      private static BufferedReader dbreader, sysin;
9
10     private CDDatabase db;
11     private Query q;
12     private CDRecord qresult;
13
14     public CDBaseApplication () throws IOException {
15        // open file "MyCDs" for stream character reading
16        dbreader = new BufferedReader(new FileReader("MyCDs"));
17
18        // Make System.in readable using readLine()
19        sysin = new BufferedReader(new InputStreamReader(System.in));
20
21        // call CDDatabase passing dbstream to create database
```

```
22          db = new CDDatabase(dbreader);
23
24          // create an unfilled query
25          q = new Query();
26      }
27
28      public void queryLoop () throws IOException {
29
30          while (true) {
31              // Prompt for query parameters.
32              System.out.print("Enter part of artist's name: ");
33              String artist = sysin.readLine();
34              System.out.print("Enter part of title: ");
35              String title = sysin.readLine();
36              System.out.print("Case matters (y,n)? ");
37              boolean caseMatters = getYesNo();
38              System.out.print("Match prefix only (y,n)? ");
39              boolean prefix = getYesNo();
40
41              // Set query parameters.
42              q.setArtist(artist);
43              q.setTitle(title);
44              q.setCase(caseMatters);
45              q.setPrefix(prefix);
46
47              // Perform the query.
48              qresult = db.doQuery(q);
49
50              if (qresult == null) {
51                  System.out.println
52                      ("Sorry, there were no matches for your query.");
53              }
54
55              while (qresult != null) {
56                  System.out.println("Result: " + qresult.toString());
57
58                  // Next query.
59                  System.out.print("Do you want to see the next match? ");
60                  if (!getYesNo()) break;
61                  qresult = db.redoQuery(q);
62                  if (qresult == null)
63                      System.out.println("No more matches for this query.");
64              }
65
66              System.out.print("Try again? ");
67              if (!getYesNo()) break;
68          }
69      }
70
71      private boolean getYesNo () throws IOException {
72          while (true) {
73              String response = sysin.readLine();
74              if (response.equalsIgnoreCase("y")
75                      || response.equalsIgnoreCase("yes"))
```

```
76        return true;
77      if (response.equalsIgnoreCase("n")
78          || response.equalsIgnoreCase("no"))
79        return false;
80      System.out.print("Please respond yes or no: ");
81      }
82    }
83  }
```

The code is straightforward. First, the constructor deserves some examination. We open the `MyCDs` file in line 16 and create a `BufferedReader` for it. In line 19, we wrap `System.in` with a `BufferedReader` so that we can read full lines of characters using `readLine`. The wrapping must be done in two pieces. `System.in` is of type `InputStream`. Referring to Figure 15.1, we see that we must first wrap `System.in` with an `InputStreamReader`, and only then can we wrap it with a `BufferedReader`.

We obtain the query parameters, set those parameters, and then perform the initial query (line 48). If that query is successful, we present the results and, if requested, perform a subsequent query (line 60).

Because the user periodically is asked to respond yes or no, we have an auxiliary method, `getYesNo`, that performs this task (lines 70 through 81).

15.6

Reading Input from the Web (*Optional*)

If programs are properly structured, there need not be a great deal of difference between an application and a corresponding applet. In this section, we turn the CD database application of Section 15.5 into an applet. Because the user interface was completely encapsulated in the class `CDBaseApplication`, this is the only class that needs to be replaced. The classes `Query`, `CDDatabase`, and `CDRecord`, which do most of the hard work, are completely unchanged. We will write a `CDBaseApplet` class and, to avoid having that class get too large, a separate `QueryManager` class to actually place the components of the GUI in the applet's window.

The applet creates one new difficulty. For security reasons, an applet that you download from a remote site is not allowed to read or write to your local file system. Therefore, we cannot download the applet and have it initialize itself from a local `MyCDs` file. This probably is exactly what we'd like it to do, and the latest versions of Java do provide mechanisms for doing that. However, the present Java security provisions are beyond the scope of this book.

So, where can we get the CD list from? Applets *are* allowed to open URLs, that is, to look at the files named by URLs. For security reasons again, Java imposes the restriction that an applet may open a remote URL only from the site

Name	Description
URL (String s)	Creates a URL from a string specification. Throws MalformedURLException if s specifies an unknown protocol.
InputStream openStream ()	Opens a connection to the URL, and returns an InputStream for reading. Throws IOException.

TABLE 15.7 Methods of the URL class.

from which the applet was downloaded. So we'll assume that both the .html file and all the applet's .class files are loaded from the site www-mickunas. cs.uiuc.edu, and the applet will open a URL from that site.

The Java API includes classes that allow one to open URLs in more or less the same way as one opens files. First, you must import java.net, which includes the class URL. Table 15.7 summarizes the URL class. The constructor URL (*url-name*) creates a URL object corresponding to the named URL. The instance method openStream() in the URL class turns a URL object into an InputStream by

```
InputStream is = new URL( url-name).openStream();
```

Notice that we must catch two kinds of exceptions that may be thrown by the openStream method. The InputStream then can be turned into an InputStreamReader and finally a BufferedReader by

```
BufferedReader dbreader
        = new BufferedReader(new InputStreamReader(is));
```

After this, characters can be read from the remote file just as from any other file.

```
1   import java.awt.*;
2   import java.awt.event.*;
3   import java.applet.*;
4   import java.io.*;
5   import java.net.*;
6
7   public class CDBaseApplet extends Applet {
8     // CD Database Search Applet
9     // Author: Samuel N. Kamin, June 1, 1996
10
11    public void init () {
12      InputStream is = null;
13      CDDatabase theDatabase = null;
14
15      // Open file for stream character reading.
16      String name = getParameter("DBURL");
17      try {
```

```
18          is = new URL(name).openStream();
19       }
20       catch (MalformedURLException e) {
21          System.out.println (name + " is not a proper URL");
22       }
23       catch (IOException e) {
24          System.out.println (
25             "Could not open " + name + " for reading.");
26       }
27
28       BufferedReader dbreader
29             = new BufferedReader(new InputStreamReader(is));
30
31       try {
32          theDatabase = new CDDatabase(dbreader);
33       }
34       catch (IOException e) {
35          System.out.println (
36             "An error occurred while reading from " + name);
37       }
38
39       // We pass "this" so the QueryManager can place components
40       // into "this" applet.  The QueryManager will be
41       // the listener for those components.
42       QueryManager qm = new QueryManager(theDatabase, this);
43       qm.createForm();
44    }
45 }
```

The `init` method of the applet opens the input file, creates the `CDDatabase`, and creates a GUI using the `QueryManager` class. We have illustrated one more feature of Java here. Instead of hard-coding the URL in the applet, it is obtained from the HTML file as a parameter. To do this, we need to add a *parameter* *parameter tag* *tag*, which is placed between the `<applet...>` tag and the corresponding `</applet>`:

```
<HTML>
<HEAD>
<TITLE>CD Database Searcher </TITLE>
</HEAD>
<BODY>

<APPLET CODE="CDBaseApplet.class" WIDTH=400 HEIGHT=400>
<param name="DBURL" value="http://www-mickunas.cs.uiuc.edu/javabook/myCDs">
</APPLET>

</BODY>
</HTML>
```

The `Applet` method `String getParameter (String s)` is used to obtain information from the various `<param>` tags. The call to `getParameter("DBURL")` in line 16 locates the `<param>` tag with `name="DBURL"` and returns as its value the string following `value=` in the tag.

The `QueryManager` is a straightforward GUI that lays out the screen as shown in Figure 15.5 and registers itself as listener for the various events. Note that any class can be a listener, not just an applet. This is called *delegating the* *delegation*

```
┌────────────────────────────────────────────────────────────────┐
│ ─            Applet Viewer: CDBaseApplet.class          □ │□│ │
├────────────────────────────────────────────────────────────────┤
│ Applet                                                         │
│                                                                │
│                        CD Search Form                          │
│                                                                │
│                                                                │
│            Fill in part of artist's name and/or CD's title     │
│                                                                │
│                                                                │
│   Artist: │                    │     Title: │                │ │
│                                                                │
│                                                                │
│                                                                │
│        Case matters:   ☐     Match prefix only:   ☐            │
│                                                                │
│                                                                │
│                                                                │
│              │ Submit query │ │ Resubmit query │               │
│                                                                │
│                                                                │
│                                                                │
│                                                                │
│ Applet started.                                                │
└────────────────────────────────────────────────────────────────┘
```

FIGURE 15.5 Appearance of the CD applet's `QueryManager`.

delegation event model — *listening responsibility*, and the Java event model is sometimes called a *delegation event model*.

Here is the code for the `QueryManager` class:

```
1   import java.awt.*;
2   import java.awt.event.*;
3   import java.applet.*;
4
5   class QueryManager implements ActionListener,
6                      ItemListener {
7
8     // Set up a query manager for a CD Database
9     // Author: Samuel N. Kamin, June 1, 1996
10
11    Applet app;     // The applet containing this form
12
```

```
13    CDDatabase db; // The database being queried
14
15    Query q;        // The query entered by the user
16
17
18    // Components of the applet window
19    TextField artist, title;
20    Checkbox caseMatters, prefix;
21    Button submitButton, resubmitButton;
22    Label result;
23
24    public QueryManager (CDDatabase db, Applet app) {
25      this.app = app;
26      this.db = db;
27      q = new Query();
28    }
29
30    public void createForm () {
31
32      // Lay out the screen
33      app.setLayout(new GridLayout(6,1));
34
35      app.add(new Label("CD Search Form", Label.CENTER));
36      app.add(
37        new Label("Fill in part of artist's name "
38                    + "and/or CD's title", Label.CENTER));
39
40      Panel p = new Panel();
41      artist = new TextField(20);
42      p.add(new Label("Artist: "));
43      p.add(artist);
44      title = new TextField(20);
45      p.add(new Label("Title: "));
46      p.add(title);
47      app.add(p);
48
49      p = new Panel();
50      caseMatters = new Checkbox();
51      p.add(new Label("Case matters: "));
52      p.add(caseMatters);
53      prefix = new Checkbox();
54      p.add(new Label("Match prefix only: "));
55      p.add(prefix);
56      app.add(p);
57
58      p = new Panel();
59      submitButton = new Button("Submit query");
60      p.add(submitButton);
61      resubmitButton = new Button("Resubmit query");
62      p.add(resubmitButton);
63      app.add(p);
64
65      result = new Label("", Label.CENTER);
66      app.add(result);
67
```

```
68      // Register listeners
69      artist.addActionListener(this);
70      title.addActionListener(this);
71      submitButton.addActionListener(this);
72      resubmitButton.addActionListener(this);
73      caseMatters.addItemListener(this);
74      prefix.addItemListener(this);
75    }
76
77    public void actionPerformed (ActionEvent e) {
78      // Four actions matter
79      // typing Enter in the artist or title textfields
80      // clicking on the submit or resubmit button
81      //
82      // The first three have the same effect,
83      //          to submit the query.
84      q.setArtist(artist.getText());
85      q.setTitle(title.getText());
86      if (e.getSource() == resubmitButton)
87        redoQuery();
88      else
89        doQuery();
90    }
91
92    public void itemStateChanged (ItemEvent e) {
93      if (e.getSource() == caseMatters)
94        q.setCase(caseMatters.getState());
95      else if (e.getSource() == prefix)
96        q.setPrefix(prefix.getState());
97    }
98
99    private void redoQuery() {
100      CDRecord qresult = db.redoQuery(q);
101      if (qresult == null) // query failed
102        result.setText("No more matches");
103      else
104        result.setText("Next match: " + qresult.toString());
105    }
106
107    private void doQuery() {
108      CDRecord qresult = db.doQuery(q);
109      if (qresult == null) // query failed
110        result.setText("No matching CD's; reformulate query");
111      else
112        result.setText("First match: " + qresult.toString());
113    }
114
115  }
```

The QueryManager responds to the actions of entering text in the text fields and clicking on the Submit button by calling the helper function void doQuery (), which sends a doQuery message to the database. The QueryManager responds to the Resubmit button by calling the helper function void redoQuery (), which sends a redoQuery message to the database. Each helper function displays an appropriate message on receiving the results of the `doQuery` or `redoQuery`.

Summary

Strings also are implemented by the mutable class `StringBuffer`, which has some of the capabilities of the `String` class as well as methods such as `StringBuffer append (String s)`, which appends a string to the string buffer.

The command line for executing a Java application may include additional parameters, which are supplied to the `main` method as an array of `Strings`.

Files that contain sequences of characters can be read by Java programs. A file with the name *filename* is made available for reading by

```
BufferedReader br
   = new BufferedReader(
         new FileReader(filename));
```

The next character in the file is obtained by

```
char c = br.read();
```

The remainder of the present line is obtained by

```
String s = br.readLine();
```

A file with the name *filename* is made available for printing by

```
PrintWriter pr
   = new PrintWriter(
         new BufferedWriter(
            new FileWriter(filename)));
```

The `PrintWriter` class has methods `print` and `println` that are capable of converting primitive types to their character representation and printing them. In addition, any object that implements the method `toString` can be printed.

A URL with the name *URLname* is made available for reading by

```
BufferedReader br
   = new BufferedReader(
         new InputStreamReader(
            new URL(URLname).openStream()));
```

Applications are permitted to open URLs on any site where they are permitted access. Absent additional security mechanisms, applets are restricted to opening only URLs that are on the site from which the applet was originally loaded.

Exercises

1. Write a program to read characters from a file (up to end of input) and calculate the number of characters that the file contains.

2. Extend the program you wrote for Exercise 1 so that it also counts the number of lines that the file contains. Do this by counting the number of new line characters that the file contains.

3. Extend the program you wrote for Exercise 2 so that it also counts the number of words that the file contains. For simplicity, you may assume that a word is a sequence of non-blank characters, where a blank character is a space, newline, or tab.

4. Write a program to print this year's calendar to a file. (Refer to Exercise 9 in Chapter 10.)

5. Modify the `Cat` class so that if it catches a `FileNotFoundException`, instead of stopping, it asks the user to type a new file name using an `InputBox`.

6. Modify Exercise 5 so that if yet another `FileNotFoundException` occurs, the program repeatedly asks the user to type a new file name. If the user enters an empty string, then the program should terminate.

7. Write a program, called `Find`, that reads a file, and prints all lines that contain some word. The program is called by

```
java Find word filename
```

8. Write a program, called `Crypt`, that reads a file, and produces a new file that is a Caesar Cipher of the original. In a Caesar Cipher, each letter of the alphabet is replaced by another, according to a rule that circularly shifts the alphabet some amount. For example, with a shift of 3, the latter "A" is replaced by "X", "B" is replaced by "Y", etc., according to the following table.

```
D E F G H I J K L M N O P Q R S T U V W X Y Z A B C
A B C D E F G H I J K L M N O P Q R S T U V W X Y Z
```

The program should be called like this:

```
java Crypt shiftamount infile outfile
```

9. Word processing programs ignore multiple spaces and line breaks in the user's input and simply place as many words on each line as possible, with one space between each pair of words. Write a program to do this line filling, with lines of length LINE_LENGTH (a symbolic constant). If a word is too big to fit on one line, break it into as many lines as necessary.

10. Extend your program from Exercise 9 to fill lines to the width of the column. Spaces should be added between words as evenly as possible.

11. The format of the input to our mail-merge application is flawed in two ways:
    (a) The character % cannot appear in the letter, and # cannot appear in any of the fields.
    (b) Because no special character separates one set of fields from the next, the accidental omission of one field would throw off the entire set of letters.

    Rectify the first problem by allowing # and % to be "escaped" in the input; that is, if the characters \# appear in the input, # appears in the output, and similarly for \%. The character \ itself must be escaped in the same way. Rectify the second problem by using % instead of # to separate fields within a single group (i.e., to separate the fields for a single customization of the letter) and # to separate groups. Be sure to test your application on an input that has missing fields.

CHAPTER 16

CASE STUDY: THE GAME
OF REVERSI

CHAPTER PREVIEW

In this chapter we develop a large applet to play the game of Reversi. In so doing, we introduce a number of advanced Java concepts, including the `Vector` class and enumerations. The applet itself implements a reasonable game-playing strategy.

"The game is done! I've won! I've won!"
Quoth she, and whistles thrice.

—Samuel Taylor Coleridge
The Ancient Mariner, part iii

In this chapter we write a large program to play an interactive game of Reversi. The program will be an applet, using the Java AWT, so this chapter depends on Chapters 10 and 12. It also uses two-dimensional arrays, so it depends on Chapter 8. The program is complex, with more than 10 different classes interacting in intricate ways. Inheritance is used to provide alternate programmed game-playing strategies.

16.1

The Game of Reversi

Reversi is a two-participant game played on an 8 × 8 square board with "stones" that are white on one side and black on the other. The white and black participants alternate moves, and during a turn, a participant places one of his or her stones on a square. Of course, only certain moves are legal. The initial configuration of the board is shown in Figure 16.1, and white has the first move.

The purpose of a move is to "capture" some of the opponent's stones, thereby *flipping* them, or turning them to one's own color.

Consider a particular square. Eight spokes emanate from that square: one in each of the directions northwest, north, northeast, east, southeast, south, southwest, and west. A move is legal if it results in flipping one or more of an opponent's stones along one or more of those spokes. To determine if a proposed move at a particular square can flip any stones along a spoke, the following algorithm is used:

1. The adjacent square and farther adjacent squares along that spoke must be occupied by the opponent's stones.
2. The first square along that spoke that is *not* occupied by the opponent's stone must be occupied by one's *own* stone.

If these two conditions are met, then the move under consideration will flip all the stones "enclosed" by one's move and the stone cited in step 2. Any stones *beyond* the one found in step 2 do not participate in the flipping process.

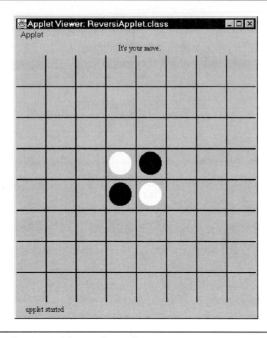

FIGURE 16.1 The initial board configuration.

Throughout our solution, we refer to the squares of the board by a coordinate system: (row, column), where (1, 1) is the upper left corner square, (1, 8) the upper right, and (8, 8) the lower right.

For example, in the configuration shown in Figure 16.2, white has only two possible moves. A move at (3, 5) flips the one black stone along the southeast spoke, leading to the white stone at (5, 7); a move at (8, 2) flips the four black stones along the northeast spoke, leading to the white stone at (3, 7). No move terminates at the white stone at (4, 7).

A move may be legal because *two or more* spokes satisfy the preceding algorithm. If that's the move chosen, then *all such spokes* flip. For example, in the configuration shown in Figure 16.3, a white stone at (6, 6) flips the black stone along its northwest spoke, as well as the black stone along its north spoke.

Notice that often spokes come close to providing a legal move but fall short on step 2 of the algorithm. In particular, if a line of the opponent's stones ends with a vacant square, step 2 is not satisfied. Likewise, if the line of opponent's stones runs to the edge of the board, step 2 is not satisfied.

Eventually, the board will fill up, and the winner is the participant with the majority of the stones.

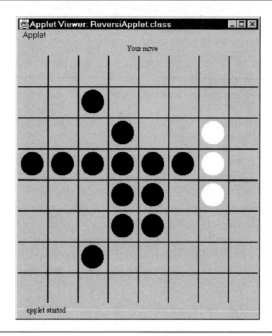

FIGURE 16.2   White has two possible moves.

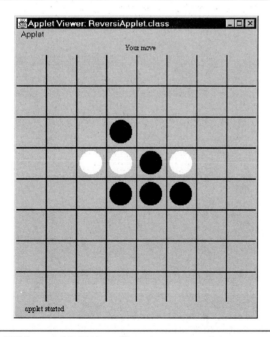

FIGURE 16.3   White at (6,6) can flip on two spokes.

Organization of the Solution

We will program the game of Reversi in a very general way, and then we particularize it to be an applet. One participant will be an interactive person (called *person*), who will make a move by making some signal. (*Hint:* Eventually we'll settle for clicking the mouse on a square.) If the move is legal, then the game board will be updated to flip the appropriate stones, and the programmed player (called *player*) will make a move. There will be some sort of "display" device, perhaps even robotic stones on a physical board. (But another hint: Eventually we'll settle for drawing the board on the computer screen.) A referee will mediate the game, keeping track of the official state of the game. Players will ask the referee to record their moves; the display device will ask the referee where the stones are on the game board; and the referee will make announcements using the "announce" device—perhaps a loudspeaker. (Yet another hint: We'll display text on the screen.)

A number of classes and objects naturally evolve in solving this problem. We can already identify some of them:

- The `PersonMoveDetector`, which detects that the person has signaled a move.
- The programmed player which is encapsulated in the class `SmartPlayer` and which will implement a particular game-playing strategy. `SmartPlayer` will be derived from an abstract class (`Player`). We assume that other strategies are possible—implemented in the derived classes `SmarterPlayer` and `ExpertPlayer`.
- The `Referee`, who keeps track of the official state of the game, accepting appropriate moves from the two participants, determining when the game is over, and making periodic announcements.
- The `Display` device, which physically shows the state of the game according to the `Referee`.
- The `Announce` device, which plays the `Referee`'s announcements.

There some other classes that are needed:

- A `Board` class to represent the state of *some* game (e.g., the status of the squares, the last move made) and to tell about the state of the game:

    - Tell if a move is legal.
    - Tell how many moves a participant has.
    - Tell if the game is over.
    - Tell how many stones a participant has.
    - Tell the status of a square.

  Given a particular state of the game, a programmed player will choose the best next move to make, usually by considering *all possible* moves, seeing where they lead, and choosing the "best" one. Seeing where a move leads will cause the programmed player to generate a number of hypothetical Boards. A Board encapsulates the complete state of the game.

- A ReversiManager is needed to tie all the objects together. The Referee needs to be told of the Announce device and the Display device (so that he can tell that device when to update itself). The Display device must be told of the Referee, so that it can ask him or her where to place the stones. The Player and PersonMoveDetector must be told of the Referee, since they submit their moves to her or him for approval. The ReversiManager needs to create all these objects, making sure that they are properly initialized.
- We will need constants for the game itself in an interface GameConstants— we'll identify Board square status as PLAYER, PERSON, VACANT, or BORDER.

Finally, there needs to be some protocol that the programmed player and the person agree upon, so that they will take turns appropriately. (Note that the Referee should not permit anyone to play out of turn. Nevertheless, we want our game to play smoothly, with each participant having a clear indication when it is time to make a move.)

The protocol will be this: As a matter of convenience, the Referee will announce when it is the person's turn. The person will make a signal, and *both* PersonMoveDetector *and* Player will be listening for that signal. The ReversiManager will set both up as listeners in such a way that PersonMoveDetector will be given the first opportunity to respond to the signal and Player will respond second. The PersonMoveDetector, responding first to the signal, will ask the Referee to make the indicated move; if it is legal, the Referee will make the move, inform Display that it should update itself, and announce that it is the programmed player's turn. Then the Player will respond to the signal, compute a move, and ask the Referee to make it.

What happens if the person attempts an illegal move? The Referee will announce that an illegal move was attempted, and it should remain the person's turn. To handle this case, the protocol has the further stipulation that when the Player responds to the signal, it first asks the Referee whose turn it is. If it is still the person's turn, then the Player does nothing. This means that the person can make another signal, attempting another move, and the whole protocol repeats itself. What happens if the programmed player attempts an illegal move? Again, the Referee will refuse the move, and it will remain the programmed player's turn.

There is yet another complication to this protocol. There are times when it's a participant's turn, but the participant has no legal move. In that case, he is said to be "stymied," and the other participant gets to make another move. The Referee will check this case after a legal move, and if the opposite participant is stymied, the Referee will indicate that and the first participant will be allowed to make another move.

Figure 16.4 is the UML class diagram for the classes described above.

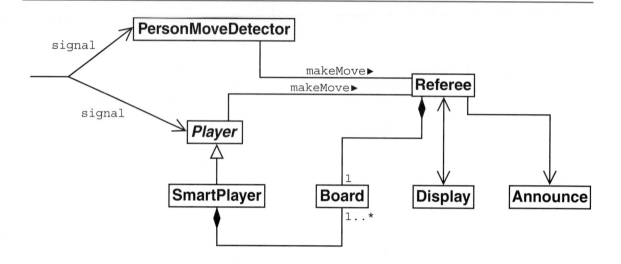

FIGURE 16.4 UML class diagram for the Reversi game.

16.3

The Classes

We'll examine each of the classes in a general way. But first we want to introduce yet another Java predefined class, the `Vector` class.

16.3.1 Java's `Vector` and `Enumeration` Classes

In Chapter 14, we developed `List` classes for storing lists of indefinite size. Java has a number of classes for storing lists of indefinite size that grow and shrink as needed, one of which is the `java.util.Vector` class. There are a number of differences between Java's `Vector` and our `List` classes, but one difference is that our `List` classes stored `int`s, whereas Java's `Vector` class stores things of type `Object`, which is Java's "mother of all classes." Every one of Java's classes is derived from the class `Object`. Therefore, `Vector` can store any of Java's predefined classes, including `Point`, which is what we will want for our Reversi game. One difficulty is that the primitive types, such as `int`, are *not* Java objects. Therefore, they cannot be stored in `Vector`s. (However, one can always "wrap" an `int` with an `Integer`, which *is* an object. See Table 13.7 on page 488.) The methods available in the `Vector` class that we use are given in Table 16.1. A newly constructed vector is considered *empty*, that is, it contains no objects; however, it has some initial *capacity*. Objects are added to a `Vector` using the `addElement` method. The number of `Object`s that have been added to a `Vector` is its *size*. If the capacity of the vector is exceeded, then Java increases it to accommodate new additions. We often need to obtain a copy of some `Vector`;

Method	Action
`Vector (int cap)`	Constructor: `cap` is the initial capacity
`Object clone ()`	Clones this vector
`void addElement (Object o)`	Adds `o` to this vector
`boolean contains (Object o)`	Tells if this vector contains `o`
`Object firstElement ()`	Retrieves the first element of this vector
`boolean isEmpty ()`	Tells if this vector is empty
`int size ()`	Tells how many elements are in this vector
`void clear ()`	Removes all elements from this vector
`Enumeration elements ()`	Returns an `Enumeration` for this vector

TABLE 16.1 Instance methods for a `Vector`.

Method	Action
`boolean hasMoreElements ()`	Tells if this enumeration is finished
`Object nextElement ()`	Retrieves the next element of this enumeration

TABLE 16.2 Instance methods for an `Enumeration`.

the `clone` method can be used for this purpose. It is important to note that the objects that the `Vector` referred to by the `Vector` are *not* copied in this process.

Notice that the method `elements` returns an `Enumeration`. `Enumeration` is yet another useful Java class that permits you systematically to run through the elements of a vector. `Enumeration` has only two methods, given in Table 16.2. The typical way of using an `Enumeration` to run through all the `Points` stored in a `Vector` is as follows:

```
Vector v;  // a vector of Points
...
Enumeration e = v.elements();
while ( e.hasMoreElements() ) {
  Point p = (Point)e.nextElement();
  ...
}
```

Notice that when retrieving the next element via `e.nextElement()`, what is returned is of type `Object`; to use it in any meaningful way, you must know what the specific type really is and cast to that type (`Point` in this case).

Remember to use `nextElement()`	**BUG ALERT 16.1**

The only way to run through the elements of a `Vector` is to use the `nextElement()` method. If you fail to call `nextElement()` inside a loop, then you will continue to access the first element, the test `hasMoreElements()` will remain true, and the loop will run forever.

BUG ALERT 16.2

You must cast `Vector` elements

When you retrieve an element of a `Vector`, you should cast the resulting `Object` to the appropriate type before you can process it.

16.4

The Reversi Classes

The Reversi classes are

- `GameConstants`
- `Player`
- `SmartPlayer`
- `PersonMoveDetector`
- `Referee`
- `Board`
- `Display`
- `Announce`

We describe each of these classes, in abbreviated form. First, we examine the `GameConstants` interface:

```
interface GameConstants {

    // values for the status of a square
    int PERSON = 0, PLAYER = 1, VACANT = 2, BORDER = 3;
}
```

This interface defines various constants that are used by a number of the classes. Recall that a variable that is declared in an `interface` is automatically made `public final static`. Next, we examine the abstract class `Player`, from which we derive the `SmartPlayer`.

```
abstract class Player implements GameConstants {

    Referee ref;

    Player (Referee ref) {
        this.ref = ref;
    }

    // Formulate a move (from a subclass).
    abstract Point getMove ();

    // Respond to the signal
```

```
    public void signal-catching method {
      // Ignore if it's the person's turn.
      while (ref.whoseTurn() == PLAYER && !ref.gameOver())
        ref.makeMove(PLAYER, getMove());
    }
  }
```

The abstract class `Player` will intercept the person's signal (after the person has made a move) and check to see if it is now the programmed player's turn. If not, then the person attempted an illegal move, so the programmed player will just return. If it *is* the programmed player's turn, then a move is formulated by calling the subclass's definition of the abstract method `getMove`. If either the attempted move is illegal or the move caused the opponent to be stymied, then it remains the programmed player's turn. The `while` loop takes care of making yet another move. Of course, this repetition should stop once the game is over.

Next, we examine the subclass `SmartPlayer`. It defines the abstract `getMove` method from the superclass `Player`.

```
    public class SmartPlayer extends Player {

      public SmartPlayer (Referee ref) {
        super(ref);
      }

      // Formulate a move.
      public Point getMove () {
        Point bestMove;
        ...
        return bestMove;
      }
    }
```

We'll see how to compute the "best" move shortly. Next, we examine the `PersonMoveDetector` class:

```
    public class PersonMoveDetector implements GameConstants {

      private Referee ref;

      public PersonMoveDetector (Referee ref) {
        this.ref = ref;
      }

      // Respond to the signal
      public void signal-catching method {
        ...
        ref.makeMove(PERSON, selectedMove);
      }
    }
```

All the `PersonMoveDetector` needs to do is to detect the "signal" and ask the `Referee` to make some indicated move. Next, we examine the `Referee` class.

```
class Referee implements GameConstants {

    private Board theBoard;    // The actual game board
    private int whoseTurn;     // Tells whose turn it is.
    private Display dev;       // The display mechanism
    private Announce msg;      // The message mechanism

    Referee (Display dev, Announce msg) {
        this.dev = dev;
        this.msg = msg;
        theBoard = new Board();
        whoseTurn = PERSON;
    }

    // Tell whose turn it is.
    public int whoseTurn () { return whoseTurn; }

    // Tell what occupies a given square.
    public int status (int row, int col) {
        ...
    }

    // Duplicate the game board.
    public Board duplicate () {
        ...
    }

    // Tell if a move is legal or not.
    public boolean isLegal (int which, Point move) {
        ...
    }

    // Tell if the game is over or not.
    public boolean gameOver () {
        ...
    }

    // Make a suggested move, if it is legal.
    public void makeMove (int participant, Point move) {
        if (!isLegal(participant, move)) {
            msg.setMessage("Illegal move.");
            return;
        }
        theBoard.makeMove (participant, move);
        if (gameOver()) {
            determine the winner
        } else {
            determine whose turn it is
        }
        // Update the display
        dev.reShow();
    }
}
```

The Referee keeps track of the *state* of the game and keeps that state information in the private instance variables—theBoard that is the official game board and whoseMove that tells whose turn it is. There are a number of methods for accessing the private instance variables—whoseTurn to access whoseTurn; status to tell what is on a particular square of theBoard; duplicate to return a clone of theBoard. Other methods do as their headers imply: isLegal allows a participant to ask the Referee if a proposed move would be legal; gameOver tells whether the game is over. The workhorse method is makeMove, which receives a proposed move from a participant, checks its legality, and, if it is legal, makes the move. If the game is over, then makeMove determines who won. Otherwise it determines which participant will be next to play. Finally, it asks the Display device to update its rendition of the game.

Next is the Board class. One instance of this is the true game board, kept by the Referee. Other versions may be created by a programmed player to test possible moves.

```
class Board implements GameConstants {

    // Clone this Board
    public Board duplicate () {
      ...
    }

    // Tell the legal moves for a participant
    public Vector tellMoves (int participant) {
      ...
    }

    // Identify the opposing participant
    public int opposite (int participant) {
      if (participant == PERSON) return PLAYER;
      else                       return PERSON;
    }

    // Tell if a move is legal
    public boolean isLegal (int participant, Point move) {
      ...
    }

    // Count the number of stones for a participant
    public int count (int participant) {
      ...
    }

    // Tell how many legal moves a participant may choose from.
    public int howManyMoves (int participant) {
      ...
    }

    // Tell what's on a square of this Board
    public int squareStatus (int row, int col) {
      ...
    }

    // Record a move on this Board
    public void makeMove (int participant, Point move) {
```

> *make the given move for the given participant*
>
> ```
>     }
>   }
> ```

The above methods do everything that you would expect, as indicated by their headers and accompanying comments. The workhorse method is `makeMove`, which actually places the stone for the indicated participant, flipping all the stones that should be flipped.

Finally come the `Display` and `Announce` classes:

```
class Display implements GameConstants {
  Referee ref;

  // Tell me who the Referee is.
  void tellReferee (Referee ref) {
    this.ref = ref;
  }

  void reShow () {
```
> *Update the Display device, asking the*
> *Referee "ref" where the stones are located.*
```
  }
}
```

and

```
class Announce {

  public void setMessage (String s) {
```
> *Make the "s" announcement*
```
  }
}
```

Hopefully you'll agree that this is a very flexible design. The programmed player will be fully specified by the subclass of `Player`, and the only thing that is required is that `Player` implement the `getMove` method. There are no constraints on how that move may be determined: by doing a cursory evaluation, or by doing a deep analysis of the game, or even by guessing! In addition, the signal that the person makes can be anything that both the person and the programmed player are able to detect. The `Display` and `Announce` devices are also very flexible—they are not constrained to be any particular kind of device.

In the next few sections, we will develop each of the classes completely. To avoid some redundancy, we'll nail down the signal, the `Display` device, and the `Announce` device now. All will use an applet area—a `Label` for the `Announce` device, a `Canvas` for the `Display` device, and mouse clicks inside the `Canvas` for the signal. It is important to realize that we are *not* forced to make these decisions at this time; we could develop our other classes while deferring these decisions, and then fill in a few small details later. But by making the decision now, we won't have to defer those tiny details. Once we've developed a class (such as `Player`), it will be complete.

We'll now develop fully all our classes. We'll start with the `Board` class, since it is used by the `Referee`, the `Display`, and perhaps by the `Player` subclass.

Variable	Meaning
`int[][] field`	Two-dimensional array that tells the board contents
`Vector[2] moves`	A pair of `Vector`s telling the allowable moves for the two participants
`Point previousMove`	The move that led to this board configuration

Method	Action
`Board duplicate ()`	Clones the board
`Vector tellMoves (int participant)`	Returns the vector of legal moves for this participant
`int opposite (int participant)`	Switches between PERSON and JAVA participants
`boolean isLegal (int participant, Point move)`	Tells if a move is legal
`int count (int participant)`	Tells how many stones participant has
`int howManyMoves (int participant)`	Tells how many moves participant has
`int squareStatus (int col, int row)`	Tells what's on a square
`private void computePossibleMoves (int participant)`	Determines the legal moves for participant
`void makeMove (int participant, Point move)`	Records a move

TABLE 16.3 Instance variables and methods for the `Board` class.

16.4.1 The `Board` Class

The complete list of the `Board` instance variables and methods is given in Table 16.3. `Board` will store the status of the board in a two-dimensional array `field[10][10]` with integer values specified by symbolic constants VACANT, PERSON, JAVA, and BORDER. One method to note is `Vector tellMoves (int participant)`; using this method, a participant can determine what the legal moves are at any point in the game. We could do things differently for this initial implementation, but the method `tellMoves` is useful for more advanced versions of Reversi. Having the `tellMoves` method implies that `Board` must compute each participant's legal moves every time a change is made to `Board`. The `Board` class is as follows:

```
1   import java.awt.*;
2   import java.util.Vector;
3
4   class Board implements GameConstants {
```

```
 5
 6    static final int
 7      B = BORDER, V = VACANT, P = PERSON, J = PLAYER;
 8    int[][] field =
 9      {
10      {B, B, B, B, B, B, B, B, B, B},
11      {B, V, V, V, V, V, V, V, V, B},
12      {B, V, V, V, V, V, V, V, V, B},
13      {B, V, V, V, V, V, V, V, V, B},
14      {B, V, V, V, P, J, V, V, V, B},
15      {B, V, V, V, J, P, V, V, V, B},
16      {B, V, V, V, V, V, V, V, V, B},
17      {B, V, V, V, V, V, V, V, V, B},
18      {B, V, V, V, V, V, V, V, V, B},
19      {B, B, B, B, B, B, B, B, B, B}
20      };
21
22    // Possible moves for each participant
23    private Vector[] moves = {new Vector(10), new Vector(10)};
24
25    // The move that led to this Board
26    Point previousMove = NULLMOVE;
27
28    public Board () {
29      computePossibleMoves(PERSON);
30      computePossibleMoves(PLAYER);
31    }
32
33    // Clone this Board
34    public Board duplicate () {
35      Board b = new Board();
36      for (int col = 0; col < 10; col++)
37        for (int row = 0; row < 10; row++)
38          b.field[row][col] = field[row][col];
39      b.moves[0] = (Vector)moves[0].clone();
40      b.moves[1] = (Vector)moves[1].clone();
41      b.previousMove = new Point(previousMove);
42      return b;
43    }
44
45    // Tell the legal moves for a participant
46    public Vector tellMoves (int participant) {
47      return (Vector)moves[participant].clone();
48    }
49
50    // Identify the opposing participant
51    public int opposite (int participant) {
52      if (participant == PERSON) return PLAYER;
53      else                      return PERSON;
54    }
55
56    // Tell if a move is legal
57    public boolean isLegal (int participant, Point move) {
58      return moves[participant].contains(move);
```

```
59        }
60
61        // Count the number of stones for a participant
62        public int count (int participant) {
63          int n = 0;
64          for (int i = 1; i < 9; i++) {
65            for (int j = 1; j < 9; j++) {
66              if ( field[i][j] == participant) n++;
67            }
68          }
69        return n;
70        }
71
72        // Tell how many legal moves a participant may choose from.
73        public int howManyMoves (int participant) {
74          return moves[participant].size();
75        }
76
77        // Tell what's on a square of this Board
78        public int squareStatus (int row, int col) {
79          return field[row][col];
80        }
81
82        // Movement deltas for NW,N,NE,W,E,SW,S,SE
83        private static Point[] spokes =
84          { new Point(-1,-1), new Point(0,-1), new Point(1,-1),
85            new Point (-1,0),                  new Point(1,0),
86            new Point (-1,1), new Point(0,1),  new Point(1,1)
87          };
88
89        // Determine the legal moves for a participant
90        private void computePossibleMoves (int participant) {
91          int op = opposite(participant);
92
93          moves[participant].clear();
94          for (int col = 1; col < 9; col++) {
95            for (int row = 1; row < 9; row++) {
96              // For this to be a valid move,
97              // this square must be vacant ...
98              if (field[row][col] == VACANT) {
99                // ... and along some spoke ...
100               boolean again = true;
101               for (int spoke = 0; spoke < 8 && again; spoke++) {
102                 int rowStep = spokes[spoke].x;
103                 int colStep = spokes[spoke].y;
104                 // ... the adjacent square must be opponent ...
105                 if (field[row+rowStep][col+colStep] == op) {
106                   // ... and subsequent must be opponent ...
107                   int colInc = col+colStep+colStep;
108                   int rowInc = row+rowStep+rowStep;
109                   while (field[rowInc][colInc] == op) {
110                     colInc = colInc + colStep;
111                     rowInc = rowInc + rowStep;
112                   }
```

```
113                    // ... and then we must find our own.
114                    if (field[rowInc][colInc] == participant) {
115                      moves[participant].addElement
116                                        (new Point(row, col));
117                      // No need to consider further spokes, since
118                      // this spoke validates this move.
119                      again = false;
120                    }
121                  }
122                }
123              }
124            }
125          }
126        }
127
128        // Record a move on this Board
129        public void makeMove (int participant, Point move) {
130
131          previousMove = move;
132          int op = opposite(participant);
133          int row = move.x, col = move.y;
134          field[row][col] = participant;
135
136          // Consider all spokes around this move.
137          for (int spoke = 0; spoke < 8; spoke++) {
138            int colStep = spokes[spoke].y;
139            int rowStep = spokes[spoke].x;
140            // Do we flip this spoke?  Only if it starts with
141            // an opponent's stone ...
142            if (field[row+rowStep][col+colStep] == op) {
143              // ... and has more opponent's stones ...
144              int colInc = col+colStep+colStep;
145              int rowInc = row+rowStep+rowStep;
146              while (field[rowInc][colInc] == op) {
147                colInc = colInc + colStep;
148                rowInc = rowInc + rowStep;
149              }
150              // ... and ends with our stone.
151              if (field[rowInc][colInc] == participant) {
152                // Flip the continuous line of opponent's
153                // stones on this spoke.
154                colInc = col+colStep;
155                rowInc = row+rowStep;
156                while (field[rowInc][colInc] == op) {
157                  field[rowInc][colInc] = participant;
158                  colInc = colInc + colStep;
159                  rowInc = rowInc + rowStep;
160                }
161              }
162            }
163          }
164          computePossibleMoves(participant);
165          computePossibleMoves(op);
166        }
167      }
```

The `field` is initialized in lines 8 through 20 with values corresponding to the initial Reversi configuration. (We have defined synonyms for the symbolic constants so that you can see the pattern of initialization.) The move that was made to arrive at this board is stored in `previousMove`.

The array `moves[2]` stores the list of legal moves for the two participants (PERSON==0 and JAVA==1), and each array element is initialized to an empty vector.

Having seen the data components of `Board`, we can now investigate its methods. The constructor is straightforward. It computes the initial set of legal moves for each participant.

The `duplicate` method (lines 33 through 43) clones the board. It must allocate a new `Board` and then copy the `field` array. The `moves` array elements cannot simply be copied, because they contain references to objects. Rather, they must also be duplicated, using `Vector`'s `clone()` method (lines 39 and 40). Notice that `clone` is a method that produces an `Object`, which must be cast back to a `Vector` before assigning to `b.moves[...]`. The `previousMove` `Point` object likewise must be duplicated.

The next six methods are quite simple. The `tellMoves` method returns a copy of the appropriate `moves` vector. The `opposite` method allows one to switch between PERSON and PLAYER. The `boolean isLegal` method (lines 56 through 59) checks to see if a given move is among those in the `moves` vector for this participant. The `count` method counts the number of stones that this participant has on the board. The method `howManyMoves` returns the size of the `moves` vector for this participant. Finally, the `squareStatus` method tells what occupies a particular square: VACANT, BORDER, JAVA, or PERSON.

We now turn to the heart of `Board`: the methods `makeMove` and `computePossibleMoves`. For each of these methods, we must move along the eight spokes that we mentioned in describing the rules of Reversi. This amounts to modifying the present column and row by ±1 in various combinations. To simplify iterating through these possibilities, we define the eight-element array of `Points`, called `spokes`, which gives the eight combinations that allow us to step in the eight directions (lines 82 through 87).

In `computePossibleMoves`, all nonborder squares of `field` are considered in a doubly nested loop (lines 94 and 95). If, on one hand, the square under consideration is not VACANT, then it cannot possibly represent a legal move, and the `if` statement causes the remainder of the inner loop to be skipped, causing us to move on to consider the next `field` element. If, on the other hand, the square *is* VACANT, then it is a candidate for a legal move and we must try to find a spoke that legalizes it.

Thus, we enter the loop in lines 100 through 121, which runs through the eight spokes. For each spoke, we obtain the amount by which we step the column and row (`colStep` and `rowStep`, respectively). We look *one step along that spoke* (line 105), and if we find no opponent's stone there, an `if` statement again causes us immediately to consider the next spoke. If we *do* find an opponent's stone adjacent to the candidate square, then we enter a `while` loop that continues to run along that spoke, starting *two steps* away, and continuing until it finds a nonopponent stone (lines 107 through 112). Eventually, this loop will find one's own stone, a VACANT square, or a BORDER square. In the `if` statement in line 114, we check to see if we stopped on our own stone. If not, the `true` part is skipped, and we again reach the end of the spoke loop (and continue to the next spoke). If, however, we *do* find that we stopped on such a stone, then we've found a spoke that legalizes the candidate move; we add that move to `moves[m]`. Then there is no need to look for further spokes once we have one that legalizes the move. So we want to terminate the spoke loop. By setting the Boolean variable `again` to `false`, we will terminate on the next iteration of the spoke loop (in the test in line 101). Leaving the spoke loop sends us to the bottom of the double loop that runs through the `field` elements, so that we can continue looking for more legal moves.

The `makeMove` method uses the `spokes` array in the same way that `computePossibleMoves` does. We are presented with a move at `field[move.x][move.y]`. We first place our stone on that square. Then we move around all eight spokes and, at each spoke, verify that

1. The square one step away is occupied by the opponent's stone.
2. Subsequent squares are occupied by the opponent's stones.
3. The "stopping" square is occupied by one's *own* stone.

The `if` statement in lines 150 through 160 verifies point 3 and runs again through the spoke, flipping the stones. We now have a differently configured board, so the last thing we do is to recompute the new moves allowed for each participant.

QUICK EXERCISE 16.1

Look at lines 39 and 40 in the `duplicate` method of class `Board`.

1. Why is the cast `(Vector)` needed?
2. Why can't the code be written as follows?

```
b.moves[0] = moves[0];
b.moves[1] = moves[1];
```

QUICK EXERCISE 16.2

Look at the method `computePossibleMoves` in class `Board`.

1. Explain why there is no danger of an array index out-of-bounds exception in the `while` loop in lines 109 through 112.
2. Explain why there is no danger of an array index out-of-bounds exception in the `if` statement in line 105.

16.4.2 The Referee Class

Let's now look at the Referee class.

```
1    import java.awt.*;
2
3    class Referee implements GameConstants {
4
5      private final static String[]
6        YOUR_MOVE = {"It's your move", "It's Reversi's move"},
7        STYMIED = {"You're stymied; it's still Reversi's move",
8                   "Reversi's stymied; it's still your move"};
9
10     private Board theBoard;    // The actual game board
11     private int whoseTurn;     // Tells whose turn it is.
12     private Display dev;       // The display mechanism
13     private Announce msg;      // The message mechanism
14
15     Referee (Display dev, Announce msg) {
16       this.dev = dev;
17       this.msg = msg;
18       theBoard = new Board();
19       whoseTurn = PERSON;
20       msg.setMessage(YOUR_MOVE[whoseTurn]);
21     }
22
23     // Tell whose turn it is.
24     public int whoseTurn () { return whoseTurn; }
25
26     // Tell what occupies a given square.
27     public int status (int row, int col) {
28       return theBoard.field[row][col];
29     }
30
31     // Duplicate the game board.
32     public Board duplicate () {
33       return theBoard.duplicate();
34     }
35
36     // Tell if a move is legal or not.
37     public boolean isLegal (int which, Point move) {
38       if (whoseTurn != which) return false;
39       return ( theBoard.isLegal(which, move) );
40     }
41
42     // Tell if the game is over or not.
43     // The game is over if no one has a move.
44     public boolean gameOver () {
45       return (theBoard.howManyMoves(PERSON)
46             + theBoard.howManyMoves(PLAYER))==0;
47     }
48
49     // Make a suggested move, if it is legal.
50     public void makeMove (int participant, Point move) {
51       if (!isLegal(participant, move)) {
```

```
52          msg.setMessage("Illegal move.");
53          return;
54       }
55       theBoard.makeMove(participant, move);
56       if (gameOver()) {
57          scoreGame();
58       } else {
59          // take turns ...
60          whoseTurn = theBoard.opposite(whoseTurn);
61          if (theBoard.howManyMoves(whoseTurn) > 0) {
62             msg.setMessage(YOUR_MOVE[whoseTurn]);
63          } else {  // ... unless the opponent is stymied
64             msg.setMessage(STYMIED[whoseTurn]);
65             whoseTurn = theBoard.opposite(whoseTurn);
66          }
67       }
68       // Update the display
69       dev.reShow();
70    }
71
72    // Tally  & report the final score of the game.
73    private void scoreGame () {
74       int
75          v1 = theBoard.count(PERSON),
76          v2 = theBoard.count(PLAYER);
77
78       msg.setMessage("Game Over");
79       if (v1<v2)
80          msg.setMessage("You lose!");
81       else if (v2<v1)
82          msg.setMessage("You win!");
83       else
84          msg.setMessage("It's a tie!");
85    }
86 }
```

This is indeed like the skeletal version we wrote earlier. This version does have some extra string constants, corresponding to the various announcements that the referee may want to make. The constructor is just as we sketched earlier, except that we make the announcement that initially it's the person's move.

The next few methods are quite straightforward: whoseTurn is an accessor for the private instance variable whoseTurn; status tells what occupies a particular square on the official game board; duplicate clones the official game board; isLegal tells if a particular move is legal; gameOver tells if the game is over. This is a little tricky—it is possible for one participant to *wipe out* the other before the board is completely filled; so a game is over when neither player has a legal move.

The main activity of the Referee is in makeMoves. The first thing done is to check whether the attempted move is legal (line 51). If the move is illegal, the referee makes an appropriate announcement and ignores the move. If the attempted move *is* legal, then it is made. This is done by a call to the Board method makeMove(int participant, Point move), which will make the indicated move for the participant. After every move, the referee must check to see if the game is over (line 56), and if it is, score the game. (When the game is over, neither participant will have a legal move.) Then, in line 60, the referee changes the whoseTurn indicator. The following if-else statement in lines 61 through 66 checks to see if a stymie has occurred and, if so, switches the turn back to the first participant, announcing the appropriate message. Since a move has been made, the official board has changed, so the referee asks the display device to update itself (line 69).

Scoring the game is easy—just count the number of stones that each participant has, and compare (lines 72 through 85).

16.4.3 The Display Class

We won't bother with the details of making our applet resizable or computing values for an arbitrary size window. Instead, we hard-code the Display to have squares that are a fixed size of 50 pixels, with lines separating them 2 pixels wide. The stones will be 40 pixels in diameter. These constants will be placed in an interface, ScreenConstants:

```
1   public interface ScreenConstants {
2
3       int SQ = 50,        // width of a board square
4           LINE = 2,       // width of dividing lines
5           DIA = 40,       // diameter of a stone
6           LINE_LEN = 8*SQ+7*LINE;  // length of dividing line
7   }
```

It is also convenient to compute another constant, the length of each line, running a length of SQ × 8 pixels for the squares, plus LINE × 7 pixels for the separating lines.

The Display class is as follows:

```
1   import java.awt.event.*;
2   import java.awt.*;
3
4   class Display extends Canvas implements GameConstants,
5                                           ScreenConstants {
6       Referee ref;
7
8       public Dimension getPreferredSize () {
9         return new Dimension(LINE_LEN, LINE_LEN);
10      }
11
12      // Tell me who the Referee is.
13      void tellReferee (Referee ref) {
14        this.ref = ref;
15      }
16
17      void reShow () {
18        repaint();
19      }
20
21      public void paint (Graphics g) {
22        for (int i=SQ; i<LINE_LEN; i=i+SQ+LINE) {
```

```
23          g.drawLine (i, 0, i, LINE_LEN-1);
24          g.drawLine (i+1, 0, i+1, LINE_LEN-1);
25          g.drawLine (0, i, LINE_LEN-1, i);
26          g.drawLine (0, i+1, LINE_LEN-1, i+1);
27        }
28      for (int col=1; col<9; col++)
29        for (int row=1; row<9; row++)
30          displaySquare(g, row, col);
31    }
32
33    private void displaySquare (Graphics g, int row, int col) {
34      // Compute upper-left corner of the stone
35      int ulx = (col-1)*(SQ+LINE)+(SQ-DIA)/2,
36          uly = (row-1)*(SQ+LINE)+(SQ-DIA)/2;
37      switch (ref.status(row, col)) {
38        case PERSON: g.setColor(Color.pink);
39                     g.fillOval(ulx, uly, DIA, DIA);
40                     break;
41        case PLAYER: g.setColor(Color.black);
42                     g.fillOval(ulx, uly, DIA, DIA);
43                     break;
44        default:  // do nothing
45      }
46    }
47  }
```

The first thing to notice is that `Display` is a subclass of `Canvas`, and it uses both constant interfaces. Since it is a `Canvas`, it will have a `paint` method for drawing the board. Moreover, recall that by default, a `Canvas` has a preferred size of zero. To override this, we define the `getPreferredSize` method in lines 8 through 10.

QUICK EXERCISE 16.3	What happens if you remove the `getPreferredSize` method from the `Display` class?

The next method, `tellReferee`, is used to communicate to the `Display` the identity of the `Referee` object. There is a good reason why we did not define a constructor to do this—the `Referee` *also* wants to know the identity of the `Display`, and we provided that information in the `Referee`'s constructor (line 15 in `Referee`). So we must construct the `Display` *before* we construct the `Referee`; therefore, at the time of construction of the `Display`, we do not know the identity of the `Referee`. That is, it would be tempting, but incorrect, to write

```
    ...
    Display d = new Display(r);        // r is not yet created!!
    Referee r = new Referee(d, ...);
    ...
```

Rather, the `Referee` object must be transmitted later:

```
. . .
Display d = new Display();
Referee r = new Referee(d, ...);
d.tellReferee(r);
. . .
```

The `reShow` method that `Referee` calls just asks for a `repaint` of the canvas. (We might have called it `repaint` to begin with; but that would have tied us too closely to a Java GUI, and we were trying to remain independent of any specific `Display` device.) The canvas's `paint` method is easy enough. It draws the 14 grid lines at the appropriate places, each 2 pixels wide. Then it fills in each of the 64 squares.

The private `displaySquare` method (lines 33 through 46) determines the status of the `Board` square at `row, col` by asking the referee about that square (line 37). The square is filled with the appropriate color stone or ignored, if it is VACANT.

16.4.4 The `PersonMoveDetector` Class

While we are thinking about the `Display` and the fact that it is a `Canvas` with a certain coordinate grid, we should look at `PersonMoveDetector`:

```
1   import java.awt.event.*;
2   import java.awt.*;
3
4   public class PersonMoveDetector implements GameConstants,
5                                              ScreenConstants,
6                                              MouseListener {
7
8       private Referee ref;
9
10      public PersonMoveDetector (Referee ref) {
11        this.ref = ref;
12      }
13
14      // Respond to the signal
15      public void mouseClicked (MouseEvent e) {
16        int col = e.getX() / (LINE+SQ) + 1,
17            row = e.getY() / (LINE+SQ) + 1;
18        ref.makeMove(PERSON, new Point(row,col));
19      }
20
21      public void mousePressed (MouseEvent e) {}
22      public void mouseReleased (MouseEvent e) {}
23      public void mouseEntered (MouseEvent e) {}
24      public void mouseExited (MouseEvent e) {}
25    }
```

As the class header shows, this class will be a listener for `MouseEvents`, so it implements the five required methods, as in Section 11.3 on page 400. The constructor is simple—saving a reference to the Referee, so that we can ask him or her to make moves for us.

The "signal" that we want to detect is the mouse click, and this is done in the mouseClicked method. Using the constants from ScreenConstants, we can determine in which of the 64 squares the click occurred (lines 16 and 17). *That* is the move that we wish to ask the Referee to make.

16.4.5   The Abstract Player Class

The Player class is even simpler than the PersonMoveDetector class.

```
1    import java.awt.*;
2    import java.awt.event.*;
3
4    abstract class Player
5              implements MouseListener, GameConstants {
6
7      Referee ref;
8
9      Player (Referee ref) {
10       this.ref = ref;
11     }
12
13     // Formulate a move.
14     abstract Point getMove ();
15
16     // Respond to the signal.
17     public void mouseClicked (MouseEvent e) {
18       // Ignore clicks if it's person's turn or if game is done.
19       while (ref.whoseTurn() == PLAYER && !ref.gameOver())
20         ref.makeMove(PLAYER, getMove());
21     }
22
23     public void mousePressed (MouseEvent e) {}
24     public void mouseReleased (MouseEvent e) {}
25     public void mouseEntered (MouseEvent e) {}
26     public void mouseExited (MouseEvent e) {}
27   }
```

It also listens for mouse clicks as the signal. When one occurs, method mouseClicked first determines if indeed it is the programmed player's turn. If not, just ignore the signal and return. If so, ask the Referee to make a move. Which move? That depends on our subclass, which must implement the abstract method getMove. The Player repeatedly makes moves, as long as it remains her or his turn and the game is still ongoing. This takes care of the case where the person is stymied by a very clever programmed player.

16.4.6   The ReversiManager Class

Before we examine the SmartPlayer class, let's see how the entire applet will be organized and laid out. First, the Announce class is just a renamed Label class, with the setText message renamed to setMessage.

```
1   import java.awt.*;
2
3   class Announce extends Label {
4
5     public Announce (String s, int justify) {
6       super(s, justify);
7     }
8
9     public void setMessage (String s) {
10      setText(s);
11    }
12  }
```

Therefore, Announce objects can be used just like Label components. The applet itself is:

```
1   import java.awt.*;
2   import java.awt.event.*;
3   import java.applet.*;
4
5   public class ReversiManager extends Applet {
6
7     Display scr = new Display();
8     Announce msg = new Announce("", Label.CENTER);
9     Referee ref = new Referee(scr, msg);
10    PersonMoveDetector person = new PersonMoveDetector(ref);
11    Player opponent = new SmartPlayer(ref);
12    Panel p = new Panel();
13
14    public void init () {
15      // Tell the display who the referee is (so the screen
16      // can access the board that the referee controls).
17      scr.tellReferee(ref);
18
19      // Lay out the screen.
20      setLayout(new BorderLayout());
21      add("North", msg);
22      add("Center", scr);
23
24      // Register component listeners.
25      scr.addMouseListener(person);
26      scr.addMouseListener(opponent);
27
28      setSize(getPreferredSize());
29      repaint();
30    }
31  }
```

The various classes are declared and created as instance variables. Then the init method tells the Display who the Referee is and next lays out the display area with the Announce label at the north and the Display canvas in the center of a BorderLayout.

Then the PersonMoveDetector object is registered as a listener for mouse activity in the Display canvas, as is the Player object. The order in which the registration occurs is the order in which the signal will be received, so the person will receive the signal before the programmed player. Finally, we set the size of the applet appropriately, and we ask that the screen be repainted.

QUICK EXERCISE 16.4	What happens if you reverse the order of registering the MouseListeners, swapping lines 25 and 26 in ReversiManager?

16.4.7 The SmartPlayer Subclass

Finally, we are able to get to the part of the program that requires some game skills: the SmartPlayer class. The SmartPlayer class is

```
1    import java.awt.*;
2    import java.util.*;
3
4    public class SmartPlayer extends Player {
5
6      public SmartPlayer (Referee ref) {
7        super(ref);
8      }
9
10     // The Referee wants PLAYER to make a move.
11     public Point getMove () {
12       Board trialBoard, presentBoard;
13       Point trialMove, bestMove=NULLMOVE;
14       int before, value, bestValue=-9999;
15
16       presentBoard = ref.duplicate();
17
18       before = presentBoard.count(PERSON) ;
19       Enumeration e = presentBoard.tellMoves(PLAYER).elements();
20       while ( e.hasMoreElements() ) {
21         trialMove = (Point)e.nextElement();
22         trialBoard = presentBoard.duplicate();
23         trialBoard.makeMove(PLAYER, trialMove);
24         value = before - trialBoard.count(PERSON);
25         if (bestValue<value) {
26           bestValue=value;
27           bestMove=trialMove;
28         }
29       }
30       return bestMove;
31     }
32   }
```

The only method in SmartPlayer is the getMove method, where the SmartPlayer determines its "best" move. Our SmartPlayer's strategy is simple: Make the move that flips the greatest number of stones! To determine which move accomplishes this, the SmartPlayer must obtain a private copy of the game board (line 16) and actually *try out* each legal move. To run through the vector of legal moves, the SmartPlayer allocates an *iterator* that will present the elements of moves [JAVA] one at a time. In Java, an iterator is called an *Enumeration*, and as we've seen, the Vector class can supply an enumeration for itself via the method elements(). This is what getMove does in lines 19 through 30.

iterator

Enumeration

The processing of each move is accomplished by

1. Duplicating our copy of the present board (line 22).
2. *Actually making the move* on the duplicate board.
3. Computing the number of stones that were flipped.

Using the knowledge of how many opponent's stones are in the present board (computed in line 18), the number of stones that are flipped is computed in line 24. The bestValue is updated in the next four lines. (The bestValue starts out at an unattainable low value.)

Summary

A two-participant game, such as Reversi, can be programmed so that an applet interacts with an interactive (presumably human) player. The interactive player makes moves by clicking the mouse, and the programmed player computes moves by evaluating game board positions.

Java's java.util.Vector class provides the ability to store an indeterminate number of objects. A Vector is expanded as necessary as new objects are added to it. The Vector class also provides a clone() method that duplicates the Vector.

Vectors can supply an Enumeration, which is yet another useful Java class. An Enumeration permits you systematically to run through the elements of a Vector using the methods hasMoreElements() and nextElement().

Exercises

1. (Requires Appendix A.) Modify the PersonMoveDetector and Player classes so that they extend MouseAdapter instead of implementing MouseListener.

2. Define a new IllegalMoveException. Modify the Board class so that it throws IllegalMoveException when there is an illegal move attempted by makeMove. Make other appropriate changes to catch the IllegalMoveException.

3. Develop a List class that stores Points instead of ints as in Chapter 14. Modify Board so that it uses the new List class instead of Vector to store legal moves.

4. Add to the Reversi program a button that will allow the Person to undo his or her most recent move (and of course undo Reversi's move that was made in response to the Person's most recent move).

5. It is convenient to be able to know which moves are available to you.
   (a) Add to the Reversi program a button that can be clicked when it is the Person's turn, that will ask Reversi to show what the possible moves are. Indicate the possible moves by coloring the relevant squares blue.
   (b) Further indicate the "best" move by determining which move the SmartPlayer would make, and color its square red.

6. The SmartPlayer isn't really so smart! Simply counting the number of stones flipped is rather shortsighted. It doesn't take into account strategies like trying to occupy the edge squares or the corner squares. Program a SmarterPlayer class that evaluates a board by computing a *weighted* count of the stones: count +24 for a corner square, +5 for an edge square, and +1 for other squares. (It is possible to devise even more complex weighting strategies, depending on whether a particular square is weak or strong in the present configuration. For example, an edge square is useless if one of the adjacent edge squares is occupied by the opponent and the other is vacant; then the opponent can immediately recapture your edge square.) Program such a SmarterPlayer.

7. (Advanced: Requires Recursion) Again, the SmarterPlayer isn't so clever! A much stronger playing strategy involves looking ahead more than one move. Each move that a player looks ahead is called a *ply*. For example, an ExpertPlayer might utilize a *two-ply look-ahead*. The evaluation of a move is determined by the situation that will exist after that move *and after the opponent makes a move in response*. Three-ply and four-ply look-aheads carry this idea even further!

   In general, an *n*-ply look-ahead involves building a *game tree*, with the present board leading to several successor boards (one for each possible move), and each of *those* boards leading to several successors, and so on.

   At the bottom of such a game tree, each board is evaluated using a static stone-counting scheme such as that used by the SmarterPlayer in Exercise 4. At the level above those terminal boards, the opponent will presumably select its best move by choosing the *minimum* value of the boards below. At the level above that, the ExpertPlayer selects the maximum, and so forth. This is the strategy if the look-ahead is an even number. If it is an odd number, then the Expert selects from bottommost boards, and the role of minimizing and maximizing is reversed.

   Thus, the ExpertPlayer implements a pair of mutually recursive evaluation methods, one to maximize results and one to minimize results:

```
int maximize(Board root, int lookAhead) {
  int bestValue=-9999;
  for each move {
    compute nextBoard, which uses that move
    value = minimize(nextBoard, lookAhead-1);
    update bestValue and bestMove
    }
  return bestValue;
  }

int minimize (Board root, int lookAhead) {
  int bestValue=9999;
  for each move {
    compute nextBoard, which uses that move
```

```
    value = maximize(nextBoard, lookAhead-1);
    update bestValue and bestMove
    }
return bestValue;
}
```

Of course, each of the mutually recursive methods must provide base cases (`lookAhead==0`).
For obvious reasons, this technique is called a *min-max game-playing strategy.*

Program such an `ExpertPlayer`.

A

OTHER JAVA FEATURES

O ur goal has been to present *principles* of programming in Java, not *language features*. Indeed, we have been rather sparing in providing language features, introducing only enough to express the principles and avoid awkward or nonidiomatic usages.

This appendix provides a reading knowledge of Java as it is used in the real world by briefly covering many of the omitted language features. With the material in this appendix and that in the text, we have covered all but its most esoteric features. The sections of this appendix can be read independently of one another. Generally, they can be read anytime after Chapter 5.

A.1

Comments

A.1.1 Old-Style Comments

Text between the symbols /* and */ (not necessarily on the same line) is ignored. However, be careful with these old-style comments, because they *do not nest*. That is, if you attempt to comment out a line that contains a comment:

```
... /* comment */ ...
```

by placing comment brackets before and after it

```
/*
... /* comment */ ...
*/
```

then the first */ ends the comment, and the ... at the end of the line is not considered to be in the comment.

A.1.2 Documentation Comments

Any comment that starts with /** and ends with */ is used by the program javadoc to produce a primitive kind of documentation from the source code of a Java program. Like old-style comments, documentation comments cannot be nested. (The javadoc comments are used in the CSLib code in Appendix E. Those comments were used to generate the online documentation for CSLib at our website, but not the documentation given in Appendix C.)

A.2

No Preprocessor

Programmers familiar with C or C++ know that those languages provide a *preprocessor* that allows such things as conditional compilation of blocks of code and inclusion of source files. Java has no such preprocessor.

A.3

Data Types

We have introduced four of the built-in data types: int, double, char, and boolean. In this section, we fill in some details about these and other types.

A.3.1 Primitive Types

The primitive types in Java are boolean, char, byte, short, int, long, float, and double. As shown in Table A.1, byte, short, and long are integer types, and float and double are floating-point types. Each type has a set of literals. We have seen the literals of type boolean (true and false), int (integers), and double (numbers in scientific notation). Literals of type byte, short, and long look like int literals, but suffixed with the letter b, s, and l, respectively. A literal of type float is a literal of type double with the letter f on the end. Character literals can be written, as we have seen, with single quotes. Alternatively, they can be notated by writing \u followed by a four-digit hexadecimal number giving the Unicode code for the character.

Every data value in a computer is represented as a binary number. The number of binary digits, or *bits*, in a given type of value depends only on the type. Table A.1 gives the sizes of the primitive types, *bit* their default values (the value given to instance variables that lack an initializer), and their minimum and maximum values.

A.3.2 Operators

We have covered all the arithmetic operators (+, -, *, /, %), comparison operators (==, !=, <, >, <=, >=), and logical operators (!, &&, ||, ^). We introduced the increment and decrement operators (++, --), but only partially. This leaves the bitwise operators, the conditional operator, and the assignment operators (including ++ and --), all of which are introduced in this section.

Type	Meaning	Default	Size	Minimum Value
				Maximum Value
boolean	true or false	false	1 bit	—
char	Unicode character	\u0000	16 bits	\u0000
				\uFFFF
byte	Integer	0	8 bits	−128
				127
short	Integer	0	16 bits	−32768
				32767
int	Integer	0	32 bits	−2147483648
				2147483647
long	Integer	0	64 bits	−9223372036854775808
				9223372036854775807
float	IEEE 754 floating-point number	0.0	32 bits	±3.40282347E+38
				±1.40239846E−45
double	IEEE 754 floating-point number	0.0	64 bits	±1.79769313486231570E+308
				±4.94065645841246544E−324

TABLE A.1 Vital statistics for the primitive types.

bitwise operators

To understand the *bitwise operators*, remember that all numbers in a computer are represented in binary. These operations combine pairs of integers on a bit-by-bit basis. They are listed and explained in Table A.2.

conditional operator

The *conditional operator* (? :) is a ternary (three-argument) operator—the only one in Java. An expression of the form

> *expr1* ?   *expr2* : *expr3*

is evaluated by evaluating *expr1* and then returning the value of either *expr2* or *expr3*, depending on whether *expr1* is true or false. For example, the expression (x==0) ? y : y/x returns the value of y if x is zero and the value of y/x otherwise. As another example, the assignment

> x = *expr1* ?   *expr2* : *expr3*;

is equivalent to

```
if ( expr1)
    x = expr2;
else
    x = expr3;
```

assignment operators

The *assignment operators* provide a simple shorthand for some common forms of assignment statement. For example,

> x += *expression*;

is equivalent to

> x = x + *expression*;

All the assignment operators work this way. If x is a variable (i.e., an expression that legally can appear on the left-hand side of an assignment statement) and e is an expression, then the following equivalences hold:

Operator	Explanation	Example (in Decimal and binary)
&: bitwise AND	Each bit in the result is obtained from the 2 corresponding bits in the arguments using the AND operation: 1 if both bits are 1; 0 otherwise	108 & 85 = 68 01101100 & 01010101 = 01000100
|: bitwise inclusive OR	Each bit in the result is obtained from the 2 corresponding bits in the arguments using the OR operation: 0 if both bits are 0; 1 otherwise	108 | 85 = 126 01101100 | 01010101 = 01111110
^: bitwise exclusive OR	Each bit in the result is obtained from the 2 corresponding bits in the arguments using the EXCLUSIVE OR operation: 0 if both bits are the same; 1 otherwise	108 ^ 85 = 57 01101100 ^ 01010101 = 00111001
~: bitwise complement	Each bit in the result is obtained from the corresponding bit in the argument using the NOT operation: 0 if the bit is 1; 1 if it is 0	~108 = 147 ~ 01101100 = 10010011
<<: left shift	Shift bits of the first argument left by the number of places indicated by the second argument (for sufficiently small numbers, m << n is equal to m $\times 2^n$)	58 << 2 = 232 00111010 << 2 = 11101000
>>>: right shift (zero fill)	Shift bits of the first argument right by the number of places indicated by the second argument (m >>> n is equal to $m/2^n$ when m is positive)	58 >>> 2 = 14 00111010 >>> 2 = 00001110
>>: right shift (sign fill)	This behaves like >>>, except the leftmost (sign) bit is replicated (m >> n is equal to $m/2^n$ when m is positive)	58 >> 2 = 14 00111010 >> 2 = 00001110

TABLE A.2 Bitwise operations of Java.

Shorthand Assignment	Equivalent Full Assignment
x += e	x = x+e
x -= e	x = x-e
x *= e	x = x*e
x /= e	x = x/e
x %= e	x = x%e
x &= e	x = x&e
x |= e	x = x|e
x ^= e	x = x^e
x <<= e	x = x<<e
x >>= e	x = x>>e
x >>>= e	x = x>>>e

Thus, x++ and x-- are equivalent to x += 1 and x -= 1, respectively.

Contrary to our use of =, ++, and -- in this book, these operators actually form expressions and can be used inside larger expressions. For example, if x has the value 10, then

```
x++*(x+5)
```

evaluates to 160. First x++ is evaluated; it *returns* 10 (the value of x) and *increments* x to 11. Next x+5 is evaluated; because x is 11, it evaluates to 16. The product of 10 and 16 is 160. Was that confusing? That's why we don't use it.

This raises the question, What values do the other assignment operators return? The answer is simple: They return the value that is assigned. In other words, x = e returns the value of e; x += e returns the value of x+e; and so on. There is one surprise, though: ++ (and similarly --) can be used both in the *postfix* form we've used before (x++) and in a *prefix* form (++x). Both increment x, but the values they return, when used in expressions, differ: x++ returns the value of x *prior to being incremented*, while ++x returns the incremented value.

Again, these values matter only when the expression appears within a larger expression. When these expressions are used as statements, their values don't matter. For example, A[i++] = 10 and A[++i] = 10 are different: The first assigns 10 to A[i], the second assigns 10 to A[i+1] (and both increment i). On the other hand, i++; A[i] = 10; is the same as ++i; A[i] = 10;. Both are equivalent to A[++i] = 10.

A typical example of the use of these operators within an expression is this loop that searches for the value x in an array A:

```
i = 0;
while (i < n && A[i++] != x) ; // : ++i would be wrong!
```

This idiom is very popular in Java.

The fact that = is an operator explains why a statement like

```
if (x = y) ...
```

is not a syntax error (provided that x and y are of type Boolean), even though it is almost certainly a mistake. As far as Java is concerned, x = y is an *expression* that returns a Boolean value. So even though the programmer probably intended to write x == y, the Java compiler cannot send an error message, because this might be legitimate.

A.4

Control Structures

A.4.1 break **and** continue **Statements**

continue statement

labeled break
labeled continue

We discussed the break statement and its ability to cause a premature termination of a loop. The statement break inside a while or for statement causes termination of the remainder of that statement. The *continue statement* is similar to break. A continue statement inside a loop causes termination of the *current* iteration of the loop without terminating the loop itself.

There are generalized versions of these statements: *labeled break* and *labeled continue* statements. If you write break label, where *label* is a label attached to an enclosing for, while, do, or switch statement, then the break breaks out of *that* statement, regardless of how deeply nested the break is inside the statement. For example, consider this code:

```
outer: for (int i=1; i<n; i++) {
           for (int j=1; j<n; j++) {
               if (maze[i][j] == MOUSE) break outer;
                 other processing
               }
                 other processing
           }
```

The statement `break outer` effectively jumps out of *both* of the loops in which it is nested.

In a similar way, the `continue` statement can be labeled. Execution of a labeled `continue` statement causes the next iteration of the labeled looping statement to be executed.

A.5

The `final` Modifier

We have seen the `final` modifier applied to data members, indicating that they are constants. This modifier also can be applied to methods, indicating that a method cannot be overridden in a derived class. It further can be applied to complete classes, indicating that a class may not be subclassed.

A.6

Inner Classes

Class definitions can be given *inside* other class definitions:

```
class C {
    ...
    class D { ... }
    ...
}
```

The inner class D is an ordinary class, with the usual syntax. It is *not* a subclass of C. There are, however, two special things about it: Only C knows about D and can create D objects; and methods in D can access the private variables and methods of C.

Inner classes are used primarily for adding event-handling code to classes. The simplest use is illustrated by the following example. Note first that the `java.awt.event` package contains the following class:

```
public abstract class MouseAdapter implements MouseListener {
    public void mouseClicked(MouseEvent e) {}
    public void mousePressed(MouseEvent e) {}
    public void mouseReleased(MouseEvent e) {}
    public void mouseEntered(MouseEvent e) {}
    public void mouseExited(MouseEvent e) {}
}
```

The `MouseAdapter` class is convenient for defining a class that handles just, say, the mouse clicking event. In our previous examples, we defined `mouseClicked` to handle this event, but we had to give trivial definitions for the other four methods. By inheriting from `MouseAdapter`, we can define just the one interesting method, and the others get their trivial definitions by inheritance.

Given the `MouseAdapter` class, we can use inner classes to define the mouse click handler:

```
class C {
    ...
    class ClickHandler extends MouseAdapter {
        public void mouseClicked(MouseEvent e) {
            ... definition of mouseClicked can refer
            ... to instance variables of C ...
        }
    }

    ...  addMouseListener(new ClickHandler()) ...

    ...
}
```

A ClickHandler object is registered as a mouse listener, so that its mouseClicked method is called whenever the mouse is clicked. Since it has access to all the variables and methods of C, it can do whatever C might have wanted to do if it had defined mouseClicked itself.

The attentive reader might ask, Why did we need to use an inner class in the last example? The alternative would be for C itself to be a subclass of MouseAdapter, to define its own version of mouseClicked, and to register itself as a mouse listener. What advantage do we gain by using inner classes? In the above example, none. However, if C already had a superclass—for example, if C were an applet, so that it was a subclass of Applet—then it could not be a subclass of MouseAdapter.

To summarize, inner classes are used when we need a class that has access to the private variables and methods of a class but needs to be a subclass of an unrelated class.

Inner classes have another special property: They can be anonymous, that is, unnamed. The above example could be written

```
class C {
    ...

    ...  addMouseListener(new MouseAdapter {
            public void mouseClicked(MouseEvent e) {
                ... definition of mouseClicked can refer
                ... to instance variables of C ...
            }
        }

    ...
}
```

Note that we have not used the ClickHandler name, but have just given the superclass of the anonymous class. Anonymous inner classes are used heavily in event-handling code for the notational convenience they provide. Other examples are in the CSLib code in Appendix E.

A.7

Concurrency-Related Features

threads

There are numerous circumstances in which two or more Java programs run simultaneously on the same computer, such as when a web page contains two applets. In Java parlance, two programs running simultaneously are called *threads*. It is often necessary for threads to communicate with one another, and this is usually accomplished by having them access the same variables. Of course, it is perfectly normal for two methods to access the same variables—that is the whole purpose of class and instance variables.

However, here we are talking about a situation where two methods are running simultaneously but in different threads and are accessing the same variables *at exactly the same time*. This situation is fraught with complications; it is studied in the area of *concurrent programming*. We mention it here because some language features can only be understood in the context of concurrent programming.

The biggest single problem in concurrent programming is controlling simultaneous access to shared variables. If two programs read the value of a variable at the same time, there is no problem; but if one writes and the other reads, then the precise order in which these events occur can be important. In the classic example, a data structure is being queried by two concurrent processes, which need to check if the structure is empty before getting an element from it; furthermore, the action of getting an element out of the structure has the side effect of removing it from the structure (so that it can be retrieved only once). If both concurrent processes read the "item available" variable simultaneously and see that there are data available, they may both attempt to access the data. Whichever one happens to get to the data first will remove them, and the second one will be accessing an empty data structure (despite having checked it for emptiness!). The two features mentioned in this section are attempts to solve aspects of this problem.

A.7.1 The synchronized Statement and Modifier

The basic method of avoiding the kinds of problems just discussed is to restrict access to variables to one thread at a time. An object can be "locked," meaning that only the thread holding the lock can access the object. A thread can lock an object in one of two ways: using a *synchronized statement* or a *synchronized method*.

synchronized statement
synchronized method

The synchronized statement has the form

```
synchronized ( object ) {
    statements
}
```

The *object*'s lock is obtained (the thread has to wait if another thread has the lock), the *statements* are executed, and then the lock is relinquished. No method in another thread can access that object while the statements are executed, because this thread has the lock. Such sections of code—in which statements have *exclusive access* to an object—are called *critical sections*.

critical section

A *synchronized method* is a method that has the synchronized modifier in its header. The entire body of a synchronized method is a critical section. That is, when the method is invoked, its receiver is locked, so that the method has exclusive access to it; the lock is relinquished when the method returns.

A.7.2 The volatile Modifier

The volatile modifier is added to a variable to indicate that this is a shared variable that might be changed by another thread at any time. This keyword does not protect the variable from changes; it just warns the Java compiler that they can happen. This prevents the compiler from generating erroneous code by assuming—as would be true, if not for concurrency—that a variable's value does not just change spontaneously.

A.8

The transient and native Modifiers

The transient modifier on a variable tells the Java compiler that the variable is not a part of its object's "persistent state" and therefore can be ignored in certain circumstances (e.g., when storing the object in a backup cache). The native modifier is applied to a method name to indicate that the method is implemented not by a Java method, but separately, in the C language or some other platform-dependent manner.

B

PRECEDENCE RULES

The following table gives the precedence levels and associativity for the Java operations. Operators are given in *decreasing order* of precedence, with operators of equal precedence grouped together. Unless otherwise indicated by parentheses, operators of higher precedence are applied before operators of lower precedence; so, for example, a*b+c is evaluated as (a*b)+c. With one exception, binary operators of equal precedence associate from left to right; for example, a/b*c is evaluated as (a/b)*c. The exception is the assignment operator = and its variants (for example, +=), which associate from right to left. All unary operators associate from right to left.

Operator	Name	Use	Page
.	Member selection	*object . member*	53, 228
[]	Subscripting	*array_name [expr]*	264
()	Function call	*expr (expr-list)*	69
++	Increment	*variable ++*	63
--	Decrement	*variable --*	64
-	Unary minus	*- expr*	115
+	Unary plus	*+ expr*	
~	Bitwise complement	*~ expr*	673
!	Boolean complement	*! expr*	110
(type)	Cast	*(type) expr*	131

Operator	Name	Use	Page
*	Multiply	*expr* * *expr*	60
/	Divide	*expr* / *expr*	60
%	Modulo (remainder)	*expr* % *expr*	60
+	Add	*expr* + *expr*	60
-	Subtract	*expr* - *expr*	60
+	Concatenate	*string* + *string*	73
<<	Left shift	*expr* << *expr*	673
>>	Right shift, sign extension	*expr* >> *expr*	673
>>>	Right shift, zero extension	*expr* >>> *expr*	673
<	Less than	*expr* < *expr*	110
<=	Less than or equal to	*expr* <= *expr*	110
>	Greater than	*expr* > *expr*	110
>=	Greater than or equal to	*expr* >= *expr*	110
instanceof	Type comparison	*expr* instanceof *type*	
==	Equal	*expr* == *expr*	110
!=	Not equal	*expr* != *expr*	110
&	Boolean AND (complete)	*expr* & *expr*	673
&	Bitwise AND	*expr* & *expr*	673
^	Boolean exclusive OR	*expr* ^ *expr*	110
^	Bitwise exclusive OR	*expr* ^ *expr*	673
|	Boolean inclusive OR (complete)	*expr* | *expr*	673
|	Bitwise inclusive OR	*expr* | *expr*	673
&&	Boolean AND (partial)	*expr* && *expr*	110
||	Boolean inclusive OR (partial)	*expr* || *expr*	110
? :	Conditional expression	*expr* ? *expr* : *expr*	672
=	Assign	*variable* = *expr*	63
*=	Multiply and assign	*variable* *= *expr*	673
/=	Divide and assign	*variable* /= *expr*	673
%=	Modulo and assign	*variable* %= *expr*	673
+=	Add and assign	*variable* += *expr*	672
-=	Subtract and assign	*variable* -= *expr*	673
<<=	Shift left and assign	*variable* <<= *expr*	673
>>=	Shift right and assign	*variable* >>= *expr*	673
>>>=	Shift right and assign	*variable* >>>= *expr*	673
&=	AND and assign	*variable* &= *expr*	673
|=	Inclusive OR and assign	*variable* |= *expr*	673
^=	Exclusive OR and assign	*variable* ^= *expr*	673

CLASSES IN CSLib
AND THE JAVA API

I n this appendix, we list the classes and interfaces used in the textbook. In most cases, these lists are expanded versions of the lists found in the tables in the text. In each case, the list contains two columns: a name and an explanation. Symbolic constants are final class variables.

The classes and interfaces that are documented here come from several packages:

Package	Page
CSLib	681
java.lang	684
java.util	687
java.awt	688
java.awt.event	695
java.applet	698
java.io	698

Within each package, classes are given in alphabetical order; within each class, the various members are given in alphabetical order.

In most cases, our lists of the variables and methods of each class are incomplete. Interfaces are given completely, as far as the instance methods go, although some symbolic constants may be omitted. The online documentation, available for browsing or download at www.javasoft.com (or, in the case of CSLib, www.mhhe.com/engcs/compsci/kamin), contains the full list of variables and methods for each class and interface.

All classes that are not declared to have a superclass have the class Object, in java.lang, as their superclass. In particular, the toString method can be used to stringify any object. (Actually toString is redefined in many classes. To save space, when a class redefines a method that it inherits, we list it only in the superclass. The online documentation includes an entry for every method definition, even if it is simply redefining an inherited method.)

Classes in the CSLib package

Class **ClosableFrame**

*ClosableFrame implements WindowListener; it should be used instead of **Frame***

Constructors	
`ClosableFrame ()`	Creates a frame with no title.
`ClosableFrame (String t)`	Creates a frame with title `t`.

Class **DrawingBox**

Constructors	
`DrawingBox ()`	Creates a drawing box with no title.
`DrawingBox (String t)`	Creates a drawing box with title `t`.

Instance methods	
`void clear ()`	Erases contents of drawing box.
`void clearRect (int x, int y, int w, int h)`	Clears (i.e. draws over in the background color) a rectangle with upper-left corner at (x, y), having width w and height h.
`void drawCircle (int x, int y, int r)`	Draws a circle with center (x, y) and radius r.
`void drawCircle (Point p, int r)`	Same as `drawCircle(p.x, p.y, r)`.
`void drawImage (Image img, int x, int y)`	Draws img at location (x, y). (Image is in java.awt, but is not documented in this appendix; see the documentation for `Applet` in java.applet.)
`void drawLine (int x0, int y0, int x1, int y1)`	Draws a line from point (x0, y0) to (x1, y1).
`void drawOval (int x, int y, int w, int h)`	Draws an oval inscribed in the rectangle with upper-left corner at (x, y), having width w and height h.
`void drawRect (int x, int y, int w, int h)`	Draws the outline of a rectangle with upper-left corner at (x, y), having width w and height h.
`void drawString (String s, int x, int y)`	Draws the string s with its baseline (bottom-left corner) at (x, y).
`void fillCircle (int x, int y, int r)`	Draws a filled circle (see `drawCircle`).
`void fillCircle (Point p, int r)`	Draws a filled circle (see `drawCircle`).
`void fillOval (int x, int y, int w, int h)`	Draws an oval as with `drawOval`, but fills it in with the current color.
`void fillRect (int x, int y, int w, int h)`	Draws a rectangle as with `drawRect`, but fills it in with the current color.
`Color getColor ()`	Gets the current drawing color. (Color is in java.awt.)
`int getDrawableHeight ()`	Gets the height of the window, in pixels.
`int getDrawableWidth ()`	Gets the width of the window, in pixels.
`void setColor (Color c)`	Sets the drawing color to c.
`void setDrawableSize (int w, int h)`	Sets the window size large enough so that the *drawable portion* is w pixels wide by h pixels high.
`void setSize (int w, int h)`	Sets the window size to w pixels wide by h pixels high.

Class **ErrorBox**

Constructors

`ErrorBox (String t)`	Pops up error box with message `t`.

Class **InputBox**

Constructors

`InputBox ()`	Creates input box with no title.
`InputBox (String t)`	Creates input box with title `t`.

Instance methods

`boolean eoi ()`	Returns true if last attempt to read hit end-of-input.
`char readChar ()`	Returns character entered by user.
`double readDouble ()`	Returns double entered by user.
`int readInt ()`	Returns integer entered by user.
`String readString ()`	Returns string entered by user.
`void setPrompt (String text)`	Makes `text` the input prompt.

Class **OutputBox**

Constructors

`OutputBox ()`	Creates output box with no title.
`OutputBox (String t)`	Creates output box with title "t".

Instance methods

`void clear ()`	Erases contents of output box.
`void print (boolean b)`	Prints the boolean `b`.
`void print (char c)`	Prints the char `c`.
`void print (double d)`	Prints the double `d`.
`void print (int i)`	Prints the integer `i`.
`void print (String s)`	Prints the string `s`.
`void print (StringBuffer sb)`	Prints the string buffer `sb`.
`void println ()`	Prints a newline.
`void println (boolean b)`	Prints the boolean `b` then a newline.
`void println (char c)`	Prints the char `c` then a newline.
`void println (double d)`	Prints the double `d` then a newline.
`void println (int i)`	Prints the integer `i` then a newline.
`void println (String s)`	Prints the string `s` then a newline.
`void println (StringBuffer sb)`	Prints the string buffer `sb` then a newline.
`void setFont (Font f)`	Future output will be in font `f`. (The Font class is in `java.awt`.)
`void setTitle (String t)`	Sets the window title to the string `t`.

Class **SFormat**

Class methods

`String sprintc (int w, double d)`	Stringifies d centered in a field of width w.
`String sprintc (int w, int i)`	Stringifies i centered in a field of width w.
`String sprintc (int w, String s)`	Centers s in a field of width w.
`String sprintr (double d)`	Stringifies d with two decimal places.
`String sprintr (int r, double d)`	Stringifies d with r decimal places.
`String sprintr (int w, int i)`	Stringifies i right-justified in a field of width w.
`String sprintr (int w, int r, double d)`	Stringifies d with r decimal places, right-justified in a field of width w.
`String sprintr (int w, String s)`	Right-justifies s in a field of width w.
`String sprintzr (int w, int i)`	Stringifies i in a field of width w, right-justified and zero-filled.

Class **Timer**

Class methods

`void pause (long t)`	Pauses for t milliseconds.

Class **TrickMouse**

Constructors

`TrickMouse ()`	Constructs a `TrickMouse`.

Class methods

`void hitWall ()`	Displays image of mouse hitting wall.
`void setTitle (String t)`	Sets title of window.
`void speak (String m)`	Shows mouse speaking message m.

C.2

Classes in the `java.lang` Package

Class **Double**

Constructors	
`Double (double v)`	Constructs a Double with value v.
`Double (String s)`	Constructs a Double with value given by the string s. It is an error if s has any nondecimal characters, including blanks.

Class Methods	
`double parseDouble (String s)`	Parses s, returning the double it represents. Equivalent to new `Double(s).doubleValue()`.

Instance Methods	
`int compareTo (Double b)`	Compares this to b; returns value as in compareTo in Integer class.
`double doubleValue ()`	Returns the double value of this Double.

Class **Integer**

Symbolic Constants	
`MAX_VALUE`	The largest value of type int.
`MIN_VALUE`	The smallest value of type int.

Constructors	
`Integer (int v)`	Constructs an Integer with value v.
`Integer (String s)`	Constructs an Integer with value given by the string s. Throws NumberFormatException if s has any noninteger characters.

Class Methods	
`int parseInt (String s)`	Parses s, returning the int it represents. Equivalent to new `Integer(s).intValue()`.

Instance Methods	
`int compareTo (Integer b)`	Compares this to b, returning 0 if equal, a number less than 0 if receiver less than b, a number greater than 0 otherwise.
`int intValue ()`	Returns the int value of this Integer.

Class **Math**

Symbolic Constants	
`double E`	Base of the natural logarithm.
`double PI`	Value of π.

Class Methods	
`double abs (double x)`	Absolute value of x (double version).
`int abs (int x)`	Absolute value of x (integer version).
`double atan2 (double y, double x)`	Angle created by right triangle with base x and height y, in radians.
`double ceil (double x)`	Ceiling (smallest integer value not less than x).
`double cos (double x)`	Cosine (x is angle, in radians).
`double exp (double x)`	Exponential (e^x).
`double floor (double x)`	Floor (largest integer value not greater than x).
`double log (double x)`	Natural logarithm (base e).
`double pow (double a, double b)`	Power (a^b).
`double random ()`	A random number between 0.0 and 1.0.
`double sin (double x)`	Sine (x is angle, in radians).
`double sqrt (double x)`	Square root.
`double tan (double x)`	Tangent (x is angle, in radians).

Class **Object**

Constructors	
`Object ()`	Creates new object.

Instance Methods	
`void toString ()`	Produces a string representation of the receiver.

Class **String**

Instance Methods
All methods are nonmutating—receiver is not altered

`char charAt (int index)`	Returns the character at the specified index. Index must be between 0 and length()-1.
`int compareTo (String s)`	Compares two strings lexicographically, returning 0 if equal, a number less than 0 if receiver less than s, a number greater than 0 otherwise.
`int compareToIgnoreCase (String s)`	Compares two strings lexicographically, ignoring case considerations; returns value as in `compareTo`.
`boolean endsWith (String s)`	True if the receiver ends with string s.
`boolean equals (String s)`	True if the strings are equal, false otherwise.
`boolean equalsIgnoreCase (String s)`	True if the strings are equal, ignoring case; false otherwise.
`int indexOf (String s)`	Returns the index within the string of the first occurrence of the string s.
`int indexOf (int c)`	Returns the index within the string of the first occurrence of the character with code c.
`int lastIndexOf (String s)`	Like `indexOf`, but returns index of last occurrence.
`int lastIndexOf (int c)`	Like `indexOf`, but returns index of last occurrence.
`int length()`	Returns the length of this string.
`String replace (char c1, char c2)`	Returns copy of receiver with all occurrences of c1 replaced by c2.
`boolean startsWith (String s)`	True if the receiver begins with string s.
`String substring (int beginx, int endx)`	Returns substring of receiver beginning at index beginx and ending at index endx-1.
`String toLowerCase()`	Converts all the characters of the string to lowercase.
`String toUpperCase()`	Converts all the characters of the string to uppercase.
`String trim ()`	Returns copy of receiver with all blanks removed from beginning and end.

Class **StringBuffer**

Constructors

`StringBuffer ()`	Creates empty string buffer.
`StringBuffer (String s)`	Creates string buffer containing characters in s.

Instance Methods
Methods that return `StringBuffer` *are mutating—receiver is altered*

`StringBuffer append (String s)`	Appends the string s.
`StringBuffer append (char ch)`	Appends the character ch.
`char charAt (int index)`	Retrieves the character at index.
`StringBuffer deleteCharAt (int index)`	Deletes the character at index.
`StringBuffer delete (int start, int end)`	Deletes the characters from position start to end-1.
`StringBuffer insert (int index, String s)`	Inserts the string s at index.
`StringBuffer insert (int index, char ch)`	Inserts the character ch at index.
`int length ()`	Returns the present length.
`StringBuffer reverse ()`	Reverses characters in this string buffer, and returns this string buffer.
`void setCharAt (int index, char ch)`	Replaces the character at index with ch.

Class **System**

Symbolic Constants

`PrintStream out`	Stream for output to command window (`PrintStream` is similar to `PrintWriter` and implements the same `print` and `println` methods).
`PrintStream err`	Similar to out, but used for printing error messages to command window.

C.3

Classes in the `java.util` Package

Abstract Class **Calendar**

Symbolic Constants

`int DAY_OF_MONTH`	Field number for day of month.
`int MONTH`	Field number for month.
`int YEAR`	Field number for year.

Class Methods

`int getInstance ()`	Return an instance of some default subclass—usually, `GregorianCalendar`—representing the current date and time.

Instance Methods

`int get (int field)`	Returns the value for a specified field.

Interface **Enumeration**

Method Declarations

`boolean hasMoreElements ()`	Tells if this enumeration is finished.
`Object nextElement ()`	Returns the next element of this enumeration. Throws `NoSuchElementException`.

Class **Vector**

Constructors

`Vector (int cap)`	`cap` is the initial capacity.

Instance Methods

`void addElement (Object o)`	Adds o to end of this vector, increasing its size by 1.
`Object clone ()`	Clones this vector.
`boolean contains (Object o)`	Tells if this vector contains o.
`Object elementAt (int i)`	Returns object at index e.
`Enumeration elements ()`	Returns an `Enumeration` for this vector.
`Object firstElement ()`	Retrieves the first element of this vector.
`boolean isEmpty ()`	Tells if this vector is empty.
`int size ()`	Tells how many elements are in this vector.

C.4

Classes in the `java.awt` Package

Class **BorderLayout** implements **LayoutManager**

Symbolic Constants

`String CENTER`	Used in add method to place component in center.
`String EAST`	Used in add method to place component at right.
`String NORTH`	Used in add method to place component on top.
`String SOUTH`	Used in add method to place component on bottom.
`String WEST`	Used in add method to place component at left.

Constructors

`BorderLayout ()`	Creates border layout object.

Class **Button** extends **Component**

Constructors

`Button ()`	Constructs a new button.
`Button (String l)`	Constructs a new button with label l.

Instance Methods

`void addActionListener (ActionListener l)`	Makes l a listener for action events from this button.
`String getLabel ()`	Gets the label for this button.
`void setLabel (String l)`	Sets the label of this button to l.

Class **Canvas** extends **Component**

Constructors

`Canvas ()`	Creates new canvas.

Instance Methods

`void paint (Graphics g)`	Repaints this canvas using g.

Class **Checkbox** extends **Component**

Constructors

`Checkbox ()`	Creates a new check box with no label.
`Checkbox (String l)`	Creates a new check box with label l.
`Checkbox (String l, boolean state)`	Creates a new check box with label l; selected if state == true.
`Checkbox (String l, CheckboxGroup g, boolean state)`	Creates a new check box as part of check box group g, with label l; selected if state == true.

Instance Methods

`void addItemListener (ItemListener l)`	Makes l a listener for item events from this check box.
`String getLabel ()`	Gets the label of this check box.
`boolean getState ()`	Gets the state of this check box (true for "on").
`void setLabel (String l)`	Sets the label of this check box.
`void setState (boolean state)`	Sets the state of this check box.

Class **CheckboxGroup**

Constructors

`CheckboxGroup ()`	Creates a new check box group.

Instance Methods

`Checkbox getSelectedCheckbox ()`	Returns the currently selected check box in this check box group.
`void setSelectedCheckbox (Checkbox box)`	Sets box as the selected check box in this check box group.

Class **Color**

Symbolic Constants	
`Color black`	The color black.
`Color blue`	The color blue.
`Color gray`	The color gray.
`Color green`	The color green.
`Color red`	The color red.
`Color white`	The color white.
`Color yellow`	The color yellow.

Constructors	
`Color (int r, int g, int b)`	Creates color with the specified red/green/blue (RGB) components; each is a value in the range 0–255.

Abstract Class **Component**

Instance Methods	
`void addMouseListener (MouseListener l)`	Makes l a listener for mouse events from this component.
`void addMouseMotionListener (MouseMotionListener l)`	Makes l a listener for mouse motion events from this component.
`Color getBackground ()`	Gets the background color of this component.
`Font getFont ()`	Gets the font of this component.
`FontMetrics getFontMetrics (Font f)`	Gets the font metrics for font f.
`Color getForeground ()`	Gets the foreground color for this component.
`Graphics getGraphics ()`	Gets the graphics context for this component.
`int getHeight ()`	Gets the height of this component.
`Dimension getMinimumSize ()`	Gets the minimum size of this component.
`Dimension getPreferredSize ()`	Gets the preferred size of this component.
`Dimension getSize ()`	Gets the size of this component.
`int getWidth ()`	Gets the width of this component.
`void paint (Graphics g)`	Paints this component.
`void paintAll (Graphics g)`	Paints this component and its subcomponents.
`void repaint ()`	Requests a repaint of this component.
`void setBackground (Color c)`	Sets the background color to c.
`void setFont (Font f)`	Sets the font of this component.
`void setForeground (Color c)`	Sets the foreground of this component.
`void setSize (int w, int h)`	Sets the size of this component.
`void setSize (Dimension d)`	Alternates version of setSize.
`void setVisible (boolean b)`	Shows or hides this component depending on b.
`void update (Graphics g)`	Updates this component (clears it and paints it).

Abstract Class **Container** extends **Component**

Instance Methods	
`Component add (Component c)`	Adds `c` to container, and returns `c`.
`Component add (Component c, int pos)`	Adds `c` to container, and returns `c`; `pos` indicates where `c` is to be placed (depending upon the layout manager).
`Component add (Component c, Object pos)`	Adds `c` to container, and returns `c`; `pos` indicates where `c` is to be placed (depending upon the layout manager).
`void setLayout (LayoutManager mgr)`	Sets layout manager for this container.

Class **Dimension**

Constructors	
`Dimension (int w, int h)`	Creates dimension (w, h).

Public Instance Variables	
`int height`	Height of the receiver.
`int width`	Width of the receiver.

Class **FlowLayout** implements **LayoutManager**

Constructors	
`FlowLayout ()`	Creates flow layout object.

Class **Font**

Symbolic Constants	
`int BOLD`	The bold style.
`int ITALIC`	The italic style.
`int PLAIN`	The plain style.

Constructors	
`Font (String name, int style, int size)`	Creates a new font with the given name, style, and size.

Instance Methods	
`String getFamily ()`	Returns the family name for this font.
`String getFontName ()`	Returns the face name for this font.
`String getName ()`	Returns the name for this font.
`int getSize ()`	Returns the size for this font.
`int getStyle ()`	Returns the style for this font.
`boolean isBold ()`	Indicates whether this font is bold.
`boolean isItalic ()`	Indicates whether this font is italic.
`boolean isPlain ()`	Indicates whether this font is plain.

Class FontMetrics

Constructors

FontMetrics (Font f)	Metrics for font f.

Instance Methods

---

int charWidth (char c)	Returns the "advance width" of character c in this font; the advance width is the offset from the start of this character to the start of the next character.
Font getFont ()	Gets the font for which this object is the metrics.
int getHeight ()	Returns standard height of a line of text in this font.
int stringWidth (String s)	Returns the advance width of s (the sum of the advance widths of the characters in s).

Abstract Class Graphics

Instance Methods

---

void clearRect (int x, int y, int w, int h)	Clears rectangle of width w and height h with upper left corner at (x, y) by filling it with background color.
void drawLine (int x1, int y1, int x2, int y2)	Draws line from (x1, y1) to (x2, y2).
void drawOval (int x, int y, int w, int h)	Draws oval that would precisely fit into the rectangle given by these arguments (see clearRect).
void drawPolygon (Polygon p)	Draws polygon.
void drawRect (int x, int y, int w, int h)	Draws outline of rectangle specified by these arguments (see clearRect).
void drawString (String s, int x, int y)	Draws s with its reference point (bottom left corner) at (x, y).
void fillOval (int x, int y, int w, int h)	Like drawOval, but fills in current color.
void fillPolygon (Polygon p)	Draws polygon, filled with current color.
void fillRect (int x, int y, int w, int h)	Like drawRect, but fills in current color.
Color getColor ()	Gets current color.
Font getFont ()	Gets current font.
FontMetrics getFontMetrics ()	Gets font metrics of current font.
void setColor (Color c)	Sets current color to c.
void setFont (Font f)	Gets current font to f.

Class GridLayout implements LayoutManager

Constructors

GridLayout ()	Creates grid layout object with one column.
GridLayout (int r, int c)	Creates grid layout object with specified number of rows and columns.
GridLayout (int r, int c, int cgap, int rgap)	Creates grid layout object with specified number of rows and columns, and an additional gap of cgap points between columns and rgap points between rows.

Class **Label** extends **Component**

Symbolic Constants

int CENTER	Indicates that the label should be centered.
int LEFT	Indicates that the label should be left-justified.
int RIGHT	Indicates that the label should be right-justified.

Constructors

Label ()	Constructs a new label.
Label (String s)	Constructs a new label with s as the text, left-justified.
Label (String s, int align)	Constructs a new label with s as the text, with the specified alignment.

Instance Methods

String getText ()	Gets the text that for this label.
void setText (String t)	Sets the text for this label to t.

Class **Panel** extends **Container**

Constructors

Panel ()	Creates panel.

Class **Point**

Constructors

Point (int x, int y)	Creates point (x, y).

Public Instance Variables

int x	x coordinate.
int y	y coordinate.

Class **Polygon**

Constructors

Polygon ()	Creates polygon with no points.

Public Instance Variables

int npoints	Number of points in the polygon.
int[] xpoints	x coordinates of points in polygon.
int[] ypoints	y coordinates of points in polygon xpoints and ypoints are parallel arrays of length npoints.

Instance Methods

void addPoint (int x, int y)	Adds point (x, y) at end of receiver.
boolean contains (Point p)	Determines whether p falls inside the polygon.

Class **Scrollbar** extends **Component**

Symbolic Constants	
`int HORIZONTAL`	Indicates a horizontal scrollbar.
`int VERTICAL`	Indicates a vertical scrollbar.

Constructors	
`Scrollbar ()`	Creates a new vertical scrollbar.
`Scrollbar (int orient)`	Creates a new scrollbar with `orient` orientation.
`Scrollbar (int orient, int value, int visible,` `int min, int max)`	Creates a new scrollbar with `orient` orientation, `value` for its initial value, `visible` for the size of the bubble, and given `min` and `max` values.

Instance Methods	
`void addAdjustmentListener` `      (AdjustmentListener l)`	Makes `l` a listener for this scrollbar's adjustment events.
`int getBlockIncrement ()`	Returns the block increment value.
`int getMaximum ()`	Returns the maximum value.
`int getMinimum ()`	Returns the minimum value.
`int getOrientation ()`	Returns the orientation.
`int getUnitIncrement ()`	Returns the unit increment.
`int getValue ()`	Returns the current value of this scrollbar.
`int getVisibleAmount ()`	Returns the size of the bubble.
`void setBlockIncrement (int i)`	Sets the block increment to `i`.
`void setMaximum (int i)`	Sets the maximum value to `i`.
`void setMinimum (int i)`	Sets the minimum value to `i`.
`void setOrientation (int i)`	Sets the orientation to `i`.
`void setUnitIncrement (int i)`	Sets the unit increment to `i`.
`void setValue (int i)`	Sets the current value to `i`.
`void setVisibleAmount (int i)`	Sets the bubble size to `i`.

Class **TextArea** extends **TextComponent**

Constructors	
`TextArea ()`	Constructs a new text area.
`TextArea (int r, int c)`	Constructs a new empty text area with `r` rows and `c` columns.
`TextArea (String s)`	Constructs a new text area with `s` as the text.
`TextArea (String s, int r, int c)`	Constructs a new text area with `r` rows and `c` columns and with `s` as the text.

Instance Methods	
`void append (String s)`	Appends `s` to the text in this text area.
`int getColumns ()`	Gets the number of columns in this text area.
`int getRows ()`	Gets the number of rows in this text area.
`void insert (String s, int p)`	Inserts `s` at position `p` in this text area.
`void replaceRange (String s, int start,` `                int end)`	Replaces text between positions `start` and `end` with `s`.
`void setColumns (int c)`	Sets the number of columns to `c`.
`void setRows (int r)`	Sets the number of rows to `r`.

Class **TextComponent** extends **Component**

Instance Methods

`void addTextListener (TextListener l)`	Adds l as a listener for text events in this component.
`String getSelectedText ()`	Gets the highlighted text in this text field.
`String getText ()`	Gets the text in this text field.
`void setText (String s)`	Sets the text in this text field to s.

Class **TextField** extends **TextComponent**

Constructors

`TextField ()`	Constructs a new text field.
`TextField (int c)`	Constructs a new empty text field with c columns.
`TextField (String s)`	Constructs a new text field with s as the text.

Instance Methods

`void addActionListener (ActionListener l)`	Makes l a listener for action events from this text field.
`void setColumns (int c)`	Sets the number of columns to c.

Classes in the `java.awt.event` Package

All event classes (`ActionEvent`, `AdjustmentEvent`, etc.) are descendants of `EventObject`, so all respond to the `getSource` message. However, most are not subclasses of `EventObject`, but instead have one or more intervening classes. These have been omitted from this list.

Interface **ActionListener**
Action events are generated by buttons and text fields.

Instance Methods

`void actionPerformed (ActionEvent e)`	Called when any action event occurs.

Class **AdjustmentEvent** extends **EventObject**

Symbolic Constants	
`int UNIT_INCREMENT`	Value increment event (i.e., click on one end of scrollbar).
`int UNIT_DECREMENT`	Value decrement event (i.e., click on other end of scrollbar).
`int BLOCK_INCREMENT`	Block increment event (i.e., click within scrollbar).
`int BLOCK_DECREMENT`	Value changed (i.e., click in other part of scrollbar).
`int TRACK`	Absolute tracking event (i.e., move selector to specific position).

Instance Methods	
`int getAdjustmentType ()`	Returns the type of adjustment (one of the values listed above).
`int getValue ()`	Returns current value of scrollbar.

Interface **AdjustmentListener**
Adjustment events are generated by scrollbars.

Instance Methods	
`void adjustmentValueChanged (AdjustmentEvent e)`	Called when any adjustment event occurs.

Class **EventObject**

Instance Methods	
`public Object getSource ()`	Returns the object on which the event initially occurred.

Class **ItemEvent**

Symbolic Constants	
`int DESELECTED`	Indicates that the item was deselected.
`int SELECTED`	Indicates that the item was selected.

Instance Methods	
`int getStateChange ()`	Returns the type of state change (one of the values `SELECTED` or `DESELECTED`).

Interface **ItemListener**
Item events are generated by check boxes.

Method Declarations	
`void itemStateChanged (ItemEvent e)`	Called when any item event occurs.

Class **MouseEvent**

Instance Methods	
`Point getPoint()`	Returns the *x*, *y* position of the event.
`int getX()`	Returns the horizontal *x* position of the event.
`int getY()`	Returns the vertical *y* position of the event.

Interface **MouseListener**

Method Declarations

`void mouseClicked (MouseEvent e)`	Called when a mouse button is clicked.
`void mouseEntered (MouseEvent e)`	Called when the mouse enters a component area.
`void mouseExited (MouseEvent e)`	Called when the mouse leaves a component area.
`void mousePressed (MouseEvent e)`	Called when a mouse button is pressed.
`void mouseReleased (MouseEvent e)`	Called when a mouse button is released.

Interface **MouseMotionListener**

Method Declarations

`void mouseDragged (MouseEvent e)`	Called when mouse moves while button is depressed.
`void mouseMoved (MouseEvent e)`	Called when mouse moves.

Interface **TextListener**
Text events are generated by text fields and text boxes.

Method Declarations

`void textValueChanged (TextEvent e)`	Called when a text event occurs (`TextEvent` adds no methods or symbolic constants to `EventObject`).

Interface **WindowListener**
Window events are generated by mouse actions on a `Window` object.

Method declarations

`void windowActivated (WindowEvent e)`	Called when a window is activated.
`void windowClosed (WindowEvent e)`	Called when a window has been closed.
`void windowClosing (WindowEvent e)`	Called when a window is being closed.
`void windowDeactivated (WindowEvent e)`	Called when a window is deactivated.
`void windowDeiconified (WindowEvent e)`	Called when a window is deiconified.
`void windowIconified (WindowEvent e)`	Called when a window is iconified.
`void windowOpened (WindowEvent e)`	Called when a window is opened.

C.6

Classes in the `java.applet` Package

<table>
<tr><td colspan="2" align="center">Class Applet</td></tr>
<tr><td colspan="2" align="center">Instance Methods</td></tr>
<tr><td><code>URL getCodeBase ()</code></td><td>Returns the base URL from where this applet was loaded.</td></tr>
<tr><td><code>Image getImage (URL url)</code></td><td>Returns an image from the given URL.</td></tr>
<tr><td><code>void init ()</code></td><td>Called by the browser to inform this applet that it has been loaded.</td></tr>
<tr><td><code>void start ()</code></td><td>Called by the browser to inform this applet that it should start its execution.</td></tr>
<tr><td><code>void stop ()</code></td><td>Called by the browser to inform this applet that it should stop its execution.</td></tr>
</table>

<table>
<tr><td colspan="2" align="center">Class URL</td></tr>
<tr><td colspan="2" align="center">Constructors</td></tr>
<tr><td><code>URL (String s)</code></td><td>Creates a URL from a string specification. Throws <code>MalformedURLException</code>.</td></tr>
<tr><td colspan="2" align="center">Instance Methods</td></tr>
<tr><td><code>InputStream openStream ()</code></td><td>Opens a connection to the URL and returns an <code>InputStream</code> for reading. Throws <code>IOException</code>.</td></tr>
</table>

C.7

Classes in the `java.io` Package

<table>
<tr><td colspan="2" align="center">Class BufferedReader extends Reader</td></tr>
<tr><td colspan="2" align="center">Constructors</td></tr>
<tr><td><code>BufferedReader (Reader in)</code></td><td>Creates a new buffered reader from the reader <code>in</code>.</td></tr>
<tr><td colspan="2" align="center">Instance Methods (All methods throw <code>IOException</code>.)</td></tr>
<tr><td><code>String readLine ()</code></td><td>Returns a line of text.</td></tr>
</table>

Class **BufferedWriter** extends **Writer**

Constructors	
`BufferedWriter (Writer out)`	Creates a new buffered writer from the writer `out`.

Instance Methods (*All methods throw IOException.*)	
`void newLine ()`	Writes a line separator.

Class **FileReader** extends **Reader** (*via* **InputStreamReader**)

Constructors	
`FileReader (String filename)`	Creates a new file reader from `filename`.

Class **FileWriter** extends **Writer** (*via* **OutputStreamWriter**)

Constructors	
`FileWriter (String filename)`	Creates a new file writer from `filename`.

Class **PrintWriter** extends **Writer**

Constructors	
`PrintWriter (Writer out)`	Creates a new print writer from the writer `out`.

Instance Methods	
`void print (type item)`	Prints the `item` according to its *type*.
`void println (type item)`	Prints the `item` according to its *type*, followed by a line separator.

Abstract Class **Reader**

Instance Methods	
`void close ()`	Closes the stream.
`int read ()`	Reads a single character.
`int read (char[] cbuf, int off, int len)`	Reads `len` characters (or until end-of-file) into `cbuf[off]` and subsequent locations.

Abstract Class **Writer**

Instance Methods	
`void close ()`	Closes the stream.
`void flush ()`	Flushes the stream.
`void write (char c)`	Writes the character `c`.
`void write (char[] cbuf, int off, int len)`	Writes `cbuf[off]` ... `cbuf[off+len-1]`.

D

UML CLASS DIAGRAMS

The Unified Modeling Language (UML) is a diagrammatic language used for illustrating the structure and semantics object-oriented systems. It has emerged as an industry standard and is promulgated by the Object Management Group. The complete specifications for UML can be found at the OMG UML resource pages: `http://www.omg.org` and in various books mentioned in the Further Readings section of this book.

As the name implies, the UML is a *language*. It has a *vocabulary* of diagrammatic *icons*, together with grammatical rules for constructing complete diagrams from the vocabulary icons. There are several types of diagrams that can be constructed to describe different aspects of systems. Classes and objects are described using *class diagrams*. High-level reactions of objects to external and internal stimuli are described using *use-case diagrams*. The interactions of objects over time are described using *sequence diagrams* and *collaboration diagrams*. And the dynamic behavior of a system is described by *statecharts*.

class diagrams
use-case diagrams
sequence diagrams

collaboration diagrams
statecharts

In this book, we have used only class diagrams. In this appendix, we summarize the icons and rules for constructing class diagrams. The UML is independent of any implementation language, but since Java is an object-oriented language, Java's features are closely reflected by the features of UML. In particular, the notions of *class* and *object* in Java correspond exactly to class and object in UML. There are some slight differences between Java's terminology and that of UML, as well as differences in the syntactic way that methods and variables are specified. We shall point out these differences as we encounter them.

UML class diagrams provide static modeling of a system by specifying both the classes and the relationships between classes, shown as links between the class icons.

D.1

Specifying a Class

Each class specifies a pattern by which objects of that class can be produced. As in Java, the state of an object is specified by the instance variables and class variables of the class; Java instance and class variables are called *attributes* in UML parlance. Further, the methods of a Java class offer services to manipulate the state of the system; Java methods are called *operations* in UML parlance.

attributes
operations

The icon for a class is a rectangle with three vertically stacked panels. The name of the class is given in the topmost panel, the attributes in the middle panel, and the operations in the bottom panel. Each attribute v is listed, together with its type T, using the form v : T. Optionally, initial values can be given for an attribute, using the form

    v : T = initial-value

Each operation is listed as a method heading, with the return type T (if any) of the method indicated by : T, and with the type of each argument shown.

Java instance variables, class variables, and methods can have visibility of public, private, or protected. The same is true of UML attributes and operations. In UML, public is indicated by a plus prefix (+), private by a minus prefix (-), and protected by a sharp prefix (#). In addition, a class variable or class method—called *static* or *class scope* in UML—is indicated by underlining. Also, a Java final instance variable or class variable is indicated by appending the *property* {frozen}.

static
class scope
UML property

For example, the Date class from Chapter 10 included

```
class Date {
...
  public final static String[]
      DAY_NAME = {"Sun", "Mon", "Tue", "Wed",
                  "Thu", "Fri", "Sat"};
...
  private int
      m, // the month of this instance of Date
      d, // the day of this instance of Date
      y; // the year of this instance of Date
...
    public static boolean leapYear (int y) {...}
...
}
```

This would have the following class diagram:

Date
+DAY_NAME: String[] = {"Sun","Mon","Tue","Wed",   "Thu","Fri"} {frozen} -m: int -d: int -y: int
+leapYear(y:int): boolean

In the Date class diagram above, the class variable DAY_NAME is public, static, and final, while the instance variables m, d, and y are private (and nonstatic). The class method leapYear is public and static.

Sometimes the names of method arguments are omitted, as in

Date
+DAY_NAME: String[] = {"Sun","Mon","Tue","Wed", "Thu","Fri"} {frozen}
-m: int -d: int -y: int
+leapYear(int): boolean

Often the attributes of a class are unknown, or of no interest, so the middle panel is sometimes left vacant, as in

Date
+leapYear(int): boolean

Sometimes the operations are also omitted; in that case, only the name panel is shown, as in

Date

D.1.1　Abstract Classes

We know that if one or more of the Java methods are abstract, then the class itself is abstract. UML distinguishes an abstract operation by italicizing the method heading and further distinguishes an abstract class by italicizing its name. The Java class

```
class MyClass {
    public int x;
    private double y;
    static protected char c;
    public static int add (int p, int q) { ... }
    private abstract void mine (double p);
}
```

would be diagrammed as

MyClass
+x: int -y: double #c: char
+add(p:int,q:int): int *-mine(p:double)*

D.1.2　Object Icons

Often it is useful to display an instance of a class, rather than the class. The object icons are like class icons, with the topmost panel containing the name of the object and its class, both underlined. Underlining indicates that we have an instance, rather than a class. (This is consistent with the underlining of class variables, since they can be viewed as class-scope instances.) Sometimes the class and instance variables are also shown, together with their values, if available. However, it is not necessary to underline them. Some modelers like to give some indication of which variables were inherited from parent classes, by adding a prefix (typically slash /). Methods are usually not shown, but they can be. Here is an example:

cat : Animal
hairless = false color = red weight = 10 domesticated = false

D.2

Associations

Associations show the static or logical relationships between pairs of classes or objects. Generally, an association exists when one object has another as an attribute. The only associations that are of interest are those that persist for a nonnegligible period of time compared to the life cycles of the instances of the associated classes. For example, an "initialize" relationship would not generally rise to the level of an association.

association

Associations are indicated by solid lines connecting classes and are often "annotated" with text and "adorned" in various ways. The name of the association may be written near the center of the connecting line. This name is often a transitive verb, with one class name used as the subject and the other used as the object. Therefore, the subject-verb-object can be read as a sentence. Usually a filled arrowhead shows the direction in which the association should be read. An example is

Each end of an association can assume a *role*, perhaps with special conditions applying to that role, with the name of the role written at the end of the line near the class that plays the role.

role

A *multiplicity* adornment shows the number of objects from one class that relates to a number of objects from the associated class. Possibilities are

multiplicity

`1`	exactly one
`1..n`	one to n
`1..*`	one or more
`*`	zero or more
`0..1`	zero or one

An example is

This indicates that one company is related to multiple persons (at least one) in the role of an employer; and conversely all employees have a single employer. (This is not to say that only one employer exists; it just says that each employee is employed by only one company. In other words, it says that a person cannot work two jobs.)

Sometimes the association has an open-arrow adornment at one end. This indicates that one class knows about the other, but not vice versa. In the absence of such a one-way arrow, an association is considered to be two-way (i.e., each class "knows about" the other).

D.3

Inheritance and Generalization

In Java, one class, C, can extend another class, P. The class C is the child, and P is the parent. In UML, this relationship is indicated by a solid line with a closed, unfilled arrowhead at the parent end, as in

D.4

Aggregations

A class may be made up of other classes—a whole-part relationship, sometimes called a *has-a* relationship. This is indicated in UML by a solid line with an unfilled diamond at the whole end, as in

Another relationship, called *composition*, is a strong form of aggregation, in which the part can "belong" to only one whole. Composition is indicated by a solid line with a *filled* diamond at the whole end, as in

composition

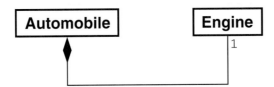

D.5

Interfaces and Realization

In UML, an interface is a fully abstract class without attributes. It is shown as a class with the designation `<<interface>>` above the name. A word enclosed in guillemets (≪≫), such as `<<interface>>`, is called a *stereotype* in UML. An interface is *implemented* by a class, indicated by a dashed line with a closed, unfilled arrowhead at the interface end. This relationship is called *realization*. An example is

stereotype
implemented
realization

In the above diagram, the class `ClickableClock` implements the interface `MouseListener`.

In Java, an interface is allowed as well to have final class variables, thereby providing symbolic constants. Strictly speaking, this is not allowed in a UML interface, but we'll show such constants in the usual UML way—public, class scope, and frozen, with initial values specified.

It often makes sense to group the methods of a class—constructors, accessors, etc., including those methods that provide the implementation for an interface. Such groups of methods can be separated by stereotypes. Then it makes sense to anchor the tail of the "realizes" association near the method(s) that actually implements the interface.

An example was the `ClickableClock` class from Chapter 11:

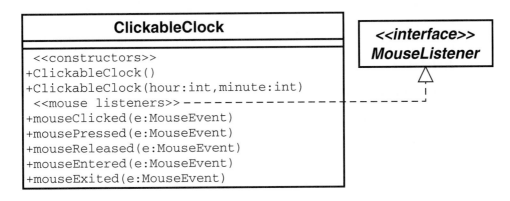

JAVADOC AND CSLIB

We are now prepared to show the details of portions of the CSLib classes. We illustrate how to use inner classes, including anonymous inner classes. We also show how the Javadoc® product from Sun Microsystems can be used to produce online documentation for your programs.

Javadoc

Javadoc reads your code files and automatically creates HTML files that contain documentation about your code. Javadoc obtains its information from your source code and from related source code, in a number of ways.

1. *Documentation comments.* These are comments that begin with the characters /** and end with the characters */.
2. *Javadoc tags.* These are special tags that are embedded within Javadoc comments and that provide the information necessary to formulate a complete description of your application. Javadoc tags have the format *@tagname further_information*—. An example is @author Sir Arthur Conan Doyle.
3. *Variable declarations.* Javadoc reads and records all information regarding declarations of class variables and instance variables. This information is used to document the types and modifiers of class and instance variables.
4. *Method declarations.* Javadoc reads and records all information in method headings. This information is used to document the return types and modifiers of class and instance methods as well as the types of a method's arguments.

We have run Javadoc on our CSLib code, and the resulting HTML documentation is linked to on the book's web site, www.mhhe.com/engcs/compsci/kamin.

E.1.1 Invoking Javadoc

Javadoc must be invoked from the command line—either the DOS prompt or a unix prompt. The (simplified) form of the command is

```
javadoc [options] [packagenames] [sourcefiles]
```

where [options] specifies an optional list of options, [packagenames] specifies an optional list of package names, and [sourcefiles] specifies an optional list of Java file names. The most commonly used options are

-help	Shows all possible options.
-public	Shows only public classes and members.
-protected	Shows only protected and public classes and members.
-private	Shows all classes and members.
-sourcepath *pathlist*	Specifies where to find source files.
-classpath *pathlist*	Specifies where to find class files.
-d *directory*	Specifies the destination directory for the HTML files.

You can specify names of packages, and Javadoc will document all classes in those packages. Those classes must be located in the appropriate directories, with the directory paths corresponding to the package names. You can also specify individual source files, using the form name.java. Either you can specify the complete path to the file (as in /home/mysrc/stuff/Secret.java), or you can run javadoc from the directory that contains the source file.

E.1.2 Documentation Comments

Javadoc comments are placed before the declarations of classes, constructors, methods, instance variables, and class variables. A Javadoc comment begins with the characters /** and ends with the characters */. In between, the comment may span several lines; it is conventional to begin each such line with the character *, indented so that the * is aligned vertically with the first * in the opening /**. The *commentary body* of the Javadoc comment consists of the text between the initial /** and the final */, while ignoring

Javadoc comments

commentary body

- Newline characters.
- On intermediate lines, all whitespace up to the initial * and the * itself.

In order for the Javadoc comment to be associated properly with a declaration, the comment must appear *immediately* ahead of the declaration. No intervening code may appear. (However, blank lines are okay.)

A Javadoc commentary body begins with a *description* consisting of some number of sentences, followed by some number of *tags*. The tags start with the first at-sign (@) that begins a line in the commentary body. The commentary body is written in HTML, using standard HTML tags to signify font changes, paragraphing, etc. Some of the standard HTML tags that you might use are

Javadoc description

Javadoc tag

`<i>text</i>`	Italicizes text.
`<b>text</b>`	Makes text boldface.
`<code>text</code>`	Sets text in the code font.
`<p>`	Starts a new paragraph.
`&amp`	Inserts the ampersand symbol.
`&lt`	Inserts the less-than symbol.
`&gt`	Inserts the greater-than symbol.

The first sentence of the Javadoc commentary body should be a concise description of the declaration being documented. This sentence is used in the *summary section* of the generated HTML documentation. This first sentence and subsequent sentences are used in the detailed documentation for the class, variable, or method.

The commentary for a class often uses complete sentences. However, for methods and attributes (instance variables and class variables), it is conventional for Javadoc comments to be formulated as phrases when a complete sentence would be unnecessarily wordy. It is also conventional for the commentary to be written using the third person rather than the second person. For example, in the `windowClosing` method in the `ClosableFrame` class detailed below, the Javadoc comment reads "Cleans up the window, and terminates the program" rather than "Clean up the window, and terminate the program." Indeed, method comments usually begin with a verb phrase in the third person.

E.1.3   Javadoc Tags

Javadoc tags are special keywords that start with the @ character. Tags have affiliated text, which includes all text from the tag name up to the next tag (or the end of the Javadoc comment). Some of the Javadoc tags that we have used in our commentary are

@author *name*	Names the author of the class or method.
@param *parameter-name description*	Describes a parameter for a method.
@return *description*	Describes what is returned by a method.
@see *package.Class#member*	Adds an entry in the "See Also" section of the documentation file, which points to the documentation for the cited member (method or instance variable or class variable).
@throws *classname description*	Describes exceptions that this method throws.

In the @see tag, there is some flexibility in how you may refer to a method. You may spell out its argument list, including the names of the arguments. Or you may spell out its argument list, including only the types of the arguments. Or you may cite only the method name; in this case, Javadoc will link to the first method in the cited class that has that name. If you omit the *package* name, then Javadoc will look for the cited class in the current and imported packages. If you also omit the *Class* name, then Javadoc will look only in the current class for the cited method, instance variable, or class variable.

E.2

The CSLib Package

E.2.1   Timer

We begin with the `Timer` class, which provides a single static method `pause(long)` that pauses a program for a specified number of milliseconds. The code is quite short, and it begins to illustrate how Javadoc comments are used:

```
1    package CSLib;
2
3    /**
4     * <code>Timer</code> is a utility class for causing a program to
5     * pause for a specified period of time.
```

```
 6      *
 7      * @author    M. Dennis Mickunas
 8      */
 9     public class Timer {
10
11       /**
12        * Pauses for a specific period of time.
13        *
14        * @see      java.lang.Thread#sleep(long)
15        *
16        * @param    msec  the specific number of milliseconds to pause.
17        */
18       public static void pause (long msec) {
19         try {Thread.sleep(msec);}
20         catch (InterruptedException e) {}
21       }
22     }
```

Examining the Javadoc class comments in lines 3 through 9, we see that they begin with the characters /** and end with the characters */. In between, it is conventional to start each line with the character * and to line up the asterisks as shown. There is another reason to use the asterisk to start the other comment lines—Javadoc ignores any spaces before the asterisk, but preserves any spaces or indentation *after* the asterisk on a line. So if you fail to begin a line with an asterisk, Javadoc will ignore any indentation that you might have provided.

In the Javadoc class comments, we see an example of embedded HTML formatting with the <code>...</code> tags. We also see examples of the @author, @see, and @param tags. In particular, the tag

    @see   java.lang.Thread#sleep(long)

refers to the sleep(long) method in class java.lang.Thread.

As for the code itself, the pause method just calls Java's Thread.sleep(long) method. Thread.sleep waits for the specified number of milliseconds, then throws an InterruptedException. By catching this exception, the pause method can resume execution.

A screen shot of the Javadoc web page for Timer class is shown in Figure E.1.

E.2.2 ClosableFrame

We have already discussed the class ClosableFrame in Chapter 13, and we saw its code in Figure 13.8 on page 490; here we present it complete with Javadoc comments. We also reiterate some observations regarding the "window-closing" event handling.

```
 1     package CSLib;
 2
 3     import java.awt.*;
 4     import java.awt.event.*;
 5
 6     /**
 7      * <code>ClosableFrame</code> is a base class that obeys the
 8      * <code>windowClosing </code> event. It is intended that the
 9      * student extend this class instead of <code>Frame</code>.
10      *
11      * @see    java.awt.Frame
12      * @see    java.awt.event.WindowListener
13      *
```

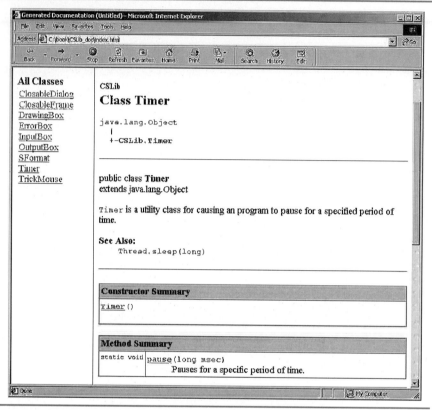

FIGURE E.1   A screen shot of Javadoc web documentation.

```
14      * @author M. Dennis Mickunas
15      */
16     public class ClosableFrame extends Frame implements WindowListener {
17
18       /**
19        * Class constructor, creating a frame that can respond to the
20        * "window closing" event; the frame will have a blank title.
21        */
22       public ClosableFrame () {
23         this("");
24       }
25
26       /**
27        * Class constructor, creating a frame that can respond to the
28        * "window closing" event; the frame will have a specific title.
29        *
30        * @param  title    the specific title for this frame.
31        */
32       public ClosableFrame (String title) {
33         super(title);
34         addWindowListener(this);
```

```
35        }
36
37        /**
38         * Cleans up the window, and terminates the program.
39         *
40         * @param   e     the specific <code>WindowEvent</code> that occurred.
41         */
42        public void windowClosing (WindowEvent e) {
43          dispose();
44          System.exit(0);
45        }
46        /**
47         * Vacuous implementation.
48         */
49        public void windowActivated (WindowEvent e) {}
50        /**
51         * Vacuous implementation.
52         */
53        public void windowClosed (WindowEvent e) {}
54        /**
55         * Vacuous implementation.
56         */
57        public void windowOpened (WindowEvent e) {}
58        /**
59         * Vacuous implementation.
60         */
61        public void windowDeactivated (WindowEvent e) {}
62        /**
63         * Vacuous implementation.
64         */
65        public void windowDeiconified (WindowEvent e) {}
66        /**
67         * Vacuous implementation.
68         */
69        public void windowIconified (WindowEvent e) {}
70
71      }
```

Recall that we wanted this code to "listen for" the "window-closing" event. To accomplish this, we have the class implement the WindowListener interface; that interface specifies methods for seven different window events, including windowClosing. Our code provides the implementation for the windowClosing method in lines 37 through 45. However, we are obliged also to implement the other six methods (in lines 46 through 69), even though we are not interested in the events that they listen for. If we insist on providing Javadoc comments for each method, then we end up with uninteresting comments like those shown.

E.2.3 ClosableDialog

The ClosableDialog class closely resembles ClosableFrame, except that it extends Dialog instead of Frame. In this class, we wish to illustrate the use of an inner class to listen for the window-closing event.

```
1       package CSLib;
2
3       import java.awt.*;
4       import java.awt.event.*;
5
```

```
6    /**
7     * <code>ClosableDialog</code> is a base class that obeys the
8     * <code>windowClosing </code> event. It is extended by various
9     * <code>CSLib</code> classes.  It uses an inner class,
10    * <code>DialogCloser</code> to implement the windowClosing listener,
11    * with <code>DialogCloser</code> extending the <code>WindowAdapter</code>
12    * class.
13    * <p>
14    * <code>ClosableDialog</code> should be compared with
15    * <code>ClosableFrame</code>, which implements the
16    * <code>WindowListener</code> methods individually.
17    *
18    * @see      ClosableFrame
19    * @see      java.awt.event.WindowAdapter
20    * @see      java.awt.Dialog
21    *
22    * @author M. Dennis Mickunas
23    */
24   public class ClosableDialog extends Dialog {
25
26     /**
27      * Constructs a non-modal dialog box in a new frame with a blank title;
28      * this dialog box can respond to the "window closing" event.
29      */
30     public ClosableDialog () {
31       this (new Frame(), "", false);
32     }
33
34     /**
35      * Constructs a dialog box in a new frame with a blank title and a
36      * specified modality; this dialog box can respond to the
37      * "window closing" event.
38      *
39      * @param modal the specified modality
40      */
41     public ClosableDialog (boolean modal) {
42       this (new Frame(), "", modal);
43     }
44
45     /**
46      * Constructs a non-modal dialog box in a new frame with a specified
47      * title; this dialog box can respond to the "window closing" event.
48      *
49      * @param title the string to use as this ClosableDialog title
50      */
51     public ClosableDialog (String title) {
52       this (new Frame(), title, false);
53     }
54
55     /**
56      * Constructs a dialog box in a new frame with a specified title and
57      * modality; this dialog box can respond to the "window closing" event.
58      *
59      * @param     title     the string to use as this ClosableDialog title
```

```
60        * @param    modal     the specified modality
61        */
62       public ClosableDialog (String title, boolean modal) {
63          this (new Frame(), title, modal);
64       }
65
66       /**
67        * Constructs a dialog box with a specified title and modality;
68        * this dialog box can respond to the "window closing" event.
69        *
70        * @param    home      a Frame to parent this Dialog Box
71        * @param    title     the string to use as this ClosableDialog title
72        * @param    modal     the specified modality
73        */
74       public ClosableDialog (Frame home, String title, boolean modal) {
75          super(home, title, modal);
76          addWindowListener(new DialogCloser());
77       }
78
79       /**
80        * <code>DialogCloser</code> is an inner class that implements the
81        * windowClosing listener for <code>ClosableDialog</code>.  It does this
82        * by extending the Java convenience wrapper <code>WindowAdapter</code>.
83        *
84        * @see    java.awt.event.WindowAdapter
85        */
86       class DialogCloser extends WindowAdapter {
87          /**
88           * Cleans up the window, and terminates the program.
89           *
90           * @param    e  The specific <code>WindowEvent</code> that occurred.
91           */
92          public void windowClosing (WindowEvent e) {
93             dispose();
94             System.exit(0);
95          }
96       }
97    }
```

The only novelty in Javadoc is the use in the Javadoc class comments of the HTML <p> tag in line 13, which starts a new paragraph in the HTML documentation.

The constructors for ClosableDialog are a bit more complicated than those for ClosableFrame. This is because the parent class, Dialog, requires more constructor arguments than Frame required. For a Dialog, we must provide a Frame to act as the "home" for the Dialog; we must also specify whether the Dialog is to be *modal* or not, that is, whether the box will block further program execution *modal* until it is closed by the user. We have a very general constructor in lines 66 through 77, which allows the programmer to specify the frame, the title, and the modality. This constructor is called (using the this(...) methodology) by the other constructors. Those other constructors provide convenient ways for the programmer to accept a default frame, or a blank title, or a default modality. We did not provide every possible combination, but provided those that made sense. (That is, we reasoned that if anything were to be optional, it would be the frame.)

One important issue to note is that we provided a zero-argument constructor. It is unlikely that any programmer would utilize this constructor; at the least, a programmer would want to specify the modality of a ClosableDialog. Nonetheless, it is considered good programming practice to supply a zero-argument constructor whenever you build a public class that *might* be extended. This constructor

> ## *Always Provide a Zero-Argument Constructor.*
>
> When you write a class that might be extended, always provide a zero-argument constructor. That way, you can be sure that all the necessary initialization will be done.

should do all the routine setup work that would be expected—in this case, creating the frame and calling the "big" constructor that adds the window listener.

Why should we provide such a constructor? Consider what would happen if a programmer were to write

```
public class MyMouseListeningClosableDialog extends ClosableDialog
                                            implements MouseListener {

  public MyClosableDialog () {
    addMouseListener(this);
  }
  ...
}
```

Do you see what would happen? Since the programmer did not supply a call to super(...) as the first statement in the constructor, Java inserts a call super(), causing ClosableDialog's zero-argument constructor to be called. Had we failed to provide a zero-argument constructor for ClosableDialog, then Java would have automatically supplied one for us—but it would not do anything except call super(), the zero-argument constructor for Dialog. In the end, we would get some sort of dialog box, *but it would not have had a window listener set up for it.*

Turning now to the way we attach a "window listener" to this class, we see that in line 76 we pass a new object, created from the class DialogCloser. Compare this to line 34 in ClosableFrame. There we passed "this" object.

The class DialogCloser *could* be written as a separate class, but it is preferable to show its implementation here, close to where it will be instantiated. We use an inner class for that—see Section A.6 on page 675. The inner class is shown in lines 79 through 96. Notice that it extends WindowAdapter, which is a Java-supplied trivial implementation of the WindowListener interface. It looks like this:

```
public abstract class WindowAdapter implements WindowListener {
    public void windowOpened(WindowEvent e) {}
    public void windowClosing(WindowEvent e) {}
    public void windowClosed(WindowEvent e) {}
    public void windowIconified(WindowEvent e) {}
    public void windowDeiconified(WindowEvent e) {}
    public void windowActivated(WindowEvent e) {}
    public void windowDeactivated(WindowEvent e) {}
}
```

The only method that we're interested in overriding is windowClosing, in lines 87 through 95.

Finally, notice that we provide Javadoc comments for the inner class DialogCloser, just as with a regular class. We also provide Javadoc comments for the methods of an inner class.

E.2.4 OutputBox

The class OutputBox is quite straightforward, but very tedious.

```
1    package CSLib;
2
```

```
3    import java.awt.*;
4
5    /**
6     * <code>OutputBox</code> is a closable frame that holds textual output.
7     * It mimics Java's <code>java.lang.System.out</code>, which is
8     * a <code>java.io.PrintStream</code>.
9     *
10    * @see        java.io.PrintStream
11    * @see        java.awt.TextArea
12    *
13    * @author    M. Dennis Mickunas
14    */
15   public class OutputBox extends ClosableFrame {
16
17      /**
18       * the area where output is printed
19       */
20      private TextArea outputArea;
21      private Font font;
22      private static final int WIDTH = 550;
23      private static final int HEIGHT = 380;
24
25      /**
26       * Constructs an OutputBox with a default title.
27       */
28      public OutputBox () {
29        this("OutputBox");
30      }
31
32      /**
33       * Constructs an OutputBox with a specific title.
34       *
35       * @param    title  the specific <code>String</code> to use as the title
36       */
37      public OutputBox (String title) {
38        super(title);
39        setResizable(true);
40        outputArea = new TextArea();
41        add(outputArea);
42        setSize(WIDTH, HEIGHT);
43        setVisible(true);
44        validate();
45        setFont(new Font("Courier", Font.PLAIN, 12));
46      }
47
48      /**
49       * Erases the text in the OutputBox.
50       */
51      public void clear () { outputArea.setText(""); }
52
53      /**
54       * Changes the font for subsequent printing.
55       *
56       * @param    font  the specific <code>Font</code> to change to.
```

```
57         */
58        public void setFont (Font font) {
59            outputArea.setFont(font);
60            this.font = font;
61        }
62
63        /**
64         * Prints a string.  The string printed is just what would be
65         * printed by <code>java.lang.System.out.print(String)</code>.
66         *
67         * @param   text   the <code>String</code> to be printed
68         */
69        public void print (String text) { outputArea.append(text); }
70
71        /**
72         * Prints an integer.  The string printed is just what would be
73         * printed by <code>java.lang.System.out.print(int)</code>.
74         *
75         * @param   number   the <code>int</code> to be printed
76         */
77        public void print (int number) { print("" + number); }
78
79        /**
80         * Prints a floating-point number.  The string printed is just what
81         * would be printed by <code>java.lang.System.out.print(float)</code>.
82         *
83         * @param   number   the <code>float</code> to be printed
84         */
85        public void print (float number) { print("" + number); }
86
87        /**
88         * Prints a double-precision floating-point number.  The string
89         * printed is just what would be printed by
90         * <code>java.lang.System.out.print(double)</code>.
91         *
92         * @param   number   the <code>double</code> to be printed
93         */
94        public void print (double number) { print("" + number); }
            ...

129       /**
130        * Terminates the current line by writing a carriage return character
131        * followed by a newline character.
132        */
133       public void println () { outputArea.append("\r\n"); }
134
135       /**
136        * Prints a String and then terminates the line.  This method
137        * invokes <code>print(String)</code> and then <code>println()</code>.
138        *
139        * @param   number   the <code>String</code> to be printed.
140        */
141       public void println (String text) { print(text); println(); }
142
```

```
143      /**
144       * Prints an integer and then terminates the line.  This method behaves as
145       * though it invokes <code>print(int)</code> and then
146       * <code>println()</code>.
147       *
148       * @param    number   the <code>int</code> to be printed.
149       */
150      public void println (int number) { println("" + number); }
151
152      /**
153       * Prints a float and then terminates the line.  This method behaves as
154       * though it invokes <code>print(float)</code> and then
155       * <code>println()</code>.
156       *
157       * @param    number   the <code>float</code> to be printed.
158       */
159      public void println (float number) { println("" + number); }
160
161      /**
162       * Prints a double and then terminates the line.  This method behaves as
163       * though it invokes <code>print(double)</code> and then
164       * <code>println()</code>.
165       *
166       * @param    number   the <code>double</code> to be printed.
167       */
168      public void println (double number) { println("" + number); }

         ...
     }
```

An OutputBox is simply a ClosableFrame into which is placed a TextArea (see Table 13.4 on page 480). Since the default layout manager for a Frame is BorderLayout, the add statement in line 41 is an abbreviation for add(outputArea, BorderLayout.CENTER), which causes the TextArea to expand to fill the entire Frame. The TextArea is manipulated directly by only a few methods.

- The clear() method (lines 48 through 51) uses setText to erase the contents of the TextArea.
- The setFont(Font) method (lines 53 through 61) calls the TextArea's corresponding setFont(Font) method.
- The print(String) method (lines 63 through 69) uses the append method to add to the contents of the TextArea.
- The println() method (lines 129 through 133) uses the append method to add to the contents of the TextArea.

All other methods of OutputBox call the foregoing print or println methods (or each other). For example, the print(int) method just converts its argument to a String by appending "", and then calls print(String).

E.2.5 ErrorBox

As we have seen with our programs, ErrorBox is a dialog box that is used when we wish to present an error message. It extends our ClosableDialog class and is modal.

```
1     package CSLib;
2
```

```java
3    import java.awt.*;
4    import java.awt.event.*;
5
6    /**
7     * <code>ErrorBox</code> is a dialog box used for presenting error
8     * messages.   It remains visible until the user dismisses it by
9     * clicking the "Dismiss" button.
10    *
11    * @author    M. Dennis Mickunas
12    */
13
14   public class ErrorBox extends ClosableDialog implements ActionListener {
15
16     /**
17      * For displaying the text of the error message
18      */
19     private Label errorMessage;
20     private Button dismissButton;
21     private Font font = new Font("Helvetica", Font.PLAIN, 12);
22     private static final int MIN_HEIGHT = 100;
23     private static final int MIN_WIDTH = 200;
24
25     /**
26      * Constructs a modal error box with a generic error message.
27      */
28     public ErrorBox () {
29       this("Error");
30     }
31
32     /**
33      * Constructs a modal error box with a specific error message.
34      *
35      * @param    errorText  the string to be used as the error message
36      */
37     public ErrorBox (String errorText) {
38       super("Error", true);
39       setResizable(false);
40       setForeground(Color.black);
41       setBackground(Color.white);
42       setLayout(new GridLayout(2, 1));
43
44       // Places the error message
45       errorMessage = new Label(" "+errorText+" ", Label.CENTER);
46       errorMessage.setFont(font);
47       add(errorMessage);
48
49       // Places the dismiss button
50       dismissButton = new Button("Dismiss");
51       dismissButton.addActionListener(this);
52       Panel p = new Panel();
53       p.add(dismissButton);
54       add(p);
55
56       // Adjusts the box size if necessary to look decent.
```

```
57      int width = getSize().width;
58      int height = getSize().height;
59      if (width < MIN_WIDTH) width = MIN_WIDTH;
60      if (height < MIN_HEIGHT) height = MIN_HEIGHT;
61      setSize(width, height);
62
63      setVisible(true);
64    }
65
66    /**
67     * Listens for the button press.  The action is to dispose of this
68     * error box, thereby returning control to the program that created
69     * this error box.
70     *
71     * @param   e  the ActionEvent that occurred
72     */
73    public void actionPerformed (ActionEvent e) {
74        dispose();
75    }
76  }
```

There is nothing in the Javadoc that we have not already seen.

The code itself is very straightforward, but provides an exercise in doing component layout. The layout is done in the constructor, in lines 42 through 54. We want the text of the error message to be placed just above the "dismiss" button. You would initially think that placing the Label and the Button directly into a simple 2 × 1 GridLayout would do the trick. The Label can indeed be added directly to the top cell. But if you place a Button in the bottom cell, it will expand to fill the entire cell! What must be done is that first the Button must be added to a Panel (where the default layout manager is FlowLayout) and then that Panel can be added to the bottom cell.

E.2.6 InputBox

The InputBox, like ErrorBox, extends ClosableDialog. In addition to the Label and Button that the ErrorBox has, the InputBox has a TextField into which the user types characters. The input can be a single character, or the characters of a string, or the characters of an integer, or the characters of a decimal number. Thus, there are four methods that return, respectively, a char, a String, an int, and a double.

```
1    package CSLib;
2
3    import java.awt.*;
4    import java.awt.event.*;
5
6    /**
7     * <code>InputBox</code> is a closable dialog box that can receive and
8     * translate textual keyword input into various Java types.  It can read
9     * and convert integers, doubles, strings, and characters.
10    * <p>
11    * The user must enter characters into a TextField, and then click on
12    * the "OK" button.  If the characters are inappropriate for the
13    * particular <code>read</code> that has been requested (for example,
14    * if a letter is entered during a call to <code>readInt</code>),
15    * then an <code>ErrorBox</code> is raised.
16    * <p>
17    * End-of-input is indicated by the user entering nothing into the
```

```
18      * TextField, and then clicking on the "OK" button.
19      *
20      * @author      M. Dennis Mickunas
21      */
22
23     public class InputBox extends ClosableDialog implements ActionListener {
24
25       private TextField inputLine;
26       private Label prompt;
27       private Button okButton;
28       private Font font = new Font("Helvetica",Font.PLAIN, 12);
29       /**
30        * set to true when end-of-input has been indicated
31        * (by the user entering an empty field).
32        */
33       private boolean eoi = false;
34
35       private static final int MIN_WIDTH = 200;
36       private static final int MIN_HEIGHT = 150;
37
38       /**
39        * Constructs an InputBox with a default title.
40        */
41       public InputBox () {
42         this("InputBox");
43       }
44
45       /**
46        * Constructs an InputBox with a specific title.
47        *
48        * @param      title  the <code>String</code> to use as the title
49        */
50       public InputBox (String title) {
51         // Creates a modal ClosableDialog with the specified title.
52         super(title, true);
53
54         setResizable(false);
55         setForeground(Color.black);
56         setBackground(Color.white);
57         setLayout(new GridLayout(3,1));
58
59         prompt = new Label("Enter Data:", Label.CENTER);
60         prompt.setFont(font);
61         add(prompt);
62
63         inputLine = new TextField(15);
64         inputLine.setFont(font);
65         Panel p = new Panel();
66         p.add(inputLine);
67         add(p);
68
69         okButton = new Button("OK");
70         okButton.addActionListener(this);
71         p = new Panel();
```

```
72        p.add(okButton);
73        add(p);
74     }
75
76     /**
77      * Sets the prompt to a particular string.
78      *
79      * @param    text  the specific <code>String</code> to use for the new prompt
80      */
81     public void setPrompt(String text) {
82        prompt.setText(text);
83     }
84
85     /**
86      * Makes the InputBox visible so that the user can enter input.
87      * The size is adjusted to accommodate the prompt, if necessary.
88      */
89     private void display() {
90        hide();
91        inputLine.setText("");
92        FontMetrics fm = Toolkit.getDefaultToolkit().getFontMetrics(font);
93        int promptWidth = fm.stringWidth(prompt.getText());
94        int inputLineWidth = inputLine.getPreferredSize().width;
95        int windowWidth = Math.max(promptWidth, inputLineWidth) + 70;
96        int width = Math.max(windowWidth, MIN_WIDTH);
97        setSize(width, MIN_HEIGHT);
98        show();
99     }
100
101     /**
102      * Catches the clicking of the OK button (presumably after text has
103      * been entered in the textfield.
104      *
105      * @param    e  the specific <code>ActionEvent</code> that occurred.
106      */
107     public void actionPerformed(ActionEvent e) {
108         hide();
109     }
110
111     /**
112      * Gets the character string that the user types.  If end-of-input
113      * had been previously satisfied, then further input is ignored.
114      *
115      * @see       #eoi
116      * @return    the <code>String</code> that was typed.
117      */
118     private String getInputLine() {
119        if (eoi) return "";
120        String s = inputLine.getText();
121        eoi = s.length() == 0;
122        return s;
123     }
124
125     /**
```

```
126        * Reads an Ascii string.
127        * End-of-input is indicated by clicking OK without entering anything.
128        *
129        * @return   the <code>String</code> value read.
130        */
131       public String readString() {
132         display();
133         return getInputLine();
134       }
135
136       /**
137        * Reads an Ascii character, and converts it to an <code>char</code>.
138        * End-of-input is indicated by clicking OK without entering anything.
139        *
140        * @see      #eoi
141        * @return   the <code>char</code> value read.
142        */
143       public char readChar() {
144         display();
145         String s = getInputLine();
146         if (eoi) return 0;
147         return s.charAt(0);
148       }
149
150       /**
151        * Reads an Ascii integer, and converts it to an <code>int</code>.
152        * Raise an ErrorBox if a non-integer is entered.
153        * End-of-input is indicated by clicking OK without entering anything.
154        *
155        * @see      #eoi
156        * @return   the <code>int</code> value read.
157        */
158       public int readInt () {
159         display();
160         while (true) {
161             String s = getInputLine();
162             if (eoi) return 0;
163             try {
164               return Integer.parseInt(s);
165             }
166             catch (NumberFormatException e) {
167               error("Integer required ");
168             }
169         };
170       }
171
172       /**
173        * Reads an Ascii real number, and converts it to a <code>double</code>.
174        * Raise an ErrorBox if a non-real number is entered.
175        * End-of-input is indicated by clicking OK without entering anything.
176        *
177        * @see      #eoi
178        * @return   the <code>double</code> value read.
179        */
```

```
180      public double readDouble() {
181        display();
182        while (true) {
183            String s = getInputLine();
184            if (eoi) return 0.0;
185            try {
186              return Double.parseDouble(s);
187            }
188            catch (NumberFormatException e) {
189                error ("Double required ");
190            }
191        };
192      }
193
194      /**
195       * Returns the end-of-input status
196       *
197       * @return    <code>true</code> if end-of-input is true
198       *
199       * @see #eoi
200       */
201      public boolean eoi() {
202        return eoi;
203      }
204
205      /**
206       * Raises an ErrorBox when the user types something inappropriate.
207       *
208       * @param    errMsg  the message presented by the ErrorBox
209       */
210      private void error (String errMsg) {
211        ErrorBox err = new ErrorBox(errMsg);
212        display();
213      }
214    }
```

As with the ErrorBox, the constructor (lines 45 through 74) lays out the InputBox. This is done with a 3×1 GridLayout, with the top cell containing the Label centered, the center cell containing a Panel that contains the TextField, and the bottom cell containing a Panel that contains the Button.

The prompt is initially set to a default value in line 59. However, the method setPrompt (lines 76 through 83) allows the user to set the prompt to some other string.

Note that the InputBox is modal. However, until it is made visible (by a call to display in lines 85 through 99), the program is able to continue executing. But once display is called, the InputBox becomes visible. The modal property of the InputBox means that the program cannot execute any further until the InputBox "loses the focus," which means that Java's runtime system turns its attention to some other component. In our program, this can be done only when the user clicks the "OK" button. Clicking the "OK" button causes the corresponding action event to be handled by the actionPerformed method (lines 101 through 109), which hides the InputBox, causing it to lose the focus.

Here's the sequence of events that happen with an InputBox:

1. The client program creates an InputBox by new InputBox().
2. The InputBox constructor is called, but the new InputBox remains hidden; so when the constructor is finished, control returns to the client program.
3. The client program eventually want to read, say, a string, so it calls String s = readString().

4. readString (lines 125 through 134) calls display, which makes the InputBox visible. Execution cannot continue to the next line until the modal InputBox has lost the focus.

5. Eventually the user clicks the "OK" button, causing actionPerformed to be called.

6. actionPerformed hides the InputBox, causing it to lose the focus.

7. Since the modal InputBox has lost the focus, execution resumes at line 133 in readString, causing getInputLine to be called.

8. getInputLine (lines 111 through 123) just picks up what the user typed in the TextField and returns that string. If that string has zero length (i.e., the user typed the empty string), then that is the signal for end of input, and eoi is set to true. One point to note is the test in the first line of getInputLine, which checks to see if eoi had been set true on a previous call. If so, eoi should remain true forever. Thus, if eoi is true, we return the null string (and leave eoi still true), regardless of what the user may have typed in the TextField.

9. When getInputLine returns the string to readString, that same string is returned by readString to the client. Notice that if eoi is true, then getInputLine and subsequently readString both return the null string, as desired.

The readChar method (lines 136 through 148) is just a little more complicated. Instead of returning the string that getInputLine produces, it returns the leading character of that string. However, if getInputLine resulted in eoi, then readChar returns zero instead. The instance variable eoi is tested by readChar, so the Javadoc method comments indicate @see #eoi. The notation #eoi generates an HTML link to the documentation for the instance variable eoi in the present (CSLib) class.

There is just a bit greater complexity involved with the method readInt. With readString and readChar, there is no input that is considered illegal. The user can type any characters whatsoever. But with readInt, the characters must form a valid integer. If we could be sure that the user would always type a correct integer, we might have written code that resembles readChar:

```
String s = getInputLine();
if (eoi) return 0;
return Integer.parseInt(s);
```

However, the user might type something illegal, and parseInt in line 164 would throw a NumberFormatException. Therefore, we are obliged to enclose line 164 inside a try-catch statement. We want to repeatedly execute the above three lines until the parseInt succeeds, and the return statement completes successfully.

The readDouble method (lines 172 through 192) is just like readInt, except that Double.parseDouble(String) is used instead of Integer.parseInt(String).

The method boolean eoi() (lines 194 through 203) allows the client to test the status of end of input.

The method error(String) is called when an input error is caught by readInt or readDouble. It just raises an ErrorBox with the supplied error message. Whichever method called error will want the user to type more input, so error causes the InputBox to reappear. (Recall, the InputBox was hidden by actionPerformed when the user clicked the "OK" button.)

E.2.7 DrawingBox

The DrawingBox class extends ClosableFrame and may be drawn upon using many of the methods that are normally used on a Graphics object. It behaves as a Canvas that occupies the drawable portion of a Frame. DrawingBox can be used as a stand-alone component for drawing, or it can be used as a teaching tool, to lead up to using the Java AWT. Many parts of DrawingBox are redundant, and we won't show them all. Here is the relevant code:

```
1    package CSLib;
2
3    import java.awt.*;
4    import java.awt.event.*;
```

```
5
6    /**
7     * <code>DrawingBox</code> is a frame upon which many of the
8     * <code>java.awt.Graphics</code> operations can be performed.  As a
9     * frame, it exists as a separate window, and the operations on it may be
10    * performed from anywhere -- not just from within a <code>paint</code>
11    * method (as is normal with a frame's <code>Graphics</code> object).
12    * (However, to be used effectively as a teaching aid, operations on a
13    * <code>DrawingBox</code> <i>should</i> be performed from within
14    * a single method, which later can be converted to a <code>paint</code>
15    * method.)
16    * <p>
17    * Care must be taken that when this frame is obscured, that
18    * subsequently it can repaint itself.  An off-screen <code>Graphics</code>
19    * context keeps an up-to-date copy of this frame's <code>Graphics</code>
20    * at all times.  The origin of the coordinate system is translated so that
21    * it is in the upper left of the <i>drawable</i> portion of the
22    * frame.  Consequently, <code>DrawingBox</code> behaves more like a
23    * <code>Canvas</code> object that occupies the drawable portion of a frame.
24    * <p>
25    * In order to distinguish the <code>Frame</code> from its drawable portion,
26    * methods <code>getDrawableWidth</code> and <code>getDrawableHeight</code>
27    * are provided.
28    * <p>
29    * <code>DrawingBox</code> uses inner classes <code>DBMouseAdapter</code>
30    * (extending <code>java.awt.event.MouseAdapter</code>) to implement mouse
31    * listeners, and <code>DBMouseMotionAdapter</code> (extending
32    * <code>java.awt.event.MouseMotionAdapter</code>) to implement mouse
33    * motion listeners.
34    *
35    * @see     ClosableFrame
36    * @see     java.awt.Graphics
37    *
38    * @author  M. Dennis Mickunas
39    *
40    */
41   public class DrawingBox extends ClosableFrame {
42
43     /**
44      * the <code>Graphics</code> object affiliated with this <code>Frame</code>
45      */
46     private Graphics g;
47     /**
48      * the size of the user's screen
49      */
50     Dimension screenSize;
51     /**
52      * an off-screen image of everything that is done to <code>g</code>
53      */
54     private Image buffer;
55     /**
56      * the <code>Graphics</code> affiliated with the off-screen image
57      */
58     private Graphics gContext;
```

```
59
60      /**
61       * Constructs a DrawingBox with the default title.
62       */
63      public DrawingBox () {
64        this ("DrawingBox");
65      }
66
67      /**
68       * Constructs a DrawingBox with a specific title.
69       *
70       * @param title the string to use as this DrawingBox title.
71       *
72       * @see     java.awt.Graphics#translate(int, int)
73       * @see     java.awt.Container#getInsets()
74       */
75      public DrawingBox (String title) {
76        super(title);
77        screenSize = Toolkit.getDefaultToolkit().getScreenSize();
78        setBackground(Color.white);
79        // By default, set size to 1/2 screen wide by 1/2 screen high.
80        setSize(screenSize.width/2, screenSize.height/2);
81        setVisible(true);
82        g = getGraphics();
83
84        // Create an off-screen image, and get its Graphics object
85        buffer = createImage(screenSize.width, screenSize.height);
86        gContext = buffer.getGraphics();
87        gContext.setColor(Color.white);
88        gContext.fillRect(0, 0, screenSize.width, screenSize.height);
89        gContext.setColor(Color.black);
90
91        // Translate the origin to the upper-left corner of the drawable area.
92        g.translate(getInsets().left, getInsets().top);
93
94        addMouseListener(new DBMouseAdapter());
95        addMouseMotionListener(new DBMouseMotionAdapter());
96
97      }
98
99      /**
100      * <code>DBMouseAdapter</code> is an inner class that implements
101      * the Mouse listener for <code>DrawingBox</code>.  It does this
102      * by extending the Java convenience wrapper <code>MouseAdapter</code>.
103      * <p>
104      * Each <code>MouseEvent</code> must be translated to correspond
105      * to the translated coordinate system of the <code>DrawingBox</code>.
106      * This translation remains in effect for any downstream mouse
107      * listeners.
108      *
109      * @see     java.awt.event.MouseAdapter
110      * @see     java.awt.event.MouseEvent#translatePoint(int int)
111      * @see     java.awt.Container#getInsets()
112      */
```

```
113      public class DBMouseAdapter extends MouseAdapter {
114        public void mouseClicked(MouseEvent e) {
115          e.translatePoint(-getInsets().left, -getInsets().top);
116        }
117        public void mouseEntered(MouseEvent e) {
118          e.translatePoint(-getInsets().left, -getInsets().top);
119        }
120        public void mouseExited(MouseEvent e) {
121          e.translatePoint(-getInsets().left, -getInsets().top);
122        }
123        public void mousePressed(MouseEvent e) {
124          e.translatePoint(-getInsets().left, -getInsets().top);
125        }
126        public void mouseReleased(MouseEvent e) {
127          e.translatePoint(-getInsets().left, -getInsets().top);
128        }
129      }
130
131      /**
132       * <code>DBMouseMotionAdapter</code> is an inner class that implements
133       * the Mouse motion listener for <code>DrawingBox</code>.  It does this
134       * by extending the Java convenience wrapper
135       * <code>MouseMotionAdapter</code>.
136       * <p>
137       * Each <code>MouseEvent</code> must be translated to correspond to the
138       * translated coordinate system of the <code>DrawingBox</code>.  This
139       * translation remains in effect for any downstream mouse motion listeners.
140       *
141       * @see    java.awt.event.MouseMotionAdapter
142       * @see    java.awt.event.MouseEvent#translatePoint(int int)
143       * @see    java.awt.Container#getInsets()
144       */
145      public class DBMouseMotionAdapter extends MouseMotionAdapter {
146        public void mouseDragged(MouseEvent e) {
147          e.translatePoint(-getInsets().left, -getInsets().top);
148        }
149        public void mouseMoved(MouseEvent e) {
150          e.translatePoint(-getInsets().left, -getInsets().top);
151        }
152      }
153
154    /**
155     * Paints the drawing box.  This will be called when the drawing box must
156     * be restored.  The off-screen image in <code>buffer</code> has a true
157     * copy of what was drawn in the drawing box.
158     *
159     * @see    java.awt.Container#getInsets()
160     */
161    public void paint (Graphics g) {
162      // Restore the DrawingBox from the offscreen cache,
163      // making sure that the insets are avoided.
164      if (buffer!=null)
165        g.drawImage(buffer, getInsets().left, getInsets().top, this);
166    }
```

```
167
168    /** Returns the current drawable width (less insets) of this drawing box.
169     *
170     * @see     java.awt.Container#getInsets()
171     *
172     * @return  the current drawable width of this drawing box.
173     */
174    public int getDrawableWidth () {
175      return getSize().width-getInsets().left-getInsets().right;
176    }
177
178    /** Returns the current drawable height (less insets) of this drawing box.
179     *
180     * @see     java.awt.Container#getInsets()
181     *
182     * @return  the current drawable height of this drawing box.
183     */
184    public int getDrawableHeight () {
185      return getSize().height-getInsets().top-getInsets().bottom;
186    }
187
188    /**
189     * Sets the drawable size of this drawing box by setting a smaller size,
190     * then increasing it by the amount of the insets.
191     *
192     * @see     java.awt.Container#getInsets()
193     *
194     * @param   width   the desired drawable width
195     * @param   height  the desired drawable height
196     */
197    public void setDrawableSize (int width, int height) {
198      super.setSize(width, height);
199      super.setSize(width+getInsets().left+getInsets().right,
200                    height+getInsets().top+getInsets().bottom);
201    }
202
203    /**
204     * Gets this drawing box's current color.
205     *
206     * @return this drawing box's current color.
207     *
208     * @see     java.awt.Color
209     * @see     java.awt.Graphics#getColor
210     */
211    public Color getColor () { return g.getColor(); }
212
213    /**
214     * Sets this drawing box's color.
215     *
216     * @param   c  the desired drawing box's color.
217     *
218     * @see     java.awt.Color
219     * @see     java.awt.Graphics#setColor
220     */
```

```
221    public void setColor (Color c) {
222      g.setColor(c);
223      gContext.setColor(c);
224    }
225
226    /**
227     * Draws a line, using the current color, between the points
228     * <i>(x1,y1)</i> and <i>(x2,y2)</i>
229     * in this drawing box's coordinate system.
230     *
231     * @param    x1   the first point's <i>x</i> coordinate.
232     * @param    y1   the first point's <i>y</i> coordinate.
233     * @param    x2   the second point's <i>x</i> coordinate.
234     * @param    y2   the second point's <i>y</i> coordinate.
235     *
236     * @see      java.awt.Graphics#drawLine
237     */
238    public void drawLine (int x1, int x2, int y1, int y2) {
239      gContext.drawLine (x1, x2, y1, y2);
240      g.drawLine (x1, x2, y1, y2);
241    }

         ...

409    /**
410     * Clears the specified rectangle by filling it with the background
411     * color of the current drawing box.
412     *
413     * @param    x the <i>x</i> coordinate of the rectangle to clear.
414     * @param    y the <i>y</i> coordinate of the rectangle to clear.
415     * @param    width the width of the rectangle to clear.
416     * @param    height the height of the rectangle to clear.
417     *
418     * @see      java.awt.Graphics#setColor
419     * @see      java.awt.Graphics#fillRect
420     * @see      java.awt.Graphics#clearRect
421     */
422    public void clearRect (int x, int y, int width, int height) {
423      gContext.setColor(Color.white);
424      gContext.fillRect (x, y, width, height);
425      gContext.setColor(g.getColor());
426      g.clearRect (x, y, width, height);
427    }
428
429    /**
430     * Clears the entire drawing box.
431     *
432     * @see      java.awt.Graphics#setColor
433     * @see      java.awt.Graphics#fillRect
434     * @see      java.awt.Graphics#clearRect
435     */
436    public void clear() {
437      gContext.setColor(Color.white);
438      gContext.fillRect (0, 0, screenSize.width, screenSize.height);
439      gContext.setColor(g.getColor());
```

```
440        g.clearRect(0, 0, getDrawableWidth(), getDrawableHeight());
441    }
442
443    /**
444     * Draws the specified image with its top-left corner at
445     * <i>(x,y)</i> in this drawing box's coordinate system.
446     * <p>
447     * This method waits for the image to be fully loaded.
448     *
449     * @param    img the specified image to be drawn.
450     * @param    x    the <i>x</i> coordinate.
451     * @param    y    the <i>y</i> coordinate.
452     *
453     * @see        java.awt.Graphics#drawImage
454     * @see        java.awt.Image
455     * @see        java.awt.MediaTracker
456     */
457    public void drawImage (Image img, int x, int y) {
458        // Wait for the image to be fully loaded.
459        MediaTracker checker = new MediaTracker(this);
460        checker.addImage(img, 0);
461        try { checker.waitForID(0);}
462        catch (InterruptedException e){};
463        // Now draw it.
464        gContext.drawImage(img, x, y, this);
465        g.drawImage(img, x, y, this);
466    }
467 }
```

One difficulty with a class like DrawingBox is that if its frame ever requires repainting, its paint(Graphics) method will be called by the AWT. To repaint the frame properly, the prior state of the DrawingBox must be remembered. One solution is to remember the sequence of calls to drawLine, drawOval, etc. that occurred (and the arguments that were passed), and to "replay" those actions within an AWT paint method. This is very awkward. Another solution (that we adopt) is to make a copy of the DrawingBox in an offline Image; then all that paint must do is to draw that Image. In lines 51 through 58 we see the declarations of this off-screen Image and the Graphics that corresponds to it. These instance variables are initialized in the constructor, in lines 85 and 86. The next three lines ensure that the off-screen image has a pure white background (since on some platforms, an image has a gray background by default).

In line 92 we translate the coordinate system of the frame so that instead of the origin being at the upper left corner of the frame, it is at the upper left corner of the *drawable* area of the frame. We have found that this is a more natural choice for the novice Java programmer.

In lines 94 and 95, we add instances of inner classes to act as mouse listeners and mouse motion listeners. As with the DialogCloser class that extended java.awt.event.WindowAdapter in ClosableDialog, here the inner class DBMouseAdapter extends java.awt.event.MouseAdapter, and the inner class DBMouseMotionAdapter extends java.awt.event.MouseMotionAdapter. Each of the methods in those inner classes must translate the MouseEvent to match the new coordinate system.

You can see that the paint method (lines 154 through 166) does exactly as we said. The image must be drawn in the untranslated coordinate system, so the insets must be accommodated. The fourth parameter, this, is an Observer parameter; its treatment is beyond the scope of this text, but supplying this does the trick in simple cases.

In lines 168 through 201, we see methods to obtain the drawable size of the DrawingBox (the overall size of the frame, minus the insets) and to set the drawable size. In lines 203 through 224, there are methods to get and set the ink color for drawing. Note that with DrawingBox, it is not possible to change the background color, since there is no convenient way to change the background color of the off-screen image.

In lines 226 through 241, we see a typical drawing method for the `DrawingBox`. The method just draws the desired line both in the `Graphics` for the frame and in the `Graphics` for the off-screen image. The other draw methods are patterned in exactly the same way.

In lines 409 through 441, we see methods for clearing a designated rectangular area, or the entire `DrawingBox`.

Finally, the `drawImage` method in lines 443 through 466 draws a GIF or JPEG image in the `DrawingBox`. This method has the same form as the `drawLine` method, except that care must be taken that the image has been fully loaded before an attempt is made to draw it. (Images are typically read from disk as GIF or JPEG files.) The Java `MediaTracker` class is used to monitor the loading of an `Image`. An explanation of `MediaTracker` is beyond the scope of this book, but the four lines 459 through 462 can be used as shown to wait for the loading of an image.

E.2.8 `SFormat`

The class `SFormat` is a utility class of methods that permit the formatting of numbers into strings. There are methods for formatting an integer in a field of specific width, either right-justified or centered. Decimals can be right-justified or centered, with the ability to specify the number of places to the right of the decimal point. An explanation of the logic for `SFormat` was given in Chapter 10, where we developed a version of this code.

The actual `CSLib` version of `SFormat` differs from what was presented in Chapter 10 only in the inclusion of complete Javadoc comments. To conserve space, we will not repeat the code here.

E.2.9 `TrickMouse`

The class `TrickMouse` was used in Chapter 2, instantiated by `HelloMorte`, `HitWall`, and `WarningMouse`.

```
1    package CSLib;
2    import java.awt.*;
3    import java.awt.event.*;
4
5    /**
6     * <code>TrickMouse</code> is a special class used as an example in the text.
7     * It should really be in a package of its own, separate from <code>CSLib</code>.
8     *
9     * @author   M. Dennis Mickunas
10    */
11   public class TrickMouse extends Frame {
12     private Image[] img = new Image[2];
13     private String message;
14     private int which;
15
16     /**
17      * Constructs a TrickMouse
18      */
19     public TrickMouse () {
20       super("Trick Mouse");
21
22       // the "hit wall" image
23       img[0] = Toolkit.getDefaultToolkit().getImage("t4.gif");
24       // the "speaking" image
25       img[1] = Toolkit.getDefaultToolkit().getImage("t1.gif");
26
```

```
27        setSize(200, 200);
28        setVisible(true);
29
30        // Use an anonymous inner class to implement the two WindowAdapter
31        // methods of interest.
32        addWindowListener(new WindowAdapter() {
33          public void windowClosing (WindowEvent e) {
34            System.exit(0);
35          }
36          public void windowActivated (WindowEvent e) {
37            repaint();
38          }
39        });
40      }
41
42      /**
43       * Sets the title of the Trick Mouse
44       *
45       * @param  title     the <code>String</code> to set the title to.
46       */
47      public void setTitle (String title) {
48        super.setTitle(title);
49      }
50
51      /**
52       * Causes the Trick Mouse to display the "hit wall" image.
53       */
54      public void hitWall () {
55        which = 0;
56        repaint();
57      }
58
59      /**
60       * Causes the Trick Mouse to display the "speak" image.
61       *
62       * @param  msg     the <code>String</code> that is "spoken."
63       */
64      public void speak (String msg) {
65        message = msg;
66        which = 1;
67        repaint();
68      }
69
70      /**
71       * Redraws the screen.  The appropriate image is drawn using
72       * <code>Graphics.drawImage(Image,...)</code>.  If this is the "speak"
73       * image, then the "spoken message" is printed using
74       * <code>Graphics.drawString(String,...)</code>.
75       *
76       * @see     java.awt.Graphics#drawImage
77       * @see     java.awt.Graphics#drawString
78       */
79
80      public void paint (Graphics g) {
```

```
81          g.drawImage(img[which], 0, 100, this);
82          if (which==1) g.drawString(message, 70, 130);
83      }
84  }
```

This class uses a number of features that we've discussed in this book. An array of images is created by reading GIF files in lines 22 through 25. An inner class is used to listen for the windowClosing and the windowActivated events. The AWT is exercised within this class, with repaint being called at appropriate times. Finally, paint illustrates the updating of Graphics that occurs whenever repaint is requested.

Index